D1451965

CCIE Security Practice Labs

Fahim Hussain Yusuf Bhaiji, CCIE No. 9305

Cisco Press

800 East 96th Street
Indianapolis, Indiana 46240 USA

CCIE Security Practice Labs

Fahim Hussain Yusuf Bhaiji

Copyright © 2004 Cisco Systems, Inc.

Cisco Press logo is a trademark of Cisco Systems, Inc.

Published by:
Cisco Press
800 East 96th Street
Indianapolis, IN 46240 USA

Printed in the United States of America 1 2 3 4 5 6 7 8 9 0

First Printing   February 2004

Library of Congress Cataloging-in-Publication Number: 2003100540

ISBN: 1-58705-134-6

Warning and Disclaimer

This book is designed to provide information to help you prepare for the CCIE Security Certification. Every effort has been made to make this book as complete and as accurate as possible, but no warranty or fitness is implied.

The information is provided on an "as is" basis. The author, Cisco Press, and Cisco Systems, Inc. shall have neither liability nor responsibility to any person or entity with respect to any loss or damages arising from the information contained in this book or from the use of the discs or programs that may accompany it.

The opinions expressed in this book belong to the author and are not necessarily those of Cisco Systems, Inc.

Trademark Acknowledgments

All terms mentioned in this book that are known to be trademarks or service marks have been appropriately capitalized. Cisco Press or Cisco Systems, Inc. cannot attest to the accuracy of this information. Use of a term in this book should not be regarded as affecting the validity of any trademark or service mark.

Feedback Information

At Cisco Press, our goal is to create in-depth technical books of the highest quality and value. Each book is crafted with care and precision, undergoing rigorous development that involves the unique expertise of members from the professional technical community.

Readers' feedback is a natural continuation of this process. If you have any comments regarding how we could improve the quality of this book, or otherwise alter it to better suit your needs, you can contact us through e-mail at feedback@ciscopress.com. Please make sure to include the book title and ISBN in your message.

We greatly appreciate your assistance.

Publisher	John Wait
Editor-in-Chief	John Kane
Executive Editor	Brett Bartow
Cisco Representative	Anthony Wolfenden
Cisco Press Program Manager	Sonia Torres Chavez
Production Manager	Patrick Kanouse
Senior Development Editor	Christopher Cleveland
Project Editor	Marc Fowler
Technical Editors	Gert De Laet, Gert Schauwers
Team Coordinator	Tammi Barnett
Book Designer	Gina Rexrode
Cover Designer	Louisa Adair
Composition	Interactive Composition Corporation

CISCO SYSTEMS

Corporate Headquarters
Cisco Systems, Inc.
170 West Tasman Drive
San Jose, CA 95134-1706
USA
www.cisco.com
Tel: 408 526-4000
    800 553-NETS (6387)
Fax: 408 526-4100

European Headquarters
Cisco Systems International BV
Haarlerbergpark
Haarlerbergweg 13-19
1101 CH Amsterdam
The Netherlands
www-europe.cisco.com
Tel: 31 0 20 357 1000
Fax: 31 0 20 357 1100

Americas Headquarters
Cisco Systems, Inc.
170 West Tasman Drive
San Jose, CA 95134-1706
USA
www.cisco.com
Tel: 408 526-7660
Fax: 408 527-0883

Asia Pacific Headquarters
Cisco Systems, Inc.
Capital Tower
168 Robinson Road
#22-01 to #29-01
Singapore 068912
www.cisco.com
Tel: +65 6317 7777
Fax: +65 6317 7799

Cisco Systems has more than 200 offices in the following countries and regions. Addresses, phone numbers, and fax numbers are listed on the
Cisco.com Web site at www.cisco.com/go/offices.

Argentina • Australia • Austria • Belgium • Brazil • Bulgaria • Canada • Chile • China PRC • Colombia • Costa Rica • Croatia • Czech Republic
Denmark • Dubai, UAE • Finland • France • Germany • Greece • Hong Kong SAR • Hungary • India • Indonesia • Ireland • Israel • Italy
Japan • Korea • Luxembourg • Malaysia • Mexico • The Netherlands • New Zealand • Norway • Peru • Philippines • Poland • Portugal
Puerto Rico • Romania • Russia • Saudi Arabia • Scotland • Singapore • Slovakia • Slovenia • South Africa • Spain • Sweden
Switzerland • Taiwan • Thailand • Turkey • Ukraine • United Kingdom • United States • Venezuela • Vietnam • Zimbabwe

About the Author

Fahim Hussain Yusuf Bhaiji, CCIE No. 9305, has been with Cisco Systems, Inc. for over three years and is currently a CCIE proctor in Cisco Systems' Sydney, Australia Lab. He has recently been charged with the management of content development for the CCIE Security. Prior to this, he was Technical Lead for the Sydney TAC Security and VPN team.

Yusuf's passion for security- and VPN-related technologies has played a dominant role in his 12 years of industry experience, from as far back as his initial master's degree in Computer Science, and since reflected in his numerous certifications.

Yusuf prides himself in his knowledge-sharing abilities, evident in the fact that he has mentored many successful CCIE candidates, as well as designing and delivering a number of security- and VPN-related courses, around the globe.

About the Technical Reviewers

Gert De Laet, CCIE No. 2657, has both CCIE Security and Routing and Switching certifications. He has more than nine years of experience in internetworking. Gert currently works for the CCIE team at Cisco in Brussels, Belgium, as CCIE Proctor/Content Engineer and Program Manager for EMEA. He also holds an Engineering degree in Electronics.

Gert Schauwers, CCIE No. 6924, has CCIE certifications in Security, Routing and Switching, and Communications and Services. He has more than four years of experience in internetworking. He is currently working for the CCIE team at Cisco in Brussels, Belgium, as CCIE Content Engineer. He has an Engineering degree in Electronics.

Dedications

I dedicate this book to my father Asghar Bhaiji for his wisdom and encouragement to succeed in life; to my late mother Khatija Bhaiji whose love is ever shining on me; to my loving aunts, Fizza and Amina, for nurturing me through my formative years; and to the rest of the family for their encouragement in every endeavor of my life.

and

To my beloved wife Farah, for her love, her continuous support, her sharing of my visions, and her part in my success.

and

To my daughter Hussaina and my son Abbas, whose love keeps me focused on the truly important aspects of life, and who help me maintain my sense of humor through the more challenging moments of my life.

Acknowledgments

I would like to take this opportunity to thank the members of the Sydney TAC Security and VPN team for their support in writing this book. I have benefited greatly from working with them and can proudly say that it has been the best team with which I have ever worked.

The wealth of knowledge and diversity of experience within the Cisco Systems, Inc. Technical Assistance Center (TAC) is equal to none. In my mind, these people are gurus. While the list of people I could mention may be endless, I would like to specifically thank Nairi Adamian, Alison Badger, David Chan, Eric Dadios, Jonathan Limbo, Bill Louis, Catherine McLachlan, and Paul Qiu.

I extend my sincere gratitude to Brett Bartow and Chris Cleveland, whose expert guidance has been a determining factor in the completion of this book.

The Technical Reviewers, Gert DeLaet and Gert Schawers, have done an amazing job. Their dedication to recreating each scenario in their own lab was extraordinary. I greatly appreciate their efforts in the accomplishment of this project.

Finally, I would like to thank you, the reader, for helping me to make this book a success.

Contents at a Glance

Table of Contents

Foreword

The CCIE program is designed to help individuals, companies, organizations, industries, and countries succeed in the networked world by distinguishing the top echelon of internetworking experts. In particular, the CCIE Security Certification is designed to identify Network Security Experts.

The first step along the CCIE Security path is for individuals to take a challenging written exam designed to assess their knowledge across a range of technologies. If their scores indicate expert-level knowledge, candidates then proceed to a performance-based CCIE Security Certification lab exam.

Why Security Certifications?

Security is one of the fastest-growing areas in the industry. The expansive development of the Internet, the increase in e-business, and the escalating threat to both public- and private-sector networks have made security and the protection of information a primary concern for all types of organizations. There is an ever-increasing demand for experts with the knowledge and skills to do it. Therefore, trained Network Security personnel will be required in the years to come.

Why CCIE Security?

CCIE Security distinguishes the top level of Network Security experts. The CCIE Security Certification enables individuals to optimize career growth, opportunity, and compensation by distinguishing themselves as being part of the Network Security experts of the world.

The CCIE Security Certification enables companies to minimize their risk by identifying the highest caliber of security personnel with the training and skills necessary to protect their critical information assets.

This book will be a valuable asset for potential CCIE Security candidates who passed the written examination and are preparing for the actual lab exam. I am positive individuals will inevitably gain extensive hands-on experience during the preparation, using this book. The main focus is on configuring the various security technologies and also on understanding and navigating the subtleties, intricacies, and potential pitfalls inherent in taking the CCIE Security lab exam.

Good luck!

Gert De Laet
Product Manager CCIE Security
Cisco Systems, Inc.

Introduction

As Vinton G. Cerf said, "The wonderful thing about the Internet is that you're connected to everyone else. The terrible thing about the Internet is that you're connected to everyone else."

The luxury of access to this wealth of information comes with its risks, and anyone on the Internet potentially is a stakeholder. The risks vary from information loss/corruption to information theft and much more. The number of security incidents is also growing dramatically.

With all this happening, there is a strong drive for network security implementations to improve security posture within every organization worldwide. Today's most complex networks require a comprehensive and integrated security solution.

The Need for Security Certification

Security is one of the fastest-growing areas in the industry. Information security is on the top of the agenda for all organizations. Companies have a need to keep information secure, and there is an ever-growing demand for IT professionals who know how to do this. Cisco Systems delivers this by offering CCIE Security certification, setting a professional benchmark in internetworking expertise.

This essential need for security in IT is undeniable. International Data Corporation predicted that the worldwide market for information security services would increase from $5.5 billion to $17.2 billion by 2004.

SANS Institute's projections estimated that less than one in 20 security professionals has the core competence and foundation knowledge to apply appropriate security measures. Equally problematic, about 50,000 IT security positions went unfilled last year.

Here are some more security stats (from Cisco Packet Magazine, First Quarter 2003 issue):

- A recent study by Riptech, a real-time information protection company, says network security breaches rose 28 percent during the first half of 2002, compared to the last half of 2001.
- A 2002 U.S. Federal Bureau of Investigation (FBI) report reveals that 85 percent of businesses have detected computer security breaches within the last 12 months.
- In a 2001 survey, the FBI found that 91 percent of respondents reported insider network abuse.

Overview of the CCIE Certification

CCIE is widely considered the industry's highest-level IT certification program, commonly referred to as the doctorate of networking. It equips candidates with excellent internetworking skills that are simply the best in the industry.

CCIE certification was recently voted #1 by IT professionals in the CertCities.com annual survey, **The Hottest Certifications for 2003**—a ranking attributed to the growing importance of certifications in a tight job market.

Furthermore, it also grabbed the title of **Most Respected High-Level Certification** in the CertCities.com Reader's Choice Awards earlier this year.

The CCIE program is designed to help individuals, companies, industries, and countries succeed in the networked world by distinguishing the top echelon of internetworking experts.

The program identifies leaders with a proven commitment to their career, the industry, and the process of ongoing learning. While individuals inevitably gain extensive product knowledge on their way to certification, product training is not the CCIE program objective. Rather, the focus is on identifying those experts capable of understanding and navigating the subtleties, intricacies, and potential pitfalls inherent in end-to-end networking regardless of technology or product brand.

True to its mission, the CCIE program evolves in step with the industry, focusing on current technologies and real-world applications to consistently identify candidates with the highest level of relevant internetworking expertise.

Currently, the CCIE certification has four tracks:

- Routing and Switching
- Security
- Communications and Services
- Voice

This book concentrates on CCIE Security Lab exam.

For more information on each individual track, refer to the following URL:

> www.cisco.com/go/ccie

Overview of the CCIE Security Exam

The CCIE Security exam covers IP and IP routing as well as specific security components.

Becoming a CCIE is a two-step process. The first step is to pass a two-hour, written qualification exam administered through Cisco-authorized testing centers. The second step is to successfully complete a hands-on lab examination at a Cisco facility demonstrating the candidate's expertise in configuring, testing, and troubleshooting real network equipment. The qualification exam is a prerequisite for attempting and scheduling the lab exam. For further details, refer to the following URL:

> www.cisco.com/warp/public/625/ccie/security/

Security Written Qualification Exam

The two-hour, multiple-choice exam is computerized and administered at Cisco authorized testing centers. The exam is closed-book and contains 100 questions. No reference materials are allowed in the exam room.

NOTE   For more details, refer to the Security written exam blueprint at
www.cisco.com/warp/public/625/ccie/security/preparing_wr_exam.html

Security Lab Exam

The Security lab exam is a one-day, eight-hour practical exam. The CCIE candidate is presented with a complex design to implement from the physical layer up. Candidates are not required to configure any end-user systems but are responsible for any device residing in the internetwork.

Each configuration scenario and problem has preassigned point values. The candidate must obtain a minimum mark of 80 percent to pass.

There are three core elements in preparing for the CCIE Lab exam:

- Your current level of work experience

- Your training level

- Your available time and equipment options for self-study

NOTE   For more details on the CCIE Lab exam, refer to

www.cisco.com/warp/public/625/ccie/security/preparing_lab_exam.html

---

Equipment List

To perform the practice labs in this book, you need the following devices:

- 8 routers—The routers can be of any model—that is, 2500, 2600 or 3600 series. But prefer modular routers so you can swap modules and adapt to different lab topologies.

- You need the following interfaces/cables for different lab topologies. For more details, refer to the Equipment list in each chapter.

  ∇ Ethernet/Fast Ethernet module/ports

  ∇ Serial module/ports

  ∇ ISDN BRI S/T module/ports

  ∇ ATM module/ports

  ∇ Straight-through cables

  ∇ Cross-over cables

  ∇ DTE-DCE back-to-back cable for serial ports

  ∇ ATM fiber cable (depending on the modules/GBIC)

NOTE   Most labs in this book require you to configure ATM. If you don't have an ATM module, use a back-to-back serial connection instead.

- 2 Catalyst 3550 switches
- 1 PIX Firewall (any model)
- 1 Cisco Intrusion Detection System (IDS) 42xx appliance
- 1 VPN-3000 concentrator
- 2 PCs:

    ▽ Windows 2000 Server with CiscoSecure ACS 3.x and Microsoft CA server installed

    ▽ Test PC with Cisco VPN Client 3.x software

Target Audience

This book is intended for candidates preparing for the CCIE Security Lab exam.

Network engineers with specialization in security can also take advantage of this book with the complex scenarios, troubleshooting tips, and solutions provided.

One of the primary objectives of this book is to assist candidates preparing for the CCIE Lab exam by providing complex practice scenarios to give the candidate a look-and-feel for the real CCIE Lab exam.

CCIE candidates can use this book as a gauging element to validate their readiness to appear for the CCIE Lab exam.

About the Book

The book has seven Practice Labs in seven chapters. The format of each chapter is the same, except that the content in each exercise section varies. The book maintains the same level of difficulty and complexity in every chapter, covering all technologies.

Each chapter starts with an overview, equipment list, general guidelines, and instructions on setting up the lab topology, including the cabling instructions, followed by 10 exercise sections:

- Section 1.0: Basic configuration
- Section 2.0: Routing configuration
- Section 3.0: ISDN configuration
- Section 4.0: PIX configuration
- Section 5.0: VPN (IPSec/GRE/L2TP/PPTP) configuration
- Section 6.0: IOS Firewall configuration
- Section 7.0: AAA configuration
- Section 8.0: Advanced Security
- Section 9.0: IP Services and Protocol-Independent Features
- Section 10.0: Security violations

Each section has further subsections related to the technology with questions broken down into various categories and respective point allocation.

Each configuration section has preassigned point values. The candidate must obtain a minimum mark of 80 percent to pass.

Following the exercise section is an important part of this book—the "Verification, Hints, and Trouble-shooting Tips" section. This section gives you hints to troubleshoot and tips to identify the hidden problem or tricks in the questions. You can use this section to verify and compare results by adapting to the trouble-shooting methods shown. This section also guides you through using the most common show and debug commands used in the verification and troubleshooting process.

Further to assist you, solutions are provided on the book's accompanying CD-ROM for the entire lab, including configurations and common **show** command outputs from all the devices in the topology.

One of the main challenges in the CCIE Lab exam is dealing with integrated technologies in one big com-plex scenario. Most of the time, candidates are very knowledgeable and proficient in configuring individual technologies as standalone, but are unable to deal with scenarios incorporating all technologies with high-level complexity. This book provides complex integrated scenarios covering all technologies in every chapter, enabling candidates to test their readiness and identify their strengths and weaknesses.

This book will serve a valuable resource for every candidate in being successful in the CCIE Security Lab exam.

Wrap-Up

Once you have successfully completed all of the Practice Labs, I am confident that you will be ready to sit for the CCIE Lab exam. It is important to remember that success will rely on a number of key elements:

- **Time management**—Read through the entire exam paper and do not start configuration before you make a plan—remember the "divide-and-conquer" technique. A well-planned approach is an important key to success.

- **Question clarity**—One of the biggest challenges in the CCIE Lab is interpretation of the ques-tions. You must learn to interpret the questions accurately and understand exactly what is required. If the question is ambiguous, always approach the proctor for clarification. Clear up any uncertain-ties and don't make any assumptions.

- **Checklist**—During the course of the exam, maintain two checklists:

  ∇ Items you think are correctly configured but need testing at a later point in time.

  ∇ Items you have been unable to address, but need to skip past for the time being to avoid wasting time, ensuring you revisit them later.

- **Point check**—Be smart in your approach. Don't waste time on noncore tasks that are not second nature to you. Address sections of the test in which you are most competent, allowing you to maxi-mize your point score, and leave those items that are more challenging or time-consuming toward the end. Try to keep tally of the number of points you may have earned so that you are always aware of where you stand in process of completion.

- **Functionality testing**—Allow time for retesting of functionality toward the end—points are awarded only for working configurations.

- **Effective troubleshooting**—Do not spend time troubleshooting uncertainties; try to move on, leaving the problem for a later stage. More often than not, this change of focus will help you on a path to resolution.

- **Memory map and packet flow**—"Memory map" the entire lab topology and see the flow of packets in your mind. This will help you clarify your troubleshooting needs and avoid looking at the wrong problem or device.

- **Destressing techniques**—Do not allow your nerves to take control. If you are feeling tense or confused, walk out of the lab and use the breakroom. Cisco facilities have a breakroom equipped with a variety of refreshments—help yourself. This will help you relax so that you can start again with a fresh mind.

Final Word

My secret formula to success is "MDC"—Motivation, Dedication, and Consistency. If you stick to these three things, I have no doubt that you will succeed too. The CCIE exam is just a test; if you don't pass, do not quit. Try again! On the positive side, an initial failure will give you the opportunity to learn more and explore things that you may not have come across earlier.

Best wishes and good luck!

Fahim Hussain Yusuf Bhaiji—CCIE No. 9305
CCIE Proctor
Sydney, Australia
Cisco Systems, Inc.

Icons Used in This Book

 Router

 Bridge

 Hub

 DSU/CSU

 Catalyst Switch

 Multilayer Switch

 ATM Switch

 ISDN/Frame Relay Switch

 Communication Server

 Gateway

 Access Server

 PC

 PC with Software

 Sun Workstation

 Macintosh

 Terminal

 File Server

 Web Server

 Cisco Works Workstation

 Modem

 Printer

 Laptop

 IBM Mainframe

 Front End Processor

 Cluster Controller

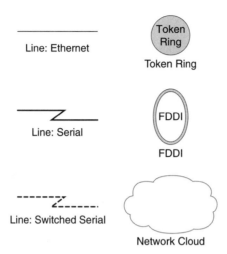

Command Syntax Conventions

The conventions used to present command syntax in this book are the same conventions used in the IOS Command Reference. The Command Reference describes these conventions as follows:

- **Boldface** indicates commands and keywords that are entered literally as shown. In actual configuration examples and output (not general command syntax), boldface indicates commands that are manually input by the user (such as a **show** command).
- *Italic* indicates arguments for which you supply actual values.
- Vertical bars (|) separate alternative, mutually exclusive elements.
- Square brackets ([ ]) indicate optional elements.
- Braces ({ }) indicate a required choice.
- Braces within brackets ([{ }]) indicate a required choice within an optional element.

CHAPTER 1

Practice Lab 1

All labs in this book are multi-protocol, multi-technology, testing you in areas such as Routing, Switching, Security, and VPN, as outlined in the CCIE Security blueprint. When you first read the questions in the lab, you might find them fairly easy, but they are carefully written to present high complexity and many hidden problems. Such is the case in the real CCIE lab exam.

To assist you, solutions are provided for the entire lab, including configurations and common **show** command outputs from all the devices in the topology. Furthermore, a "Verification, Hints, and Troubleshooting Tips" section is provided, which gives you tips and hints to troubleshoot and identify the hidden problem or trick in the question.

This is the first lab of seven in this book. Each lab is 8 hours and weighs 100 marks, passing of which is 80 marks. The objective is to complete the lab within 8 hours and obtain a minimum of 80 marks to pass. This test has been written such that you should be able to complete all questions, including initial configuration (such as IP addressing), within 8 hours; this excludes cabling time. Allow up to 1 hour for cabling, use the cabling instructions, and observe the instructions in the general guidelines. You can use any combination of routers as long as you fulfill the topology diagram in Figure 1-1. It is not compulsory to use the same model of routers.

NOTE   Cabling and IP addressing are already completed on the real CCIE Lab. You are not required to do any cabling or the IP addressing.

Equipment List

- 6 routers with the following specifications (all routers are to be loaded with the latest Cisco IOS version in 12.1(T) train):

    R1 — 4 serial, 1 BRI (with IP Plus image)

    R2 — 2 serial, 1 Ethernet (with IP Plus + Firewall image)

    R3 — 2 serial, 1 Ethernet, 1 BRI (with IP Plus + IPSec 56 image)

    R4 — 1 serial, 1 Ethernet (with IP Plus + Firewall + IPSec 56 image)

    R5 — 1 serial, 1 Ethernet (with IP Plus image)

    R6 — 5 serial, 3 Ethernet (with IP Plus + IPSec 56 image)

- 1 switch 3550
- 1 PIX — 2 interfaces (with version 6.x)
- 1 PC with Windows 2000 Server with CiscoSecure ACS 3.x+
- The IDS device in the topology is not required; it is there to give you an idea to configure other aspects of this lab. Subsequent chapters do require a Network IDS appliance.

Figure 1-1 *Lab Topology Diagram*

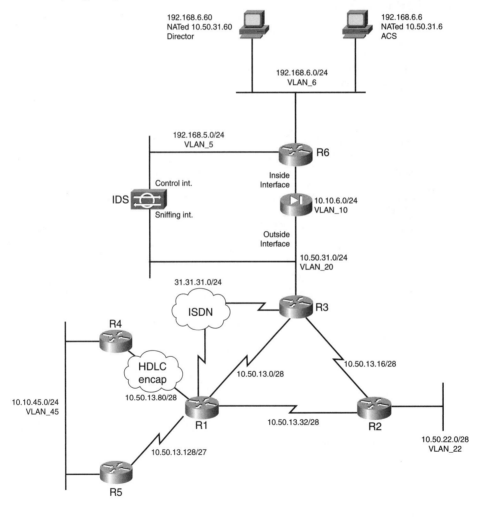

General Guidelines

- Please read the whole lab before you start.
- Do not configure any static/default routes unless otherwise specified/required.

- Use DLCIs provided in the diagram.

- Use the IP addressing scheme provided in the diagram; do not change any IP addressing unless otherwise specified. In the CCIE Lab, initial configurations are loaded, and therefore IP addresses are not to be changed. In this book, each chapter has a separate lab topology with different IP addressing, so each chapter needs to be recabled and all IP addresses need to be redone from the previous chapter.

- Use **cisco** as the password for any authentication string, enable-password, and TACACS+/RADIUS key or for any other purpose.

- Add additional loopbacks as specified during this lab.

- Configure VLANs on Switch1 as per Figure 1-1.

- All routers should be able to ping any interface in the network using the *optimal* path.

- You must time yourself to complete this lab in 8 hours.

- Do not use any external resources or answers provided in this book when attempting the lab.

- Configure a backdoor for any of the AAA questions below to the local database. If you don't, you will lose all points for that question.

- Do not configure any authentication or authorization on the console and aux ports.

Setting Up the Lab

You can use any combination of routers as long as you fulfill the topology diagram outlined in Figure 1-1. It is not compulsory to use the same model of routers.

Frame Relay DLCI Information

Only DLCIs indicated in Figure 1-2 should be mapped on the routers.

Figure 1-2   *Frame Relay DLCI Diagram*

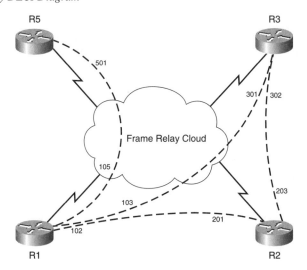

Routing Protocol Information

Use Figure 1-3 to configure routing protocols for the exercises to follow.

Figure 1-3   *Routing Protocol Information*

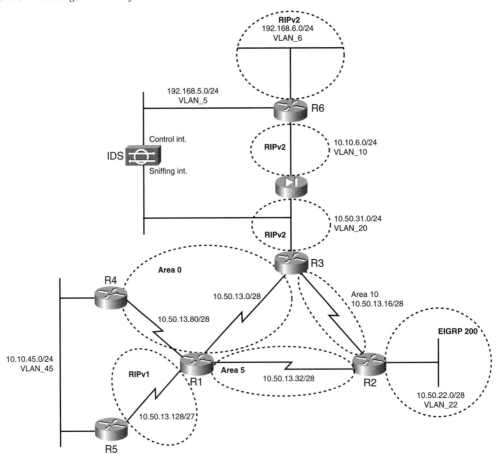

BGP Information

Use Figure 1-4 to configure BGP.

Cabling Instructions

Use Tables 1-1 and 1-2 for cabling all devices in your topology. It is not a must to use same type or sequence of interface. You may use any combination of interface(s) as long as you fulfill the requirement.

Figure 1-4   *BGP Information*

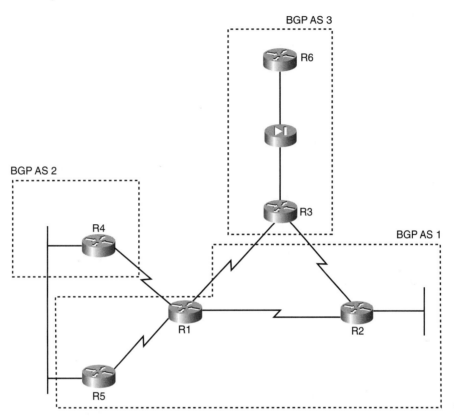

Table 1-1   *Cabling Instructions (Ethernet)*

Ethernet Cabling	Switch1
R2-ethernet0/0	Port 1
R3-fastethernet0/0	Port 2
R4-fastethernet2/0	Port 3
R5-ethernet0	Port 4
R6-ethernet0/0 to VLAN6	Port 5
R6-ethernet0/1 to PIX	Port 6
PIX-inside-ethernet1	Port 7
PIX-outside-ethernet0	Port 8

continues

Table 1-1   *Cabling Instructions (Ethernet) (Continued)*

Ethernet Cabling	Switch1
IDS-control-interface	Port 9
IDS-sniffing-interface	Port 10
AAA server	Port 11

Table 1-2   *Cabling Instructions (Serial)*

Back-to-Back Cabling	DTE-End	DCE-End
R1-to-frsw* (to R2/R3)	R1-serial2/0	R6-serial1/0
R1-to-frsw* (to R5)	R1-serial2/1	R6-serial1/1
R1-to-R4	R1-serial2/2	R4-serial3/0
R2-to-frsw* (to R1/R3)	R2-serial1/0	R6-serial1/2
R3-to-frsw* (to R1/R2)	R3-serial1/0	R6-serial1/3
R5-to-frsw* (to R1)	R5-serial0	R6-serial1/4

*frsw = Frame Relay Switch R6

Practice Lab 1 Exercises

Section 1.0: Basic Configuration (10 points)

1.1: IP Addressing (2 points)

1   Redraw a detailed topology with all necessary information.

2   Configure IP addressing as per the diagram.

3   Do not configure any static or default routes anywhere on the network unless otherwise specified. Configure a default route on R2. Your routing table should have an entry as follows: "Gateway of last resort is 0.0.0.0." Populate this default route to all the routers.

4   Create the following loopbacks:

Loopback-1 11.11.11.11/24 on R1

Loopback-2 111.111.111.111/24 on R1

Loopback-1 12.12.12.12/24 on R2

Loopback-2 122.122.122.122/24 on R2

Loopback-1 13.13.13.13/24 on R3

Loopback-2 133.133.133.133/24 on R3

Loopback-3 192.168.3.1/24 on R3

Loopback-1 14.14.14.14/24 on R4

Loopback-2 144.144.144.144/24 on R4

Loopback-1 16.16.16.16/24 on R6

Loopback-2 166.166.166.166/24 on R6

1.2: Frame Relay Configuration (4 points)

1 Configure R6 as a Frame Relay switch. Use the DLCI information provided for Frame Relay routing as per Figure 1-2.

2 Configure Frame Relay between R1, R2, R3, and R5. Configure point-to-point subinterfaces on all routers. Do not configure a subinterface on R1 for serial connection to R5. Use only the DLCIs provided in the DLCI information diagram. Use LMI type Cisco. The speed should be set to 56 KB on the DCE ends.

1.3: LAN Switch Configuration (4 points)

1 Configure Switch1 with the VLAN information provided in the diagram shown in Figure 1-1. Also make sure that it is easier for the network administrator to troubleshoot port/VLAN identification.

2 Configure security such that network devices are operational on allocated ports only. In the event of a security breach, the administrator should take strict action.

3 Configure the management interface of the switch with IP address 10.10.45.45. Only R4, R5, and R1 should have Telnet access to the switch. Configure redundancy such that the management interface is reachable from R1 if the serial link is down between R1 and R4. Configure a static route on R1 for the 10.10.45.0/24 network. Do not configure any routing protocol on Switch1 to achieve this task; you can use static routes as required.

4 Configure port 9 on the switch to be in VLAN 5. There is an IDS sensor deployed off r6. It has been preconfigured. The aim is to protect the PIX outside interface, so configure accordingly.

Section 2.0: Routing Configuration (25 points)

2.1: Core Routing OSPF/EIGRP/RIP (5 points)

1 Configure OSPF, EIGRP, and RIP as shown in Figure 1-3. All routing/update traffic should be encrypted. Mutually redistribute between IGPs only where necessary.

2.2: OSPF (4 points)

1 Configure a loopback on R3 10.50.13.97/28 in Area 66. R5 should see this network in the routing table. Do not use any summarization technique to achieve this task. Performance should not be compromised.

2 Configure the following loopbacks on R3; put them in Area 30 on R3.

30.30.1.0/24

30.30.2.0/24

30.30.3.0/24

30.30.4.0/24

30.30.5.0/24

30.30.6.0/24

2.3: EIGRP (3 points)

1 Configure three null routes on R2 to appear in the EIGRP-200 database for the following subnets: 10.50.22.16/28 10.50.22.32/28 10.50.22.64/28. Redistribute EIGRP-200 on R2 into OSPF. All other routers should see these routes as *one* route with a cost of 10.

2.4: RIP (3 points)

1 Configure RIPv2 on PIX to peer with inside router R6 and outside router R3. Use strong encryption. Do not configure a static default route. PIX should learn all routes via RIP. You must ensure that no other device can establish adjacency with the PIX and that routing updates are secured.

2 Configure RIP version 1 between R1 and R5. R5 should be able to ping all parts of the network.

3 Advertise VLAN 6 network 192.168.6.0/24 on R6 in RIPv2. Make sure you can ping the AAA server from the PIX.

2.5: BGP (10 points)

2.5.1: Basic BGP Configuration (2 points)

1 Configure the BGP peers as follows using Figure 1-4.

R2 – R3 eBGP

R2 – R1 iBGP

R1 – R3 eBGP

R1 – R5 iBGP

R5 – R4 eBGP

R3 – R6 iBGP (configure static NAT 10.10.6.2 to 10.50.31.22 on PIX to achieve this task)

NOTE   You can use "no sync" on all BGP peers.

2.5.2: BGP Connections (2 points)

1 Ensure that eBGP connection state on R6 shows local port as 179 always.

2.5.3: BGP and OSPF (2 points)

1 Advertise loopback2 on R2 and R4 in BGP. Redistribute BGP into OSPF on these routers so that BGP routes on all OSPF routers are seen as OSPF (E1) and not through BGP. Ensure all routers can ping these loopbacks using the optimal path. Do not use the **distance** command to achieve this task.

2.5.4: BGP and RIP (2 points)

1 Advertise loopback2 on R1 in BGP and RIPv1. Advertise loopback1 in RIPv1 only. R5 should be able to ping all routers in the network and vice versa.

2.5.5: BGP Attributes (2 points)

1 Advertise loopback1 and loopback2 on R6 in BGP. Do not use the **network** statement to advertise loopback2. R3 should see both loopbacks as internal. Ensure all routers in the network can ping these loopbacks using the optimal path.

Section 3.0: ISDN Configuration (8 points)

3.1: Basic ISDN (4 points)

1 Configure ISDN on R1 and R3. Use network 31.31.31.0/24. Advertise this network in OSPF area0.

ISDN information:

BRI number on R3 is 99281766

BRI number on R1 is 99281764

Switch-type = basic-ts013

> **2** Configure redundancy such that if there is a change in backbone database on R3, BRI comes up and all traffic continues normally.

3.2: PPP Callback (4 points)

> **1** R1 should call back R3 using TACACS+. Configure static NAT translation on PIX for AAA server behind R6 to achieve this task, as shown in topology diagram Figure 1-1.

Section 4.0: PIX Configuration (5 points)

4.1: Basic PIX Configuration (2 points)

> **1** Configure PIX inside and outside interface 10.10.6.1 and 10.50.31.1 respectively. Do not configure a default route on PIX. All routes should be learned via RIP as per Section 2.4.
>
> **2** You should be able to ping all routers in the network from the PIX, including the AAA server and R6 networks behind the PIX.

4.2: Network Address Translation (NAT) (2 points)

> **1** Configure static NAT translation and an access list on PIX to receive reliable syslog messages for a server behind R6. NAT 192.168.6.65 as 10.50.31.65.

4.3: Advanced Configuration (1 point)

> **1** A workstation on VLAN 6 is failing to ping a server on the same VLAN. Both PCs are in the same VLAN. Upon investigating, it is determined that the workstation is seeing the PIX inside MAC address for the server. When ethernet1 on PIX is shut down, the workstation can ping successfully. Resolve this without shutting down the ethernet1.

Section 5.0: IPSec/GRE Configuration (10 points)

5.1: IPSec (5 points)

5.1.1: IPSec LAN-to-LAN Using Preshared (2 points)

> **1** Encrypt IDS traffic between PIX and R4 in Section 6.2.1. Use a preshared key and SHA for message authentication and DES for encryption. Configure all other parameters as you feel appropriate.

5.1.2: Advanced IPSec LAN-to-LAN (3 points)

1 Configure IPSec to encrypt GRE traffic between R6 and R3 in Section 5.2.

2 Use preshared keys. Configure all other parameters as you feel appropriate.

3 If there is a loss of connectivity between two IPSec peers, terminate the sessions.

4 You are allowed to put one static route but not a default route on the PIX to achieve this task.

5.2: GRE (5 points)

1 Configure GRE through PIX; R6 should see all loopbacks in area 30 created on R3 in Section 2.2. R6 should ping even networks through GRE and odd networks through PIX. Run EIGRP-100 on GRE. Any ACL used to accomplish this task should not be more than one line.

Section 6.0: IOS Firewall + IOS IDS Configuration (10 points)

6.1: CBAC (6 points)

6.1.1: Basic CBAC Configuration (2 points)

1 Configure IOS Firewall on R2 to protect the EIGRP network. Ensure it can reach the rest of the network.

6.1.2: Firewall Filtering (2 points)

1 No access but ICMP is allowed to R2.

2 R1 should be able to Telnet to R2 using its loopback2 address as source. Configure ingress ACL on WAN links, including anti-spoofing technique. Do not deny RFC1918 address space.

6.1.3: Advanced CBAC Configuration (2 points)

1 Configure prevention against TCP host-specific denial-of-service on R2. Set the threshold to 200 before the firewall engine starts deleting half-open sessions to the host.

6.2: Intrusion Detection System (IDS) (4 points)

6.2.1: Basic IDS Configuration (2 points)

1 Configure IDS on R4 to protect the Ethernet network from internal intrusion, and configure to send an alarm for info and attack matching signatures.

2 Use the following details:

Director Host id 5, Sensor Host-id 4

Org id 100, Org name cisco

Director IP is 192.168.6.60 (create NAT on PIX to 10.50.31.60 to achieve this task)

6.2.2: Signature Tuning (1 point)

1 The message in the following line is received on the syslog server:

```
Jun 28 10:52:25.538: %IDS-4-TCP_SYN_ATTACK_SIG: Sig:3050:Half-Open Syn
    Flood - from 10.50.16.5 to 144.144.144.144
```

Upon investigation it was discovered that there is a specific application running on this machine. Consider these as false alarms; configure the IDS not to send such alarms in the future.

6.2.3: Spam Attack (1 point)

1 R4 is experiencing a spam attack. An alarm should only be generated if the spam attack has more than 500 recipients in a mail message.

Section 7.0: AAA (7 points)

7.1: AAA on the Router (4 points)

1 Configure router authentication and authorization on R4 using TACACS+. Configure two users on ACS, "user1" and "user2." User1 should have privilege level 10 and user2 privilege level 15. Configure such that User1 is able to run the command **show running-configuration** only, and user2 is able to run all commands.

2 Configure redundancy such that in the event the TACACS+ server is down, both users are able to log in using the local database and maintaining the same authorization.

3 When user1 or user2 logs in, they should get the # prompt with their respective privilege level without entering the **enable** command.

4   Configure fallback to local in the event the AAA server is down. Do not configure any authentication or authorization for console and auxiliary ports.

7.2: AAA on PIX (3 points)

1   Users should be able to Telnet to R6 loopback1 from anywhere on the network. Configure username "r6telnet" on ACS with the necessary parameters. Configure authentication and port authorization on PIX to achieve this task.

Section 8.0: Advanced Security (10 points)

8.1: Password Protection (2 points)

1   Make sure when users see the configuration of the router, all passwords are secured and not readable.

8.2: EXEC Authentication (4 points)

1   Encrypt the enable password on R2 with a nonreversible algorithm denoted by the number 5 in the configuration.

2   R2 should prompt for a username/password for privilege access and authenticate with the TACACS server. Do not use any AAA commands to achieve this task. In the event when the TACACS server is down, allow users to log in successfully. Do not use the **tacacs-server last-resort** command to achieve this task.

8.3: Access Control (4 points)

1   Configure such that a username **testconfig** with password **testconfig** is able to see the current configuration of R3 from anywhere on the network without having login access to the router.

2   Configure R5 vty line so that only loopback2 of R3 is able to Telnet.

Section 9.0: IP Services and Protocol-Independent Features (10 points)

9.1: NAT (4 points)

1   Create a loopback on R3 with 192.168.3.1/24. Configure NAT translation on R3 for this network to be translated to interface IP address with overload. You should be able to

ping anywhere in the network from R3 sourcing from this loopback and get NATed to the corresponding egress interface.

9.2: NTP (2 points)

1 Configure R1 clock polling from NTP server R2. All NTP packets should be encrypted. Update the system.

9.3: SNMP (2 points)

1 Configure R3 to report the BGP configuration to Network Management System 192.168.6.99 (NATed 10.50.31.99). Configure the appropriate static/ACL on the PIX to achieve this task.

9.4: Policy Routing (2 points)

1 There is a mail server 10.50.31.98 and a web server 10.50.31.99 on VLAN20. Configure such that networks behind and from R1

Traverse via R2 to reach the mail server

Traverse via R3 to reach the web server

Section 10.0: Security Violations (5 points)

10.1: Denial of Service—DoS (3 points)

1 R3 is experiencing an ICMP DoS attack on the WAN links. Take necessary action to prevent this. Do not deny ICMP.

10.2: IP Spoofing (2 points)

1 Configure PIX to perform a route lookup based on the source address to protect from an IP spoofing attack using network ingress and egress filtering, as described in RFC 2267.

Verification, Hints, and Troubleshooting Tips

As mentioned in the Overview, this section is primarily important when you're configuring the exercise and it is not working for you. You can use this section to verify and compare results by adapting the troubleshooting methods shown. Also provided are hints needed to configure and complete the respective exercises. Sometimes, it is easy to misinterpret the question, which has hidden and tricky elements required to be configured.

This section also guides you in using the most common **show** and **debug** commands used for verification and troubleshooting, which are very handy. Learn to use them and to read the outputs and when to use them.

There are several key elements to pass the exam, one of which is to troubleshoot effectively.

Section 1.0: Basic Configuration

1.1: IP Addressing

1 Configure IP addresses as per the topology diagram shown in Figure 1-1.

2 Configure all the loopbacks and advertise them as per the instructions in different sections of the exercise.

3 Configure a default route on R2 to Ethernet 0/0. This will show "Gateway of last resort is 0.0.0.0" in your routing table. Propagate the default route to all other routers.

4 Configure **default-information originate always** on R2. Do not configure any static routes unless otherwise specified.

1.2: Frame Relay Configuration

1 Map only DLCIs specified in the diagram. Do **show frame-relay map** and check to see if there are any additional DLCIs dynamically populated that are not required. If so, turn off inverse-arp on that interface using the **no frame-relay inverse-arp** command.

1.3: LAN Switch Configuration

1 Configure IP address 10.10.45.45 on VLAN 45.

2 Configure a port description on the interface for identification.

3 Configure VLAN names as per the topology diagram.

4 Configure port security on all ports except port 10 (span destination port).

5 Configure a default route to 10.10.45.4 and a floating static route to 10.10.45.5 with higher admin distance for redundancy.

6 Configure an access list to permit R4, R5, and R1 and apply to vty lines. Note that you have to put two host entries for R1 for redundancy, one through R4 and another through R5; see switch configuration in the Solutions section. Test by sourcing the Telnet with Serial 2/1 and Serial 2/2 from R1 as follows:

```
r1#telnet 10.10.45.45 /source-interface Serial 2/1
r1#telnet 10.10.45.45 /source-interface Serial 2/2
```

7 Configured SPAN session and specify ports to monitor: source port 8 (PIX outside interface) and destination port 10 (sniffing interface).

8 Static route for 10.10.45.0/24 network on R1 should not be seen on any other routers.

Section 2.0: Routing Configuration

2.1: Core Routing OSPF/EIGRP/RIP

1 Configure core routing for all the above protocols on all routers in the network. Redistribute only where necessary; you must use your judgement. See the solutions below where required.

2.2: OSPF

1 There is a loopback on R3 10.50.13.97/28 in Area66. You will see this route on all participating OSPF routers but not on R5, which is running RIPv1. The RIP network between R5 and R1 is a /27. You are redistributing OSPF into RIP on R1, but it will not redistribute the /28 since it has a different mask belonging to the same major net.

2 The workaround is to summarize this in RIP on R1 to /27. Since you are restricted not to use a summarization technique, another technique to achieve this is to create a loopback on R1 with a /27 mask; this will automatically get into the RIP database, as it is the same major net. You can check this in the RIP database with **show ip rip database** on R1, and you will find the loopback as directly connected and not redistributed. This is not a good practice in real life but you can use this in lab setup.

3 It is always a good idea to hardcode the router IDs on each OSPF speaker. This way, it is easier to identify the router sending/receiving updates and troubleshoot any problems with the OSPF peers.

4 On R5, you need to enable **split-horizon** on the serial link to R1, as it is advertising the 30.0.0.0/8 route back to R1 (see the following debug output):

```
r1#debug ip routing
04:08:11: RT: network 144.144.0.0 is now variably masked
04:08:11: RT: add 144.144.0.0/16 via 10.50.13.130, rip metric [120/3]
04:08:11: RT: network 122.0.0.0 is now variably masked
04:08:11: RT: add 122.0.0.0/8 via 10.50.13.130, rip metric [120/3]
```

```
04:08:11: RT: network 13.0.0.0 is now variably masked
04:08:11: RT: add 13.0.0.0/8 via 10.50.13.130, rip metric [120/3]
04:08:11: RT: network 133.133.0.0 is now variably masked
04:08:11: RT: add 133.133.0.0/16 via 10.50.13.130, rip metric [120/3]
04:08:11: RT: network 30.0.0.0 is now variably masked
04:08:11: RT: add 30.0.0.0/8 via 10.50.13.130, rip metric [120/3]

04:08:39: RT: metric change to 144.144.0.0 via 10.50.13.130, rip metric [120/3]
           new metric [120/4]
04:08:39: RT: metric change to 122.0.0.0 via 10.50.13.130, rip metric [120/3]
           new metric [120/4]
04:08:39: RT: metric change to 13.0.0.0 via 10.50.13.130, rip metric [120/3]
           new metric [120/4]
04:08:39: RT: metric change to 133.133.0.0 via 10.50.13.130, rip metric [120/3]
           new metric [120/4]
04:08:39: RT: metric change to 30.0.0.0 via 10.50.13.130, rip metric [120/3]
           new metric [120/4]
```

Fix this by enabling split-horizon on Serial0 on R5.

Snip from R5 config:

```
interface Serial0
  ip address 10.50.13.130 255.255.255.224
  ip split-horizon
  no frame-relay inverse-arp
```

2.3: EIGRP

1 Configure EIGRP with the null routes, redistribute EIGRP into OSPF with a metric of 10, and then summarize them in OSPF to a /25 to advertise one route to all OSPF neighbors.

2.4: RIP

1 Basic RIP configuration to be done on R3, R6, and PIX using MD5 authentication. Do not configure any default route on PIX and R6. You should configure RIP on PIX to inject a default route for R3 using **rip inside default version 2 authentication md5 cisco 1**.

2 Make sure you can ping the AAA server from the PIX.

2.5: BGP

2.5.1: Basic BGP Configuration

1 Configure R1 as route-reflector server for BGP connection to R5, as it is not fully meshed. Also configure next-hop-self for R5 peer, as R1 will advertise all routes learned by iBGP peers and forward to R5 without changing the next hop, and this could cause reachability problems at times if you don't have proper routes on R5.

2 For iBGP between R3 and R6, you need to create static NAT for R6 Ethernet 10.10.6.2 to 10.50.31.22 and permit TCP port 49 on PIX for inbound connections. You will use 10.50.31.22 on R3 for BGP peer configuration.

3 It is always a good idea to hardcode the router IDs on each BGP speaker just like in the OSPF process for troubleshooting.

2.5.2: BGP Connections

1 This is a tricky one. The objective is to always build a BGP connection from outside-to-inside only. That is, R6 should not be able to build a BGP connection to R3, which it can by default since packets are going from a higher security level interface to a lower interface.

2 To achieve this task, you need to configure an ACL on the inside interface and deny R6 BGP connection to R3:

```
access-list inside deny tcp host 10.10.6.2 host 10.50.31.2 eq bgp (hitcnt=4)
```

See also the PIX output in the Solutions section.

2.5.3: BGP and OSPF

1 Another tricky question. It seems very straightforward to create loopbacks on R2 and R4. Advertise them in BGP using the **network** command, and redistribute into OSPF. All OSPF routers should see these routes.

2 Well, it is not so simple. After doing the above, check from R3 and R4 and see if you can ping using the optimal path. If you do traceroute from routers R3 and R4, you will notice that they are not taking the optimal path.

For example:

Traceroute 122.122.122.122 from R4 and you will find that it is going through R5, whereas the optimal path is via R1.

Traceroute 144.144.144.144 or 122.122.122.122 from R3 and you will find that it is not using the optimal path either.

3 The solution is to use the BGP **network backdoor** command. You can also use the **distance** command, but you are restricted to use this to achieve this task. See solutions for R3 and R4.

NOTE   Note that there is a bug with the BGP **network backdoor** command in Cisco IOS Software Release 12.1T. When you apply the command it will not take effect. See bug id CSCdr12571 for more details. The workaround is to remove using the **no network backdoor** command and reapply back in. No need to clear BGP.

2.5.4: BGP and RIP

1 Traceroute 111.111.111.111 (loopback2) from R4. You will notice that the next hop is R5 10.10.45.5 and not R1 10.50.13.81 as it is for 11.11.11.11 (loopback1). Why?

Because we advertised 111.111.111.111 in RIP and BGP on R1, which made to BGP table on R5, and since R5 was peering eBGP with R4, it overwrote the route learned on R4 via OSPF as better admin distance. To confirm, turn on **debug ip routing** on R4 and **clear ip route *** as demonstrated in the following ip routing debug snippet from R4.

```
5d23h: RT: add 111.111.111.0/24 via 10.50.13.81, ospf metric [110/5]
5d23h: RT: closer admin distance for 111.111.111.0, flushing 1 routes
5d23h: RT: add 111.111.111.0/24 via 10.10.45.5, bgp metric [20/0]
```

As you can see, it overwrites the 111.111.111.111 route learned via OSPF with BGP.

To fix this, you need to tweak the eBGP admin distance from 20 to 120 (something higher than OSPF) as follows.

Configure the **distance bgp 120 200 200** command on R4 in BGP.

Then **clear ip route *** and you will see that the OSPF route stays, as demonstrated in the following ip routing debug from R4.

```
5d23h: RT: add 111.111.111.0/24 via 10.50.13.81, ospf metric [110/5]
```

NOTE   You will not notice this problem if you have BGP "synchronization" enabled on R4; do "no sync" on R4 BGP and you will run into this problem.

2.5.5: BGP Attributes

1 Advertise loopback1 using the **network** command on R6. You are restricted to use the **network** command to advertise loopback2; you will need to redistribute connected in BGP. Create an access list and a route map to redistribute loopback2 only. After doing so, do a **show ip bgp** on R6 and you will find that the origin-code for loopback2 is incomplete, denoted by a **?**, because it has been redistributed and BGP hasn't learned this internally. To change the origin-code to denote **i**, use the **set origin igp** command in your route map:

```
access-list 16 permit 166.166.166.0 0.0.0.255
!
route-map loop2 permit 10
 match ip address 16
 set origin igp
!
router bgp 3
 no synchronization
 bgp router-id 6.6.6.6
 bgp cluster-id 2795939494
 bgp log-neighbor-changes
 network 16.16.16.0 mask 255.255.255.0
 redistribute connected metric 2 route-map loop2
```

Done? No, not yet.

Check the routing table on R3 to see if you see the R6 Loopback1 and Loopback2. Check its next hop, and which routing protocol is it learning from:

```
r3#show ip route
      16.0.0.0/24 is subnetted, 1 subnets
O E2    16.16.16.0 [110/5] via 10.50.13.1, 00:00:07, Serial1/0.1
      166.166.0.0/24 is subnetted, 1 subnets
O E2    166.166.166.0 [110/5] via 10.50.13.1, 00:00:07, Serial1/0.1
O*E2 0.0.0.0/0 [110/1] via 10.50.13.17, 00:00:07, Serial1/0.3
```

See the following debugs, which show Loopback1 and Loopback2 being learned via OSPF (10.50.13.1) and not iBGP (10.50.31.22). This is because R3 is peering eBGP with R1 and redistributing BGP into OSPF on R1. Because OSPF is peering with R3, it is learning the route via OSPF and overwriting the iBGP route learned via R6. Very complex loop!

```
r3#debug ip routing
IP routing debugging is on
r3#
4d23h: RT: closer admin distance for 16.16.16.0, flushing 1 routes
4d23h: RT: add 16.16.16.0/24 via 10.50.13.1, ospf metric [110/5]
4d23h: RT: add 122.122.122.0/24 via 10.50.13.17, ospf metric [110/786]
4d23h: RT: add 144.144.144.0/24 via 10.50.13.1, ospf metric [110/834]
4d23h: RT: closer admin distance for 166.166.166.0, flushing 1 routes
4d23h: RT: add 166.166.166.0/24 via 10.50.13.1, ospf metric [110/5]
```

To fix this, create an access list and filter the two loopbacks using distribute-list inbound in OSPF:

```
r3# show running-config
! <snip>
router ospf 110
 router-id 3.3.3.3
 distribute-list 16 in
!
r3#show access-lists
Standard IP access list 16
    deny   16.16.16.0, wildcard bits 0.0.0.255
    deny   166.166.166.0, wildcard bits 0.0.0.255
    permit any

r3#
r3#debug ip routing
IP routing debugging is on
r3# <snip>
4d23h: RT: add 16.16.16.0/24 via 10.50.31.22, bgp metric [200/2]
4d23h: RT: add 166.166.166.0/24 via 10.50.31.22, bgp metric [200/2]
```

Routes are now being learned via iBGP and not OSPF.

Ping and traceroute to verify.

Section 3.0: ISDN Configuration

3.1: Basic ISDN

1 Configure legacy BRI on R1 and R3. Configure OSPF demand circuit for redundancy on R3.

3.2: PPP Callback

1 Configure R1 as callback server and R3 as callback client. Do not configure dialer-map on R1, as it will retrieve the callback number from the AAA server.

2 Configure AAA server with username "r3" and its callback attributes. Refer to Figure 1-5 for PPP callback user profile settings on ACS.

3 As a fallback, configure PPP authentication to local and a username "r3" on R1 with callback string:

```
aaa new-model
aaa authentication ppp default group tacacs+ local
aaa authorization network default group tacacs+ local
!
username r3 callback-dialstring 99281766 password 7 094F471A1A0A
```

Figure 1-5   *PPP Callback Settings on CiscoSecure ACS*

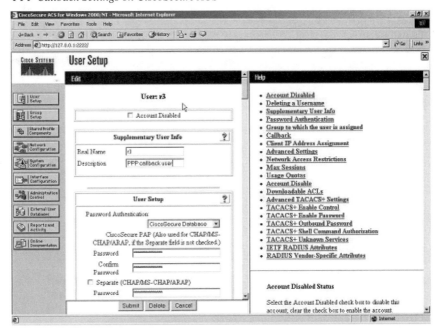

Figure 1-5 *PPP Callback Settings on CiscoSecure ACS (Continued)*

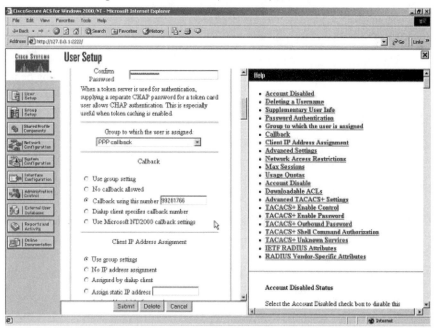

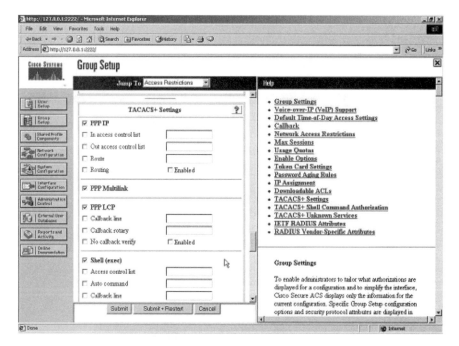

Section 4.0: PIX Configuration

4.1: Basic PIX Configuration

1 As stated earlier, do not configure a default route on PIX. It should learn it from R3 via RIP. Make sure you are able to ping all parts of the network including behind PIX.

4.2: Network Address Translation (NAT)

1 Configure a static NAT on PIX for the syslog server behind PIX.

2 Configure outside access list to open TCP port 1468 for TCP-based reliable syslog server:

```
static (inside,outside) 10.50.31.65 192.168.6.65 netmask 255.255.255.255 0 0
access-list outside permit tcp any host 10.50.31.65 eq 1468 (hitcnt=0)
```

4.3: Advanced Configuration

1 The problem is that PIX is replying for ARP request for the server mentioned. This could be due to a global or alias configured for the same IP address. The fix is to turn off proxy-arp for this interface. **sysopt noproxyarp inside** stops PIX answering for the ARP requests coming from the inside interface.

Section 5.0: IPSec/GRE Configuration

5.1: IPSec

5.1.1: IPSec LAN-to-LAN Using Preshared

1 Configure a LAN-to-LAN IPSec between the PIX and R4. The key is the interesting traffic for IPSec—the IPSec access list, which should be for UDP port 45000, the postoffice protocol communication between the IDS and Director. You can also configure an access list for UDP traffic from host to host—10.50.13.82 to 10.50.31.60.

5.1.2: Advanced IPSec LAN-to-LAN

1 Configure GRE traffic in section 5.2. IPSec access list should be host-to-host and use tunnel mode. Configure ISAKMP keepalive to check the connectivity. If the peer does not respond, phase1 SA will go down and this will also take down the phase 2 SAs.

2 Also remember to configure **no ip route-cache** on all GRE tunnels and physical interfaces where crypto map is applied.

5.2: GRE

1 This is a tricky one. Configure GRE between R3 and R6. You need to configure static translation on PIX for loopback2 to the same address for GRE tunnel on R3 to peer as the GRE destination.

2 Furthermore, modify the outside access list on PIX to allow ESP and UDP/500 from host 133.133.133.133 to 166.166.166.166. You do not need to allow GRE since the packets will be encrypted as per section 5.1.2:

```
access-list outside permit esp host 133.133.133.133 host 166.166.166.166
   (hitcnt=79166)
access-list outside permit udp host 133.133.133.133 host 166.166.166.166
   eq isakmp (hitcnt=99)
static (inside,outside) 166.166.166.166 166.166.166.166
```

3 Redistribute OSPF into EIGRP 100 with a route map to match only loopbacks in area30. The example that follows is for the redistribution configuration on R3:

```
router eigrp 100
  redistribute ospf 110 route-map o2e.
!
access-list 2 permit 30.30.1.0
access-list 2 permit 30.30.2.0
access-list 2 permit 30.30.3.0
access-list 2 permit 30.30.4.0
access-list 2 permit 30.30.5.0
access-list 2 permit 30.30.6.0
!
route-map o2e permit 10
 match ip address 2
```

We are not done yet.

Now, if you do a **show ip route** on R6, you will see that it is learning all the routes via the GRE tunnel interface as expected. See the routing table on R6:

```
r6#show ip route
Codes: C - connected, S - static, I - IGRP, R - RIP, M - mobile, B - BGP
       D - EIGRP, EX - EIGRP external, O - OSPF, IA - OSPF inter area
       N1 - OSPF NSSA external type 1, N2 - OSPF NSSA external type 2
       E1 - OSPF external type 1, E2 - OSPF external type 2, E - EGP
       i - IS-IS, L1 - IS-IS level-1, L2 - IS-IS level-2, ia - IS-IS inter area
       * - candidate default, U - per-user static route, o - ODR
       P - periodic downloaded static route

Gateway of last resort is 10.10.6.1 to network 0.0.0.0

D EX    30.30.1.0 [170/297270016] via 36.36.36.3, 00:13:47, Tunnel63
D EX    30.30.2.0 [170/297270016] via 36.36.36.3, 00:13:47, Tunnel63
D EX    30.30.3.0 [170/297270016] via 36.36.36.3, 00:13:47, Tunnel63
```

```
D EX    30.30.4.0 [170/297270016] via 36.36.36.3, 00:13:47, Tunnel63
D EX    30.30.5.0 [170/297270016] via 36.36.36.3, 00:13:47, Tunnel63
D EX    30.30.6.0 [170/297270016] via 36.36.36.3, 00:13:47, Tunnel63
R*   0.0.0.0/0 [120/1] via 10.10.6.1, 00:00:16, Ethernet0/1
```

The question requires pinging the even networks via the tunnel and odd networks via the PIX. In doing so, it is allowed to use an ACL with one line only.

The solution is "policy routing." You need to create a policy route to match the odd networks and set the next hop to the PIX inside interface—that is, 10.10.6.1—and apply it in global mode, as packets will originate from R6 when testing:

```
ip local policy route-map next-hop
!
access-list 102 permit ip any 30.30.1.0 0.0.254.255
!
route-map next-hop permit 10
  match ip address 102
  set ip next-hop 10.10.6.1
```

The way to confirm if it is working is to turn on **debug icmp trace** on PIX, and ping the odd networks. You will see the packets flowing through, but when you ping even networks, it won't show, as they will be traversing as GRE/IPSec packets and not ICMP traffic. The following example demonstrates this procedure.

```
pix# debug icmp trace
ICMP trace on
Warning: this may cause problems on busy networks

r6#ping 30.30.1.1
Type escape sequence to abort.
Sending 5, 100-byte ICMP Echos to 30.30.1.1, timeout is 2 seconds:
!!!!!
Success rate is 100 percent (5/5), round-trip min/avg/max = 104/179/200 ms

r6#ping 30.30.2.2
Type escape sequence to abort.
Sending 5, 100-byte ICMP Echos to 30.30.2.2, timeout is 2 seconds:
!!!!!
Success rate is 100 percent (5/5), round-trip min/avg/max = 8/8/8 ms

pix# debug icmp trace
ICMP trace on
Warning: this may cause problems on busy networks
pix# 190: Outbound ICMP echo request (len 72 id 58378 seq 1947) 36.36.36.6 >
    10.50.31.1 >30.30.1.1
191: Inbound  ICMP echo reply (len 72 id 17920 seq 1947) 30.30.1.1 >
    10.50.31.1 > 36.36.36.6
192: Outbound ICMP echo request (len 72 id 58634 seq 1947) 36.36.36.6 >
    10.50.31.1 > 30.30.1.1
```

```
193: Inbound  ICMP echo reply (len 72 id 18176 seq 1947) 30.30.1.1 >
     10.50.31.1 > 36.36.36.6
194: Outbound ICMP echo request (len 72 id 58890 seq 1947) 36.36.36.6 >
     10.50.31.1 > 30.30.1.1
195: Inbound  ICMP echo reply (len 72 id 18432 seq 1947) 30.30.1.1 >
     10.50.31.1 > 36.36.36.6
196: Outbound ICMP echo request (len 72 id 59146 seq 1947) 36.36.36.6 >
     10.50.31.1 > 30.30.1.1
197: Inbound  ICMP echo reply (len 72 id 18688 seq 1947) 30.30.1.1 >
     10.50.31.1 > 36.36.36.6
198: Outbound ICMP echo request (len 72 id 59402 seq 1947) 36.36.36.6 >
     10.50.31.1 > 30.30.1.1
199: Inbound  ICMP echo reply (len 72 id 18944 seq 1947) 30.30.1.1 >
     10.50.31.1 > 36.36.36.6
```

As you can see, that ping works for both the odd and even networks from R6, but ICMP packets are only seen when pinging the *odd* network, not the *even* network.

Note that the return echo-reply packets are sent back to the 36.36.36.6 IP address, which is the tunnel IP on R6.

You need to create a static route on PIX for this network, or you will notice that the odd network pings are unsuccessful.

Section 6.0: IOS Firewall Configuration

6.1: CBAC

6.1.1: Basic CBAC Configuration

1 Configure basic IOS Firewall **ip inspect** commands and inspect TCP/UDP/HTTP only. Apply inspect outbound on serial links and ingress ACL for filtering.

6.1.2: Firewall Filtering

1 Inbound ACL on serial links, permit ICMP, OSPF, BGP, and replies from TACACS+ server and host 111.111.111.111 to be able to Telnet to R2.

2 For anti-spoofing, do a **show ip route connected**. Whichever networks are listed should be denied in the ACL for source network:

```
r2#show access-lists 120
Extended IP access list 120
    deny ip 12.12.12.0 0.0.0.255 any
    deny ip 122.122.122.0 0.0.0.255 any
    deny ip 10.50.22.0 0.0.0.15 any
    permit ospf any any (73740 matches)
    permit tcp any any eq bgp (29682 matches)
```

```
permit tcp any eq bgp any (5155 matches)
permit icmp any any (314 matches)
permit tcp host 10.50.31.6 eq tacacs any (100 matches)
permit tcp host 111.111.111.111 any eq telnet (636 matches)
```

6.1.3: Advanced CBAC Configuration

1 Configure TCP embryonic (half-open) connections as follows:

`ip inspect tcp max-incomplete host 200 block-time 0`

6.2: Intrusion Detection System (IDS)

6.2.1: Basic IDS Configuration

1 Configure basic IDS on R4 using the **ip audit** command set. Use the first example that follows to configure IDS, and use the second example for logs generated when you detect an attack/signature.

NOTE   Note that communication between IDS and Director is on UDP port 45000.

```
ip audit name lab1 info action alarm
ip audit name lab1 attack action alarm
!
interface FastEthernet2/0
 ip address 10.10.45.4 255.255.255.0
 ip audit lab1 in
 ip audit lab1 out
 duplex half
```

```
6d23h: %IDS-4-ICMP_FRAGMENT_SIG: Sig:2150:Fragmented ICMP Traffic - from
    10.10.45.5 to 10.10.45.4
```

6.2.2: Signature Tuning

1 If you receive false positive alarms from the IDS on R4, you need to disable signature 3050 for host 10.50.16.5 on R4. The following example demonstrates tuning IDS signatures on R4:

```
ip audit signature 3050 list 5
!
access-list 5 deny    10.50.16.5
access-list 5 permit any
```

6.2.3: Spam Attack

1 Configure R4 protection against SMTP mail spamming using the following command:

```
ip audit smtp spam 500
```

Section 7.0: AAA

7.1: AAA on the Router

1 Configure AAA on R4 to use the TACACS+ server.

2 Configure authentication, EXEC authorization, and command-level 1/10/15 authorization.

3 Move the **show running-config** command to level 10 for user1 to be able to invoke it.

4 Configure fallback to local in the event the AAA server goes down.

5 Make sure you use a named method list and apply it to vty lines. Do not configure any authentication or authorization for console or auxiliary ports, or you will lose all marks.

6 Use the following example to configure all of the above.

```
aaa new-model
aaa authentication login vtyline group tacacs+ local
aaa authentication login con-none none
aaa authorization exec vtyexec group tacacs+ local
aaa authorization exec conexec none
aaa authorization commands 1 comm1 group tacacs+ local
aaa authorization commands 1 comm-con-none none
aaa authorization commands 10 comm10 group tacacs+ local
aaa authorization commands 10 comm-con-none none
aaa authorization commands 15 comm15 group tacacs+ local
aaa authorization commands 15 comm-con-none none
!
username user1 privilege 10 password 7 044E18031D70
username user2 privilege 15 password 7 13100417195E
!
privilege exec level 10 show run
privilege exec level 15 show!
line con 0
 exec-timeout 0 0
 authorization commands 1 comm-con-none
 authorization commands 10 comm-con-none
 authorization commands 15 comm-con-none
 authorization exec conexec
 login authentication con-none
line aux 0
 authorization commands 1 comm-con-none
```

```
      authorization commands 10 comm-con-none
      authorization commands 15 comm-con-none
      authorization exec conexec
      login authentication con-none
line vty 0 4
      authorization commands 1 comm1
      authorization commands 10 comm10
      authorization commands 15 comm15
      authorization exec vtyexec
      login authentication vtyline
      !
      end
```

7 Configure ACS with two users as follows.

User1 with privilege level 10 and permit the **show run** command. See Figure 1-6 for user settings on CiscoSecure ACS.

User2 with privilege level 15 with all commands permitted. See Figure 1-7 for user settings on CiscoSecure ACS.

8 Configure CiscoSecure ACS users above with corresponding privilege levels, so when they log in, they land in enable mode and don't need to enter **enable**. You need to configure exec authorization to achieve this task. Refer to Figure 1-6 for user1 and Figure 1-7 for user2 profile settings on ACS.

Figure 1-6 *User1 Settings on CiscoSecure ACS*

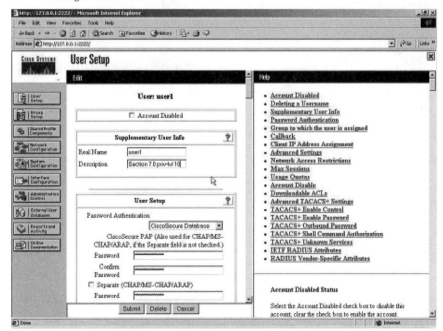

Figure 1-6 *User1 Settings on CiscoSecure ACS (Continued)*

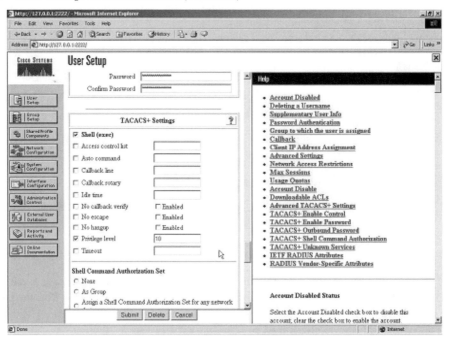

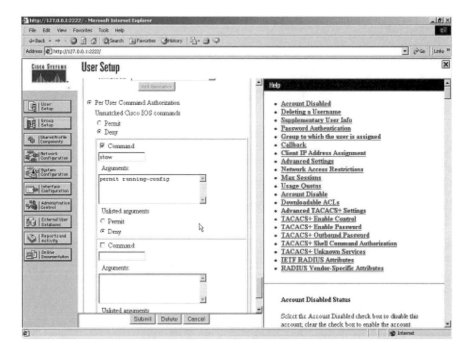

Figure 1-7   *User2 Settings on CiscoSecure ACS*

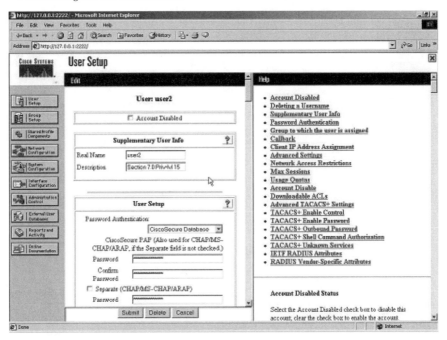

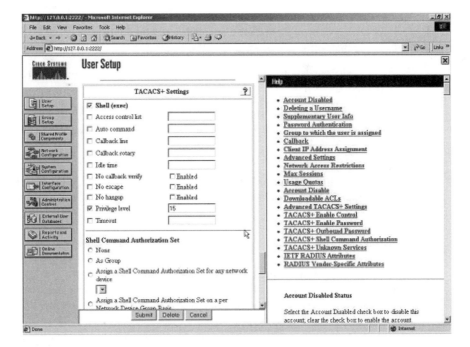

Figure 1-7 *User2 Settings on CiscoSecure ACS (Continued)*

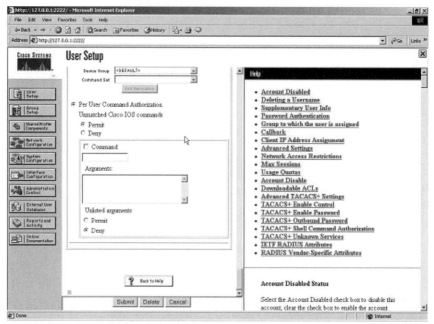

7.2: AAA on PIX

1 Configure TACACS+ authentication and authorization for Telnet service on PIX (refer to the example that follows item 3).

2 Configure static translation for Loopback1 of R6. (Refer to the example that follows item 3 to configure the PIX.)

3 Configure username **r6telnet** on ACS with Per User Command Authorization set to permit Telnet service for R6 Loopback1 only. Refer to Figure 1-8 for **r6telnet** profile settings on ACS.

```
pix# show aaa
aaa authentication include telnet outside 0.0.0.0 0.0.0.0 0.0.0.0 0.0.0.0 ACS
aaa authorization include telnet outside 0.0.0.0 0.0.0.0 0.0.0.0 0.0.0.0 ACS
pix#
pix# show aaa-server
aaa-server ACS (inside) host 192.168.6.6 cisco timeout 10
pix#
pix(config)# show access-list outside
access-list outside permit tcp any host 10.50.31.6 eq tacacs (hitcnt=103)
access-list outside permit tcp any host 16.16.16.16 eq telnet (hitcnt=7)
pix(config)# show static
static (inside,outside) 16.16.16.16 16.16.16.16 netmask 255.255.255.255 0 0
```

```
! Login capture from R3 telnetting to R6 loopback1:
r3#telnet 16.16.16.16
Trying 16.16.16.16 ... Open

Username: r6telnet
Password: r6telnet

User Access Verification
Password:
r6>en
Password:
r6#
r6#
! After successfully logging on to R6, confirm that
! authentication/authorization is working on pix;
pix# show uauth
                        Current    Most Seen
Authenticated Users        1           1
Authen In Progress         0           1
user 'r6telnet' at 10.50.31.2, authorized to:
    port 16.16.16.16/telnet
    absolute   timeout: 0:05:00
    inactivity timeout: 0:00:00
```

Figure 1-8   r6telnet *Settings on CiscoSecure ACS*

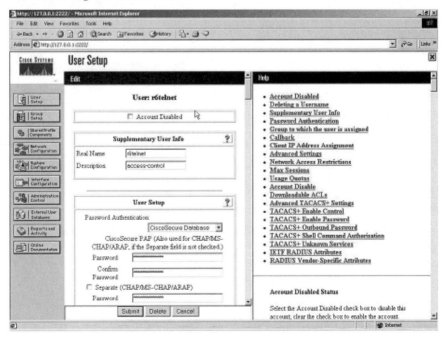

Figure 1-8 **r6telnet** *Settings on CiscoSecure ACS (Continued)*

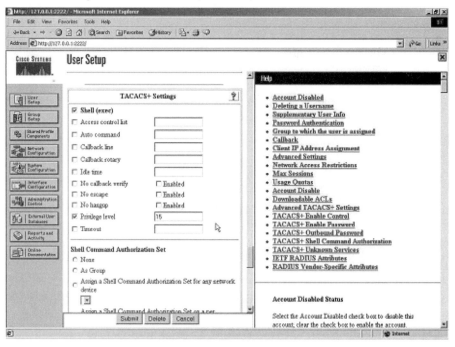

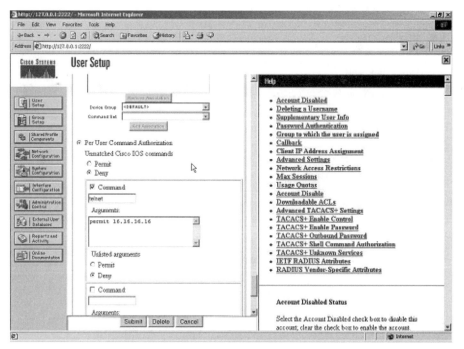

NOTE   If Shell Command Authorization Set does not appear in User Setup in ACS, go to Interface
Configuration and select TACACS+ and tick the User column for Shell (exec). See Figure 1-9.

Figure 1-9   *Interface Configuration on ACS*

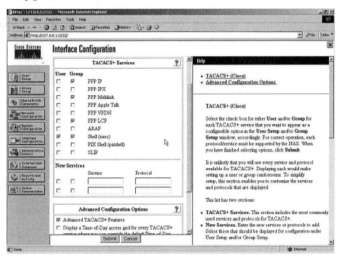

NOTE   The Reports and Activity section in CiscoSecure ACS is very useful for troubleshooting. Verify
FAILED/PASSED attempts in Reports, as shown in Figure 1-10.

Figure 1-10   *Reports and Activity in ACS*

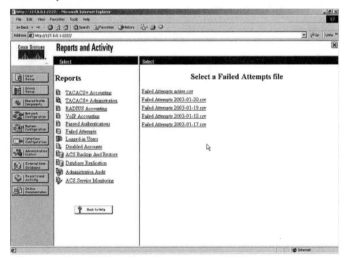

Section 8.0: Advanced Security

8.1: Password Protection

   1 Configure **service password-encryption** on all the routers to encrypt the enable password; otherwise, they will appear in clear text in the configuration.

8.2: EXEC Authentication

   1 Configure **enable secret** on R2.

   2 Configure authentication for shell EXEC without using the AAA engine using the **enable use-tacacs** command. Note that this is not TACACS+ but TACACS server (without the +). CiscoSecure ACS is not a TACACS server but TACACS+ only.

   3 Configure fallback to pass authentication in the event the TACACS server is down or not found using **enable last-resort succeed**.

8.3: Access Control

   1 In this case, you can configure **autocommand** for a user to Telnet to the router. **autocommand** will execute the required command and exit the session. This way the user will not be able to keep its Telnet session:

```
username testconfig privilege 15 password 7 15060E1F1029242A2E3A32
username testconfig autocommand show run
!
line vty 0 4
 privilege level 15
 password 7 110A1016141D
 login local
!
end
```

Test by Telnetting from R1 to 10.50.13.2.

```
r1#telnet 10.50.13.2
Trying 10.50.13.2 ... Open

User Access Verification

Username: testconfig
Password: testconfig
Building configuration...
```

```
Current configuration : 7022 bytes
!
! Last configuration change at 23:46:49 AEDT Sun Jan 19 2003
! NVRAM config last updated at 00:15:25 AEDT Mon Jan 20 2003
!
version 12.1
no service single-slot-reload-enable
service timestamps debug uptime
service timestamps log uptime
service password-encryption
!
hostname r3
!
snipped
!
end

[Connection to 10.50.13.2 closed by foreign host]
r1#
```

As you can see, as soon as the **show run** command output finished, the session was closed.

2 Configure R5 Telnet access to permit host 133.133.133.133 only:

```
access-list 3 permit 133.133.133.133
!
line vty 0 4
 access-class 3 in
 password 7 13061E010803
 login
!
end
```

Section 9.0: IP Services and Protocol-Independent Features

9.1: NAT

1 Configure NAT for Loopback3 192.168.3.1/24.

2 The objective is that when sourced from Loopback3 to anywhere on the network, it should be translated using the egress interface. For example, if you ping 122.122.122.122, it will use egress interface Serial1/0.3, whereas if you ping 144.144.144.144, it will use egress interface Serial1/0.1. If you ping 166.166.166.166, it will use egress interface FastEthernet0/0. To configure this multihomed NAT, enter the following:

```
ip nat inside source route-map fastethernet0/0 interface FastEthernet0/0
   overload
ip nat inside source route-map serial1/0.1 interface Serial1/0.1 overload
ip nat inside source route-map serial1/0.3 interface Serial1/0.3 overload
!
access-list 102 permit ip 192.168.3.0 0.0.0.255 any
!
route-map serial1/0.1 permit 10
 match ip address 102
 match interface Serial1/0.1
!
route-map serial1/0.3 permit 10
 match ip address 102
 match interface Serial1/0.3
!
route-map fastethernet0/0 permit 10
 match ip address 102
 match interface FastEthernet0/0
```

To test multihomed NAT, enter the following:

```
! "Debug ip nat" on R3 and ping 122.122.122.122, 144.144.144.144 and
   166.166.166.166
! sourcing from Loopback3:
r3#ping ip
Target IP address: 122.122.122.122
Repeat count [5]:
Datagram size [100]:
Timeout in seconds [2]:
Extended commands [n]: y
Source address or interface: loopback3
Type of service [0]:
Set DF bit in IP header? [no]:
Validate reply data? [no]:
Data pattern [0xABCD]:
Loose, Strict, Record, Timestamp, Verbose[none]:
Sweep range of sizes [n]:
Type escape sequence to abort.
Sending 5, 100-byte ICMP Echos to 122.122.122.122, timeout is 2 seconds:
!!!!!
```

```
Success rate is 100 percent (5/5), round-trip min/avg/max = 68/68/68 ms
r3#
r3#
4d14h: NAT: s=192.168.3.1->10.50.13.18, d=122.122.122.122 [195]
4d14h: NAT*: s=122.122.122.122, d=10.50.13.18->192.168.3.1 [195]
4d14h: NAT: s=192.168.3.1->10.50.13.18, d=122.122.122.122 [196]
4d14h: NAT*: s=122.122.122.122, d=10.50.13.18->192.168.3.1 [196]
4d14h: NAT: s=192.168.3.1->10.50.13.18, d=122.122.122.122 [197]
4d14h: NAT*: s=122.122.122.122, d=10.50.13.18->192.168.3.1 [197]
4d14h: NAT: s=192.168.3.1->10.50.13.18, d=122.122.122.122 [198]
4d14h: NAT*: s=122.122.122.122, d=10.50.13.18->192.168.3.1 [198]
4d14h: NAT: s=192.168.3.1->10.50.13.18, d=122.122.122.122 [199]
4d14h: NAT*: s=122.122.122.122, d=10.50.13.18->192.168.3.1 [199]
r3#
r3#
r3#ping ip
Target IP address: 144.144.144.144
Repeat count [5]:
Datagram size [100]:
Timeout in seconds [2]:
Extended commands [n]: y
Source address or interface: loopback3
Type of service [0]:
Set DF bit in IP header? [no]:
Validate reply data? [no]:
Data pattern [0xABCD]:
Loose, Strict, Record, Timestamp, Verbose[none]:
Sweep range of sizes [n]:
Type escape sequence to abort.
Sending 5, 100-byte ICMP Echos to 144.144.144.144, timeout is 2 seconds:
!!!!!
Success rate is 100 percent (5/5), round-trip min/avg/max = 96/99/101 ms
r3#
r3#
4d14h: NAT: s=192.168.3.1->10.50.13.2, d=144.144.144.144 [210]
4d14h: NAT*: s=144.144.144.144, d=10.50.13.2->192.168.3.1 [210]
4d14h: NAT: s=192.168.3.1->10.50.13.2, d=144.144.144.144 [211]
4d14h: NAT*: s=144.144.144.144, d=10.50.13.2->192.168.3.1 [211]
4d14h: NAT: s=192.168.3.1->10.50.13.2, d=144.144.144.144 [212]
4d14h: NAT*: s=144.144.144.144, d=10.50.13.2->192.168.3.1 [212]
4d14h: NAT: s=192.168.3.1->10.50.13.2, d=144.144.144.144 [213]
4d14h: NAT*: s=144.144.144.144, d=10.50.13.2->192.168.3.1 [213]
```

```
4d14h: NAT: s=192.168.3.1->10.50.13.2, d=144.144.144.144 [214]
4d14h: NAT*: s=144.144.144.144, d=10.50.13.2->192.168.3.1 [214]
r3#
r3#
r3#ping ip
Target IP address: 166.166.166.166
Repeat count [5]:
Datagram size [100]:
Timeout in seconds [2]:
Extended commands [n]: y
Source address or interface: loopback3
Type of service [0]:
Set DF bit in IP header? [no]:
Validate reply data? [no]:
Data pattern [0xABCD]:
Loose, Strict, Record, Timestamp, Verbose[none]:
Sweep range of sizes [n]:
Type escape sequence to abort.
Sending 5, 100-byte ICMP Echos to 166.166.166.166, timeout is 2 seconds:
!!!!!
Success rate is 100 percent (5/5), round-trip min/avg/max = 4/4/4 ms
r3#
r3#
4d14h: NAT: s=192.168.3.1->10.50.31.2, d=166.166.166.166 [205]
4d14h: NAT*: s=166.166.166.166, d=10.50.31.2->192.168.3.1 [205]
4d14h: NAT: s=192.168.3.1->10.50.31.2, d=166.166.166.166 [206]
4d14h: NAT*: s=166.166.166.166, d=10.50.31.2->192.168.3.1 [206]
4d14h: NAT: s=192.168.3.1->10.50.31.2, d=166.166.166.166 [207]
4d14h: NAT*: s=166.166.166.166, d=10.50.31.2->192.168.3.1 [207]
4d14h: NAT: s=192.168.3.1->10.50.31.2, d=166.166.166.166 [208]
4d14h: NAT*: s=166.166.166.166, d=10.50.31.2->192.168.3.1 [208]
4d14h: NAT: s=192.168.3.1->10.50.31.2, d=166.166.166.166 [209]
4d14h: NAT*: s=166.166.166.166, d=10.50.31.2->192.168.3.1 [209]
```

The preceding test from R3 confirms NATing loopback3 with respective egress interface as per the route map:

Ping 122.122.122.122 NATed with 10.50.13.18 egress Serial1/0.3

Ping 144.144.144.144 NATed with 10.50.13.2 egress Serial1/0.1

Ping 166.166.166.166 NATed with 10.50.31.2 egress FastEthernet0/0

9.2: NTP

1 Configure R2 as NTP Server and R1 as NTP Client.

2 Configure authentication using the md5 key. NTP status and authentication on R2 is as follows:

```
r1# show ntp status
Clock is synchronized, stratum 9, reference is 10.50.13.34
nominal freq is 250.0000 Hz, actual freq is 250.0000 Hz, precision is 2**24
reference time is C1D5BFAA.20689871 (00:22:02.126 UTC Mon Jan 20 2003)
clock offset is 1.6778 msec, root delay is 64.39 msec
root dispersion is 126.82 msec, peer dispersion is 0.12 msec
r1#
r1#
r1#show ntp associations detail
10.50.13.34 configured, authenticated, our_master, sane, valid, stratum 8
ref ID 127.127.7.1, time C1D5BF88.FE740124 (00:21:28.993 UTC Mon Jan 20 2003)
our mode client, peer mode server, our poll intvl 64, peer poll intvl 64
root delay 0.00 msec, root disp 125.03, reach 377, sync dist 157.349
delay 64.39 msec, offset 1.6778 msec, dispersion 0.12
precision 2**16, version 3
org time C1D5BFAA.188E6A78 (00:22:02.095 UTC Mon Jan 20 2003)
rcv time C1D5BFAA.20689871 (00:22:02.126 UTC Mon Jan 20 2003)
xmt time C1D5BFAA.0FC3685F (00:22:02.061 UTC Mon Jan 20 2003)
filtdelay =    64.67    64.39    64.50    64.45    64.67    64.39    64.80    67.99
filtoffset =    1.66     1.68     1.60     1.55     1.57     1.55     1.66    -0.13
filterror =     0.02     0.03     0.05     0.06     0.08     0.09     0.11     0.12
r1#
r1#
r1#show clock
00:25:19.586 UTC Mon Jan 20 2003
r1#
r1#
```

3 In some IOS it is necessary to enter the NTP authentication commands in a particular order. Below is the exact order that confirms operation:

For R2 (master) enter commands in the following sequence:

```
ntp authentication-key 1 md5 cisco
ntp master 2
```

For R1 (Client) enter commands in the following sequence:

```
ntp authentication-key 1 md5 cisco
ntp authenticate
```

```
ntp trusted-key 1
ntp server 10.50.13.34 key 1
```

4 Remember that you have an inbound access list applied to the serial link on R2; you need
to allow NTP.

9.3: SNMP

1 Configure R3 to send SNMP traps when a configuration change happens for BGP:

```
snmp-server community public RO
snmp-server community private RW
snmp-server enable traps config
snmp-server enable traps bgp
snmp-server host 10.50.31.99 public  config bgp


! snip from R3 test using debug snmp packet;

r3#debug snmp packets
SNMP packet debugging is on
r3#
r3#config terminal
Enter configuration commands, one per line.  End with CNTL/Z.
r3(config)#
r3(config)#
5d00h: SNMP: Queuing packet to 10.50.31.99
5d00h: SNMP: V1 Trap, ent ciscoConfigManMIB.2, addr 10.50.31.2, gentrap 6,
    spectrap 1
 ccmHistoryEventEntry.3.162 = 1
 ccmHistoryEventEntry.4.162 = 2
 ccmHistoryEventEntry.5.162 = 3
5d00h: SNMP: Packet sent via UDP to 10.50.31.99
r3(config)#
r3(config)#end
r3#
r3#clear ip bgp *
r3#
5d00h: %BGP-5-ADJCHANGE: neighbor 10.50.13.1 Down User reset
5d00h: SNMP: Queuing packet to 10.50.31.99
5d00h: SNMP: V1 Trap, ent bgp, addr 10.50.31.2, gentrap 6, spectrap 2
 bgpPeerEntry.14.10.50.13.1 = 00 00
 bgpPeerEntry.2.10.50.13.1 = 1
5d00h: %BGP-5-ADJCHANGE: neighbor 10.50.13.17 Down User reset
```

```
5d00h: SNMP: Queuing packet to 10.50.31.99
5d00h: SNMP: V1 Trap, ent bgp, addr 10.50.31.2, gentrap 6, spectrap 2
 bgpPeerEntry.14.10.50.13.17 = 00 00
 bgpPeerEntry.2.10.50.13.17 = 1
5d00h: %BGP-5-ADJCHANGE: neighbor 10.50.31.22 Down User reset
r3#
5d00h: SNMP: Queuing packet to 10.50.31.99
5d00h: SNMP: V1 Trap, ent bgp, addr 10.50.31.2, gentrap 6, spectrap 2
 bgpPeerEntry.14.10.50.31.22 = 04 00
 bgpPeerEntry.2.10.50.31.22 = 1
5d00h: SNMP: Packet sent via UDP to 10.50.31.99
5d00h: SNMP: Packet sent via UDP to 10.50.31.99
5d00h: SNMP: Packet sent via UDP to 10.50.31.99
r3#
r3#
! Snip from PIX config and ACL;
pix# show access-list outside
access-list outside permit udp host 10.50.31.2 host 10.50.31.99 eq snmptrap
  (hitcnt=44)
pix# show static
static (inside,outside) 10.50.31.99 192.168.6.99 netmask 255.255.255.255 0 0
pix#
```

9.4: Policy Routing

1 Configure policy routing on R1 to change the next hop for mail and web server off R3:

```
interface Serial2/0.2 point-to-point
 ip address 10.50.13.33 255.255.255.240
 ip policy route-map server
!
interface Serial2/0.3 point-to-point
 ip address 10.50.13.1 255.255.255.240
 ip policy route-map server
!
!
ip local policy route-map server
!
access-list 101 permit ip any host 10.50.31.98
access-list 102 permit ip any host 10.50.31.99
!
route-map server permit 10
```

```
 match ip address 101
 set ip next-hop 10.50.13.34
 !
route-map server permit 20
 match ip address 102
 set ip next-hop 10.50.13.2
 !
route-map server permit 30
```

```
! Verify with traceroute;
r1#traceroute 10.50.31.98
Type escape sequence to abort.
Tracing the route to 10.50.31.98

  1 10.50.13.34 !A  *   !A
```

```
r1#traceroute 10.50.31.99
Type escape sequence to abort.
Tracing the route to 10.50.31.99

  1 10.50.13.2 32 msec 32 msec 32 msec
  2 *  *  *
```

Section 10.0: Security Violations

10.1: Denial of Service—DoS

   1 Configure CAR (rate-limit) on R3 to prevent ICMP flooding:

```
interface Serial1/0.1 point-to-point
 ip address 10.50.13.2 255.255.255.240
 rate-limit input access-group 110 560000 256000 384000 conform-action
   continue exceed-action drop
 !
interface Serial1/0.3 point-to-point
 ip address 10.50.13.18 255.255.255.240
 rate-limit input access-group 110 560000 256000 384000 conform-action
   continue exceed-action drop
    !
access-list 110 permit icmp any any
```

10.2: IP Spoofing

1 Configure Unicast RPF IP spoofing protection on PIX for inside and outside interfaces:

```
pix# show ip verify
ip verify reverse-path interface outside
ip verify reverse-path interface inside
```

CHAPTER 2

Practice Lab 2

Now that you have completed the first lab in Chapter 1, Practice Lab 1, you might have a fair understanding of how the CCIE test is laid out and how to approach it. But, of course, this is just a practice test, and you should not assume that the questions, design, layout, or structure of the test match the real CCIE test. These labs are close to the real labs, but not exactly the same.

This lab is also a multiprotocol, multitechnology lab, just as in Chapter 1, and you will be tested on all areas. The degree of complexity in each lab has been maintained at the same level.

The lab topology is different than Chapter 1, with two more routers added to this lab.

Use the "Verification, Hints, and Troubleshooting Tips" section to build up troubleshooting skills and learn how to identify problems and resolve them.

The lab is composed of 100 marks. To pass the lab, you must complete the lab within 8 hours and obtain a minimum of 80 marks to pass. As with all other labs, this test has been written such that you should be able to complete all questions, including initial configuration (such as IP addressing), within 8 hours; this excludes cabling time. Allow up to 1 hour for cabling, and follow the cabling instructions in the "Cabling Instructions" section and observe the instructions in the "General Guidelines" section. You can use any combination of routers as long as you fulfill the topology diagram in Figure 2-1. It is not compulsory to use the same model of routers.

NOTE	The real CCIE Lab does not require you to do any cabling or the IP addressing.

Equipment List

- 8 routers with the following specifications (all routers are to be loaded with the latest Cisco IOS version in 12.1(T) train):

    R1 — 2 serial, 1 Ethernet (with IP Plus image)

    R2 — 1 serial, 2 Ethernet (with IP Plus image)

    R3 — 2 Ethernet (with IP Plus image)

    R4 — 1 serial, 1 BRI (with IP Plus + IPSec 56 image)

    R5 — 1 serial, 1 Ethernet (with IP Plus + Firewall image)

> R6 — 1 serial, 1 Ethernet, 1 BRI (with IP Plus + IPSec 56 image)
>
> R7 — 1 Ethernet (with IP Plus image)
>
> R8 — 3 serial, 1 Ethernet (with IP Plus + IPSec 56 image)

- 1 3550 switch
- 1 PIX: 2 interfaces (with version 6.1.4 with DES enabled)
- 2 PCs:

  Windows 2000 Server with CiscoSecure ACS 3.0+ installed

  Test PC (Windows 95/98/2000) with CiscoSecure VPN Client 3.x installed

General Guidelines

- Do not configure any static/default routes unless otherwise specified/required.
- Use DLCIs provided in the diagram.
- Use the IP addressing scheme provided in the diagram; do not change any IP addressing unless otherwise specified. In the CCIE Lab, initial configurations are loaded, and therefore IP addresses are not to be changed. In this book, each chapter has a separate lab topology with different IP addressing, so each chapter needs to be recabled and all IP addresses need to be redone from the previous chapter.
- Use **cisco** as the password for any authentication string, enable-password, and TACACS+/ RADIUS key or for any other purpose unless otherwise specified.
- Add additional loopbacks as specified during this lab.
- Configure VLANs on Switch1 as per the diagram.
- All routers should be able to ping any interface in the network using the *optimal* path.
- You must time yourself to complete this lab in 8 hours.
- The lab has 100 marks total, and you require 80 marks to pass. Each section is indicated with marks.
- Do not use any external resources or answers provided in this book when attempting the lab.
- Configure fallback for any of the AAA questions below to the local database. If you don't, you will lose all points for that question.
- Do not configure any authentication or authorization on the console and aux ports.

NOTE   The real CCIE lab exams are hands-on structures similar to this book. Each configuration exercise has preassigned point values. The candidate must obtain a minimum mark of 80% to pass. This book provides you with a similar structure to give you a better understanding and experience. For more information on CCIE exam structure, refer to the following URLs:

www.cisco.com/en/US/partner/learning/le3/le2/le23/learning_certification_level_home.html

www.cisco.com/warp/customer/625/ccie/exam_preparation/preparation.html

---

Setting Up the Lab

You can use any combination of routers as long as you fulfill the topology diagram outlined in Figure 2-1. It is not compulsory to use the same model of routers.

Figure 2-1 *Lab Topology Diagram*

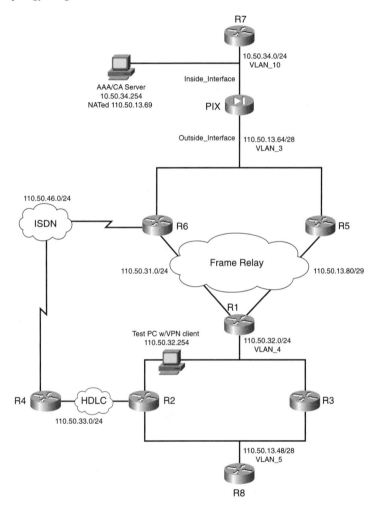

Frame Relay DLCI Information

Configure R8 as a Frame Relay switch and use Figure 2-2 for DLCI information. Only DLCIs indicated in Figure 2-2 should be mapped on the routers.

Routing Protocol Information

Use Figure 2-3 to configure routing protocols for the exercises to follow.

Figure 2-2 *Frame Relay DLCI Diagram*

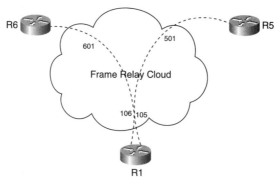

Figure 2-3 *Routing Protocol Information*

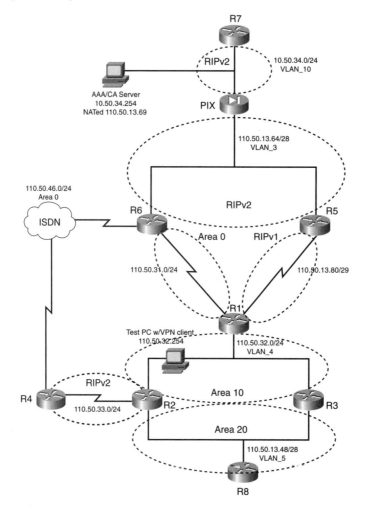

BGP Information

Use Figure 2-4 to configure BGP.

Figure 2-4   *BGP Information*

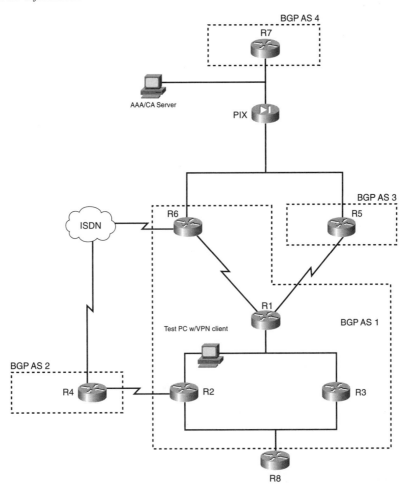

Cabling Instructions

Use Tables 2-1 and 2-2 for cabling all devices in your topology. It is not a must to use the same type or sequence of interface. You may use any combination of interfaces as long as you fulfill the requirement.

Table 2-1   *Cabling Instructions (Ethernet)*

Ethernet Cabling	Switch1
R1-fastethernet2/0	Port 1
R2-ethernet0/0 VLAN_4	Port 2
R2-ethernet0/1 VLAN_5	Port 3
R3-ethernet0/0 VLAN_4	Port 4
R3-ethernet0/1 VLAN_5	Port 5
R5-ethernet0	Port 6
R6-fastethernet0/0	Port 7
PIX-outside-ethernet0	Port 8
PIX-inside-ethernet1	Port 9
R7-fastethernet0/0	Port 10
AAA server	Port 11
R8-ethernet0/0	Port 12
Test PC	Port 13

Table 2-2   *Cabling Instructions (Serial)*

Back-to-Back Cabling	DTE-End	DCE-End
R1-to-frsw* (to r5/r6)	R1-serial3/0	R8-serial1/0
R5-to-frsw* (to r1)	R5-serial0	R8-serial1/1
R6-to-frsw* (to r1)	R6-serial1/0	R8-serial1/2
R2-to-R4	R4-serial2/0	R2-serial1/0

*frsw = Frame Relay switch R8

Practice Lab 2 Exercises

As you start Lab 2, remember that each section is indicated with corresponding points. Gauge the value of the question by its points and complexity, and spend adequate time on it. Do not waste time on a section when you get stuck; you must learn to move on and attend to problem sections later on.

The steps in each exercise are not necessarily intended to be completed in order. They can be done in any order of preference or as you feel appropriate. There may be situations where intentionally the steps have been written in incorrect order to cause a problem. You have to identify the best approach and fulfill all the requirements.

Section 1.0: Basic Configuration (10 points)

1.1: IP Addressing (2 points)

1 Redraw a detailed topology with all the necessary information.

2 Configure IP addressing as per the topology diagram in Figure 2-1.

3 Do not configure any static or default routes anywhere on the network unless otherwise specified. Configure a default route on R8 to null0. R8 is the perimeter router in this network. Populate this default route to all the routers.

4 Create the following loopbacks:

Loopback-1 11.11.11.11/24 on R1

Loopback-1 12.12.12.12/24 on R2

Loopback-1 13.13.13.13/24 on R3

Loopback-2 13.14.13.13/24 on R3

Loopback-1 14.14.14.14/24 on R4

Loopback-2 144.144.144.144/24 on R4

Loopback-1 15.15.15.15/24 on R5

Loopback-1 16.16.16.16/24 on R6

Loopback-1 17.17.17.17/24 on R7

Loopback-1 18.18.18.18/24 on R8

1.2: Frame Relay Configuration (4 points)

1 Configure R8 as a Frame Relay switch, using the DLCI information provided for Frame Relay routing in Figure 2-2.

2 Configure Frame Relay between R1, R5, and R6.

3 Configure subinterfaces on R1.

4 Do not configure subinterface on R5 and R6.

5 Use only the DLCIs provided in Figure 2-2. No dynamic DLCIs are allowed for this exercise.

1.3: LAN Switch Configuration (4 points)

1 Configure Switch1 with the VLAN information provided in the topology diagram in Figure 2-1.

2 Configure the switch management interface to be in VLAN_10 with IP address 10.50.34.10. All devices on the network should be able to ping the management interface.

3 Configure static NAT to 110.50.13.68 on PIX to achieve this task.

4 Configure MAC restriction such that only PIX interfaces e0 and e1 are connected to ports 8 and 9 of the switch. If any device other than PIX is connected to these ports, the switch should shut down the ports.

5 R2 and R3 are experiencing a broadcast storm on VLAN_4. Packets are flooding the LAN, creating excessive traffic and degrading network performance. Configure traffic suppression level 50 on the switch to prevent this.

Section 2.0: Routing Configuration (25 points)

2.1: OSPF (7 points)

1 Configure OSPF as shown in Figure 2-3.

2 Configure strong authentication for all areas.

3 Configure R1-R6 and Loopback1 on R6 in Area0. All routers should see this loopback.

4 Configure R1-R2-R3 in Area10.

5 Configure R2-R3-R8 in Area20. Add Loopback1 on R8 in Area20.

6 This is already configured as of point 15.

7 Configure OSPF redundancy and high availability for Area10 such that R1 has connectivity to R8 in the event of failure of R2 or R3. R1 should form adjacency to one router only in Area10 at any given time (such as R2 or R3), as the other router is supposed to be Standby. Verify OSPF adjacency and the routing table on R1 and R8 when you shut down Ethernet0/1 on R2. Do not use any static routes to achieve this task.

8 Ensure that the Area20 network appears in the routing table on all routers.

9 Redistribute OSPF/RIP as appropriate on R1, R2, and R6.

10 Filter on R1 such that R3 can ping the loopback-1 on R5 but not the Ethernet. The route for Ethernet should be visible. All other traffic should pass normally. Do not configure ACL on R3 or R5 to achieve this task.

2.2: EIGRP (3 points)

1 Configure loopback-1 and loopback-2 on R3 in EIGRP-200. Summarize such that all routers see only one route for these. All routers should see the summarized route.

2 Redistribute EIGRP into OSPF with a metric of 10 on all routers. All routers should see this route in the routing table.

2.3: RIP (5 points)

1 Configure RIPv2 between R2-R4. Put Loopback-1 and Loopback-2 on R4 in RIP.

2 Configure RIPv1 between R1 and R5.

3 Configure RIPv2 between R7 and PIX.

4 Configure RIPv2 between R5, R6, and PIX.

5 Configure simple authentication for RIPv2 peers.

6 Advertise the default route to all peers in the network.

7 Advertise loopback-1 on R5 and R7.

8 Redistribute between RIP/OSPF where necessary.

9 All routers should be able to ping above loopbacks using the optimal path.

2.4: BGP (10 points)

2.4.1: Basic BGP Configuration (4 points)

1 Configure BGP as shown in the BGP information diagram in Figure 2-4.

2 Configure AS1 peers R1, R2, R3, and R6. Only one neighbor statement is allowed on R2, R3, and R6. Use private AS-numbers to achieve this task.

3 Private AS-numbers should not appear on AS2, AS3, and AS4 peers.

4 Configure authentication in AS1.

5 Configure R4 to peer with R6 using Loopback1 on each end.

6 Configure R1 to peer with R5. R5 should receive a default route via BGP only.

7 Redistribute BGP into OSPF on R2 and R3.

2.4.2: Multi-Homed BGP Setup (2 points)

1 Configure R7 to peer with two different service providers, such as R5 and R6. Use Loopback-1 as the source. You may put a static route on R5 and R6 for R7 Loopback-1. Create static translation and ACL on PIX to achieve this task.

2 Take necessary measures to prevent any route leaking between service providers.

2.4.3: BGP Route Filtering (2 points)

1 Advertise loopback-2 on R4 in BGP and RIPv2.

2 AS3 should not see any routes from AS2. Do not use as-path, filter-list, or prefix-list on any peers to achieve this task.

3 Do not configure any method on R4 to achieve this task.

2.4.4: BGP Route Selection (2 points)

1 Advertise loopback-1 on R1 and R2 in BGP.

2 AS4 should prefer R5 to reach loopback-1 on R1 and R6 to reach loopback-1 on R2. Do not use weight or MED to achieve this task.

3 Advertise loopback-1 on R7 in BGP; do not use the **network** command to achieve this task.

4 All routers should be able to ping these loopbacks.

Section 3.0: ISDN Configuration (7 points)

3.1: Basic ISDN (4 points)

1 Configure ISDN on R4 and R6.

2 Use network 110.50.46.0/24.

3 Advertise the ISDN network in OSPF Area0.

4 Do not configure any legacy commands on R4.

ISDN information:

BRI number on R4 is 99047132

BRI number on R6 is 99047265

Switch-type = basic-net3

3.2: PPP Authentication and Multilink (3 points)

1 Configure PPP authentication and authorization using the local database on the router. Do not configure AAA on R6.

2 R6 should use host name "LAB2" for CHAP authentication.

3 Configure ISDN to bring up a second B channel on 1 percent for load in any direction.

Section 4.0: PIX Configuration (5 points)

4.1: Basic PIX Configuration (3 points)

1 Configure host name PIX.

2 Configure outside IP address 110.50.13.67/28.

3 Configure inside IP address 10.50.34.1/24.

4 Configure RIP on inside and outside interfaces as shown in the diagram.

5 Configure simple authentication for RIPv2.

6 You should be able to ping Loopback1 on R7.

7 Make sure you can ping the AAA server and the switch management interface.

8 Do not use conduit statements on PIX.

4.2: Network Address Translation (NAT) (2 points)

1 You should receive RIP route(s) from R7. Configure network address translation such that devices on the outside of PIX can ping this loopback1 address of R7 as is. You are allowed to add a static route for this on R5 and R6 only. R1 should learn this route via BGP.

2 Configure static NAT for AAA server 10.50.34.254 to 110.50.13.69.

3 Configure static NAT for Switch Management Interface 10.50.34.10 to 110.50.13.68.

4 All networks behind PIX should be able to go out to the Internet. Hide these networks with the IP address of the outside interface.

Section 5.0: IPSec/GRE Configuration (15 points)

5.1: IPSec (10 points)

5.1.1: IPSec Remote Access Using Preshared Key (3 points)

1 Configure the remote-access VPN on PIX for clients coming from the outside network.

2 Configure extended authentication using RADIUS.

3 Assign the IP address, WINS, and DNS from PIX.

4 Assign IP from VPNPool of 172.16.1.0/24.

    5 Assign WINS server IP is 200.200.200.200.

    6 Assign DNS server IP is 200.200.200.201.

    7 Configure group name **lab2** and password **cisco.**

    8 Test PC should use the tunnel to reach networks behind PIX only.

    9 Verify from Test PC in VLAN-4 by pinging AAA server 10.50.34.254.

    10 Make sure you have a route on Test PC for 110.50.13.64/28 pointing to 110.50.32.1.

5.1.2: IPSec LAN-to-LAN Using Preshared Key (3 points)

    1 Encrypt GRE traffic in section 5.2.

    2 Use the preshared authentication method. Configure all other parameters as you feel appropriate.

5.1.3: IPSec Redundancy (4 points)

    1 Configure IPSec redundancy such that if any interface(s) on R6 goes down, IPSec traffic continues normally via the ISDN link.

    2 R6 should not trigger the call.

    3 R4 must call R6 and maintain a connection.

5.2: GRE (5 points)

    1 Configure the following private networks on R4, R6, and R8:

    Loopback-10 on R4: 10.1.4.1/24

    Loopback-10 on R6: 10.1.6.1/24

    Loopback-10 on R8: 10.1.8.1/24

    2 Configure GRE between R4, R6, and R8. Run EIGRP-100 to advertise private networks. These networks should not be visible on any other routers.

Section 6.0: IOS Firewall Configuration (8 points)

6.1: Context-Based Access Control (CBAC) (4 points)

    1 Configure the firewall on R5 to protect VLAN_3 for TCP and UDP traffic.

2 Use Network Ingress Filtering and anti-spoofing techniques defeating DoS attacks as per RFC 1918 and 2267.

3 Configure CBAC to inspect the custom application traffic in Section 6.2.

6.2: Port to Application Mapping (PAM) (4 points)

1 Your organization has a custom HTTP-based application server on VLAN_5, which is listening on ports 8080 through 8083. It has built-in security to listen to different ports for requests from different source IPs.

2 Configure R5 such that hosts 110.50.13.70 and 110.50.13.71 are able to use ports 8080, 8081 and ports 8082, 8083, respectively, to access this application.

Section 7.0: AAA (7 points)

7.1: AAA on the Router (3 points)

1 Configure R2 authentication and authorization using TACACS+.

2 Use Loopback-1 as source.

3 Configure username **r2-telnet** on ACS with privilege level 5.

4 Configure command authorization for level 5 users to be able to configure interface-specific commands. Log all commands for level 5 user.

5 Console and Aux should not be affected by any of the authentication/authorization process.

7.2: AAA on the Switch (4 points)

1 Configure Telnet access to the switch from anywhere on the network.

2 Configure authentication, authorization, and accounting using RADIUS.

3 Configure accounting such that we can bill user **sw2** for the time logged onto the switch.

4 Log all commands.

5 Configure username **sw2** on ACS with privilege level 15.

6 Verify ACS logs that you see logged-in user(s) and the commands being used.

7 Console and Aux should not be affected by any of the authentication/authorization process.

Section 8.0: Advanced Security (8 points)

8.1: Perimeter Security (3 points)

1 The Internet uplink on R8 is under heavy load, resulting in less time allocation to handle the routing protocols, and priority to system-level processes. Upon investigation, it seems some fast packet flood is causing this condition. Your task is to lower this effect by configuring 20 percent of the CPU available to process system-level tasks.

2 Users on VLAN_5 are complaining of slow response for TCP-based connections. At the same time, UDP-based connections are good and having no problems. As per RFC 896, configure Nagle congestion control algorithm on R8 to alleviate the small-packet problem in TCP.

8.2: Router Management Using HTTP (3 points)

1 Configure HTTP for router management on R1. Restrict access to Test PC in VLAN_4 only.

2 Configure TACACS+ to authenticate username **r1-http** for this.

3 Source all TACACS+ requests with Loopback-1.

8.3: Access Control (2 points)

1 Configure access control on R3 such that the router administrator always has the ability to Telnet, using password **cisco123**.

2 Do not use the **ip access-class** command to achieve this task.

3   All other users should continue to have Telnet access to R3. Note that all other users must use the default password **cisco** for Telnet.

4 Do not configure AAA or define any local username to achieve this task.

Section 9.0: IP Services and Protocol-Independent Features (10 points)

9.1: NAT (3 points)

1 Configure network address translation on R4, R6, and R8 for private networks to communicate with public networks.

2 Configure PAT using the next IP address of the egress interface subnet.

3 No network address translation should occur when communicating between private networks.

9.2: NTP (3 points)

1   R1 should update its clock from R2.

2   R3 should dynamically synchronize with R1. Do not configure any NTP server statement on R3 to achieve this task.

3   Configure strong authentication between NTP peers.

4   Use Loopback-1 for NTP updates.

9.3: Traffic Shaping (2 points)

1   The Frame Relay link on R1 with DLCI 106 is experiencing heavy congestion. This is resulting in OSPF losing neighbor relationships.

2   Configure R1 such that the Frame Relay provider does not drop any OSPF packets during congestion.

9.4: HSRP (2 points)

1   Configure secure HSRP on VLAN_4.

2   R2 should be ACTIVE with a higher priority than R3.

3   Configure such that if Ethernet0/1 of VLAN_5 on R2 goes down, HSRP fails over to R3. When the Ethernet comes UP, R2 should take the active role immediately.

Section 10.0: Security Violations (6 points)

10.1: Denial of Service (DoS) (3 points)

1   R1 is experiencing a Denial-of-Service attack from the Internet. Upon investigation by collecting sniffer traces on VLAN_4, it was found that the packets arriving are noninitial IP fragments; packets have FO > 0 with the MF bit set, to a web server 110.50.13.72 in VLAN_3 on port 80. You do not want to allow any fragments to reach the web server. Allow only nonfragmented packets to reach the web server.

10.2: IP Spoofing (3 points)

1   Simulate a DoS attack from R3 to R8 with ICMP floods, using R2 as a reflector. Use the necessary Loopback-1 for source and destination address as appropriate.

2 Once you are successful in the above penetration test, configure such that the attack is blocked and make sure you are unsuccessful when you attempt an attack again. Do not use CAR or anti-spoofing ACL methods to achieve this task.

Verification, Hints, and Troubleshooting Tips

This is a very important section in this book. It helps you troubleshoot problems and verify answers. There are lots of hidden tricks and problems within the exercise for which there are numerous methods to troubleshoot, as there is no set formula or way to do this. The best method to use is the one you feel comfortable using. Having said that, you can use the troubleshooting methodology in this book. Get familiar with the **debug** and **show** commands used in this section, as they are very handy.

The hints provided in each section below are not necessarily in order of the question. They have been provided as a guideline and address some or all parts of the corresponding exercise question. The key element to succeess is to quickly and easily ensure you get it right the first time.

Section 1.0: Basic Configuration

1.1: IP Addressing

1 Configure IP addressing as shown in the topology diagram in Figure 2-1.

2 Configure all the loopbacks and advertise them as per instructions in different sections of the exercise.

3 Configure a default route on R8 to null0. Propagate the default route to all other routers. Configure "default-information originate always" on R8. Do not configure any static routes unless otherwise specified.

1.2: Frame Relay Configuration

1 Configure R8 as a Frame Relay switch.

2 Do not configure subinterfaces on R5 and R6. By default, Frame Relay inverse-arp is enabled. Since R5 and R6 are using the main interface, they will map dynamic DLCIs along with the static DLCI. You need to disable inverse-arp on these interfaces.

3 No additional DLCIs should be mapped on R5 and R6 other than the static configured on the serial interface. Example 2-1 shows a comparison between inverse-arp enabled and disabled.

Example 2-1   **show** *Outputs from R5 and R6*

```
! DLCI mapping(s) when Inverse-arp enabled on R5 (by default)
r5# show frame-relay map
Serial0 (up): ip 0.0.0.0 dlci 501(0x1F5,0x7C50)
                broadcast,
                CISCO, status defined, active
Serial0 (up): ip 110.50.13.81 dlci 501(0x1F5,0x7C50), static,
                broadcast,
                CISCO, status defined, active
! DLCI mapping(s) after Inverse-arp disabled using "no frame-relay inverse-arp" on R5
r5# show frame-relay map
Serial0 (up): ip 110.50.13.81 dlci 501(0x1F5,0x7C50), static,
                broadcast,
                CISCO, status defined, active
! DLCI mapping(s) when Inverse-arp enabled on R6 (by default)
r6#show frame-relay map
Serial1/0 (up): ip 110.50.31.1 dlci 601(0x259,0x9490), static,
                broadcast,
                CISCO, status defined, active
Serial1/0 (up): ip 0.0.0.0 dlci 601(0x259,0x9490)
                broadcast,
                CISCO, status defined, active
! DLCI mapping(s) after Inverse-arp disabled using "no frame-relay inverse-arp" on R6
r6#show frame-relay map
Serial1/0 (up): ip 110.50.31.1 dlci 601(0x259,0x9490), static,
                broadcast,
                CISCO, status defined, active
! DLCI mapping(s) on R1, having point-to-point sub-interfaces.
r1#show frame-relay map
Serial0/0.5 (up): point-to-point dlci, dlci 105(0x69,0x1890), broadcast
            status defined, active
Serial0/0.6 (up): point-to-point dlci, dlci 106(0x6A,0x18A0), broadcast
            status defined, active
```

NOTE   You need to **shut** and **no shut** after disabling inverse-arp for changes to take effect.

1.3: LAN Switch Configuration

1 Configure all VLANs on the switch as per the topology diagram in Figure 2-1.

2 Configure the switch management interface in VLAN_10 with IP address 10.50.34.10/24.

3 Configure static NAT and ACL entries on PIX to 110.50.13.68 for all devices in the network to be able to Telnet the switch.

4 Configure port security on Fastethernet 0/8 and 0/9 for PIX outside and inside MAC addresses. Verify the MAC address on PIX. See Example 2-2.

5 Configure storm control on Fastethernet 0/2 and 0/4. See Example 2-2.

NOTE	For more info on the **storm-control** command, see www.cisco.com/univercd/cc/td/doc/product/lan/c3550/12112cea/3550scg/swtrafc.htm#xtocid1

Example 2-2 *Snip from Switch1 Configuration*

```
interface FastEthernet0/2
 switchport access vlan 4
 switchport mode access
 no ip address
 storm-control broadcast level 50.00
!
interface FastEthernet0/4
 switchport access vlan 4
 switchport mode access
 no ip address
 storm-control broadcast level 50.00
!
interface FastEthernet0/8
 switchport access vlan 3
 switchport mode access
 switchport port-security
 switchport port-security mac-address 0007.5057.e27e
 no ip address
!
interface FastEthernet0/9
 switchport access vlan 10
 switchport mode access
 switchport port-security
 switchport port-security mac-address 0007.5057.e27f
 no ip address
!
interface Vlan10
 ip address 10.50.34.10 255.255.255.0
!
ip default-gateway 10.50.34.1
!
```

Section 2.0: Routing Configuration

2.1: OSPF

    1 Configure OSPF areas as shown in the Routing Protocol Information diagram in Figure 2-3 with MD5 authentication.

    2 OSPF redundancy is a tricky question; the pointers that follow advise you on what you need to do. See Example 2-3.

3 You need to configure HSRP in VLAN_4 on R2 and R3. R1 should form OSPF adjacency to the HSRP Virtual IP address. See Section 9.4 for more details.

4 Configure GRE Tunnel on R1, R2, and R3 with any subnet not used thus far (such as 21.21.21.0/24). Make sure you change the OSPF network type to point-to-multipoint, as by default tunnel interface is point-to-point. Tunnel source should be Loopback1 on R1 and HSRP Virtual IP on R2 and R3.

5 Advertise the tunnel network 21.21.21.0 in OSPF process on R1, R2, and R3 in Area 10. To achieve this task, you do not advertise 110.50.32.0 network in OSPF.

6 Configure Area 10 as a virtual link for Area20. You need to configure two virtual-link statements on R1 for redundancy—one pointing to R2 router-id and another to R3 router-id.

7 Virtual links between R1, R2, and R3 use router-id and not physical interface IP.

8 R2 and R3 must have area0 authentication configured for virtual-link to work.

9 Configure ingress ACL on R1 Fastethernet2/0 (VLAN4) to deny ICMP from R3 to R5-Ethernet0.

10 Redistribute network 110.50.33.0/24 on R2 into OSPF as connected.

Example 2-3 provides a snip from the R1, R2, and R3 configurations and **show** commands to explain how this works. This was obtained before shutting down Ethernet0/1 on R2, which means that R1 OSPF adjacency is formed with R2 and all routes including the default route are learned via R2 and R3 is in Standby mode.

Example 2-3 *How OSPF Redundancy Works*

```
r1#show running-config
Building configuration...

Current configuration : 3380 bytes
<snip>
!
interface Loopback1
 ip address 11.11.11.11 255.255.255.0
!
interface Tunnel12
 ip address 21.21.21.1 255.255.255.0
 ip ospf message-digest-key 1 md5 cisco
 ip ospf network point-to-multipoint
 ip ospf hello-interval 2
 ip ospf dead-interval 4
 tunnel source Loopback1
 tunnel destination 110.50.32.10
!
router ospf 110
 router-id 1.1.1.1
 log-adjacency-changes
 area 0 authentication message-digest
 area 0 virtual-link 2.2.2.2
```

continues

Example 2-3 *How OSPF Redundancy Works (Continued)*

```
 area 10 authentication message-digest
 area 10 virtual-link 3.3.3.3 message-digest-key 1 md5 cisco
 area 10 virtual-link 2.2.2.2 message-digest-key 1 md5 cisco
 redistribute rip metric 5 subnets
 network 21.21.21.0 0.0.0.255 area 10
 network 110.50.31.0 0.0.0.255 area 0
 !

r1#show ip ospf neighbor

Neighbor ID     Pri   State         Dead Time   Address       Interface
6.6.6.6           1   FULL/  -      00:00:32    110.50.31.2   Serial3/0.6
2.2.2.2           1   FULL/  -      00:00:03    21.21.21.2    Tunnel12
3.3.3.3           1   INIT/  -      00:00:02    21.21.21.3    Tunnel12

r1#show ip route ospf
      16.0.0.0/8 is variably subnetted, 2 subnets, 2 masks
O        16.16.16.0/24 [110/65] via 110.50.31.2, 00:16:57, Serial3/0.6
      21.0.0.0/8 is variably subnetted, 2 subnets, 2 masks
O        21.21.21.2/32 [110/11111] via 21.21.21.2, 00:17:57, Tunnel12
      110.0.0.0/8 is variably subnetted, 5 subnets, 3 masks
O E2     110.50.13.64/28 [110/5] via 110.50.31.2, 00:03:07, Serial3/0.6
O IA     110.50.13.48/28 [110/11121] via 21.21.21.2, 00:03:07, Tunnel12
O*E2 0.0.0.0/0 [110/1] via 21.21.21.2, 00:03:07, Tunnel12
r2#show running-config
<snip>

interface Loopback1
 ip address 12.12.12.12 255.255.255.0
 !
interface Tunnel21
 ip address 21.21.21.2 255.255.255.0
 no ip route-cache cef
 ip ospf message-digest-key 1 md5 7 104D000A0618
 ip ospf network point-to-multipoint
 ip ospf hello-interval 2
 ip ospf dead-interval 4
 tunnel source 110.50.32.10
 tunnel destination 11.11.11.11
 !
interface Ethernet0/0
 ip address 110.50.32.2 255.255.255.0
 ip verify unicast reverse-path
 no ip redirects
 half-duplex
 standby 1 priority 105 preempt
 standby 1 authentication cisco
 standby 1 ip 110.50.32.10
 standby 1 track Et0/1
 !
interface Ethernet0/1
 ip address 110.50.13.49 255.255.255.240
```

Example 2-3 *How OSPF Redundancy Works (Continued)*

```
 ip ospf message-digest-key 1 md5 7 070C285F4D06
 half-duplex
!
router ospf 110
 router-id 2.2.2.2
 log-adjacency-changes
 area 0 authentication message-digest
 area 10 authentication message-digest
 area 10 virtual-link 1.1.1.1 message-digest-key 1 md5 7 030752180500
 area 20 authentication message-digest
 network 21.21.21.0 0.0.0.255 area 10
 network 110.50.13.48 0.0.0.15 area 20
 network 110.50.33.0 0.0.0.255 area 20
 default-information originate always
!


r2#show ip ospf neighbor

Neighbor ID     Pri   State          Dead Time   Address       Interface
1.1.1.1          1    FULL/  -       00:00:03    21.21.21.1    Tunnel21
8.8.8.8          1    FULL/DR        00:00:31    110.50.13.51  Ethernet0/1
3.3.3.3          1    FULL/BDR       00:00:31    110.50.13.50  Ethernet0/1


r2#show ip route ospf
      16.0.0.0/8 is variably subnetted, 2 subnets, 2 masks
O        16.16.16.0/24 [110/11176] via 21.21.21.1, 00:20:38, Tunnel21
O E2     16.0.0.0/8 [110/5] via 21.21.21.1, 00:06:50, Tunnel21
      21.0.0.0/8 is variably subnetted, 2 subnets, 2 masks
O        21.21.21.1/32 [110/11111] via 21.21.21.1, 00:21:38, Tunnel21
      110.0.0.0/8 is variably subnetted, 5 subnets, 3 masks
O E2     110.50.13.80/29 [110/5] via 21.21.21.1, 00:06:50, Tunnel21
O E2     110.50.13.64/28 [110/5] via 21.21.21.1, 00:06:50, Tunnel21
O        110.50.31.0/24 [110/11175] via 21.21.21.1, 00:20:38, Tunnel21
O E2 15.0.0.0/8 [110/5] via 21.21.21.1, 00:06:50, Tunnel21


r2#sh ip ro os
      16.0.0.0/8 is variably subnetted, 2 subnets, 2 masks
O        16.16.16.0/24 [110/11176] via 21.21.21.1, 1d05h, Tunnel21
O E2     16.0.0.0/8 [110/5] via 21.21.21.1, 1d05h, Tunnel21
      18.0.0.0/8 is variably subnetted, 2 subnets, 2 masks
O        18.18.18.0/24 [110/2] via 110.50.13.51, 1d05h, FastEthernet0/1
O E2     18.0.0.0/8 [110/5] via 21.21.21.1, 1d05h, Tunnel21
      21.0.0.0/8 is variably subnetted, 2 subnets, 2 masks
O        21.21.21.1/32 [110/11111] via 21.21.21.1, 1d05h, Tunnel21
      110.0.0.0/8 is variably subnetted, 5 subnets, 3 masks
O E2     110.50.13.80/29 [110/5] via 21.21.21.1, 1d05h, Tunnel21
O E2     110.50.13.64/28 [110/5] via 21.21.21.1, 1d05h, Tunnel21
O        110.50.31.0/24 [110/11175] via 21.21.21.1, 1d05h, Tunnel21
```

continues

Example 2-3 *How OSPF Redundancy Works (Continued)*

```
        13.0.0.0/8 is variably subnetted, 2 subnets, 2 masks
O E2    13.12.0.0/14 [110/10] via 110.50.13.50, 1d05h, FastEthernet0/1
O E2    13.0.0.0/8 [110/5] via 21.21.21.1, 1d05h, Tunnel21
O E2  15.0.0.0/8 [110/5] via 21.21.21.1, 1d05h, Tunnel21
O*E2  0.0.0.0/0 [110/1] via 110.50.13.51, 1d05h, FastEthernet0/1
r2#


r2#show standby
Ethernet0/0 - Group 1
  Local state is Active, priority 105, may preempt
  Hellotime 3 holdtime 10
  Next hello sent in 00:00:01.920
  Hot standby IP address is 110.50.32.10 configured
  Active router is local
  Standby router is 110.50.32.3 expires in 00:00:09
  Standby virtual mac address is 0000.0c07.ac01
  20 state changes, last state change 00:24:26
  Tracking interface states for 1 interface, 1 up:
    Up   Ethernet0/1
r3#show running-config
<snip>
!
interface Loopback1
 ip address 13.13.13.13 255.255.255.0
!
interface Tunnel31
 ip address 21.21.21.3 255.255.255.0
 ip ospf message-digest-key 1 md5 7 110A1016141D
 ip ospf network point-to-multipoint
 ip ospf hello-interval 2
 ip ospf dead-interval 4
 tunnel source 110.50.32.10
 tunnel destination 11.11.11.11
!
interface Ethernet0/0
 ip address 110.50.32.3 255.255.255.0
 no ip redirects
 half-duplex
 standby 1 ip 110.50.32.10
 standby 1 preempt
 standby 1 track Ethernet0/1
!
interface Ethernet0/1
 ip address 110.50.13.50 255.255.255.240
 ip ospf message-digest-key 1 md5 7 060506324F41
 half-duplex
!
router ospf 110
 router-id 3.3.3.3
 log-adjacency-changes
 area 0 authentication message-digest
```

Example 2-3   *How OSPF Redundancy Works (Continued)*

```
      area 10 authentication message-digest
      area 10 virtual-link 1.1.1.1 message-digest-key 1 md5 7 030752180500
      area 20 authentication message-digest
      network 21.21.21.0 0.0.0.255 area 10
      network 110.50.13.48 0.0.0.15 area 20
      default-information originate always
      !

      r3#show ip ospf neighbor

      Neighbor ID     Pri   State          Dead Time   Address        Interface
      2.2.2.2           1   FULL/DROTHER   00:00:32    110.50.13.49   Ethernet0/1
      8.8.8.8           1   FULL/DR        00:00:32    110.50.13.51   Ethernet0/1

      r3#show ip route ospf
           16.0.0.0/8 is variably subnetted, 2 subnets, 2 masks
      O IA    16.16.16.0/24 [110/11186] via 110.50.13.49, 00:23:06, Ethernet0/1
      O E2    16.0.0.0/8 [110/5] via 110.50.13.49, 00:08:39, Ethernet0/1
           21.0.0.0/8 is variably subnetted, 3 subnets, 2 masks
      O IA    21.21.21.1/32 [110/11121] via 110.50.13.49, 00:23:21, Ethernet0/1
      O IA    21.21.21.2/32 [110/10] via 110.50.13.49, 00:23:21, Ethernet0/1
           110.0.0.0/8 is variably subnetted, 5 subnets, 3 masks
      O E2    110.50.13.80/29 [110/5] via 110.50.13.49, 00:08:39, Ethernet0/1
      O E2    110.50.13.64/28 [110/5] via 110.50.13.49, 00:08:39, Ethernet0/1
      O IA    110.50.31.0/24 [110/11185] via 110.50.13.49, 00:23:06, Ethernet0/1
      O E2 15.0.0.0/8 [110/5] via 110.50.13.49, 00:08:39, Ethernet0/1

      r3#sh ip ro ospf
           17.0.0.0/24 is subnetted, 1 subnets
      O E2    17.17.17.0 [110/10] via 110.50.13.49, 06:11:42, FastEthernet0/1
           16.0.0.0/8 is variably subnetted, 2 subnets, 2 masks
      O IA    16.16.16.0/24 [110/11177] via 110.50.13.49, 1d05h, FastEthernet0/1
      O E2    16.0.0.0/8 [110/5] via 110.50.13.49, 1d05h, FastEthernet0/1
           18.0.0.0/8 is variably subnetted, 2 subnets, 2 masks
      O E2    18.0.0.0/8 [110/5] via 110.50.13.49, 1d05h, FastEthernet0/1
      O       18.18.18.0/24 [110/2] via 110.50.13.51, 1d05h, FastEthernet0/1
           21.0.0.0/8 is variably subnetted, 3 subnets, 2 masks
      O IA    21.21.21.1/32 [110/11112] via 110.50.13.49, 1d05h, FastEthernet0/1
      O IA    21.21.21.2/32 [110/1] via 110.50.13.49, 1d05h, FastEthernet0/1
           110.0.0.0/8 is variably subnetted, 5 subnets, 3 masks
      O E2    110.50.13.80/29 [110/5] via 110.50.13.49, 1d05h, FastEthernet0/1
      O E2    110.50.13.64/28 [110/5] via 110.50.13.49, 1d05h, FastEthernet0/1
      O IA    110.50.31.0/24 [110/11176] via 110.50.13.49, 1d05h, FastEthernet0/1
           13.0.0.0/8 is variably subnetted, 4 subnets, 3 masks
      O       13.12.0.0/14 is a summary, 1d06h, Null0
      O E2    13.0.0.0/8 [110/5] via 110.50.13.49, 1d05h, FastEthernet0/1
      O E2 15.0.0.0/8 [110/5] via 110.50.13.49, 1d05h, FastEthernet0/1
      O*E2 0.0.0.0/0 [110/1] via 110.50.13.51, 1d05h, FastEthernet0/1
      r3#
```

continues

Example 2-3 *How OSPF Redundancy Works (Continued)*

```
r3#show standby
Ethernet0/0 - Group 1
  State is Standby
    22 state changes, last state change 00:24:48
  Virtual IP address is 110.50.32.10
  Active virtual MAC address is 0000.0c07.ac01
    Local virtual MAC address is 0000.0c07.ac01 (default)
  Hello time 3 sec, hold time 10 sec
    Next hello sent in 0.452 secs
  Preemption enabled
  Active router is 110.50.32.2, priority 105 (expires in 8.205 sec)
  Standby router is local
  Priority 100 (default 100)
    Track interface Ethernet0/1 state Up decrement 10
  IP redundancy name is "hsrp-Et0/0-1" (default)
```
```
r8#show ip route ospf
O E2 16.0.0.0/8 [110/5] via 110.50.13.49, 00:00:03, Ethernet0/0
     21.0.0.0/32 is subnetted, 1 subnets
O IA    21.21.21.2 [110/10] via 110.50.13.49, 00:00:03, Ethernet0/0
     110.0.0.0/8 is variably subnetted, 4 subnets, 3 masks
O E2    110.50.13.80/29 [110/5] via 110.50.13.49, 00:00:03, Ethernet0/0
O E2    110.50.13.64/28 [110/5] via 110.50.13.49, 00:00:03, Ethernet0/0
O E2    110.50.32.0/24 [110/5] via 110.50.13.49, 00:00:03, Ethernet0/0
O E2 15.0.0.0/8 [110/5] via 110.50.13.49, 00:00:03, Ethernet0/0
r8#
```
```
! After shutting down Ethernet 0/1 on R2; R1 forms adjacency with R3 instead of R2, all
! routes are converged via R3. R2 looses its adjacency with R1 and all routes are cleared.
! Furthermore, R8 converges with R3 too.
```
```
r1#show ip ospf neighbor

Neighbor ID    Pri   State       Dead Time   Address       Interface
6.6.6.6          1   FULL/ -     00:00:35    110.50.31.2   Serial3/0.6
2.2.2.2          1   INIT/ -     00:00:03    21.21.21.2    Tunnel12
3.3.3.3          1   FULL/ -     00:00:03    21.21.21.3    Tunnel12
r1#
r1#

r1#show ip route ospf
     16.0.0.0/8 is variably subnetted, 2 subnets, 2 masks
O       16.16.16.0/24 [110/65] via 110.50.31.2, 00:02:11, Serial3/0.6
     21.0.0.0/8 is variably subnetted, 2 subnets, 2 masks
O       21.21.21.3/32 [110/11111] via 21.21.21.3, 00:02:21, Tunnel12
     110.0.0.0/8 is variably subnetted, 5 subnets, 3 masks
O E2    110.50.13.64/28 [110/5] via 110.50.31.2, 00:02:01, Serial3/0.6
O IA    110.50.13.48/28 [110/11121] via 21.21.21.3, 00:02:01, Tunnel12
O*E2 0.0.0.0/0 [110/1] via 21.21.21.3, 00:02:01, Tunnel12
r1#
```
```
r2#show standby
Ethernet0/0 - Group 1
  Local state is Standby, priority 95, may preempt
```

Example 2-3 *How OSPF Redundancy Works (Continued)*

```
     Hellotime 3 holdtime 10
     Next hello sent in 00:00:01.374
     Hot standby IP address is 110.50.32.10 configured
     Active router is 110.50.32.3 expires in 00:00:09, priority 100
     Standby router is local
     22 state changes, last state change 00:03:17
     Tracking interface states for 1 interface, 0 up:
       Down Ethernet0/1

r2#show ip ospf neighbor
<Nil>
r2#
r2#
r2#show ip route ospf
<Nil>
r2#
r2#
r3#show standby
Ethernet0/0 - Group 1
  State is Active
     23 state changes, last state change 00:03:53
  Virtual IP address is 110.50.32.10
  Active virtual MAC address is 0000.0c07.ac01
    Local virtual MAC address is 0000.0c07.ac01 (default)
  Hello time 3 sec, hold time 10 sec
    Next hello sent in 0.387 secs
  Preemption enabled
  Active router is local
  Standby router is 110.50.32.2, priority 95 (expires in 7.283 sec)
  Priority 100 (default 100)
    Track interface Ethernet0/1 state Up decrement 10
  IP redundancy name is "hsrp-Et0/0-1" (default)

r3#show ip ospf neighbor

Neighbor ID     Pri   State         Dead Time   Address        Interface
1.1.1.1          1    FULL/  -      00:00:03    21.21.21.1     Tunnel31
8.8.8.8          1    FULL/DR       00:00:35    110.50.13.51   Ethernet0/1

r3#show ip route ospf
       16.0.0.0/8 is variably subnetted, 2 subnets, 2 masks
O        16.16.16.0/24 [110/11176] via 21.21.21.1, 00:03:28, Tunnel31
O E2     16.0.0.0/8 [110/5] via 21.21.21.1, 00:03:08, Tunnel31
       21.0.0.0/8 is variably subnetted, 2 subnets, 2 masks
O        21.21.21.1/32 [110/11111] via 21.21.21.1, 00:03:38, Tunnel31
       110.0.0.0/8 is variably subnetted, 5 subnets, 3 masks
O E2     110.50.13.80/29 [110/5] via 21.21.21.1, 00:03:08, Tunnel31
O E2     110.50.13.64/28 [110/5] via 21.21.21.1, 00:03:08, Tunnel31
O        110.50.31.0/24 [110/11175] via 21.21.21.1, 00:03:28, Tunnel31
O E2 15.0.0.0/8 [110/5] via 21.21.21.1, 00:03:08, Tunnel31
```

continues

Example 2-3 *How OSPF Redundancy Works (Continued)*

```
r8#show ip route ospf
      16.0.0.0/8 is variably subnetted, 2 subnets, 2 masks
O IA    16.16.16.0/24 [110/11186] via 110.50.13.50, 00:03:40, Ethernet0/0
O E2    16.0.0.0/8 [110/5] via 110.50.13.50, 00:03:40, Ethernet0/0
      21.0.0.0/32 is subnetted, 2 subnets
O IA    21.21.21.1 [110/11121] via 110.50.13.50, 00:03:40, Ethernet0/0
O IA    21.21.21.3 [110/10] via 110.50.13.50, 00:03:40, Ethernet0/0
      110.0.0.0/8 is variably subnetted, 5 subnets, 3 masks
O E2    110.50.13.80/29 [110/5] via 110.50.13.50, 00:03:40, Ethernet0/0
O E2    110.50.13.64/28 [110/5] via 110.50.13.50, 00:03:40, Ethernet0/0
O IA    110.50.31.0/24 [110/11185] via 110.50.13.50, 00:03:40, Ethernet0/0
O E2    110.50.32.0/24 [110/5] via 110.50.13.50, 00:03:40, Ethernet0/0
O E2 15.0.0.0/8 [110/5] via 110.50.13.50, 00:03:40, Ethernet0/0
```

2.2: EIGRP

1 Advertise Loopback1 and Loopback2 on R3 in EIGRP-200.

2 Redistribute EIGRP-200 into OSPF with metric 10.

3 Summarize these routes in OSPF as 13.12.0.0 255.252.0.0.

2.3: RIP

1 Configure RIPv2 between R2-R4.

2 Put Loopback-1 and Loopback-2 on R4 in RIP.

3 Configure RIPv1 between R1 and R5.

4 Configure RIPv2 between R7 and PIX.

5 Configure RIPv2 between R5, R6, and PIX.

6 Configure simple authentication for RIPv2 peers.

7 Advertise the default route to all peers in the network.

8 Advertise loopback-1 on R5 and R7.

9 All routers should be able to ping the above loopbacks using the optimal path.

10 Configure all RIPv2 with clear-text authentication.

11 PIX should learn all routes via RIP.

12 Configure PIX to advertise the default route to R7.

13 Redistribute OSPF/RIP mutually on R2.

2.4: BGP

2.4.1: Basic BGP Configuration

1   Configure BGP confederation in AS1. Use private AS number 65xxx on all routers with confederation identifier AS1. Private AS numbers are in the range of 64512 to 65535.

2   Configure password **cisco** to authenticate BGP peers in AS1 only.

3   R4 and R6 are peering eBGP. Note that they are multiple hops away.

4   R5 should learn the default route through BGP from R1. This will cause problems on R7; DG learned via RIP from PIX is overwritten. Change the external BGP Admin Distance on R7 from 20 to 130 so that RIP route with Admin Distance of 120 gets preferred. R7 should not propagate this default route further to any BGP peer; this is taken care of by the filter applied in Section 2.4.2 for route leaking.

TIP   Be careful in using the BGP **neighbor default-originate** command, as it can cause issues in many cases. Always rely on the default gateway learned via IGP.

2.4.2: Multi-Homed BGP Setup

1   Configure two eBGP statements on R7 to peer with R5 and R6.

2   Configure a static route on R5 and R6 for Loopback1 of R7 and use this for BGP updates.

3   For R5 and R6 to peer with Loopback1 of R7, redistribute Loopback1 on R7 in BGP (see Example 2-4).

4   Filter updates such that only routes originating in AS4 are advertised to R5 and R6. This prevents any route leaking. That is, we do not advertise any routes traversing AS4—for example, Loopback1. See Example 2-4 on how to do this.

Example 2-4   *Snip from R7 Configuration*

```
router bgp 4
 bgp router-id 7.7.7.7
 bgp cluster-id 286331153
 bgp log-neighbor-changes
 redistribute connected metric 1 route-map loopback1
 neighbor 15.15.15.15 remote-as 3
 neighbor 15.15.15.15 ebgp-multihop 255
 neighbor 15.15.15.15 update-source Loopback1
 neighbor 15.15.15.15 filter-list 7 out
 neighbor 16.16.16.16 remote-as 1
 neighbor 16.16.16.16 ebgp-multihop 255
 neighbor 16.16.16.16 update-source Loopback1
```

continues

Example 2-4 *Snip from R7 Configuration (Continued)*

```
 neighbor 16.16.16.16 filter-list 7 out
 distance bgp 130 200 200
 no auto-summary
 !
 ip as-path access-list 7 permit ^$
 !
 access-list 17 permit 17.17.17.0 0.0.0.255
 route-map loopback1 permit 10
  match ip address 17
```

2.4.3: BGP Route Filtering

1 Configure the route map on R6 to set community to **no-export** for Loopback-2 of R4 so that it does not get propagated to external AS3 via R1. See Example 2-5.

2 Apply the route map to AS1 peer statement only. See Example 2-5.

3 Redistribute BGP on R2 and R3 into OSPF so that R8 learns all the routes.

Example 2-5 *Snip from R6 Configuration*

```
router bgp 65006
 no synchronization
 bgp router-id 6.6.6.6
 bgp cluster-id 269488144
 bgp log-neighbor-changes
 bgp confederation identifier 1
 bgp confederation peers 65001
 neighbor 110.50.31.1 remote-as 65001
 neighbor 110.50.31.1 password 7 121A0C041104
 neighbor 110.50.31.1 send-community
 neighbor 110.50.31.1 route-map noexport out
 no auto-summary
 !
 access-list 14 permit 144.144.144.0 0.0.0.255
 !
 route-map noexport permit 10
  match ip address 14
  set community no-export
```

2.4.4: BGP Route Selection

1 Configure AS-PATH prepend on R5 and R6 to advertise network(s) with longer as-path. See Example 2-6.

Example 2-6 *Snip from R5 and R6 Configuration (Also Check the R7 BGP Table)*

```
R5#show running-config
<snip>
router bgp 3
 no synchronization
```

Example 2-6 *Snip from R5 and R6 Configuration (Also Check the R7 BGP Table) (Continued)*

```
 bgp router-id 5.5.5.5
 bgp cluster-id 252645135
 bgp log-neighbor-changes
 neighbor 17.17.17.17 remote-as 4
 neighbor 17.17.17.17 ebgp-multihop 255
 neighbor 17.17.17.17 update-source Loopback1
 neighbor 17.17.17.17 route-map set-next-hop in
 neighbor 17.17.17.17 route-map set-prepend out
 neighbor 110.50.13.81 remote-as 1
 no auto-summary
!
access-list 1 permit 12.12.12.0 0.0.0.255

route-map set-next-hop permit 10
 set ip next-hop 110.50.13.67
!
route-map set-prepend permit 10
 match ip address 1
 set as-path prepend 3 3
!
route-map set-prepend permit 20
r6# show running-config
<snip>

!
router bgp 65006
 no synchronization
 bgp router-id 6.6.6.6
 bgp cluster-id 269488144
 bgp log-neighbor-changes
 bgp confederation identifier 1
 bgp confederation peers 65001
 neighbor 14.14.14.14 remote-as 2
 neighbor 14.14.14.14 ebgp-multihop 255
 neighbor 14.14.14.14 update-source Loopback1
 neighbor 14.14.14.14 remove-private-AS
 neighbor 17.17.17.17 remote-as 4
 neighbor 17.17.17.17 ebgp-multihop 255
 neighbor 17.17.17.17 update-source Loopback1
 neighbor 17.17.17.17 remove-private-AS
 neighbor 17.17.17.17 route-map set-prepend out
 neighbor 110.50.31.1 remote-as 65001
 neighbor 110.50.31.1 password 7 121A0C041104
 neighbor 110.50.31.1 send-community
 neighbor 110.50.31.1 route-map noexport out
 no auto-summary
!
access-list 1 permit 11.11.11.0 0.0.0.255
!
```

continues

Example 2-6 *Snip from R5 and R6 Configuration (Also Check the R7 BGP Table) (Continued)*

```
route-map set-prepend permit 10
 match ip address 1
 set as-path prepend 1 1
!
route-map set-prepend permit 20
! On R7, you will notice that Loopback-1 of R1 is best via R5 and Loopback-1 of R2 is
  best via R6.
```

```
r7#show ip bgp
BGP table version is 98, local router ID is 7.7.7.7
Status codes: s suppressed, d damped, h history, * valid, > best, i - internal
Origin codes: i - IGP, e - EGP, ? - incomplete

   Network          Next Hop            Metric LocPrf Weight Path
*> 0.0.0.0          15.15.15.15                        0 3 1 i
*> 11.11.11.0/24    15.15.15.15                        0 3 1 i
*                   16.16.16.16                        0 1 1 1 i
*  12.12.12.0/24    15.15.15.15                        0 3 3 3 1 i
*>                  16.16.16.16                        0 1 i
*> 17.17.17.0/24    0.0.0.0               1        32768 ?
*> 144.144.144.0/24 16.16.16.16                        0 1 2 i
r7#
```

Section 3.0: ISDN Configuration

3.1: Basic ISDN

1   Configure ISDN on R4 and R6.

2   Configure legacy commands on R6 and dialer interface on R4.

3   Do not configure dial number on R6 in the dialer-map statement, as R6 is not supposed to make the call to R4; only R4 is to call R6. Refer to Section 5.1.3 on IPSec redundancy.

4   Configure ISDN network in Area0.

NOTE   ISDN switch-type varies from providers in different parts of the world. For a list of valid ISDN switch types, see

www.cisco.com/univercd/cc/td/doc/product/software/ios113ed/113t/113t_3
/multisdn.htm#15611

3.2: PPP Authentication and Multilink

1   Configure **chap hostname** on R6 as LAB2.

2 Configure **username** LAB2 on R4 for CHAP authentication.

3 Configure **ppp multilink** on R4 and R6.

4 Configure **dialer load-threshold** on R4.

Section 4.0: PIX Configuration

4.1: Basic PIX Configuration

1 Configure basic parameters to bootstrap PIX.

2 Make sure you can ping R5, R6, R7, Loopback1 on R7 and AAA server.

3 Configure RIPv2 with clear text authentication on both interfaces e0 and e1. See Example 2-7.

4 Configure PIX to advertise the default route to R7 via RIP. See Example 2-7.

Tip   This gets overwritten by eBGP from R5; refer to Section 2.4.1.

---

5 Configure an access list for the outside interface to allow necessary traffic as required for the whole lab. See Example 2-7 in the next section.

4.2: Network Address Translation (NAT)

1 Configure static NAT for AAA server, Switch1 Management interface, and Loopback1 of R7. See Example 2-7.

2 Configure NAT/GLOBAL for any internal network to go to the Internet. Use outside interface IP address for PAT. See Example 2-7.

Example 2-7 *Snip from PIX Configuration*

```
PIX(config)# show rip
rip outside passive version 2 authentication text cisco 1
rip inside passive version 2 authentication text cisco 1
rip inside default version 2 authentication text cisco 1

PIX(config)# show static
static (inside,outside) 17.17.17.17 17.17.17.17 netmask 255.255.255.255 0 0
static (inside,outside) 110.50.13.68 10.50.34.10 netmask 255.255.255.255 0 0
static (inside,outside) 110.50.13.69 10.50.34.254 netmask 255.255.255.255 0 0
```

continues

Example 2-7 *Snip from PIX Configuration (Continued)*

```
PIX(config)# show nat
nat (inside) 0 access-list 101
nat (inside) 1 0.0.0.0 0.0.0.0 0 0

PIX(config)# show global
global (outside) 1 interface

PIX(config show access-list
access-list 101; 2 elements
access-list 101 permit ip 10.50.34.0 255.255.255.0 172.16.1.0 255.255.255.0
  (hitcnt=20)
access-list 101 permit ip 17.17.17.0 255.255.255.0 10.50.34.0 255.255.255.0 (hitcnt=0)
access-list outside; 6 elements
access-list outside permit tcp host 15.15.15.15 host 17.17.17.17 eq bgp (hitcnt=2)
access-list outside permit tcp host 16.16.16.16 host 17.17.17.17 eq bgp (hitcnt=4)
access-list outside permit icmp any any (hitcnt=918)
access-list outside permit gre host 15.15.15.15 host 17.17.17.17 (hitcnt=39569)
access-list outside permit tcp any host 110.50.13.69 eq tacacs (hitcnt=53)
access-list outside permit tcp any host 110.50.13.68 eq telnet (hitcnt=5)
```

Section 5.0: IPSec/GRE Configuration

5.1: IPSec

5.1.1: IPSec Remote Access Using Preshared Key

1 Configure the VPN client to terminate on PIX using the preshared key. Refer to Figure 2-5 for setting up the VPN client on Test_PC.

2 Configure extended authentication and assign IP address, WINS, DNS. Refer to Figure 2-6 for screen shots of the Cisco VPN client when establishing the connection.

3 Configure split tunneling for the client to use tunnel for networks behind PIX only, such as 10.50.34.0 and 17.17.17.0 only. See split-tunnel ACL 101 on PIX. See Figure 2-7 to verify the statistics of the connection. The way to tell if split tunnel is working is that the networks listed will be those configured in split-tunnel ACL on PIX and will have a key on the side. There will be no 0.0.0.0 network when doing split tunneling, which indicates that it will not use the tunnel for any traffic other than the networks with the key indication beside it.

TIP   Refer to the sample configuration on Cisco.com for VPN Client with external authentication using RADIUS:

www.cisco.com/warp/customer/110/cvpn3k_pix_ias.html

Figure 2-5   *Properties for Cisco VPN Client 3.x for Windows*

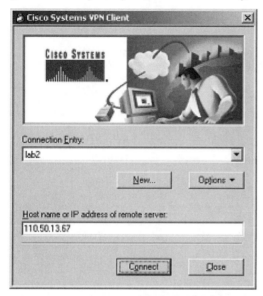

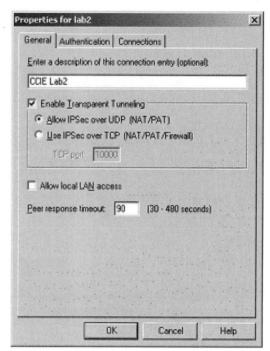

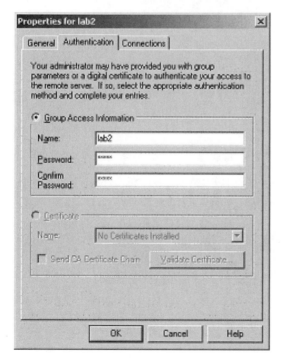

Figure 2-6   *Establishing a VPN Connection*

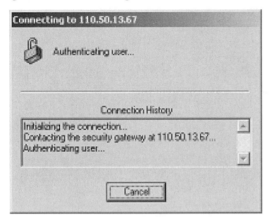

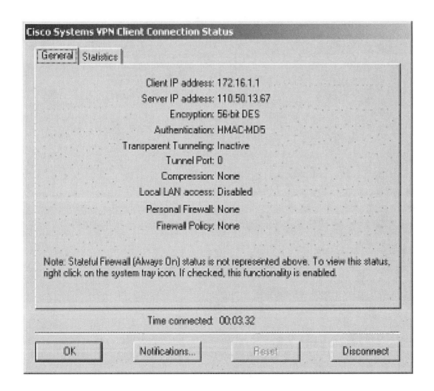

Figure 2-7   *Connection Statistics and Split-Tunnel Verification*

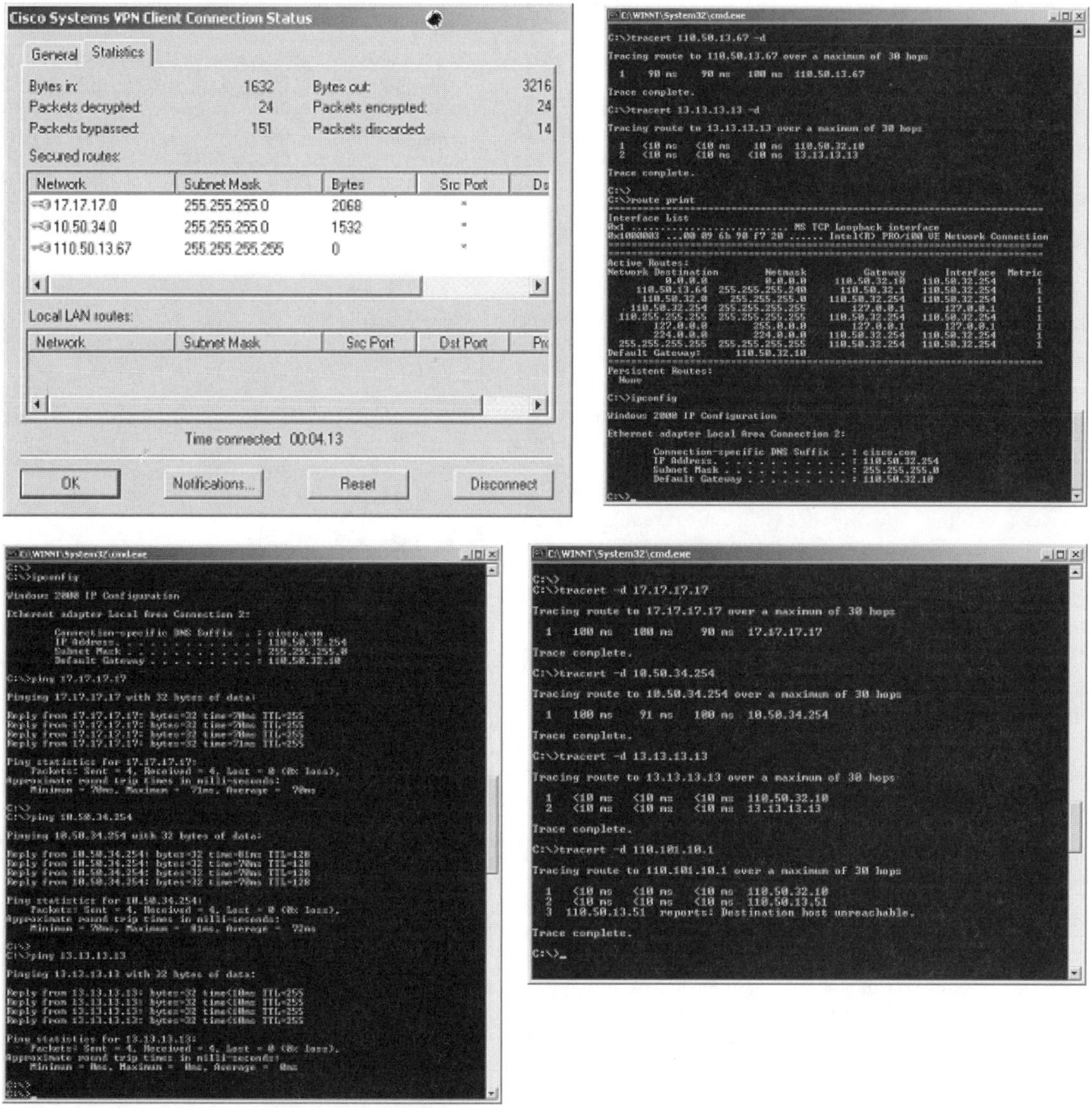

5.1.2: IPSec LAN-to-LAN Using Preshared Key

1 Configure IPSec for GRE traffic in Section 5.2. See Example 2-8 of a working GRE/IPSec tunnel between R4, R6, and R8.

2 Configure ISAKMP policy using preshared keys.

3 Make sure IPSec works after adding NAT and IPSec redundancy in the sections to come.

Example 2-8 *GRE/IPSec—Snip from R4, R6, and R8*

```
r4# show crypto engine connections active

   ID Interface       IP-Address       State  Algorithm             Encrypt  Decrypt
   17 <none>          <none>           set    HMAC_MD5+DES_56_CB          0        0
   18 Serial2/0       110.50.33.4      set    HMAC_MD5+DES_56_CB          0        0
 2172 Serial2/0       110.50.33.4      set    HMAC_MD5+DES_56_CB          0      430
 2173 Serial2/0       110.50.33.4      set    HMAC_MD5+DES_56_CB        425        0
 2174 Tunnel46        46.46.46.1       set    HMAC_MD5+DES_56_CB          0      320
 2175 Tunnel46        46.46.46.1       set    HMAC_MD5+DES_56_CB        320        0

r4#show crypto isakmp sa
     dst            src            state        conn-id   slot
 14.14.14.14    16.16.16.16     QM_IDLE           18       0
 18.18.18.18    14.14.14.14     QM_IDLE           17       0


r4#show ip route eigrp
      68.0.0.0/24 is subnetted, 1 subnets
D        68.68.68.0 [90/310044416] via 48.48.48.2, 15:55:49, Tunnel48
                    [90/310044416] via 46.46.46.2, 15:55:49, Tunnel46
      10.0.0.0/24 is subnetted, 3 subnets
D        10.1.8.0 [90/297372416] via 48.48.48.2, 15:55:49, Tunnel48
D        10.1.6.0 [90/297372416] via 46.46.46.2, 15:55:49, Tunnel46


r4# show ip eigrp neighbors
IP-EIGRP neighbors for process 200
IP-EIGRP neighbors for process 100
H    Address               Interface    Hold Uptime   SRTT   RTO  Q  Seq Type
                                        (sec)         (ms)        Cnt Num
1    46.46.46.2            Tu46          12 15:55:54 1059   5000  0  40
0    48.48.48.2            Tu48          12 16:28:18   43   5000  0  71
```

```
r6# show crypto engine connections active

   ID Interface       IP-Address       State  Algorithm             Encrypt  Decrypt
    1 <none>          <none>           set    HMAC_MD5+DES_56_CB          0        0
    2 Serial1/0       110.50.31.2      set    HMAC_MD5+DES_56_CB          0        0
 2174 Tunnel64        46.46.46.2       set    HMAC_MD5+DES_56_CB          0      423
 2175 Tunnel64        46.46.46.2       set    HMAC_MD5+DES_56_CB        427        0
 2176 Tunnel64        46.46.46.2       set    HMAC_MD5+DES_56_CB          0      325
 2177 Tunnel64        46.46.46.2       set    HMAC_MD5+DES_56_CB        324        0

r6#show crypto isakmp sa
dst            src            state        conn-id   slot
 14.14.14.14    16.16.16.16     QM_IDLE           1        0
 16.16.16.16    18.18.18.18     QM_IDLE           2        0
```

Example 2-8 *GRE/IPSec—Snip from R4, R6, and R8 (Continued)*

```
r6#show ip route eigrp
     48.0.0.0/24 is subnetted, 1 subnets
D       48.48.48.0 [90/310044416] via 68.68.68.1, 15:56:00, Tunnel68
                   [90/310044416] via 46.46.46.1, 15:56:00, Tunnel64
     10.0.0.0/24 is subnetted, 3 subnets
D       10.1.8.0 [90/297372416] via 68.68.68.1, 15:56:00, Tunnel68
D       10.1.4.0 [90/297372416] via 46.46.46.1, 15:56:00, Tunnel64
r6#
r6#
r6#show ip eigrp neighbors
IP-EIGRP neighbors for process 100
H   Address                 Interface       Hold Uptime   SRTT   RTO  Q  Seq Type
                                            (sec)         (ms)       Cnt Num
1   46.46.46.1              Tu64             14 15:56:07  164   5000  0  50
0   68.68.68.1              Tu68             13 16:00:07  125   5000  0  69
r6#
```

```
r8# show crypto engine connections active

   ID Interface        IP-Address       State   Algorithm              Encrypt  Decrypt
    4 <none>           <none>           set     HMAC_MD5+DES_56_CB           0        0
    5 <none>           <none>           set     HMAC_MD5+DES_56_CB           0        0
 2250 Ethernet0/0      110.50.13.51     set     HMAC_MD5+DES_56_CB           0      412
 2251 Ethernet0/0      110.50.13.51     set     HMAC_MD5+DES_56_CB         415        0
 2252 Ethernet0/0      110.50.13.51     set     HMAC_MD5+DES_56_CB           0      319
 2253 Ethernet0/0      110.50.13.51     set     HMAC_MD5+DES_56_CB         321        0

r8#show crypto isakmp sa
     dst             src            state          conn-id   slot
 18.18.18.18    14.14.14.14        QM_IDLE            4        6
 16.16.16.16    18.18.18.18        QM_IDLE            5        6


r8#show ip route eigrp
     10.0.0.0/24 is subnetted, 3 subnets
D       10.1.6.0 [90/297372416] via 68.68.68.2, 15:56:05, Tunnel86
D       10.1.4.0 [90/297372416] via 48.48.48.1, 15:56:06, Tunnel84
     46.0.0.0/24 is subnetted, 1 subnets
D       46.46.46.0 [90/310044416] via 48.48.48.1, 16:00:07, Tunnel84
                   [90/310044416] via 68.68.68.2, 16:00:07, Tunnel86


r8#show ip eigrp neighbors
IP-EIGRP neighbors for process 100
H   Address                 Interface       Hold Uptime   SRTT   RTO  Q  Seq Type
                                            (sec)         (ms)       Cnt Num
1   68.68.68.2              Tu86             10 16:00:13  172   5000  0  41
0   48.48.48.1              Tu84             10 16:28:32   82   5000  0  51
```

5.1.3: IPSec Redundancy

1   Configure **dialer-watch** on R4, and watch route 16.16.16.0/24 or any other route originating from R6.

2   Configure process switch **no ip route-cache** on all tunnel and physical interfaces.

3   Advertise ISDN network on R4 and R6 in OSPF Area0.

4   Configure **default-information originate always** on R4 to push a default route to R6 for redundancy when ISDN comes up.

5   Apply the crypto map statement on interfaces Dialer1 and Tunnel interfaces on R4 and Serial1/0, Tunnel interfaces and Fastethernet 0/0 on R6.

TIP   See Example 2-9 on Cisco.com to configure IPSec redundancy over ISDN using Dialer Watch. Read carefully the "Verify" section in the following URL, which explains how this works:

www.cisco.com/warp/public/707/ipsec_dialerwatch.html

Example 2-9   *IPSec Redundancy—Snip from R4 and R6*

```
! Before shutting down all interfaces on R6, the watched route is learnt via Serial
  link;
r4#show ip route 16.0.0.0
Routing entry for 16.0.0.0/8, 2 known subnets
  Variably subnetted with 2 masks
  Redistributing via rip

R        16.16.16.0/24 [100/2] via 110.50.33.2, 00:00:06, Serial2/0
R        16.0.0.0/8 [100/2] via 110.50.33.2, 00:00:06, Serial2/0
r4#
! After shutting down Fastethernet0/0 and Serial1/0 (all interfaces) on R6,
! Dialer Watch detects a loss route and brings up the ISDN link. PPP multilink
! is working also.

r4#show debug
Dial on demand:
  Dial on demand events debugging is on
r4#

1d01h: DDR: Dialer Watch: watch-group = 1
1d01h: DDR:        network 16.16.16.0/255.255.255.0 DOWN,
1d01h: DDR:        primary DOWN
1d01h: DDR: Dialer Watch: Dial Reason: Primary of group 1 DOWN
1d01h: DDR: Dialer Watch: watch-group = 1,
1d01h: BR1/0 DDR: rotor dialout [priority]
1d01h: DDR:        dialing secondary by dialer string 99047265 on Di1
1d01h: BR1/0 DDR: Attempting to dial 99047265
r4#
```

Example 2-9 *IPSec Redundancy—Snip from R4 and R6 (Continued)*

```
r4#
1d01h: %LINK-3-UPDOWN: Interface BRI1/0:1, changed state to up
1d01h: BR1/0:1 DDR: Dialer Watch: resetting call in progress
1d01h: BR1/0:1: interface must be fifo queue, force fifo
1d01h: %DIALER-6-BIND: Interface BR1/0:1 bound to profile Di1
1d01h: Di1 DDR: Authenticated host LAB2 with no matching dialer map
1d01h: Di1 DDR: dialer protocol up
1d01h: BR1/0 DDR: rotor dialout [priority]
1d01h: BR1/0 DDR: Attempting to dial 99047265
1d01h: %LINEPROTO-5-UPDOWN: Line protocol on Interface BRI1/0:1, changed state to up
1d01h: %LINK-3-UPDOWN: Interface BRI1/0:2, changed state to up
1d01h: BR1/0:2: interface must be fifo queue, force fifo
1d01h: %DIALER-6-BIND: Interface BR1/0:2 bound to profile Di1
1d01h: %ISDN-6-CONNECT: Interface BRI1/0:1 is now connected to 99047265 LAB2
1d01h: %LINEPROTO-5-UPDOWN: Line protocol on Interface BRI1/0:2, changed state to up
1d01h: %ISDN-6-CONNECT: Interface BRI1/0:2 is now connected to 99047265 LAB2
1d01h: %OSPF-5-ADJCHG: Process 110, Nbr 6.6.6.6 on Dialer1 from LOADING to FULL,
  Loading Done
r4#
r4#
r4#
r4#show isdn active
------------------------------------------------------------------------------
                           ISDN ACTIVE CALLS
------------------------------------------------------------------------------
Call    Calling      Called       Remote  Seconds Seconds Seconds Charges
Type    Number       Number       Name    Used    Left    Idle    Units/Currency
------------------------------------------------------------------------------
Out                  99047265     LAB2        17 Unavail   -          0
Out                  99047265     LAB2        16 Unavail   -          0
------------------------------------------------------------------------------

r4#
r4#
r4#show dialer

BRI1/0 - dialer type = ISDN

Dial String      Successes    Failures    Last DNIS   Last status
0 incoming call(s) have been screened.
0 incoming call(s) rejected for callback.

BRI1/0:1 - dialer type = ISDN
Idle timer (120 secs), Fast idle timer (20 secs)
Wait for carrier (30 secs), Re-enable (15 secs)
Dialer state is data link layer up
Dial reason: Dialing on watched route loss
Interface bound to profile Di1
Current call connected 00:01:22
Connected to 99047265 (LAB2)
```

continues

Example 2-9 *IPSec Redundancy—Snip from R4 and R6 (Continued)*

```
BRI1/0:2 - dialer type = ISDN
Idle timer (120 secs), Fast idle timer (20 secs)
Wait for carrier (30 secs), Re-enable (15 secs)
Dialer state is multilink member
Dial reason: Multilink bundle overloaded
Interface bound to profile Di1
Current call connected 00:01:22
Connected to 99047265 (LAB2)


r4#
r4#
r4#show ppp multilink

Dialer1, bundle name is LAB2
  0 lost fragments, 0 reordered, 0 unassigned
  0 discarded, 0 lost received, 1/255 load
  0x133 received sequence, 0x10A sent sequence
  Member links: 2 (max not set, min not set)
    BRI1/0:1
    BRI1/0:2
r4#

r4#show ip route 16.0.0.0
Routing entry for 16.0.0.0/8, 2 known subnets
  Variably subnetted with 2 masks
  Redistributing via rip

R       16.16.16.0/24 [100/1] via 110.50.46.2, 00:00:00, Dialer1
R       16.0.0.0/8 [100/2] via 110.50.33.2, 00:00:05, Serial2/0
r4#


r6#
r6#show isdn active
--------------------------------------------------------------------------
                          ISDN ACTIVE CALLS
--------------------------------------------------------------------------
Call   Calling      Called      Remote Seconds Seconds Seconds Charges
Type   Number       Number      Name   Used    Left    Idle    Units/Currency
--------------------------------------------------------------------------
In     ---N/A---    99047265      r4     38 Unavail    -
In     ---N/A---    99047265      r4     36 Unavail    -
--------------------------------------------------------------------------

r6#
r6#
r6#show dialer

BRI0/0 - dialer type = ISDN
```

Example 2-9 *IPSec Redundancy—Snip from R4 and R6 (Continued)*

```
Dial String       Successes    Failures    Last DNIS    Last status
0 incoming call(s) have been screened.
0 incoming call(s) rejected for callback.

BRI0/0:1 - dialer type = ISDN
Idle timer (120 secs), Fast idle timer (20 secs)
Wait for carrier (30 secs), Re-enable (15 secs)
Dialer state is multilink member
Connected to <unknown phone number> (r4)

BRI0/0:2 - dialer type = ISDN
Idle timer (120 secs), Fast idle timer (20 secs)
Wait for carrier (30 secs), Re-enable (15 secs)
Dialer state is multilink member
Connected to <unknown phone number> (r4)
r6#
r6#
r6#show ppp multilink

Virtual-Access1, bundle name is r4
  Bundle up for 00:00:59
  Dialer interface is BRI0/0
  0 lost fragments, 0 reordered, 0 unassigned
  0 discarded, 0 lost received, 1/255 load
  0x43 received sequence, 0x48 sent sequence
  Member links: 2 (max not set, min not set)
    BRI0/0:1, since 00:00:59, last rcvd seq 000042
    BRI0/0:2, since 00:00:57, last rcvd seq 000041
```

5.2: GRE

1 Configure fully-meshed GRE tunnels on R4, R6, and R8. You need to create two tunnels on each router. Use Loopback1 for GRE source and destination on all routers.

2 Encrypt GRE traffic as per Section 5.1.2.

3 Configure process switching on all tunnel and physical interfaces.

NOTE Refer to the following sample configurations on Cisco.com as a template to configure fully meshed GRE/IPSec topology:

www.cisco.com/warp/public/707/ios_meshed.html

www.cisco.com/warp/public/707/33.shtml

Section 6.0: IOS Firewall Configuration

6.1: Context-Based Access Control (CBAC)

  1 Configure CBAC on R5. Inspect TCP, UDP, and HTTP traffic.

  2 Configure inspection inbound on Ethernet0 (VLAN_3) on R5. See Example 2-11 for testing CBAC from R7.

  3 Configure anti-spoofing inbound ACL on Serial0 on R5 for dynamic entries. See Example 2-10 to test anti-spoofing ACL.

TIP   Refer to the following URL for more on configuring anti-spoofing ACL:

www.cisco.com/warp/public/707/21.html#anti_spoofing

Example 2-10 *Anti-Spoofing Test from R1*

```
! Create a Loopback with IP address that of VLAN3, do an Extended Ping from R1 to R5
! sourcing from this loopback;

r1#show ip interface brief loopback 99
Interface               IP-Address      OK? Method Status            Protocol
Loopback99              110.50.13.73    YES manual up                up
r1#

r1#ping 17.17.17.17
Type escape sequence to abort.
Sending 5, 100-byte ICMP Echos to 17.17.17.17, timeout is 2 seconds:
!!!!!
Success rate is 100 percent (5/5), round-trip min/avg/max = 64/66/68 ms
r1#
r1#
r1#ping ip
Target IP address: 17.17.17.17
Repeat count [5]:
Datagram size [100]:
Timeout in seconds [2]:
Extended commands [n]: y
Source address or interface: loopback 99
Type of service [0]:
Set DF bit in IP header? [no]:
Validate reply data? [no]:
Data pattern [0xABCD]:
Loose, Strict, Record, Timestamp, Verbose[none]:
Sweep range of sizes [n]:
Type escape sequence to abort.
Sending 5, 100-byte ICMP Echos to 17.17.17.17, timeout is 2 seconds:
.....
```

Example 2-10 *Anti-Spoofing Test from R1 (Continued)*

```
Success rate is 0 percent (0/5)
r1#
r1#
r1#
! Snip from R5 anti-spoofing ACL 101 applied ingress in Serial interface;

r5#show access-lists 101
Extended IP access list 101
    deny ip 110.50.13.64 0.0.0.15 any (10 matches)
    deny ip 17.17.17.0 0.0.0.255 any
    deny ip 15.15.15.0 0.0.0.255 any
    deny ip 10.0.0.0 0.255.255.255 any
    deny ip 172.16.0.0 0.15.255.255 any
    deny ip 192.168.0.0 0.0.255.255 any
    deny ip 127.0.0.0 0.255.255.255 any
    deny ip 224.0.0.0 31.255.255.255 any
    deny ip host 0.0.0.0 any
    deny icmp any any redirect
    permit ip any any (62 matches)
```

Example 2-11 *Testing CBAC from R7*

```
! Telnet to R2 Loopback-1 from R7, and a dynamic ACL entry in ACL 101 on R5 for
! return traffic and TCP session in CBAC is created.

r5#show ip inspect sessions
Half-open Sessions
 Session 7B43E4 (110.50.13.67:1027)=>(12.12.12.12:23) tcp SIS_OPENING

r5#show access-lists 101
Extended IP access list 101
    permit tcp host 12.12.12.12 eq telnet host 110.50.13.67 eq 1027
    deny ip 110.50.13.64 0.0.0.15 any (10 matches)
    deny ip 17.17.17.0 0.0.0.255 any
    deny ip 15.15.15.0 0.0.0.255 any
    deny ip 10.0.0.0 0.255.255.255 any
    deny ip 172.16.0.0 0.15.255.255 any
    deny ip 192.168.0.0 0.0.255.255 any
    deny ip 127.0.0.0 0.255.255.255 any
    deny ip 224.0.0.0 31.255.255.255 any
    deny ip host 0.0.0.0 any
    deny icmp any any redirect
    permit ip any any (111 matches)
r5#
```

6.2: Port to Application Mapping (PAM)

1 Configure PAM on R5 for HTTP traffic on ports 8081 through 8084 for specific hosts
   using ACL as shown in Example 2-12.

    2 Configure HTTP inspection in CBAC.

    3 CBAC will inspect nonstandard HTTP ports mapped in the PAM table.

    4 This technique is also very useful to prevent against DoS attacks on common well-known
       ports such as port 80.

Example 2-12 *Configuring PAM—Snip from R5 Configuration*

```
access-list 70 permit host 110.50.13.70
access-list 71 permit host 110.50.13.71
ip port-map http port 8081 list 70
ip port-map http port 8082 list 70
ip port-map http port 8083 list 71
ip port-map http port 8084 list 71

r5#show ip port-map  http
Host specific:    http            port 8081    in list 70    user defined
Host specific:    http            port 8082    in list 70    user defined
Host specific:    http            port 8083    in list 71    user defined
Default mapping: http             port 80                    system defined
Host specific:    http            port 8084    in list 71    user defined
```

Section 7.0: AAA

Configure NAS entries for all AAA clients used in this lab (see Figure 2-8).

Figure 2-8 *NAS Entries in CiscoSecure ACS*

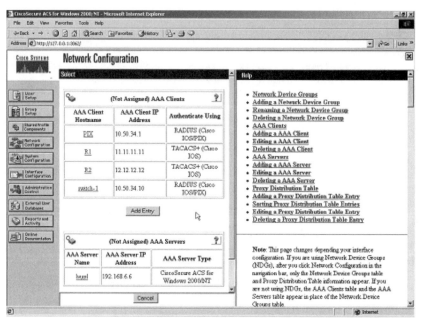

7.1: AAA on the Router

1 Configure TACACS+ for Telnet authentication and authorization on R2.

2 Make sure you use a named method list and apply it only to the vty line.

3 Create a separate named method list with no authentication and no authorization for console and aux.

4 Configure accounting for Level 1 and Level 5 commands and apply to the vty line. Refer to Figure 2-10 for Accounting Logs from CiscoSecure ACS.

5 Source TACACS+ with Loopback-1 as ACS is configured with IP 12.12.12.12 in Network settings.

6 Create a user **r2-telnet** in ACS with the necessary settings. Refer to Figure 2-9 for user **r2-telnet** settings on ACS.

7 Create a fallback to the local database and create a username with priv_lvl 5.

8 Move the **config term** and **interface** commands to Lvl_5.

9 Refer to Example 2-13 for R2 configuration and sample debug outputs for all the above.

Figure 2-9   *User **r2-telnet** Settings on CiscoSecure ACS*

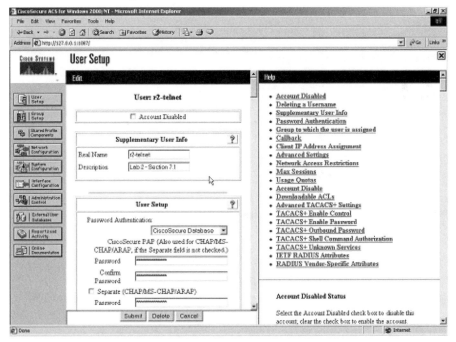

Figure 2-10 *Accounting Logs from CiscoSecure ACS*

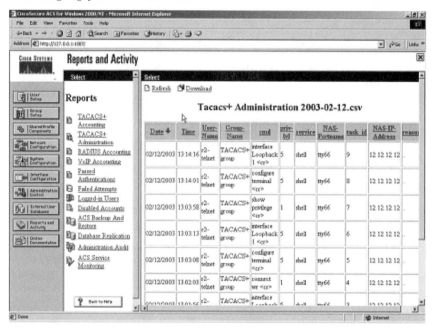

Example 2-13 *AAA Configuration and Sample Debug Outputs from R2*

```
aaa new-model
aaa authentication login lab2 group tacacs+ local
aaa authentication login no-authen none
aaa authorization exec lab2 group tacacs+ local
aaa authorization exec no-author none
aaa accounting commands 1 lab2 start-stop group tacacs+
aaa accounting commands 5 lab2 start-stop group tacacs+
username r2-telnet privilege 5 password cisco
ip tacacs source-interface Loopback1
tacacs-server host 110.50.13.69
tacacs-server key cisco
!
privilege configure level 5 interface
privilege exec level 5 config term
!
line con 0
 exec-timeout 0 0
 authorization exec no-author
 login authentication no-authen
 transport input none
line aux 0
 authorization exec no-author
 login authentication no-authen
```

Example 2-13 *AAA Configuration and Sample Debug Outputs from R2 (Continued)*

```
line vty 0 4
 password 7 070C285F4D06
 authorization exec lab2
 accounting commands 1 lab2
 accounting commands 5 lab2
 login authentication lab2
!
end
! Snip of good debugs from R2. Telnet was done from R7 to R2, and tried different
! commands such as "config term" and "interface loopback 1". Note that the requests
! are sourced as 12.12.12.12

r2#show debug
General OS:
  TACACS access control debugging is on
  AAA Authentication debugging is on
  AAA Authorization debugging is on
  AAA Accounting debugging is on

6d22h: AAA: parse name=tty66 idb type=-1 tty=-1
6d22h: AAA: name=tty66 flags=0x11 type=5 shelf=0 slot=0 adapter=0 port=66 channel=0
6d22h: AAA/MEMORY: create_user (0x82434810) user='' ruser='' port='tty66'
  rem_addr='110.50.13.67' authen_type=ASCII service=LOGIN priv=1
6d22h: AAA/AUTHEN/START (4016652159): port='tty66' list='lab2' action=LOGIN
  service=LOGIN
6d22h: AAA/AUTHEN/START (4016652159): found list lab2
6d22h: AAA/AUTHEN/START (4016652159): Method=tacacs+ (tacacs+)
6d22h: TAC+: send AUTHEN/START packet ver=192 id=4016652159
6d22h: TAC+: Using default tacacs server-group "tacacs+" list.
6d22h: TAC+: Opening TCP/IP to 110.50.13.69/49 timeout=5
6d22h: TAC+: Opened TCP/IP handle 0x82443D84 to 110.50.13.69/49 using source 12.12.12.12
6d22h: TAC+: 110.50.13.69 (4016652159) AUTHEN/START/LOGIN/ASCII queued
6d22h: TAC+: (4016652159) AUTHEN/START/LOGIN/ASCII processed
6d22h: TAC+: ver=192 id=4016652159 received AUTHEN status = GETUSER
6d22h: AAA/AUTHEN (4016652159): status = GETUSER
6d22h: AAA/AUTHEN/CONT (4016652159): continue_login (user='(undef)')
6d22h: AAA/AUTHEN (4016652159): status = GETUSER
6d22h: AAA/AUTHEN (4016652159): Method=tacacs+ (tacacs+)
6d22h: TAC+: send AUTHEN/CONT packet id=4016652159
6d22h: TAC+: 110.50.13.69 (4016652159) AUTHEN/CONT queued
6d22h: TAC+: (4016652159) AUTHEN/CONT processed
6d22h: TAC+: ver=192 id=4016652159 received AUTHEN status = GETPASS
6d22h: AAA/AUTHEN (4016652159): status = GETPASS
6d22h: AAA/AUTHEN/CONT (4016652159): continue_login (user='r2-telnet')
6d22h: AAA/AUTHEN (4016652159): status = GETPASS
6d22h: AAA/AUTHEN (4016652159): Method=tacacs+ (tacacs+)
6d22h: TAC+: send AUTHEN/CONT packet id=4016652159
6d22h: TAC+: 110.50.13.69 (4016652159) AUTHEN/CONT queued
6d22h: TAC+: (4016652159) AUTHEN/CONT processed
6d22h: TAC+: ver=192 id=4016652159 received AUTHEN status = PASS
6d22h: AAA/AUTHEN (4016652159): status = PASS
```

continues

Example 2-13 *AAA Configuration and Sample Debug Outputs from R2 (Continued)*

```
6d22h: TAC+: Closing TCP/IP 0x82443D84 connection to 110.50.13.69/49
6d22h: tty66 AAA/AUTHOR/EXEC (2993023776): Port='tty66' list='lab2' service=EXEC
6d22h: AAA/AUTHOR/EXEC: tty66 (2993023776) user='r2-telnet'
6d22h: tty66 AAA/AUTHOR/EXEC (2993023776): send AV service=shell
6d22h: tty66 AAA/AUTHOR/EXEC (2993023776): send AV cmd*
6d22h: tty66 AAA/AUTHOR/EXEC (2993023776): found list "lab2"
6d22h: tty66 AAA/AUTHOR/EXEC (2993023776): Method=tacacs+ (tacacs+)
6d22h: AAA/AUTHOR/TAC+: (2993023776): user=r2-telnet
6d22h: AAA/AUTHOR/TAC+: (2993023776): send AV service=shell
6d22h: AAA/AUTHOR/TAC+: (2993023776): send AV cmd*
6d22h: TAC+: using previously set server 110.50.13.69 from group tacacs+
6d22h: TAC+: Opening TCP/IP to 110.50.13.69/49 timeout=5
6d22h: TAC+: Opened TCP/IP handle 0x82444208 to 110.50.13.69/49 using source 12.12.12.12
6d22h: TAC+: Opened 110.50.13.69 index=1
6d22h: TAC+: 110.50.13.69 (2993023776) AUTHOR/START queued
6d22h: TAC+: (2993023776) AUTHOR/START processed
6d22h: TAC+: (2993023776): received author response status = PASS_ADD
6d22h: TAC+: Closing TCP/IP 0x82444208 connection to 110.50.13.69/49
6d22h: AAA/AUTHOR (2993023776): Post authorization status = PASS_ADD
6d22h: AAA/AUTHOR/EXEC: Processing AV service=shell
6d22h: AAA/AUTHOR/EXEC: Processing AV cmd*
6d22h: AAA/AUTHOR/EXEC: Processing AV priv-lvl=5
6d22h: AAA/AUTHOR/EXEC: Authorization successful
r2#
6d22h: AAA/ACCT/CMD: User r2-telnet, Port tty66, Priv 5:
       "configure terminal <cr>"
6d22h: AAA/ACCT/CMD: Found list "lab2"
6d22h: AAA/ACCT: user r2-telnet, acct type 3 (2678723592): Method=tacacs+ (tacacs+)
6d22h: TAC+: using previously set server 110.50.13.69 from group tacacs+
6d22h: TAC+: Opening TCP/IP to 110.50.13.69/49 timeout=5
6d22h: TAC+: Opened TCP/IP handle 0x8244468C to 110.50.13.69/49 using source
  12.12.12.12
6d22h: TAC+: Opened 110.50.13.69 index=1
6d22h: TAC+: 110.50.13.69 (2678723592) ACCT/REQUEST/STOP queued
6d22h: TAC+: (2678723592) ACCT/REQUEST/STOP processed
6d22h: TAC+: (2678723592): received acct response status = SUCCESS
6d22h: TAC+: Closing TCP/IP 0x8244468C connection to 110.50.13.69/49
6d22h: AAA/ACCT/CMD: User r2-telnet, Port tty66, Priv 5:
       "interface Loopback 1 <cr>"
6d22h: AAA/ACCT/CMD: Found list "lab2"
6d22h: AAA/ACCT: user r2-telnet, acct type 3 (4048033009): Method=tacacs+ (tacacs+)
6d22h: TAC+: using previously set server 110.50.13.69 from group tacacs+
6d22h: TAC+: Opening TCP/IP to 110.50.13.69/49 timeout=5
6d22h: TAC+: Opened TCP/IP handle 0x82444B10 to 110.50.13.69/49 using source
  12.12.12.12
6d22h: TAC+: Opened 110.50.13.69 index=1
6d22h: TAC+: 110.50.13.69 (4048033009) ACCT/REQUEST/STOP queued
6d22h: TAC+: (4048033009) ACCT/REQUEST/STOP processed
6d22h: TAC+: (4048033009): received acct response status = SUCCESS
6d22h: TAC+: Closing TCP/IP 0x82444B10 connection to 110.50.13.69/49
```

7.2: AAA on the Switch

1 Configure Authentication, Exec Authorization, and Accounting for Exec and Commands on the switch. Refer to Example 2-14 for the AAA configuration on the switch. Refer to Figure 2-11 for the Accounting logs.

2 No need to create ACL on PIX for RADIUS requests, as Switch-1 and AAA are on the same VLAN.

3 Do not configure any authentication/authorization for Console and Aux ports. Verify by Telnetting to the switch from any device in the network. Refer to Example 2-15 for good debugs from Switch1. Telnet was done from R7 to Switch1, and tried different commands such as **show run**, **wr mem**, **config term**, and so on.

4 Configure username **sw2** on CiscoSecure ACS with appropriate settings. Refer to Figure 2-12 for user **sw2** settings on ACS.

Example 2-14 *AAA Configuration on the Switch*

```
hostname Switch1
!
aaa new-model
aaa authentication login lab2 group radius local
aaa authentication login no-authen none
aaa authorization exec lab2 group radius local
aaa authorization exec no-author none
aaa accounting exec lab2 start-stop group radius
aaa accounting commands 1 lab2 start-stop group radius
aaa accounting commands 15 lab2 start-stop group radius
enable password 7 070C285F4D06
!
username sw2 password 7 cisco
!
radius-server host 10.50.34.254 auth-port 1812 acct-port 1813
radius-server retransmit 3
radius-server key cisco
!
line con 0
 exec-timeout 0 0
 authorization exec no-author
 login authentication no-authen
line vty 0 4
 authorization exec lab2
 accounting commands 1 lab2
 accounting commands 15 lab2
 accounting exec lab2
 login authentication lab2
line vty 5 15
!
end
```

Example 2-15 *Snip of Good Debugs from Switch1*

```
! Telnet was done from R7 to Switch1, and tried different commands such as
! "show run", "wr mem" and "config term", etc.
Switch1#show debug
General OS:
  AAA Authentication debugging is on
  AAA Authorization debugging is on
  AAA Accounting debugging is on
Radius protocol debugging is on

1w4d: AAA: parse name=tty1 idb type=-1 tty=-1
1w4d: AAA: name=tty1 flags=0x11 type=5 shelf=0 slot=0 adapter=0 port=1 channel=0
1w4d: AAA/MEMORY: create_user (0xE021B8) user='' ruser='' port='tty1'
  rem_addr='10.50.34.2' authen_type=ASCII service=LOGIN priv=1
1w4d: AAA/AUTHEN/START (887515695): port='tty1' list='lab2' action=LOGIN service=LOGIN
1w4d: AAA/AUTHEN/START (887515695): found list lab2
1w4d: AAA/AUTHEN/START (887515695): Method=radius (radius)
1w4d: AAA/AUTHEN (887515695): status = GETUSER
1w4d: AAA/AUTHEN/CONT (887515695): continue_login (user='(undef)')
1w4d: AAA/AUTHEN (887515695): status = GETUSER
1w4d: AAA/AUTHEN (887515695): Method=radius (radius)
1w4d: AAA/AUTHEN (887515695): status = GETPASS
1w4d: AAA/AUTHEN/CONT (887515695): continue_login (user='sw2')
1w4d: AAA/AUTHEN (887515695): status = GETPASS
1w4d: AAA/AUTHEN (887515695): Method=radius (radius)
1w4d: RADIUS: ustruct sharecount=1
1w4d: RADIUS: Initial Transmit tty1 id 7 10.50.34.254:1812, Access-Request, len 73
1w4d:        Attribute 4 6 0A32220A
1w4d:        Attribute 5 6 00000001
1w4d:        Attribute 61 6 00000005
1w4d:        Attribute 1 5 7377321F
1w4d:        Attribute 31 12 31302E35
1w4d:        Attribute 2 18 C0BD009D
1w4d: RADIUS: Received from id 7 10.50.34.254:1812, Access-Accept, len 32
1w4d:        Attribute 6 6 00000001
1w4d:        Attribute 8 6 FFFFFFFF
1w4d: RADIUS: saved authorization data for user E021B8 at DFDDE4
1w4d: AAA/AUTHEN (887515695): status = PASS
1w4d: tty1 AAA/AUTHOR/EXEC (1143158904): Port='tty1' list='lab2' service=EXEC
1w4d: AAA/AUTHOR/EXEC: tty1 (1143158904) user='sw2'
1w4d: tty1 AAA/AUTHOR/EXEC (1143158904): send AV service=shell
1w4d: tty1 AAA/AUTHOR/EXEC (1143158904): send AV cmd*
1w4d: tty1 AAA/AUTHOR/EXEC (1143158904): found list "lab2"
1w4d: tty1 AAA/AUTHOR/EXEC (1143158904): Method=radius (radius)
1w4d: AAA/AUTHOR (1143158904): Post authorization status = PASS_ADD
1w4d: AAA/AUTHOR/EXEC: Authorization successful
1w4d: AAA/ACCT/EXEC/START User sw2, port tty1
1w4d: AAA/ACCT/EXEC: Found list "lab2"
1w4d: AAA/ACCT/EXEC/START User sw2, Port tty1,
        task_id=6 timezone=UTC service=shell
```

Example 2-15 *Snip of Good Debugs from Switch1 (Continued)*

```
1w4d: AAA/ACCT: user sw2, acct type 0 (400129182): Method=radius (radius)
1w4d: RADIUS: ustruct sharecount=3
1w4d: RADIUS: Initial Transmit tty1 id 8 10.50.34.254:1813, Accounting-Request, len 89
1w4d:          Attribute 4 6 0A32220A
1w4d:          Attribute 5 6 00000001
1w4d:          Attribute 61 6 00000005
1w4d:          Attribute 1 5 7377321F
1w4d:          Attribute 31 12 31302E35
1w4d:          Attribute 40 6 00000001
1w4d:          Attribute 45 6 00000001
1w4d:          Attribute 6 6 00000007
1w4d:          Attribute 44 10 30303030
1w4d:          Attribute 41 6 00000000
1w4d: RADIUS: Received from id 8 10.50.34.254:1813, Accounting-response, len 20
1w4d: AAA/ACCT/CMD: User sw2, Port tty1, Priv 15:
         "show running-config <cr>"
1w4d: AAA/ACCT/CMD: Found list "lab2"
1w4d: AAA/ACCT: user sw2, acct type 3 (2621678809): Method=radius (radius)
Switch1#
Switch1#
Switch1#
1w4d: AAA/ACCT/CMD: User sw2, Port tty1, Priv 15:
          "write memory <cr>"
1w4d: AAA/ACCT/CMD: Found list "lab2"
1w4d: AAA/ACCT: user sw2, acct type 3 (2377841683): Method=radius (radius)
Switch1#
Switch1#
1w4d: AAA/ACCT/CMD: User sw2, Port tty1, Priv 15:
          "configure terminal <cr>"
1w4d: AAA/ACCT/CMD: Found list "lab2"
1w4d: AAA/ACCT: user sw2, acct type 3 (3679197411): Method=radius (radius)
Switch1#
1w4d: %SYS-5-CONFIG_I: Configured from console by sw2 on vty0 (10.50.34.2)
Switch1#
Switch1#
1w4d: AAA/ACCT/CMD: User sw2, Port tty1, Priv 1:
           "show clock <cr>"
1w4d: AAA/ACCT/CMD: Found list "lab2"
1w4d: AAA/ACCT: user sw2, acct type 3 (248650303): Method=radius (radius)
1w4d: AAA/ACCT/EXEC/STOP User sw2, Port tty1:
          task_id=6 timezone=UTC service=shell disc-cause=1 disc-cause-ext=1020
          elapsed_time=442 nas-rx-speed=0 nas-tx-speed=0
1w4d: AAA/ACCT: user sw2, acct type 0 (598855493): Method=radius (radius)
1w4d: RADIUS: ustruct sharecount=2
1w4d: RADIUS: Initial Transmit tty1 id 9 10.50.34.254:1813, Accounting-Request, len 101
1w4d:          Attribute 4 6 0A32220A
1w4d:          Attribute 5 6 00000001
1w4d:          Attribute 61 6 00000005
1w4d:          Attribute 1 5 7377321F
```

continues

Example 2-15 *Snip of Good Debugs from Switch1 (Continued)*

```
1w4d:          Attribute 31 12 31302E35
1w4d:          Attribute 40 6 00000002
1w4d:          Attribute 45 6 00000001
1w4d:          Attribute 6 6 00000007
1w4d:          Attribute 44 10 30303030
1w4d:          Attribute 49 6 00000001
1w4d:          Attribute 46 6 000001BA
1w4d:          Attribute 41 6 00000000
1w4d: RADIUS: Received from id 9 10.50.34.254:1813, Accounting-response, len 20
1w4d: AAA/MEMORY: free_user (0xE021B8) user='sw2' ruser='' port='tty1'
  rem_addr='10.50.34.2' authen_type=ASCII service=LOGIN priv=1
```

Figure 2-11 *Exec Accounting Logs from CiscoSecure ACS*

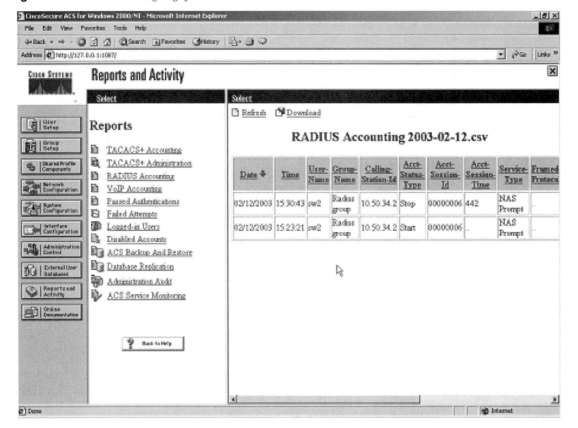

Figure 2-12 *User sw2 Settings on CiscoSecure ACS*

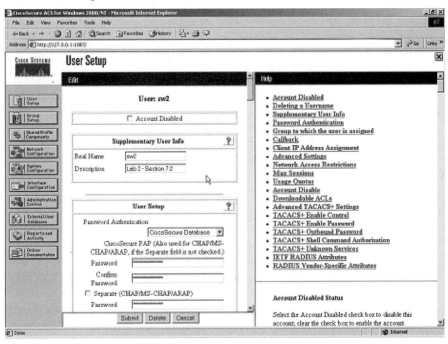

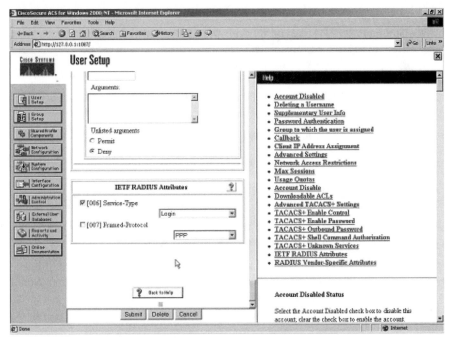

Section 8.0: Advanced Security

8.1: Perimeter Security

1 If the network is under a heavy load, and it does not give adequate CPU time to process system-level tasks such as handling routing protocols, configure the **scheduler** command to allocate CPU times efficiently. Configure R8 with **scheduler allocate 2000 500**.

NOTE   For more info on the **scheduler** command, see the following URL:

www.cisco.com/univercd/cc/td/doc/product/software/ios121/121cgcr
/fun_r/frprt3/frd3003.htm#1019339

---

2 Configure **service nagle** on R8.

NOTE   For more info on **service nagle**, see

www.cisco.com/univercd/cc/td/doc/product/software/ios121/121cgcr
/fun_r/frprt3/frd3003.htm#1019550

8.2: Router Management Using HTTP

1 Configure HTTP server on R1 with AAA authentication and Exec authorization using TACACS+. Refer to Example 2-16.

2 Use Loopback-1 to source TACACS+ requests. Refer to Example 2-16.

3 Configure fallback to the local database in the event the TACACS+ server is down. Refer to Example 2-16.

4 Note that HTTP users need priv_lvl 15.

5 Configure local username **r1-http** on R1 with priv_lvl 15 for AAA fallback. Refer to Example 2-16.

6 Configure ACL to permit Test_PC only for HTTP. Refer to Example 2-16.

7 Configure username **r1-http** in ACS with priv_lvl 15, allow Shell (exec), and enable all Undefined Services. See Figure 2-13 for ACS settings.

8 Verify this by browsing R1 (110.50.32.1) from the Test_PC. Refer to Figure 2-14 for Authentication Logs from CiscoSecure ACS. Refer to Figure 2-15 for router management via HTTP.

TIP See the following URL for more info on configuring TACACS+ authentication for HTTP users: www.cisco.com/warp/public/480/http-2.html

Example 2-16 *HTTP Configuration and* **debug** *Output from R1*

```
r1#show running-config
Building configuration...

Current configuration : 3706 bytes
<snip>
!
aaa new-model
aaa authentication login default group tacacs+ local
aaa authentication login noauthen none
aaa authorization exec default group tacacs+
aaa authorization exec noexec none
!
 username r1-http privilege 15 password 0 cisco
!
ip http server
ip http access-class 1
ip http authentication aaa
ip tacacs source-interface Loopback1
!
access-list 1 permit 110.50.32.254
!
tacacs-server host 110.50.13.69
tacacs-server key cisco
!
!
line con 0
 exec-timeout 0 0
 authorization exec noexec
 login authentication noauthen
 transport input none
line aux 0
 authorization exec noexec
 login authentication noauthen
line vty 0 4
 authorization exec default
 login authentication default
line vty 5 15
 authorization exec default
 login authentication default
!
end
! Debug output from R1, note that source IP is 11.11.11.11 (Loopback1).
r1#show debug
```
continues

Example 2-16 *HTTP Configuration and* **debug** *Output from R1 (Continued)*

```
General OS:
  TACACS access control debugging is on
  AAA Authentication debugging is on
  AAA Authorization debugging is on
r1#
r1#
r1#
r1#
1d08h: AAA: parse name=tty2 idb type=-1 tty=-1
1d08h: AAA: name=tty2 flags=0x11 type=5 shelf=0 slot=0 adapter=0 port=2 channel=0
1d08h: AAA/MEMORY: create_user (0x631EC8D8) user='' ruser='' port='tty2'
  rem_addr='110.50.32.254' authen_type=ASCII service=LOGIN priv=0
1d08h: AAA/AUTHEN/START (1455966780): port='tty2' list='' action=LOGIN service=LOGIN
1d08h: AAA/AUTHEN/START (1455966780): using "default" list
1d08h: AAA/AUTHEN/START (1455966780): Method=tacacs+ (tacacs+)
1d08h: TAC+: send AUTHEN/START packet ver=192 id=1455966780
1d08h: TAC+: Using default tacacs server-group "tacacs+" list.
1d08h: TAC+: Opening TCP/IP to 110.50.13.69/49 timeout=5
1d08h: TAC+: Opened TCP/IP handle 0x631EB85C to 110.50.13.69/49 using source 11.11.11.11
1d08h: TAC+: 110.50.13.69 (1455966780) AUTHEN/START/LOGIN/ASCII queued
1d08h: TAC+: (1455966780) AUTHEN/START/LOGIN/ASCII processed
1d08h: TAC+: ver=192 id=1455966780 received AUTHEN status = GETUSER
1d08h: AAA/AUTHEN (1455966780): status = GETUSER
1d08h: AAA/AUTHEN/CONT (1455966780): continue_login (user='(undef)')
1d08h: AAA/AUTHEN (1455966780): status = GETUSER
1d08h: AAA/AUTHEN (1455966780): Method=tacacs+ (tacacs+)
1d08h: TAC+: send AUTHEN/CONT packet id=1455966780
1d08h: TAC+: 110.50.13.69 (1455966780) AUTHEN/CONT queued
1d08h: TAC+: (1455966780) AUTHEN/CONT processed
1d08h: TAC+: ver=192 id=1455966780 received AUTHEN status = GETPASS
1d08h: AAA/AUTHEN (1455966780): status = GETPASS
1d08h: AAA/AUTHEN/CONT (1455966780): continue_login (user='r1-http')
1d08h: AAA/AUTHEN (1455966780): status = GETPASS
1d08h: AAA/AUTHEN (1455966780): Method=tacacs+ (tacacs+)
1d08h: TAC+: send AUTHEN/CONT packet id=1455966780
1d08h: TAC+: 110.50.13.69 (1455966780) AUTHEN/CONT queued
1d08h: TAC+: (1455966780) AUTHEN/CONT processed
1d08h: TAC+: ver=192 id=1455966780 received AUTHEN status = PASS
1d08h: AAA/AUTHEN (1455966780): status = PASS
1d08h: TAC+: Closing TCP/IP 0x631EB85C connection to 110.50.13.69/49
1d08h: tty2 AAA/AUTHOR/HTTP (2051807032): Port='tty2' list='' service=EXEC
1d08h: AAA/AUTHOR/HTTP: tty2 (2051807032) user='r1-http'
1d08h: tty2 AAA/AUTHOR/HTTP (2051807032): send AV service=shell
1d08h: tty2 AAA/AUTHOR/HTTP (2051807032): send AV cmd*
1d08h: tty2 AAA/AUTHOR/HTTP (2051807032): found list "default"
1d08h: tty2 AAA/AUTHOR/HTTP (2051807032): Method=tacacs+ (tacacs+)
1d08h: AAA/AUTHOR/TAC+: (2051807032): user=r1-http
1d08h: AAA/AUTHOR/TAC+: (2051807032): send AV service=shell
1d08h: AAA/AUTHOR/TAC+: (2051807032): send AV cmd*
1d08h: TAC+: using previously set server 110.50.13.69 from group tacacs+
```

Example 2-16 *HTTP Configuration and* **debug** *Output from R1 (Continued)*

```
1d08h: TAC+: Opening TCP/IP to 110.50.13.69/49 timeout=5
1d08h: TAC+: Opened TCP/IP handle 0x631EBCE0 to 110.50.13.69/49 using source 11.11.11.11
1d08h: TAC+: Opened 110.50.13.69 index=1
1d08h: TAC+: 110.50.13.69 (2051807032) AUTHOR/START queued
1d08h: TAC+: (2051807032) AUTHOR/START processed
1d08h: TAC+: (2051807032): received author response status = PASS_ADD
1d08h: TAC+: Closing TCP/IP 0x631EBCE0 connection to 110.50.13.69/49
1d08h: AAA/AUTHOR (2051807032): Post authorization status = PASS_ADD
1d08h: AAA/MEMORY: free_user (0x631EC8D8) user='r1-http' ruser='' port='tty2'
  rem_addr='110.50.32.254' authen_type=ASCII service=LOGIN priv=0
r1#
r1#
```

Figure 2-13 *User* **r1-http** *Settings on CiscoSecure ACS*

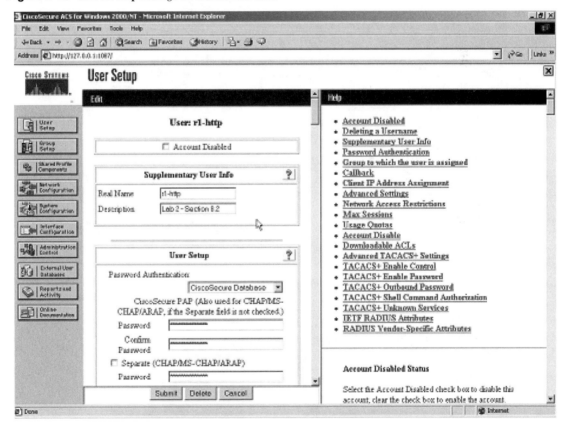

Figure 2-13 *User* **r1-http** *Settings on CiscoSecure ACS (Continued)*

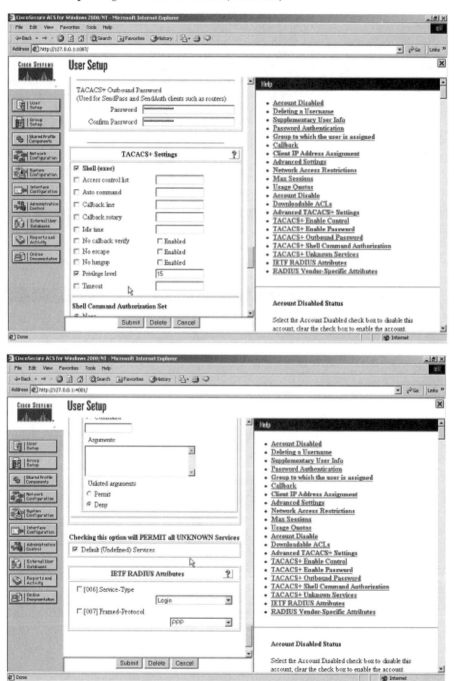

Figure 2-14 *Passed Authentication Logs from CiscoSecure ACS*

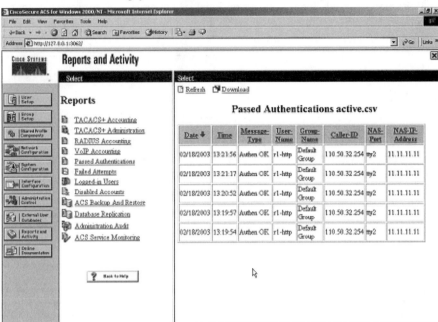

Figure 2-15 *Router Management Using a Browser*

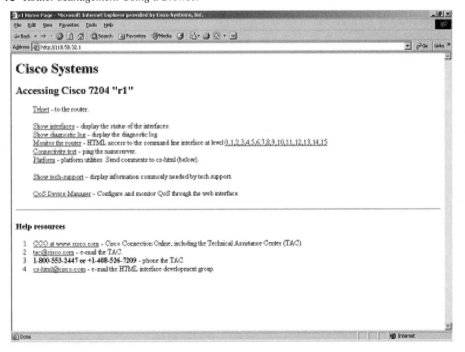

| **NOTE** | If the Default (Undefined) Services option does not appear, go to Interface Configuration and select TACACS+ and then Advanced Configuration Options. Choose Display enable default (undefined) service configuration. |

8.3: Access Control

1 Configure vty password **cisco** for lines 0 through 3 and password **cisco123** for line 5.

2 Test this by Telnetting to R3 from R2 (five times). The fifth time, you should use the **cisco123** password to get in. See Example 2-17 for configuration and sample debug output.

Example 2-17 *R3 Configuration and Debug Output*

```
R3#show running-config
<snip>
line vty 0 3
  password cisco
line vty 4
  password cisco123
```

```
r2#ping 13.13.13.13
Type escape sequence to abort.
Sending 5, 100-byte ICMP Echos to 13.13.13.13, timeout is 2 seconds:
!!!!!
Success rate is 100 percent (5/5), round-trip min/avg/max = 4/4/4 ms

r2#telnet 13.13.13.13
Trying 13.13.13.13 ... Open

User Access Verification

Password: cisco
r3>
! Repeat the above 4 times, and you will occupy 4 vty lines, see below;
r3#who
    Line       User       Host(s)            Idle       Location
*  0 con 0               idle           00:00:00
  66 vty 0               idle           00:03:14 110.50.32.2
  67 vty 1               idle           00:02:58 110.50.32.2
  68 vty 2               idle           00:02:54 110.50.32.2
  69 vty 3               idle           00:02:50 110.50.32.2
! Now, if you try the telnet 5th time, you will hit vty line #5, where the
! password is not "cisco".
r2#telnet 13.13.13.13
Trying 13.13.13.13 ... Open

User Access Verification
```

Example 2-17 *R3 Configuration and Debug Output (Continued)*

```
Password: cisco  ⇐---invalid as we are now hitting vty line 5
Password: cisco123  ⇐ correct password "cisco123" for vty 5 lets you in
r3>
r3>
```

Section 9.0: IP Services and Protocol-Independent Features

9.1: NAT

1 Create multiple route maps to NAT to the corresponding egress interface. See Example 2-18.

TIP See the following sample config to configure GRE/IPSec with NAT:

www.cisco.com/warp/public/707/quicktip.html

Example 2-18 *NAT Configuration from R4 (R6 and R8 Look Similar Except for the ACL; See Solutions)*

```
interface Loopback10
 ip address 10.1.4.1 255.255.255.0
 ip nat inside
!
interface Serial2/0
 ip address 110.50.33.4 255.255.255.0
 ip nat outside
!
interface Dialer1
 ip address 110.50.46.1 255.255.255.0
 ip nat outside
!
ip nat inside source route-map dialer1 interface Dialer1 overload
ip nat inside source route-map serial2/0 interface Serial2/0 overload
!
access-list 104 deny   ip 10.1.4.0 0.0.0.255 10.1.6.0 0.0.0.255
access-list 104 deny   ip 10.1.4.0 0.0.0.255 10.1.8.0 0.0.0.255
access-list 104 permit ip 10.1.4.0 0.0.0.255 any
!
route-map dialer1 permit 10
 match ip address 104
 match interface Dialer1
!
route-map serial2/0 permit 10
 match ip address 104
 match interface Serial2/0
```

9.2: NTP

1 Configure R2 as the NTP server.

2 Configure R2 to broadcast NTP on Ethernet0/0.

3 Configure R1 as the NTP client.

4 Configure authentication using password **cisco**.

5 Configure R3 as the Dynamic NTP client by receiving NTP broadcasts on Ethernet0/0.

6 See Example 2-19 to configure all the above.

7 Verify that clocks on all routers are synced and authenticated. See Example 2-20.

Example 2-19 *NTP Configuration on R1, R2, and R3*

```
! Snip from R2 (master)
interface Ethernet0/0
 ip address 110.50.32.2 255.255.255.0
 ntp broadcast
!
ntp authentication-key 1 md5 121A0C041104 7
ntp source Loopback1
ntp master
end
! Snip from R1 (Client)
ntp authentication-key 1 md5 cisco
ntp authenticate
ntp trusted-key 1
ntp clock-period 17179861
ntp source Loopback1
ntp update-calendar
ntp server 110.50.32.2 key 1
! Snip from R3 (Dynamic client);
interface Ethernet0/0
 ip address 110.50.32.3 255.255.255.0
 ntp broadcast client
```

Example 2-20 *NTP Verification on R1, R2, and R3*

```
r2#show ntp status
Clock is synchronized, stratum 8, reference is 127.127.7.1
nominal freq is 249.5901 Hz, actual freq is 249.5901 Hz, precision is 2**16
reference time is C1F84AFB.A60B88C8 (05:13:31.648 UTC Sat Feb 15 2003)
clock offset is 0.0000 msec, root delay is 0.00 msec
root dispersion is 0.02 msec, peer dispersion is 0.02 msec


r2#show ntp associations detail
127.127.7.1 configured, our_master, sane, valid, stratum 7
ref ID 127.127.7.1, time C1F84AFB.A60B88C8 (05:13:31.648 UTC Sat Feb 15 2003)
our mode active, peer mode passive, our poll intvl 64, peer poll intvl 64
root delay 0.00 msec, root disp 0.00, reach 377, sync dist 0.015
```

Example 2-20 *NTP Verification on R1, R2, and R3 (Continued)*

```
delay 0.00 msec, offset 0.0000 msec, dispersion 0.02
precision 2**18, version 3
org time C1F84AFB.A60B88C8 (05:13:31.648 UTC Sat Feb 15 2003)
rcv time C1F84AFB.A60B88C8 (05:13:31.648 UTC Sat Feb 15 2003)
xmt time C1F84AFB.A60AAC64 (05:13:31.648 UTC Sat Feb 15 2003)
filtdelay =    0.00    0.00    0.00    0.00    0.00    0.00    0.00    0.00
filtoffset =   0.00    0.00    0.00    0.00    0.00    0.00    0.00    0.00
filterror =    0.02    0.99    1.97    2.94    3.92    4.90    5.87    6.85
Reference clock status:  Running normally
Timecode:

r2#show clock
05:14:06.661 UTC Sat Feb 15 2003


! Snip from R1 NTP Client

r1#show ntp status
Clock is synchronized, stratum 9, reference is 110.50.32.2
nominal freq is 250.0000 Hz, actual freq is 250.0000 Hz, precision is 2**24
reference time is C1F84B14.B52A5542 (05:13:56.707 UTC Sat Feb 15 2003)
clock offset is -3.6984 msec, root delay is 2.66 msec
root dispersion is 4.44 msec, peer dispersion is 0.70 msec

r1#show ntp associations detail
110.50.32.2 configured, authenticated, our_master, sane, valid, stratum 8
ref ID 127.127.7.1, time C1F84AFB.A60B88C8 (05:13:31.648 UTC Sat Feb 15 2003)
our mode client, peer mode server, our poll intvl 64, peer poll intvl 64
root delay 0.00 msec, root disp 0.03, reach 377, sync dist 2.060
delay 2.66 msec, offset -3.6984 msec, dispersion 0.70
precision 2**16, version 3
org time C1F84B14.B3E08EB9 (05:13:56.702 UTC Sat Feb 15 2003)
rcv time C1F84B14.B52A5542 (05:13:56.707 UTC Sat Feb 15 2003)
xmt time C1F84B14.B465C21F (05:13:56.704 UTC Sat Feb 15 2003)
filtdelay =    2.66    2.38    2.47    2.43    2.47    2.47    2.46    2.46
filtoffset =  -3.70   -3.45   -3.05   -2.60   -2.01   -1.12   -0.26   -0.20
filterror =    0.02    0.99    1.97    2.94    3.92    4.90    5.87    5.89

r1#show clock
05:14:19.932 UTC Sat Feb 15 2003


! Snip from R3 Dynamic NTP Client;

r3#show ntp status
Clock is synchronized, stratum 9, reference is 110.50.32.2
nominal freq is 249.5901 Hz, actual freq is 249.5901 Hz, precision is 2**18
reference time is C1F84AE3.4C14D938 (05:13:07.297 UTC Sat Feb 15 2003)
clock offset is 0.0197 msec, root delay is 3.68 msec
root dispersion is 15875.06 msec, peer dispersion is 15875.02 msec
```

continues

Example 2-20 *NTP Verification on R1, R2, and R3 (Continued)*

```
r3#show ntp associations detail
110.50.32.2 dynamic, our_master, sane, valid, stratum 8
ref ID 127.127.7.1, time C1F84AFB.A60B88C8 (05:13:31.648 UTC Sat Feb 15 2003)
our mode bdcast client, peer mode bdcast, our poll intvl 64, peer poll intvl 64
root delay 0.00 msec, root disp 0.03, reach 6, sync dist 15876.877
delay 3.68 msec, offset 0.0197 msec, dispersion 15875.02
precision 2**16, version 3
org time C1F84B1B.A62B3F5A (05:14:03.649 UTC Sat Feb 15 2003)
rcv time C1F84B1B.87D2622B (05:14:03.530 UTC Sat Feb 15 2003)
xmt time C1F84AE3.4B1EA196 (05:13:07.293 UTC Sat Feb 15 2003)
filtdelay =    3.68    0.00    0.00    0.00    0.00    0.00    0.00    0.00
filtoffset =   0.02    0.00    0.00    0.00    0.00    0.00    0.00    0.00
filterror =    0.02 16000.0 16000.0 16000.0 16000.0 16000.0 16000.0 16000.0


r3#show clock
05:14:31.022 UTC Sat Feb 15 2003
```

9.3: Traffic Shaping

1   Configure the Frame Relay Discard Eligible (DE) list and apply this to DLCI 106 on subinterface Serial 3/0.6 on R1.

2   Configure ACL to deny OSPF packets for getting tagged for discard eligible by Frame Relay so that they do get dropped by the Frame Relay switch. See Example 2-21.

Example 2-21 *Frame Relay Traffic Shaping*

```
! Snip from R1 configuration and output from show command.
frame-relay de-list 1 protocol ip list 102
!
interface Serial3/0.6 point-to-point
 ip address 110.50.31.1 255.255.255.0
 frame-relay de-group 1 106
 frame-relay interface-dlci 106
!
access-list 102 deny    ospf any any
access-list 102 permit ip any any


r1#show frame-relay pvc 106

PVC Statistics for interface Serial3/0 (Frame Relay DTE)

DLCI = 106, DLCI USAGE = LOCAL, PVC STATUS = ACTIVE, INTERFACE = Serial3/0.6

   input pkts 43          output pkts 53         in bytes 4622
   out bytes 5455         dropped pkts 0         in FECN pkts 0
   in BECN pkts 0         out FECN pkts 0        out BECN pkts 0
   in DE pkts 0           out DE pkts 43
   out bcast pkts 13      out bcast bytes 1525
```

Example 2-21 *Frame Relay Traffic Shaping (Continued)*

```
     pvc create time 2d06h, last time pvc status changed 00:03:32


r1#show access-lists 102
Extended IP access list 102
     deny ospf any any (9 matches)
     permit ip any any (43 matches)
```

9.4: HSRP

1 Configure HSRP peers R2 and R3 with Virtual IP address 110.50.32.10.

2 R2 should be Active. R3 is always Standby.

3 Configure authentication using password **cisco.**

4 Configure HSRP tracking for Ethernet0/1 of R2.

5 Configure R2 with priority 105 and preempt option.

6 See Example 2-22 to configure HSRP as above.

7 This section plays an important role in solving OSPF Redundancy in Section 2.1.

Example 2-22 *HSRP Configuration Snip and Output from the* **show** *Command from R2 and R3*

```
!
hostname r2
!
interface Ethernet0/0
 ip address 110.50.32.2 255.255.255.0
 ip verify unicast reverse-path
 no ip redirects
 half-duplex
 ntp broadcast
 standby 1 priority 105 preempt
 standby 1 authentication cisco
 standby 1 ip 110.50.32.10
 standby 1 track Et0/1


!
hostname r3
!
interface Ethernet0/0
 ip address 110.50.32.3 255.255.255.0
 no ip redirects
 half-duplex
 ntp broadcast client
 standby 1 ip 110.50.32.10
 standby 1 preempt
```

continues

Example 2-22 *HSRP Configuration Snip and Output from the* **show** *Command from R2 and R3 (Continued)*

```
  standby 1 track Ethernet0/1

r2#show standby
Ethernet0/0 - Group 1
  Local state is Active, priority 105, may preempt
  Hellotime 3 holdtime 10
  Next hello sent in 00:00:02.091
  Hot standby IP address is 110.50.32.10 configured
  Active router is local
  Standby router is 110.50.32.3 expires in 00:00:07
  Standby virtual mac address is 0000.0c07.ac01
  2 state changes, last state change 3d11h
  Tracking interface states for 1 interface, 1 up:
    Up    Ethernet0/1
r2#

r3#show standby
Ethernet0/0 - Group 1
  State is Standby
    1 state change, last state change 3d11h
  Virtual IP address is 110.50.32.10
  Active virtual MAC address is 0000.0c07.ac01
    Local virtual MAC address is 0000.0c07.ac01 (default)
  Hello time 3 sec, hold time 10 sec
    Next hello sent in 1.534 secs
  Preemption enabled
  Active router is 110.50.32.2, priority 105 (expires in 9.375 sec)
  Standby router is local
  Priority 100 (default 100)
    Track interface Ethernet0/1 state Up decrement 10
  IP redundancy name is "hsrp-Et0/0-1" (default)
r3#
```

Section 10.0: Security Violations

10.1: Denial of Service (DoS)

1 An ACL is already configured on the R1 Fastethernet2/0 (VLAN4) interface to fulfill the requirement for Section 2.1.

2 You need to merge ACLs for this. See Example 2-23.

3 ACL 101 configured in Example 2-23 will not allow noninitial fragments through to the server because of the first line. A noninitial fragment to the server is denied when it encounters the first ACL line because Layer 3 information in the packet matches the Layer 3 information in the ACL line.

4 Initial or nonfragments to port 80 on the server also match the first line of the ACL for Layer 3 information, but because the fragments keyword is present, the next ACL entry (the second line) is processed. The second line of the ACL permits the initial or nonfragments because they match the ACL line for Layer 3 and Layer 4 information.

Example 2-23 *DoS ACL: Snip from R1 Configuration*

```
access-list 101 deny ip any host 110.50.13.72 fragments
access-list 101 permit tcp any host 110.50.13.72 eq 80
access-list 101 deny   icmp host 110.50.32.3 host 110.50.13.65
access-list 101 deny   icmp host 13.13.13.13 host 110.50.13.65
access-list 101 deny   icmp host 110.50.13.50 host 110.50.13.65
access-list 101 permit icmp any any
access-list 101 permit ip any any
```

10.2: IP Spoofing

1 To simulate and verify the DoS attack, perform the following steps:

  a. Create Loopback-20 with IP address 18.18.18.18 on R3 (this is spoofing Loopback1 on R8).

  b. Do an extended ping from R3; source from Loopback-20 to destination 12.12.12.12 of R2.

  c. The result is that ICMP echo-replies are sent to R8 and not back to R3.

  d. Create an ICMP ACL on R2 as follows to confirm that packets from source 18.18.18.18 to destination 12.12.12.12 are arriving on VLAN 4 ingress interface ethernet0/0. You can check hit counts to prove that the attack is successful.

  e. access-list 101 permit icmp host 18.18.18.18 host 12.12.12.12.

  f. Do a **debug ip packet detail 101** and **debug ip icmp** on R2.

  g. Do a **debug ip icmp** on R8.

  h. You will see echo-replies being sent to R8 from R2.

  i. See Example 2-24.

Example 2-24 *IP Spoofing Simulation*

```
! Ping R2 loopback-1 using spoofed source IP address of R8
r3#ping ip
Target IP address: 12.12.12.12
Repeat count [5]:
Datagram size [100]:
Timeout in seconds [2]:
Extended commands [n]: y
Source address or interface: loopback20
Type of service [0]:
Set DF bit in IP header? [no]:
Validate reply data? [no]:
Data pattern [0xABCD]:
Loose, Strict, Record, Timestamp, Verbose[none]:
Sweep range of sizes [n]:
```

continues

Example 2-24 *IP Spoofing Simulation (Continued)*

```
Type escape sequence to abort.
Sending 5, 100-byte ICMP Echos to 12.12.12.12, timeout is 2 seconds:
Packet sent with a source address of 18.18.18.18
.....
Success rate is 0 percent (0/5)
r3#
! On R2 do a "debug ip packet detail 101" and" debug ip icmp; you will notice that
! the packet is arriving on Ethernet0/0 on VLAN_4. This confirms that R3 is sending it.
! R2 is sending all the echo-replies to R8 and not R3.
! This is called anti-spoofing attack where R2 is used as a reflector to attack R8.
r2#show debug
Generic IP:
  ICMP packet debugging is on
  IP packet debugging is on (detailed) for access list 101
r2#
1w0d: IP: s=18.18.18.18 (Ethernet0/0), d=12.12.12.12, len 100, rcvd 4
1w0d:     ICMP type=8, code=0
1w0d: ICMP: echo reply sent, src 12.12.12.12, dst 18.18.18.18
1w0d: IP: s=18.18.18.18 (Ethernet0/0), d=12.12.12.12, len 100, rcvd 4
1w0d:     ICMP type=8, code=0
1w0d: ICMP: echo reply sent, src 12.12.12.12, dst 18.18.18.18
1w0d: IP: s=18.18.18.18 (Ethernet0/0), d=12.12.12.12, len 100, rcvd 4
1w0d:     ICMP type=8, code=0
1w0d: ICMP: echo reply sent, src 12.12.12.12, dst 18.18.18.18
1w0d: IP: s=18.18.18.18 (Ethernet0/0), d=12.12.12.12, len 100, rcvd 4
1w0d:     ICMP type=8, code=0
1w0d: ICMP: echo reply sent, src 12.12.12.12, dst 18.18.18.18
1w0d: IP: s=18.18.18.18 (Ethernet0/0), d=12.12.12.12, len 100, rcvd 4
1w0d:     ICMP type=8, code=0
1w0d: ICMP: echo reply sent, src 12.12.12.12, dst 18.18.18.18
r2#
r2#show access-lists 101
Extended IP access list 101
    permit icmp host 18.18.18.18 host 12.12.12.12 (5 matches)
r2#


On R8 receiving all the echo-replies from R2
r8#
r8#
1w2d: ICMP: echo reply rcvd, src 12.12.12.12, dst 18.18.18.18
1w2d: ICMP: echo reply rcvd, src 12.12.12.12, dst 18.18.18.18
1w2d: ICMP: echo reply rcvd, src 12.12.12.12, dst 18.18.18.18
1w2d: ICMP: echo reply rcvd, src 12.12.12.12, dst 18.18.18.18
1w2d: ICMP: echo reply rcvd, src 12.12.12.12, dst 18.18.18.18
r8#
r8#
! To fix this, configure "ip verify unicast reverse-path" on Ethernet0/0.
! Note that Cisco express forwarding (CEF) must be enabled on the R2 for this.
! Unicast RPF does this by doing a reverse lookup in the CEF table.
! Ping again from R3 sourcing from Loopback20 and you will not receive any
```

Example 2-24 *IP Spoofing Simulation (Continued)*

```
! icmp echo-replies on R8. This is because of Unicast RPF is dropping all
! packets on ethernet0/0 which has invalid source IP that is not validating with
! R2's routing table. To confirm if Unicast RPF is working, use
! "show ip traffic" command and look for Unicast RPF drop count.
! Non-zero count indicates Unicast RPF is working.
! For more on Unicast RPF, see http://www.cisco.com/univercd/cc/td/doc/product/
  software/ios121/121cgcr/secur_c/scprt5/scdrpf.htm
r2#show ip traffic
IP statistics:
  Rcvd:  2852995 total, 611157 local destination
         0 format errors, 0 checksum errors, 638 bad hop count
         0 unknown protocol, 1 not a gateway
         0 security failures, 0 bad options, 0 with options
  Opts:  0 end, 0 nop, 0 basic security, 0 loose source route
         0 timestamp, 0 extended security, 0 record route
         0 stream ID, 0 strict source route, 0 alert, 0 cipso, 0 ump
         0 other
  Frags: 0 reassembled, 0 timeouts, 0 couldn't reassemble
         0 fragmented, 0 couldn't fragment
  Bcast: 14 received, 9 sent
  Mcast: 561632 received, 440927 sent
  Sent:  483569 generated, 2240772 forwarded
  Drop:  672 encapsulation failed, 0 unresolved, 0 no adjacency
         4 no route, 5 unicast RPF, 0 forced drop
```

CHAPTER 3

Practice Lab 3

One of the key elements for success in passing the CCIE exam is time management. A well-planned approach will go a long way in assisting you to achieve this. The elements of perfection and accuracy will come with much practice. Do not be discouraged if you have found the previous labs difficult. Your aim should be to move on through these exercises, making improvements in your approach and identifying areas of development.

Following the previous chapters, this lab is a multiprotocol, multitechnology exercise. You will be tested on all areas, and the degree of complexity in each lab is the same.

The topology is of a new design, and the VPN3000 Concentrator has been added to the scenario.

Again, you should aim to use the "Verification, Hints, and Troubleshooting Tips" section to build your troubleshooting skills and learn how to identify and resolve the problems.

The lab is marked out of 100. You must complete the lab within 8 hours and obtain a minimum of 80 marks to pass. As with all labs, this test has been written such that you should be able to complete all questions, including initial configuration (that is, IP addressing), within 8 hours, excluding cabling time. Allow up to 1 hour for cabling, using the provided instructions and observing the general guidelines. You can use any combination of routers as long as you fulfill the needs of the topology in Figure 3-1. It is not compulsory to use routers of the same model.

| NOTE | The real CCIE Lab does not require you to do any cabling or IP addressing. |

Equipment List

- 8 routers with the following specifications (all routers are to be loaded with the latest Cisco IOS version in 12.1(T) train):

    R1 — 2 Ethernet, 1 BRI (with IP Plus + IPSec 56 image)

    R2 — 2 Ethernet (with IP Plus image)

    R3 — 2 Ethernet (with IP Plus image)

    R4 — 1 serial, 1 Ethernet, 1 BRI (with IP Plus image)

    R5 — 1 serial, 1 Ethernet (with IP Plus + Firewall image)

R6 — 4 Ethernet (with IP Plus + Firewall image)

R7 — 2 Ethernet (with IP Plus + IPSec 56 image)

R8 — 1 Ethernet (with IP Plus image)

- 1 Switch 3550
- 1 PIX with 2 interfaces (version 6.x with DES enabled)
- 1 VPN3000 Concentrator (version 3.6.x)
- 3 PCs:

  Windows 2000 Server with CiscoSecure ACS 3.x installed

  Test PC with CiscoSecure VPN Client 3.x installed

  Test PC (any OS)

General Guidelines

- Do not configure any static/default routes unless otherwise specified/required.
- Use DLCIs provided in the diagram.
- Use the IP addressing scheme provided in the diagram; do not change any IP addressing unless otherwise specified. In the CCIE Lab, initial configurations are loaded, and therefore IP addresses are not to be changed. In this book, each chapter has a separate lab topology with different IP addressing, so each chapter needs to be recabled and all IP addresses need to be redone from the previous chapter.
- Use **cisco** as the password for any authentication string, enable-password, and TACACS+/RADIUS key or for any other purpose unless otherwise specified.
- Add additional loopbacks as specified during this lab.
- Configure VLANs on Switch1 as per the diagram.
- All routers should be able to ping any interface in the network using the *optimal* path.
- Do not use any external resources or answers provided in this book when attempting the lab.
- Configure fallback for any of the AAA questions below to the local database. If you don't, you will lose all points for that question.
- Do not configure any authentication or authorization on the console and aux ports.

NOTE   The real CCIE lab exams are hands-on structures similar to this book. Each configuration exercise has preassigned point values. The candidate must obtain a minimum mark of 80% to pass. This book provides you with a similar structure to give you a better understanding and experience. For more information on CCIE exam structure, refer to the following URLs:

www.cisco.com/en/US/partner/learning/le3/le2/le23/learning_certification_level_home.html

www.cisco.com/warp/customer/625/ccie/exam_preparation/preparation.html

---

Setting Up the Lab

You can use any combination of routers as long as you fulfill the topology diagram outlined in Figure 3-1. It is not compulsory to use the same model of routers.

Figure 3-1   *Lab Topology*

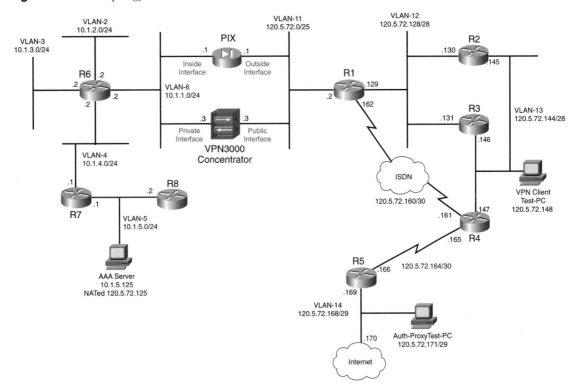

Routing Protocol Information

Use Figure 3-2 to configure all routing protocols.

BGP Information

Use Figure 3-3 to configure BGP.

Figure 3-2 *Routing Protocol Information*

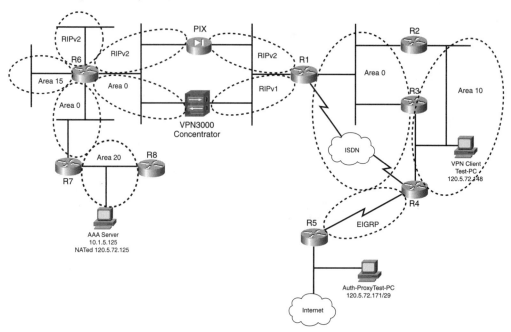

Figure 3-3 *BGP Information*

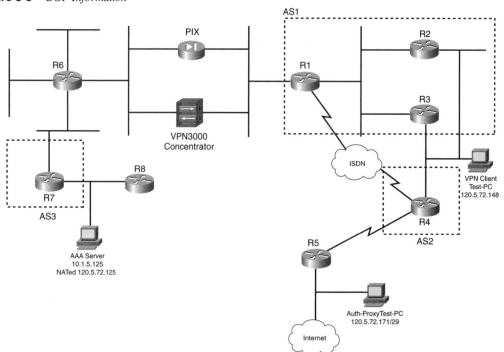

Cabling Instructions

Use Tables 3-1 and 3-2 for cabling all devices in your topology. It is not a must to use the same type or sequence of interface. You may use any combination of interface(s) as long as you fulfill the requirement.

Table 3-1   *Cabling Instructions (Ethernet)*

Ethernet Cabling	Switch1
R1-Fastethernet0/0	Port 1
R1-Fastethernet0/1	Port 2
R2-Ethernet0/0	Port 3
R2- Ethernet 0/1	Port 4
R3- Ethernet 0/0	Port 5
R3- Ethernet0/1	Port 6
R4-Fastethernet0/0	Port 7
R5- Ethernet 0	Port 8
R6- Ethernet 1/0	Port 9
R6- Ethernet 1/1	Port 10
R6- Ethernet 1/2	Port 11
R6- Ethernet 1/3	Port 12
R7- Ethernet 0/0	Port 13
R7- Ethernet 0/1	Port 14
R8-Fastethernet0/0	Port 15
PIX-outside-E0	Port 16
PIX-inside-E1	Port 17
VPN3000-inside	Port 18
VPN3000-outside	Port 19
AAA server	Port 20
Test-PC-VPN-Client	Port 21
Test-PC-for-Auth-Proxy	Port 22

Table 3-2   *Cabling Instructions (Serial)*

Back-to-Back Cabling	DTE-End	DCE-End
R4-to-R5	R4-serial2/0	R5-serial0

Practice Lab 3 Exercises

As you start Lab 3, remember that each section is indicated with corresponding points. Gauge the value of the question by its points and complexity, and spend adequate time on it. Do not waste time on a section when you get stuck; you must learn to move on and attend to problem sections later on.

The steps in each exercise are not necessarily intended to be completed in order. They can be done in any order of preference or as you feel appropriate. There may be situations where the steps have intentionally been written in incorrect order to cause a problem. You have to identify the best approach and fulfill all the requirements.

Section 1.0: Basic Configuration (8 points)

1.1: IP Addressing (2 points)

1 Redraw a detailed topology with all the necessary information.

2 Configure IP addressing as per the topology diagram shown in Figure 3-1.

3 Do not configure any static or default routes anywhere on the network unless otherwise specified. Configure a default route on R5 to ISP next-hop address 120.5.72.170.

4 Create the following loopbacks:

Loopback-1 11.11.11.11/24 on R1

Loopback-1 12.12.12.12/24 on R2

Loopback-2 122.122.122.122/24 on R2

Loopback-1 13.13.13.13/24 on R3

Loopback-2 133.133.133.133/24 on R3

Loopback-1 14.14.14.14/24 on R4

Loopback-2 144.144.144.144/24 on R4

Loopback-1 15.15.15.15/24 on R5

Loopback-10 155.155.155.155/24 on R5

Loopback-11 156.156.156.156/24 on R5

Loopback-1 16.16.16.16/24 on R6

Loopback-1 17.17.17.17/24 on R7

Loopback-2 177.177.177.177/24 on R7

Loopback-1 18.18.18.18/24 on R8

1.2: Serial Links Configuration (2 points)

1 Configure the R4 and R5 serial link for PPP.

2 Use CHAP authentication.

3 R5 should use host name **Router5** password **cisco** for CHAP authentication.

1.3: LAN Switch Configuration (4 points)

1 Configure VLANs on Switch1 as shown in Figure 3-1.

2 Configure the Switch1 management interface in VLAN-3. Assign IP address 10.1.3.10. Only devices in VLAN-4 and VLAN-5 should be able to access the switch, excluding the AAA server.

3 Configure the default gateway to be R6. Do not use any static routes.

Section 2.0: Routing Configuration (27 points)

1 Configure routing protocols as per the following instructions using Figure 3-2.

2.1: OSPF (8 points)

1 Configure the network between R1-R2-R3 and the ISDN network in OSPF Area0.

2 Configure OSPF load balancing in Area0. R1 must round-robin between R2 and R3 to send/receive traffic.

3 Put VLAN-13 interfaces on R2 and R3 in OSPF Area10.

4 Configure R6-R7 in Area0. Note that there is a separate OSPF process running for networks behind PIX/VPN3000.

5 Networks behind PIX/VPN3000 should not be visible on devices outside PIX/VPN3000. Do not use distribute-list or any filtering methods to achieve this task.

6 Networks in front of PIX/VPN3000 should not be visible on devices behind PIX/VPN3000. You can use distribute-list to filter them as necessary.

7 Configure Loopback-1 on R2, R3, R6, and R7 in Area0.

8 Configure Loopback-2 on R7 in Area0.

9 Configure R6 and VPN3000 Concentrator Private Interface in Area0. Ensure Concentrator learns all routes via OSPF; do not configure any static routes.

10 Configure VLAN-3 on R6 in OSPF Area15.

11 Configure R7-R8 in OSPF Area20. R8 should not see any internal or external OSPF routers.

12 Configure strong authentication for all OSPF areas. Use password **cisco**.

13 Propagate the default route to all participating OSPF devices. Do not propagate the default route if R4 does not receive a default route from downstream.

14 R8 should not receive any external OSPF routes. Make sure R8 learns a default route via OSPF.

2.2: EIGRP (5 points)

1 Configure EIGRP 100 between R4 and R5.

2 Configure Loopback-1 on R4 and R5 in EIGRP-100.

3 Redistribute EIGRP/OSPF mutually on R4.

4 Propagate the default route configured on R5 to R4. Do not use any static route on R4.

5 Advertise Loopback-10 and Loopback-11 on R5 in EIGRP-100. R4 should not advertise Loopback-10 to OSPF when redistributing. Only Loopback-11 should be seen on routers beyond R4. Do not use distribute-list or summarization to achieve this task.

2.3: RIP (4 points)

1 Configure RIPv2 between the PIX inside interface and R6.

2 Configure RIPv2 between the PIX outside interface and R1.

3 Advertise Loopback1 on R1 in RIPv2.

4 Configure R1 and VPN3000 Concentrator Public Interface RIPv1. Ensure R1 does not receive any routes from the Concentrator. Do not use distribute-list on R1 to achieve this task.

5 Use MD5 authentication.

6 Configure Loopback-1 on R8 in RIPv2. Ensure you see this network on all devices, including the PIX.

7 Redistribute RIP/OSPF mutually on R1, R6, and R8.

8 Configure PIX to advertise a default route to R6. Do not configure a default route on PIX or anywhere except on R5. All routers should learn the default route through respective routing protocols.

2.4: BGP (10 points)

2.4.1: Basic BGP Configuration (3 points)

1 Configure BGP peers as follows; use Figure 3-3.

2 iBGP between R1 and R2 in AS1.

3 iBGP between R1 and R3 in AS1.

4 R2 and R3 in AS1 should not peer to each other. Next hop for all routes should be 11.11.11.11.

5 Configure R4 to peer eBGP connections two times to R2 and R3.

6 eBGP between R1 and R7. Configure static translation and ACL on PIX to achieve this task. You may add a static route on R7 for Loopback-1 of R1.

7 Use Loopback-1 for BGP source on all peers. Ensure that peers in AS1 (R1, R2, and R3) have the next hop set to the Loopback1. Do not use **neighbor next-hop-self** or **set ip next-hop A.B.C.D** in the route-map on any routers.

8 Advertise Loopback-2 on R2, R3, and R4 in BGP. Make sure all devices can ping these loopbacks. Ensure all routers outside the PIX have these loopbacks in its routing table.

9 Advertise Loopback-2 on R7. Configure a static translation and ACL on PIX.

10 Redistribute BGP into RIP on R1, and ensure that PIX and VPN3000 learn all BGP routes.

2.4.2: BGP Route Summarization (3 points)

1 Configure null routes as follows and advertise in BGP accordingly. Configure community no-export for network 1.1.4.0 on R7 only and propagate communities to all AS. Configure summarization on R2 and R3 such that AS2 peers see this as one Class B route. Make sure that AS3 has all the AS-PATH information in the summarized route. Do not use any filtering method to exclude the 1.1.4.0 network from summarization.

On R1:

```
ip route 1.1.1.0 255.255.255.0 null0
ip route 1.1.2.0 255.255.255.0 null0
ip route 1.1.3.0 255.255.255.0 null0
```

On R7:

```
ip route 1.1.4.0 255.255.255.0 null0
ip route 1.1.5.0 255.255.255.0 null0
ip route 1.1.6.0 255.255.255.0 null0
```

2.4.3: BGP Path Selection (4 points)

1 Configure AS1 such that R1 prefers R2 to reach routes from AS2. Do not use weight to achieve this task.

2 Configure AS1 transitive such that routes to AS3 are preferred via R3 and routes to AS1 are preferred via R2. Do not use local-preference or weight to achieve this task. Do not use IP Network ACL.

Section 3.0: ISDN Configuration (7 points)

3.1: Basic ISDN (4 points)

1 Configure ISDN on R1 and R4.

2 Use network 120.5.72.160/30 and advertise in OSPF Area0.

3 Do not send passwords in clear text.

4 Configure ISDN to come up if there is a change in the OSPF domain. Do not use the backup interface command to achieve this task.

5 All routes should be converged via ISDN.

ISDN information:

BRI number on R1 is 99047265

BRI number on R4 is 99047132

Switch-type = basic-net3

3.2: PPP Multilink (3 points)

1 Configure ISDN to bring up both B channels to have more bandwidth.

2 Verify this by bringing up the ISDN by disabling the switch port for R1 in VLAN-12.

Section 4.0: PIX Configuration (10 points)

4.1: Basic PIX Configuration (4 points)

1 Configure host name PIX.

2 Configure outside IP address 120.5.72.1/25.

3 Configure inside IP address 10.1.1.1/24.

4 Configure RIP on the inside and outside interfaces as shown in the routing protocol information in Figure 3-2.

5 Configure strong authentication for RIPv2 peers.

6 Make sure you can ping AAA server, loopback(s), and all networks in the topology.

4.2: Network Address Translation (NAT) (4 points)

1 You should receive RIP route(s) from R6. Configure network address translation for all internal networks to their corresponding octets with the first octet to be 110. For example, translate 10.1.1.1 to 110.1.1.1.

2 All Loopback1(s) on devices behind PIX should be visible on devices outside the PIX.

3 Add static routes on R1 for all 110.x.x.x networks and Loopback1(s) to PIX. All devices in the network outside the PIX should be able to ping these networks.

4 Configure static NAT and ACL for AAA server 10.1.5.125 to 120.5.72.125.

5 All networks behind PIX should be able to go out to the Internet. Hide these networks with the IP address of the outside interface.

4.3: Advanced PIX Configuration (2 points)

1 Configure a static translation and ACL for web server 10.1.4.120 in VLAN-4 to the 120.5.72.120 address. Customers are complaining of connectivity problems with the web server. Company policy documentation shows that a firewall is installed on this web server, which is randomizing TCP sequence numbers. You do not have admin privileges for the web server to disable the firewall; your task is to fix this issue on the PIX.

Section 5.0: IPSec Configuration (10 points)

5.1: IPSec Remote Access to VPN3000 Concentrator (6 points)

1 Configure the IPSec client in VLAN-13 to the VPN3000 concentrator. Use the following parameters.

2 Configure Group-name **lab3-users** with password **cisco.**

3 Configure internal user authentication. Configure username **cisco123** password **cisco123** on the concentrator.

4 Create a VPN-pool of 10.1.6.0/24 for VPN clients.

5 Configure NAT transparent mode.

6 Make sure VPN client Test-PC in VLAN-13 can ping all internal networks behind the VPN3000 concentrator through the IPSec tunnel. Do not configure any static route(s) to achieve this task. Configure default-route to 120.5.72.2.

5.2: IPSec LAN-to-LAN Using Preshared (4 points)

1   Encrypt BGP traffic between AS1 and AS3. Use Loopack1 for BGP and IPSec peering. Configure all other parameters as appropriate.

Section 6.0: IOS Firewall Configuration (8 points)

6.1: Context-Based Access Control (CBAC) (4 points)

1   Configure the firewall on R5 for all traffic going to the Internet. Configure the ingress ACL on the Internet link to protect from RFC1918.

2   Modify settings such that TCP and UDP idle-time are 30 minutes and 15 seconds, respectively.

3   Configure the firewall to start deleting TCP/UDP half-open sessions at 1000, and continue to delete until the connection drops to 800 sessions.

6.2: Proxy Authentication (4 points)

1   Configure R6 for proxy authentication for users in VLAN-14 to a web server behind PIX.

2   Configure inbound ACL on R6 VLAN-6 interface (Ethernet1/0) to download per-user auth-proxy ACL from the AAA server.

3   Configure R8 with HTTP service to act as a web server for this exercise. Configure static NAT and ACL on PIX for 10.1.5.2 to 120.5.72.22.

4   Download a user profile from the AAA server. Authentication should be triggered on the HTTP connection to R8 from VLAN-14 users only.

5   Configure username **web-user** on CiscoSecure ACS with appropriate settings.

6   Make sure the R6 console and aux ports are not affected by AAA settings.

Section 7.0: AAA (8 points)

7.1: AAA on the Router (4 points)

1   Configure R4 authentication for Telnet to local database and fallback to line password.

2   Configure console authentication to line password **cisco123** only.

3 Configure two users on the router as follows: User5 and User11 with privilege level 5 and 11, respectively, with password **cisco**. Ensure that the user gets dropped into the respective privilege level by default. Usernames must be case-sensitive.

4 User5 should be able to configure routing protocol-related configuration, and User11 should be able to configure interface-specific configurations.

5 Configure command accounting for both users to the TACACS+ server.

6 Configure CiscoSecure ACS for R4 Loopback1 with preshared key **cisco** to receive accounting updates.

7.2: AAA on PIX (4 points)

1 Configure SSH on PIX for TestPC 120.5.72.148 in VLAN-13.

2 Configure SSH authentication using TACACS+.

3 Configure username **ssh-user** on CiscoSecure ACS.

Section 8.0: Advanced Security (6 points)

8.1: Perimeter Security (3 points)

1 Prevent R5 from large ICMP packet floods from the Internet.

2 Configure traffic policing using Modular Quality of Service (QoS) and a two-token bucket algorithm to eliminate this.

3 Do not use CAR to achieve this task.

4 Do not deny ICMP completely using ACL; normal ICMP pings should work fine.

8.2: Web Server Security (3 points)

1 Web server 120.5.72.120 in VLAN-4 is getting increased embryonic TCP half-open attack.

2 This attack is causing the server to exhaust its memory in maintaining state information on these connections. One of the things to minimize this is by controlling the number of TCP half-open sessions that the web server can handle.

3 Configure the PIX to prevent the flood of embryonic connections by setting the limit to 5000 for this server.

Section 9.0: IP Services and Protocol-Independent Features (10 points)

9.1: NAT (4 points)

1 Configure TCP NAT load distribution on R4 for Telnet traffic between R2 and R3 to Virtual IP 120.5.72.150.

2 Use Destination NAT.

3 When the user from R5 Telnets to Virtual IP, the Telnet prompt should load balance between R2 and R3.

9.2: NTP (3 points)

1 Configure R7 as the NTP server.

2 Use Loopback1 as the source interface for NTP updates.

3 Update the system calendar with NTP.

4 Configure strong authentication.

5 Configure R4 to synchronize its clock with the NTP server.

9.3: Policy-Based Routing (3 points)

1 Configure R5 with Policy-Based Routing for packets arriving from R3 with no explicit route for the packet's destination to black-hole it instead of using the default gateway. Verify by pinging from R3 to any network not used in this lab.

Section 10.0: Security Violations (6 points)

10.1: Denial of Service (DoS) (4 points)

1 A worm is spreading on the intranet, and all devices are being affected. The point of entrance for this worm is through VLAN-2, and it moves to other parts of the network.

2 The worm spreads using HTTP protocol.

3 Mitigate this attack using NBAR.

4 Variations of patterns are found in the sniffer captures. The following are some snips:

http://<IP_ADDRESS>/scripts/..%255c../winnt/system32/cmd.exe?/c+dir%20c:

http://<IP_ADDRESS>/scripts/..%255c../winnt/system32/cmd.exe?/c+dir%20c:%5c

http://<IP_ADDRESS>/scripts/..%255c../winnt/system32/cmd.exe?/c+dir%20c:
%5ciis%5c

http://<IP_ADDRESS>/scripts/..%255c../winnt/system32/cmd.exe?/c+type%20c:
%5ciis%5clicense.txt

5 Use a unique pattern identified in the URL and mark all packets that match this pattern with DSCP value of 1.

6 Use ACL to discard all packets with DSCP value of 1.

10.2: IP Fragment Attack (2 points)

1 Configure PIX firewall to secure against IP fragment type attacks such as teardrop and land as per RFC 1858.

Verification, Hints, and Troubleshooting Tips

It is important for you to use this section to assist you in troubleshooting problems and verifying answers. The exercises in this chapter include some hidden tricks that this section will help you identify.

The hints provided here are to be used as a guideline and address some or all parts of the corresponding exercise question. They are not listed in any order.

Section 1.0: Basic Configuration

1.1: IP Addressing

1 You must have noticed that in each chapter, I have asked you to redraw a detailed topology diagram including everything. Why?

2 The answer is, because the topology diagram provided is not a complete picture of the network. There are all sorts of information in the exercise that are very important—for example, where are the ACLs configured, which direction, which router has the NAT configured, which router is the NTP server, and so on.

3 All these pieces of information need to be collated into one piece of sheet.

4 This helps very much in troubleshooting your own problems as you move through the exercise.

1.2: Serial Links Configuration

1 Configure serial links on R4 and R5 with PPP encapsulation. Remember, default encapsulation on serial links is HDLC.

2 Configure CHAP authentication and R5 to send CHAP host name Router5.

3 Configure username on R4 for CHAP host name for R5, and vice versa. Note that the CHAP host name for R5 is different than the default router host name.

1.3: LAN Switch Configuration

1 Configure Switch1 management by adding ACL and applying it to the VLAN-3 interface on the switch. See Example 3-1.

2 Test by extended Telnet from various Ethernets on R6. See Example 3-2.

3 Configure the default gateway to be R6. Do not use any static routes.

Example 3-1 *Snip from Switch Configuration*

```
interface Vlan3
 ip address 10.1.3.10 255.255.255.0
 ip access-group 1 in
!
ip default-gateway 10.1.3.2
!
access-list 1 deny    10.1.5.125
access-list 1 permit 10.1.4.0 0.0.0.255
access-list 1 permit 10.1.5.0 0.0.0.255
access-list 1 permit 10.1.3.0 0.0.0.255
access-list 1 deny    any
```

Example 3-2 *Telnet Test from R6 Sourcing from Different Ethernet Interfaces*

```
r6#telnet 10.1.3.10
Trying 10.1.3.10 ... Open


User Access Verification

Password: cisco
Switch1>exit

[Connection to 10.1.3.10 closed by foreign host]

r6#telnet 10.1.3.10 /source-interface ethernet 1/1
Trying 10.1.3.10 ...
% Destination unreachable; gateway or host down



r6#telnet 10.1.3.10 /source-interface ethernet 1/2
Trying 10.1.3.10 ... Open
```

Example 3-2   *Telnet Test from R6 Sourcing from Different Ethernet Interfaces (Continued)*

```
User Access Verification

Password: cisco
Switch1>exit

[Connection to 10.1.3.10 closed by foreign host]



r6#telnet 10.1.3.10 /source-interface ethernet 1/0
Trying 10.1.3.10 ...
% Destination unreachable; gateway or host down

r6#

Verify successful attempts on Switch ACL 1.

Switch1#show access-lists 1
Standard IP access list 1
    deny   10.1.5.125 (2 matches)
    permit 10.1.4.0, wildcard bits 0.0.0.255 (10 matches)
    permit 10.1.5.0, wildcard bits 0.0.0.255 (10 matches)
    permit 10.1.3.0, wildcard bits 0.0.0.255 (141 matches)
    deny   any
Switch1#
```

Section 2.0: Routing Configuration

2.1: OSPF

1 Configure OSPF areas as indicated in Figure 3-2.

2 OSPF load balancing in Area0 will be automatic when configuring R4 to peer with R2/R3 and R1 with R2/R3. OSPF supports equal-cost load balancing by default.

3 Configure separate OSPF processes on routers behind the PIX/VPN3000. They should not have any link whatsoever.

4 For R8 not to receive external OSPF routes, we could configure Area20 as **stub**. Since we are advertising Loopback1 on R8 in RIP and redistributing RIP into OSPF, we need to configure Area20 as NSSA. See Example 3-3.

Example 3-3   *Snip from R8 Configuration*

```
router ospf 110
 router-id 8.8.8.8
 area 20 authentication message-digest
 area 20 nssa
 redistribute rip metric 10 subnets
```

continues

Example 3-3 *Snip from R8 Configuration (Continued)*

```
 network 10.1.5.0 0.0.0.255 area 20
 !
router rip
 version 2
 network 18.0.0.0
 no auto-summary
```

5 If Area 20 was defined as a stub area, RIP routes would not be propagated into the OSPF domain because redistribution isn't allowed in the stub area. The only solution here is to define area 20 as NSSA, which will convert Type 5 LSA into Type 7 and inject RIP routes into the OSPF NSSA domain. See Example 3-4.

6 Configure MD5 authentication for all areas.

7 R7 will not propagate the default route to R8, as Area20 is NSSA. The NSSA border router does not, by default, originate a default route into the NSSA.

8 Configure the **area nssa default-information originate** command to inject the default route into the NSSA domain. See Example 3-5.

NOTE   Refer to the following URL for more information on default route into an NSSA:

www.cisco.com/warp/public/104/ospfdb11.html

---

9 Do not use the **always** keyword in default-information on R4 and R6, as the objective is to advertise a default route only if there is one in the routing table.

10 Configure static routes on R1 for all internal networks (NATed/non-NATed) behind PIX, and redistribute into OSPF on R1. See Section 4.2 for more details.

Example 3-4 *Routing Table from R7 and R8*

```
!Snip from R7:
r7#show ip route ospf
     16.0.0.0/24 is subnetted, 1 subnets
O       16.16.16.0 [110/11] via 10.1.4.2, 03:16:46, Ethernet0/0
     18.0.0.0/24 is subnetted, 1 subnets
O N2    18.18.18.0 [110/10] via 10.1.5.2, 00:03:36, Ethernet0/1
     10.0.0.0/24 is subnetted, 5 subnets
O IA    10.1.3.0 [110/20] via 10.1.4.2, 00:03:36, Ethernet0/0
O E1    10.1.2.0 [110/20] via 10.1.4.2, 00:03:36, Ethernet0/0
O E1    10.1.1.0 [110/20] via 10.1.4.2, 00:03:36, Ethernet0/0
O*E2 0.0.0.0/0 [110/1] via 10.1.4.2, 00:03:36, Ethernet0/0

r8#show ip route
Codes: C - connected, S - static, I - IGRP, R - RIP, M - mobile, B - BGP
       D - EIGRP, EX - EIGRP external, O - OSPF, IA - OSPF inter area
       N1 - OSPF NSSA external type 1, N2 - OSPF NSSA external type 2
```

Example 3-4 *Routing Table from R7 and R8 (Continued)*

```
              E1 - OSPF external type 1, E2 - OSPF external type 2, E - EGP
              i - IS-IS, L1 - IS-IS level-1, L2 - IS-IS level-2, ia - IS-IS inter area
              * - candidate default, U - per-user static route, o - ODR
              P - periodic downloaded static route

Gateway of last resort is 10.1.5.1 to network 0.0.0.0

       17.0.0.0/24 is subnetted, 1 subnets
O IA     17.17.17.0 [110/2] via 10.1.5.1, 06:02:00, FastEthernet0/0
       16.0.0.0/24 is subnetted, 1 subnets
O IA     16.16.16.0 [110/12] via 10.1.5.1, 06:02:00, FastEthernet0/0
       18.0.0.0/24 is subnetted, 1 subnets
C        18.18.18.0 is directly connected, Loopback1
       10.0.0.0/24 is subnetted, 4 subnets
O IA     10.1.3.0 [110/21] via 10.1.5.1, 06:02:00, FastEthernet0/0
O IA     10.1.1.0 [110/21] via 10.1.5.1, 06:02:00, FastEthernet0/0
C        10.1.5.0 is directly connected, FastEthernet0/0
O IA     10.1.4.0 [110/11] via 10.1.5.1, 06:02:01, FastEthernet0/0
       177.177.0.0/32 is subnetted, 1 subnets
O IA     177.177.177.177 [110/2] via 10.1.5.1, 06:02:01, FastEthernet0/0
O*N2 0.0.0.0/0 [110/1] via 10.1.5.1, 06:02:01, FastEthernet0/0
!The ABR converts Type 7 to Type 5 and propagates further. See route as follows on R6:
r6#show ip route ospf
       17.0.0.0/24 is subnetted, 1 subnets
O        17.17.17.0 [110/11] via 10.1.4.1, 00:21:38, Ethernet1/3
       18.0.0.0/24 is subnetted, 1 subnets
O E2     18.18.18.0 [110/10] via 10.1.4.1, 00:14:22, Ethernet1/3
       10.0.0.0/24 is subnetted, 5 subnets
O IA     10.1.5.0 [110/20] via 10.1.4.1, 00:22:08, Ethernet1/3
       177.177.0.0/32 is subnetted, 1 subnets
O        177.177.177.177 [110/11] via 10.1.4.1, 00:21:41, Ethernet1/3
```

Example 3-5 *Snip from R7 Configuration*

```
router ospf 110
 router-id 7.7.7.7
 area 0 authentication message-digest
 area 20 authentication message-digest
 area 20 nssa default-information-originate
 !
```

2.2: EIGRP

1 Inject the default route into EIGRP. There are two ways to inject a default route into EIGRP: redistribute a static route or summarize to 0.0.0.0/0.

2 Summarization will cause issues, as we also want to advertise specific routes followed in the exercise. The solution is to redistribute static into EIGRP. See Example 3-6.

See the following URL for more details:

www.cisco.com/warp/public/103/eigrp-toc.html#defaultrouting

Example 3-6 *Snip from R5*

```
router eigrp 100
 redistribute static route-map default-route
 network 120.5.72.164 0.0.0.3
 no auto-summary
 no eigrp log-neighbor-changes
 !
 ip route 0.0.0.0 0.0.0.0 120.5.72.170
 !
 access-list 2 permit 0.0.0.0
 !
 route-map default-route permit 10
 match ip address 2
!On R4, Default Route seen
r4#show ip route eigrp
     155.155.0.0/24 is subnetted, 1 subnets
D EX    155.155.155.0 [170/1889792] via 120.5.72.166, 00:12:34, Serial2/0
     156.156.0.0/24 is subnetted, 1 subnets
D EX    156.156.156.0 [170/1889792] via 120.5.72.166, 00:12:34, Serial2/0
     15.0.0.0/24 is subnetted, 1 subnets
D       15.15.15.0 [90/1889792] via 120.5.72.166, 06:06:11, Serial2/0D*EX 0.0.0.0/0
[170/1787392] via 120.5.72.166, 00:12:34, Serial2/0
r4#
```

3 Use the tagging method to filter routes without using a distribute list. See Example 3-7.

Example 3-7 *Filtering Routes Using Tags*

```
!Snip from R5, tagging routes that will needs to be filtered:
router eigrp 100
 redistribute connected route-map tag-loops
 redistribute static route-map default-route
 network 120.5.72.164 0.0.0.3
 no auto-summary
 no eigrp log-neighbor-changes
 !
 access-list 15 permit 155.155.155.0 0.0.0.255
 access-list 16 permit 156.156.156.0 0.0.0.255
 route-map tag-loops permit 10
 match ip address 15
 set tag 15
 !
 route-map tag-loops permit 20
 match ip address 16
 !

r5#
r5#show ip eigrp topology
<snip>
IP-EIGRP Topology Table for AS(100)/ID(120.5.72.169)

Codes: P - Passive, A - Active, U - Update, Q - Query, R - Reply,
       r - reply Status, s - sia Status
```

Example 3-7 *Filtering Routes Using Tags (Continued)*

```
P 0.0.0.0/0, 1 successors, FD is 281600
        via Rstatic (281600/0)
P 120.5.72.0/25, 1 successors, FD is 2195456
        via 120.5.72.165 (2195456/281600), Serial0
P 120.5.72.165/32, 1 successors, FD is 2169856
        via Rconnected (2169856/0)
P 120.5.72.164/30, 1 successors, FD is 2169856
        via Connected, Serial0
P 120.5.72.166/32, 0 successors, FD is Inaccessible
        via 120.5.72.165 (2681856/1761792), Serial0
P 155.155.155.0/24, 1 successors, FD is 128256, tag is 15
        via Rconnected (128256/0)
P 156.156.156.0/24, 1 successors, FD is 128256
        via Rconnected (128256/0)
P 120.5.72.144/28, 1 successors, FD is 2195456
        via 120.5.72.165 (2195456/281600), Serial0
P 120.5.72.128/28, 1 successors, FD is 2195456
        via 120.5.72.165 (2195456/281600), Serial0
r5#
!Snip from R4, filtering tagged routes when redistributing to OSPF.
router eigrp 100
 redistribute ospf 110
 network 120.5.72.164 0.0.0.3
 default-metric 10000 100 255 1 1500
 no auto-summary
 no eigrp log-neighbor-changes
!
router ospf 110
 router-id 4.4.4.4
 log-adjacency-changes
 area 10 authentication message-digest
 redistribute eigrp 100 metric 1 subnets route-map filter-tagged-routes
 network 120.5.72.144 0.0.0.15 area 10
 default-information originate
!
route-map filter-tagged-routes deny 10
 match tag 15
!
route-map filter-tagged-routes permit 20
!


r4#show ip eigrp topology
IP-EIGRP Topology Table for AS(100)/ID(120.5.72.165)

Codes: P - Passive, A - Active, U - Update, Q - Query, R - Reply,
       r - reply Status, s - sia Status

P 0.0.0.0/0, 1 successors, FD is 1787392
        via 120.5.72.166 (1787392/281600), Serial2/0
```

continues

Example 3-7 *Filtering Routes Using Tags (Continued)*

```
P 120.5.72.0/25, 1 successors, FD is 281600
        via Redistributed (281600/0)
P 120.5.72.165/32, 0 successors, FD is Inaccessible
        via 120.5.72.166 (2681856/2169856), Serial2/0
P 120.5.72.164/30, 1 successors, FD is 1761792
        via Connected, Serial2/0
P 120.5.72.166/32, 1 successors, FD is 1761792
        via Rconnected (1761792/0)
P 155.155.155.0/24, 1 successors, FD is 1889792, tag is 15
        via 120.5.72.166 (1889792/128256), Serial2/0
P 156.156.156.0/24, 1 successors, FD is 1889792
        via 120.5.72.166 (1889792/128256), Serial2/0
P 120.5.72.144/28, 1 successors, FD is 281600
        via Redistributed (281600/0)
P 120.5.72.128/28, 1 successors, FD is 281600
        via Redistributed (281600/0)
!See Routing Table on R2, network 155.155.155.0 is absent, only Network
!156.156.156.0 is visible:
r2#show ip rou ospf
     17.0.0.0/24 is subnetted, 1 subnets
O E2    17.17.17.0 [110/1] via 120.5.72.129, 01:17:34, Ethernet0/0
     16.0.0.0/24 is subnetted, 1 subnets
O E2    16.16.16.0 [110/1] via 120.5.72.129, 01:17:34, Ethernet0/0
     18.0.0.0/24 is subnetted, 1 subnets
O E2    18.18.18.0 [110/1] via 120.5.72.129, 01:17:34, Ethernet0/0
     156.156.0.0/24 is subnetted, 1 subnets
O E2    156.156.156.0 [110/1] via 120.5.72.147, 01:17:34, Ethernet0/1
     110.0.0.0/24 is subnetted, 5 subnets
O E2    110.1.5.0 [110/1] via 120.5.72.129, 01:17:34, Ethernet0/0
O E2    110.1.4.0 [110/1] via 120.5.72.129, 01:17:34, Ethernet0/0
O E2    110.1.3.0 [110/1] via 120.5.72.129, 01:17:34, Ethernet0/0
O E2    110.1.2.0 [110/1] via 120.5.72.129, 01:17:34, Ethernet0/0
O E2    110.1.1.0 [110/1] via 120.5.72.129, 01:17:35, Ethernet0/0
     11.0.0.0/24 is subnetted, 1 subnets
O E2    11.11.11.0 [110/2] via 120.5.72.129, 01:17:35, Ethernet0/0
     13.0.0.0/24 is subnetted, 1 subnets
O       13.13.13.0 [110/11] via 120.5.72.131, 01:17:45, Ethernet0/0
     14.0.0.0/24 is subnetted, 1 subnets
O E2    14.14.14.0 [110/1] via 120.5.72.147, 01:17:36, Ethernet0/1
     120.0.0.0/8 is variably subnetted, 5 subnets, 4 masks
O E2    120.5.72.0/25 [110/2] via 120.5.72.129, 01:17:36, Ethernet0/0
O E2    120.5.72.164/30 [110/1] via 120.5.72.147, 01:17:36, Ethernet0/1
O E2    120.5.72.166/32 [110/1] via 120.5.72.147, 01:17:36, Ethernet0/1
     15.0.0.0/24 is subnetted, 1 subnets
O E2    15.15.15.0 [110/1] via 120.5.72.147, 01:17:36, Ethernet0/1
O*E2 0.0.0.0/0 [110/1] via 120.5.72.147, 01:17:36, Ethernet0/1
r2#
```

TIP   See the following URL for more information:

www.cisco.com/warp/public/103/eigrp-toc.html#admintags

2.3: RIP

1 Some hidden tricks and problems are in the RIP section.

2 Three important things to watch out for:

— Redistributing BGP on R1 requires the **bgp redistribute-internal** command. See Example 3-8. Also read the explanation of this issue in Section 2.4.1 with Example 3-12.

— Filter the BGP-to-RIP redistribution on R1 for the routes learned from R7 (behind PIX). These should not be propagated to PIX/VPN3000. Use a route map to filter. See Example 3-9.

— VPN3k is configured for RIP version 1 and will advertise routes to R1; you need to filter them. VPN3k is not a passive device like the PIX. We do not want to learn any network(s) from behind PIX/VPN3000 on R1. This is achievable by using distribute-list, but since you are not to use this method, the workaround is to configure Fastethernet0/0 on R1 to listen to RIPv2 updates only. This way we will not accept/receive inbound RIPv1 routes from VPN3000. It is also known that the PIX is a passive device and is not going to send any RIPv2 updates, so we are now in a situation where no routes are being learned via fastethernet0/0 through RIP. See Example 3-10.

Example 3-8 *Snip from R1 Configuration*

```
router bgp 1
 bgp redistribute-internal
 bgp router-id 1.1.1.1
```

Example 3-9 *PIX Routing Table Before and After Applying the Route Map on R1*

```
pix(config)# show route
        outside 0.0.0.0 0.0.0.0 120.5.72.2 2 RIP
        inside 10.1.1.0 255.255.255.0 10.1.1.1 1 CONNECT static
        inside 10.1.2.0 255.255.255.0 10.1.1.2 1 RIP
        inside 10.1.3.0 255.255.255.0 10.1.1.2 1 RIP
        inside 10.1.4.0 255.255.255.0 10.1.1.2 1 RIP
        inside 10.1.5.0 255.255.255.0 10.1.1.2 5 RIP
        outside 11.11.11.0 255.255.255.0 120.5.72.2 1 RIP
        outside 12.12.12.0 255.255.255.0 120.5.72.2 2 RIP
        outside 13.13.13.0 255.255.255.0 120.5.72.2 2 RIP
        outside 14.14.14.0 255.255.255.0 120.5.72.2 2 RIP
        outside 15.15.15.0 255.255.255.0 120.5.72.2 2 RIP
        inside 16.16.16.0 255.255.255.0 10.1.1.2 5 RIP
        inside 17.17.17.0 255.255.255.0 10.1.1.2 5 RIP
        inside 18.18.18.0 255.255.255.0 10.1.1.2 5 RIP
        outside 120.5.72.0 255.255.255.128 120.5.72.1 1 CONNECT static
        outside 120.5.72.128 255.255.255.240 120.5.72.2 1 RIP
        outside 120.5.72.144 255.255.255.240 120.5.72.2 2 RIP
        outside 120.5.72.164 255.255.255.252 120.5.72.2 2 RIP
        outside 120.5.72.166 255.255.255.255 120.5.72.2 2 RIP
        outside 122.122.122.0 255.255.255.0 120.5.72.2 1 RIP
```

continues

Example 3-9 *PIX Routing Table Before and After Applying the Route Map on R1 (Continued)*

```
         outside 133.133.133.0 255.255.255.0 120.5.72.2 1 RIP
         outside 144.144.144.0 255.255.255.0 120.5.72.2 1 RIP
         outside 156.156.156.0 255.255.255.0 120.5.72.2 2 RIP
         outside 177.177.177.0 255.255.255.0 120.5.72.2 1 RIP
         inside 177.177.177.177 255.255.255.255 10.1.1.2 5 RIP
pix(config)#
!Snip from R1:
access-list 1 permit 17.17.17.17
!
route-map routes-from-r7 deny 10
 match ip next-hop 1
!
route-map routes-from-r7 permit 20

r1#show access-lists 1
Standard IP access list 1
    permit 17.17.17.17 (6 matches)
r1#
!After applying the route-map on R1:
pix(config)# show route
         outside 0.0.0.0 0.0.0.0 120.5.72.2 2 RIP
         inside 10.1.1.0 255.255.255.0 10.1.1.1 1 CONNECT static
         inside 10.1.2.0 255.255.255.0 10.1.1.2 1 RIP
         inside 10.1.3.0 255.255.255.0 10.1.1.2 1 RIP
         inside 10.1.4.0 255.255.255.0 10.1.1.2 1 RIP
         inside 10.1.5.0 255.255.255.0 10.1.1.2 5 RIP
         outside 11.11.11.0 255.255.255.0 120.5.72.2 1 RIP
         outside 12.12.12.0 255.255.255.0 120.5.72.2 2 RIP
         outside 13.13.13.0 255.255.255.0 120.5.72.2 2 RIP
         outside 14.14.14.0 255.255.255.0 120.5.72.2 2 RIP
         outside 15.15.15.0 255.255.255.0 120.5.72.2 2 RIP
         inside 16.16.16.0 255.255.255.0 10.1.1.2 5 RIP
         inside 17.17.17.0 255.255.255.0 10.1.1.2 5 RIP
         inside 18.18.18.0 255.255.255.0 10.1.1.2 5 RIP
         outside 120.5.72.0 255.255.255.128 120.5.72.1 1 CONNECT static
         outside 120.5.72.128 255.255.255.240 120.5.72.2 1 RIP
         outside 120.5.72.144 255.255.255.240 120.5.72.2 2 RIP
         outside 120.5.72.164 255.255.255.252 120.5.72.2 2 RIP
         outside 120.5.72.166 255.255.255.255 120.5.72.2 2 RIP
         outside 122.122.122.0 255.255.255.0 120.5.72.2 1 RIP
         outside 133.133.133.0 255.255.255.0 120.5.72.2 1 RIP
         outside 144.144.144.0 255.255.255.0 120.5.72.2 1 RIP
         outside 156.156.156.0 255.255.255.0 120.5.72.2 2 RIP
         inside 177.177.177.177 255.255.255.255 10.1.1.2 5 RIP
pix(config)#
```

Example 3-10 *Filtering Networks on R1 from VPN3000*

```
!To filter networks behind PIX/VPN3000 not to be visible on devices
!outside PIX/VPN3000, configure to receive RIPv2 updates only.
!Snip from R1 configuration:
interface FastEthernet0/0
```

Example 3-10 *Filtering Networks on R1 from VPN3000 (Continued)*

```
ip address 120.5.72.2 255.255.255.128
ip rip send version 1 2
ip rip receive version 2
ip rip authentication mode md5
ip rip authentication key-chain lab3
duplex auto
speed auto
```

Confirm the preceding configuration with the following command, and you should see no routes from the VPN3000 hop 120.5.72.3:

```
r1#show ip route ospf | include via 120.5.72.3
```

2.4: BGP

2.4.1: Basic BGP Configuration

1 BGP peers as indicated; use Figure 3-3.

2 R2 and R3 in AS1 should not peer to each other, only peer to R1 in AS1 and R4 in AS2.

3 On AS1 peers, you are restricted to use **neighbor next-hop-self** or the **set ip next-hop A.B.C.D** in the route map on any routers. The workaround is to configure the **set ip next-hop peer-address** statement in the route map and apply inbound on *all* AS1 peers. This sets the next hop to the address used for peering in the neighbor statement, which is Loopback1 in our case. See Example 3-11.

Example 3-11 *BGP Next Hop on R1, R2, and R3*

```
!Snip from R1 configuation
router bgp 1
 bgp router-id 1.1.1.1
 neighbor 12.12.12.12 remote-as 1
 neighbor 12.12.12.12 update-source Loopback1
 neighbor 12.12.12.12 route-reflector-client
 neighbor 12.12.12.12 send-community
 neighbor 12.12.12.12 route-map set-next-hop in
 neighbor 13.13.13.13 remote-as 1
 neighbor 13.13.13.13 update-source Loopback1
 neighbor 13.13.13.13 route-reflector-client
 neighbor 13.13.13.13 send-community
 neighbor 13.13.13.13 route-map set-next-hop in
!
route-map set-next-hop permit 10
 set ip next-hop peer-address

!Snip from R2 configuration
router bgp 1
 bgp router-id 2.2.2.2
```

continues

Example 3-11 *BGP Next Hop on R1, R2, and R3 (Continued)*

```
 neighbor 11.11.11.11 remote-as 1
 neighbor 11.11.11.11 update-source Loopback1
 neighbor 11.11.11.11 route-map set-next-hop in
!
route-map set-next-hop permit 10
 set ip next-hop peer-address
!

!Snip from R3 configuration
router bgp 1
 bgp router-id 3.3.3.3
 neighbor 11.11.11.11 remote-as 1
 neighbor 11.11.11.11 update-source Loopback1
 neighbor 11.11.11.11 route-map set-next-hop in
!
route-map set-next-hop permit 10
 set ip next-hop peer-address
```

4 To ensure PIX and VPN3000, see Loopback2 of R2, R3, and R4; you need to redistribute BGP into RIP on R1. Default behavior is that BGP will not redistribute iBGP derived routes into IGP (RIP). To force it, use the **bgp redistribute-internal** command. See Example 3-12.

5 If you read the whole exercise you will notice Section 5.1 requires you to peer BGP using Loopback1 and encrypt (IPSec) all BGP traffic.

Example 3-12 *BGP Redistribution on R1*

```
!snip from R1 configuration
router rip
 version 2
 redistribute bgp 1 metric 1 route-map routes-from-r7
 no auto-summary
!
router bgp 1
 no synchronization
 bgp redistribute-internal
 bgp router-id 1.1.1.1
```

2.4.2: BGP Route Summarization

1 Configure community no-export for network 1.1.4.0 on R7. See Example 3-13.

2 Advertise communities to all BGP peers. See Example 3-14.

3 You must use as-set and attribute-map to get the summarized route to AS2 (R4). See Example 3-15.

4 Remove community noexport originated from R7 on network 1.1.4.0 using attribute-map in the aggregate command. See Example 3-15 from R2 and R3.

Example 3-13 *BGP Community Setting*

```
!snip from R7 setting community for 1.1.4.0

router bgp 3
 bgp router-id 7.7.7.7
 network 1.1.4.0 mask 255.255.255.0
 network 1.1.5.0 mask 255.255.255.0
 network 1.1.6.0 mask 255.255.255.0
 neighbor 11.11.11.11 remote-as 1
 neighbor 11.11.11.11 ebgp-multihop 255
 neighbor 11.11.11.11 update-source Loopback1
 neighbor 11.11.11.11 send-community
 neighbor 11.11.11.11 route-map set-noexport out
!
access-list 4 permit 1.1.4.0 0.0.0.255
!
route-map set-noexport permit 10
 match ip address 4
 set community no-export
!
route-map set-noexport permit 20
!
```

Example 3-14 *BGP Sending Communities*

```
!Snip from R1 sending communities to R2 and R3
router bgp 1
 bgp router-id 1.1.1.1
 network 1.1.1.0 mask 255.255.255.0
 network 1.1.2.0 mask 255.255.255.0
 network 1.1.3.0 mask 255.255.255.0
 neighbor 12.12.12.12 remote-as 1
 neighbor 12.12.12.12 update-source Loopback1
 neighbor 12.12.12.12 route-reflector-client
 neighbor 12.12.12.12 next-hop-self
 neighbor 12.12.12.12 send-community
 neighbor 13.13.13.13 remote-as 1
 neighbor 13.13.13.13 update-source Loopback1
 neighbor 13.13.13.13 route-reflector-client
 neighbor 13.13.13.13 next-hop-self
 neighbor 13.13.13.13 send-community
```

Example 3-15 *BGP as-set and attribute-map*

```
!Snip from R2 config advertise with as-set and removing community.
router bgp 1
 no synchronization
 bgp router-id 2.2.2.2
 aggregate-address 1.1.0.0 255.255.0.0 as-set summary-only attribute-map remove-
   community-noexport
!
route-map remove-community-noexport permit 10
 set community none
```

continues

Example 3-15 *BGP as-set and attribute-map (Continued)*

```
!Before removing the community
r2#show ip bgp 1.1.0.0
BGP routing table entry for 1.1.0.0/16, version 171
Paths: (1 available, best #1, table Default-IP-Routing-Table, not advertised to
  EBGP peer)
  Advertised to non peer-group peers:
  11.11.11.11
  3, (aggregated by 1 2.2.2.2)
    0.0.0.0 from 0.0.0.0 (2.2.2.2)
      Origin IGP, localpref 100, weight 32768, valid, aggregated, local, best
      Community: no-export
r2#

!After removing community
r2#show ip bgp 1.1.0.0
BGP routing table entry for 1.1.0.0/16, version 12
Paths: (1 available, best #1, table Default-IP-Routing-Table)
  Advertised to non peer-group peers:
  11.11.11.11 14.14.14.14
  3, (aggregated by 1 2.2.2.2)
    0.0.0.0 from 0.0.0.0 (2.2.2.2)
      Origin IGP, localpref 100, weight 32768, valid, aggregated, local, best
r2#

!Snip from R3 config advertise with as-set and removing community
router bgp 1
 no synchronization
 bgp router-id 3.3.3.3
 aggregate-address 1.1.0.0 255.255.0.0 as-set summary-only attribute-map remove-
   community-noexport
!
route-map remove-community-noexport permit 10
 set community none
!

!Before removing the community
r3#show ip bgp 1.1.0.0
BGP routing table entry for 1.1.0.0/16, version 188
Paths: (2 available, best #2, table Default-IP-Routing-Table, not advertised to EBGP peer)
  Advertised to non peer-group peers:
  11.11.11.11
  3, (aggregated by 1 2.2.2.2)
    12.12.12.12 (metric 11) from 11.11.11.11 (2.2.2.2)
      Origin IGP, localpref 100, valid, internal
      Originator: 2.2.2.2, Cluster list: 11.11.11.11
  3, (aggregated by 1 3.3.3.3)
    0.0.0.0 from 0.0.0.0 (3.3.3.3)
      Origin IGP, localpref 100, weight 32768, valid, aggregated, local, best
      Community: no-export

!After removing community:
r3#show ip bgp 1.1.0.0
BGP routing table entry for 1.1.0.0/16, version 10
```

Example 3-15 *BGP as-set and attribute-map (Continued)*

```
Paths: (2 available, best #2, table Default-IP-Routing-Table)
  Advertised to non peer-group peers:
  11.11.11.11 14.14.14.14
  3, (aggregated by 1 2.2.2.2)
    12.12.12.12 (metric 11) from 11.11.11.11 (2.2.2.2)
      Origin IGP, localpref 100, valid, internal
      Originator: 2.2.2.2, Cluster list: 11.11.11.11
  3, (aggregated by 1 3.3.3.3)
    0.0.0.0 from 0.0.0.0 (3.3.3.3)
      Origin IGP, localpref 100, weight 32768, valid, aggregated, local, best
r3#


!Summarized route with as-path successfully added to R4


r4#show ip bgp
BGP table version is 20, local router ID is 4.4.4.4
Status codes: s suppressed, d damped, h history, * valid, > best, i - internal
Origin codes: i - IGP, e - EGP, ? - incomplete

   Network          Next Hop          Metric LocPrf Weight Path
*  1.1.0.0/16       12.12.12.12          60             0 1 3 i
*>                  13.13.13.13          50             0 1 3 i
*> 122.122.122.0/24 12.12.12.12          50             0 1 i
*                   13.13.13.13          60             0 1 i
*> 133.133.133.0/24 12.12.12.12          50             0 1 i
*                   13.13.13.13          60             0 1 i
*> 144.144.144.0/24 0.0.0.0               0         32768 i
*  177.177.177.0/24 12.12.12.12          60             0 1 3 i
*>                  13.13.13.13          50             0 1 3 i
r4#
```

2.4.3: BGP Path Selection

1 Use local-preference to configure AS1 such that R1 prefers R2 to reach routes from AS2. Do not use weight. See Example 3-16.

Example 3-16 *BGP Local-Preference*

```
!Snip from R2 config
router bgp 1
 no synchronization
 bgp router-id 2.2.2.2
 neighbor 11.11.11.11 remote-as 1
 neighbor 11.11.11.11 ebgp-multihop 255
 neighbor 11.11.11.11 update-source Loopback1
 neighbor 11.11.11.11 next-hop-self
 neighbor 11.11.11.11 route-map setpref out
!
access-list 1 permit 144.144.144.0 0.0.0.255
!
route-map setpref permit 10
 match ip address 1
```

continues

Example 3-16 *BGP Local-Preference (Continued)*

```
 set local-preference 200
 !
route-map setpref permit 20


r1#show ip bgp
BGP table version is 43, local router ID is 1.1.1.1
Status codes: s suppressed, d damped, h history, * valid, > best, i - internal,
              r RIB-failure
Origin codes: i - IGP, e - EGP, ? - incomplete

   Network          Next Hop          Metric LocPrf Weight Path
*>i122.122.122.0/24 12.12.12.12            0    100      0 i
*>i133.133.133.0/24 13.13.13.13            0    100      0 i
*>i144.144.144.0/24 12.12.12.12            0    200      0 2 i
*> 177.177.177.0/24 17.17.17.17            0             0 3 i
r1#
r1#ping 144.144.144.144

Type escape sequence to abort.
Sending 5, 100-byte ICMP Echos to 144.144.144.144, timeout is 2 seconds:
!!!!!
Success rate is 100 percent (5/5), round-trip min/avg/max = 1/3/4 ms
r1#traceroute 144.144.144.144

Type escape sequence to abort.
Tracing the route to 144.144.144.144

  1 120.5.72.130 0 msec 0 msec 4 msec
  2 120.5.72.147 0 msec *  0 msec
```

2 Use MED to configure AS1 transitive such that routes to AS3 are preferred via R3 and routes to AS1 are preferred via R2. See Example 3-17.

Example 3-17 *BGP MED*

```
!Snip from R2 configuration
router bgp 1
 no synchronization
 bgp router-id 2.2.2.2
 neighbor 14.14.14.14 remote-as 2
 neighbor 14.14.14.14 ebgp-multihop 255
 neighbor 14.14.14.14 update-source Loopback1
 neighbor 14.14.14.14 route-map setmed out
 no auto-summary
 !
ip as-path access-list 1 permit _3_
ip as-path access-list 2 permit ^$
 !
 !
access-list 1 permit 144.144.144.0 0.0.0.255
 !
```

Example 3-17 *BGP MED (Continued)*

```
route-map setmed permit 10
 match as-path 1
 set metric 60
!
route-map setmed permit 20
 match as-path 2
 set metric 50
!
route-map setmed permit 30
!
route-map setpref permit 10
 match ip address 1
 set local-preference 200
!

!Snip from R3:
router bgp 1
 no synchronization
 bgp router-id 3.3.3.3
 neighbor 14.14.14.14 remote-as 2
 neighbor 14.14.14.14 ebgp-multihop 255
 neighbor 14.14.14.14 update-source Loopback1
 neighbor 14.14.14.14 route-map setmed out
!
no ip http server
ip as-path access-list 1 permit _3_
ip as-path access-list 2 permit ^$
!
route-map setmed permit 10
 match as-path 1
 set metric 50
!
route-map setmed permit 20
 match as-path 2
 set metric 60
!
route-map setmed permit 30
!


!BGP Table on R4 and Test from R4.
r4#show ip bgp
BGP table version is 10, local router ID is 4.4.4.4
Status codes: s suppressed, d damped, h history, * valid, > best, i - internal
Origin codes: i - IGP, e - EGP, ? - incomplete

   Network          Next Hop          Metric LocPrf Weight Path
*  122.122.122.0/24 13.13.13.13          60             0 1 i
*>                  12.12.12.12          50             0 1 i
*> 133.133.133.0/24 12.12.12.12          50             0 1 i
*                   13.13.13.13          60             0 1 i
*> 144.144.144.0/24 0.0.0.0               0         32768 i
```

continues

Example 3-17 *BGP MED (Continued)*

```
*   177.177.177.0/24 12.12.12.12          60              0 1 3 i
*>                   13.13.13.13          50              0 1 3 i


r4#ping 133.133.133.133


Type escape sequence to abort.
Sending 5, 100-byte ICMP Echos to 133.133.133.133, timeout is 2 seconds:
!!!!!
Success rate is 100 percent (5/5), round-trip min/avg/max = 1/2/4 ms

r4#traceroute 133.133.133.133

Type escape sequence to abort.
Tracing the route to 133.133.133.133

  1 120.5.72.145 4 msec 0 msec 0 msec
  2 120.5.72.131 4 msec *  0 msec

r4#ping 177.177.177.177

Type escape sequence to abort.
Sending 5, 100-byte ICMP Echos to 177.177.177.177, timeout is 2 seconds:
!!!!!
Success rate is 100 percent (5/5), round-trip min/avg/max = 4/4/8 ms
r4#
r4#traceroute 177.177.177.177

Type escape sequence to abort.
Tracing the route to 177.177.177.177

  1 120.5.72.146 4 msec 0 msec 4 msec
  2 120.5.72.129 0 msec 4 msec 0 msec
  3 *  *  *
  4 *
r4#
```

Section 3.0: ISDN Configuration

3.1: Basic ISDN

1 Configure ISDN as indicated.

2 Advertise in OSPF Area0.

3 Configure OSPF demand-circuit to bring up the ISDN if there is a change in the database. See Example 3-18 for ISDN working when switch1 port 2 was disabled for R1 in VLAN-12.

4 Example 3-18 also shows that OSPF converges when ISDN comes up and all routes are learned via BRI.

3.2: PPP Multilink

1 Configure PPP multilink and load threshold. See Example 3-18, where both B channels are up.

Example 3-18 *ISDN with OSPF Demand-Circuit and PPP Multilink*

```
r1#show dialer

BRI0/0 - dialer type = ISDN

Dial String      Successes   Failures    Last DNIS   Last status
99047132              7          0        00:00:14      successful
0 incoming call(s) have been screened.
0 incoming call(s) rejected for callback.

BRI0/0:1 - dialer type = ISDN
Idle timer (900 secs), Fast idle timer (20 secs)
Wait for carrier (30 secs), Re-enable (15 secs)
Dialer state is multilink member
Dial reason: ip (s=120.5.72.162, d=224.0.0.5)
Connected to 99047132 (r4)

BRI0/0:2 - dialer type = ISDN
Idle timer (900 secs), Fast idle timer (20 secs)
Wait for carrier (30 secs), Re-enable (15 secs)
Dialer state is multilink member
Dial reason: Multilink bundle overloaded
Connected to 99047132 (r4)
r1#
r1#
r1#
r1#show isdn active
--------------------------------------------------------------------------------
                            ISDN ACTIVE CALLS
--------------------------------------------------------------------------------
Call    Calling      Called       Remote  Seconds Seconds Seconds Charges
Type    Number       Number       Name    Used    Left    Idle    Units/Currency
--------------------------------------------------------------------------------
Out     ---N/A---    99047132       r4      80   Unavail    -        0
Out     ---N/A---    99047132       r4      15   Unavail    -        0
--------------------------------------------------------------------------------


r1#show ip ospf neighbor

Neighbor ID     Pri   State          Dead Time   Address        Interface
4.4.4.4          1    FULL/  -           -        120.5.72.161   BRI0/0


r1#show ip route
Codes: C - connected, S - static, I - IGRP, R - RIP, M - mobile, B - BGP
       D - EIGRP, EX - EIGRP external, O - OSPF, IA - OSPF inter area
       N1 - OSPF NSSA external type 1, N2 - OSPF NSSA external type 2
```

continues

Example 3-18 *ISDN with OSPF Demand-Circuit and PPP Multilink (Continued)*

```
            E1 - OSPF external type 1, E2 - OSPF external type 2, E - EGP
            i - IS-IS, L1 - IS-IS level-1, L2 - IS-IS level-2, ia - IS-IS inter area
            * - candidate default, U - per-user static route, o - ODR
            P - periodic downloaded static route

Gateway of last resort is 120.5.72.161 to network 0.0.0.0

     17.0.0.0/24 is subnetted, 1 subnets
S       17.17.17.0 [1/0] via 120.5.72.1
     16.0.0.0/24 is subnetted, 1 subnets
S       16.16.16.0 [1/0] via 120.5.72.1
     1.0.0.0/24 is subnetted, 6 subnets
S       1.1.1.0 is directly connected, Null0
S       1.1.2.0 is directly connected, Null0
S       1.1.3.0 is directly connected, Null0
B       1.1.4.0 [20/0] via 17.17.17.17, 23:57:02
B       1.1.5.0 [20/0] via 17.17.17.17, 23:57:03
B       1.1.6.0 [20/0] via 17.17.17.17, 23:57:04
     18.0.0.0/24 is subnetted, 1 subnets
S       18.18.18.0 [1/0] via 120.5.72.1
     156.156.0.0/24 is subnetted, 1 subnets
O E2    156.156.156.0 [110/1] via 120.5.72.161, 00:01:57, BRI0/0
     110.0.0.0/24 is subnetted, 5 subnets
S       110.1.5.0 [1/0] via 120.5.72.1
S       110.1.4.0 [1/0] via 120.5.72.1
S       110.1.3.0 [1/0] via 120.5.72.1
S       110.1.2.0 [1/0] via 120.5.72.1
S       110.1.1.0 [1/0] via 120.5.72.1
     177.177.0.0/24 is subnetted, 1 subnets
B       177.177.177.0 [20/0] via 17.17.17.17, 23:57:19
     11.0.0.0/24 is subnetted, 1 subnets
C       11.11.11.0 is directly connected, Loopback1
     14.0.0.0/24 is subnetted, 1 subnets
O E2    14.14.14.0 [110/1] via 120.5.72.161, 00:01:57, BRI0/0
     120.0.0.0/8 is variably subnetted, 6 subnets, 4 masks
C       120.5.72.0/25 is directly connected, FastEthernet0/0
O E2    120.5.72.164/30 [110/1] via 120.5.72.161, 00:01:57, BRI0/0
O E2    120.5.72.166/32 [110/1] via 120.5.72.161, 00:01:57, BRI0/0
C       120.5.72.161/32 is directly connected, BRI0/0
C       120.5.72.160/30 is directly connected, BRI0/0
O IA    120.5.72.144/28 [110/1572] via 120.5.72.161, 00:01:58, BRI0/0
     15.0.0.0/24 is subnetted, 1 subnets
O E2    15.15.15.0 [110/1] via 120.5.72.161, 00:01:58, BRI0/0
O*E2 0.0.0.0/0 [110/1] via 120.5.72.161, 00:01:58, BRI0/0


r1#show ppp multilink

Virtual-Access1, bundle name is r4
  Bundle up for 00:01:46
  Dialer interface is BRI0/0
```

Example 3-18 *ISDN with OSPF Demand-Circuit and PPP Multilink (Continued)*

```
       0 lost fragments, 0 reordered, 0 unassigned
       0 discarded, 0 lost received, 1/255 load
       0x0 received sequence, 0x2 sent sequence
       Member links: 2 (max not set, min not set)
         BRI0/0:1, since 00:01:46, no frags rcvd
         BRI0/0:2, since 00:00:42, no frags rcvd
r1#



r4#show dialer

BRI1/0 - dialer type = ISDN

Dial String      Successes   Failures    Last DNIS    Last status
99047265                 3          0    00:01:39              successful
0 incoming call(s) have been screened.
0 incoming call(s) rejected for callback.

BRI1/0:1 - dialer type = ISDN
Idle timer (900 secs), Fast idle timer (20 secs)
Wait for carrier (30 secs), Re-enable (15 secs)
Dialer state is multilink member
Connected to 99047265 (r1)

BRI1/0:2 - dialer type = ISDN
Idle timer (900 secs), Fast idle timer (20 secs)
Wait for carrier (30 secs), Re-enable (15 secs)
Dialer state is multilink member
Connected to 99047265 (r1)


r4#show isdn active
--------------------------------------------------------------------------
                          ISDN ACTIVE CALLS
--------------------------------------------------------------------------
Call    Calling      Called      Remote  Seconds Seconds Seconds Charges
Type    Number       Number      Name    Used    Left    Idle    Units/Currency
--------------------------------------------------------------------------
In      ---N/A---    99047132      r1        93  Unavail   -
In      ---N/A---    99047132      r1        29  Unavail   -
--------------------------------------------------------------------------


r4#show ip ospf neighbor

Neighbor ID     Pri   State          Dead Time   Address        Interface
1.1.1.1           1   FULL/  -           -        120.5.72.162   BRI1/0
2.2.2.2           1   FULL/BDR       00:00:38     120.5.72.145   FastEthernet0/0
3.3.3.3           1   FULL/DR        00:00:31     120.5.72.146   FastEthernet0/0
```

continues

Example 3-18 *ISDN with OSPF Demand-Circuit and PPP Multilink (Continued)*

```
r4#show ip route
Codes: C - connected, S - static, I - IGRP, R - RIP, M - mobile, B - BGP
       D - EIGRP, EX - EIGRP external, O - OSPF, IA - OSPF inter area
       N1 - OSPF NSSA external type 1, N2 - OSPF NSSA external type 2
       E1 - OSPF external type 1, E2 - OSPF external type 2, E - EGP
       i - IS-IS, L1 - IS-IS level-1, L2 - IS-IS level-2, ia - IS-IS inter area
       * - candidate default, U - per-user static route, o - ODR
       P - periodic downloaded static route

Gateway of last resort is 120.5.72.166 to network 0.0.0.0

     17.0.0.0/24 is subnetted, 1 subnets
O E2    17.17.17.0 [110/1] via 120.5.72.162, 00:01:21, BRI1/0
     16.0.0.0/24 is subnetted, 1 subnets
O E2    16.16.16.0 [110/1] via 120.5.72.162, 00:01:21, BRI1/0
     1.0.0.0/24 is subnetted, 3 subnets
O E2    1.1.1.0 [110/1] via 120.5.72.162, 00:01:21, BRI1/0
O E2    1.1.2.0 [110/1] via 120.5.72.162, 00:01:21, BRI1/0
O E2    1.1.3.0 [110/1] via 120.5.72.162, 00:01:21, BRI1/0
     155.155.0.0/24 is subnetted, 1 subnets
D EX    155.155.155.0 [170/1889792] via 120.5.72.166, 06:06:10, Serial2/0
     18.0.0.0/24 is subnetted, 1 subnets
O E2    18.18.18.0 [110/1] via 120.5.72.162, 00:01:22, BRI1/0
     156.156.0.0/24 is subnetted, 1 subnets
D EX    156.156.156.0 [170/1889792] via 120.5.72.166, 06:06:10, Serial2/0
     110.0.0.0/24 is subnetted, 5 subnets
O E2    110.1.5.0 [110/1] via 120.5.72.162, 00:01:22, BRI1/0
O E2    110.1.4.0 [110/1] via 120.5.72.162, 00:01:22, BRI1/0
O E2    110.1.3.0 [110/1] via 120.5.72.162, 00:01:22, BRI1/0
O E2    110.1.2.0 [110/1] via 120.5.72.162, 00:01:22, BRI1/0
O E2    110.1.1.0 [110/1] via 120.5.72.162, 00:01:22, BRI1/0
     144.144.0.0/24 is subnetted, 1 subnets
C       144.144.144.0 is directly connected, Loopback2
     11.0.0.0/24 is subnetted, 1 subnets
O E2    11.11.11.0 [110/2] via 120.5.72.162, 00:01:22, BRI1/0
     14.0.0.0/24 is subnetted, 1 subnets
C       14.14.14.0 is directly connected, Loopback1
     120.0.0.0/8 is variably subnetted, 6 subnets, 4 masks
O E2    120.5.72.0/25 [110/2] via 120.5.72.162, 00:01:23, BRI1/0
C       120.5.72.164/30 is directly connected, Serial2/0
C       120.5.72.166/32 is directly connected, Serial2/0
C       120.5.72.160/30 is directly connected, BRI1/0
C       120.5.72.162/32 is directly connected, BRI1/0
C       120.5.72.144/28 is directly connected, FastEthernet0/0
     15.0.0.0/24 is subnetted, 1 subnets
D       15.15.15.0 [90/1889792] via 120.5.72.166, 06:06:11, Serial2/0
D*EX 0.0.0.0/0 [170/1787392] via 120.5.72.166, 06:06:12, Serial2/0


r4#show ppp multilink
```

Example 3-18 *ISDN with OSPF Demand-Circuit and PPP Multilink (Continued)*

```
Virtual-Access1, bundle name is r1
  Dialer interface is BRI1/0
  0 lost fragments, 0 reordered, 0 unassigned
  0 discarded, 0 lost received, 1/255 load
  0x2 received sequence, 0x2 sent sequence
  Member links: 2 (max not set, min not set)
    BRI1/0:1
    BRI1/0:2
```

Section 4.0: PIX Configuration

4.1: Basic PIX Configuration

1 Configure PIX host name, IP addresses, and so on.

2 Do not configure any default or static route.

3 Configure RIP and authentication for v2 as shown in Figure 3-2.

4 Make sure you can ping AAA server, Loopback(s), and all networks in the topology.

4.2: Network Address Translation (NAT)

1 Configure static NAT translation for all internal private address ranges. Change the first octet to 110. For example, translate 10.1.1.1 to 110.1.1.1. See Example 3-19.

2 Do not translate Loopback1(s) on devices behind PIX; they should be visible on devices outside. See Example 3-19.

3 Configure NAT for AAA server 10.1.5.125 to 120.5.72.125. See Example 3-19.

4 Configure the **nat** and **global** commands to translate all other networks to use the outside interface—that is, PAT. See Example 3-20.

Example 3-19 *PIX Static Translations*

```
PIX(config)# show static
static (inside,outside) 110.1.1.0 10.1.1.0 netmask 255.255.255.0 0 0
static (inside,outside) 110.1.2.0 10.1.2.0 netmask 255.255.255.0 0 0
static (inside,outside) 110.1.3.0 10.1.3.0 netmask 255.255.255.0 0 0
static (inside,outside) 110.1.4.0 10.1.4.0 netmask 255.255.255.0 0 0
static (inside,outside) 110.1.5.0 10.1.5.0 netmask 255.255.255.0 0 0
static (inside,outside) 16.16.16.16 16.16.16.16 netmask 255.255.255.255 0 0
static (inside,outside) 17.17.17.17 17.17.17.17 netmask 255.255.255.255 0 0
static (inside,outside) 18.18.18.18 18.18.18.18 netmask 255.255.255.255 0 0
static (inside,outside) 177.177.177.177 177.177.177.177 netmask 255.255.255.255 0 0
static (inside,outside) 120.5.72.125 10.1.5.125 netmask 255.255.255.255 0 0
```

Example 3-20 *PIX* **nat** *and* **global**

```
!Snip from PIX configuration
nat (inside) 1 0.0.0.0 0.0.0.0 0 0
global (outside) 1 interface
```

4.3: Advanced PIX Configuration

1 PIX ASA randomizes TCP sequence numbers. Configure PIX not to randomize the TCP/IP packet's sequence number by using option **norandomseq** in the static command for web server 10.1.4.120. See Example 3-21.

Example 3-21 *PIX Static Translation*

```
static (inside,outside) 120.5.72.120 10.1.4.120 netmask 255.255.255.255 0 0  norandomseq
```

Section 5.0: IPSec Configuration

5.1: IPSec Remote Access to VPN3000 Concentrator

1 Configure the VPN3000 interface setting as per the topology diagram in Figure 3-1.

2 Configure OSPF on the private interface and RIPv1 on the public interface. See Figure 3-4 for interface and routing protocol settings.

3 Configure group and user information as shown in Figure 3-5.

4 Configure IP pool 10.1.6.0/24 for clients.

5 For the VPN client Test PC to be able to ping all networks behind the VPN3000 concentrator, the router (r6) needs a route for VPN client pool 10.1.6.0 pointing to the VPN3000 concentrator. Since we are not allowed to configure any static routes, the solution is to configure RRI (Reverse Route Injection) on VPN3000. See Figure 3-6.

6 RRI dynamically pushes the remote-access network to R6 via OSPF upon a VPN client connection. See Example 3-23.

NOTE You need to tick the Autonomous System check box under the VPN3000 menu to indicate that this is an Autonomous System boundary (ASBR) device as follows:

Configuration | System | IP Routing | OSPF

---

7 By selecting the Autonomous System check box, you will also advertise routes to R6 which again we don't want. Do a **show ip route ospf | include via 10.1.1.3** and you will

see all the routes learned from the VPN3000. All these networks should use PIX next hop and not the concentrator. Filter them using a distribute list, except for the one generated by RRI for our VPN client address pool. See Example 3-22.

8   Connect from Test-PC 120.5.72.148 in VLAN-13. See Figure 3-7 for the client connection.

9   After successfully connecting, verify the routing table on R6 and VPN3000 to see if the 10.1.6.x route was populated. See Figure 3-8 for a capture of the routing table on the VPN3000 and Example 3-23 for the routing table on R6.

10 You can also verify client status from the VPN3000 from the Monitoring | Session option. See Figure 3-9.

11 Configure the VPN client with Group-name **lab3-users** password **cisco**. Make sure you enable Transparent mode using UDP. See Figure 3-10 for VPN Client settings on the Test-PC.

Example 3-22 *Filter Incorrect Routes on R6 Learned Via VPN3000*

```
r6#show ip route ospf | include via 10.1.1.3
O E2 1.0.0.0/8 [110/20] via 10.1.1.3, 03:59:30, Ethernet1/0
O E2 156.156.0.0/16 [110/20] via 10.1.1.3, 00:21:03, Ethernet1/0
O E2 11.0.0.0/8 [110/20] via 10.1.1.3, 03:59:30, Ethernet1/0
O E2 12.0.0.0/8 [110/20] via 10.1.1.3, 03:59:30, Ethernet1/0
O E2 13.0.0.0/8 [110/20] via 10.1.1.3, 03:59:30, Ethernet1/0
O E2 14.0.0.0/8 [110/20] via 10.1.1.3, 00:29:21, Ethernet1/0
O E2    120.5.72.166 [110/20] via 10.1.1.3, 00:21:08, Ethernet1/0
O E2 15.0.0.0/8 [110/20] via 10.1.1.3, 00:21:03, Ethernet1/0

!Snip from R6 config:
router ospf 110
 router-id 6.6.6.6
distribute-list 1 in Ethernet1/0
!
access-list 1 permit 10.1.6.0 0.0.0.255
```

After applying the distribute list above, all the routes are dropped except the 10.1.6.0 network.

Example 3-23 *VPN Client Connection*

```
!After connecting the VPN client, the route is added

2w3d: RT: network 10.0.0.0 is now variably masked
2w3d: RT: add 10.1.6.1/32 via 10.1.1.3, ospf metric [110/20]
!Routing table from R6 when client connected, dynamic route populated for
!10.1.6.1/32 which is the IP address assigned to the VPN client.

r6#show ip route
Codes: C - connected, S - static, I - IGRP, R - RIP, M - mobile, B - BGP
       D - EIGRP, EX - EIGRP external, O - OSPF, IA - OSPF inter area
       N1 - OSPF NSSA external type 1, N2 - OSPF NSSA external type 2
```

continues

Example 3-23 *VPN Client Connection (Continued)*

```
            E1 - OSPF external type 1, E2 - OSPF external type 2, E - EGP
            i - IS-IS, L1 - IS-IS level-1, L2 - IS-IS level-2, ia - IS-IS inter area
            * - candidate default, U - per-user static route, o - ODR
            P - periodic downloaded static route

Gateway of last resort is 10.1.1.1 to network 0.0.0.0

     17.0.0.0/24 is subnetted, 1 subnets
O        17.17.17.0 [110/11] via 10.1.4.1, 00:21:38, Ethernet1/3
     16.0.0.0/24 is subnetted, 1 subnets
C        16.16.16.0 is directly connected, Loopback1
     18.0.0.0/24 is subnetted, 1 subnets
O E2     18.18.18.0 [110/1] via 10.1.4.1, 00:21:38, Ethernet1/3
     10.0.0.0/8 is variably subnetted, 6 subnets, 2 masks
C        10.1.3.0/24 is directly connected, Ethernet1/2
C        10.1.2.0/24 is directly connected, Ethernet1/1
C        10.1.1.0/24 is directly connected, Ethernet1/0
O E2     10.1.6.1/32 [110/20] via 10.1.1.3, 00:13:49, Ethernet1/0
O IA     10.1.5.0/24 [110/20] via 10.1.4.1, 00:21:39, Ethernet1/3
C        10.1.4.0/24 is directly connected, Ethernet1/3
     177.177.0.0/32 is subnetted, 1 subnets
O        177.177.177.177 [110/11] via 10.1.4.1, 00:21:41, Ethernet1/3
R*   0.0.0.0/0 [120/1] via 10.1.1.1, 00:00:16, Ethernet1/0


!After disconnecting the VPN client, the route is deleted

2w3d: RT: del 10.1.6.1/32 via 10.1.1.3, ospf metric [110/20]
2w3d: RT: delete subnet route to 10.1.6.1/32
r6#
```

TIP   For more information on configuring VPN3000, see the following URLs:

- When RRI is used, either RIP or OSPF can be used to advertise these routes:

  www.cisco.com/warp/public/471/rri.html#usingospfwithrri

  or

  www.cisco.com/en/US/products/hw/vpndevc/ps2284/products_configuration_
  example09186a0080094a6b.shtml

- Configuring IPSec—Cisco VPN 3000 Client to VPN 3000 Concentrator:

  www.cisco.com/warp/public/471/ipsec_3000.html

- NAT Transparent mode:

  www.cisco.com/warp/public/471/nat_trans.html

Figure 3-4 *Interface and Routing Protocol Settings on VPN3000*

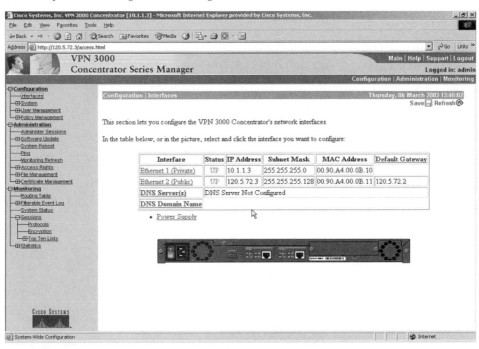

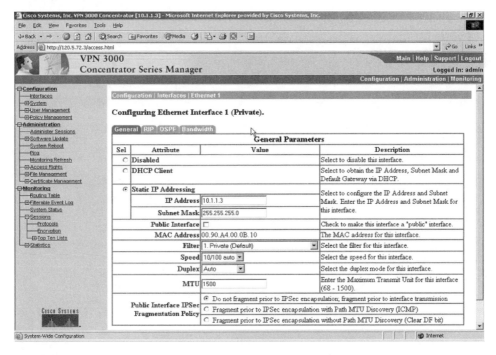

Figure 3-4 *Interface and Routing Protocol Settings on VPN3000 (Continued)*

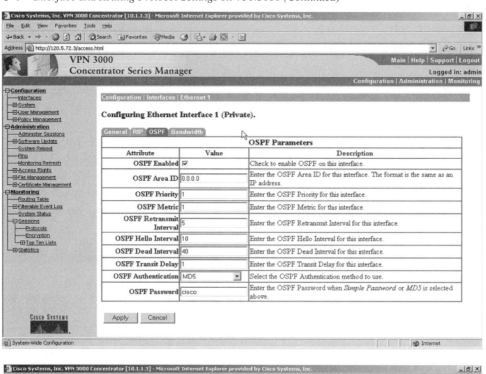

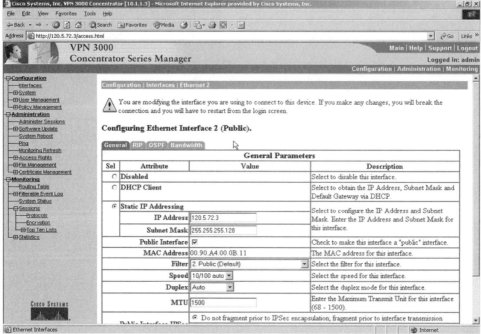

Figure 3-4   *Interface and Routing Protocol Settings on VPN3000 (Continued)*

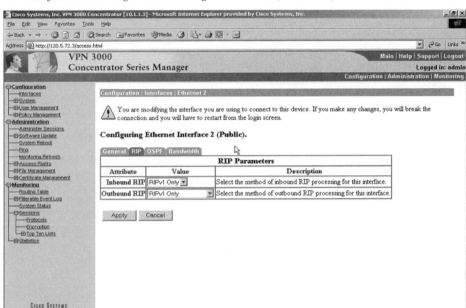

Figure 3-5   *Group and User Information on VPN3000*

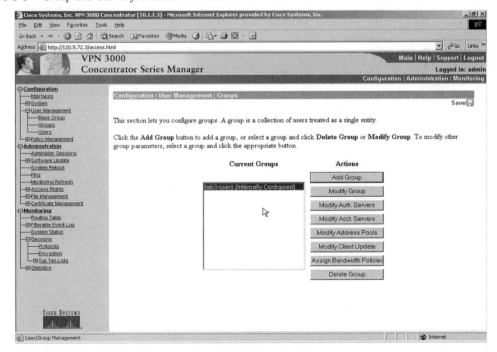

Figure 3-5 *Group and User Information on VPN3000 (Continued)*

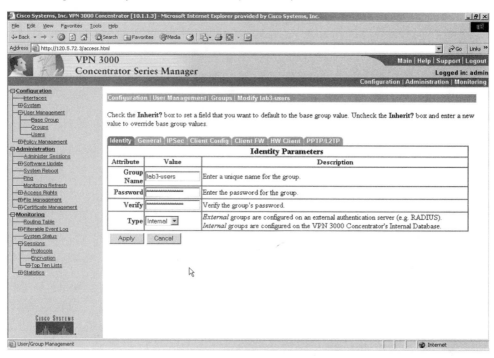

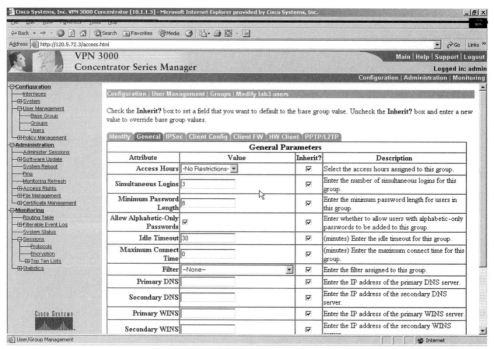

Figure 3-5   *Group and User Information on VPN3000 (Continued)*

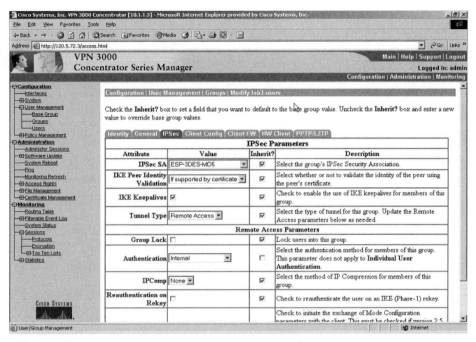

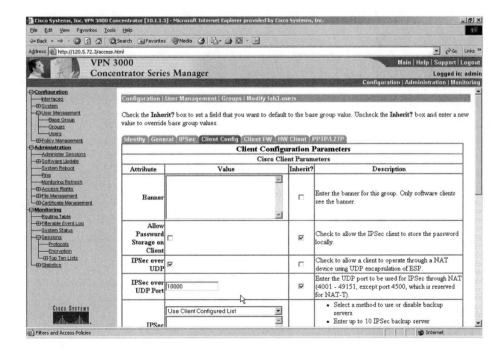

Figure 3-5 *Group and User Information on VPN3000 (Continued)*

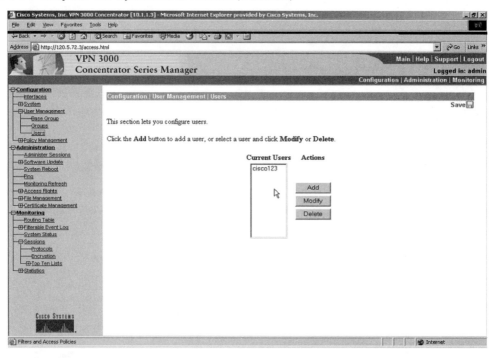

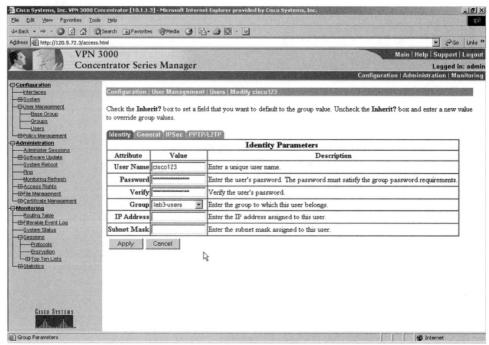

Figure 3-6   *RRI (Reverse Route Injection) on VPN3000*

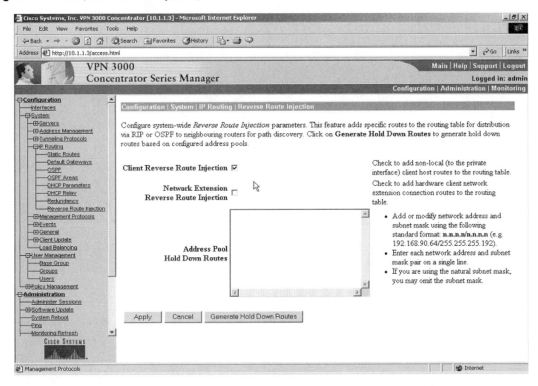

Figure 3-7   *VPN Client Connection*

Figure 3-7 *VPN Client Connection (Continued)*

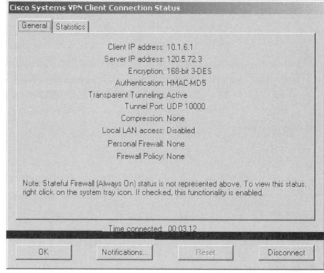

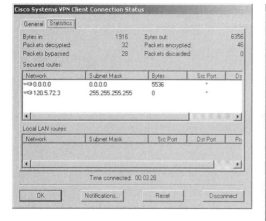

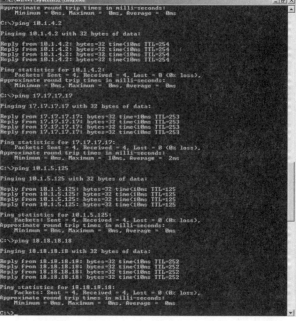

Figure 3-8   *Routing Table from the VPN3000*

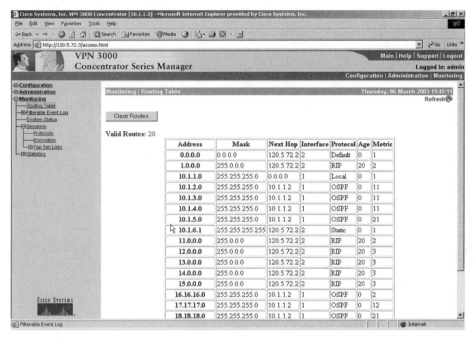

Figure 3-9   *Monitor VPN Client Status from the VPN3000*

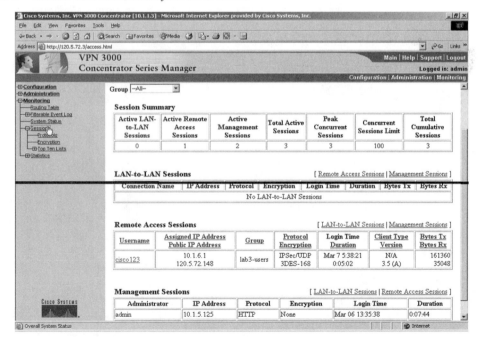

Figure 3-9 *Monitor VPN Client Status from the VPN3000 (Continued)*

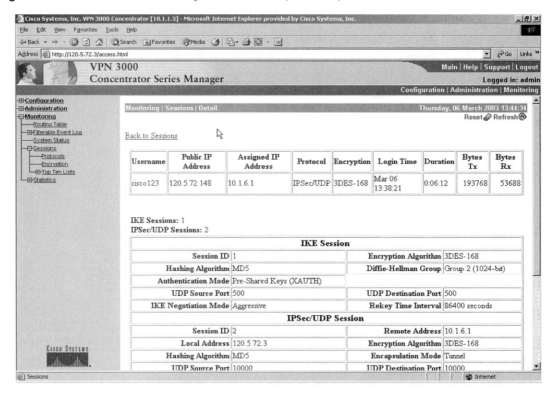

Figure 3-10 *VPN Client Settings on Test-PC in VLAN-13*

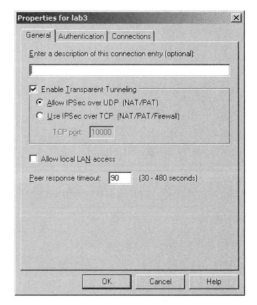

Figure 3-10 *VPN Client Settings on Test-PC in VLAN-13 (Continued)*

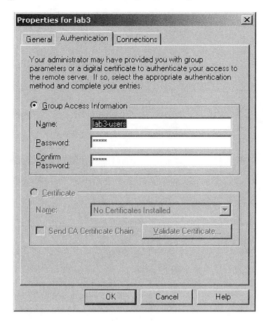

5.2: IPSec LAN-to-LAN Using Preshared

1 Encrypt BGP traffic between R1 and R7 using loopback1(s). See Example 3-24.

2 Use preshared authentication and choose all other parameters as appropriate.

3 You need to create a static NAT on PIX and ACL to permit IPSec and ISAKMP traffic.
See Example 3-25.

Example 3-24 *IPSec Configuration on R1 and R7*

```
!Snip from R1:
crypto isakmp policy 10
 hash md5
 authentication pre-share
 group 2
crypto isakmp key cisco address 17.17.17.17
!
!
crypto ipsec transform-set lab3 esp-des esp-md5-hmac
!
crypto map lab3 local-address Loopback1
crypto map lab3 10 ipsec-isakmp
 set peer 17.17.17.17
 set transform-set lab3
 match address 101
!
```

continues

Example 3-24 *IPSec Configuration on R1 and R7 (Continued)*

```
interface FastEthernet0/0
 ip address 120.5.72.2 255.255.255.128
 crypto map lab3
!
access-list 101 permit tcp host 11.11.11.11 eq bgp host 17.17.17.17
access-list 101 permit tcp host 11.11.11.11 host 17.17.17.17 eq bgp

r1#show crypto engine connection active

  ID Interface       IP-Address       State  Algorithm           Encrypt  Decrypt
   1 <none>          <none>           set    HMAC_MD5+DES_56_CB         0        0
2002 FastEthernet0/0 120.5.72.2       set    HMAC_MD5+DES_56_CB         0       84
2003 FastEthernet0/0 120.5.72.2       set    HMAC_MD5+DES_56_CB       114        0

r1#
r1#show access-lists 101
Extended IP access list 101
    permit tcp host 11.11.11.11 eq bgp host 17.17.17.17
    permit tcp host 11.11.11.11 host 17.17.17.17 eq bgp (414 matches)
r1#




!Snip from R7:
crypto isakmp policy 10
 hash md5
 authentication pre-share
 group 2
crypto isakmp key cisco address 11.11.11.11
!
!
crypto ipsec transform-set lab3 esp-des esp-md5-hmac
!
crypto map lab3 local-address Loopback1
crypto map lab3 10 ipsec-isakmp
 set peer 11.11.11.11
 set transform-set lab3
 match address 101
!
interface Ethernet0/0
 ip address 10.1.4.1 255.255.255.0
 crypto map lab3

!
access-list 101 permit tcp host 17.17.17.17 host 11.11.11.11 eq bgp
access-list 101 permit tcp host 17.17.17.17 eq bgp host 11.11.11.11


r7# show crypto engine connection active
```

Example 3-24 *IPSec Configuration on R1 and R7 (Continued)*

```
ID Interface        IP-Address      State  Algorithm            Encrypt  Decrypt
 2 <none>           <none>          set    HMAC_MD5+DES_56_CB         0        0
 3 <none>           <none>          set    HMAC_MD5+DES_56_CB         0        0
2002 Ethernet0/0    10.1.4.1        set    HMAC_MD5+DES_56_CB         0      114
2003 Ethernet0/0    10.1.4.1        set    HMAC_MD5+DES_56_CB        84        0

r7#show access-lists 101
Extended IP access list 101
    permit tcp host 17.17.17.17 host 11.11.11.11 eq bgp
    permit tcp host 17.17.17.17 eq bgp host 11.11.11.11 (411 matches)
r7#
```

Example 3-25 *NAT Translation and ACL on PIX*

```
!Snip from PIX.
PIX(config)# show static
static (inside,outside) 17.17.17.17 17.17.17.17 netmask 255.255.255.255 0 0

PIX(config)# show access-list
access-list outside permit udp host 11.11.11.11 host 17.17.17.17 eq isakmp (hitcnt=30)
access-list outside permit esp host 11.11.11.11 host 17.17.17.17 (hitcnt=5798)
PIX(config)#
```

Section 6.0: IOS Firewall Configuration

6.1: Context-Based Access Control (CBAC)

1   Configure CBAC on R5 for traffic going to the Internet. Apply outbound inspection on Ethernet0.

2   Configure ingress ACL 101 on Internet link Ethernet0 to protect from RFC1918. See Example 3-26.

3   Modify CBAC thresholds for TCP and UDP idle-time to 30 minutes and 15 seconds respectively. See Example 3-26.

4   Tune the firewall to start deleting half-open sessions at 1000 and stop when the connection drops to 800 sessions. See Example 3-26.

Example 3-26 *CBAC Configuration on R5*

```
!Snip from R5
ip inspect max-incomplete high 1000
ip inspect max-incomplete low 800
ip inspect one-minute high 1000
ip inspect one-minute low 800
ip inspect udp idle-time 15
ip inspect tcp idle-time 1800
```

continues

Example 3-26 *CBAC Configuration on R5 (Continued)*

```
ip inspect name lab3 tcp
ip inspect name lab3 udp
ip inspect name lab3 http
ip inspect name lab3 smtp
!
interface Ethernet0
 ip address 120.5.72.169 255.255.255.248
 ip access-group 101 in
 ip inspect lab3 out
!
access-list 101 deny   ip 10.0.0.0 0.255.255.255 any
access-list 101 deny   ip 172.16.0.0 0.15.255.255 any
access-list 101 deny   ip 192.168.0.0 0.0.255.255 any
access-list 101 deny   ip host 0.0.0.0 any
access-list 101 deny   ip 224.0.0.0 31.255.255.255 any
access-list 101 deny   ip 127.0.0.0 0.255.255.255 any
access-list 101 permit ip any any
```

6.2: Proxy Authentication

1 Configure proxy authentication on R6 for VLAN-14 users when browsing to web server R8 behind PIX. See Example 3-27.

2 Configure the ingress ACL on Ethernet 1/0 on R6. It's very important to remember that this ACL needs to open holes for all other traffic traversing through R6 in other exercises—for example, OSPF, BGP, IPSec, NTP, ICMP, and so on. See Example 3-27 for what the ACL looks like.

3 Configure static NAT and ACL on PIX for R8 Loopback1. See Example 3-28.

4 Enable HTTP server on R8 so users in VLAN-14 can browse to it. Note that users need to browse to the NATed address 120.5.72.22.

5 See Figure 3-11 for the HTTP connection from a Test-PC in VLAN-14 to R8 120.5.72.22.

Example 3-27 *Proxy Authentication on R6*

```
!snip from R6 config
hostname r6
!
aaa new-model
aaa authentication login default group tacacs+ local
aaa authentication login console none
aaa authorization exec default group tacacs+ local
aaa authorization exec console none
aaa authorization auth-proxy default group tacacs+
!
ip auth-proxy auth-proxy-banner
ip auth-proxy auth-cache-time 10
ip auth-proxy name lab3 http auth-cache-time 60
!
interface Ethernet1/0
 ip address 10.1.1.2 255.255.255.0
```

Example 3-27 *Proxy Authentication on R6 (Continued)*

```
 ip access-group 101 in
 ip rip authentication mode md5
 ip rip authentication key-chain lab3
 ip auth-proxy lab3
 ip ospf message-digest-key 1 md5 7 1511021F0725
 duplex half
!
access-list 1 permit 120.5.72.168 0.0.0.7
access-list 101 permit icmp any any
access-list 101 permit ospf any any
access-list 101 permit udp any any eq rip
access-list 101 permit esp any any
access-list 101 permit udp any any eq isakmp
tacacs-server host 10.1.5.125
tacacs-server key cisco
!Test from VLAN-14. User browsing to the Web Server (R8). Auth-proxy engine
!maintaining session information.
r6#show ip auth-proxy cache
Authentication Proxy Cache
 Client IP 120.5.72.171 Port 1203, timeout 60, state HTTP_ESTAB
!ACL dynamically being populated, opening holes for remote host. (Pay attention
!to the first 3 lines in ACL which are !downloaded from AAA server)
r6#show access-lists 101
Extended IP access list 101
    permit udp host 120.5.72.171 any
    permit tcp host 120.5.72.171 any (336 matches)
    permit icmp host 120.5.72.171 any
    permit icmp any any (40 matches)
    permit ospf any any (6 matches)
    permit udp any any eq rip (4 matches)
    permit esp any any (9 matches)
    permit udp any any eq isakmp (10 matches)
```

Example 3-28 *Snip from PIX*

```
access-list outside permit tcp 120.5.72.168 255.255.255.248 host 120.5.72.22 eq
  www (hitcnt=15)
static (inside,outside) 120.5.72.22 10.1.5.2 netmask 255.255.255.255 0 0
```

TIP   See the following URLs for more information on auth-proxy configuration:

- Auth-proxy Authentication Inbound (CBAC, no NAT) Configuration

  www.cisco.com/warp/public/793/ios_fw/auth4.html

- Implementing Authentication Proxy (steps to do on ACS)

  www.cisco.com/warp/public/793/ios_fw/auth_intro.html

- Feature Overview—How the Authentication Proxy Works

  www.cisco.com/univercd/cc/td/doc/product/software/ios120/120newft/120t
  /120t5/iosfw2/iosfw2_1.htm

Figure 3-11 *HTTP Connection from Test-PC in VLAN-14*

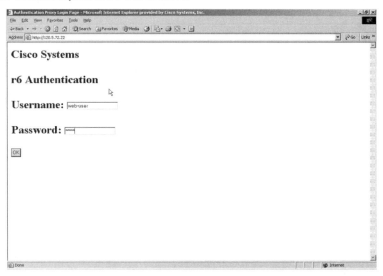

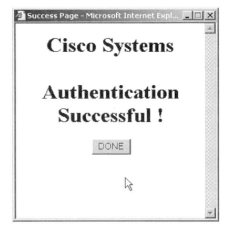

Section 7.0: AAA

7.1: AAA on the Router

1 Configure R4 vty and console authentication using the local database. AAA server is not used for any authentication or authorization process.

2 Configure separate VTY and Console line passwords as per the requirement.

3 For usernames to be case-sensitive, configure login authentication for **local-case**. See Example 3-29.

4 Configure command authorization with privilege levels as per the exercise. You don't need to configure privilege shell exec for Level 11, as it inherits from Level 5.

5 Configure Accounting for Commands to AAA server. Define the TACACS+ server. See Example 3-29.

Example 3-29 *AAA Configuration on R4*

```
!Snip from R4 config
!
hostname r4
!
logging rate-limit console 10 except errors
aaa new-model
aaa authentication login lab3 local-case line
aaa authentication login console line
aaa authorization exec lab3 local
aaa authorization exec console none
aaa accounting commands 1 lab3 start-stop group tacacs+
aaa accounting commands 5 lab3 start-stop group tacacs+
aaa accounting commands 11 lab3 start-stop group tacacs+
aaa accounting commands 15 lab3 start-stop group tacacs+
!
username User11 privilege 11 password cisco
username User5 privilege 5 password cisco
!
tacacs-server host 120.5.72.125
tacacs-server key cisco
!
privilege configure level 11 interface
privilege configure level 5 router
privilege exec level 5 config term
!
line con 0
 exec-timeout 0 0
 privilege level 15
 password cisco123
 authorization exec console
 login authentication console
 transport input none
line vty 0 4
 password cisco
 authorization exec lab3
 accounting commands 5 lab3
 accounting commands 11 lab3
 login authentication lab3
!
```

7.2: AAA on PIX

1 Configure SSH on PIX with TACACS+ authentication. See Example 3-30.

2 Generate RSA keys before configuring SSH.

3 Configure username **ssh-user** with password **cisco** on CiscoSecure ACS.

TIP	For more information on configuring SSH on PIX using AAA, refer to the following URL: Configuring AAA Authenticated SSH www.cisco.com/warp/public/110/authtopix.shtml#aaaauthsshconfig

Example 3-30 *Snip from PIX Configuration*

```
PIX(config)# show ssh
120.5.72.148 255.255.255.255 outside

PIX(config)# show aaa
aaa authentication ssh console ACS

PIX(config)# show aaa-server
aaa-server TACACS+ protocol tacacs+
aaa-server RADIUS protocol radius
aaa-server LOCAL protocol local
aaa-server ACS protocol tacacs+
aaa-server ACS (inside) host 10.1.5.125 cisco timeout 10

PIX(config)# show ca mypubkey rsa
% Key pair was generated at: 13:05:34 UTC Mar 4 2003
Key name: PIX.cisco.com
 Usage: General Purpose Key
 Key Data:
  30819f30 0d06092a 864886f7 0d010101 05000381 8d003081 89028181 00a7ef49
  c17efa2f 58d39d48 de35a744 4da799bd 997f3caf 7d8177af e0df84f8 fd7b3a36
  70ec51f9 af40e51f af1836ad f5919311 5f9da522 fbc8e7f6 ebf067d1 148da98d
  2e71f65c fab5bbad 23c14f0b 97a48a51 fbe3f385 3ae221a5 78fba8a2 c7bd6124
  88747d9a 0a67efb3 6534fc2c f2007751 428e1a5a 0cd13330 ec2063a2 95020301 0001
```

Section 8.0: Advanced Security

8.1: Perimeter Security

1 To prevent R5 from large ICMP packet floods, configure traffic policing. See Example 3-31.

2 Verify by doing large ICMP packet pings and regular ICMP pings from a host in VLAN-14 to 120.5.72.169. See Example 3-32.

For more information, see the following URL:

www.cisco.com/univercd/cc/td/doc/product/software/ios122/122cgcr/fqos_c/fqcprt1/qcfpbr.htm

3 The traffic policing feature works with a token bucket mechanism. There are currently two types of token bucket algorithms: a single-token bucket algorithm and a two-token bucket algorithm.

A single-token bucket system is used when the violate-action option is not specified.

A two-token bucket system is used when the violate-action option is specified.

For more information on token bucket, see the following URL:

www.cisco.com/univercd/cc/td/doc/product/software/ios122/122cgcr/fqos_c/fqcprt4/qcfpolsh.htm#19709

Example 3-31 *Configuring Traffic Policing*

```
!Snip from R5 config

class-map match-any icmp-attack
  match access-group 111
!
policy-map police
  class icmp-attack
    police 8000 4000 6000 conform-action transmit exceed-action drop violate-action
drop
!
interface Ethernet0
 ip address 120.5.72.169 255.255.255.248
 ip access-group 101 in
 service-policy input police
!
access-list 101 deny    ip 10.0.0.0 0.255.255.255 any
access-list 101 deny    ip 172.16.0.0 0.15.255.255 any
access-list 101 deny    ip 192.168.0.0 0.0.255.255 any
access-list 101 deny    ip host 0.0.0.0 any
access-list 101 deny    ip 224.0.0.0 31.255.255.255 any
access-list 101 deny    ip 127.0.0.0 0.255.255.255 any
access-list 101 permit ip any any
access-list 111 permit icmp any any
```

Example 3-32 *Verify Traffic Policy Is Working*

```
!To verify if Traffic Policy is working, do large ICMP packet pings from a host in
!VLAN-14 to 120.5.72.169

C:\>ping 120.5.72.169 -t -l 5000

Pinging 120.5.72.169 with 5000 bytes of data:

Request timed out.
Request timed out.
Request timed out.
Request timed out.
```

continues

Example 3-32 *Verify Traffic Policy Is Working (Continued)*

```
Ping statistics for 120.5.72.169:
    Packets: Sent = 4, Received = 0, Lost = 4 (100% loss),
Approximate round trip times in milli-seconds:
    Minimum = 0ms, Maximum =  0ms, Average =  0ms
Control-C
^C
C:\>

!Normal ping works fine.

C:\>ping 120.5.72.169

Pinging 120.5.72.169 with 32 bytes of data:

Reply from 120.5.72.169: bytes=32 time<10ms TTL=253
Reply from 120.5.72.169: bytes=32 time<10ms TTL=253
Reply from 120.5.72.169: bytes=32 time<10ms TTL=253
Reply from 120.5.72.169: bytes=32 time<10ms TTL=253

Ping statistics for 120.5.72.169:
    Packets: Sent = 4, Received = 4, Lost = 0 (0% loss),
Approximate round trip times in milli-seconds:
    Minimum = 0ms, Maximum =  0ms, Average =  0ms

C:\>

r5#show policy-map interface
 Ethernet0

  Service-policy input: police (1071)

    Class-map: icmp-attack (match-any) (1073/2)
      172 packets, 176056 bytes
      5 minute offered rate 0 bps, drop rate 0 bps
      Match: access-group 111 (1077)
        172 packets, 176056 bytes
        5 minute rate 0 bps
      police:
        8000 bps, 4000 limit, 6000 extended limit
        conformed 78 packets, 53876 bytes; action: transmit
        exceeded 16 packets, 21776 bytes; action: drop
        violated 78 packets, 100404 bytes; action: drop
        conformed 0 bps, exceed 0 bps violate 0 bps

    Class-map: class-default (match-any) (1081/0)
      6 packets, 552 bytes
      5 minute offered rate 0 bps, drop rate 0 bps
      Match: any  (1085)
r5#
r5#show access-lists 111
Extended IP access list 111
    permit icmp any any (172 matches)
r5#
```

8.2: Web Server Security

1 Configure the embryonic connection limit on static translation on PIX for web server 120.5.72.120. See Example 3-33.

Example 3-33 *Embryonic Connection Limit on PIX*

```
!Snip from PIX
static (inside,outside) 120.5.72.120 10.1.4.120 netmask 255.255.255.255 0 5000
  norandomseq
```

TIP   For more information, see the PIX Command Reference URL:

www.cisco.com/univercd/cc/td/doc/product/iaabu/pix/pix_61/cmd_ref/s.htm#xtocid20

Section 9.0: IP Services and Protocol-Independent Features

9.1: NAT

1 Configure TCP load distribution using destination NAT. See Example 3-34.

2 The pool defines the addresses of the real hosts.

3 The access list defines the virtual address.

4 Verify by Telnetting to virtual IP from R5 two times. Each time you should land on different routers—that is, load balance between R2 and R3. See Example 3-35.

Example 3-34 *TCP Load Distribution Using Destination NAT*

```
!Snip from R4 config
interface FastEthernet0/0
 ip address 120.5.72.147 255.255.255.240
 ip nat inside
!
interface Serial2/0
 ip address 120.5.72.165 255.255.255.252
 ip nat outside
!
ip nat pool real-hosts 120.5.72.145 120.5.72.146 prefix-length 28 type rotary
ip nat inside destination list 1 pool real-hosts
!
access-list 1 permit 120.5.72.150
```

Example 3-35 *Verify Destination NAT*

```
!Test by telnetting 2 times to Virtual IP 120.5.72.150 from R5 as follows:

r5#telnet 120.5.72.150
Trying 120.5.72.150 ... Open


                                                                    continues
```

Example 3-35 *Verify Destination NAT (Continued)*

```
User Access Verification

Password: cisco
r3>
r3>
r3>exit

[Connection to 120.5.72.150 closed by foreign host]
r5#telnet 120.5.72.150
Trying 120.5.72.150 ... Open


User Access Verification

Password: cisco
r2>
r2>
r2>exit

[Connection to 120.5.72.150 closed by foreign host]
r5#
!As you can see, after the test above, each time telnet was to a different router
!load-balancing between r2 and r3. Also check the NAT translation table on R4 which
!validates the test

r4#show ip nat translations
Pro Inside global     Inside local     Outside local      Outside global
tcp 120.5.72.150:23   120.5.72.146:23  120.5.72.166:11003 120.5.72.166:11003
tcp 120.5.72.150:23   120.5.72.145:23  120.5.72.166:11004 120.5.72.166:11004
```

9.2: NTP

1 Configure R7 as the NTP server and R4 as the client. See Example 3-36.

2 Use Loopback1 on R4 and R7 for NTP updates.

3 Configure MD5 authentication for NTP clients to authenticate with the NTP server.

4 The problem here can happen if you forget to punch a hole for NTP on R6 ACL on interface Ethernet1/0 and PIX. See Example 3-37.

Example 3-36 *NTP Server and Client Configuration*

```
!Snip from R7
ntp authentication-key 1 md5 045802150C2E 7
ntp source Loopback1
ntp master
ntp update-calendar

r7#show ntp status
Clock is synchronized, stratum 8, reference is 127.127.7.1
```

Example 3-36 *NTP Server and Client Configuration (Continued)*

```
nominal freq is 250.0000 Hz, actual freq is 250.0000 Hz, precision is 2**24
reference time is C20EE6FA.9BAA6AF4 (18:48:58.608 AST Tue Mar 4 2003)
clock offset is 0.0000 msec, root delay is 0.00 msec
root dispersion is 0.02 msec, peer dispersion is 0.02 msec

r7#show ntp associations detail
127.127.7.1 configured, our_master, sane, valid, stratum 7
ref ID 127.127.7.1, time C20EE6FA.9BAA6AF4 (18:48:58.608 AST Tue Mar 4 2003)
our mode active, peer mode passive, our poll intvl 64, peer poll intvl 64
root delay 0.00 msec, root disp 0.00, reach 377, sync dist 0.015
delay 0.00 msec, offset 0.0000 msec, dispersion 0.02
precision 2**24, version 3
org time C20EE6FA.9BAA6AF4 (18:48:58.608 AST Tue Mar 4 2003)
rcv time C20EE6FA.9BAA6AF4 (18:48:58.608 AST Tue Mar 4 2003)
xmt time C20EE6FA.9BA992DD (18:48:58.608 AST Tue Mar 4 2003)
filtdelay =     0.00    0.00    0.00    0.00    0.00    0.00    0.00    0.00
filtoffset =    0.00    0.00    0.00    0.00    0.00    0.00    0.00    0.00
filterror =     0.02    0.99    1.97    2.94    3.92    4.90    5.87    5.89
Reference clock status:  Running normally
Timecode:

r7#show clock
18:49:45.983 AST Tue Mar 4 2003

!Snip from R4
ntp authentication-key 1 md5 070C285F4D06 7
ntp authenticate
ntp trusted-key 1
ntp clock-period 17178258
ntp source Loopback1
ntp server 17.17.17.17 key 1

r4#show ntp status
Clock is synchronized, stratum 9, reference is 17.17.17.17
nominal freq is 250.0000 Hz, actual freq is 250.0001 Hz, precision is 2**24
reference time is C20EE6E4.7A6D879F (18:48:36.478 AST Tue Mar 4 2003)
clock offset is -7.7662 msec, root delay is 4.61 msec
root dispersion is 7884.29 msec, peer dispersion is 7876.50 msec

r4# show ntp associations detail
17.17.17.17 configured, authenticated, our_master, sane, valid, stratum 8
ref ID 127.127.7.1, time C20EE6BA.9BAB793F (18:47:54.608 AST Tue Mar 4 2003)
our mode client, peer mode server, our poll intvl 64, peer poll intvl 64
root delay 0.00 msec, root disp 0.03, reach 3, sync dist 7878.830
delay 4.61 msec, offset -7.7662 msec, dispersion 7876.50
precision 2**24, version 3
org time C20EE6E4.77D9382D (18:48:36.468 AST Tue Mar 4 2003)
rcv time C20EE6E4.7A6D879F (18:48:36.478 AST Tue Mar 4 2003)
xmt time C20EE6E4.792AD297 (18:48:36.473 AST Tue Mar 4 2003)
filtdelay =     4.61    4.71    0.00    0.00    0.00    0.00    0.00    0.00
```

continues

Example 3-36 *NTP Server and Client Configuration (Continued)*

```
filtoffset =   -7.77   -4.79    0.00    0.00    0.00    0.00    0.00    0.00
filterror =     0.02    0.99 16000.0 16000.0 16000.0 16000.0 16000.0 16000.0

r4#show clock
18:49:22.505 AST Tue Mar 4 2003
```

Example 3-37 *ACL Snip on R6 and PIX*

```
r6#show access-lists 101
Extended IP access list 101
    permit icmp any any (131 matches)
    permit ospf any any (9183 matches)
    permit udp any any eq rip (5724 matches)
    permit esp any any (2862 matches)
    permit udp any any eq isakmp (74 matches)
    permit udp any any eq ntp (4 matches)

PIX(config)# show access-list
access-list outside; 6 elements
access-list outside permit icmp any any (hitcnt=106)
access-list outside permit udp host 11.11.11.11 host 17.17.17.17 eq isakmp (hitcnt=18)
access-list outside permit esp host 11.11.11.11 host 17.17.17.17 (hitcnt=2900)
access-list outside permit tcp any host 120.5.72.120 eq www (hitcnt=0)
access-list outside permit tcp 120.5.72.168 255.255.255.248 host 120.5.72.22 eq www
  (hitcnt=15)
access-list outside permit udp host 14.14.14.14 host 17.17.17.17 eq ntp (hitcnt=1)
```

9.3: Policy-Based Routing

1 Configure Policy-Based Routing using a route map and set the default interface to null0. See Example 3-38.

2 An important thing to remember is to apply policy on the ingress interface (Serial0) where packets arrive from R3.

3 Ping to any unknown networks/hosts from R3 that are not used in this lab. Ping a couple of times and verify on R5 with **show route-map black-hole**. See Example 3-39.

Example 3-38 *Policy-Based Routing on R5*

```
!Snip from R5 config
interface Serial0
 ip address 120.5.72.166 255.255.255.252
 ip policy route-map black-hole
!
access-list 1 permit 120.5.72.146
!
route-map black-hole permit 10
 match ip address 1
 set default interface Null0
!
route-map black-hole permit 20
```

Example 3-39 *Verify on R5 After Pinging Unknown Hosts from R3*

```
r5#show route-map black-hole
route-map black-hole, permit, sequence 10
  Match clauses:
    ip address (access-lists): 1
  Set clauses:
    default interface Null0
  Policy routing matches: 15 packets, 1560 bytes
route-map black-hole, permit, sequence 20
  Match clauses:
  Set clauses:
  Policy routing matches: 23 packets, 1402 bytes

r5#show ip policy
Interface       Route map
Serial0         black-hole
r5#
```

Section 10.0: Security Violations

10.1: Denial of Service (DoS)

1 Classify inbound packets for the worm using NBAR and the class-based marking feature in IOS. This feature looks inside HTTP URLs and matches any of the specified strings.

2 Using NBAR and class-based marking, classify bad packets by setting the DSCP value 1. Use the unique pattern ***cmd.exe*** in the URL to mark all packets. **cmd.exe** is a command shell access on Windows NT.

3 These attacks can be blocked on the router using three methods:

Using ACL

Using Policy-Based Routing

Using Class-Based Policing

4 Use the ACL method as required for this task. ACL needs to apply outbound toward the target.

5 Policy needs to apply inbound on the interface where the worm enters.

6 See Example 3-40 to mitigate this attack.

Example 3-40 *Mitigating DoS*

```
!Snip from R6 config
class-map match-any http-worm
  match protocol http url "*cmd.exe*"
!
!
```
continues

Example 3-40 *Mitigating DoS (Continued)*

```
policy-map mark-http-worm
  class http-worm
    set ip dscp 1
!
interface Ethernet1/0
 ip address 10.1.1.2 255.255.255.0
 ip access-group 101 in
 ip access-group 199 out
!
interface Ethernet1/1
 ip address 10.1.2.2 255.255.255.0
 service-policy input mark-http-worm
!
interface Ethernet1/2
 ip address 10.1.3.2 255.255.255.0
 ip access-group 199 out
!
interface Ethernet1/3
 ip address 10.1.4.2 255.255.255.0
 ip access-group 199 out
!
access-list 199 deny   ip any any dscp 1
access-list 199 permit ip any any
!



r6#show class-map
 Class Map match-any class-default (id 0)
   Match any

 Class Map match-any http-worm (id 2)
   Match protocol http url "*cmd.exe*"

r6#show policy-map
  Policy Map mark-http-worm
    Class http-worm
      set ip dscp 1

r6#show access-lists 199
Extended IP access list 199
    deny ip any any dscp 1
    permit ip any any (16 matches)
```

10.2: IP Fragment Attack

1   Configure the IP Frag Guard feature with the **sysopt security fragguard** command on
     the PIX.

2 This feature enforces two security checks:

First, each noninitial IP fragment is required to be associated with an already seen valid initial IP fragment.

Second, IP fragments are rated to 100 full IP fragmented packets per second to each internal host.

TIP   For information on the IP Frag Guard feature, see the following URL:

www.cisco.com/univercd/cc/td/doc/product/iaabu/pix/pix_61/cmd_ref/s.htm#xtocid22

CHAPTER 4

Practice Lab 4

Every candidate working toward the CCIE exam has one goal: Passing the CCIE lab exam and getting a CCIE number. The answer to get there is simple: practice, practice, practice. As someone said, "Practice makes perfect," but the problem is, practice what? Where can you get practice labs and scenarios? Most people are confident in technologies as standalone. For example, someone could be expert in firewalls but wouldn't know what can go wrong if BGP runs through the firewall. The CCIE exam is spread on wide syllabi and includes a range of technologies—all integrated, making a complex setup. The challenge is to work toward building this complex network from "scratch to perfection" in 8 hours. Keeping this challenge in mind, this book was written to assist candidates by providing close to real CCIE Lab exam scenarios with a high level of complexity and integrating all technologies possibly tested.

The lab is marked out of 100. You must complete the lab within 8 hours and obtain a minimum of 80 marks to pass. As with all labs, this test has been written such that you should be able to complete all questions, including initial configuration (that is, IP addressing), within 8 hours, excluding cabling time. Allow up to 1 hour for cabling, using the provided instructions and observing the general guidelines. You can use any combination of routers as long as you fulfill the needs of the topology diagram in Figure 4-1. It is not compulsory to use routers of the same model.

| NOTE | The real CCIE Lab does not require you to do any cabling or IP addressing. |

Equipment List

- 8 routers with the following specifications (all routers are to be loaded with the latest Cisco IOS version in 12.1(T) train).

    R1 — 4 Ethernet (with Enterprise + IPSec 56 image)

    R2 — 1 Ethernet (with IP Plus image)

    R3 — 2 Ethernet, 1 BRI (with IP Plus image)

R4 — 2 Ethernet (with IP Plus image)

R5 — 1 Ethernet, 1 serial (with IP Plus + IPSec 56 image)

R6 — 1 Ethernet, 1 serial, 1 BRI (with IP Plus image)

R7 — 1 Ethernet, 1 serial (with IP Plus image)

R8 — 1 Ethernet, 1 serial (with IP Plus image)

- 2 switches (3550)
- 1 PIX with 2 interfaces (version 6.x with DES enabled)
- 1 PC: Windows 2000 Server with CiscoSecure ACS 3.0+ and Microsoft CA Server installed

General Guidelines

- Do not configure any static/default routes unless otherwise specified/required.
- Use DLCIs provided in the diagram.
- Use the IP addressing scheme provided in the diagram; do not change any IP addressing unless otherwise specified. In the CCIE Lab, initial configurations are loaded, and therefore IP addresses are not to be changed. In this book, each chapter has a separate lab topology with different IP addressing, so each chapter needs to be recabled and all IP addresses need to be redone from the previous chapter.
- Use **cisco** as the password for any authentication string, enable-password, and TACACS+/ RADIUS key or for any other purpose unless otherwise specified.
- Add additional loopbacks as specified during this lab.
- Configure VLANs on both Switch1 and Switch2 as per the diagram.
- All routers should be able to ping any interface in the network using the *optimal* path.
- You must time yourself to complete this lab in 8 hours.
- The lab is of 100 marks total, and you require 80 marks to pass. Each section is indicated with marks.
- Do not use any external resources or answers provided in this book when attempting the lab.
- Do not configure any authentication or authorization on the console and aux ports.

NOTE   The real CCIE Lab exams are hands-on structures similar to this book. Each configuration exercise has preassigned point values. The candidate must obtain a minimum mark of 80% to pass. This book provides you with a similar structure to give you a better understanding and experience. For more information on CCIE exam structure, see the following URL:

www.cisco.com/en/US/partner/learning/le3/le2/le23/learning_certification_ level_home.html

www.cisco.com/warp/customer/625/ccie/exam_preparation/preparation.html

---

Setting Up the Lab

You can use any combination of routers as long as you fulfill the topology diagram, outlined in Figure 4-1. It is not compulsory to use the same model of routers.

Figure 4-1 *Lab Topology*

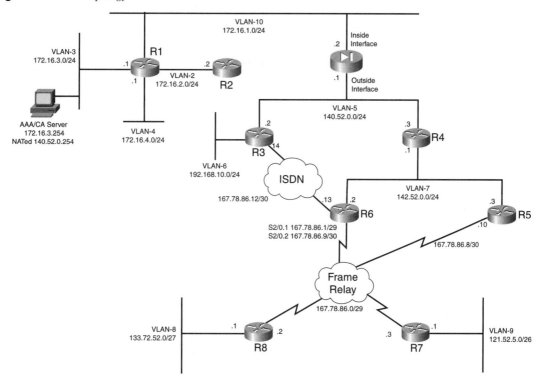

Frame Relay DLCI Information

Configure R3 as a Frame Relay switch and use Figure 4-2 for DLCI information. Only DLCIs indicated in Figure 4-2 should be mapped on the routers.

Routing Protocol Information

Use Figure 4-3 to configure all routing protocols.

Figure 4-2 *Frame Relay DLCI*

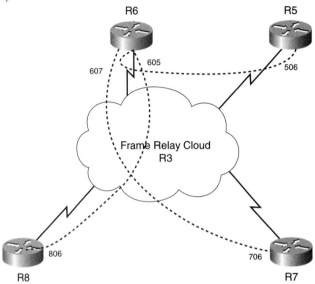

Figure 4-3 *Routing Protocol Information*

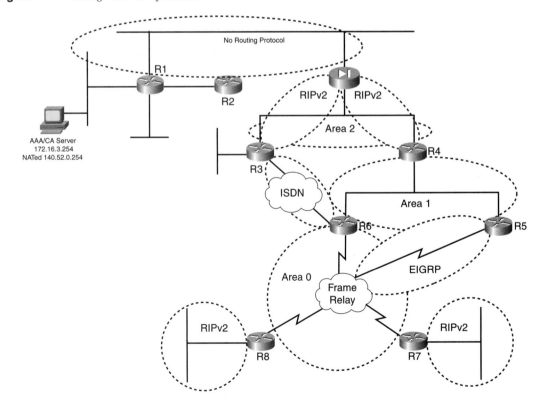

BGP Information

Use Figure 4-4 to configure BGP.

Figure 4-4 *BGP Information*

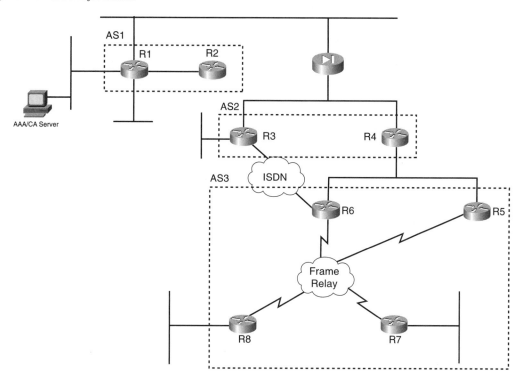

Cabling Instructions

Use Tables 4-1 and 4-2 for cabling all devices in your topology. It is not a must to use the same type or sequence of interface. You may use any combination of interfaces as long as you fulfill the requirement.

Table 4-1 *Cabling Instructions (Ethernet)*

Ethernet Cabling	VLAN	Switch1	Switch2
Trunk port		Port 1	Port 1
R1-Ethernet1/0	10	Port 2	
R1-Ethernet1/1	2	Port 3	
R1-Ethernet1/2	3		Port 2

continues

Table 4-1   *Cabling Instructions (Ethernet) (Continued)*

Ethernet Cabling	VLAN	Switch1	Switch2
R1-Ethernet1/3	4		Port 3
R2-Fastethernet0/0	2	Port 4	
R3-Fastethernet0/0	5		Port 4
R3-Fastethernet0/1	6	Port 5	
R4-Ethernet0/0	5		Port 5
R4-Ethernet0/1	7	Port 6	
R5-Ethernet0	7	Port 7	
R6-Fastethernet0/0	7		Port 6
R7-Ethernet0/0	9	Port 8	
R8-Ethernet0/0	8		Port 7
PIX-inside-E1	10		Port 8
PIX-outside-E0	5	Port 9	
AAA server	3	Port 10	

Table 4-2   *Cabling Instructions (Serial)*

Back-to-Back Cabling	DTE-End	DCE-End
R5-to-frsw*	R5-serial0	R3-serial1/3
R6-to-frsw*	R6-serial2/0	R3-serial1/2
R7-to-frsw*	R7-serial1/0	R3-serial1/0
R8-to-frsw*	R8-serial1/0	R3-serial1/1

*frsw = Frame Relay switch R3

Practice Lab 4 Exercises

The exercises in this lab assist you in understanding the core elements in the CCIE Lab exam and train you to configure and troubleshoot the most complex scenarios in simple ways.

The steps in each exercise are not necessarily intended to be completed in order. They can be done in any order of preference or as you feel appropriate. There may be situations where the steps have intentionally been written in incorrect order to cause a problem. You have to identify the best approach and fulfill all the requirements.

Section 1.0: Basic Configuration (10 points)

1.1: IP Addressing (2 points)

1 Redraw a detailed topology with all necessary information.

2 Originate a default route from R6 OSPF/EIGRP to all OSPF/EIGRP peers.

3 Do not configure any IGP routing protocols on R1, R2, and PIX inside interface for networks behind PIX. You can configure RIPv2 on PIX outside interface only. Do not configure a static default route on any other routers.

4 All devices behind PIX should be routing through Switch1. Configure Switch1 as the routing device for VLAN 2, 3, 4, and 10. See Section 2.5.

5 Make sure you can ping the AAA server from R2 and PIX.

6 Configure the following loopback interfaces:

Loopback-1 11.11.11.11/24 on R1

Loopback-10 10.10.10.1/24 on R1

Loopback-1 13.13.13.13/24 on R3

Loopback-10 10.10.10.1/24 on R5 (this is not a typo; overlap with Loopback-10 on R1 is on purpose)

Loopback-9 10.9.6.1/24 on R6

Loopback-5 17.17.17.17/24 on R7

Loopback-9 10.9.7.1/24 on R7

Loopback-1 133.72.52.33/27 on R8

Loopback-2 133.72.52.65/27 on R8

Loopback-5 18.18.18.18/24 on R8

Loopback-9 10.9.8.1/24 on R8

1.2: Frame Relay Configuration (4 points)

1 Configure R3 as a Frame Relay switch; use the DLCI information provided for Frame Relay routing in Figure 4-2.

2 Configure Frame Relay between R5, R6, R7, and R8.

3 Configure subinterfaces on R6.

4 Do not configure subinterfaces on R5, R7, and R8.

5 Only DLCIs in Figure 4-2 should populate the Frame Relay map table on all routers. No additional dynamic DLCIs are allowed for this exercise.

1.3: LAN Switch Configuration (4 points)

1 Configure the Catalyst switches with VLAN information provided in the topology diagram in Figure 4-1. Note that there are two Catalyst switches. Refer to Table 4-1 for port details.

2 Configure trunking between the two Catalyst switches with ISL encapsulation.

3 Configure VTP domain name **lab4** with strong authentication.

4 The Configuration Revision number should be the same on both switches.

5 Two servers connected to Switch1 ports 15 and 16 need to be protected such that no traffic is forwarded between the two servers. Servers should not be able to communicate with each other, but should be able to communicate with other devices. Do not use ACL or port-security to achieve this task.

6 Configure Switch1 and Switch2 management interface for VLAN-4. Assign IP addresses 172.16.4.10 and 172.16.4.20, respectively. All devices on the network should be able to ping and Telnet to both switches. Configure PIX accordingly. You may add a static route for 172.16.4.0 on R3 and R4 to achieve this task.

Section 2.0: Routing Configuration (26 points)

2.1: OSPF (5 points)

1 Configure OSPF as shown in Figure 4-3.

2 Configure MD5 authentication for all areas.

3 Configure Area 0 in the Frame Relay network. Do not use the **ip ospf network** command on any routers.

4 Configure Area 1 and Area 2 as per Figure 4-3. Make sure PIX learns all routes.

5 Advertise Loopback-1 on R3 in OSPF.

6 All OSPF routers should see one route for network(s) 133.72.52.x from R8. Do not configure summarization on R6.

7 R3 should learn all routes from R4 via RIP and not OSPF. Do not use the **distance** command to change Admin distances. Do not use distribute-list to filter routes into OSPF.

2.2: EIGRP (3 points)

1 Configure EIGRP AS-4 between R5 and R6.

2 Originate a default route from the R6 EIGRP process to R5. The default route must appear as EIGRP external on the R5 routing table.

3 Configure strong authentication for EIGRP AS-4.

4 Network 167.78.86.8/30 should be visible on all routers including PIX.

2.3: RIP (3 points)

1 Configure RIPv2 between the PIX outside interface and R3 and R4.

2 Configure MD5 authentication.

3 Do not configure RIP for the inside interface.

4 Advertise VLAN-8 and VLAN-9 networks in RIPv2 respectively on R8 and R7.

5 Create two loopbacks on R8: Loopback1 with 133.72.52.32/27 and Loopback2 with 133.72.52.64/27. Advertise these in RIPv2.

2.4: BGP (11 points)

2.4.1: Basic BGP Configuration (4 points)

1 Configure BGP as shown in the BGP information diagram in Figure 4-4.

2 Make R1 in AS1 peer with R2 and R4. Configure static NAT translation for R1 172.16.1.1 to 140.52.0.100.

3 Make R4 in AS2 peer with R1, R3, R5, and R6.

4 Do not use Route-Reflector for R7 and R8 in AS3. Do not use any Confederation command(s) on R5. R4 must peer with R5 using AS3.

2.4.2: BGP Through the Firewall (2 points)

1 Configure Loopback1 on R1 with IP 11.11.11.11/24. Configure a static NAT, ACL, and static route on PIX for Loopback1. Advertise Loopback1 in BGP on R1.

2.4.3: BGP Route Filtering (2 points)

1 R3 in AS2 should not see any routes from AS1. Do not use distribute-list, prefix-list, or route-map to achieve this task. Use a filtering method which is best to filter any range of networks advertised from AS1 in the future.

2.4.4: BGP Route Coloring (3 points)

1 Configure Loopback5 on R7 and R8 with IP 17.17.17.17/24 and 18.18.18.18/24 respectively. Advertise them in AS3.

    2 Configure Loopback5(s) with Community 5 on both routers.

    3 AS1 should see the Loopback5(s) with Community 10. All other peers should continue seeing Community 5.

    4 Make sure all routers can ping these loopbacks.

2.5: Layer 3 Switching (4 points)

    1 Configure Inter-VLAN routing for VLAN(s) 2, 3, 4, and 10 on Switch1.

    2 Do not configure any routing protocol(s) on Switch1, R1, R2, and PIX inside interface.

    3 Configure default route(s) on R1, R2, and PIX inside interface to Switch1. Do not configure the default route on PIX outside interface.

Section 3.0: ISDN Configuration (5 points)

3.1: Basic ISDN (3 points)

    1 Configure ISDN on R3 and R6.

    2 Use network 167.78.86.12/30.

    3 Advertise ISDN network in OSPF Area2.

    4 Do not configure any dial string on R6.

    5 ISDN should bring up the link after 10 seconds of VLAN-5 link on R3 going down.

    6 ISDN should remain up for 1 minute after VLAN-5 link recovers.

    7 R3 should converge with OSPF, and all routes must learn through OSPF, including the default route.

    ISDN information:

    BRI number on R3 is 99047132

    BRI number on R6 is 99047265

    Switch-type = basic-net3

3.2: PPP Authentication and Load Balancing (2 points)

    1 Configure PPP authentication. Do not configure AAA.

    2 R6 should send host name R6 for PPP authentication.

    3 ISDN should bring up the link if the VLAN-5 link load exceeds 75 percent, and tear down when the aggregate load is 5 percent.

Section 4.0: PIX Configuration (8 points)

4.1: Basic PIX Configuration (3 points)

1 Configure host name PIX.

2 Configure outside IP address 140.52.0.1/24.

3 Configure inside IP address 172.16.1.2/24.

4 Configure RIP on the outside interface as shown in Figure 4-3.

5 Configure simple authentication for RIPv2.

6 Configure the default route for the inside network to Switch1.

7 Configure static NAT and ACL for CA server 172.16.3.254 to 140.52.0.254.

8 Configure static NAT and ACL for Switch1 and Switch2 Management Interface 172.16.4.10 and 172.16.4.20, respectively.

9 Configure static NAT for Loopback1 of R1 to 11.11.11.11.

10 Configure a static NAT and ACL for a mail server with IP address 172.16.4.251 to 140.52.0.251.

11 Make sure you can ping the CA server and both switch management interfaces. PIX should be able to ping all devices on the network.

4.2: Advanced PIX Configuration (5 points)

1 Configure the following advanced features on PIX.

2 E-mail users are unable to send/receive mail. Upon investigation, it was found that the mail server is using Extended SMTP protocol. Configure PIX to allow ESMTP protocol mail through.

3 Block all Java applets from the Internet returning in web pages.

Section 5.0: IPSec/GRE Configuration (10 points)

5.1: IPSec LAN-to-LAN Through the Firewall Using CA (5 points)

1 Configure IPSec between R1 and R5 for Loopback10(s). Use Digital Certificates for authentication. Configure all other parameters as appropriate. If necessary, you can add one static route on R5 to achieve this task.

5.2: Multipoint GRE (5 points)

1 Configure secure GRE tunnels on R3, R6, R7, and R8.

2 Do not use the tunnel destination command on any routers.

3 Use subnet 10.1.1.0/24 for tunnel interface(s).

4 Configure only one tunnel interface on each router.

5 Configure EIGRP AS 1 on tunnel interface(s).

6 Advertise Loopback-9 on R6, R7, and R8 and VLAN-6 in EIGRP AS 1.

7 No other routers should see these loopbacks.

Section 6.0: IOS Firewall Configuration (8 points)

6.1: IOS Firewall (4 points)

1 Configure R5 and R6 as firewalls such that all TCP traffic from LAN to Internet (Frame Relay) is allowed only if originating from LAN and not vice versa. Allow routing protocols where necessary and UDP traffic for domain name resolution. For testing purposes, allow pings from anywhere.

2 Do not use CBAC to achieve this task.

6.2: Intrusion Detection System (IDS) (4 points)

1 Configure IDS on PIX to monitor the outside network and drop all attack signatures and alarm both attack and informational signatures.

2 Send alerts to Syslog server 172.16.1.10 in VLAN-10.

3 Disable the ICMP echo signature that is causing the high volume of alarms.

4 Ensure that all IDS logs have the correct timestamp for tracking attacks as they occur.

Section 7.0: AAA (7 points)

7.1: AAA on the Switch (3 points)

1 Configure both switches for RADIUS authentication.

2 Configure RADIUS for privileged access authorization.

3 Configure fallback to the local database in case the AAA server is unavailable.

4 Console port(s) should not be affected.

5 Configure accounting for all sessions.

6 Configure username **switch-user** password **cisco** in ACS with appropriate settings to achieve this task.

7.2: AAA on PIX (4 points)

1 Configure PIX to authenticate and authorize any Telnet traffic through to R2 in VLAN-2.

2 Users must be prompted for login credentials by PIX using TACACS+ server in VLAN-3 before they can log on to R2.

3 Configure double authentication, first with TACACS+ by PIX (if successful), and second by R2 itself locally.

4 Configure username **telnet-user** password **cisco** in ACS with appropriate settings for the first phase of authentication.

5 Configure username **r2telnet-user** password **cisco** on R2 for the second phase of authentication.

6 Verify Telnet to R2 from any router outside PIX.

Section 8.0: Advanced Security (10 points)

8.1: Perimeter Security (2 points)

1 Configure R4 to block all Java applets within HTTP from the Internet.

8.2: IP Fragmentation (2 points)

1 Internal networks have had increasing fragmentation issues mostly due to misconfiguration and vulnerabilities in the application servers. Configure PIX not to allow any fragmented packets through. Do not disable the floodguard feature on PIX.

8.3: Traffic Filtering Using Lock-and-Key (3 points)

1 Configure an access list on the R1 (VLAN-2) interface to deny all traffic except Telnet.

2 Configure R1 to dynamically open a hole for all traffic in this ACL when R2 authenticates with valid credentials.

    3 Configure AAA on R1 using TACACS+ for authentication. The console should not be affected.

    4 Configure username **locknkey-user** password **cisco** in CiscoSecure ACS.

8.4: Key Management (3 points)

    1 Configure different keys for RIP authentication in Section 2.3 on R3 and R4.

    2 Between the hours of 1:00 p.m. and 4:00 p.m., accept key string strict, and accept cisco for all other hours.

    3 Allow overlap of up to 1 hour for discrepancies in the peer's time when sending.

Section 9.0: IP Services and Protocol-Independent Features (10 points)

9.1: Network Monitoring and Management (3 points)

    1 Send SNMP traps for any changes in Frame Relay and configuration changes on R7 and R8 to server 140.52.0.55 in VLAN-5.

    2 Only server 140.52.0.55 should be authorized to retrieve and modify Management Information Base (MIB) objects.

    3 Use community strings **lab4-read** and **lab4-write** for read-only and write permission, respectively.

9.2: Time-Based Policy Routing (3 points)

    1 Between the hours of 9:00 a.m. and 5:00 p.m. Monday through Friday, R4 should reach R7 Loopback-5 via R5.

    2 For all other hours it should use R6.

9.3: Load Sharing Using HSRP (3 points)

    1 Configure load sharing in VLAN-7 for all traffic to load balance between R5 and R6.

    2 Half the workstations in VLAN-7 will be configured to R5 Virtual IP 142.52.0.50 for the default gateway, and half of the workstations will be configured to R6 Virtual IP 142.52.0.51 for the default gateway.

    3 When any of the router(s) in the pair is down, the other router takes 100% of the traffic for the router that is unavailable.

9.4: Multiple Paths (1 point)

1 Change the maximum number of paths on R4 so that two equal-cost routes are installed in the routing table.

Section 10.0: Security Violations (6 points)

10.1: TCP SYN DoS Attack (3 points)

1 An attacker from random source IP addresses is flooding a high number of connections to TCP-based application server(s) in VLAN-4. This is causing the servers to maintain high numbers of half-open connections, and they are getting overwhelmed, resulting in denying service to legitimate users.

2 Configure R1 to monitor TCP traffic to servers in VLAN-7, and drop any half-open connections that do not complete within 15 seconds, hence protecting the TCP SYN-flooding attacks.

3 Do not use IOS FW CBAC or CAR to achieve this task.

10.2: ARP Spoofing (3 points)

1 Many techniques exist in tricking a system into modifying its MAC table and sending the data to the attacker. A number of ARP spoofing tools available can craft an ARP reply packet that provides the switch with false information.

2 With our critical network infrastructure, extreme measures need to be taken to prevent ARP spoofing. A list of all the MAC addresses of every device in the network is available.

NOTE   ARP spoofing can result in a denial of service (DoS). Another possible use can be session hijacking, where an attacker acts as a man-in-the-middle on an ongoing session and takes over the MAC and IP address of one of the hosts to gain access to the network and pretend to be a trusted host for activities such as theft of information or corrupting transmitting data or to inject new information in the network.

Verification, Hints, and Troubleshooting Tips

This section has some important and useful hints for hidden tricks in some of the sections. Furthermore, detailed information on configuring IPSec using CA certificates is provided. A complete enrollment process and testing IPSec using CA is explained in detail.

The hints provided here are to be used as a guideline and address some or all parts of the corresponding exercise question. They are not listed in any order.

Section 1.0: Basic Configuration

1.1: IP Addressing

    1 Redraw a detailed topology with all necessary information, such as subnet information, routing protocol zones, ACLs, DLCIs, firewall, CBAC inspection, IDS inspection, and so on.

    2 Do not configure any IGP routing protocols on R1, R2, and PIX inside interface for networks behind PIX. You can configure RIPv2 on PIX outside interface only in the following sections.

    3 Switch1 will be the routing device for VLAN 2, 3, 4, and 10. See Section 2.5.

    4 Make sure you can ping the AAA server from R2 and PIX.

1.2: Frame Relay Configuration

    1 Configure multipoint subinterface on R6 for network 167.78.86.0/29 and point-to-point subinterface for network 167.78.86.8/30.

    2 Configure point-to-point subinterface(s) on R5, R7, and R8.

    3 Configure DLCIs as per Figure 4-2.

    4 Enable split horizon on serial links on R5, R7, and R8.

1.3: LAN Switch Configuration

    1 Configure the trunk between switch1 and switch2 port 1 as per Table 4-1.

    2 Configure VTP domain lab4 on both switches.

    3 Configure VTP authentication using MD5 password **cisco**. See Example 4-1.

    4 Configure both switches in server mode for the Configuration Revision number to sync. See Example 4-1.

    5 Configure ports 15 and 16 as protected ports. See Example 4-2.

TIP   For more information on configuring protected ports, refer to the following URL:

www.cisco.com/univercd/cc/td/doc/product/lan/c3550/1214ea1
/3550scg/swbcsup.htm#xtocid147587

---

    6 The use of protected ports ensures that there is no exchange of unicast, broadcast, or multicast traffic between ports configured as protected on the switch. A protected port does not forward any traffic (unicast, multicast, or broadcast) to any other port that is also a protected port.

7 Configure the management interface on Switch1 VLAN-4 as 172.16.4.10, but point the default gateway to PIX 172.16.1.2—that is, hanging off on VLAN10 interface on Switch1.

8 Configure the management interface on Switch2 VLAN-4 as 172.16.4.20. Point the default gateway to 172.16.4.10 of Switch1, as it is the Layer3 default gateway.

9 Set the line password on both switches to **cisco.**

10 Telnet from anywhere on the network to management IP of both switches: 172.16.4.10 and 172.16.4.20. See Example 4-5.

11 Configure static translation on PIX for 172.16.4.10 and 172.16.4.20 and allow ICMP and Telnet in ACL. See Example 4-3.

12 Configure a static route on R3 and R4 for network 172.16.4.0 to PIX.

13 Verify all VLAN assignments. See Example 4-4.

Example 4-1   *VTP Status from Switch1 and Switch2 Showing MD5 Authentication*

```
Switch1#show vtp status
VTP Version                      : 2
Configuration Revision           : 11
Maximum VLANs supported locally  : 1005
Number of existing VLANs         : 15
VTP Operating Mode               : Server
VTP Domain Name                  : lab4
VTP Pruning Mode                 : Disabled
VTP V2 Mode                      : Disabled
VTP Traps Generation             : Disabled
MD5 digest                       : 0xDD 0x22 0xC4 0x13 0x14 0xF7 0x2C 0xF1
Configuration last modified by 0.0.0.0 at 3-11-03 00:43:58
Local updater ID is 172.16.2.10 on interface Vl2 (lowest numbered VLAN interface found)
Switch1#


Switch2#show vtp status
VTP Version                      : 2
Configuration Revision           : 11
Maximum VLANs supported locally  : 1005
Number of existing VLANs         : 15
VTP Operating Mode               : Server
VTP Domain Name                  : lab4
VTP Pruning Mode                 : Disabled
VTP V2 Mode                      : Disabled
VTP Traps Generation             : Disabled
MD5 digest                       : 0xDD 0x22 0xC4 0x13 0x14 0xF7 0x2C 0xF1
Configuration last modified by 0.0.0.0 at 3-11-03 00:43:58
Local updater ID is 172.16.1.20 on interface Vl10 (lowest numbered VLAN interface
  found)
Switch2#
```

Example 4-2 *Configuring Protected Ports on Switch1*

```
interface FastEthernet0/15
 switchport mode access
 switchport protected
 no ip address
!
interface FastEthernet0/16
 switchport mode access
 switchport protected
 no ip address
!

Switch#show interfaces fa0/15 switchport
Name: Fa0/15
Switchport: Enabled
Administrative Mode: static access
Operational Mode: down
Administrative Trunking Encapsulation: negotiate
Negotiation of Trunking: Off
Access Mode VLAN: 1 (default)
Trunking Native Mode VLAN: 1 (default)
Administrative private-vlan host-association: none
Administrative private-vlan mapping: none
Operational private-vlan: none
Trunking VLANs Enabled: ALL
Pruning VLANs Enabled: 2-1001
Protected: true
Unknown unicast blocked: disabled
Unknown multicast blocked: disabled


Voice VLAN: none (Inactive)
Appliance trust: none


Switch#show interfaces fa0/16 switchport
Name: Fa0/16
Switchport: Enabled
Administrative Mode: static access
Operational Mode: down
Administrative Trunking Encapsulation: negotiate
Negotiation of Trunking: Off
Access Mode VLAN: 1 (default)
Trunking Native Mode VLAN: 1 (default)
Administrative private-vlan host-association: none
Administrative private-vlan mapping: none
Operational private-vlan: none
Trunking VLANs Enabled: ALL
Pruning VLANs Enabled: 2-1001
Protected: true
Unknown unicast blocked: disabled
Unknown multicast blocked: disabled
```

Example 4-2 *Configuring Protected Ports on Switch1 (Continued)*

```
Voice VLAN: none (Inactive)
Appliance trust: none
Switch#
```

Example 4-3 *Snip from PIX for Management Interface of Switches*

```
pix(config)# show static
static (inside,outside) 172.16.4.10 172.16.4.10 netmask 255.255.255.255 0 0
static (inside,outside) 172.16.4.20 172.16.4.20 netmask 255.255.255.255 0 0

pix(config)# show access-list
access-list outside; 3 elements
access-list outside permit icmp any any (hitcnt=50)
access-list outside permit tcp any host 172.16.4.10 eq telnet (hitcnt=3)
access-list outside permit tcp any host 172.16.4.20 eq telnet (hitcnt=3)
```

Example 4-4 *VLAN Assignments on Switch1 and Switch2*

```
Switch1#show vlan brief

VLAN Name                             Status    Ports
---- -------------------------------- --------- -------------------------------
1    default                          active    Fa0/11, Fa0/12, Fa0/13, Fa0/14
                                                Fa0/15, Fa0/16, Fa0/17, Fa0/18
                                                Fa0/19, Fa0/20, Fa0/21, Fa0/22
                                                Fa0/23, Fa0/24, Gi0/1, Gi0/2
2    VLAN-2                           active    Fa0/3, Fa0/4
3    VLAN-3                           active    Fa0/10
4    VLAN-4                           active
5    VLAN-5                           active    Fa0/9
6    VLAN-6                           active    Fa0/5
7    VLAN-7                           active    Fa0/6, Fa0/7
8    VLAN-8                           active
9    VLAN-9                           active    Fa0/8
10   VLAN-10                          active    Fa0/2
15   VLAN0015                         active
1002 fddi-default                     active
1003 token-ring-default               active
1004 fddinet-default                  active
1005 trnet-default                    active
Switch1#


Switch2#show vlan brief

VLAN Name                             Status    Ports
---- -------------------------------- --------- -------------------------------
1    default                          active    Fa0/9, Fa0/10, Fa0/11, Fa0/12
                                                Fa0/13, Fa0/14, Fa0/15, Fa0/16
                                                Fa0/17, Fa0/18, Fa0/19, Fa0/20
                                                Fa0/21, Fa0/22, Fa0/23, Fa0/24
                                                Gi0/1, Gi0/2
```

continues

Example 4-4 *VLAN Assignments on Switch1 and Switch2 (Continued)*

```
2     VLAN-2                        active
3     VLAN-3                        active    Fa0/2
4     VLAN-4                        active    Fa0/3
5     VLAN-5                        active    Fa0/4, Fa0/5
6     VLAN-6                        active
7     VLAN-7                        active    Fa0/6
8     VLAN-8                        active    Fa0/7
9     VLAN-9                        active
10    VLAN-10                       active    Fa0/8
15    VLAN0015                      active
1002  fddi-default                  active
1003  token-ring-default            active
1004  fddinet-default               active
1005  trnet-default                 active
Switch2#
```

Example 4-5 *Telnet from R3 to Both Switch(s) Management Interface*

```
r3#telnet 172.16.4.10
Trying 172.16.4.10 ... Open


User Access Verification

Password: cisco
Switch1>
Switch1>exit

[Connection to 172.16.4.10 closed by foreign host]
r3#



r3#telnet 172.16.4.20
Trying 172.16.4.20 ... Open


User Access Verification

Password: cisco
Switch2>
Switch2>
Switch2>exit

[Connection to 172.16.4.20 closed by foreign host]
r3#
r3#
```

Section 2.0: Routing Configuration

2.1: OSPF

1   Configure OSPF as shown in Figure 4-3 with MD5 authentication for all areas.

2   If you do a **show ip ospf interface** on R6, R7, and R8, you will see the network type is NON-BROADCAST and NBMA does not form adjacency without changing this network type. As you are not to use the **ip ospf network** command, configure R6 in Area 0 using the **neighbor** command—that is, unicast OSPF. See Example 4-6.

3   Summarize RIP external routes on R8 for network(s) 133.72.52.x in OSPF using the **summary-address** command. See Example 4-7.

4   Area 2 is not connected to OSPF backbone. Create a virtual link in Area 1 to interconnect Area 2 with MD5 authentication. See Example 4-8.

5   Redistribute OSPF into RIP on R3 and R4.

6   Redistribute RIP into OSPF on R7 and R8.

7   For R3 to learn all routes from R4 via RIP and not OSPF, configure the **ip ospf database-filter** command on R4 to filter all outbound routes to R3. See Example 4-9.

Example 4-6   *OSPF Point-to-Multipoint Network with Nonbroadcast*

```
!Configure neighbor command on R6 for peer R7 and R8.
Snip from R6:
router ospf 110
 router-id 6.6.6.6
 log-adjacency-changes
 area 0 authentication message-digest
 area 1 authentication message-digest
 area 1 virtual-link 4.4.4.4 message-digest-key 1 md5 cisco
 network 142.52.0.0 0.0.0.255 area 1
 network 167.78.86.0 0.0.0.7 area 0
 neighbor 167.78.86.2
 neighbor 167.78.86.3
 default-information originate always

r6#show ip ospf interface
Serial2/0.1 is up, line protocol is up
  Internet Address 167.78.86.1/29, Area 0
  Process ID 110, Router ID 6.6.6.6, Network Type NON_BROADCAST, Cost: 48
  Transmit Delay is 1 sec, State DR, Priority 100
  Designated Router (ID) 6.6.6.6, Interface address 167.78.86.1
  No backup designated router on this network
  Timer intervals configured, Hello 30, Dead 120, Wait 120, Retransmit 5
    Hello due in 00:00:04
  Index 1/1, flood queue length 0
  Next 0x0(0)/0x0(0)
```

continues

Example 4-6 *OSPF Point-to-Multipoint Network with Nonbroadcast (Continued)*

```
    Last flood scan length is 1, maximum is 4
    Last flood scan time is 0 msec, maximum is 0 msec
    Neighbor Count is 2, Adjacent neighbor count is 2
      Adjacent with neighbor 8.8.8.8
      Adjacent with neighbor 7.7.7.7
    Suppress hello for 0 neighbor(s)
    Message digest authentication enabled
      Youngest key id is 1
  FastEthernet0/0 is up, line protocol is up
    Internet Address 142.52.0.2/24, Area 1
    Process ID 110, Router ID 6.6.6.6, Network Type BROADCAST, Cost: 1
    Transmit Delay is 1 sec, State DROTHER, Priority 1
    Designated Router (ID) 4.4.4.4, Interface address 142.52.0.1
    Backup Designated router (ID) 5.5.5.5, Interface address 142.52.0.3
    Timer intervals configured, Hello 10, Dead 40, Wait 40, Retransmit 5
      Hello due in 00:00:06
    Index 1/2, flood queue length 0
    Next 0x0(0)/0x0(0)
    Last flood scan length is 0, maximum is 9
    Last flood scan time is 0 msec, maximum is 0 msec
    Neighbor Count is 2, Adjacent neighbor count is 2
      Adjacent with neighbor 5.5.5.5  (Backup Designated Router)
      Adjacent with neighbor 4.4.4.4  (Designated Router)
    Suppress hello for 0 neighbor(s)
    Message digest authentication enabled
      Youngest key id is 1

r7#show ip ospf interface
  Serial1/0 is up, line protocol is up
    Internet Address 167.78.86.3/29, Area 0
    Process ID 110, Router ID 7.7.7.7, Network Type NON_BROADCAST, Cost: 64
    Transmit Delay is 1 sec, State DROTHER, Priority 0
    Designated Router (ID) 6.6.6.6, Interface address 167.78.86.1
    No backup designated router on this network
    Timer intervals configured, Hello 30, Dead 120, Wait 120, Retransmit 5
      Hello due in 00:00:07
    Index 1/1, flood queue length 0
    Next 0x0(0)/0x0(0)
    Last flood scan length is 1, maximum is 1
    Last flood scan time is 0 msec, maximum is 0 msec
    Neighbor Count is 1, Adjacent neighbor count is 1
      Adjacent with neighbor 6.6.6.6  (Designated Router)
    Suppress hello for 0 neighbor(s)
    Message digest authentication enabled
      Youngest key id is 1
  r7#

r8#show ip ospf interface
  Serial1/0 is up, line protocol is up
    Internet Address 167.78.86.2/29, Area 0
    Process ID 110, Router ID 8.8.8.8, Network Type NON_BROADCAST, Cost: 781
    Transmit Delay is 1 sec, State DROTHER, Priority 0
```

Example 4-6 *OSPF Point-to-Multipoint Network with Nonbroadcast (Continued)*

```
    Designated Router (ID) 6.6.6.6, Interface address 167.78.86.1
    No backup designated router on this network
    Timer intervals configured, Hello 30, Dead 120, Wait 120, Retransmit 5
      Hello due in 00:00:13
    Index 1/1, flood queue length 0
    Next 0x0(0)/0x0(0)
    Last flood scan length is 1, maximum is 4
    Last flood scan time is 0 msec, maximum is 0 msec
    Neighbor Count is 1, Adjacent neighbor count is 1
      Adjacent with neighbor 6.6.6.6  (Designated Router)
    Suppress hello for 0 neighbor(s)
    Message digest authentication enabled
      Youngest key id is 1
r8#
```

Example 4-7 *OSPF Summarization on R8*

```
router ospf 110
 router-id 8.8.8.8
 log-adjacency-changes
 area 0 authentication message-digest
 summary-address 133.72.52.0 255.255.255.128
 redistribute rip metric 1 subnets
 network 167.78.86.0 0.0.0.7 area 0
```

Example 4-8 *OSPF Virtual Link with MD5 Authentication*

```
!Snip from R6 config
router ospf 110
 router-id 6.6.6.6
 log-adjacency-changes
 area 0 authentication message-digest
 area 1 authentication message-digest
 area 1 virtual-link 4.4.4.4 message-digest-key 1 md5 cisco
 network 142.52.0.0 0.0.0.255 area 1
 network 167.78.86.0 0.0.0.7 area 0
 neighbor 167.78.86.2
 neighbor 167.78.86.3
 default-information originate always

r6#show ip ospf virtual-links
Virtual Link OSPF_VL0 to router 4.4.4.4 is up
  Run as demand circuit
  DoNotAge LSA allowed.
  Transit area 1, via interface FastEthernet0/0, Cost of using 1
  Transmit Delay is 1 sec, State POINT_TO_POINT,
  Timer intervals configured, Hello 10, Dead 40, Wait 40, Retransmit 5
    Hello due in 00:00:03
    Adjacency State FULL (Hello suppressed)
    Index 3/5, retransmission queue length 0, number of retransmission 2
```
                                                                    continues

Example 4-8   *OSPF Virtual Link with MD5 Authentication (Continued)*

```
         First 0x0(0)/0x0(0) Next 0x0(0)/0x0(0)
         Last retransmission scan length is 2, maximum is 2
         Last retransmission scan time is 0 msec, maximum is 0 msec
      Message digest authentication enabled
         Youngest key id is 1
   r6#


   !Snip from R4 config
   router ospf 110
    router-id 4.4.4.4
    log-adjacency-changes
    area 0 authentication message-digest
    area 1 authentication message-digest
    area 1 virtual-link 6.6.6.6 message-digest-key 1 md5 cisco
    area 2 authentication message-digest
    redistribute static metric 1 subnets
    network 140.52.0.0 0.0.0.255 area 2
    network 142.52.0.0 0.0.0.255 area 1

   r4#show ip ospf virtual-links
   Virtual Link OSPF_VL0 to router 6.6.6.6 is up
      Run as demand circuit
      DoNotAge LSA allowed.
      Transit area 1, via interface Ethernet0/1, Cost of using 10
      Transmit Delay is 1 sec, State POINT_TO_POINT,
      Timer intervals configured, Hello 10, Dead 40, Wait 40, Retransmit 5
         Hello due in 00:00:04
         Adjacency State FULL (Hello suppressed)
         Index 1/4, retransmission queue length 0, number of retransmission 0
         First 0x0(0)/0x0(0) Next 0x0(0)/0x0(0)
         Last retransmission scan length is 0, maximum is 0
         Last retransmission scan time is 0 msec, maximum is 0 msec
      Message digest authentication enabled
         Youngest key id is 1
```

Example 4-9   *OSPF Database Filtering on R4*

```
   interface Ethernet0/0
    ip address 140.52.0.3 255.255.255.0
    ip rip authentication mode md5
    ip rip authentication key-chain lab4
    ip ospf message-digest-key 1 md5 cisco
    ip ospf priority 100
    ip ospf database-filter all out
    half-duplex
   !Enable debug ip routing on R4. When you configure database-filtering on R4 as
   !shown in Example 4-9, you will see that all OSPF routes are deleted and learnt
   !via RIP on R3.
   r3#show debug
   IP routing:
     IP routing debugging is on
```

Example 4-9   *OSPF Database Filtering on R4 (Continued)*

```
2d02h: RT: del 167.78.86.0/29 via 140.52.0.3, ospf metric [110/59]
2d02h: RT: delete subnet route to 167.78.86.0/29
2d02h: RT: delete network route to 167.78.0.0
2d02h: RT: del 142.52.0.0/24 via 140.52.0.3, ospf metric [110/11]
2d02h: RT: delete subnet route to 142.52.0.0/24
2d02h: RT: delete network route to 142.52.0.0
2d02h: RT: del 133.72.52.0/25 via 140.52.0.3, ospf metric [110/1]
2d02h: RT: delete subnet route to 133.72.52.0/25
2d02h: RT: delete network route to 133.72.0.0
2d02h: RT: del 121.52.5.0/26 via 140.52.0.3, ospf metric [110/1]
2d02h: RT: delete subnet route to 121.52.5.0/26
2d02h: RT: delete network route to 121.0.0.0
2d02h: RT: del 0.0.0.0 via 140.52.0.3, ospf metric [110/1]
2d02h: RT: delete network route to 0.0.0.0
r3#
2d02h: RT: add 0.0.0.0/0 via 140.52.0.3, rip metric [120/1]
2d02h: RT: default path is now 0.0.0.0 via 140.52.0.3
2d02h: RT: new default network 0.0.0.0
2d02h: RT: add 121.52.5.0/26 via 140.52.0.3, rip metric [120/1]
2d02h: RT: add 133.72.52.0/25 via 140.52.0.3, rip metric [120/1]
2d02h: RT: add 142.52.0.0/24 via 140.52.0.3, rip metric [120/1]
2d02h: RT: add 167.78.86.0/29 via 140.52.0.3, rip metric [120/1]
```

TIP   See the following URL for more information on OSPF database filtering:

www.cisco.com/univercd/cc/td/doc/product/software/ios121/121cgcr/ip_r/iprprt2
/1rdospf.htm#1018116

2.2: EIGRP

1 Configure R5-R6 in EIGRP AS 4.

2 EIGRP does not originate default routes like OSPF. The only way to inject a default route
   to EIGRP peers is to redistribute static or summarization.

3 Configure a default route on R6 to null 0 and redistribute static in EIGRP AS 4. See
   Example 4-10.

4 Configure MD5 authentication for EIGRP AS 4. See Example 4-10.

Example 4-10 *Snip from R5 and R6 EIGRP Config and Default Route*

```
!Snip from R6:
hostname r6
!
key chain lab4
 key 1
  key-string cisco
!
```
                                                                           continues

Example 4-10 *Snip from R5 and R6 EIGRP Config and Default Route (Continued)*

```
interface Serial2/0.2 point-to-point
 ip address 167.78.86.9 255.255.255.252
 ip authentication mode eigrp 4 md5
 ip authentication key-chain eigrp 4 lab4
 frame-relay interface-dlci 605
!
router eigrp 4
 redistribute static
 network 167.78.86.8 0.0.0.3
 default-metric 10000 1000 255 1 1500
 no auto-summary
 no eigrp log-neighbor-changes
!
ip route 0.0.0.0 0.0.0.0 Null0

!Snip from R5:
hostname r5
!
key chain lab4
 key 1
  key-string cisco
!
interface Serial0
 ip address 167.78.86.10 255.255.255.252
 ip authentication mode eigrp 4 md5
 ip authentication key-chain eigrp 4 lab4
 frame-relay map ip 167.78.86.9 506 broadcast
 no frame-relay inverse-arp
 frame-relay lmi-type cisco

r5#show ip route eigrp
D*EX 0.0.0.0/0 [170/2425856] via 167.78.86.9, 00:02:22, Serial0
r5#
```

2.3: RIP

1 Configure RIPv2 on the PIX outside interface and R3 and R4 with MD5 authentication.

2 Configure multiple keys on R3 and R4; see Section 8.4.

3 Do not configure RIP for the inside interface. Configure the inside default gateway to the VLAN-10 IP-address of Switch1.

4 Advertise VLAN-8 and VLAN-9 networks in RIPv2.

5 Advertise Loopback1 and Loopback2 on R8 in RIPv2. See Section 2.1 OSPF to summarize network(s) 133.72.52.x.

6 Redistribute OSPF into RIP on R3 and R4 so PIX learns all the routes.

2.4: BGP

2.4.1: Basic BGP Configuration

1 Configure BGP peers as per Figure 4-4.

2 R1 should peer with R2, R3, and R4. Configure static NAT and ACL on PIX. See Example 4-11.

3 For R1 to peer with R2, make sure you punch a hole in the Lock-and-Key ACL on R1, configured in Section 8.3.

4 Redistribute BGP into RIP on R3 and R4 so PIX learns all the routes.

5 AS3 iBGP is not fully meshed. Do not configure full-mesh iBGP sessions. Configure BGP confederation between R6-R7-R8.

6 Do not configure any confederation commands on R5. Use BGP AS 65006 on R5 and configure R6 to peer with R5 as route-reflector-client.

7 The hidden problem here is that you need R4 to peer with R5 with AS 3 and not 65006. Configure **bgp local-as** on R5 for the R4 neighbor. See the R4 and R5 configuration in Example 4-12.

Example 4-11 *PIX NAT and ACL*

```
pix(config)# show static
static (inside,outside) 140.52.0.100 172.16.1.1 netmask 255.255.255.255 0 0

pix(config)# show access-list
access-list outside permit icmp any any (hitcnt=317)
access-list outside permit tcp host 140.52.0.3 host 140.52.0.100 eq bgp (hitcnt=85)
```

Example 4-12 *AS3 iBGP Using Confederation and Route Reflector*

```
!Snip from R6:
router bgp 65006
 no synchronization
 bgp router-id 6.6.6.6
 bgp log-neighbor-changes
 bgp confederation identifier 3
 bgp confederation peers 65007 65008
 neighbor 142.52.0.1 remote-as 2
 neighbor 142.52.0.1 send-community
 neighbor 167.78.86.2 remote-as 65008
 neighbor 167.78.86.2 send-community
 neighbor 167.78.86.3 remote-as 65007
 neighbor 167.78.86.3 send-community
 neighbor 167.78.86.10 remote-as 65006
 neighbor 167.78.86.10 route-reflector-client
 neighbor 167.78.86.10 send-community
 no auto-summary
```

continues

Example 4-12 *AS3 iBGP Using Confederation and Route Reflector (Continued)*

```
!Snip from R4:
router bgp 2
 no synchronization
 bgp redistribute-internal
 bgp router-id 4.4.4.4
 bgp log-neighbor-changes
 neighbor 140.52.0.2 remote-as 2
 neighbor 140.52.0.2 send-community
 neighbor 140.52.0.100 remote-as 1
 neighbor 140.52.0.100 ebgp-multihop 255
 neighbor 140.52.0.100 send-community
 neighbor 140.52.0.100 route-map set-next-hop in
 neighbor 140.52.0.100 route-map change-community out
 neighbor 142.52.0.2 remote-as 3
 neighbor 142.52.0.2 send-community
 neighbor 142.52.0.3 remote-as 3
 neighbor 142.52.0.3 send-community
 maximum-paths 2
 no auto-summary

!Snip from R5, no BGP Confederation command used.
router bgp 65006
 no synchronization
 bgp router-id 5.5.5.5
 bgp log-neighbor-changes
 neighbor 142.52.0.1 remote-as 2
 neighbor 142.52.0.1 local-as 3
 neighbor 167.78.86.9 remote-as 65006
 no auto-summary

!Snip from R7
router bgp 65007
 no synchronization
 bgp router-id 7.7.7.7
 bgp log-neighbor-changes
 bgp confederation identifier 3
 bgp confederation peers 65006
 neighbor 167.78.86.1 remote-as 65006
 no auto-summary

!Snip from R8
router bgp 65008
 no synchronization
 bgp router-id 8.8.8.8
 bgp log-neighbor-changes
 bgp confederation identifier 3
 bgp confederation peers 65006
 neighbor 167.78.86.1 remote-as 65006
 no auto-summary
```

2.4.2: BGP Through the Firewall

1 Inbound BGP updates from R1 will have a next hop of 172.16.1.1 (private address).
Configure the next hop using a route map on R4 for inbound updates from R1. See
Example 4-13.

Example 4-13 *BGP Next-Hop Modification for Inbound Updates from R1 Behind PIX*

```
!Snip from R4:
router bgp 2
 no synchronization
 bgp router-id 4.4.4.4
 neighbor 140.52.0.100 remote-as 1
 neighbor 140.52.0.100 ebgp-multihop 255
 neighbor 140.52.0.100 route-map set-next-hop in
!
route-map set-next-hop permit 10
 set ip next-hop 140.52.0.100
!

!BGP Table before applying route-map:
r4#show ip bgp
BGP table version is 2, local router ID is 4.4.4.4
Status codes: s suppressed, d damped, h history, * valid, > best, i - internal,
              r RIB-failure
Origin codes: i - IGP, e - EGP, ? - incomplete

   Network          Next Hop          Metric LocPrf Weight Path
*> 11.11.11.0/24    172.16.1.1             0            0 1 i

!BGP Table after applying the route-map:
r4#show ip bgp
BGP table version is 2, local router ID is 4.4.4.4
Status codes: s suppressed, d damped, h history, * valid, > best, i - internal,
              r RIB-failure
Origin codes: i - IGP, e - EGP, ? - incomplete

   Network          Next Hop          Metric LocPrf Weight Path
*> 11.11.11.0/24    140.52.0.100           0            0 1 i
r4#
```

2.4.3: BGP Route Filtering

1 Filter AS1 updates on R3 using as-path access-list. See Example 4-14. AS-PATH ACL
is effective, as it checks the AS number in the AS-PATH and not the Layer-3 network.

2 Use BGP Regular Expressions _1_ to deny any update that has AS number 1 in the
AS-PATH. The permit .* regular expression means permit any or all.

Example 4-14 *Filtering AS1 Updates Using AS-PATH Access List*

```
router bgp 2
 no synchronization
 bgp router-id 3.3.3.3
 bgp log-neighbor-changes
 neighbor 140.52.0.3 remote-as 2
 neighbor 140.52.0.3 filter-list 1 in
 no auto-summary
!
ip as-path access-list 1 deny _1_
ip as-path access-list 1 permit .*

!BGP Table before applying the filter-list:

r3#show ip bgp
BGP table version is 32, local router ID is 3.3.3.3
Status codes: s suppressed, d damped, h history, * valid, > best, i - internal,
              r RIB-failure
Origin codes: i - IGP, e - EGP, ? - incomplete

   Network          Next Hop          Metric LocPrf Weight Path
*>i11.11.11.0/24    140.52.0.100           0    100      0 1 i
*>i17.17.17.0/24    142.52.0.2                  100      0 3 i
*>i18.18.18.0/24    142.52.0.2                  100      0 3 i

!BGP Table after applying the filter-list:

r3#show ip bgp
BGP table version is 3, local router ID is 3.3.3.3
Status codes: s suppressed, d damped, h history, * valid, > best, i - internal,
              r RIB-failure
Origin codes: i - IGP, e - EGP, ? - incomplete

   Network          Next Hop          Metric LocPrf Weight Path
*>i17.17.17.0/24    142.52.0.2                  100      0 3 i
*>i18.18.18.0/24    142.52.0.2                  100      0 3 i
```

2.4.4: BGP Route Coloring

1 Configure BGP community on R7 and R8 for Loopback5(s) as 10. See Example 4-15.

2 Change this community on R4 to 5 for Loopback5(s) from R7 and R8. See Example 4-16.

3 Another hidden issue is that R7 and R8 will not be able to ping Loopback5 (s) and/or any routes learned from each other. The solution is to set the next hop to hub router R6 IP 167.78.86.1. See Example 4-17 for verifying this and Example 4-18 for the solution.

Example 4-15 *BGP Route Coloring Using Community on R7 and R8*

```
!Snip from R7 config:
router bgp 65007
 no synchronization
 bgp router-id 7.7.7.7
```

Example 4-15 *BGP Route Coloring Using Community on R7 and R8 (Continued)*

```
 bgp confederation identifier 3
 bgp confederation peers 65006
 network 17.17.17.0 mask 255.255.255.0
 neighbor 167.78.86.1 remote-as 65006
 neighbor 167.78.86.1 send-community
 neighbor 167.78.86.1 route-map set-community out
 no auto-summary
!
access-list 5 permit 17.17.17.0 0.0.0.255
route-map set-community permit 10
 match ip address 5
 set community 5
!
route-map set-community permit 20

!Snip from R8 config:
router bgp 65008
 no synchronization
 bgp router-id 8.8.8.8
 bgp confederation identifier 3
 bgp confederation peers 65006
 network 18.18.18.0 mask 255.255.255.0
 neighbor 167.78.86.1 remote-as 65006
 neighbor 167.78.86.1 send-community
 neighbor 167.78.86.1 route-map set-community out
 no auto-summary
!
access-list 5 permit 18.18.18.0 0.0.0.255
!
route-map set-community permit 10
 match ip address 5
 set community 5
!
route-map set-community permit 20
```

Example 4-16 *BGP Changing Route Coloring Using Community*

```
!Snip from R4:
router bgp 2
 no synchronization
 bgp router-id 4.4.4.4
 neighbor 140.52.0.2 remote-as 2
 neighbor 140.52.0.2 send-community
 neighbor 140.52.0.100 remote-as 1
 neighbor 140.52.0.100 ebgp-multihop 255
 neighbor 140.52.0.100 send-community
 neighbor 140.52.0.100 route-map set-next-hop in
 neighbor 140.52.0.100 route-map change-community out
 neighbor 142.52.0.2 remote-as 3
 neighbor 142.52.0.3 remote-as 3
 no auto-summary
```

continues

Example 4-16 *BGP Changing Route Coloring Using Community (Continued)*

```
!
ip community-list 1 permit 5
!
route-map change-community permit 10
 match community 1
 set community 10
!
route-map change-community permit 20

!BGP Table on R1 before changing community on R4:
r1#show ip bgp 17.17.17.17
BGP routing table entry for 17.17.17.0/24, version 15
Paths: (1 available, best #1, table Default-IP-Routing-Table)
  Advertised to non peer-group peers:
  172.16.2.2
  2 3
    140.52.0.3 from 140.52.0.3 (4.4.4.4)
      Origin IGP, localpref 100, valid, external, best
      Community: 5

r1#show ip bgp 18.18.18.0
BGP routing table entry for 18.18.18.0/24, version 16
Paths: (1 available, best #1, table Default-IP-Routing-Table)
  Advertised to non peer-group peers:
  172.16.2.2
  2 3
    140.52.0.3 from 140.52.0.3 (4.4.4.4)
      Origin IGP, localpref 100, valid, external, best
      Community: 5

!BGP Table on R1 after changing community on R4:
r1#show ip bgp 17.17.17.17
BGP routing table entry for 17.17.17.0/24, version 19
Paths: (1 available, best #1, table Default-IP-Routing-Table)
Flag: 0x208
  Advertised to non peer-group peers:
  172.16.2.2
  2 3
    140.52.0.3 from 140.52.0.3 (4.4.4.4)
      Origin IGP, localpref 100, valid, external, best
      Community: 10

r1#show ip bgp 18.18.18.0
BGP routing table entry for 18.18.18.0/24, version 20
Paths: (1 available, best #1, table Default-IP-Routing-Table)
Flag: 0x208
  Advertised to non peer-group peers:
  172.16.2.2
  2 3
    140.52.0.3 from 140.52.0.3 (4.4.4.4)
      Origin IGP, localpref 100, valid, external, best
      Community: 10
```

Example 4-17 *Next-Hop Issue on R7 and R8*

```
!See routing table for R7 below, there are 2 routes learnt from R8
!(167.78.86.2). R7 cannot ping either of them.
r7#show ip route | include 167.78.86.2
B       18.18.18.0 [200/0] via 167.78.86.2, 23:31:45
O E2    133.72.52.0 [110/1] via 167.78.86.2, 1d02h, Serial1/0
r7#

r7#ping 18.18.18.18

Type escape sequence to abort.
Sending 5, 100-byte ICMP Echos to 18.18.18.18, timeout is 2 seconds:
.....
Success rate is 0 percent (0/5)
r7#
r7#ping 133.72.52.1

Type escape sequence to abort.
Sending 5, 100-byte ICMP Echos to 133.72.52.1, timeout is 2 seconds:
.....
Success rate is 0 percent (0/5)
r7#

!Enable following debug:
r7#debug ip packet detail
IP packet debugging is on (detailed)
r7#
r7#show debugging
Generic IP:
  IP packet debugging is on (detailed)
r7#
3d17h: IP: s=167.78.86.3 (local), d=133.72.52.1, len 100, cef process switched
3d17h:     ICMP type=8, code=0
3d17h: IP: s=167.78.86.3 (local), d=133.72.52.1 (Serial1/0), len 100, sending
3d17h:     ICMP type=8, code=0
3d17h: IP: s=167.78.86.3 (local), d=133.72.52.1 (Serial1/0), len 100,
   encapsulation failed
!Encapsulation failed means, it does not have Layer-2 mapping for 167.78.86.2.
!This is because we have only mapped frame-relay to hub router R6 and not R8.
!To fix the problem, set the next-hop to the hub router 167.78.86.1 using local
!policy. See Example 4-18 below.
!Ping successful after applying local policy on both routers as per Example 4-18
!below.
r7#ping 18.18.18.18

Type escape sequence to abort.
Sending 5, 100-byte ICMP Echos to 18.18.18.18, timeout is 2 seconds:
!!!!!
Success rate is 100 percent (5/5), round-trip min/avg/max = 132/135/148 ms
r7#
r7#traceroute 18.18.18.18
```

continues

Example 4-17 *Next-Hop Issue on R7 and R8 (Continued)*

```
Type escape sequence to abort.
Tracing the route to 18.18.18.18

  1 167.78.86.1 32 msec 32 msec 32 msec
  2 167.78.86.2 76 msec *  64 msec
r7#


r7#ping 133.72.52.1

Type escape sequence to abort.
Sending 5, 100-byte ICMP Echos to 133.72.52.1, timeout is 2 seconds:
!!!!!
Success rate is 100 percent (5/5), round-trip min/avg/max = 128/130/132 ms
r7#
r7#traceroute 133.72.52.1

Type escape sequence to abort.
Tracing the route to 133.72.52.1

  1 167.78.86.1 36 msec 32 msec 32 msec
  2 167.78.86.2 64 msec *  64 msec
r7#
r7#
```

Example 4-18 *Set Next Hop on R7 and R8 to Hub Router R6*

```
!Snip from R7. Do the same on R8.
interface Ethernet0/0
 ip policy route-map next-hop
!
ip local policy route-map next-hop
!
route-map next-hop permit 10
 set ip next-hop 167.78.86.1
!

r7#show route-map next-hop
route-map next-hop, permit, sequence 10
  Match clauses:
  Set clauses:
    ip next-hop 167.78.86.1
  Policy routing matches: 61 packets, 5478 bytes
r7#
```

2.5: Layer 3 Switching

1 Enable **ip routing** on Switch1.

2 Configure four VLAN interfaces and give IP address(es) to each VLAN interface. See
   Example 4-19.

3 Configure the default gateway on Switch1 to the PIX inside interface.

4 Configure the default gateway on R1, R2, and PIX to the VLAN interface IP address on Switch1.

TIP   See the following URLs for more information on inter-VLAN routing:

www.cisco.com/univercd/cc/td/doc/product/software/ios121/121cgcr/switch_c/xcprt7/xcdvl.htm

www.cisco.com/univercd/cc/td/doc/product/lan/c3550/1214ea1/3550scg/swiprout.htm#24886

Example 4-19 *Inter-VLAN Routing on Switch1*

```
Switch#show running-config | begin interface Vlan
interface Vlan1
 no ip address
 shutdown
!
interface Vlan2
 ip address 172.16.2.10 255.255.255.0
!
interface Vlan3
 ip address 172.16.3.10 255.255.255.0
!
interface Vlan4
 ip address 172.16.4.10 255.255.255.0
!
interface Vlan10
 ip address 172.16.1.10 255.255.255.0
!

Switch#show ip inter brief | include Vlan
Vlan1                   unassigned      YES NVRAM  administratively down down
Vlan2                   172.16.2.10     YES manual up                    up
Vlan3                   172.16.3.10     YES manual up                    up
Vlan4                   172.16.4.10     YES manual up                    up
Vlan10                  172.16.1.10     YES manual up                    up


Switch1#show ip route
Codes: C - connected, S - static, I - IGRP, R - RIP, M - mobile, B - BGP
       D - EIGRP, EX - EIGRP external, O - OSPF, IA - OSPF inter area
       N1 - OSPF NSSA external type 1, N2 - OSPF NSSA external type 2
       E1 - OSPF external type 1, E2 - OSPF external type 2, E - EGP
       i - IS-IS, L1 - IS-IS level-1, L2 - IS-IS level-2, ia - IS-IS inter area
       * - candidate default, U - per-user static route, o - ODR
       P - periodic downloaded static route
```

continues

Example 4-19 *Inter-VLAN Routing on Switch1 (Continued)*

```
Gateway of last resort is 172.16.1.2 to network 0.0.0.0

     172.16.0.0/24 is subnetted, 4 subnets
C       172.16.4.0 is directly connected, Vlan4
C       172.16.1.0 is directly connected, Vlan10
C       172.16.2.0 is directly connected, Vlan2
C       172.16.3.0 is directly connected, Vlan3
S*   0.0.0.0/0 [1/0] via 172.16.1.2
Switch1#
```

Section 3.0: ISDN Configuration

3.1: Basic ISDN

1   Configure ISDN on R3 and R6 using network 167.78.86.12/30. See Example 4-20.

2   Configure the ISDN network in OSPF Area2 with MD5 authentication. By advertising the ISDN network in Area 2, R3 should converge with OSPF, and all routes will be learned via OSPF, including the default route.

3   Do not configure the dial-string on the R6 dialer map statement. See Example 4-20.

4   Configure the dial backup scenario using the **backup interface** command on the VLAN-5 Ethernet interface on R3. See Example 4-20.

5   Configure the **backup delay** command to bring up the link after 10 seconds of the VLAN-5 link on R3 going down, and tear down after 1 minute of the VLAN-5 link coming up. See Example 4-20.

6   Verify by disconnecting the cable for VLAN-5 interface Fastethernet 0/0 on R3 or shutting the port on switch. ISDN should activate in 10 seconds, and the OSPF neighbor forms adjacency and routes converge via OSPF. See Example 4-21.

Example 4-20 *ISDN Configuration on R3 and R6*

```
!Snip from R3 config:
hostname r3
!
username R6 password 0 cisco
!
interface FastEthernet0/0
 backup delay 10 60
 backup interface BRI0/0
 backup load 75 5
 ip address 140.52.0.2 255.255.255.0
 ip ospf message-digest-key 1 md5 cisco
!
interface BRI0/0
 ip address 167.78.86.13 255.255.255.252
```

Example 4-20 *ISDN Configuration on R3 and R6 (Continued)*

```
 encapsulation ppp
 ip ospf message-digest-key 1 md5 cisco
 ip ospf cost 999
 dialer map ip 167.78.86.14 name r6 broadcast 99047132
 dialer-group 1
 isdn switch-type basic-net3
 no peer neighbor-route
 ppp authentication chap
!
dialer-list 1 protocol ip permit

!Snip from R6 cconfig:
hostname r6
!
username r3 password 0 cisco
!
interface BRI1/0
 ip address 167.78.86.14 255.255.255.252
 encapsulation ppp
 ip ospf message-digest-key 1 md5 cisco
 ip ospf cost 999
 dialer map ip 167.78.86.13 name r3 broadcast
 dialer-group 1
 isdn switch-type basic-net3
 no peer neighbor-route
 ppp authentication chap
 ppp chap hostname R6
!
dialer-list 1 protocol ip permit
!
```

Example 4-21 *ISDN Link Activating When VLAN-5 Interface Fastethernet0/0 Down*

```
r3#show ip ospf neighbor

Neighbor ID     Pri   State      Dead Time   Address       Interface
4.4.4.4         100   FULL/DR    00:00:34    140.52.0.3    FastEthernet0/0


r3#debug dialer
Dial on demand events debugging is on

r3#show debug
Dial on demand:
  Dial on demand events debugging is on

1w3d: %LINEPROTO-5-UPDOWN: Line protocol on Interface FastEthernet0/0, changed state
  to down
1w3d: %OSPF-5-ADJCHG: Process 110, Nbr 4.4.4.4 on FastEthernet0/0 from FULL to DOWN,
  Neighbor Down: Interface down or detached
1w3d: %LINK-3-UPDOWN: Interface BRI0/0:1, changed state to down
```
continues

Example 4-21 *ISDN Link Activating When VLAN-5 Interface Fastethernet0/0 Down (Continued)*

```
1w3d: %LINK-3-UPDOWN: Interface BRI0/0:2, changed state to down
1w3d: BR0/0:1 DDR: disconnecting call
1w3d: BR0/0:2 DDR: disconnecting call
1w3d: BR0/0 DDR: place call
1w3d: BR0/0 DDR: Dialing cause ip (s=167.78.86.13, d=224.0.0.5)
1w3d: BR0/0 DDR: Attempting to dial 99047132
1w3d: %LINK-3-UPDOWN: Interface BRI0/0, changed state to up
1w3d: %ISDN-6-LAYER2UP: Layer 2 for Interface BR0/0, TEI 65 changed to up
1w3d: %LINK-3-UPDOWN: Interface BRI0/0:1, changed state to up
1w3d: BR0/0:1 DDR: Remote name for R6
1w3d: BR0/0:1 DDR: Authenticated host R6 with no matching dialer map
1w3d: BR0/0:1 DDR: dialer protocol up
1w3d: %LINEPROTO-5-UPDOWN: Line protocol on Interface BRI0/0:1, changed state to up
1w3d: %ISDN-6-CONNECT: Interface BRI0/0:1 is now connected to 99047132 R6
1w3d: %OSPF-5-ADJCHG: Process 110, Nbr 6.6.6.6 on BRI0/0 from LOADING to FULL, Loading
  Done

r3#show isdn active
--------------------------------------------------------------------------
                         ISDN ACTIVE CALLS
--------------------------------------------------------------------------
Call   Calling      Called        Remote Seconds Seconds Seconds Charges
Type   Number       Number        Name   Used    Left    Idle    Units/Currency
--------------------------------------------------------------------------
Out    ---N/A---    99047132      R6     15      119     0       0
--------------------------------------------------------------------------

r3#show dialer

BRI0/0 - dialer type = ISDN

Dial String      Successes   Failures   Last DNIS   Last status
99047132              5          0       00:00:20       successful
0 incoming call(s) have been screened.
0 incoming call(s) rejected for callback.

BRI0/0:1 - dialer type = ISDN
Idle timer (120 secs), Fast idle timer (20 secs)
Wait for carrier (30 secs), Re-enable (15 secs)
Dialer state is data link layer up
Dial reason: ip (s=167.78.86.13, d=224.0.0.5)
Time until disconnect 119 secs
Connected to 99047132 (R6)

BRI0/0:2 - dialer type = ISDN
Idle timer (120 secs), Fast idle timer (20 secs)
Wait for carrier (30 secs), Re-enable (15 secs)
Dialer state is idle

r3#show ip ospf neighbor
```

Example 4-21 *ISDN Link Activating When VLAN-5 Interface Fastethernet0/0 Down (Continued)*

```
Neighbor ID      Pri   State          Dead Time   Address       Interface
6.6.6.6            1   FULL/  -        00:00:35    167.78.86.14  BRI0/0

r3#show ip route
Codes: C - connected, S - static, I - IGRP, R - RIP, M - mobile, B - BGP
       D - EIGRP, EX - EIGRP external, O - OSPF, IA - OSPF inter area
       N1 - OSPF NSSA external type 1, N2 - OSPF NSSA external type 2
       E1 - OSPF external type 1, E2 - OSPF external type 2, E - EGP
       i - IS-IS, L1 - IS-IS level-1, L2 - IS-IS level-2, ia - IS-IS inter area
       * - candidate default, U - per-user static route, o - ODR
       P - periodic downloaded static route

Gateway of last resort is 167.78.86.14 to network 0.0.0.0

C      192.168.10.0/24 is directly connected, FastEthernet0/1
       172.16.0.0/24 is subnetted, 1 subnets
S         172.16.4.0 [1/0] via 140.52.0.1
       10.0.0.0/24 is subnetted, 1 subnets
C         10.1.1.0 is directly connected, Tunnel1
       133.72.0.0/25 is subnetted, 1 subnets
O E2      133.72.52.0 [110/1] via 167.78.86.14, 00:00:05, BRI0/0
       167.78.0.0/16 is variably subnetted, 3 subnets, 2 masks
C         167.78.86.12/30 is directly connected, BRI0/0
O E2      167.78.86.8/30 [110/1] via 167.78.86.14, 00:00:06, BRI0/0
O IA      167.78.86.0/29 [110/1047] via 167.78.86.14, 00:00:06, BRI0/0
       13.0.0.0/24 is subnetted, 1 subnets
C         13.13.13.0 is directly connected, Loopback1
       121.0.0.0/26 is subnetted, 1 subnets
O E2      121.52.5.0 [110/1] via 167.78.86.14, 00:00:06, BRI0/0
O*E2   0.0.0.0/0 [110/1] via 167.78.86.14, 00:00:06, BRI0/0
r3#
!After VLAN-5 interface Fastethernet0/0 recovers, ISDN tearing down in 60 seconds,
!OSPF adjacency deleted via BRI and forming via Fastethernet0/0 again. See also
!the routing table change to learn all the routes via RIP and not OSPF to satisfy
!question in Section 2.1.
1w3d: %LINEPROTO-5-UPDOWN: Line protocol on Interface FastEthernet0/0, changed state
  to up
1w3d: %OSPF-5-ADJCHG: Process 110, Nbr 4.4.4.4 on FastEthernet0/0 from LOADING to FULL,
  Loading Done
r3#
1w3d: BR0/0:1 DDR: disconnecting call
1w3d: BR0/0:2 DDR: disconnecting call
1w3d: %ISDN-6-DISCONNECT: Interface BRI0/0:1 disconnected from 99047132 R6, call lasted
  367 seconds
1w3d: %LINK-3-UPDOWN: Interface BRI0/0:1, changed state to down
1w3d: %ISDN-6-LAYER2DOWN: Layer 2 for Interface BRI0/0, TEI 65 changed to down
1w3d: %LINK-3-UPDOWN: Interface BRI0/0:1, changed state to down
1w3d: %ISDN-6-LAYER2DOWN: Layer 2 for Interface BR0/0, TEI 65 changed to down
1w3d: BR0/0:1 DDR: disconnecting call
1w3d: BR0/0:1 DDR: disconnecting call
1w3d: %OSPF-5-ADJCHG: Process 110, Nbr 6.6.6.6 on BRI0/0 from FULL to DOWN, Neighbor
  Down: Interface down or detached
```

continues

Example 4-21 *ISDN Link Activating When VLAN-5 Interface Fastethernet0/0 Down (Continued)*

```
1w3d: %LINK-5-CHANGED: Interface BRI0/0, changed state to standby mode
1w3d: %LINK-3-UPDOWN: Interface BRI0/0:2, changed state to down
1w3d: %LINEPROTO-5-UPDOWN: Line protocol on Interface BRI0/0:1, changed state to down
1w3d: %BGP-5-ADJCHANGE: neighbor 140.52.0.3 Up

r3#show ip route
Codes: C - connected, S - static, I - IGRP, R - RIP, M - mobile, B - BGP
       D - EIGRP, EX - EIGRP external, O - OSPF, IA - OSPF inter area
       N1 - OSPF NSSA external type 1, N2 - OSPF NSSA external type 2
       E1 - OSPF external type 1, E2 - OSPF external type 2, E - EGP
       i - IS-IS, L1 - IS-IS level-1, L2 - IS-IS level-2, ia - IS-IS inter area
       * - candidate default, U - per-user static route, o - ODR
       P - periodic downloaded static route

Gateway of last resort is 140.52.0.3 to network 0.0.0.0

     17.0.0.0/24 is subnetted, 1 subnets
R       17.17.17.0 [120/1] via 140.52.0.3, 00:00:03, FastEthernet0/0
     18.0.0.0/24 is subnetted, 1 subnets
R       18.18.18.0 [120/1] via 140.52.0.3, 00:00:03, FastEthernet0/0
     140.52.0.0/24 is subnetted, 1 subnets
C       140.52.0.0 is directly connected, FastEthernet0/0
C    192.168.10.0/24 is directly connected, FastEthernet0/1
     172.16.0.0/24 is subnetted, 1 subnets
S       172.16.4.0 [1/0] via 140.52.0.1
     142.52.0.0/24 is subnetted, 1 subnets
R       142.52.0.0 [120/1] via 140.52.0.3, 00:00:05, FastEthernet0/0
     10.0.0.0/24 is subnetted, 2 subnets
D       10.9.6.0 [90/297372416] via 10.1.1.1, 00:01:48, Tunnel1
C       10.1.1.0 is directly connected, Tunnel1
     11.0.0.0/24 is subnetted, 1 subnets
R       11.11.11.0 [120/1] via 140.52.0.100, 00:00:05, FastEthernet0/0
     133.72.0.0/25 is subnetted, 1 subnets
R       133.72.52.0 [120/1] via 140.52.0.3, 00:00:05, FastEthernet0/0
     167.78.0.0/16 is variably subnetted, 3 subnets, 2 masks
R       167.78.86.12/30 [120/1] via 140.52.0.3, 00:00:05, FastEthernet0/0
R       167.78.86.8/30 [120/1] via 140.52.0.3, 00:00:05, FastEthernet0/0
R       167.78.86.0/29 [120/1] via 140.52.0.3, 00:00:05, FastEthernet0/0
     13.0.0.0/24 is subnetted, 1 subnets
C       13.13.13.0 is directly connected, Loopback1
     121.0.0.0/26 is subnetted, 1 subnets
R       121.52.5.0 [120/1] via 140.52.0.3, 00:00:05, FastEthernet0/0
R*   0.0.0.0/0 [120/1] via 140.52.0.3, 00:00:05, FastEthernet0/0
r3#
```

3.2: PPP Authentication and Load Balancing

1 Configure PPP authentication on R3 and R6 BRI(s). Configure a username on both
   routers. Note that R6 is sending CHAP host name R6 (case-sensitive). Configure
   username **R6** on R3 and username **r3** on R6. See Example 4-20 in Section 3.1.

2 Configure the **backup load** command on R3 to bring up the ISDN link if the VLAN-5 link load exceeds 75 percent, and tear down when the aggregate load is 5 percent. See Example 4-20 in Section 3.1.

Section 4.0: PIX Configuration

4.1: Basic PIX Configuration

1 Configure host name and IP addresses as defined.

2 Configure RIP with MD5 on the outside interface as shown in Figure 4-3. See Example 4-22.

3 Configure the default route for the inside network to Switch1 VLAN-10 IP address 172.16.1.10. See Example 4-24.

4 Configure static NAT for CA server 172.16.3.254 to 140.52.0.254. See Example 4-23.

5 Configure static NAT for Switch1 and Switch2 management interface 172.16.4.10 and 172.16.4.20, respectively. See Example 4-23.

6 Configure static NAT for Loopback1 of R1 to 11.11.11.11. See Example 4-23.

7 Configure a static NAT and ACL for a mail server with IP address 172.16.4.251 to 140.52.0.251. See Example 4-23.

8 Make sure you can ping AAA server and both switch management interfaces. PIX should be able to ping all devices on the network.

Example 4-22 *RIP on PIX*

```
pix# show rip
rip outside passive version 2 authentication md5 cisco 1
```

Example 4-23 *Static Translations on PIX*

```
pix# show static
static (inside,outside) 172.16.4.10 172.16.4.10 netmask 255.255.255.255 0 0
static (inside,outside) 172.16.4.20 172.16.4.20 netmask 255.255.255.255 0 0
static (inside,outside) 140.52.0.254 172.16.3.254 netmask 255.255.255.255 0 0
static (inside,outside) 140.52.0.100 172.16.1.1 netmask 255.255.255.255 0 0
static (inside,outside) 11.11.11.11 11.11.11.11 netmask 255.255.255.255 0 0
static (inside,outside) 140.52.0.250 172.16.2.2 netmask 255.255.255.255 0 0
static (inside,outside) 140.52.0.251 172.16.4.251 netmask 255.255.255.255 0 0
```

Example 4-24 *Routing Table on PIX*

```
pix# show route
        inside 0.0.0.0 0.0.0.0 172.16.1.10 1 OTHER static
        inside 11.11.11.0 255.255.255.0 172.16.1.1 1 OTHER static
        outside 13.13.13.0 255.255.255.0 140.52.0.2 2 RIP
```

continues

Example 4-24 *Routing Table on PIX (Continued)*

```
          outside 13.13.13.13 255.255.255.255 140.52.0.2 1 RIP
          outside 17.17.17.0 255.255.255.0 140.52.0.3 1 RIP
          outside 18.18.18.0 255.255.255.0 140.52.0.3 1 RIP
          outside 121.52.5.0 255.255.255.192 140.52.0.3 1 RIP
          outside 133.72.52.0 255.255.255.128 140.52.0.3 1 RIP
          outside 140.52.0.0 255.255.255.0 140.52.0.1 1 CONNECT static
          outside 142.52.0.0 255.255.255.0 140.52.0.3 1 RIP
          outside 167.78.86.0 255.255.255.248 140.52.0.3 1 RIP
          outside 167.78.86.8 255.255.255.252 140.52.0.3 1 RIP
          outside 167.78.86.12 255.255.255.252 140.52.0.3 1 RIP
          inside 172.16.1.0 255.255.255.0 172.16.1.2 1 CONNECT static
```

4.2: Advanced PIX Configuration

1 ESMTP uses port 25, the same as Simple SMTP. ESMTP mail is blocked by PIX due to the fixup SMTP, which only permits RFC 821 commands — HELO, MAIL, RCPT, DATA, RSET, NOOP, and QUIT. All other commands are rejected. To allow mail servers using ESMPT, disable fixup protocol for SMTP on PIX. See Example 4-25.

2 Filter all Java applets in web traffic using the **filter** command on PIX from any host connecting to any host on the Internet. See Example 4-25.

Example 4-25 *Snip from PIX*

```
pix(config)# show fixup
fixup protocol ftp 21
fixup protocol http 80
fixup protocol h323 h225 1720
fixup protocol h323 ras 1718-1719
fixup protocol ils 389
fixup protocol rsh 514
fixup protocol rtsp 554
fixup protocol sqlnet 1521
fixup protocol sip 5060
fixup protocol skinny 2000
no fixup protocol smtp 25

 pix(config)# show filter
filter java 80 0.0.0.0 0.0.0.0 0.0.0.0 0.0.0.0
```

Section 5.0: IPSec/GRE Configuration

5.1: IPSec LAN-to-LAN Through the Firewall Using CA

1 This is a tricky question. Overlapping networks on R1 and R5 — 10.1.1.0/24 — need to be encrypted.

2 IPSec access list cannot be configured for this. The solution is to create NAT on both ends and use the NATed address for IPSec ACL. See Example 4-26. On an ingress IPSec packet, NAT is performed first, followed by IPSec ACL.

TIP   See the following URL for more information about the order of operation:

NAT Order of Operation

www.cisco.com/warp/public/556/5.html

---

3 Static NAT on PIX is already configured for R1 as 140.52.0.100. Use this on R5 for IPSec peering. Create ACL on PIX for ESP, UDP/500 (ISAKMP), and TCP/80 (for CA enrollment). See Example 4-27.

4 Configure IPSec on both peers using CA certificates for authentication. See the configs in Example 4-28.

5 Configure two IKE policies, one with rsa-sig (certs) and another with preshared. See Example 4-29 for the CA enrollment process.

6 Remember the identity needs to be the host name for the certificate to work using **crypto isakmp identity hostname**.

7 Install a CA server on 172.16.3.254 (Microsoft CA server is used in this lab).

8 Install add-on MSCEP.dll on the CA server for Cisco routers to enroll.

TIP   Install Certificate Services MSCEP Add-on (Microsoft Simple Certificate Enrollment Protocol) on the CA server. MSCEP.DLL is a Certificate Services add-on ISAPI dynamic-link library (DLL) that enables enrollment for Cisco routers for IPSec authentication certificates from a Microsoft Windows 2000 Certificate Authority (CA) using the Simple Certificate Enrollment Protocol (SCEP).

For further information, refer to

www.tburke.net/info/reskittools/topics/mscep.htm

www.tburke.net/info/reskittools/topics/mscep_installing.htm

---

9 Remember to configure CA to issue certificates automatically when a request comes in (default is manual). See Figure 4-5.

10 Verify by pinging the NAT address from one of the peers. See Example 4-30 for testing IPSec and bringing up the tunnel. Also verify IKE uses certificates and not preshared keys. See Figure 4-6 for valid certificates issued to both routers.

Figure 4-5 *Configure CA to Issue Certificates Automatically Upon Valid Request*

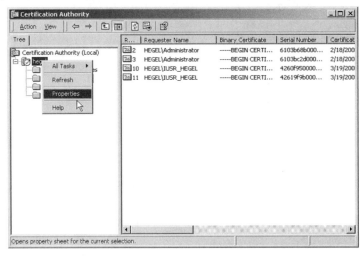

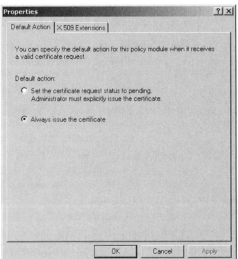

Example 4-26 *NAT Configuration on R1 and R5 for Overlapping Networks*

```
!Snip from R1:
interface Loopback10
 ip address 10.10.10.1 255.255.255.0
 ip nat inside
!
interface Ethernet1/0
 ip address 172.16.1.1 255.255.255.0
 ip nat outside
 crypto map lab4
!
ip nat pool natpool 192.168.1.1 192.168.1.254 netmask 255.255.255.0
```

Example 4-26 *NAT Configuration on R1 and R5 for Overlapping Networks (Continued)*

```
ip nat inside source list 10 pool natpool
!
access-list 10 permit 10.10.10.0 0.0.0.255
!

r1#show ip nat translations
Pro Inside global     Inside local      Outside local      Outside global
--- 192.168.1.1       10.10.10.1        ---                ---
r1#

!Snip from R5:
interface Loopback10
 ip address 10.10.10.1 255.255.255.0
 ip nat inside
!
interface Ethernet0
 ip address 142.52.0.3 255.255.255.0
 ip nat outside
 crypto map lab4
!
ip nat pool natpool 192.168.2.1 192.168.2.254 netmask 255.255.255.0
ip nat inside source list 10 pool natpool
!
access-list 10 permit 10.10.10.0 0.0.0.255


r5#show ip nat translations
Pro Inside global     Inside local      Outside local      Outside global
--- 192.168.2.1       10.10.10.1        ---                ---
r5#
```

Example 4-27 *Static NAT and ACL on PIX for IPSec*

```
static (inside,outside) 140.52.0.100 172.16.1.1 netmask 255.255.255.255 0 0
!
access-list outside permit esp host 142.52.0.3 host 140.52.0.100 (hitcnt=48)
access-list outside permit udp host 142.52.0.3 host 140.52.0.100 eq isakmp (hitcnt=15)
access-list outside permit tcp host 142.52.0.3 host 140.52.0.254 eq www (hitcnt=14)
```

TIP   Configure two IKE policies, one with rsa-sig (certs) and another with preshared. Before configuring CA certificates, it is a good practice to always test your config with preshared keys. If the tunnel is up and you can verify that IPSec is working, enroll with CA server and add a new IKE policy to use certs above the preshared. In this case, IKE using preshared is policy 20, and IKE using CA is policy 10.

Example 4-28 *IPSec Configuration on R1 and R5*

```
!Snip from R1 config:
crypto ca identity ca-server
 enrollment mode ra
```

continues

Example 4-28 *IPSec Configuration on R1 and R5 (Continued)*

```
 enrollment url http://172.16.3.254:80/certsrv/mscep/mscep.dll
 crl optional
!
!
crypto isakmp policy 10
 hash md5
 group 2
!
crypto isakmp policy 20
 authentication pre-share
crypto isakmp key cisco address 142.52.0.3
crypto isakmp identity hostname
!
!
crypto ipsec transform-set lab4 esp-des esp-md5-hmac
!
crypto map lab4 10 ipsec-isakmp
 set peer 142.52.0.3
 set transform-set lab4
 match address 101
!
!
interface Ethernet1/0
 ip address 172.16.1.1 255.255.255.0
 ip nat outside
 half-duplex
 crypto map lab4
!
access-list 101 permit ip 192.168.1.0 0.0.0.255 192.168.2.0 0.0.0.255
!Snip from R5 config:
crypto ca identity ca-server
 enrollment mode ra
 enrollment url http://140.52.0.254:80/certsrv/mscep/mscep.dll
 crl optional
!
crypto isakmp policy 10
 hash md5
 group 2
!
crypto isakmp policy 20
 authentication pre-share
crypto isakmp key cisco address 140.52.0.100
crypto isakmp identity hostname
!
!
crypto ipsec transform-set lab4 esp-des esp-md5-hmac
!
crypto map lab4 10 ipsec-isakmp
 set peer 140.52.0.100
 set transform-set lab4
 match address 101
```

Example 4-28 *IPSec Configuration on R1 and R5 (Continued)*

```
!
!
interface Ethernet0
 ip address 142.52.0.3 255.255.255.0
 ip nat outside
 crypto map lab4
!
access-list 101 permit ip 192.168.2.0 0.0.0.255 192.168.1.0 0.0.0.255
```

Example 4-29 *CA Enrollment Process on R1 and R5*

```
!Enrolling R5
r5#show clock
22:50:51.343 AEST Wed Mar 19 2003
r5#
r5#conf t
Enter configuration commands, one per line.  End with CNTL/Z.
r5(config)#ip domain name cisco.com
r5(config)#crypto key generate rsa
The name for the keys will be: r5.cisco.com
Choose the size of the key modulus in the range of 360 to 2048 for your
  General Purpose Keys. Choosing a key modulus greater than 512 may take
  a few minutes.

How many bits in the modulus [512]:
Generating RSA keys ...
[OK]
4d20h: %SSH-5-ENABLED: SSH 1.5 has been enabledrypto ca identity

r5(config)#crypto ca identity ca-server
r5(ca-identity)#enrollment url http://140.52.0.254/certsrv/mscep/mscep.dll
r5(ca-identity)#crl optional
r5(ca-identity)#crypto ca authenticate ca-server

Certificate has the following attributes:
Fingerprint: 044E6386 D685E0AD 3999E792 840F1AE4
% Do you accept this certificate? [yes/no]: yes

r5(config)#
r5(config)#
r5(config)#crypto ca enroll ca-server
%
% Start certificate enrollment ..
% Create a challenge password. You will need to verbally provide this
    password to the CA Administrator in order to revoke your certificate.
    For security reasons your password will not be saved in the configuration.
    Please make a note of it.

Password:
Re-enter password:

% The subject name in the certificate will be: r5.cisco.com
```

continues

Example 4-29 *CA Enrollment Process on R1 and R5 (Continued)*

```
% Include the router serial number in the subject name? [yes/no]: n
% Include an IP address in the subject name? [yes/no]: n
Request certificate from CA? [yes/no]: yes
% Certificate request sent to Certificate Authority
% The certificate request fingerprint will be displayed.
% The 'show crypto ca certificate' command will also show the fingerprint.

r5(config)#
r5(config)#
r5(config)#    Fingerprint:  3D27D2A5 50E4C360 47E2507B 62B7ADA9


4d21h: %CRYPTO-6-CERTRET: Certificate received from Certificate Authority


r5#show crypto ca certificate
Certificate
  Status: Available
  Certificate Serial Number: 42619F9B00000000000B
  Key Usage: General Purpose
  Issuer:
    CN = hegel
     OU = hegel
     O = hegel
     L = Sydney
     ST = NSW
     C = AU
     EA =<16> labs@labs.com
  Subject Name Contains:
    Name: r5.cisco.com
  CRL Distribution Point:
    http://hegel.scs.cisco.com/CertEnroll/hegel.crl
  Validity Date:
    start date: 10:43:07 AEST Mar 19 2003
    end   date: 10:53:07 AEST Mar 19 2004

RA Signature Certificate
  Status: Available
  Certificate Serial Number: 6103B68B000000000002
  Key Usage: Signature
  Issuer:
    CN = hegel
     OU = hegel
     O = hegel
     L = Sydney
     ST = NSW
     C = AU
     EA =<16> labs@labs.com
  Subject:
    CN = hegel
     OU = hegel
     O = hegel
     L = Sydney
     ST = NSW
```

Example 4-29 *CA Enrollment Process on R1 and R5 (Continued)*

```
      C = AU
      EA =<16> hegel@hegel
    CRL Distribution Point:
      http://hegel.scs.cisco.com/CertEnroll/hegel.crl
    Validity Date:
      start date: 12:23:15 AEST Feb 18 2003
      end   date: 12:33:15 AEST Feb 18 2004

CA Certificate
  Status: Available
  Certificate Serial Number: 2288F45842C63A844FE73D976DDC35B1
  Key Usage: Signature
  Issuer:
    CN = hegel
     OU = hegel
     O = hegel
     L = Sydney
     ST = NSW
     C = AU
     EA =<16> labs@labs.com
  Subject:
    CN = hegel
     OU = hegel
     O = hegel
     L = Sydney
     ST = NSW
     C = AU
     EA =<16> labs@labs.com
  CRL Distribution Point:
    http://hegel.scs.cisco.com/CertEnroll/hegel.crl
  Validity Date:
    start date: 12:16:21 AEST Feb 18 2003
    end   date: 12:23:53 AEST Feb 18 2005

RA KeyEncipher Certificate
  Status: Available
  Certificate Serial Number: 6103BC2D000000000003
  Key Usage: Encryption
  Issuer:
    CN = hegel
     OU = hegel
     O = hegel
     L = Sydney
     ST = NSW
     C = AU
     EA =<16> labs@labs.com
  Subject:
    CN = hegel
     OU = hegel
     O = hegel
     L = Sydney
     ST = NSW
```

continues

Example 4-29 *CA Enrollment Process on R1 and R5 (Continued)*

```
     C = AU
     EA =<16> hegel@hegel
  CRL Distribution Point:
    http://hegel.scs.cisco.com/CertEnroll/hegel.crl
  Validity Date:
    start date: 12:23:17 AEST Feb 18 2003
    end   date: 12:33:17 AEST Feb 18 2004


!Enrolling R1
r1#show clock
22:50:19.547 AEST Wed Mar 19 2003

r1#conf t
Enter configuration commands, one per line.  End with CNTL/Z.
r1(config)#ip domain name cisco.com
r1(config)#crypto key generate rsa
The name for the keys will be: r1.cisco.com
Choose the size of the key modulus in the range of 360 to 2048 for your
  General Purpose Keys. Choosing a key modulus greater than 512 may take
  a few minutes.

How many bits in the modulus [512]:
Generating RSA keys ...
[OK]
00:22:21: %SSH-5-ENABLED: SSH 1.5 has been enabled


r1(config)#crypto ca identity ca-server
r1(ca-identity)#enrollment url http://172.16.3.254/certsrv/mscep/mscep.dll
r1(ca-identity)#crl opt
r1(ca-identity)#crl optional
r1(ca-identity)#exit
r1(config)#crypto ca authenticate ca-server
Certificate has the following attributes:
Fingerprint: 044E6386 D685E0AD 3999E792 840F1AE4
% Do you accept this certificate? [yes/no]: yes

r1#conf t
Enter configuration commands, one per line.  End with CNTL/Z.
r1(config)#crypto ca enroll ca-server
%
% Start certificate enrollment ..
% Create a challenge password. You will need to verbally provide this
    password to the CA Administrator in order to revoke your certificate.
    For security reasons your password will not be saved in the configuration.
    Please make a note of it.

Password:
Re-enter password:

% The subject name in the certificate will be: r1.cisco.com
% Include the router serial number in the subject name? [yes/no]: no
% Include an IP address in the subject name? [yes/no]: no
```

Example 4-29 *CA Enrollment Process on R1 and R5 (Continued)*

```
Request certificate from CA? [yes/no]: yes
% Certificate request sent to Certificate Authority
% The certificate request fingerprint will be displayed.
% The 'show crypto ca certificate' command will also show the fingerprint.

r1(config)#    Fingerprint:  19CC0DC5 EC72211C 7E2FE923 22FDC762

00:26:54: %CRYPTO-6-CERTRET: Certificate received from Certificate Authority

r1#show crypto ca certificates
Certificate
  Status: Available
  Certificate Serial Number: 4260F95000000000000A
  Key Usage: General Purpose
  Issuer:
    CN = hegel
    OU = hegel
    O = hegel
    L = Sydney
    ST = NSW
    C = AU
    EA =<16> labs@labs.com
  Subject Name Contains:
    Name: r1.cisco.com
  CRL Distribution Point:
    http://hegel.scs.cisco.com/CertEnroll/hegel.crl
  Validity Date:
    start date: 10:42:24 AEST Mar 19 2003
    end   date: 10:52:24 AEST Mar 19 2004
  Associated Identity: ca-server

RA Signature Certificate
  Status: Available
  Certificate Serial Number: 6103B68B000000000002
  Key Usage: Signature
  Issuer:
    CN = hegel
    OU = hegel
    O = hegel
    L = Sydney
    ST = NSW
    C = AU
    EA =<16> labs@labs.com
  Subject:
    CN = hegel
    OU = hegel
    O = hegel
    L = Sydney
    ST = NSW
    C = AU
    EA =<16> hegel@hegel
```

continues

Example 4-29 *CA Enrollment Process on R1 and R5 (Continued)*

```
      CRL Distribution Point:
        http://hegel.scs.cisco.com/CertEnroll/hegel.crl
      Validity Date:
        start date: 12:23:15 AEST Feb 18 2003
        end   date: 12:33:15 AEST Feb 18 2004
      Associated Identity: ca-server

RA KeyEncipher Certificate
  Status: Available
  Certificate Serial Number: 6103BC2D000000000003
  Key Usage: Encryption
  Issuer:
    CN = hegel
     OU = hegel
     O = hegel
     L = Sydney
     ST = NSW
     C = AU
     EA =<16> labs@labs.com
  Subject:
    CN = hegel
     OU = hegel
     O = hegel
     L = Sydney
     ST = NSW
     C = AU
     EA =<16> hegel@hegel
  CRL Distribution Point:
    http://hegel.scs.cisco.com/CertEnroll/hegel.crl
  Validity Date:
    start date: 12:23:17 AEST Feb 18 2003
    end   date: 12:33:17 AEST Feb 18 2004
  Associated Identity: ca-server

CA Certificate
  Status: Available
  Certificate Serial Number: 2288F45842C63A844FE73D976DDC35B1
  Key Usage: Signature
  Issuer:
    CN = hegel
     OU = hegel
     O = hegel
     L = Sydney
     ST = NSW
     C = AU
     EA =<16> labs@labs.com
  Subject:
    CN = hegel
     OU = hegel
     O = hegel
     L = Sydney
     ST = NSW
```

Example 4-29 *CA Enrollment Process on R1 and R5 (Continued)*

```
      C = AU
      EA =<16> labs@labs.com
  CRL Distribution Point:
    http://hegel.scs.cisco.com/CertEnroll/hegel.crl
  Validity Date:
    start date: 12:16:21 AEST Feb 18 2003
    end   date: 12:23:53 AEST Feb 18 2005
  Associated Identity: ca-server



!Good debug from R1 when enrolling to CA.
r1#debug crypto pki transactions
Crypto PKI Trans debugging is on
r1#
r1#
r1#show debug
Cryptographic Subsystem:
  Crypto PKI Trans debugging is on

00:26:52: CRYPTO_PKI: transaction PKCSReq completed
00:26:52: CRYPTO_PKI: status:
00:26:52: CRYPTO_PKI: can not resolve server name/IP address
00:26:52: CRYPTO_PKI: Using unresolved IP Address 172.16.3.254
00:26:52: CRYPTO_PKI: http connection opened
00:26:54: CRYPTO_PKI:  received msg of 1984 bytes
00:26:54: CRYPTO_PKI: HTTP response header:
 HTTP/1.1 200 OK
Server: Microsoft-IIS/5.0
Date: Wed, 19 Mar 2003 00:52:24 GMT
Content-Length: 1838
Content-Type: application/x-pki-message


00:26:54: CRYPTO_PKI: WARNING: Certificate, private key or CRL was not found while
selecting CRL

00:26:54: CRYPTO_PKI: status = 100: certificate is granted
00:26:54: CRYPTO_PKI: WARNING: Certificate, private key or CRL was not found while
selecting CRL

00:26:54: CRYPTO_PKI: All enrollment requests completed.
00:26:54: CRYPTO_PKI: All enrollment requests completed.
00:26:54: CRYPTO_PKI: All enrollment requests completed.
00:26:54: CRYPTO_PKI: WARNING: Certificate, private key or CRL was not found while
  selecting CRL
```

NOTE   If CA enrollment is successful, you should get the following message on the console:

%CRYPTO-6-CERTRET: Certificate received from Certificate Authority

Figure 4-6 *Valid Certificates Issued by CA to Both Routers*

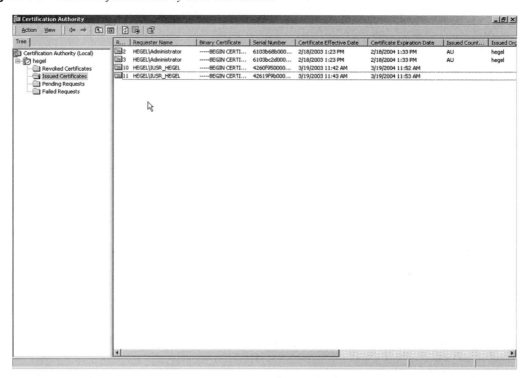

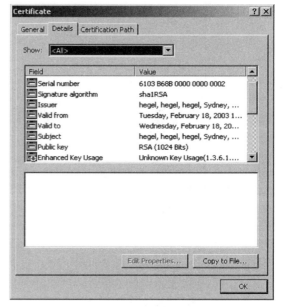

Figure 4-6   *Valid Certificates Issued by CA to Both Routers (Continued)*

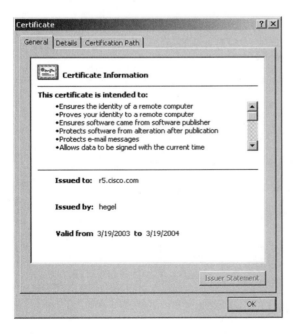

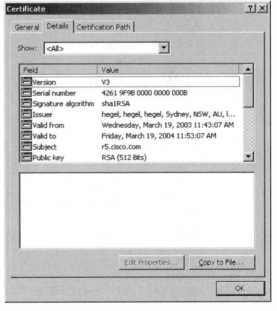

Example 4-30 *Test Process with Good Debugs to Verify Tunnel Comes up Using Certificates*

```
!Ping from R5 the NATed IP 192.168.1.1 (local IP 10.10.10.1 of R1) sourcing from
!Loopback10 to bring up the tunnel.
r5#ping ip
Target IP address: 192.168.1.1
Repeat count [5]:
Datagram size [100]:
Timeout in seconds [2]:
Extended commands [n]: y
Source address or interface: loopback10
Type of service [0]:
Set DF bit in IP header? [no]:
Validate reply data? [no]:
Data pattern [0xABCD]:
Loose, Strict, Record, Timestamp, Verbose[none]:
Sweep range of sizes [n]:
Type escape sequence to abort.
Sending 5, 100-byte ICMP Echos to 192.168.1.1, timeout is 2 seconds:
....
Success rate is 0 percent (0/5)
r5#
!First few pings will be lost when the tunnel is coming UP, try again and it
!should be fine.
r5#ping ip
Target IP address: 192.168.1.1
Repeat count [5]:
Datagram size [100]:
Timeout in seconds [2]:
Extended commands [n]: y
Source address or interface: loopback10
Type of service [0]:
Set DF bit in IP header? [no]:
Validate reply data? [no]:
Data pattern [0xABCD]:
Loose, Strict, Record, Timestamp, Verbose[none]:
Sweep range of sizes [n]:
Type escape sequence to abort.
Sending 5, 100-byte ICMP Echos to 192.168.1.1, timeout is 2 seconds:
!!!!!
Success rate is 100 percent (5/5), round-trip min/avg/max = 28/28/28 ms

!Good debugs from R1 when tunnel is coming UP using certs.
r1#show debugging
Cryptographic Subsystem:
  Crypto ISAKMP debugging is on
  Crypto IPSEC debugging is on


00:40:33: ISAKMP (0:0): received packet from 142.52.0.3 (N) NEW SA
00:40:33: ISAKMP: local port 500, remote port 500
00:40:33: ISAKMP (0:1): processing SA payload. message ID = 0
00:40:33: ISAKMP (0:1): found peer pre-shared key matching 142.52.0.3
```

Example 4-30 *Test Process with Good Debugs to Verify Tunnel Comes up Using Certificates (Continued)*

```
00:40:33: ISAKMP (0:1): Checking ISAKMP transform 1 against priority 10 policy
00:40:33: ISAKMP:      encryption DES-CBC
00:40:33: ISAKMP:      hash MD5
00:40:33: ISAKMP:      default group 2
00:40:33: ISAKMP:      auth RSA sig
00:40:33: ISAKMP (0:1): atts are acceptable. Next payload is 3
00:40:33: ISAKMP (0:1): SA is doing RSA signature authentication using id type ID_FQDN
00:40:33: ISAKMP (0:1): sending packet to 142.52.0.3 (R) MM_SA_SETUP
00:40:35: ISAKMP (0:1): received packet from 142.52.0.3 (R) MM_SA_SETUP
00:40:35: ISAKMP (0:1): processing KE payload. message ID = 0
00:40:36: ISAKMP (0:1): processing NONCE payload. message ID = 0
00:40:36: ISAKMP (0:1): SKEYID state generated
00:40:36: ISAKMP (0:1): processing CERT_REQ payload. message ID = 0
00:40:36: ISAKMP (0:1): peer wants a CT_X509_SIGNATURE cert
00:40:36: ISAKMP (0:1): peer want cert issued by CN = hegel, OU = hegel, O = hegel, L
= Sydney, ST = NSW, C = AU, EA =<16> labs@labs.com
00:40:36: ISAKMP (0:1): processing vendor id payload
00:40:36: ISAKMP (0:1): speaking to another IOS box!
00:40:36: ISAKMP (0:1): sending packet to 142.52.0.3 (R) MM_KEY_EXCH
00:40:42: ISAKMP (0:1): received packet from 142.52.0.3 (R) MM_KEY_EXCH
00:40:42: ISAKMP (0:1): processing ID payload. message ID = 0
00:40:42: ISAKMP (0:1): processing CERT payload. message ID = 0
00:40:42: ISAKMP (0:1): processing a CT_X509_SIGNATURE cert
00:40:42: ISAKMP (0:1): cert approved with warning
00:40:42: ISAKMP (0:1): processing SIG payload. message ID = 0
00:40:42: ISAKMP (1): sa->peer.name = , sa->peer_id.id.id_fqdn.fqdn = r5.cisco.com
00:40:42: ISAKMP (0:1): SA has been authenticated with 142.52.0.3
00:40:42: ISAKMP (1): ID payload
        next-payload : 6
        type         : 2
        protocol     : 17
        port         : 500
        length       : 16
00:40:42: ISAKMP (1): Total payload length: 20
00:40:43: ISKAMP: growing send buffer from 1024 to 3072
00:40:43: ISAKMP (0:1): sending packet to 142.52.0.3 (R) QM_IDLE
00:40:44: ISAKMP (0:1): received packet from 142.52.0.3 (R) QM_IDLE
00:40:44: ISAKMP (0:1): processing HASH payload. message ID = 372832242
00:40:44: ISAKMP (0:1): processing SA payload. message ID = 372832242
00:40:44: ISAKMP (0:1): Checking IPSec proposal 1
00:40:44: ISAKMP: transform 1, ESP_DES
00:40:44: ISAKMP:    attributes in transform:
00:40:44: ISAKMP:       encaps is 1
00:40:44: ISAKMP:       SA life type in seconds
00:40:44: ISAKMP:       SA life duration (basic) of 3600
00:40:44: ISAKMP:       SA life type in kilobytes
00:40:44: ISAKMP:       SA life duration (VPI) of  0x0 0x46 0x50 0x0
00:40:44: ISAKMP:       authenticator is HMAC-MD5
00:40:44: ISAKMP (0:1): atts are acceptable.
00:40:44: IPSEC(validate_proposal_request): proposal part #1,
  (key eng. msg.) INBOUND local= 172.16.1.1, remote= 142.52.0.3,
```

continues

Example 4-30 *Test Process with Good Debugs to Verify Tunnel Comes up Using Certificates (Continued)*

```
          local_proxy= 192.168.1.0/255.255.255.0/0/0 (type=4),
          remote_proxy= 192.168.2.0/255.255.255.0/0/0 (type=4),
          protocol= ESP, transform= esp-des esp-md5-hmac ,
          lifedur= 0s and 0kb,
          spi= 0x0(0), conn_id= 0, keysize= 0, flags= 0x4
00:40:44: ISAKMP (0:1): processing NONCE payload. message ID = 372832242
00:40:44: ISAKMP (0:1): processing ID payload. message ID = 372832242
00:40:44: ISAKMP (0:1): processing ID payload. message ID = 372832242
00:40:44: ISAKMP (0:1): asking for 1 spis from ipsec
00:40:44: IPSEC(key_engine): got a queue event...
00:40:44: IPSEC(spi_response): getting spi 4213612989 for SA
          from 172.16.1.1      to 142.52.0.3      for prot 3
00:40:44: ISAKMP: received ke message (2/1)
00:40:44: ISAKMP (0:1): sending packet to 142.52.0.3 (R) QM_IDLE
00:40:44: ISAKMP (0:1): received packet from 142.52.0.3 (R) QM_IDLE
00:40:44: ISAKMP (0:1): Creating IPSec SAs
00:40:44:          inbound SA from 142.52.0.3 to 172.16.1.1
          (proxy 192.168.2.0 to 192.168.1.0)
00:40:44:          has spi 0xFB26A1BD and conn_id 2000 and flags 4
00:40:44:          lifetime of 3600 seconds
00:40:44:          lifetime of 4608000 kilobytes
00:40:44:        outbound SA from 172.16.1.1      to 142.52.0.3      (proxy 192.168.1.0
to 192.168.2.0    )
00:40:44:          has spi 1774136193 and conn_id 2001 and flags C
00:40:44:          lifetime of 3600 seconds
00:40:44:          lifetime of 4608000 kilobytes
00:40:44: ISAKMP (0:1): deleting node 372832242 error FALSE reason "quick mode done
(await()"
00:40:44: IPSEC(key_engine): got a queue event...
00:40:44: IPSEC(initialize_sas): ,
  (key eng. msg.) INBOUND local= 172.16.1.1, remote= 142.52.0.3,
    local_proxy= 192.168.1.0/255.255.255.0/0/0 (type=4),
    remote_proxy= 192.168.2.0/255.255.255.0/0/0 (type=4),
    protocol= ESP, transform= esp-des esp-md5-hmac ,
    lifedur= 3600s and 4608000kb,
    spi= 0xFB26A1BD(4213612989), conn_id= 2000, keysize= 0, flags= 0x4
00:40:44: IPSEC(initialize_sas): ,
  (key eng. msg.) OUTBOUND local= 172.16.1.1, remote= 142.52.0.3,
    local_proxy= 192.168.1.0/255.255.255.0/0/0 (type=4),
    remote_proxy= 192.168.2.0/255.255.255.0/0/0 (type=4),
    protocol= ESP, transform= esp-des esp-md5-hmac ,
    lifedur= 3600s and 4608000kb,
    spi= 0x69BF2B81(1774136193), conn_id= 2001, keysize= 0, flags= 0xC
00:40:44: IPSEC(create_sa): sa created,
  (sa) sa_dest= 172.16.1.1, sa_prot= 50,
    sa_spi= 0xFB26A1BD(4213612989),
    sa_trans= esp-des esp-md5-hmac , sa_conn_id= 2000
00:40:44: IPSEC(create_sa): sa created,
  (sa) sa_dest= 142.52.0.3, sa_prot= 50,
    sa_spi= 0x69BF2B81(1774136193),
    sa_trans= esp-des esp-md5-hmac , sa_conn_id= 2001
```

Example 4-30 *Test Process with Good Debugs to Verify Tunnel Comes up Using Certificates (Continued)*

```
!Verify packets using the tunnel with stats from following show commands.
r1#show crypto engine connections active

  ID Interface       IP-Address      State  Algorithm          Encrypt  Decrypt
   1 Ethernet1/0     172.16.1.1      set    HMAC_MD5+DES_56_CB        0        0
2000 Ethernet1/0     172.16.1.1      set    HMAC_MD5+DES_56_CB        0        5
2001 Ethernet1/0     172.16.1.1      set    HMAC_MD5+DES_56_CB        5        0


r1#show crypto isakmp sa
dst             src             state          conn-id    slot
172.16.1.1      142.52.0.3      QM_IDLE              1      0



r1#show crypto ipsec sa

interface: Ethernet1/0
    Crypto map tag: lab4, local addr. 172.16.1.1

   local  ident (addr/mask/prot/port): (192.168.1.0/255.255.255.0/0/0)
   remote ident (addr/mask/prot/port): (192.168.2.0/255.255.255.0/0/0)
   current_peer: 142.52.0.3
     PERMIT, flags={origin_is_acl,}
    #pkts encaps: 5, #pkts encrypt: 5, #pkts digest 5
    #pkts decaps: 5, #pkts decrypt: 5, #pkts verify 5
    #pkts compressed: 0, #pkts decompressed: 0
    #pkts not compressed: 0, #pkts compr. failed: 0, #pkts decompress failed: 0
    #send errors 0, #recv errors 0

    local crypto endpt.: 172.16.1.1, remote crypto endpt.: 142.52.0.3
    path mtu 1500, media mtu 1500
    current outbound spi: 69BF2B81

    inbound esp sas:
     spi: 0xFB26A1BD(4213612989)
       transform: esp-des esp-md5-hmac ,
       in use settings ={Tunnel, }
       slot: 0, conn id: 2000, flow_id: 1, crypto map: lab4
       sa timing: remaining key lifetime (k/sec): (4607999/3389)
       IV size: 8 bytes
       replay detection support: Y

    inbound ah sas:

    inbound pcp sas:

    outbound esp sas:
     spi: 0x69BF2B81(1774136193)
       transform: esp-des esp-md5-hmac ,
       in use settings ={Tunnel, }
       slot: 0, conn id: 2001, flow_id: 2, crypto map: lab4
```

continues

Example 4-30 *Test Process with Good Debugs to Verify Tunnel Comes up Using Certificates (Continued)*

```
                   sa timing: remaining key lifetime (k/sec): (4607999/3389)
                   IV size: 8 bytes
                   replay detection support: Y

              outbound ah sas:

              outbound pcp sas:

!Good debugs from R5 when tunnel is coming UP using certs.
r5#show debugging
Cryptographic Subsystem:
  Crypto ISAKMP debugging is on
  Crypto IPSEC debugging is on
r5#
4d21h: IPSEC(sa_request): ,
  (key eng. msg.) src= 142.52.0.3, dest= 140.52.0.100,
    src_proxy= 192.168.2.0/255.255.255.0/0/0 (type=4),
    dest_proxy= 192.168.1.0/255.255.255.0/0/0 (type=4),
    protocol= ESP, transform= esp-des esp-md5-hmac ,
    lifedur= 3600s and 4608000kb,
    spi= 0x69BF2B81(1774136193), conn_id= 0, keysize= 0, flags= 0x4004
4d21h: ISAKMP: received ke message (1/1)
4d21h: ISAKMP: local port 500, remote port 500
4d21h: ISAKMP (0:1): beginning Main Mode exchange
4d21h: ISAKMP (0:1): sending packet to 140.52.0.100 (I) MM_NO_STATE
4d21h: ISAKMP (0:1): received packet from 140.52.0.100 (I) MM_NO_STATE
4d21h: ISAKMP (0:1): processing SA payload. message ID = 0
4d21h: ISAKMP (0:1): found peer pre-shared key matching 140.52.0.100
4d21h: ISAKMP (0:1): Checking ISAKMP transform 1 against priority 10 policy
4d21h: ISAKMP:       encryption DES-CBC
4d21h: ISAKMP:       hash MD5
4d21h: ISAKMP:       default group 2
4d21h: ISAKMP:       auth RSA sig
4d21h:. ISAKMP (0:1): atts are acceptable. Next payload is 0
4d21h: ISAKMP (0:1): SA is doing RSA signature authentication using id type ID_FQDN
4d21h: ISAKMP (0:1): sending packet to 140.52.0.100 (I) MM_SA_SETUP.
4d21h: ISAKMP (0:1): received packet from 140.52.0.100 (I) MM_SA_SETUP
4d21h: ISAKMP (0:1): processing KE payload. message ID = 0
4d21h: ISAKMP (0:1): processing NONCE payload. message ID = 0
4d21h: ISAKMP (0:1): SKEYID state generated
4d21h: ISAKMP (0:1): processing CERT_REQ payload. message ID = 0
4d21h: ISAKMP (0:1): peer wants a CT_X509_SIGNATURE cert
4d21h: ISAKMP (0:1): peer want cert issued by CN = hegel, OU = hegel, O = hegel, L =
Sydney, ST = NSW, C = AU, EA =<16> labs@labs.com
4d21h: ISAKMP (0:1): processing vendor id payload
4d21h: ISAKMP (0:1): speaking to another IOS box!
4d21h: ISAKMP (1): ID payload
            next-payload : 6
            type         : 2
            protocol     : 17
            port         : 500
            length       : 16
```

Example 4-30 *Test Process with Good Debugs to Verify Tunnel Comes up Using Certificates (Continued)*

```
4d21h: ISAKMP (1): Total payload length: 20..
4d21h: ISKAMP: growing send buffer from 1024 to 3072
4d21h: ISAKMP (0:1): sending packet to 140.52.0.100 (I) MM_KEY_EXCH
4d21h: ISAKMP (0:1): received packet from 140.52.0.100 (I) MM_KEY_EXCH
4d21h: ISAKMP (0:1): processing ID payload. message ID = 0
4d21h: ISAKMP (0:1): processing CERT payload. message ID = 0
4d21h: ISAKMP (0:1): processing a CT_X509_SIGNATURE cert
4d21h: ISAKMP (0:1): cert approved with warning
4d21h: ISAKMP (0:1): processing SIG payload. message ID = 0
4d21h: ISAKMP (1): sa->peer.name = 140.52.0.100, sa->peer_id.id.id_fqdn.fqdn =
  r1.cisco.com
4d21h: ISAKMP (0:1): SA has been authenticated with 140.52.0.100
4d21h: ISAKMP (0:1): beginning Quick Mode exchange, M-ID of 372832242
4d21h: ISAKMP (0:1): sending packet to 140.52.0.100 (I) QM_IDLE
4d21h: ISAKMP (0:1): received packet from 140.52.0.100 (I) QM_IDLE
4d21h: ISAKMP (0:1): processing HASH payload. message ID = 372832242
4d21h: ISAKMP (0:1): processing SA payload. message ID = 372832242
4d21h: ISAKMP (0:1): Checking IPSec proposal 1
4d21h: ISAKMP: transform 1, ESP_DES
4d21h: ISAKMP:    attributes in transform:
4d21h: ISAKMP:       encaps is 1
4d21h: ISAKMP:       SA life type in seconds
4d21h: ISAKMP:       SA life duration (basic) of 3600
4d21h: ISAKMP:       SA life type in kilobytes
4d21h: ISAKMP:       SA life duration (VPI) of  0x0 0x46 0x50 0x0
4d21h: ISAKMP:       authenticator is HMAC-MD5
4d21h: ISAKMP (0:1): atts are acceptable.
4d21h: IPSEC(validate_proposal_request): proposal part #1,
  (key eng. msg.) dest= 140.52.0.100, src= 142.52.0.3,
    dest_proxy= 192.168.1.0/255.255.255.0/0/0 (type=4),
    src_proxy= 192.168.2.0/255.255.255.0/0/0 (type=4),
    protocol= ESP, transform= esp-des esp-md5-hmac ,
    lifedur= 0s and 0kb,
    spi= 0x0(0), conn_id= 0, keysize= 0, flags= 0x4
4d21h: ISAKMP (0:1): processing NONCE payload. message ID = 372832242
4d21h: ISAKMP (0:1): processing ID payload. message ID = 372832242
4d21h: ISAKMP (0:1): processing ID payload. message ID = 372832242
4d21h: ISAKMP (0:1): Creating IPSec SAs
4d21h:        inbound SA from 140.52.0.100 to 142.52.0.3
       (proxy 192.168.1.0 to 192.168.2.0)
4d21h:        has spi 0x69BF2B81 and conn_id 2000 and flags 4
4d21h:        lifetime of 3600 seconds
4d21h:        lifetime of 4608000 kilobytes
4d21h:        outbound SA from 142.52.0.3     to 140.52.0.100    (proxy 192.168.2.0
  to 192.168.1.0    )
4d21h:        has spi -81354307 and conn_id 2001 and flags 4
4d21h:        lifetime of 3600 seconds
4d21h:        lifetime of 4608000 kilobytes
4d21h: ISAKMP (0:1): sending packet to 140.52.0.100 (I) QM_IDLE
4d21h: ISAKMP (0:1): deleting node 372832242 error FALSE reason ""
4d21h: IPSEC(key_engine): got a queue event...
```

continues

Example 4-30 *Test Process with Good Debugs to Verify Tunnel Comes up Using Certificates (Continued)*

```
4d21h: IPSEC(initialize_sas): ,
  (key eng. msg.) dest= 142.52.0.3, src= 140.52.0.100,
    dest_proxy= 192.168.2.0/255.255.255.0/0/0 (type=4),
    src_proxy= 192.168.1.0/255.255.255.0/0/0 (type=4),
    protocol= ESP, transform= esp-des esp-md5-hmac ,
    lifedur= 3600s and 4608000kb,
    spi= 0x69BF2B81(1774136193), conn_id= 2000, keysize= 0, flags= 0x4
4d21h: IPSEC(initialize_sas): ,
  (key eng. msg.) src= 142.52.0.3, dest= 140.52.0.100,
    src_proxy= 192.168.2.0/255.255.255.0/0/0 (type=4),
    dest_proxy= 192.168.1.0/255.255.255.0/0/0 (type=4),
    protocol= ESP, transform= esp-des esp-md5-hmac ,
    lifedur= 3600s and 4608000kb,
    spi= 0xFB26A1BD(4213612989), conn_id= 2001, keysize= 0, flags= 0x4
4d21h: IPSEC(create_sa): sa created,
  (sa) sa_dest= 142.52.0.3, sa_prot= 50,
    sa_spi= 0x69BF2B81(1774136193),
    sa_trans= esp-des esp-md5-hmac , sa_conn_id= 2000
4d21h: IPSEC(create_sa): sa created,
  (sa) sa_dest= 140.52.0.100, sa_prot= 50,
    sa_spi= 0xFB26A1BD(4213612989),
    sa_trans= esp-des esp-md5-hmac , sa_conn_id= 2001

!Verify packets used the tunnel with stats from following show commands.
r5#show crypto engine connections active

   ID Interface       IP-Address      State Algorithm            Encrypt  Decrypt
    1 <none>          <none>          set   HMAC_MD5+DES_56_CB          0        0
 2000 Ethernet0       142.52.0.3      set   HMAC_MD5+DES_56_CB          0        5
 2001 Ethernet0       142.52.0.3      set   HMAC_MD5+DES_56_CB          5        0

r5#show crypto isakmp sa
    dst             src            state        conn-id   slot
140.52.0.100    142.52.0.3         QM_IDLE         1        0


r5#show crypto ipsec sa

interface: Ethernet0
    Crypto map tag: lab4, local addr. 142.52.0.3

   local  ident (addr/mask/prot/port): (192.168.2.0/255.255.255.0/0/0)
   remote ident (addr/mask/prot/port): (192.168.1.0/255.255.255.0/0/0)
   current_peer: 140.52.0.100
     PERMIT, flags={origin_is_acl,}
    #pkts encaps: 5, #pkts encrypt: 5, #pkts digest 5
    #pkts decaps: 5, #pkts decrypt: 5, #pkts verify 5
    #pkts compressed: 0, #pkts decompressed: 0
    #pkts not compressed: 0, #pkts compr. failed: 0, #pkts decompress failed: 0
    #send errors 5, #recv errors 0
```

Example 4-30 *Test Process with Good Debugs to Verify Tunnel Comes up Using Certificates (Continued)*

```
      local crypto endpt.: 142.52.0.3, remote crypto endpt.: 140.52.0.100
      path mtu 1500, media mtu 1500
      current outbound spi: FB26A1BD

      inbound esp sas:
       spi: 0x69BF2B81(1774136193)
         transform: esp-des esp-md5-hmac ,
         in use settings ={Tunnel, }
         slot: 0, conn id: 2000, flow_id: 1, crypto map: lab4
         sa timing: remaining key lifetime (k/sec): (4607999/3219)
         IV size: 8 bytes
         replay detection support: Y

      inbound ah sas:

      inbound pcp sas:

      outbound esp sas:
       spi: 0xFB26A1BD(4213612989)
         transform: esp-des esp-md5-hmac ,
         in use settings ={Tunnel, }
         slot: 0, conn id: 2001, flow_id: 2, crypto map: lab4
         sa timing: remaining key lifetime (k/sec): (4607999/3219)
         IV size: 8 bytes
         replay detection support: Y

      outbound ah sas:

      outbound pcp sas:
```

TIP   For more information on configuring certs and duplicate subnets, refer to the following URLs:

Configuring an IPSec Tunnel Between Routers with Duplicate LAN Subnets

www.cisco.com/warp/public/707/same-ip.html

Configure a LAN-to-LAN IPSec using Digital Certificates

www.cisco.com/warp/public/707/lan_to_lan_ipsec_pix_rtr_cert.html

5.2: Multipoint GRE

1 Configure one GRE tunnel with 10.1.1.0/24 subnet on each router: R3, R6, R7, and R8.

2 Configure GRE tunnel mode as multipoint. See Example 4-31.

3 Do not configure the tunnel destination command on any routers. Configure NHRP (Next Hop Resolution Protocol) to map spokes; use static map or dynamic (optional).

> **4** Configure tunnel authentication using password **cisco**.
>
> **5** Configure EIGRP AS-1 on tunnel interface(s) and advertise Loopback9(s) and VLAN-6 networks.
>
> **6** Do not redistribute EIGRP-1 into any protocol.

Example 4-31 *Multipoint GRE Configuration on R6, R3, R7, and R8 Using NHRP*

```
r6#show running-config interface tunnel 1
Building configuration...

Current configuration : 502 bytes
!
interface Tunnel1
 ip address 10.1.1.1 255.255.255.0
 ip mtu 1400
 ip nhrp authentication cisco
 ip nhrp map 10.1.1.2 167.78.86.2
 ip nhrp map 10.1.1.3 167.78.86.3
 ip nhrp map multicast 167.78.86.3
 ip nhrp map multicast 167.78.86.2
 ip nhrp map 10.1.1.4 140.52.0.2
 ip nhrp map multicast 140.52.0.2
 ip nhrp network-id 1010
 ip nhrp holdtime 600
 no ip route-cache cef
 no ip split-horizon eigrp 1
 no ip split-horizon
 tunnel source Serial2/0.1
 tunnel mode gre multipoint
 tunnel key 101010
end

r3#show running-config interface tunnel 1
Building configuration...

Current configuration : 503 bytes
!
interface Tunnel1
 ip address 10.1.1.4 255.255.255.0
 no ip redirects
 ip mtu 1440
 ip nhrp authentication cisco
 ip nhrp map 10.1.1.1 167.78.86.1
 ip nhrp map multicast 167.78.86.1
 ip nhrp map 10.1.1.2 167.78.86.2
 ip nhrp map multicast 167.78.86.2
 ip nhrp map 10.1.1.3 167.78.86.3
 ip nhrp map multicast 167.78.86.3
 ip nhrp network-id 1010
 ip nhrp holdtime 600
 ip nhrp nhs 10.1.1.1
```

Example 4-31 *Multipoint GRE Configuration on R6, R3, R7, and R8 Using NHRP (Continued)*

```
 no ip split-horizon eigrp 1
 tunnel source FastEthernet0/0
 tunnel mode gre multipoint
 tunnel key 101010
end

r7#show running-config interface tunnel 1
Building configuration...

Current configuration : 495 bytes
!
interface Tunnel1
 ip address 10.1.1.3 255.255.255.0
 no ip redirects
 ip mtu 1440
 ip nhrp authentication cisco
 ip nhrp map 10.1.1.1 167.78.86.1
 ip nhrp map multicast 167.78.86.1
 ip nhrp map 10.1.1.2 167.78.86.2
 ip nhrp map multicast 167.78.86.2
 ip nhrp map 10.1.1.4 140.52.0.2
 ip nhrp map multicast 140.52.0.2
 ip nhrp network-id 1010
 ip nhrp holdtime 600
 ip nhrp nhs 10.1.1.1
 no ip split-horizon eigrp 1
 tunnel source Serial1/0
 tunnel mode gre multipoint
 tunnel key 101010
end

r8#show running-config interface tunnel 1
Building configuration...

Current configuration : 495 bytes
!
interface Tunnel1
 ip address 10.1.1.2 255.255.255.0
 no ip redirects
 ip mtu 1400
 ip nhrp authentication cisco
 ip nhrp map 10.1.1.1 167.78.86.1
 ip nhrp map multicast 167.78.86.1
 ip nhrp map 10.1.1.3 167.78.86.3
 ip nhrp map multicast 167.78.86.3
 ip nhrp map 10.1.1.4 140.52.0.2
 ip nhrp map multicast 140.52.0.2
 ip nhrp network-id 1010
 ip nhrp holdtime 600
```

continues

Example 4-31 *Multipoint GRE Configuration on R6, R3, R7, and R8 Using NHRP (Continued)*

```
 ip nhrp nhs 10.1.1.1
 no ip split-horizon eigrp 1
 tunnel source Serial1/0
 tunnel mode gre multipoint
 tunnel key 101010
end


r6#show ip nhrp static
10.1.1.2/32 via 10.1.1.2, Tunnel1 created 03:07:20, never expire
  Type: static, Flags: authoritative used
  NBMA address: 167.78.86.2
10.1.1.3/32 via 10.1.1.3, Tunnel1 created 03:11:24, never expire
  Type: static, Flags: authoritative used
  NBMA address: 167.78.86.3
10.1.1.4/32 via 10.1.1.4, Tunnel1 created 00:17:03, never expire
  Type: static, Flags: authoritative used
  NBMA address: 140.52.0.2


r3#show ip nhrp detail
10.1.1.1/32 via 10.1.1.1, Tunnel1 created 00:17:32, never expire
  Type: static, Flags: authoritative used
  NBMA address: 167.78.86.1
10.1.1.2/32 via 10.1.1.2, Tunnel1 created 00:17:32, never expire
  Type: static, Flags: authoritative used
  NBMA address: 167.78.86.2
10.1.1.3/32 via 10.1.1.3, Tunnel1 created 00:16:54, never expire
  Type: static, Flags: authoritative used
  NBMA address: 167.78.86.3


r7#show ip nhrp detail
10.1.1.1/32 via 10.1.1.1, Tunnel1 created 03:11:30, never expire
  Type: static, Flags: authoritative used
  NBMA address: 167.78.86.1
10.1.1.2/32 via 10.1.1.2, Tunnel1 created 02:49:31, never expire
  Type: static, Flags: authoritative
  NBMA address: 167.78.86.2
10.1.1.4/32 via 10.1.1.4, Tunnel1 created 00:16:21, never expire
  Type: static, Flags: authoritative
  NBMA address: 140.52.0.2


r8#show ip nhrp detail
10.1.1.1/32 via 10.1.1.1, Tunnel1 created 03:09:57, never expire
  Type: static, Flags: authoritative used
  NBMA address: 167.78.86.1
10.1.1.3/32 via 10.1.1.3, Tunnel1 created 02:49:20, never expire
  Type: static, Flags: authoritative used
  NBMA address: 167.78.86.3
10.1.1.4/32 via 10.1.1.4, Tunnel1 created 00:16:03, never expire
  Type: static, Flags: authoritative
  NBMA address: 140.52.0.2
```

Section 6.0: IOS Firewall Configuration

6.1: IOS Firewall

1 Configure R5 and R6 as firewall using ACLs.

2 Use the **established** keyword to permit return TCP traffic from LAN to Frame Relay.

3 The established is used for the TCP protocol only: Indicates an established connection. A match occurs if the TCP datagram has the ACK or RST bits set. The nonmatching case is that of the initial TCP datagram that has a SYN bit to form a connection.

4 Telnet from any router behind R5/R6 should be successful, but Telnet from R7/R8 to any routers behind R5/R6 will not be successful. See Example 4-32.

Example 4-32 *ACL on R6 Ingress on Frame Relay Link*

```
!After applying ACL on R5/R6 Frame Relay Link as shown below, telnet not
!successful from R7 to R3, but successful from R3 to R7.
r6# show access-lists 110
Extended IP access list 110
    permit tcp any any established (4122 matches)
    permit udp any any eq domain
    permit icmp any any (90 matches)
    permit ospf any any (4969 matches)
    permit eigrp any any (30490 matches)
    permit tcp any any eq bgp (8 matches)
    permit tcp any eq bgp any
    permit gre any host 167.78.86.1 (55950 matches)
    permit udp any any eq snmp
    permit udp any any eq snmptrap (70 matches)

r5# show access-lists 110
Extended IP access list 110
    permit tcp any any established (28 matches)
    permit udp any any eq domain
    permit icmp any any (40 matches)
    permit ospf any any
    permit eigrp any any (27810 matches)
    permit tcp any any eq bgp (535 matches)
    permit tcp any eq bgp any
    permit udp any any eq snmp
    permit udp any any eq snmptrap

r7#ping 13.13.13.13

Type escape sequence to abort.
Sending 5, 100-byte ICMP Echos to 13.13.13.13, timeout is 2 seconds:
!!!!!
Success rate is 100 percent (5/5), round-trip min/avg/max = 68/68/68 ms
```

continues

Example 4-32 *ACL on R6 Ingress on Frame Relay Link (Continued)*

```
r7#telnet 13.13.13.13
Trying 13.13.13.13 ...
% Destination unreachable; gateway or host down

r7#
r3#ping 17.17.17.17

Type escape sequence to abort.
Sending 5, 100-byte ICMP Echos to 17.17.17.17, timeout is 2 seconds:
!!!!!
Success rate is 100 percent (5/5), round-trip min/avg/max = 64/67/68 ms

r3#telnet 17.17.17.17
Trying 17.17.17.17 ... Open


User Access Verification

Password: cisco
r7>
r7>
```

6.2: Intrusion Detection System (IDS)

1 Configure IDS on PIX using the **ip audit** command set.

2 Configure Syslog server.

3 Configure action drop and alarm for attack signatures. See Example 4-33.

4 Configure action alarm only for informational signatures. See Example 4-33.

5 Configure logging host 172.16.1.10 to send the alarms when a signature triggers.

6 Configure log timestamps.

7 To disable ICMP echo signature, you need to find out SigID. Configure buffer logging on PIX and ping from R4 to PIX outside interface. Then do a **show log** to see the Signature ID for ICMP echo request. See Example 4-34.

8 Use the SigID 2004 in Syslog to disable ICMP echo signature.

Example 4-33 *IDS Configuration on PIX*

```
logging on
logging timestamp
logging buffered debugging
logging trap debugging
logging host inside 172.16.1.10
ip audit name lab4-attack attack action alarm drop
ip audit name lab4-info info action alarm
```

Example 4-33 *IDS Configuration on PIX (Continued)*

```
ip audit interface outside lab4-info
ip audit interface outside lab4-attack
ip audit info action alarm
ip audit attack action alarm
ip audit signature 2004 disable
```

Example 4-34 *Syslog from PIX to Identify SigID for ICMP Echo Signature*

```
pix(config)# show log
Syslog logging: enabled
     Facility: 20
     Timestamp logging: enabled
     Standby logging: disabled
     Console logging: disabled
     Monitor logging: disabled
     Buffer logging: level debugging, 13 messages logged
     Trap logging: level debugging, facility 20, 45 messages logged
          Logging to inside 172.16.1.10
     History logging: disabled
111008: User 'enable_15' executed the 'logging buff debug' command.
111008: User 'enable_15' executed the 'logging on' command.
400014: IDS:2004 ICMP echo request from 140.52.0.3 to 140.52.0.1 on interface outside
400014: IDS:2004 ICMP echo request from 140.52.0.3 to 140.52.0.1 on interface outside
400014: IDS:2004 ICMP echo request from 140.52.0.3 to 140.52.0.1 on interface outside
400014: IDS:2004 ICMP echo request from 140.52.0.3 to 140.52.0.1 on interface outside
400014: IDS:2004 ICMP echo request from 140.52.0.3 to 140.52.0.1 on interface outside
400014: IDS:2004 ICMP echo request from 140.52.0.3 to 140.52.0.1 on interface outside
400014: IDS:2004 ICMP echo request from 140.52.0.3 to 140.52.0.1 on interface outside
400014: IDS:2004 ICMP echo request from 140.52.0.3 to 140.52.0.1 on interface outside
400014: IDS:2004 ICMP echo request from 140.52.0.3 to 140.52.0.1 on interface outside
400014: IDS:2004 ICMP echo request from 140.52.0.3 to 140.52.0.1 on interface outside
```

TIP   For more information on IDS on PIX, refer to

www.cisco.com/univercd/cc/td/doc/product/iaabu/pix/pix_sw/v_61/config
/sysmgmt.htm#1002309

Section 7.0: AAA

7.1: AAA on the Switch

1 Configure AAA on both switches using RADIUS. See Example 4-35.

2 Configure EXEC authorization using RADIUS.

3 Configure Network entries on ACS for Switch1 IP 172.16.3.10 and Switch2 IP 172.16.4.20 with key **cisco**. This is because Switch1 has a VLAN3 interface and all AAA requests will be sourced using the VLAN3 interface IP address. This is not the case in Switch2, since it has only one VLAN interface—the Management VLAN4 with IP address 172.16.4.20 See Figure 4-7 for ACS configuration.

4 Configure the AAA fallback method to local and configure a local username on both switches.

5 Configure a separate method list that does not authenticate or authorize, and apply it to the Console port.

6 Configure username **switch-user** password **cisco** in ACS and configure Attribute 6 Service Type=Login. See Figure 4-8 for ACS configuration.

7 Verify by Telnetting from any router to both switches' Management IP. See Example 4-36.

8 Configure accounting for Exec. See Example 4-37 for good accounting debugs. You may also verify on ACS RADIUS Accounting report. See Figure 4-9.

TIP For more information on configuring switch access with RADIUS, refer to the following URL: www.cisco.com/univercd/cc/td/doc/product/lan/c3550/12113ea1/3550scg /swauthen.htm#1091098

Example 4-35 *AAA Configuration on Switch1 and Switch2*

```
!Snip from Switch1 config
hostname Switch1
!
aaa new-model
aaa authentication login vty group radius local
aaa authentication login con none
aaa authorization exec vty group radius local
aaa authorization exec con none
aaa accounting exec vty start-stop group radius
enable password cisco
!
username switch-user privilege 15 password 0 cisco
!
radius-server host 172.16.3.254 auth-port 1812 acct-port 1813
radius-server retransmit 3
radius-server key cisco
!
line con 0
 exec-timeout 0 0
 authorization exec con
```

Example 4-35 *AAA Configuration on Switch1 and Switch2 (Continued)*

```
 login authentication con
 escape-character 27
line vty 0 4
 password cisco
 authorization exec vty
 accounting exec vty
 login authentication vty
line vty 5 15
 password cisco
 authorization exec vty
 accounting exec vty
 login authentication vty
 !
end
!Snip from Switch2 config
hostname Switch2
!
aaa new-model
aaa authentication login vty group radius local
aaa authentication login con none
aaa authorization exec vty group radius local
aaa authorization exec con none
aaa accounting exec vty start-stop group radius
enable password cisco
!
username switch-user privilege 15 password 0 cisco
!
radius-server host 172.16.3.254 auth-port 1812 acct-port 1813
radius-server retransmit 3
radius-server key cisco
!
line con 0
 exec-timeout 0 0
 authorization exec con
 login authentication con
 escape-character 27
line vty 0 4
 password cisco
 authorization exec vty
 accounting exec vty
 login authentication vty
line vty 5 15
 password cisco
 authorization exec vty
 accounting exec vty
 login authentication vty
 !
end
```

Example 4-36 *Telnet to Both Switches' Management IP*

```
r1#telnet 172.16.4.10
Trying 172.16.4.10 ... Open


User Access Verification

Username: switch-user
Password: cisco

Switch1>exit

[Connection to 172.16.4.10 closed by foreign host]


r1#telnet 172.16.4.20
Trying 172.16.4.20 ... Open


User Access Verification

Username: switch-user
Password: cisco

Switch2>
Switch2>exit

[Connection to 172.16.4.20 closed by foreign host]
r1#
r1#
```

Example 4-37 *AAA Accounting Debugs from Switch1*

```
Switch1#show debugging
General OS:
  AAA Accounting debugging is on
Switch1#
Switch1#
1w2d: AAA: parse name=tty1 idb type=-1 tty=-1
1w2d: AAA: name=tty1 flags=0x11 type=5 shelf=0 slot=0 adapter=0 port=1 channel=0
1w2d: AAA/MEMORY: create_user (0xDFC114) user='' ruser='' port='tty1'
rem_addr='172.16.4.1' authen_type=ASCII service=LOGIN priv=1
1w2d: AAA/ACCT/EXEC/START User switch-user, port tty1
1w2d: AAA/ACCT/EXEC: Found list "vty"
1w2d: AAA/ACCT/EXEC/START User switch-user, Port tty1,
        task_id=8 timezone=UTC service=shell
1w2d: AAA/ACCT: user switch-user, acct type 0 (1315242846): Method=radius (radius)
Switch1#
Switch1#
1w2d: AAA/ACCT/ACCT_DISC: Found list "vty"
```

Example 4-37 *AAA Accounting Debugs from Switch1 (Continued)*

```
1w2d: tty1 AAA/DISC: 1/"User Request"
1w2d: AAA/ACCT/ACCT_DISC: Found list "vty"
1w2d: tty1 AAA/DISC/EXT: 1020/"User Request"
1w2d: AAA/ACCT/ACCT_DISC: Found list "vty"
1w2d: tty1 AAA/DISC: 9/"NAS Error"
1w2d: AAA/ACCT/ACCT_DISC: Found list "vty"
1w2d: tty1 AAA/DISC/EXT: 1002/"Unknown"
1w2d: AAA/ACCT: no attribute "elapsed_time" to replace, adding it
1w2d: AAA/ACCT/EXEC/STOP: cannot retrieve modem speed
1w2d: AAA/ACCT/EXEC/STOP User switch-user, Port tty1:
        task_id=8 timezone=UTC service=shell disc-cause=1 disc-cause-ext=1020
elapsed_time=8 nas-rx-speed=0 nas-tx-speed=0
1w2d: AAA/ACCT: user switch-user, acct type 0 (143614545): Method=radius (radius)
1w2d: AAA/MEMORY: free_user (0xDFC114) user='switch-user' ruser='' port='tty1'
  rem_addr='172.16.4.1' authen_type=ASCII service=LOGIN priv=1
Switch1#
```

Figure 4-7   *NAS Settings on ACS*

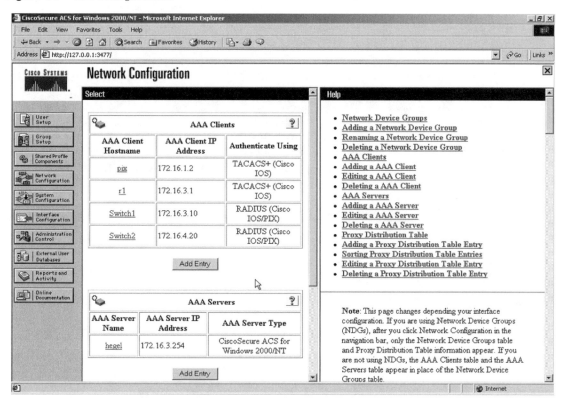

Figure 4-8 *User switch-user Settings on ACS*

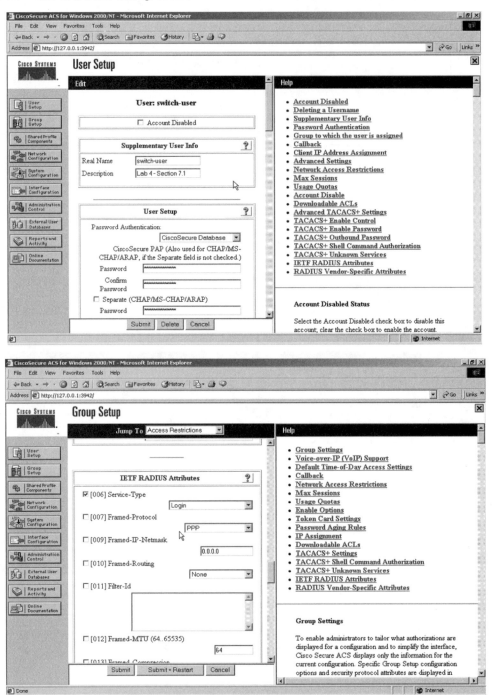

Figure 4-9   *Accounting Reports on ACS*

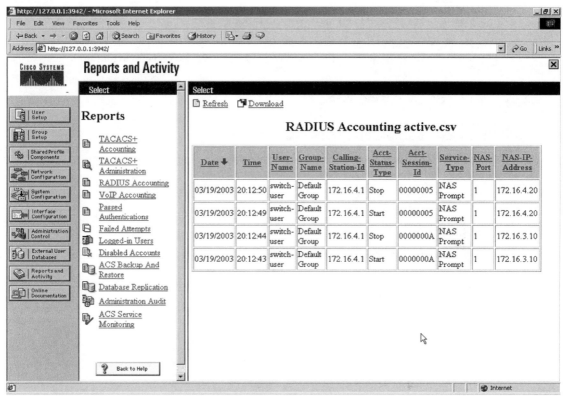

7.2: AAA on PIX

1   Configure AAA for Telnet traffic through the PIX to authenticate and authorize each session using TACACS+. See Example 4-38.

2   Configure AAA on R2 for Telnet/vty authentication using the local database. This is the second (double) authentication phase. See Example 4-39.

3   Configure CiscoSecure ACS for **telnet-user** password **cisco** with Shell Command Authorization. See Figure 4-10 for settings on ACS.

4   Hidden trick. There is an ACL on the Ethernet interface (VLAN-2) on R1 for Section 8.3. You need to punch a hole for all return Telnet traffic from R2. See Example 4-40.

5   Verify Telnet from R4 to NATed address of R2 140.52.0.250. See Example 4-41.

Example 4-38 *AAA Config on PIX*

```
pix(config)# show static
static (inside,outside) 140.52.0.250 172.16.2.2 netmask 255.255.255.255 0 0

pix(config)# show access-list
access-list outside permit tcp any host 140.52.0.250 eq telnet (hitcnt=6)

pix(config)# show aaa-server
aaa-server ACS (inside) host 172.16.3.254 cisco timeout 10

pix(config)# show aaa
aaa authentication include telnet outside 0.0.0.0 0.0.0.0 0.0.0.0 0.0.0.0 ACS
aaa authorization include telnet outside 0.0.0.0 0.0.0.0 0.0.0.0 0.0.0.0 ACS
```

Example 4-39 *AAA Config on R2*

```
hostname r2
!
aaa new-model
aaa authentication login vty local
enable password cisco
!
username r2telnet-user password 0 cisco
!
line vty 0 4
 privilege level 15
 password cisco
 login authentication vty
!
end
```

Example 4-40 *ACL on R1 for Return Telnet Traffic from R2*

```
r1#show access-lists 103
Extended IP access list 103
    permit tcp any host 172.16.2.1 eq telnet
    permit tcp host 172.16.2.2 eq telnet any (56 matches)
    Dynamic lab4 permit ip any any
```

Example 4-41 *Verify Telnet to R2 from R4*

```
!Below you can see the double authentication. The first one is by PIX using
!TACACS+, and the second is by R2 using local.
r4#telnet 140.52.0.250
Trying 140.52.0.250 ... Open

Username: telnet-user

Password: cisco
```

Example 4-41 *Verify Telnet to R2 from R4 (Continued)*

```
User Access Verification

Username: r2telnet-user
Password: cisco

r2#
r2#exit

[Connection to 140.52.0.250 closed by foreign host]
r4#
r4#
```

```
!Verify on PIX using 'show uauth' that user has been authorized for telnet
!traffic only.
pix(config)# show uauth
                        Current    Most Seen
Authenticated Users        1           1
Authen In Progress         0           1
user 'telnet-user' at 140.52.0.3, authorized to:
   port 172.16.2.2/telnet
   absolute   timeout: 0:05:00
   inactivity timeout: 0:00:00
pix(config)#
pix(config)#
```

```
!Good AAA authentication debugs from R2 local (second phase) authentication.
r2#show debug
General OS:
  AAA Authentication debugging is on
r2#
r2#
1w3d: AAA: parse name=tty66 idb type=-1 tty=-1
1w3d: AAA: name=tty66 flags=0x11 type=5 shelf=0 slot=0 adapter=0 port=66 channel=0
1w3d: AAA/MEMORY: create_user (0x80E7B60C) user='' ruser='' port='tty66'
rem_addr='140.52.0.3' authen_type=ASCII service=LOGIN priv=15
1w3d: AAA/AUTHEN/START (2908502432): port='tty66' list='vty' action=LOGIN
   service=LOGIN
1w3d: AAA/AUTHEN/START (2908502432): found list vty
1w3d: AAA/AUTHEN/START (2908502432): Method=LOCAL
1w3d: AAA/AUTHEN (2908502432): status = GETUSER
1w3d: AAA/AUTHEN/CONT (2908502432): continue_login (user='(undef)')
1w3d: AAA/AUTHEN (2908502432): status = GETUSER
1w3d: AAA/AUTHEN/CONT (2908502432): Method=LOCAL
1w3d: AAA/AUTHEN (2908502432): status = GETPASS
1w3d: AAA/AUTHEN/CONT (2908502432): continue_login (user='r2telnet-user')
1w3d: AAA/AUTHEN (2908502432): status = GETPASS
1w3d: AAA/AUTHEN/CONT (2908502432): Method=LOCAL
1w3d: AAA/AUTHEN (2908502432): status = PASS
r2#
1w3d: AAA/MEMORY: free_user (0x80E7B60C) user='r2telnet-user' ruser='' port='tty66'
  rem_addr='140.52.0.3' authen_type=ASCII service=LOGIN priv=15
r2#
```

Figure 4-10 *User telnet-user Settings with Command Authorization Set on ACS*

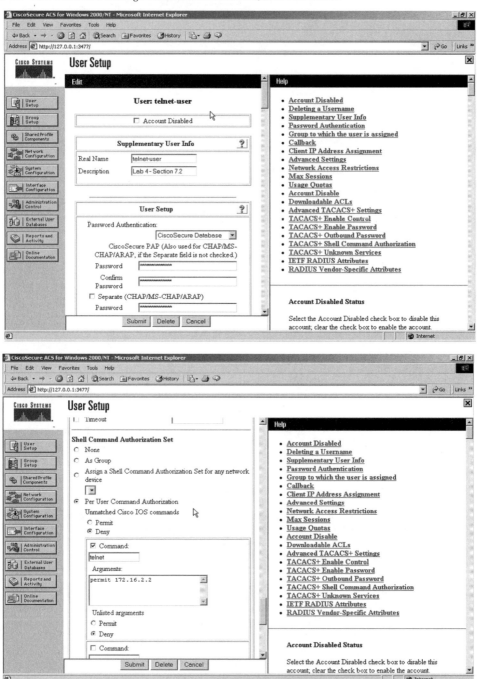

Section 8.0: Advanced Security

8.1: Perimeter Security

1 Configure HTTP inspection on R4 to block all Java applets. See Example 4-42.

2 Use the java-list option to specify an access list from sites to permit/deny downloading Java applets.

3 Configure TCP inspection to test if CBAC is working; see Example 4-43.

Example 4-42 *HTTP Inspection with Java Filtering on R4*

```
ip inspect name lab4 http java-list 1
!
access-list 1 deny    any
!

r4#show ip inspect all
Session audit trail is disabled
Session alert is enabled
one-minute (sampling period) thresholds are [400:500] connections
max-incomplete sessions thresholds are [400:500]
max-incomplete tcp connections per host is 50. Block-time 0 minute.
tcp synwait-time is 30 sec -- tcp finwait-time is 5 sec
tcp idle-time is 3600 sec -- udp idle-time is 30 sec
dns-timeout is 5 sec
Inspection Rule Configuration
 Inspection name lab4
    http java-list 1 alert is on audit-trail is off timeout 3600
    tcp alert is on audit-trail is off timeout 3600

Interface Configuration
 Interface Ethernet0/1
  Inbound inspection rule is not set
  Outgoing inspection rule is lab4
    http java-list 1 alert is on audit-trail is off timeout 3600
    tcp alert is on audit-trail is off timeout 3600
  Inbound access list is not set
  Outgoing access list is not set
```

Example 4-43 *Test if CBAC Is Working on R4*

```
!Test CBAC by telnetting from R3 anywhere beyond R4. Verify using following show
!command on R4.
r4#show ip inspect sessions
Established Sessions
 Session 82BBC490 (140.52.0.2:11009)=>(167.78.86.2:23) tcp SIS_OPEN
r4#
```

TIP	For more information on Java applets, see the following URL:
	www.cisco.com/warp/partner/synchronicd/cc/pd/iosw/ioft/iofwft/tech /firew_wp.htm#xtocid15

8.2: IP Fragmentation

1 Use the **fragment chain 1** command to specify the maximum number of packets into which a full IP packet can be fragmented. Setting the limit to 1 means that all packets must be whole—that is, unfragmented. See Example 4-44.

Example 4-44 *Snip from PIX*

```
pix(config)# show fragment
Interface: outside
    Size: 200, Chain: 1, Timeout: 5
    Queue: 0, Assemble: 0, Fail: 0, Overflow: 0
Interface: inside
    Size: 200, Chain: 1, Timeout: 5
    Queue: 0, Assemble: 0, Fail: 0, Overflow: 0
```

TIP	For more information, see the following URL:
	www.cisco.com/univercd/cc/td/doc/product/iaabu/pix/pix_61/cmd_ref/df.htm#xtocid16

8.3: Traffic Filtering Using Lock-and-Key

1 Configure Lock-and-Key (dynamic ACL) on R1 for all traffic to R1 from R2 on the VLAN-2 interface. See Example 4-45.

2 Configure AAA authentication using TACACS+ for the Lock-and-key user.

3 Lock-and-key security is a traffic filtering security feature that uses dynamic access lists.

4 Lock-and-key is available for IP traffic only.

5 Configure username **locknkey-user** password **cisco** on CiscoSecure ACS. No special attributes need to be configured on ACS for this user. Only a valid username and password are sufficient.

6 Verify first by pinging 172.16.2.1 (R1 interface) from R2; this should fail. Telnet to R1 and authenticate. Ping again; it should be successful. Verify dynamic ACL on R1. See Example 4-46.

TIP   For more details on Lock-and-Key, refer to the following URLs:

www.cisco.com/warp/partner/synchronicd/cc/pd/iosw/ioft/iolk/tech/landk_wp.htm

www.cisco.com/univercd/cc/td/doc/product/software/ios121/121cgcr/secur_c/scprt3
/scdlock.htm

Example 4-45 *Lock-and-Key Config on R1*

```
hostname r1
!
aaa new-model
aaa authentication login vty group tacacs+ local
!
username cisco password 0 cisco
!
interface Ethernet1/1
 ip address 172.16.2.1 255.255.255.0
 ip access-group 103 in
!
access-list 103 permit tcp any host 172.16.2.1 eq telnet
access-list 103 dynamic lab4 timeout 120 permit ip any any
!
tacacs-server host 172.16.3.254
tacacs-server key cisco
!
line vty 0 4
 login authentication vty
 autocommand  access-enable timeout 2
!
end
```

Example 4-46 *Verify Lock-and-Key Works*

```
!Ping from R2 to R1 172.16.2.1, it will fail in the first instance. Once you
!telnet and authenticate, R1 will dynamically open hole in ACL 103. Ping again
!from R2 with success.
r2#ping 172.16.2.1

Type escape sequence to abort.
Sending 5, 100-byte ICMP Echos to 172.16.2.1, timeout is 2 seconds:
U.U.U
Success rate is 0 percent (0/5)
r2#
r2#
r2#telnet 172.16.2.1
Trying 172.16.2.1 ... Open
```

continues

Example 4-46 *Verify Lock-and-Key Works (Continued)*

```
User Access Verification

Username: locknkey-user
Password: cisco
[Connection to 172.16.2.1 closed by foreign host]
r2#
r2#
r2#ping 172.16.2.1

Type escape sequence to abort.
Sending 5, 100-byte ICMP Echos to 172.16.2.1, timeout is 2 seconds:
!!!!!
Success rate is 100 percent (5/5), round-trip min/avg/max = 1/3/4 ms
r2#
r2#
r2#ping 172.16.2.1

Type escape sequence to abort.
Sending 5, 100-byte ICMP Echos to 172.16.2.1, timeout is 2 seconds:
!!!!!
Success rate is 100 percent (5/5), round-trip min/avg/max = 4/4/4 ms
r2#

!ACL 103 on R1 dynamically punches hole and starts timeout.
r1#show access-lists 103
Extended IP access list 103
    permit tcp any host 172.16.2.1 eq telnet (46 matches)
    Dynamic lab4 permit ip any any
      permit ip any any (14 matches) (time left 107)

r1#show access-lists 103
Extended IP access list 103
    permit tcp any host 172.16.2.1 eq telnet (46 matches)
    Dynamic lab4 permit ip any any
      permit ip any any (22 matches) (time left 101)

r1#show access-lists 103
Extended IP access list 103
    permit tcp any host 172.16.2.1 eq telnet (46 matches)
    Dynamic lab4 permit ip any any
      permit ip any any (26 matches) (time left 18)

r1#show access-lists 103
Extended IP access list 103
    permit tcp any host 172.16.2.1 eq telnet (46 matches)
    Dynamic lab4 permit ip any any
      permit ip any any (31 matches)

!Good debugs from R1 for authentication process.
r1#show debugging
```

Example 4-46 *Verify Lock-and-Key Works (Continued)*

```
General OS:
  TACACS access control debugging is on
  AAA Authentication debugging is on

17:58:35: AAA: parse name=tty66 idb type=-1 tty=-1
17:58:35: AAA: name=tty66 flags=0x11 type=5 shelf=0 slot=0 adapter=0 port=66 channel=0
17:58:35: AAA/MEMORY: create_user (0x629A7D24) user='' ruser='' port='tty66'
rem_addr='172.16.2.2' authen_type=ASCII service=LOGIN priv=1
17:58:35: AAA/AUTHEN/START (99183976): port='tty66' list='vty' action=LOGIN
  service=LOGIN
17:58:35: AAA/AUTHEN/START (99183976): found list vty
17:58:35: AAA/AUTHEN/START (99183976): Method=tacacs+ (tacacs+)
17:58:35: TAC+: send AUTHEN/START packet ver=192 id=99183976
17:58:35: TAC+: Using default tacacs server-group "tacacs+" list.
17:58:35: TAC+: Opening TCP/IP to 172.16.3.254/49 timeout=5
17:58:35: TAC+: Opened TCP/IP handle 0x62810560 to 172.16.3.254/49
17:58:35: TAC+: 172.16.3.254 (99183976) AUTHEN/START/LOGIN/ASCII queued
17:58:35: TAC+: (99183976) AUTHEN/START/LOGIN/ASCII processed
17:58:35: TAC+: ver=192 id=99183976 received AUTHEN status = GETUSER
17:58:35: AAA/AUTHEN (99183976): status = GETUSER
17:58:40: AAA/AUTHEN/CONT (99183976): continue_login (user='(undef)')
17:58:40: AAA/AUTHEN (99183976): status = GETUSER
17:58:40: AAA/AUTHEN (99183976): Method=tacacs+ (tacacs+)
17:58:40: TAC+: send AUTHEN/CONT packet id=99183976
17:58:40: TAC+: 172.16.3.254 (99183976) AUTHEN/CONT queued
17:58:40: TAC+: (99183976) AUTHEN/CONT processed
17:58:40: TAC+: ver=192 id=99183976 received AUTHEN status = GETPASS
17:58:40: AAA/AUTHEN (99183976): status = GETPASS
17:58:42: AAA/AUTHEN/CONT (99183976): continue_login (user='locknkey-user')
17:58:42: AAA/AUTHEN (99183976): status = GETPASS
17:58:42: AAA/AUTHEN (99183976): Method=tacacs+ (tacacs+)
17:58:42: TAC+: send AUTHEN/CONT packet id=99183976
17:58:42: TAC+: 172.16.3.254 (99183976) AUTHEN/CONT queued
17:58:42: TAC+: (99183976) AUTHEN/CONT processed
17:58:42: TAC+: ver=192 id=99183976 received AUTHEN status = PASS
17:58:42: AAA/AUTHEN (99183976): status = PASS
17:58:42: TAC+: Closing TCP/IP 0x62810560 connection to 172.16.3.254/49
17:58:42: AAA/MEMORY: free_user (0x629A7D24) user='locknkey-user' ruser=''
  port='tty66' rem_addr='172.16.2.2' authen_type=ASCII service=LOGIN priv=1
```

8.4: Key Management

1 Configure two keys on R3 and R4, one default key cisco and another "strict" key for a specific time range. See Example 4-47.

2 Make sure your clock is synchronized on both routers. No need to configure NTP. Manually configure the clocks.

3 To verify if keys are working in the hours specified, change the clock manually and shut/unshut the interface(s) in RIP to reconverge with new keys. See Example 4-48.

Example 4-47 *Snip from R3 Configuration (Same Config on R4)*

```
key chain lab4
 key 1
  key-string cisco
 key 2
  key-string strict
  accept-lifetime 13:00:00 Mar 18 2003 duration 10800
  send-lifetime 14:00:00 Mar 18 2003 duration 3600
!
interface FastEthernet0/0
 ip address 140.52.0.2 255.255.255.0
 ip rip authentication mode md5
 ip rip authentication key-chain lab4
 ip ospf message-digest-key 1 md5 cisco
 duplex auto
 speed auto
!
```

Example 4-48 *RIP Keys Verification and Testing*

```
!Verify by shutting and un-shutting interfaces to force RIP to re-converge.
r3#show clock
14:10:58.399 UTC Tue Mar 18 2003

r3#config term
Enter configuration commands, one per line.  End with CNTL/Z.
r3(config)#interface fa0/0
r3(config-if)#shutdown
1w1d: %OSPF-5-ADJCHG: Process 110, Nbr 4.4.4.4 on FastEthernet0/0 from FULL to DOWN,
Neighbor Down: Interface down or detached
1w1d: %LINK-5-CHANGED: Interface FastEthernet0/0, changed state to administratively
down
1w1d: %LINEPROTO-5-UPDOWN: Line protocol on Interface FastEthernet0/0, changed state
  to down

r3#show ip rip database
0.0.0.0/0 is possibly down
0.0.0.0/0 is possibly down
121.0.0.0/8 is possibly down
121.52.5.0/26 is possibly down
133.72.0.0/16 is possibly down
133.72.52.0/25 is possibly down
140.52.0.0/16 is possibly down
140.52.0.0/24 is possibly down
142.52.0.0/16 is possibly down
142.52.0.0/24 is possibly down
167.78.0.0/16 is possibly down
167.78.86.0/29 is possibly down

!Now, unshut the interface
r3(config)#interface fa0/0
```

Example 4-48 *RIP Keys Verification and Testing (Continued)*

```
r3(config-if)#no shutdown
1w1d: %LINK-3-UPDOWN: Interface FastEthernet0/0, changed state to up
r3#
r3#
1w1d: %LINEPROTO-5-UPDOWN: Line protocol on Interface FastEthernet0/0, changed state
  to up
r3#
1w1d: %OSPF-5-ADJCHG: Process 110, Nbr 4.4.4.4 on FastEthernet0/0 from LOADING to FULL,
  Loading Done
r3#
r3#
r3#
r3#show clock
14:11:43.043 UTC Tue Mar 18 2003

r3#show ip route rip
     142.52.0.0/24 is subnetted, 1 subnets
R       142.52.0.0 [120/1] via 140.52.0.3, 00:00:14, FastEthernet0/0
     133.72.0.0/25 is subnetted, 1 subnets
R       133.72.52.0 [120/1] via 140.52.0.3, 00:00:14, FastEthernet0/0
     167.78.0.0/29 is subnetted, 1 subnets
R       167.78.86.0 [120/1] via 140.52.0.3, 00:00:14, FastEthernet0/0
     121.0.0.0/26 is subnetted, 1 subnets
R       121.52.5.0 [120/1] via 140.52.0.3, 00:00:14, FastEthernet0/0
R*   0.0.0.0/0 [120/1] via 140.52.0.3, 00:00:14, FastEthernet0/0
```

Section 9.0: IP Services and Protocol-Independent Features

9.1: Network Monitoring and Management

1 Configure SNMP v1 on R7 and R8.

2 Configure community strings with ACL to allow host 140.52.0.55 only. See Example 4-49.

3 Hidden trick. You need to punch hole in ingress ACL on R6 for UDP port 162 for snmptraps. See Example 4-50.

Example 4-49 *SNMP Configuration on R7 and R8*

```
snmp-server community lab4-read RO 6
snmp-server community lab4-write RW 6
snmp-server enable traps config
```

continues

Example 4-49 *SNMP Configuration on R7 and R8 (Continued)*

```
snmp-server enable traps frame-relay
snmp-server host 140.52.0.55 frame-relay  config
access-list 6 permit host 140.52.0.55
!Enable debug snmp packet on R7 and try making any changes in config mode.
3d03h: SNMP: Queuing packet to 140.52.0.55
3d03h: SNMP: V1 Trap, ent ciscoConfigManMIB.2, addr 167.78.86.3, gentrap 6, spectrap 1
 ccmHistoryEventEntry.3.58 = 1
 ccmHistoryEventEntry.4.58 = 2
 ccmHistoryEventEntry.5.58 = 3
3d03h: SNMP: Packet sent via UDP to 140.52.0.55

!Verify with following show command on R7 and R8.
r7#show snmp
0 SNMP packets input
    0 Bad SNMP version errors
    0 Unknown community name
    0 Illegal operation for community name supplied
    0 Encoding errors
    0 Number of requested variables
    0 Number of altered variables
    0 Get-request PDUs
    0 Get-next PDUs
    0 Set-request PDUs
8 SNMP packets output
    0 Too big errors (Maximum packet size 1500)
    0 No such name errors
    0 Bad values errors
    0 General errors
    0 Response PDUs
    8 Trap PDUs

SNMP logging: enabled
    Logging to 140.52.0.55.162, 0/10, 8 sent, 0 dropped.
r7#

r8#show snmp
Chassis: JAB024802D7 (1682508901)
0 SNMP packets input
    0 Bad SNMP version errors
    0 Unknown community name
    0 Illegal operation for community name supplied
    0 Encoding errors
    0 Number of requested variables
    0 Number of altered variables
    0 Get-request PDUs
    0 Get-next PDUs
    0 Set-request PDUs
6 SNMP packets output
    0 Too big errors (Maximum packet size 1500)
```

Example 4-49 *SNMP Configuration on R7 and R8 (Continued)*

```
    0 No such name errors
    0 Bad values errors
    0 General errors
    0 Response PDUs
    6 Trap PDUs

SNMP logging: enabled
    Logging to 140.52.0.55.162, 0/10, 6 sent, 0 dropped.
```

Example 4-50 *Snip of ACL on R6*

```
r6#show access-lists
Extended IP access list 110
    permit tcp any any established (267 matches)
    permit udp any any eq domain
    permit icmp any any (10 matches)
    permit ospf any any (343 matches)
    permit eigrp any any (3170 matches)
    permit tcp any any eq bgp (7 matches)
    permit tcp any eq bgp any
    permit gre any host 167.78.86.1 (3344 matches)
    permit udp any any eq snmp
    permit udp any any eq snmptrap (38 matches)
r6#
```

9.2: Time-Based Policy Routing

1 Configure Time-Based Access Lists on R6 and apply to the policy route and set the next hop to R5. See Example 4-51.

2 Verify by changing the clock on R5, and traceroute to 17.17.17.17 to see if Policy Routing with Time-Based ACL is working. See Example 4-52.

Example 4-51 *Policy Routing with Time-Based ACL on R4*

```
ip local policy route-map time-based-pbr
!
access-list 170 permit ip any host 17.17.17.17 time-range pbr
!
route-map time-based-pbr permit 10
 match ip address 170
 set ip next-hop 142.52.0.3
!
```
continues

Example 4-51 *Policy Routing with Time-Based ACL on R4 (Continued)*

```
route-map time-based-pbr permit 20
!
time-range pbr
 periodic weekdays 9:00 to 17:00
 !
```

Example 4-52 *Verify if Policy Routing with Time-Based ACL Is Working*

```
!Change the clock to be between 9:00 am to 5:00 pm, and trace.
r4#show clock
14:48:51.291 UTC Tue Mar 18 2003


r4#traceroute 17.17.17.17

Type escape sequence to abort.
Tracing the route to 17.17.17.17

  1 142.52.0.3 4 msec 4 msec 4 msec
  2 167.78.86.9 13 msec 16 msec 12 msec
  3 167.78.86.3 44 msec *  44 msec


r4#show time-range
time-range entry: pbr (active)
   periodic weekdays 9:00 to 17:00
   used in: IP ACL entry


r4#show access-lists 170
Extended IP access list 170
    permit ip any host 17.17.17.17 time-range pbr (active) (9 matches)
!Change the clock not to be between 9:00 am to 5:00 pm, and trace again.
r4#clock set 8:00:00 Mar 18 2003
r4#show clock
08:00:02.552 UTC Tue Mar 18 2003


r4#traceroute 17.17.17.17

Type escape sequence to abort.
Tracing the route to 17.17.17.17

  1 142.52.0.2 0 msec 0 msec 4 msec
  2 167.78.86.3 32 msec *  32 msec


r4#show time-range
```

Example 4-52 *Verify if Policy Routing with Time-Based ACL Is Working (Continued)*

```
time-range entry: pbr (inactive)
   periodic weekdays 9:00 to 17:00
   used in: IP ACL entry


r4#show access-lists 170
Extended IP access list 170
    permit ip any host 17.17.17.17 time-range pbr (inactive) (9 matches)
```

9.3: Load Sharing Using HSRP

1 Configure two HSRP groups on R5 and R6 for load balancing traffic in VLAN-7. See Example 4-53.

2 Configure preempt for both groups to fail over in the event Active is Dead for any group. Test HSRP failover by shutting the Ethernet0 on R5. See Example 4-54.

Example 4-53 *Two HSRP Groups Between R5 and R6 for Load Balancing*

```
!Snip configuration from R6:
interface Fast 0/0 0
standby 1 ip 142.52.0.50
standby 1 priority 110
standby 1 preempt
standby 2 ip 142.52.0.51
standby 2 preempt

!Snip configuration from R5:
interface Ethernet 0/0
standby 1 ip 142.52.0.50
standby 1 preempt
standby 2 ip 142.52.0.51
standby 2 priority 110
standby 2 preempt

r5#show standby
Ethernet0 - Group 1
  Local state is Standby, priority 100, may preempt
  Hellotime 3 holdtime 10
  Next hello sent in 00:00:02.298
  Hot standby IP address is 142.52.0.50 configured
  Active router is 142.52.0.2 expires in 00:00:07, priority 110
  Standby router is local
  1 state changes, last state change 00:02:36
Ethernet0 - Group 2
  Local state is Active, priority 110, may preempt
```

continues

Example 4-53 *Two HSRP Groups Between R5 and R6 for Load Balancing (Continued)*

```
  Hellotime 3 holdtime 10
  Next hello sent in 00:00:02.396
  Hot standby IP address is 142.52.0.51 configured
  Active router is local
  Standby router is 142.52.0.2 expires in 00:00:07
  Standby virtual mac address is 0000.0c07.ac02
  1 state changes, last state change 00:01:58
r5#

r6#show standby
FastEthernet0/0 - Group 1
  Local state is Active, priority 110, may preempt
  Hellotime 3 holdtime 10
  Next hello sent in 00:00:01.730
  Hot standby IP address is 142.52.0.50 configured
  Active router is local
  Standby router is 142.52.0.3 expires in 00:00:08
  Standby virtual mac address is 0000.0c07.ac01
  2 state changes, last state change 00:02:51
FastEthernet0/0 - Group 2
  Local state is Standby, priority 100, may preempt
  Hellotime 3 holdtime 10
  Next hello sent in 00:00:02.360
  Hot standby IP address is 142.52.0.51 configured
  Active router is 142.52.0.3 expires in 00:00:08, priority 110
  Standby router is local
  4 state changes, last state change 00:01:43
r6#
```

Example 4-54 *Test HSRP Failover by Shutting the Ethernet0 on R5*

```
r5#conf t
Enter configuration commands, one per line.  End with CNTL/Z.
r5(config)#interface ethernet 0
r5(config-if)#shutdown
4d04h: %OSPF-5-ADJCHG: Process 110, Nbr 6.6.6.6 on Ethernet0 from FULL to DOWN,
  Neighbor Down: Interface down or detached
4d04h: %OSPF-5-ADJCHG: Process 110, Nbr 4.4.4.4 on Ethernet0 from FULL to DOWN,
  Neighbor Down: Interface down or detached
4d04h: %BGP-5-ADJCHANGE: neighbor 142.52.0.1 Down Interface flap
4d04h: %LINK-5-CHANGED: Interface Ethernet0, changed state to administratively down
4d04h: %STANDBY-6-STATECHANGE: Standby: 1: Ethernet0 state Standby       -> Init
4d04h: %STANDBY-6-STATECHANGE: Standby: 2: Ethernet0 state Active        -> Init
4d04h: %LINEPROTO-5-UPDOWN: Line protocol on Interface Ethernet0, changed state to down

!R6 is now Active for both HSRP groups.
r6#4d02h: %STANDBY-6-STATECHANGE: Standby: 2: FastEthernet0/0 state Standby -> Active
```

Example 4-54 *Test HSRP Failover by Shutting the Ethernet0 on R5 (Continued)*

```
r6#show standby
FastEthernet0/0 - Group 1
  Local state is Active, priority 110, may preempt
  Hellotime 3 holdtime 10
  Next hello sent in 00:00:01.292
  Hot standby IP address is 142.52.0.50 configured
  Active router is local
  Standby router is unknown expired
  Standby virtual mac address is 0000.0c07.ac01
  2 state changes, last state change 00:03:41
FastEthernet0/0 - Group 2
  Local state is Active, priority 100, may preempt
  Hellotime 3 holdtime 10
  Next hello sent in 00:00:00.010
  Hot standby IP address is 142.52.0.51 configured
  Active router is local
  Standby router is unknown expired
  Standby virtual mac address is 0000.0c07.ac02
  5 state changes, last state change 00:00:05
```

TIP   For more information on load sharing using HSRP, see the following URL:

www.cisco.com/univercd/cc/td/doc/cisintwk/ics/cs009.htm#xtocid122335

9.4: Multiple Paths

   1 Configure the maximum-paths command under each routing protocol configured on R4.
   See Example 4-55.

Example 4-55 *Snip of Config from R4*

```
router ospf 110
 router-id 4.4.4.4
 log-adjacency-changes
 area 0 authentication message-digest
 area 1 authentication message-digest
 area 1 virtual-link 6.6.6.6 message-digest-key 1 md5 cisco
 area 2 authentication message-digest
 redistribute static metric 1 subnets
 network 140.52.0.0 0.0.0.255 area 2
 network 142.52.0.0 0.0.0.255 area 1
 maximum-paths 2
```

continues

Example 4-55 *Snip of Config from R4 (Continued)*

```
!
router rip
 version 2
 redistribute ospf 110 metric 1
 network 140.52.0.0
 neighbor 140.52.0.1
 maximum-paths 2
 no auto-summary
!
router bgp 2
 no synchronization
 bgp router-id 4.4.4.4
 bgp log-neighbor-changes
 neighbor 140.52.0.2 remote-as 2
 neighbor 140.52.0.2 send-community
 neighbor 140.52.0.100 remote-as 1
 neighbor 140.52.0.100 ebgp-multihop 255
 neighbor 140.52.0.100 send-community
 neighbor 140.52.0.100 route-map set-next-hop in
 neighbor 140.52.0.100 route-map change-community out
 neighbor 142.52.0.2 remote-as 3
 neighbor 142.52.0.2 send-community
 neighbor 142.52.0.3 remote-as 3
 neighbor 142.52.0.3 send-community
 maximum-paths 2
 no auto-summary
```

By default, most IP routing protocols install a maximum of four parallel routes in a routing table.

TIP For more information, see the following URL:

www.cisco.com/univercd/cc/td/doc/product/software/ios121/121cgcr/ip_c/ipcprt2
/1cdindep.htm#1001036

Section 10.0: Security Violations

10.1: TCP SYN DoS Attack

1 Configure the TCP Intercept feature on R1 to protect TCP servers from TCP SYN-flooding attacks.

2 Configure ACL to protect only network 172.16.4.0 with TCP Intercept. See Example 4-56.

3 Configure TCP Intercept in Watch mode where all TCP connections passed through are watched by the router. If any connection does not complete the three-way handshake within the time specified, it will drop the connection by sending a reset. See Example 4-56.

Example 4-56 *Snip from R1 Config*

```
ip tcp intercept list 102
ip tcp intercept watch-timeout 15
ip tcp intercept mode watch
access-list 102 permit tcp any 172.16.4.0 0.0.0.255
```

TIP   For more information about TCP Intercept (preventing DoS), refer to the following URL:

www.cisco.com/univercd/cc/td/doc/product/software/ios121/121cgcr/secur_c/scprt3/scddenl.htm

NOTE   This feature is not available in IOS Firewall or IPSec feature sets.

The TCP Intercept feature is only available in Enterprise, Service Provider, or Telco feature sets.

10.2: ARP Spoofing

1 Use the Port Security feature on both switches to combat ARP spoofing by locking down each Ethernet port on the switch with the corresponding MAC address of the device connected on each port. See Example 4-57.

2 Enabling this feature will restrict the switch such that only one (default) MAC address is allowed per physical port.

3 Do not configure port security for trunk port and HSRP interfaces on R5 and R6 in VLAN-7.

Example 4-57 *Port Security on Switch1 and Switch2*

```
Switch1#show port-security address
          Secure Mac Address Table
-------------------------------------------------------------------
Vlan    Mac Address       Type              Ports    Remaining Age
                                                      (mins)

----    -----------       ----              -----    -------------
  10    0002.b933.eb10    SecureConfigured  Fa0/2    -
   2    0002.b933.eb11    SecureConfigured  Fa0/3    -
```
continues

Example 4-57 *Port Security on Switch1 and Switch2 (Continued)*

```
     2    0004.4dbb.e340    SecureConfigured    Fa0/4     -
     6    0007.85aa.ad61    SecureConfigured    Fa0/5     -
     7    0050.7346.31c1    SecureConfigured    Fa0/6     -
     9    00e0.1e18.ea00    SecureConfigured    Fa0/8     -
     5    0007.5057.e27e    SecureConfigured    Fa0/9     -
     3    0090.2742.fd94    SecureConfigured    Fa0/10    -
------------------------------------------------------------------------
Total Addresses in System : 8
Max Addresses limit in System : 128


Switch1#show port-security
Secure Port      MaxSecureAddr   CurrentAddr    SecurityViolation   Security Action
                  (Count)         (Count)        (Count)

------------------------------------------------------------------------
      Fa0/2          1               1                0             Shutdown
      Fa0/3          1               1                0             Shutdown
      Fa0/4          1               1                0             Shutdown
      Fa0/5          1               1                0             Shutdown
      Fa0/6          1               1                0             Shutdown
      Fa0/8          1               1                0             Shutdown
      Fa0/9          1               1                0             Shutdown
      Fa0/10         1               1                0             Shutdown
      Fa0/15         1               0                0             Shutdown
      Fa0/16         1               0                0             Shutdown
------------------------------------------------------------------------
Total Addresses in System : 8
Max Addresses limit in System : 128


Switch2#show port-security address
          Secure Mac Address Table
------------------------------------------------------------------------
Vlan    Mac Address     Type            Ports    Remaining Age
                                                  (mins)
----    -----------     ----            -----    -------------
     3    0002.b933.eb12   SecureConfigured    Fa0/2     -
     4    0002.b933.eb13   SecureConfigured    Fa0/3     -
     5    0007.85aa.ad60   SecureConfigured    Fa0/4     -
     5    0050.7346.31c0   SecureConfigured    Fa0/5     -
     7    0004.9af2.8180   SecureConfigured    Fa0/6     -
     8    0050.7325.6fe0   SecureConfigured    Fa0/7     -
    10    0007.5057.e27f   SecureConfigured    Fa0/8     -
------------------------------------------------------------------------
Total Addresses in System : 7
Max Addresses limit in System : 128
```

Example 4-57 *Port Security on Switch1 and Switch2 (Continued)*

```
Switch2#show port-security
Secure Port     MaxSecureAddr  CurrentAddr  SecurityViolation Security Action
                  (Count)        (Count)       (Count)
-----------------------------------------------------------------------------
      Fa0/2         1              1            0               Shutdown
      Fa0/3         1              1            0               Shutdown
      Fa0/4         1              1            0               Shutdown
      Fa0/5         1              1            0               Shutdown
      Fa0/7         1              1            0               Shutdown
      Fa0/8         1              1            0               Shutdown
-----------------------------------------------------------------------------
Total Addresses in System : 7
Max Addresses limit in System : 128
```

CHAPTER 5

Practice Lab 5

This chapter gives you an extensive broad view of the CCIE Lab exam, giving you an opportunity to gauge yourself in one of the most complex scenarios. Each of these chapters has been carefully written to cover the topics in CCIE Security blueprint.

Preparing for the CCIE Lab exam is a very individual process. Conquering the lab exam requires lots of practice and hard work. The main objective of these labs is to provide you with sample scenarios for practice so that you can master the little skills to succeed on the real exam.

The lab is marked out of 100 points. You must complete the lab within 8 hours and obtain a minimum of 80 points to pass. As with all labs, this test has been written such that you should be able to complete all questions, including initial configuration (that is, IP addressing), within 8 hours, excluding cabling time. Allow up to 1 hour for cabling, using the provided instructions and observing the general guidelines. You can use any combination of routers as long as you fulfill the needs of the topology diagram. It is not compulsory to use routers of the same model.

NOTE   The real CCIE Lab does not require you to do any cabling or IP addressing.

Equipment List

- 8 routers with the following specifications (all routers are to be loaded with the latest Cisco IOS Software Release 12.1(T) train):

    R1 — 1 Ethernet, 1 BRI (with IP Plus image)

    R2 — 1 Ethernet, 1 BRI, 1 ATM (with IP Plus image)

    R3 — 1 Ethernet, 1 serial (with IP Plus image)

    R4 — 1 ATM (with IP Plus image)

    R5 — 2 serials (with IP Plus + IPSec 56 image)

    R6 — 1 Ethernet, 1 serial (with IP Plus + IPSec 56 image)

    R7 — 1 Ethernet, 1 serial (with IP Plus image)

    R8 — 1 Ethernet (with IP Plus image)

- 2 Switches (3550)
- 1 PIX with 2 interfaces (version 6.x with DES enabled)
- 1 Cisco Intrusion Detection System (IDS) 42xx appliance (version 3.x)
- 2 PCs:

    Windows 2000 Server with CiscoSecure ACS 3.x+

    Test PC with Cisco VPN Client 3.x software

General Guidelines

- Do not configure any static/default routes unless otherwise specified/required.
- Use DLCIs provided in the diagram.
- Use the IP addressing scheme provided in the diagram; do not change any IP addressing unless otherwise specified. In the CCIE Lab, initial configurations are loaded, and therefore IP addresses are not to be changed. In this book, each chapter has a separate lab topology with different IP addressing, so each chapter needs to be recabled and all IP addresses need to be redone from the previous chapter.
- Use **cisco** as the password for any authentication string, enable-password, and TACACS+/RADIUS key or for any other purpose unless otherwise specified.
- Add additional loopbacks as specified during this lab.
- Configure VLANs on Switch1 and Switch2 as per the diagram.
- All routers should be able to ping any interface in the network using the *optimal* path.
- You must time yourself to complete this lab in 8 hours.
- Do not use any external resources or answers provided in this book when attempting the lab.
- Do not configure any authentication or authorization on the console and aux ports.

NOTE   The real CCIE Lab exams are hands-on structures similar to this book. Each configuration exercise has preassigned point values. The candidate must obtain a minimum mark of 80% to pass. This book provides you with a similar structure to give you a better understanding and experience. For more information on CCIE exam structure, consult the following URL:

www.cisco.com/warp/customer/625/ccie/exam_preparation/preparation.html

---

Setting Up the Lab

You can use any combination of routers as long as you fulfill the topology diagram outlined in Figure 5-1. It is not compulsory to use the same model of routers.

Figure 5-1   *Lab Topology Diagram*

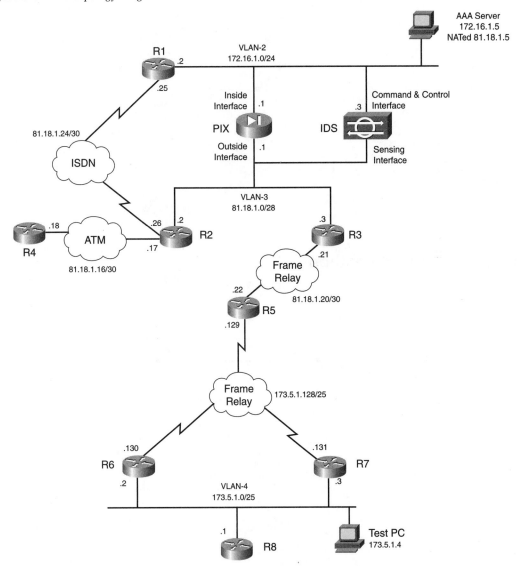

Frame Relay DLCI Information

Configure R1 as the Frame Relay switch and use Figure 5-2 for DLCI information. Only DLCIs indicated in Figure 5-2 should be mapped on the routers.

Figure 5-2 *Frame Relay DLCI Diagram*

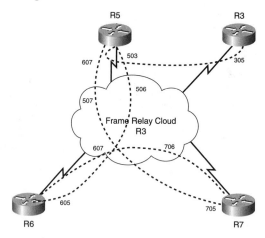

Routing Protocol Information

Use Figure 5-3 to configure all routing protocols.

Figure 5-3 *Routing Protocol Information*

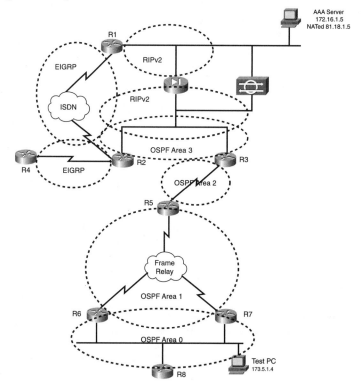

BGP Information

Use Figure 5-4 to configure BGP.

Figure 5-4   *BGP Information*

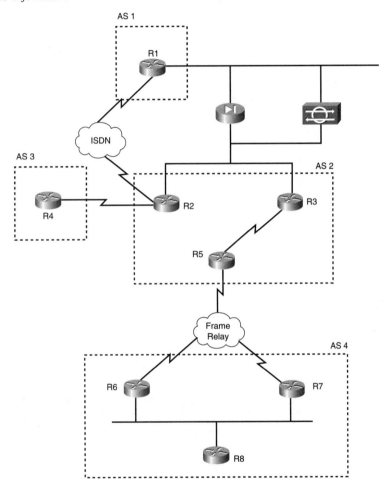

Cabling Instructions

Use Tables 5-1 and 5-2 for cabling all devices in your topology. It is not a must to use the same type or sequence of interface. You may use any combination of interface(s) as long as you fulfill the requirement.

Table 5-1   *Cabling Instructions (Ethernet)*

Ethernet Cabling	VLAN	Switch1	Switch2
Trunk port		Port 1	Port 1
R1-Ethernet0/0	2	Port 2	
PIX-inside-E1	2	Port 3	
PIX-outside-E0	3		Port 2
AAA server	2	Port 4	
R2-Fastethernet0/0	3		Port 3
R3-Ethernet0	3	Port 5	
R6-Ethernet0/0	4		Port 4
R7-Ethernet0/0	4	Port 6	
R8-Fastethernet0/0	4		Port 5
IDS Command and Control	2		Port 6
IDS Sensing	3	Port 7	
Test PC	4	Port 8	

Table 5-2   *Cabling Instructions (Serial)*

Back-to-Back Cabling	DTE-End	DCE-End
R5-to-frsw*	R5-serial1/0	R1-serial1/0
R5-to-frsw*	R5-serial1/1	R1-serial1/3
R6-to-frsw*	R6-serial1/0	R1-serial1/2
R7-to-frsw*	R7-serial0/0	R1-serial1/1
R3-to-frsw*	R3-serial0	R1-serial1/4

*frsw = Frame Relay switch R1

Practice Lab 5 Exercises

Read each exercise carefully before attempting it. Note that some parts of the exercise affect other parts, so it is very important to read the whole test before you begin.

This chapter has new additions in the topology (ATM and the IDS). The ATM switch is not required; ATM can be connected back-to-back for lab purposes. See Section 1.4 for ATM.

The steps in each exercise are not necessarily intended to be completed in order. They can be done in any order of preference or as you feel appropriate. There may be situations where the steps have intentionally been written in incorrect order to cause a problem. You have to identify the best approach and fulfill all the requirements.

Section 1.0: Basic Configuration (13 points)

1.1: IP Addressing (2 points)

1   Redraw a detailed topology with all necessary information.

2   Configure IP addressing as shown in Figure 5-1.

3   There should be no default gateway on any router except R1. R1 should only learn the default route via PIX and no other device. Do not advertise or originate the default gateway using any routing protocol.

4   Make sure you can ping all devices toward the end of the lab.

5   Configure the following loopbacks:

Loopback-1 11.11.11.11 on R1

Loopback-1 12.12.12.12 on R2

Loopback-1 13.13.13.13 on R3

Loopback-1 14.14.14.14 on R4

Loopback-2 14.14.1.1 on R4

Loopback-3 14.14.2.1 on R4

Loopback-1 15.15.15.15 on R5

Loopback-2 155.155.155.155 on R5

Loopback-5 192.168.1.0 on R5

Loopback-1 16.16.16.16 on R6

Loopback-5 192.168.2.0 on R6

Loopback-1 17.17.17.17 on R7

Loopback-1 18.18.18.18 on R8

Loopback-2 188.188.188.188 on R8

1.2: Frame Relay Configuration (5 points)

1 Configure R1 as a Frame Relay switch using the DLCI information provided for Frame Relay routing in Figure 5-2.

2 Configure a full-mesh Frame Relay network between R5, R6, and R7.

3 Do not configure subinterfaces on any router.

4 Configure static frame maps on all routers.

5 Configure Frame Relay routers to verify end-to-end communication. Local PVC status should be active only if the PVC status on the other end is active.

6 Configure three consecutive end-to-end confirmations received and sent before the interface status is changed from down to up.

1.3: LAN Switch Configuration (3 points)

1 Configure both switches with VLANs as shown in Table 5-1.

2 Configure ISL Trunking between the two switches. Port 1 on both switches is connected for trunking.

3 Configure VTP domain lab5 with strong authentication.

4 Switch1 should not be able to make any changes in the VLAN database.

5 Configure Switch2 management IP 172.16.1.52. Only VLAN-2 should be allowed to manage Switch2.

1.4: ATM Configuration (3 points)

1 Configure back-to-back ATM between R2 and R4.

2 Configure ATM PVC on both ends to be the same, as there is no ATM switch in between. Configure VPI=0 and VCI=101.

3 Configure LLC SNAP encapsulation.

4 Do not configure any subinterface.

NOTE   Define transmit clock source on one end using **atm clock INTERNAL**.

Section 2.0: Routing Configuration (25 points)

2.1: OSPF (7 points)

1   Configure OSPF as shown in Figure 5-3.

2   Configure simple authentication for all areas.

3   Area 1 should have full redundancy to the OSPF backbone if any router in Frame Relay goes down.

4   Do not configure any OSPF Virtual Link in Area 2 or Area 3.

5   All routers should see the Area 2 network.

6   R5 should do per-packet load balancing for VLAN-4 network in Area 0. Do not use any static routes to achieve this task.

7   Advertise Loopback-1 on R2, R3, R5, R6, R7, and R8 in OSPF.

8   Configure null routes for the following networks on R5 (major net should appear as one route on every device):

   151.151.151.0/24

   151.151.152.0/24

   151.151.153.0/24

2.2: EIGRP (3 points)

1   Configure EIGRP AS5 between the ATM network on R2 and R4.

2   Configure MD5 authentication in AS5.

3   Advertise Loopback-1, Loopback-2, and Loopback-3 on R4 in EIGRP AS5.

4   Configure and advertise the following null routes in EIGRP AS5 on R4:

   141.1.1.0/24

   141.1.2.0/24

   141.1.3.0/24

   141.1.5.0/24

   141.1.8.0/24

5   All routers including PIX should see networks advertised in AS5.

6   Null routes on R4 should be seen as one single route on all routers/PIX beyond R2.

2.3: RIP (3 points)

 1 Configure RIP between PIX, R1, R2, and R3 as shown in Figure 5-3.

 2 Use strong authentication.

 3 Do not configure a default route on PIX.

 4 Advertise Loopback-1 and Loopback-2 on R1 in RIPv2.

 5 Make sure all devices in VLAN-2 including AAA server can ping 11.11.11.11.

 6 Redistribute BGP into RIP on R3 so that PIX learns all BGP routes.

2.4: BGP (12 points)

2.4.1: Basic BGP Configuration (4 points)

 1 Configure BGP peers as shown in Figure 5-4.

 2 Configure R1 to peer with R2 and R3.

 3 All eBGP peers should use Loopback-1 for updates.

 4 Configure R2, R3, and R5 peers in AS2.

 5 Configure R2 to peer with R4.

 6 Configure R5 to peer with R6 and R7.

 7 Configure R8 to peer with R6 and R7 in AS4. R8 should learn all eBGP routes via R6 and R7 with the external next hop not visible.

 8 Advertise Loopback-2 on R5 and R8 in BGP.

2.4.2: BGP Authentication (2 points)

 1 Configure all BGP peers with strong authentication using password **cisco**.

2.4.3: BGP Path Selection (4 points)

 1 R8 should reach all AS2 routes via R7. Do not use Local Preference, MED, or Weight to achieve this task. Do not configure any methods on R8 to achieve this task.

 2 R1 should choose R2 to reach Loopback-2 of R8. For all other destinations, it should use normal BGP path selection criteria. Do not use MED, Prepend, or Local Preference to achieve this task. Do not configure any methods on R2/R3 to achieve this task.

2.4.4: BGP Route Filtering (2 points)

1 R4 should not receive any updates originating on AS4.

2 Do not configure a prefix list, community, or distribute list to achieve this task.

3 Do not use any route maps or IP ACL to achieve this task.

Section 3.0: ISDN Configuration (7 points)

3.1: Basic ISDN (3 points)

1 Configure ISDN on R1 and R2.

2 Use network 81.18.1.24/30.

3 Advertise ISDN network in EIGRP AS12 using strong authentication.

4 Redistribute EIGRP-12 into OSPF on R2.

ISDN information:

BRI number on R1 is 99047265

BRI number on R2 is 99047132

Switch-type = basic-net3

3.2: Advanced ISDN (4 points)

1 Configure R1 such that if the PIX outside interface goes down, R1 should route all traffic through ISDN via R2 and not PIX. In other words, if the PIX loses connectivity to the outside network, R1 should trigger ISDN as a redundant path.

2 All routes on R1 should converge via EIGRP.

3 Do not use dialer watch, HSRP, or any static routes to achieve this task.

Section 4.0: PIX Configuration (8 points)

4.1: Basic PIX Configuration (4 points)

1 Configure host name PIX with an inside/outside IP address as shown in Figure 5-1.

2 Configure RIP for inside and outside interfaces using MD5 authentication.

3 Configure RIP to advertise a default route to inside (R1) but not outside.

4 Configure global PAT translation for all networks behind PIX to be able to ping any networks outside the PIX.

5 PIX receives a RIP route for Loopback-2 on R1. Configure translation for the 22.22.22.0/24 network to 122.122.122.0/24. Do not use the **static** command to achieve this task. Configure a static route on R3 for 122.122.122.0/24 and advertise to the rest of the network.

6 Configure static NAT translation for R1 Loopback-1 11.11.11.11 to the same for BGP peering. Configure ACL accordingly. Configure the static route on R3 and redistribute accordingly.

4.2: Advanced PIX Configuration (4 points)

1 R3 should not be able to ping the PIX outside interface. Do not configure any ACL on R3.

2 Configure PIX for a simultaneous close TCP terminating sequence instead of a normal shutdown sequence as per RFC 793.

Section 5.0: IPSec Configuration (10 points)

5.1: IPSec LAN-to-LAN Router-to-Router (5 points)

1 Configure IPSec LAN-to-LAN between R5 and R6 for Loopback5 networks.

2 Configure a 56-bit encryption algorithm and no authentication.

3 Configure **cisco** as the preshared key.

4 Do not configure the **set peer** statement on R6.

5 Do not use an IPSec dynamic map on R5.

6 Configure a static route for Loopback5 on both ends.

5.2: L2TP over IPSec Using Certificates (5 points)

1 Configure L2TP over IPSec between PIX and Windows 2000 Test PC in VLAN-4 using certificates.

2 Obtain certificate(s) on PIX and Test PC from CA server 172.16.1.5 in VLAN-2.

3 Test PC in VLAN-4 is running Windows 2000 native IPSec/L2TP client to establish an encrypted L2TP tunnel to the PIX firewall.

4 Configure an IP address pool of 70.70.70.0/24 on PIX for L2TP users.

5   Configure L2TP group name **lab5** on PIX.

6   Configure external authentication using RADIUS.

7   Configure IPSec on PIX to encrypt L2TP traffic using a certificate.

8   Configure 56-bit encryption an all other parameters as appropriate.

9   Configure username **l2tp-user** password **cisco** on CiscoSecure ACS with necessary settings.

Section 6.0: Intrusion Detection System (IDS) (6 points)

6.1: Intrusion Detection System (IDS) (3 points)

1   Configure Cisco IDS sensor as shown in Figure 5-1.

2   Configure the Command and Control interface with IP address 172.16.1.3 in VLAN-2.

3   Configure the Sensing interface to monitor VLAN-3 and VLAN 4.

4   Use IDM (IDS Device Manager) to configure sensor parameters and IEV (IDS Event Viewer) to receive alarms from the sensor.

6.2: Advanced Intrusion Detection System (IDS) (3 points)

1   Change the ICMP echo signature to HIGH severity. Ping any device in VLAN 3 or 4 and make sure you receive alarms in IEV.

2   Configure a custom signature 55055 to trigger HIGH severity when any Telnet session tries to change the password on any device monitored.

Section 7.0: AAA (6 points)

7.1: AAA on the Switch (3 points)

1   Configure RADIUS authentication and authorization for Switch2 management.

2   Configure AAA to fall back local in the event the AAA server is not available.

3   Configure switch2 to send all authentication requests to RADIUS server 172.16.1.5 only.

4   Configure switch2 to send all accounting requests to RADIUS server 172.16.1.6 only.

5   Configure user **switch-telnet** password **cisco** on CiscoSecure ACS and switch2.

7.2: AAA on PIX (3 points)

1 Configure PIX management for Telnet authentication using TACACS+.

2 PIX management should be allowed from VLAN-2 only.

3 Configure user **pix-telnet** password **cisco** in CiscoSecure ACS.

4 PIX console should not be affected with AAA.

Section 8.0: Advanced Security (7 points)

8.1: Perimeter Security (3 points)

1 Deny all traceroute through R5 inbound toward PIX.

2 Traceroute through R5 toward Frame Relay network to R6, R7, and VLAN4 and R8 should work.

3 Configure egress ACL on Frame Relay link (173.5.1.128/25) toward R6 and R7.

8.2: Access Restriction (2 points)

1 Configure an effective method on R8 to restrict access to network 181.1.1.0/24 destination(s).

2 Do not use ACL to achieve this task.

8.3: Access Control (2 points)

1 Configure PIX to prevent web browsers from sending embedded commands in FTP requests. Each FTP command must be acknowledged before a new command is allowed.

2 All FTP connections sending any embedded commands should be dropped.

Section 9.0: IP Services and Protocol-Independent Features (12 points)

9.1: Network Address Translation (NAT) (4 points)

1 Configure NAT on Frame Relay routers R6 and R7 such that if they receive a packet on their outside interface (FR) with a destination address of 173.5.1.135, the destination address is translated to 173.5.1.40.

2 Configure NAT on Frame Relay routers R6 and R7 such that if they receive receive a packet on their inside interface (VLAN-4) with a destination address of 173.5.1.41, the destination address is translated to 173.5.1.136.

9.2: DHCP (3 points)

1 Configure R1 as a DHCP server for clients in VLAN-2 using 172.16.1.0/24 subnet.

2 Exclude static IP addresses already used in the topology diagram as per Figure 5-1.

3 Disable recording of address conflicts on the DHCP server.

4 Configure the DHCP server to assign IP address 172.16.1.100 to a specific application server in VLAN-2 based on its host name **LAB5**. This means that any workstation on VLAN-2 with host name **LAB5** should always obtain IP 172.16.1.100.

9.3: UDP Broadcast Forwarding (3 points)

1 Configure UDP broadcast forwarding for a server 173.5.1.52 located in VLAN-4 for custom application on port 2050.

2 UDP broadcast for NetBIOS name service should be denied.

9.4: Traffic-Based Accounting (2 points)

1 Configure R1 for accounting all IP inbound/outbound traffic on VLAN-2.

2 The accounting information is required for billing departments for network usage on a per-host per-byte basis.

Section 10.0: Security Violations (6 points)

10.1: Smurf Attack (3 points)

1 AAA/CA server in VLAN-2 is getting a smurf attack.

2 Configure access restriction to prevent this from happening again in the future.

3 You do not have access to the PIX, IDS, or any router in the network to secure this.

4 You do not have access to the AAA/CA server to configure anything on it.

5 With these limitations, your task is to secure this.

10.2: Basic VLAN Hopping Attack (3 points)

1 An unknown device can spoof switch2 to believe it is a valid switch that needs trunking.

2 If the attacker succeeds in negotiating the trunk with switch2, it can send and receive traffic on all VLANs configured.

3 Protect switch2 to prevent this type of attack.

Verification, Hints, and Troubleshooting Tips

This chapter contains some good hidden issues, which you will see in the sections to follow. Some tasks might not be clear as to what solution or method is required. It is very important to understand the question's requirement and the restriction given. If it isn't clear, ask the proctor for clarification.

The hints provided here are to be used as a guideline and address some or all parts of the corresponding exercise question. They are not listed in any order.

Section 1.0: Basic Configuration

1.1: IP Addressing

1 Redraw a detailed topology with all necessary information to assist you throughout the lab.

2 Configure IP addressing as shown in Figure 5-1. Do not change any subnet masks.

3 Do not configure default gateway on any router except R1. R1 should learn the default route via PIX only. In the event ISDN comes up on R1 for Section 3.2, it should not learn any default route via ISDN. R1 should converge all individual network routes via ISDN. Do not advertise or originate default-gateway on any other router using any routing protocol. All other routers should have **Gateway of last resort is not set** in the routing table.

4 Make sure you can ping all devices including AAA server.

5 Configure loopback(s) as indicated to be used in the exercises to follow.

1.2: Frame Relay Configuration

1 Configure R1 as a Frame Relay switch, and route DLCIs as shown in Figure 5-2.

2 Configure a full-mesh Frame Relay network between R5, R6, and R7. Do not configure subinterfaces on any router.

3 Configure static frame maps on all routers.

4 Configure a Frame Relay map class for end-to-end bidirectional KEEPALIVE. Apply the map class to all serial interfaces on FR routers where DLCI maps are configured:

```
map-class frame-relay lab5
 frame-relay end-to-end keepalive mode bidirectional
 frame-relay end-to-end keepalive success-events send 3
 frame-relay end-to-end keepalive success-events recv 3
 no frame-relay adaptive-shaping
```

5 Configure three end-to-end success-events for send/receive before the interface status is changed from down to up as demonstrated in the preceding configuration.

1.3: LAN Switch Configuration

1 Configure VLAN assignment on both switches as per Table 5-1.

2 Configure ISL trunking between the two switches on Port 1.

3 Configure VTP domain **lab5** with password **cisco**.

4 Configure Switch2 as VTP server; add/delete VLANs as necessary.

5 Configure Switch1 as VTP client for it not to be able to make any changes in the VLAN database.

6 Configure Switch2 management IP 172.16.1.52 on the VLAN-2 interface and configure ACL for network 172.16.1.0/24 to allow VTY access:

```
interface Vlan1
 no ip address
 shutdown
!
interface Vlan2
 ip address 172.16.1.52 255.255.255.0
!
access-list 1 permit 172.16.1.0 0.0.0.255
!
line con 0
 exec-timeout 0 0
 escape-character 27
line vty 0 4
 access-class 1 in
 password cisco
line vty 5 15
 access-class 1 in
 password cisco
!
end
```

1.4: ATM Configuration

1   Configure back-to-back ATM between R2 and R4.

2   Configure the same PVC mappings on both routers, as they are connected back-to-back, no ATM switch in between, as shown in the example following item 5.

3   Configure ATM PVC on both ends to be the same, as there is no ATM switch in between. Configure VPI=0 and VCI=101, as shown in the example following item 5.

4   Configure aal5snap encapsulation, as shown in the example following item 5.

5   Do not configure any subinterface.

```
<snip from R2 config>

interface ATM3/0
 ip address 81.18.1.17 255.255.255.252
 atm clock INTERNAL
 no atm ilmi-keepalive
 pvc 0 0/101
  protocol ip 81.18.1.18 broadcast
  broadcast
  encapsulation aal5snap


<snip from R4 config>
interface ATM0/0
 ip address 81.18.1.18 255.255.255.252
 no atm ilmi-keepalive
 pvc 0 0/101
  protocol ip 81.18.1.17 broadcast
  broadcast
  encapsulation aal5snap


! Verify ATM using following commands;

R2#show atm map
Map list 0_ATM3/0 : PERMANENT
ip 81.18.1.18 maps to VC 1, VPI 0, VCI 101, ATM3/0
        , broadcast


R2#show atm vc
             VCD /                                    Peak  Avg/Min Burst
  Interface  Name     VPI  VCI Type  Encaps  SC  Kbps Kbps  Cells  Sts
  3/0        0          0  101 PVC   SNAP    UBR 155000             UP
```

```
R4#show atm map
Map list 0_ATM0/0 : PERMANENT
ip 81.18.1.17 maps to VC 1, VPI 0, VCI 101, ATM0/0
        , broadcast

R4#show atm vc
              VCD /                                  Peak  Avg/Min Burst
Interface     Name    VPI   VCI  Type  Encaps   SC   Kbps  Kbps    Cells  Sts
0/0           0       0     101  PVC   SNAP     UBR  155000                UP
```

Section 2.0: Routing Configuration

2.1: OSPF

1 Configure OSPF as shown in Figure 5-3.

2 Configure simple authentication for all areas.

3 Tricky question for Area 3. The problem is you cannot configure Area 2 as a virtual link area.

4 The workaround is to configure a GRE tunnel between R3 and R5 and advertise it in Area 0. This way, you are extending Area 0 to R3, and Area 3 converges without configuring a virtual link.

5 This solution is very common when you have to address discontiguous Area 0s and you want to merge them:

```
! <snip from R5>
interface Tunnel1
 ip address 10.1.1.1 255.255.255.0
 ip ospf authentication-key cisco
 tunnel source Serial1/1
 tunnel destination 81.18.1.21
!
interface Serial1/0
 ip address 173.5.1.129 255.255.255.128
 encapsulation frame-relay
 no ip route-cache
 ip ospf authentication-key cisco
 ip ospf network point-to-multipoint
 no ip mroute-cache
 frame-relay map ip 173.5.1.130 506 broadcast
 frame-relay map ip 173.5.1.131 507 broadcast
 no frame-relay inverse-arp
!
interface Serial1/1
 ip address 81.18.1.22 255.255.255.252
```

```
 encapsulation frame-relay
 ip ospf authentication-key cisco
 ip ospf network point-to-point
 frame-relay map ip 81.18.1.21 503 broadcast
 no frame-relay inverse-arp
!
router ospf 110
 router-id 5.5.5.5
 log-adjacency-changes
 area 0 authentication
 area 1 authentication
 area 1 virtual-link 6.6.6.6 authentication-key cisco
 area 1 virtual-link 7.7.7.7 authentication-key cisco
 area 2 authentication
 summary-address 151.151.0.0 255.255.0.0
 redistribute static metric 1 subnets route-map null-routes
 network 10.1.1.0 0.0.0.255 area 0
 network 81.18.1.20 0.0.0.3 area 2
 network 173.5.1.128 0.0.0.127 area 1
!
ip route 151.151.151.0 255.255.255.0 Null0
ip route 151.151.152.0 255.255.255.0 Null0
ip route 151.151.153.0 255.255.255.0 Null0
!
access-list 15 permit 151.151.151.0 0.0.0.255
access-list 15 permit 151.151.152.0 0.0.0.255
access-list 15 permit 151.151.153.0 0.0.0.255
!
route-map null-routes permit 10
 match ip address 15
!

! <snip from R3>
interface Tunnel1
 ip address 10.1.1.2 255.255.255.0
 ip ospf authentication-key cisco
 tunnel source Serial0
 tunnel destination 81.18.1.22
!
interface Ethernet0
 ip address 81.18.1.10 255.255.255.240 secondary
 ip address 81.18.1.3 255.255.255.240
 ip ospf authentication-key cisco
!
interface Serial0
 ip address 81.18.1.21 255.255.255.252
```

```
encapsulation frame-relay
ip ospf authentication-key cisco
ip ospf network point-to-point
frame-relay map ip 81.18.1.22 305 broadcast
no frame-relay inverse-arp
!
router ospf 110
router-id 3.3.3.3
area 0 authentication
area 2 authentication
area 3 authentication
network 10.1.1.0 0.0.0.255 area 0
network 81.18.1.0 0.0.0.7 area 3
network 81.18.1.20 0.0.0.3 area 2
```

6   You will still require configuring virtual link in Area 1 for all other areas to learn Area 0 routes plus for Area 1 redundancy. Extending the Area 0 using Tunnel will not help because no networks (other than Tunnel) are advertised in Area 0 on R3 and R5.

7   R5 will learn two routes for the VLAN-4 network, one via R6 and another via R7. By default OSPF supports six equal-cost paths. Per-destination or per-packet load balancing depends on the switching type. By default, all interfaces are Fastswitch enabled which does per-destination load balancing. Configure process switching for per-packet load balancing using the **no ip route-cache** command:

```
R5#show ip route
Codes: C - connected, S - static, I - IGRP, R - RIP, M - mobile, B - BGP
       D - EIGRP, EX - EIGRP external, O - OSPF, IA - OSPF inter area
       N1 - OSPF NSSA external type 1, N2 - OSPF NSSA external type 2
       E1 - OSPF external type 1, E2 - OSPF external type 2, E - EGP
       i - IS-IS, L1 - IS-IS level-1, L2 - IS-IS level-2, ia - IS-IS inter area
       * - candidate default, U - per-user static route, o - ODR
       P - periodic downloaded static route

Gateway of last resort is not set

     81.0.0.0/8 is variably subnetted, 2 subnets, 2 masks
O IA    81.18.1.0/28 [110/11121] via 10.1.1.2, 00:15:08, Tunnel1
C       81.18.1.20/30 is directly connected, Serial1/1
     173.5.0.0/16 is variably subnetted, 4 subnets, 2 masks
C       173.5.1.128/25 is directly connected, Serial1/0
O       173.5.1.131/32 [110/781] via 173.5.1.131, 00:22:39, Serial1/0
O       173.5.1.130/32 [110/781] via 173.5.1.130, 00:22:39, Serial1/0
O       173.5.1.0/25 [110/791] via 173.5.1.130, 00:15:08, Serial1/0
                      [110/791] via 173.5.1.131, 00:15:09, Serial1/0
     10.0.0.0/24 is subnetted, 1 subnets
C       10.1.1.0 is directly connected, Tunnel1
```

```
R5#show ip interface serial 1/0
Serial1/0 is up, line protocol is up
  Internet address is 173.5.1.129/25
  Broadcast address is 255.255.255.255
  Address determined by non-volatile memory
  MTU is 1500 bytes
  Helper address is not set
  Directed broadcast forwarding is disabled
  Multicast reserved groups joined: 224.0.0.5 224.0.0.6
  Outgoing access list is not set
  Inbound  access list is not set
  Proxy ARP is enabled
  Local Proxy ARP is disabled
  Security level is default
  Split horizon is disabled
  ICMP redirects are always sent
  ICMP unreachables are always sent
  ICMP mask replies are never sent
  IP fast switching is enabled
  IP fast switching on the same interface is enabled
  IP Flow switching is disabled
  IP Fast switching turbo vector
  IP multicast fast switching is enabled
  IP multicast distributed fast switching is disabled
  IP route-cache flags are Fast
  Router Discovery is disabled
  IP output packet accounting is disabled
  IP access violation accounting is disabled
  TCP/IP header compression is disabled
  RTP/IP header compression is disabled
  Probe proxy name replies are disabled
  Policy routing is disabled
  Network address translation is disabled
  WCCP Redirect outbound is disabled
  WCCP Redirect inbound is disabled
  WCCP Redirect exclude is disabled
  BGP Policy Mapping is disabled

! Configure Process switching on R5 Serial 1/0 for per-packet load balancing:

<snip from R5>
interface Serial1/0
 ip address 173.5.1.129 255.255.255.128
 encapsulation frame-relay
 no ip route-cache
```

```
R5#show ip interface serial 1/0
Serial1/0 is up, line protocol is up
  Internet address is 173.5.1.129/25
  Broadcast address is 255.255.255.255
  Address determined by non-volatile memory
  MTU is 1500 bytes
  Helper address is not set
  Directed broadcast forwarding is disabled
  Multicast reserved groups joined: 224.0.0.5 224.0.0.6
  Outgoing access list is not set
  Inbound  access list is not set
  Proxy ARP is enabled
  Local Proxy ARP is disabled
  Security level is default
  Split horizon is disabled
  ICMP redirects are always sent
  ICMP unreachables are always sent
  ICMP mask replies are never sent
  IP fast switching is disabled
  IP fast switching on the same interface is disabled
  IP Flow switching is disabled
  IP Fast switching turbo vector
  IP multicast fast switching is disabled
  IP multicast distributed fast switching is disabled
  IP route-cache flags are None
  Router Discovery is disabled
  IP output packet accounting is disabled
  IP access violation accounting is disabled
  TCP/IP header compression is disabled
  RTP/IP header compression is disabled
  Probe proxy name replies are disabled
  Policy routing is disabled
  Network address translation is disabled
  WCCP Redirect outbound is disabled
  WCCP Redirect inbound is disabled
  WCCP Redirect exclude is disabled
  BGP Policy Mapping is disabled



R5#show ip route 173.5.1.0
Routing entry for 173.5.1.0/25
  Known via "ospf 110", distance 110, metric 791, type intra area
  Last update from 173.5.1.131 on Serial1/0, 00:15:14 ago
  Routing Descriptor Blocks:
    173.5.1.130, from 8.8.8.8, 00:15:14 ago, via Serial1/0
```

```
              Route metric is 791, traffic share count is 1
       * 173.5.1.131, from 8.8.8.8, 00:15:14 ago, via Serial1/0
              Route metric is 791, traffic share count is 1

R5#ping 173.5.1.1

Type escape sequence to abort.
Sending 5, 100-byte ICMP Echos to 173.5.1.1, timeout is 2 seconds:
!!!!!
Success rate is 100 percent (5/5), round-trip min/avg/max = 64/66/68 ms

R5#show ip route 173.5.1.0
Routing entry for 173.5.1.0/25
  Known via "ospf 110", distance 110, metric 791, type intra area
  Last update from 173.5.1.131 on Serial1/0, 00:15:26 ago
  Routing Descriptor Blocks:
  * 173.5.1.130, from 8.8.8.8, 00:15:26 ago, via Serial1/0
       Route metric is 791, traffic share count is 1
    173.5.1.131, from 8.8.8.8, 00:15:26 ago, via Serial1/0
       Route metric is 791, traffic share count is 1

R5#ping 173.5.1.1

Type escape sequence to abort.
Sending 5, 100-byte ICMP Echos to 173.5.1.1, timeout is 2 seconds:
!!!!!
Success rate is 100 percent (5/5), round-trip min/avg/max = 64/67/68 ms
R5#show ip route 173.5.1.0
Routing entry for 173.5.1.0/25
  Known via "ospf 110", distance 110, metric 791, type intra area
  Last update from 173.5.1.131 on Serial1/0, 00:15:29 ago
  Routing Descriptor Blocks:
    173.5.1.130, from 8.8.8.8, 00:15:29 ago, via Serial1/0
       Route metric is 791, traffic share count is 1
  * 173.5.1.131, from 8.8.8.8, 00:15:29 ago, via Serial1/0
       Route metric is 791, traffic share count is 1
```

8 Configure null routes on R5 for 151.151.151.0, 151.151.152.0, and 151.151.153.0.
Redistribute statics in OSPF and summarize to /16. See the R5 in the example for item 5.

NOTE   See this URL for more info on OSPF Authentication on a Virtual Link:

www.cisco.com/warp/public/104/27.html

See this URL for more info on OSPF Load Balancing:

www.cisco.com/warp/public/105/46.html

2.2: EIGRP

1 Configure EIGRP AS 5 between the ATM network on R2 and R4.

2 Advertise Loopback-1 and Loopback-2 on R4 in EIGRP AS 5 and advertise the null routes in EIGRP AS 5 on R4.

3 Redistribute EIGRP in OSPF and RIP on R2.

4 Remember, there is no three-way redistribution on the router—EIGRP redistributing into OSPF and OSPF into RIP. OSPF cannot be used as transit protocol for EIGRP routes to get into RIP. RIP will not inherit EIGRP routes because OSPF will not advertise EIGRP derived routes to RIP; it will advertise OSFP derived routes only. Therefore, you must think of redistribution as two-way only and not three-way.

5 All routers including PIX should see networks advertised in AS 5. Refer to the example following item 7.

6 Null routes on R4 need to be summarized, but not on R4. Summarize them on R2 in OSPF and RIP, as the question requires summarization beyond R2, which means R2 must see all individual routes. Refer to the example following item 7.

7 Configure MD5 authentication. Note that it is important to enter EIGRP authentication commands in the right order. For example, configure the authentication mode before defining the key-chain under the interface. If you do not get the right steps, you will find that the adjacency will not form. To troubleshoot such issues, remove authentication entirely and see if adjacency is OK; that way you can rule out any authentication issues. Refer to the following URL and the configuration example that follows:

EIGRP Route Authentication: www.cisco.com/univercd/cc/td/doc/product/software /ios112/eigrpmd5.htm#xtocid161894

```
! <Snip from R2 config>
key chain lab5
 key 1
  key-string cisco
!
interface FastEthernet0/0
 ip address 81.18.1.2 255.255.255.240
 ip rip authentication mode md5
 ip rip authentication key-chain lab5
 ip summary-address rip 141.1.0.0 255.255.240.0
!
interface ATM3/0
 ip address 81.18.1.17 255.255.255.252
 ip authentication mode eigrp 5 md5
 ip authentication key-chain eigrp 5 lab5
 atm clock INTERNAL
```

```
 no atm ilmi-keepalive
 pvc 0 0/101
  protocol ip 81.18.1.18 broadcast
  broadcast
  encapsulation aal5snap
!
router eigrp 5
 redistribute ospf 110
 network 81.18.1.16 0.0.0.3
 default-metric 1000 100 255 1 1500
 no auto-summary
 no eigrp log-neighbor-changes
!
router ospf 110
 router-id 2.2.2.2
 log-adjacency-changes
 area 3 authentication
 summary-address 141.1.0.0 255.255.240.0
 redistribute eigrp 5 metric 1 subnets
 network 81.18.1.0 0.0.0.7 area 3
!
router rip
 version 2
 redistribute eigrp 5 metric 1
 network 81.0.0.0
 no auto-summary
!


! <Snip from R4 config>
key chain lab5
 key 1
   key-string cisco
!
interface Loopback1
 ip address 14.14.1.1 255.255.255.0
!
interface Loopback2
 ip address 14.14.2.1 255.255.255.0
!
interface ATM0/0
 ip address 81.18.1.18 255.255.255.252
 ip authentication mode eigrp 5 md5
```

```
ip authentication key-chain eigrp 5 lab5
no atm ilmi-keepalive
pvc 0 0/101
  protocol ip 81.18.1.17 broadcast
  broadcast
  encapsulation aal5snap
!
router eigrp 5
 redistribute static
 network 14.14.1.0 0.0.0.255
 network 14.14.2.0 0.0.0.255
 network 81.18.1.16 0.0.0.3
 default-metric 10000 100 255 1 1500
 no auto-summary
 no eigrp log-neighbor-changes
!
ip route 141.1.1.0 255.255.255.0 Null0
ip route 141.1.2.0 255.255.255.0 Null0
ip route 141.1.3.0 255.255.255.0 Null0
ip route 141.1.5.0 255.255.255.0 Null0
ip route 141.1.8.0 255.255.255.0 Null0
```

2.3: RIP

1 Configure RIP between PIX, R1, R2, and R3 using MD5 authentication.

2 Push the default route to inside R1, but not on the outside.

3 Advertise Loopback-1 and Loopback-2 on R1 in RIPv2.

4 All devices in VLAN-2 will be able to ping 11.11.11.11 only if the default gateway is set to R1 and not PIX. Remember, PIX is not a routing device; therefore, it will not reroute any packets arriving on an interface out the same interface.

5 To show you an example, see Figure 5-5a and Figure 5-5b, captured from an AAA/CA server where the default gateway was set to PIX and was not able to ping 11.11.11.11. After changing the default gateway to R1, you can ping 11.11.11.11 and all other networks outside the PIX.

6 Redistribute BGP into RIP on R3 so that PIX learns all BGP routes. Remember to configure **bgp redistribute-internal**, as iBGP routes do not get redistributed into IGP unless forced to use this command.

Figure 5-5a *IP Configuration Settings on AAA Server with Default Gateway Set to PIX*

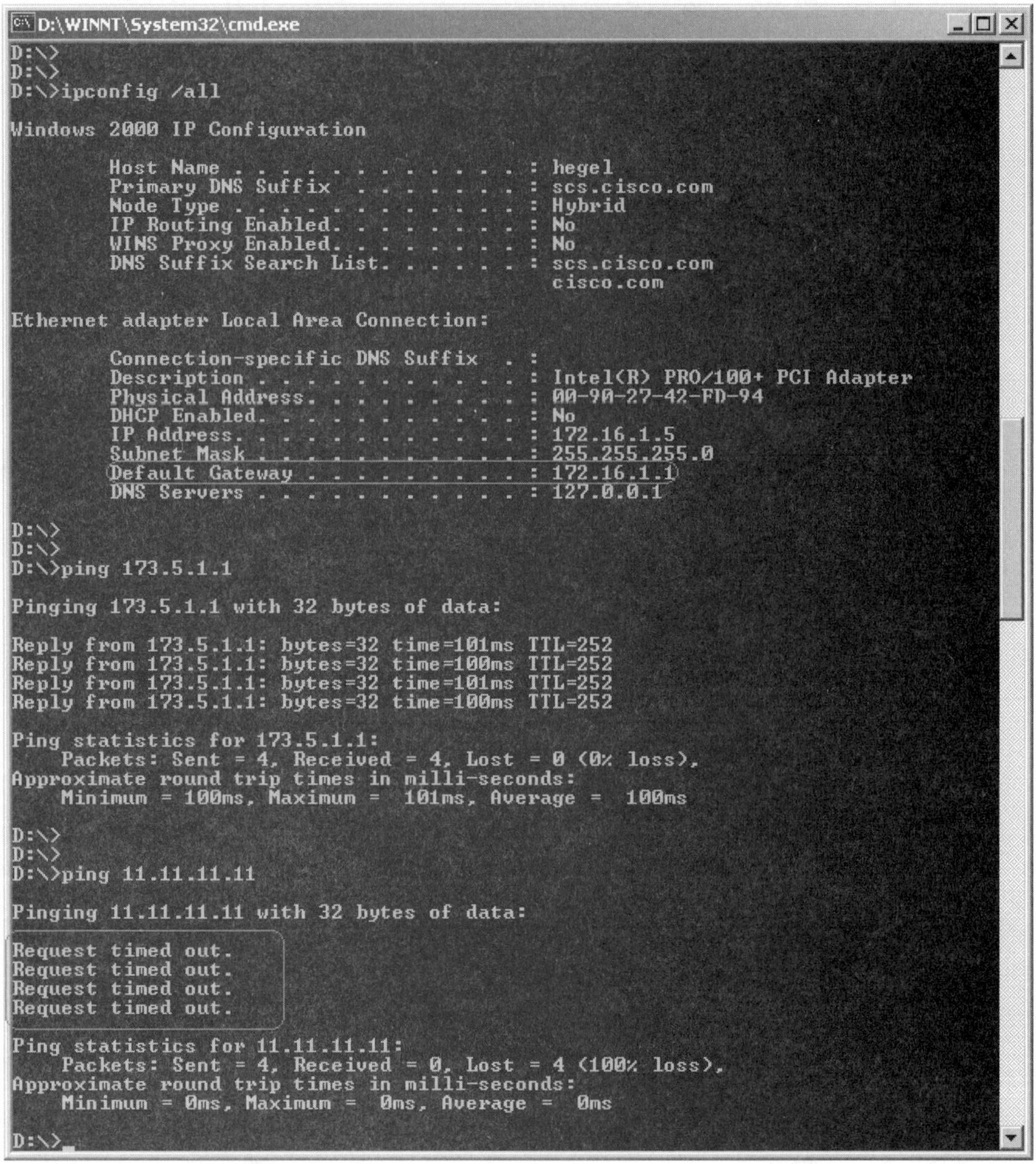

```
D:\WINNT\System32\cmd.exe                                              _ □ ×
D:\>
D:\>
D:\>ipconfig /all

Windows 2000 IP Configuration

        Host Name . . . . . . . . . . . . . : hegel
        Primary DNS Suffix  . . . . . . . . : scs.cisco.com
        Node Type . . . . . . . . . . . . . : Hybrid
        IP Routing Enabled. . . . . . . . . : No
        WINS Proxy Enabled. . . . . . . . . : No
        DNS Suffix Search List. . . . . . . : scs.cisco.com
                                              cisco.com

Ethernet adapter Local Area Connection:

        Connection-specific DNS Suffix  . :
        Description . . . . . . . . . . . . : Intel(R) PRO/100+ PCI Adapter
        Physical Address. . . . . . . . . . : 00-90-27-42-FD-94
        DHCP Enabled. . . . . . . . . . . . : No
        IP Address. . . . . . . . . . . . . : 172.16.1.5
        Subnet Mask . . . . . . . . . . . . : 255.255.255.0
        Default Gateway . . . . . . . . . . : 172.16.1.1
        DNS Servers . . . . . . . . . . . . : 127.0.0.1

D:\>
D:\>
D:\>ping 173.5.1.1

Pinging 173.5.1.1 with 32 bytes of data:

Reply from 173.5.1.1: bytes=32 time=101ms TTL=252
Reply from 173.5.1.1: bytes=32 time=100ms TTL=252
Reply from 173.5.1.1: bytes=32 time=101ms TTL=252
Reply from 173.5.1.1: bytes=32 time=100ms TTL=252

Ping statistics for 173.5.1.1:
    Packets: Sent = 4, Received = 4, Lost = 0 (0% loss),
Approximate round trip times in milli-seconds:
    Minimum = 100ms, Maximum =  101ms, Average =  100ms

D:\>
D:\>
D:\>ping 11.11.11.11

Pinging 11.11.11.11 with 32 bytes of data:

Request timed out.
Request timed out.
Request timed out.
Request timed out.

Ping statistics for 11.11.11.11:
    Packets: Sent = 4, Received = 0, Lost = 4 (100% loss),
Approximate round trip times in milli-seconds:
    Minimum = 0ms, Maximum =  0ms, Average =  0ms

D:\>
```

Figure 5-5b *IP Configuration Settings on AAA Server with Default Gateway Set to R1*

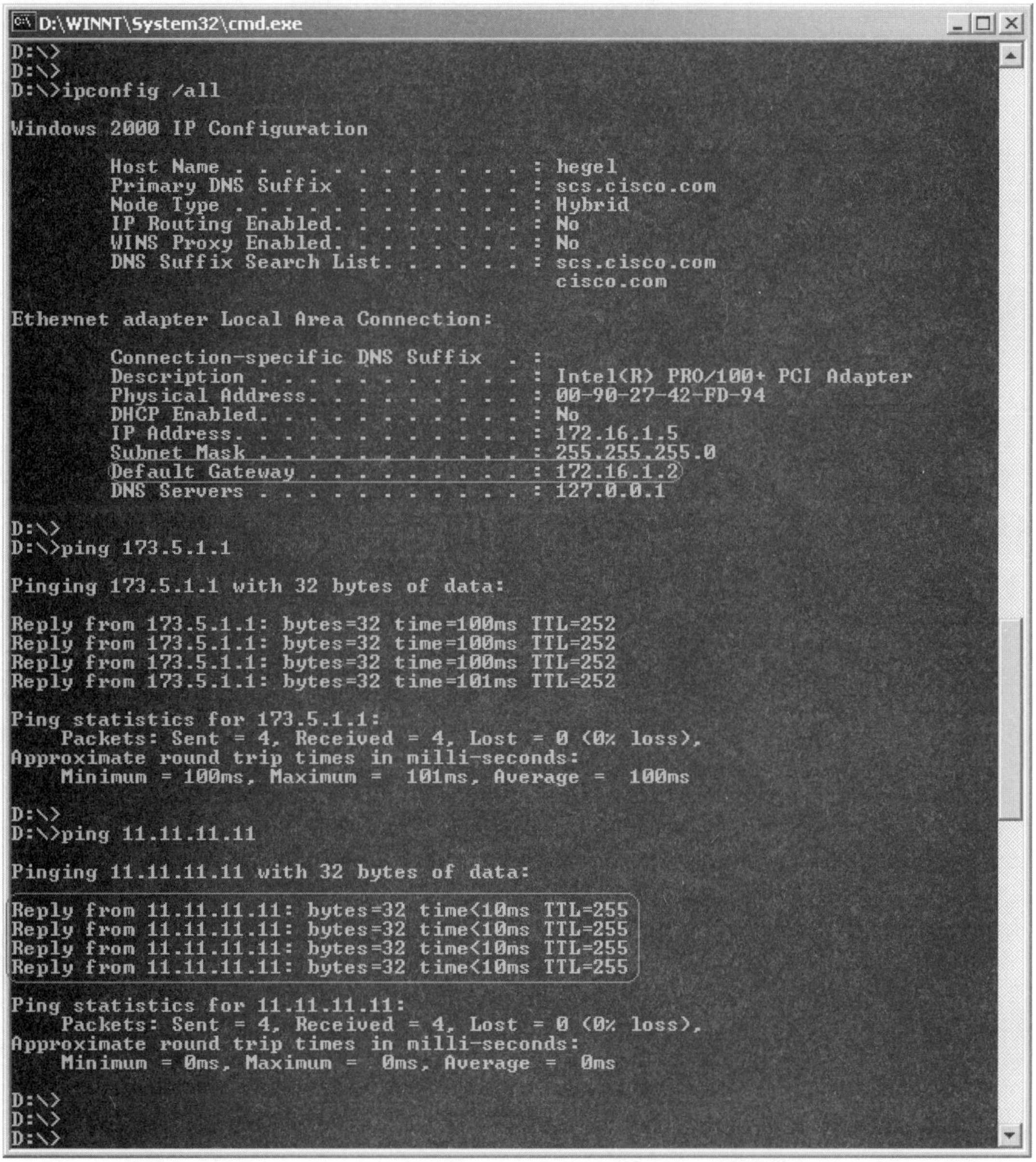

```
D:\WINNT\System32\cmd.exe                                                    _ □ ×
D:\>
D:\>
D:\>ipconfig /all

Windows 2000 IP Configuration

        Host Name . . . . . . . . . . . . : hegel
        Primary DNS Suffix  . . . . . . . : scs.cisco.com
        Node Type . . . . . . . . . . . . : Hybrid
        IP Routing Enabled. . . . . . . . : No
        WINS Proxy Enabled. . . . . . . . : No
        DNS Suffix Search List. . . . . . : scs.cisco.com
                                            cisco.com

Ethernet adapter Local Area Connection:

        Connection-specific DNS Suffix  . :
        Description . . . . . . . . . . . : Intel(R) PRO/100+ PCI Adapter
        Physical Address. . . . . . . . . : 00-90-27-42-FD-94
        DHCP Enabled. . . . . . . . . . . : No
        IP Address. . . . . . . . . . . . : 172.16.1.5
        Subnet Mask . . . . . . . . . . . : 255.255.255.0
        Default Gateway . . . . . . . . . : 172.16.1.2
        DNS Servers . . . . . . . . . . . : 127.0.0.1

D:\>
D:\>ping 173.5.1.1

Pinging 173.5.1.1 with 32 bytes of data:

Reply from 173.5.1.1: bytes=32 time=100ms TTL=252
Reply from 173.5.1.1: bytes=32 time=100ms TTL=252
Reply from 173.5.1.1: bytes=32 time=100ms TTL=252
Reply from 173.5.1.1: bytes=32 time=101ms TTL=252

Ping statistics for 173.5.1.1:
    Packets: Sent = 4, Received = 4, Lost = 0 (0% loss),
Approximate round trip times in milli-seconds:
    Minimum = 100ms, Maximum =  101ms, Average =  100ms

D:\>
D:\>ping 11.11.11.11

Pinging 11.11.11.11 with 32 bytes of data:

Reply from 11.11.11.11: bytes=32 time<10ms TTL=255
Reply from 11.11.11.11: bytes=32 time<10ms TTL=255
Reply from 11.11.11.11: bytes=32 time<10ms TTL=255
Reply from 11.11.11.11: bytes=32 time<10ms TTL=255

Ping statistics for 11.11.11.11:
    Packets: Sent = 4, Received = 4, Lost = 0 (0% loss),
Approximate round trip times in milli-seconds:
    Minimum = 0ms, Maximum =  0ms, Average =  0ms

D:\>
D:\>
D:\>
```

2.4: BGP

2.4.1: Basic BGP Configuration

1 Configure BGP peers as shown in Figure 5-4.

2 Configure only the eBGP peer to use Loopback-1 for the update source, not for iBGP peering.

3 Configure R1 to peer with R2 and R3.

4 Configure R2, R3, and R5 peers in AS2. Configure R3 as route reflector in AS2.

5 Configure R2 to peer with R4.

6 Configure R5 to peer with R6 and R7.

7 Configure R8 to peer with R6 and R7 in AS4. Configure next-hop-self on R6 and R7 for R8 peering so that the external next hop is not visible to R8.

8 Advertise Loopback-2 on R5 and R8 in BGP for tasks to follow.

2.4.2: BGP Authentication

1 Configure all BGP peers with MD5 authentication using password **cisco**.

2 A hidden problem. BGP through PIX with MD5 authentication will not work. When the PIX is translating the packet back on to itself on the outside/inside interface, the TCP sequence number is randomized as a security measure through its adaptive security algorithm (ASA). The changing of the sequence number affects the MD5 hashing used by the BGP peers to match the passwords. So, one peer uses the proper sequence number to encrypt the password and sends the packet off to the PIX. The PIX translates this packet (to itself) and changes the sequence number on the packet. The other BGP peer gets the packet and uses this new sequence number to decrypt the password. This process causes the decrypting peer to see a different password, which it logs as the BGP MD5 failed attempt.

3 The solution is to disable the sequence number randomization using the **norandomseq** option in the **static** command as follows:

```
PIX(config)# show static
static (inside,outside) 11.11.11.11 11.11.11.11
  netmask 255.255.255.255 0 0 norandomseq,nailed
```

2.4.3: BGP Path Selection

1 Configure R6 to prepend AS-PATH for all inbound AS2 routes from R5. R8 will then choose R7 to reach AS2 routes, as demonstrated in the following example:

```
<snip from R6 config>
router bgp 4
 bgp router-id 6.6.6.6
```

```
 neighbor 15.15.15.15 remote-as 2
 neighbor 15.15.15.15 ebgp-multihop 255
 neighbor 15.15.15.15 update-source Loopback1
 neighbor 15.15.15.15 route-map AS2-prepend in
!
ip as-path access-list 1 permit _2_
!
route-map AS2-prepend permit 10
 match as-path 1
 set as-path prepend 2 2
!
route-map AS2-prepend permit 20
!
```

```
R8#show ip bgp
BGP table version is 3, local router ID is 8.8.8.8
Status codes: s suppressed, d damped, h history, * valid, > best, i - internal
Origin codes: i - IGP, e - EGP, ? - incomplete
```

Network	Next Hop	Metric	LocPrf	Weight	Path
* i155.155.155.0/24	173.5.1.2	0	100	0	2 2 2 i
*>i	173.5.1.3	0	100	0	2 i
*> 188.188.188.0/24	0.0.0.0	0		32768	i

2 Configure weight on R1 to choose R2 to reach Loopback-2 of R8, as demonstrated in the following example:

```
<snip from R1 config>
router bgp 1
 bgp router-id 1.1.1.1
 neighbor 12.12.12.12 remote-as 2
 neighbor 12.12.12.12 ebgp-multihop 255
 neighbor 12.12.12.12 update-source Loopback1
 neighbor 12.12.12.12 route-map R8-Loopback2 in
!
access-list 1 permit 188.188.188.0
!
route-map R8-Loopback2 permit 10
 match ip address 1
 set weight 100
!
route-map R8-Loopback2 permit 20
!
```

```
R1#show ip bgp
```

```
BGP table version is 4, local router ID is 1.1.1.1
Status codes: s suppressed, d damped, h history, * valid, > best,
  i - internal,
               r RIB-failure
Origin codes: i - IGP, e - EGP, ? - incomplete

   Network          Next Hop          Metric LocPrf Weight Path
*> 155.155.155.0/24 13.13.13.13                        0 2 i
*                   12.12.12.12                         0 2 i
*> 188.188.188.0/24 12.12.12.12                      100 2 4 i
*                   13.13.13.13                         0 2 4 i
```

2.4.4: BGP Route Filtering

1 Configure AS-PATH access-list with filter-list on R2 to filter AS4 updates to R4, as demonstrated in the following example:

```
<snip from R2 config>
router bgp 2
 bgp router-id 2.2.2.2
neighbor 14.14.14.14 remote-as 3
 neighbor 14.14.14.14 ebgp-multihop 255
 neighbor 14.14.14.14 password cisco
 neighbor 14.14.14.14 update-source Loopback1
 neighbor 14.14.14.14 filter-list 1 out
 !
ip as-path access-list 1 deny _4_
ip as-path access-list 1 permit .*
! BGP table on R4 before applying filter-list on R2.
R4#show ip bgp
BGP table version is 7, local router ID is 14.14.14.14
Status codes: s suppressed, d damped, h history, * valid, > best, i - internal
Origin codes: i - IGP, e - EGP, ? - incomplete

   Network          Next Hop          Metric LocPrf Weight Path
*> 155.155.155.0/24 12.12.12.12                        0 2 i
*> 188.188.188.0/24 12.12.12.12                        0 2 4 i


! BGP table on R4 after applying filter-list on R2.
R4#show ip bgp
BGP table version is 2, local router ID is 4.4.4.4
Status codes: s suppressed, d damped, h history, * valid, > best, i - internal
Origin codes: i - IGP, e - EGP, ? - incomplete

   Network          Next Hop          Metric LocPrf Weight Path
*> 155.155.155.0/24 12.12.12.12                        0 2 i
```

Section 3.0: ISDN Configuration

3.1: Basic ISDN

1 Configure legacy ISDN on R1 and R2. Use network 81.18.1.24/30.

2 Configure EIGRP AS 12 using MD5 authentication on both routers and advertise the ISDN network.

3 Redistribute EIGRP-12 into OSPF on R2.

4 Redistribute connected into EIGRP 12 on R1 for all devices to learn loopback(s).

5 Redistribute connected into OSPF on R2 for all devices to learn ISDN network 81.18.1.24/30.

3.2: Advanced ISDN

1 Very tricky question. To enable redundancy for R1 to use ISDN if the outside interface of PIX is down, the only solution is to configure a GRE tunnel between R1 and R3, and configure the R1 BRI interface as the backup interface for the Tunnel interface, as demonstrated in the following example:

```
interface Tunnel3
 ip address 10.3.3.1 255.255.255.0
 backup interface BRI0/0
 keepalive 2 3
 tunnel source Loopback1
 tunnel destination 13.13.13.13
!
interface BRI0/0
 ip address 81.18.1.25 255.255.255.252
 ip authentication mode eigrp 12 md5
 ip authentication key-chain eigrp 12 lab5
 encapsulation ppp
 ip ospf cost 999
 dialer idle-timeout 600
 dialer map ip 81.18.1.26 name R2 broadcast 99047132
 dialer-group 1
 isdn switch-type basic-net3
 no peer neighbor-route
 ppp authentication chap
!
```

2 Configure keepalives on the R1 tunnel to 2 seconds, so if it missed three keepalives, it will trigger ISDN for backup.

3 By advertising the ISDN network in EIGRP AS12, all routes will converge via BRI, as demonstrated in the example following item 4.

4 Verify by shutting down switch2 port for PIX Ethernet0, which brings down the tunnel interface on R1, causing ISDN to come up, as demonstrated in the following example:

```
R1#show debug
Dial on demand:
  Dial on demand events debugging is on

*Mar  2 21:27:35.179: %LINEPROTO-5-UPDOWN: Line protocol on Interface
   Tunnel3, changed state to down
*Mar  2 21:27:35.183: %LINK-3-UPDOWN: Interface BRI0/0:1, changed state to
   down
*Mar  2 21:27:35.183: %LINK-3-UPDOWN: Interface BRI0/0:2, changed state to
   down
*Mar  2 21:27:35.191: BR0/0:1 DDR: disconnecting call
*Mar  2 21:27:35.191: BR0/0:2 DDR: disconnecting call
*Mar  2 21:27:35.235: %LINK-3-UPDOWN: Interface BRI0/0, changed state to up
*Mar  2 21:27:35.940: BR0/0 DDR: Dialing cause ip (s=81.18.1.25,
   d=224.0.0.10)
*Mar  2 21:27:35.940: BR0/0 DDR: Attempting to dial 99047132
*Mar  2 21:27:36.201: %ISDN-6-LAYER2UP: Layer 2 for Interface BR0/0, TEI 67
   changed to up
*Mar  2 21:27:37.932: %LINK-3-UPDOWN: Interface BRI0/0:1, changed state to up
*Mar  2 21:27:37.988: BR0/0:1 DDR: Remote name for R2
*Mar  2 21:27:38.004: BR0/0:1 DDR: dialer protocol up
*Mar  2 21:27:38.989: %LINEPROTO-5-UPDOWN: Line protocol on Interface BRI0/
   0:1, changed state to up
*Mar  2 21:27:39.414: %DUAL-5-NBRCHANGE: IP-EIGRP 12: Neighbor 81.18.1.26
   (BRI0/0) is up: new adjacency
*Mar  2 21:27:43.933: %ISDN-6-CONNECT: Interface BRI0/0:1 is now connected
   to 99047132 R2


R1#show dialer

BRI0/0 - dialer type = ISDN

Dial String      Successes    Failures    Last DNIS    Last status
99047132                 4           2     00:01:01       successful
0 incoming call(s) have been screened.
0 incoming call(s) rejected for callback.
```

```
BRI0/0:1 - dialer type = ISDN
Idle timer (600 secs), Fast idle timer (20 secs)
Wait for carrier (30 secs), Re-enable (15 secs)
Dialer state is data link layer up
Dial reason: ip (s=81.18.1.25, d=224.0.0.10)
Time until disconnect 599 secs
Connected to 99047132 (R2)

BRI0/0:2 - dialer type = ISDN
Idle timer (600 secs), Fast idle timer (20 secs)
Wait for carrier (30 secs), Re-enable (15 secs)
Dialer state is idle


R1#show isdn active
-----------------------------------------------------------------------
                          ISDN ACTIVE CALLS
-----------------------------------------------------------------------
Call  Calling   Called   Remote  Seconds Seconds Seconds  Charges
Type  Number    Number   Name    Used    Left    Idle     Units/Currency
-----------------------------------------------------------------------
Out   ---N/A--- 99047132 R2      318     599     0              0
-----------------------------------------------------------------------


R1#show ip route
Codes: C - connected, S - static, R - RIP, M - mobile, B - BGP
       D - EIGRP, EX - EIGRP external, O - OSPF, IA - OSPF inter area
       N1 - OSPF NSSA external type 1, N2 - OSPF NSSA external type 2
       E1 - OSPF external type 1, E2 - OSPF external type 2
       i - IS-IS, L1 - IS-IS level-1, L2 - IS-IS level-2, ia - IS-IS inter area
       * - candidate default, U - per-user static route, o - ODR
       P - periodic downloaded static route

Gateway of last resort is 172.16.1.1 to network 0.0.0.0

     17.0.0.0/32 is subnetted, 1 subnets
D EX    17.17.17.17 [170/40537600] via 81.18.1.26, 00:01:28, BRI0/0
     16.0.0.0/32 is subnetted, 1 subnets
D EX    16.16.16.16 [170/40537600] via 81.18.1.26, 00:01:28, BRI0/0
     155.155.0.0/24 is subnetted, 1 subnets
B       155.155.155.0 [20/0] via 13.13.13.13, 00:00:09
     18.0.0.0/32 is subnetted, 1 subnets
```

```
D EX    18.18.18.18 [170/40537600] via 81.18.1.26, 00:01:28, BRI0/0
        81.0.0.0/8 is variably subnetted, 4 subnets, 2 masks
D EX    81.18.1.0/28 [170/40537600] via 81.18.1.26, 00:01:29, BRI0/0
D EX    81.18.1.16/30 [170/40537600] via 81.18.1.26, 00:01:29, BRI0/0
D EX    81.18.1.20/30 [170/40537600] via 81.18.1.26, 00:01:29, BRI0/0
C       81.18.1.24/30 is directly connected, BRI0/0
        141.1.0.0/20 is subnetted, 1 subnets
D EX    141.1.0.0 [170/40537600] via 81.18.1.26, 00:01:29, BRI0/0
        172.16.0.0/24 is subnetted, 1 subnets
C       172.16.1.0 is directly connected, Ethernet0/0
        22.0.0.0/24 is subnetted, 1 subnets
C       22.22.22.0 is directly connected, Loopback2
        188.188.0.0/24 is subnetted, 1 subnets
B       188.188.188.0 [20/0] via 13.13.13.13, 00:00:11
        173.5.0.0/16 is variably subnetted, 4 subnets, 2 masks
D EX    173.5.1.129/32 [170/40537600] via 81.18.1.26, 00:01:29, BRI0/0
D EX    173.5.1.131/32 [170/40537600] via 81.18.1.26, 00:01:29, BRI0/0
D EX    173.5.1.130/32 [170/40537600] via 81.18.1.26, 00:01:29, BRI0/0
D EX    173.5.1.0/25 [170/40537600] via 81.18.1.26, 00:01:30, BRI0/0
        10.0.0.0/24 is subnetted, 1 subnets
D EX    10.1.1.0 [170/40537600] via 81.18.1.26, 00:01:30, BRI0/0
        11.0.0.0/24 is subnetted, 1 subnets
C       11.11.11.0 is directly connected, Loopback1
        12.0.0.0/24 is subnetted, 1 subnets
D EX    12.12.12.0 [170/40537600] via 81.18.1.26, 00:01:30, BRI0/0
        122.0.0.0/24 is subnetted, 1 subnets
D EX    122.122.122.0 [170/40537600] via 81.18.1.26, 00:01:30, BRI0/0
        13.0.0.0/8 is variably subnetted, 2 subnets, 2 masks
D EX    13.13.13.13/32 [170/40537600] via 81.18.1.26, 00:01:30, BRI0/0
D EX    13.13.13.0/24 [170/40537600] via 81.18.1.26, 00:01:30, BRI0/0
D EX 151.151.0.0/16 [170/40537600] via 81.18.1.26, 00:01:30, BRI0/0
        15.0.0.0/32 is subnetted, 1 subnets
D EX    15.15.15.15 [170/40537600] via 81.18.1.26, 00:01:30, BRI0/0
R*   0.0.0.0/0 [120/1] via 172.16.1.1, 00:00:26, Ethernet0/0


R1#traceroute 173.5.1.1

Type escape sequence to abort.
Tracing the route to 173.5.1.1

  1 81.18.1.26 16 msec 16 msec 16 msec
  2 81.18.1.3 24 msec 20 msec 20 msec
  3 10.1.1.1 68 msec 65 msec 64 msec
  4 173.5.1.131 100 msec
    173.5.1.130 100 msec
```

```
   173.5.1.131 100 msec
 5 173.5.1.1 100 msec *  100 msec
R1#
```

Section 4.0: PIX Configuration

4.1: Basic PIX Configuration

1 Configure RIP for inside/outside interface using MD5 authentication.

2 Configure two separate NAT/global instances, one for Loopback-2 on R1 and the other for all networks (0.0.0.0) to PAT on the outside interface, as demonstrated in the folllowing example:

```
PIX# show nat
nat (inside) 2 22.22.22.0 255.255.255.0 0 0
nat (inside) 1 0.0.0.0 0.0.0.0 0 0

PIX# show global
global (outside) 2 122.122.122.1-122.122.122.254 netmask 255.255.255.0
global (outside) 1 interface
```

3 Configure static routes for network 11.11.11.0/24 and 122.122.122.0/24 on R3.

4.2: Advanced PIX Configuration

1 Configure ICMP filtering for the PIX outside interface such that R3 cannot ping and configure implicit permit, as demonstrated in the following example:

```
PIX(config)# show icmp
icmp deny host 81.18.1.3 outside
icmp permit any outside
```

2 The ICMP command defines the control list for traffic that terminates on the PIX interface.

3 Configure PIX for simultaneous close TCP terminating sequence instead of normal close using the **sysopt connection timewait** command.

4 In a simultaneous close, both ends of the transaction initiate the closing sequence, as opposed to the normal sequence where one end closes and the other end acknowledges prior to initiating its own closing sequence. By default, PIX tracks the normal shutdown sequence and releases the connection after two FINs and the Acknowledgment of the last FIN segment.

NOTE   For more information on the **sysopt** command for the TCP terminating sequence on PIX, see www.cisco.com/univercd/cc/td/doc/product/iaabu/pix/pix_61/cmd_ref/s.htm#xtocid22

Section 5.0: IPSec Configuration

5.1: IPSec LAN-to-LAN Router-to-Router

1 Configure a LAN-to-LAN tunnel between R5 and R6 for Loopback5 networks, as demonstrated in the following example:

```
! <snip from R5 config>
hostname R5
!
crypto isakmp policy 10
 authentication pre-share
crypto isakmp key cisco address 173.5.1.130
!
!
crypto ipsec transform-set lab5 esp-des
!
!
!
crypto map lab5 10 ipsec-isakmp
 set peer 173.5.1.130
 set transform-set lab5
 match address 101
!
interface Loopback5
 ip address 192.168.1.1 255.255.255.0
!
!
interface Serial1/0
 ip address 173.5.1.129 255.255.255.128
 crypto map lab5
!
ip route 192.168.2.0 255.255.255.0 Serial1/0
!
access-list 101 permit icmp 192.168.1.0 0.0.0.255 192.168.2.0 0.0.0.255
!


<snip from R6 config>
hostname R6
!
crypto isakmp policy 10
 authentication pre-share
crypto isakmp key cisco address 0.0.0.0
```

```
!
!
crypto ipsec transform-set lab5 esp-des
!
crypto dynamic-map lab5-ted 10
 set transform-set lab5
 match address 101
!
crypto map lab5 10 ipsec-isakmp dynamic lab5-ted discover
!
interface Loopback5
 ip address 192.168.2.1 255.255.255.0
 no ip directed-broadcast
!
!
interface Serial1/0
 ip address 173.5.1.130 255.255.255.128
 crypto map lab5
!
ip route 192.168.1.0 255.255.255.0 Serial1/0
!
access-list 101 permit icmp 192.168.2.0 0.0.0.255 192.168.1.0 0.0.0.255
```

```
! Verify with:
```

R5#show crypto engine connections active

ID	Interface	IP-Address	State	Algorithm	Encrypt	Decrypt
1	\<none\>	\<none\>	set	HMAC_SHA+DES_56_CB	0	0
2000	Serial1/0	173.5.1.129	set	DES_56_CBC	0	109
2001	Serial1/0	173.5.1.129	set	DES_56_CBC	109	0

R6#show crypto engine connections active

ID	Interface	IP-Address	State	Algorithm	Encrypt	Decrypt
1	\<none\>	\<none\>	set	HMAC_SHA+DES_56_CB	0	0
2000	Serial1/0	173.5.1.130	set	DES_56_CBC	0	109
2001	Serial1/0	173.5.1.130	set	DES_56_CBC	109	0

Crypto adjacency count : Lock: 0, Unlock: 0

2   Configure DES algorithm in the transform set, no authentication. Configure **cisco** as the preshared key.

3   Configure TED (Tunnel End-Point Discovery) on R6, a feature that allows routers to discover IPSec endpoints. Do not configure the **set peer** statement on R6. Refer to the example following item 1.

4   Configure a static route for Loopback5 on both ends.

NOTE   To read more about TED, refer to the following URL:

www.cisco.com/warp/public/707/tedpreshare.html

There is a known bug in Cisco IOS for TED not working—bug ID CSCdt76326. The following is the Release-note from the bug. Use version 12.0 or 12.2(T) instead.

Release-note: In versions 12.1T and 12.2 of IOS, the tunnel endpoint discovery (TED) protocol does not work. There is no workaround.

5.2: L2TP over IPSec Using Certificates

1   Configure PIX for L2TP over IPSec using CA, as demonstrated in the following example:

```
! <Snip from PIX config>
ip local pool l2tp 70.70.70.0-70.70.70.254
sysopt connection permit-l2tp
crypto ipsec transform-set l2tp esp-des esp-md5-hmac
crypto ipsec transform-set l2tp mode transport
crypto ipsec security-association lifetime seconds 3600
crypto dynamic-map lab5-dyna 10 match address l2tp
crypto dynamic-map lab5-dyna 10 set transform-set l2tp
crypto map lab5 10 ipsec-isakmp dynamic lab5-dyna
crypto map lab5 client authentication RADIUS
crypto map lab5 interface outside
isakmp enable outside
isakmp policy 10 authentication rsa-sig
isakmp policy 10 encryption des
isakmp policy 10 hash md5
isakmp policy 10 group 1
isakmp policy 10 lifetime 86400
ca identity lab5 172.16.1.5:/certsrv/mscep/mscep.dll
ca configure lab5 ra 1 20 crloptional
vpdn group lab5 accept dialin l2tp
vpdn group lab5 ppp authentication chap
vpdn group lab5 ppp authentication mschap
```

```
vpdn group lab5 client configuration address local l2tp
vpdn group lab5 client configuration dns 70.70.70.1
vpdn group lab5 client configuration wins 70.70.70.1
vpdn group lab5 client authentication aaa RADIUS
vpdn group lab5 client accounting RADIUS
vpdn group lab5 l2tp tunnel hello 60
vpdn enable outside
: end
```

2 Obtain certificate(s) on PIX and Test PC from CA server 172.16.1.5 in VLAN-2, as demonstrated in the following example:

```
! <CA enrollment steps on PIX>
PIX(config)# ca authenticate lab5

Certificate has the following attributes:

PIX(config)# 044e6386 d685e0ad 3999e792 840f1ae4
PIX(config)#
PIX(config)# ca enroll lab5 cisco serial
%
% Start certificate enrollment ..

% The subject name in the certificate will be: PIX.cisco.com

% Certificate request sent to Certificate Authority
% The certificate request fingerprint will be displayed.
PIX(config)#
PIX(config)#      Fingerprint:  7d9b8fec 95c4e0a6 59fb2dc7 1da69418

The certificate has been granted by CA!

PIX(config)#
PIX(config)# show ca certificate
Certificate
  Status: Available
  Certificate Serial Number: 42ef23d500000000000c
  Key Usage: General Purpose
  Subject Name
    Name: PIX.cisco.com
    Serial Number: 1829c362
  Validity Date:
    start date: 05:08:40 UTC Apr 1 2003
    end   date: 05:18:40 UTC Apr 1 2004

RA Signature Certificate
```

```
Status: Available
Certificate Serial Number: 6103b68b000000000002
Key Usage: Signature
  CN = hegel
  OU = hegel
  O = hegel
  L = Sydney
  ST = NSW
  C = AU
  EA =<16> hegel@hegel
Validity Date:
  start date: 02:23:15 UTC Feb 18 2003
  end   date: 02:33:15 UTC Feb 18 2004

CA Certificate
  Status: Available
  Certificate Serial Number: 2288f45842c63a844fe73d976ddc35b1
  Key Usage: Signature
    CN = hegel
    OU = hegel
    O = hegel
    L = Sydney
    ST = NSW
    C = AU
    EA =<16> labs@labs.com
  Validity Date:
    start date: 02:16:21 UTC Feb 18 2003
    end   date: 02:23:53 UTC Feb 18 2005

RA KeyEncipher Certificate
  Status: Available
  Certificate Serial Number: 6103bc2d000000000003
  Key Usage: Encryption
    CN = hegel
    OU = hegel
    O = hegel
    L = Sydney
    ST = NSW
    C = AU
    EA =<16> hegel@hegel
  Validity Date:
    start date: 02:23:17 UTC Feb 18 2003
    end   date: 02:33:17 UTC Feb 18 2004
```

3   Configure an IP address pool of 70.70.70.0/24 on PIX for L2TP users.

4   Configure group name **lab5** on PIX for L2TP connections.

5   Configure external authentication using RADIUS.

6   Configure username **l2tp-user** password **cisco** on CiscoSecure ACS with the necessary settings.

7   Configure a Dial-up Network connection on the Test PC for the IPSec/L2TP tunnel. Configure IPSec policy parameters on the Test PC.

NOTE	To enroll Test PC with the CA, refer to the following document:
	How to: Install a Certificate for Use with IP Security
	http://support.microsoft.com/default.aspx?scid=kb;EN-US;253498

NOTE	Use the following URLs for reference:
	Configure L2TP over IPSec:
	www.cisco.com/warp/public/110/l2tp-ipsec.html
	www.cisco.com/en/US/tech/tk801/tk703/technologies_configuration_example09186a00800946f5.shtml
	Description of the IPSec Policy Created for L2TP/IPSec:
	http://support.microsoft.com/default.aspx?scid=kb;EN-US;248750
	How to Configure an L2TP/IPSec Connection Using Pre-shared Key Authentication:
	http://support.microsoft.com/default.aspx?scid=kb;EN-US;240262
	Refer to Step-by-Step Guide for Setting up a Certification Authority:
	www.microsoft.com/windows2000/techinfo/planning/security/casetupsteps.asp

Section 6.0: Intrusion Detection System (IDS)

6.1: Intrusion Detection System (IDS)

1   Configure IDS from the console; log in as **root** and default password **attack**.

2   Use the **sysconfig-sensor** utility on the sensor to configure IP address, mask, default route, and ACL to allow the **172.** network to be able to manage it. By default the ACL allows for network **10.** only. See Figure 5-6.

Figure 5-6 *Sensor Initialization Using Sysconfig-Sensor*

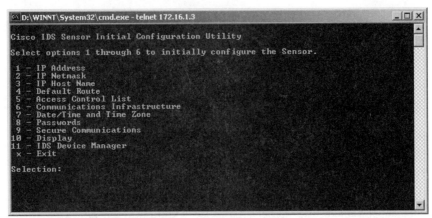

3 Use any workstation (AAA/CA server in this case) to browse to the sensor. That is, use IDM (IDS Device Manager) to configure the rest of the parameters. See Figures 5-7a through 5-7d.

Figure 5-7a *Sensor Setup Using IDM*

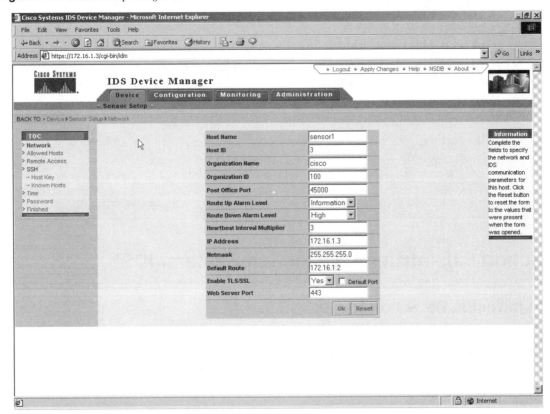

Figure 5-7b *Configuring Communication Parameters for Remote (IEV) Host Using IDM*

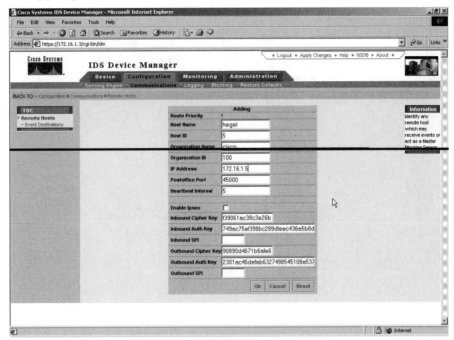

Figure 5-7c *Adding Remote (IEV) Host for Event Destination Using IDM*

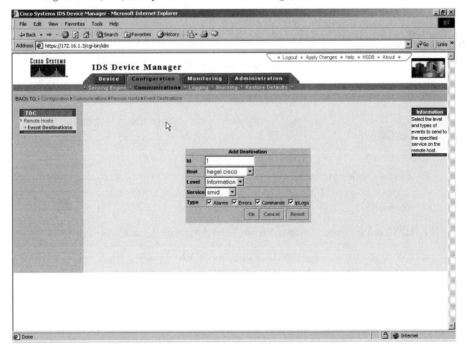

Figure 5-7d *Applying Changes to Write to Sensor*

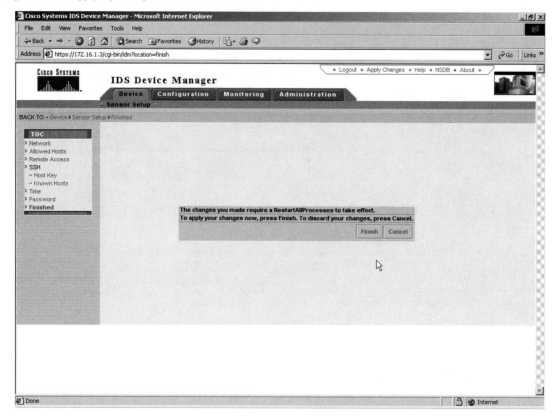

4 IDM is a web-based application that allows you to configure and manage your sensor. The web server for the IDS Device Manager resides on the sensor. You can access it through the Netscape or Internet Explorer web browsers.

5 Install IEV on the AAA/CA server. IEV can be installed by downloading the installation file from the sensor using IDM. Go to IDM, Monitoring, IDS Event Viewer, and download the file.

6 IEV is a Java-based application that enables you to view and manage alarms for up to three sensors. With the IDS Event Viewer you can connect to and view alarms in real time or in imported log files.

7 IDM and IEV are supported from Sensor version 3.1 and above only.

8 Configure the sensing interface to monitor VLAN-3 and VLAN-4 on switch1 as per Table 5-1. Refer to the following example for the configuration:

```
hostname sw1
!
monitor session 1 source vlan 3 - 4 rx
```

```
monitor session 1 destination interface Fa0/7

sw1#show monitor session 1
Session 1
- - - - - - - - -
 Type        : Local Session
Source Ports:
    RX Only:       None
    TX Only:       None
    Both:          None
Source VLANs:
    RX Only:       3-4
    TX Only:       None
    Both:          None
Source RSPAN VLAN: None
Destination Ports: Fa0/7
    Encapsulation: Native
           Ingress: Disabled
Reflector Port:    None
Filter VLANs:      None
Dest RSPAN VLAN:   None
```

NOTE   See the following URL for step-by-step instructions to initialize the sensor. Do not configure Option 6 (Communications Infrastructure); use IDM to do this:

www.cisco.com/univercd/cc/td/doc/product/iaabu/csids/csids8/13870_01.htm#xtocid13

See this URL for step-by-step instructions to configure IDM:

www.cisco.com/univercd/cc/td/doc/product/iaabu/csids/csids8/13876_01.htm

See this URL for step-by-step instructions to configure IEV:

www.cisco.com/univercd/cc/td/doc/product/iaabu/csids/csids8/13877_01.htm

See this URL to configure Switched Port Analyzer (SPAN) on the Catalyst 3550 switch:

www.cisco.com/univercd/cc/td/doc/product/lan/c3550/12112cea/3550scg/swspan.htm

6.2: Advanced Intrusion Detection System (IDS)

1   Change ICMP echo signature 2004 as HIGH severity using IDM. See Figure 5-8. Ping any device in VLAN 3 or 4 and make sure you receive alarms in IEV. See Figures 5-9a through 5-9c for IEV.

Figure 5-8 *Signature Tuning Using IDM*

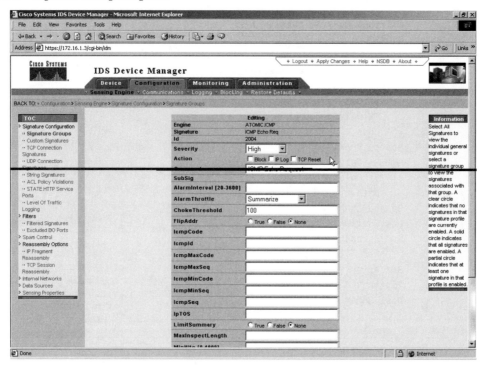

Figure 5-9a *IEV (IDS Event Viewer)*

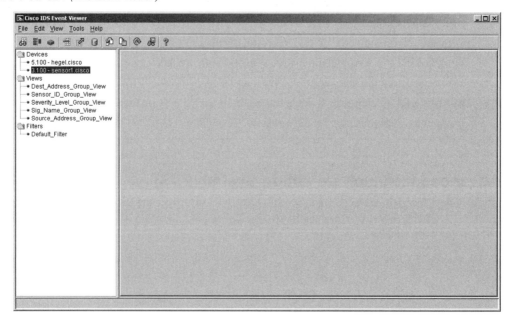

Figure 5-9b *Viewing Alarms Using IEV (View Sorted by Signature Name)*

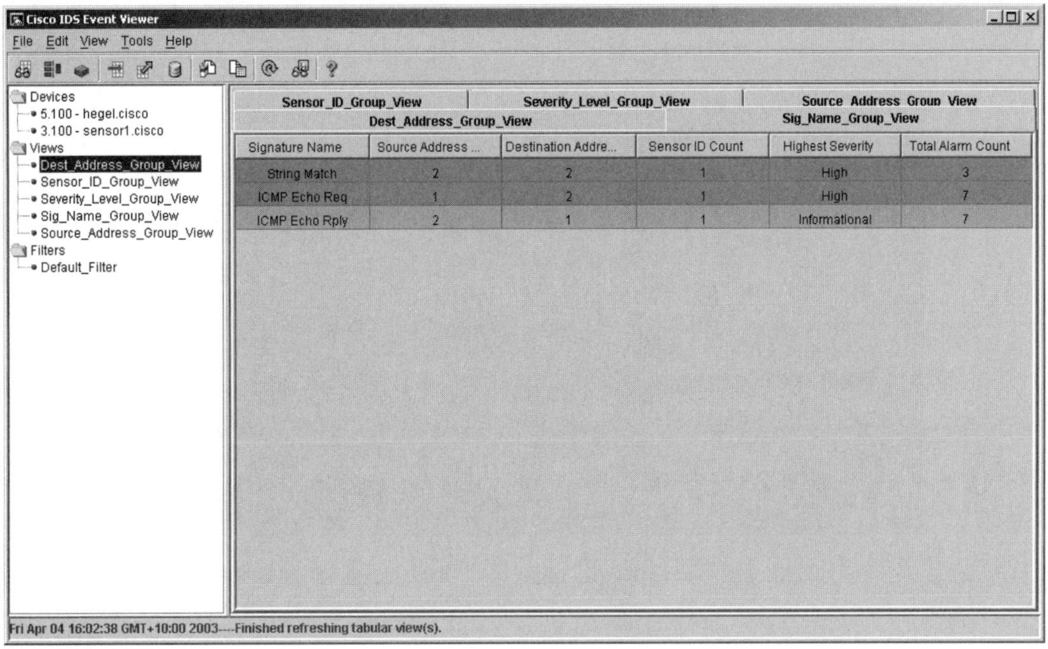

Figure 5-9c *Viewing Alarms Using IEV (View Sorted by Destination IP)*

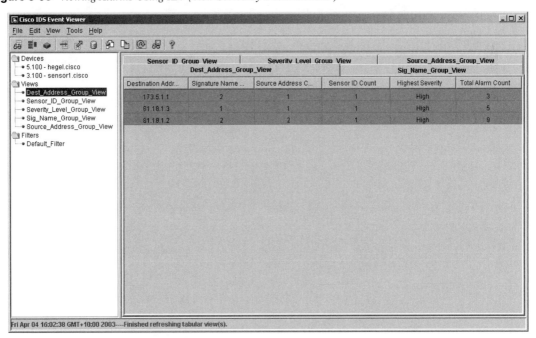

2 If you are not receiving alarms in IEV, verify if the IEV host can ping the sensor, and then use the **snoop** command to check if the sensing (sniffing) interface is receiving SPANed traffic. See Figure 5-10a.

Figure 5-10a *Using the* **snoop** *Command on the Sensor*

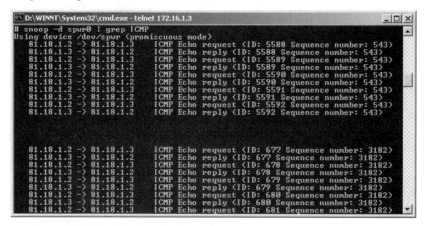

3 From IDM, verify sensor information and connection status. See Figure 5-10b.

Figure 5-10b *Verifying Sensor Information and Connection Status in IDM*

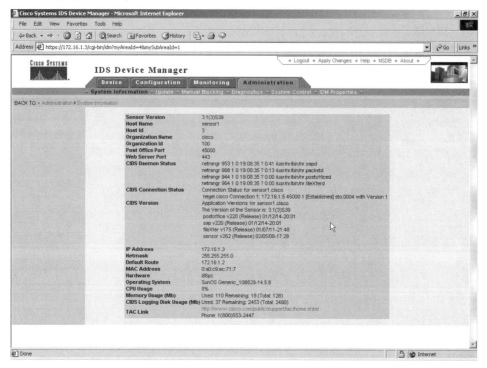

4 Configure a custom signature 55055 using IDM as HIGH severity for any Telnet session to match the string **password**. See Figure 5-11. Telnet to any router(s) in VLAN 3 or 4, and enter the string **password**. Verify alarms in IEV. Refer to Figures 5-9a through 5-9c for IEV.

Figure 5-11 *Adding Custom Signature 55055 Using IDM*

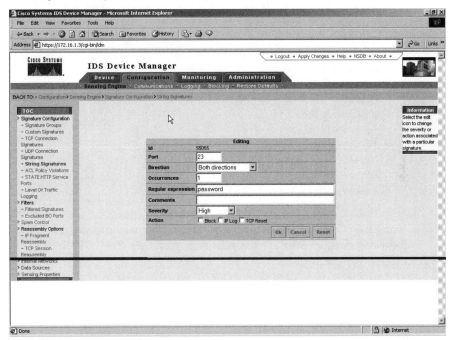

Section 7.0: AAA

7.1: AAA on the Switch

1 Configure RADIUS authentication and accounting for Switch2 management.

2 Configure AAA to fallback local in the event the AAA server is not available.

3 Configure switch2 to send all authentication requests to RADIUS server 172.16.1.5 and all accounting requests to RADIUS server 172.16.1.6 only. You can do this by configuring the auth-port or acct-port to **0** for not sending, as shown in the example that follows:

```
hostname sw2
!
aaa new-model
aaa authentication login vty group radius local
```

```
aaa accounting exec vty start-stop group radius
enable password cisco
!
username switch-telnet password 0 cisco
!
radius-server host 172.16.1.5 auth-port 1812 acct-port 0
radius-server host 172.16.1.6 auth-port 0 acct-port 1813
radius-server retransmit 3
radius-server key cisco
!
line vty 0 4
 access-class 1 in
 password cisco
 accounting exec vty
 login authentication vty
line vty 5 15
 access-class 1 in
 password cisco
 accounting exec vty
 login authentication vty
```

4 Verify the switch2 configuration by enabling debugs on the switch, as demonstrated in the
following example, where authentication requests are sent to 172.16.1.5 and accounting
requests are sent to 172.16.1.6:

```
sw2#show debug
General OS:
  AAA Authentication debugging is on
  AAA Accounting debugging is on
RADIUS protocol debugging is on
sw2#
sw2#
sw2#
1w0d: AAA: parse name=tty1 idb type=-1 tty=-1
1w0d: AAA: name=tty1 flags=0x11 type=5 shelf=0 slot=0 adapter=0 port=1
  channel=0
1w0d: AAA/MEMORY: create_user (0xF312D8) user='' ruser='' port='tty1'
  rem_addr='172.16.1.2' authen_type=ASCII service=LOGIN priv=1
1w0d: AAA/AUTHEN/START (3388747900): port='tty1' list='vty' action=LOGIN
  service=LOGIN
1w0d: AAA/AUTHEN/START (3388747900): found list vty
1w0d: AAA/AUTHEN/START (3388747900): Method=radius (radius)
1w0d: AAA/AUTHEN (3388747900): status = GETUSER
1w0d: AAA/AUTHEN/CONT (3388747900): continue_login (user='(undef)')
1w0d: AAA/AUTHEN (3388747900): status = GETUSER
1w0d: AAA/AUTHEN (3388747900): Method=radius (radius)
1w0d: AAA/AUTHEN (3388747900): status = GETPASS
```

```
1w0d: AAA/AUTHEN/CONT (3388747900): continue_login (user='switch-telnet')
1w0d: AAA/AUTHEN (3388747900): status = GETPASS
1w0d: AAA/AUTHEN (3388747900): Method=radius (radius)
1w0d: RADIUS: ustruct sharecount=1
1w0d: RADIUS: Initial Transmit tty1 id 3 172.16.1.5:1812, Access-Request,
  len 83
1w0d:         Attribute 4 6 AC100134
1w0d:         Attribute 5 6 00000001
1w0d:         Attribute 61 6 00000005
1w0d:         Attribute 1 15 73776974
1w0d:         Attribute 31 12 3137322E
1w0d:         Attribute 2 18 8F05811F
1w0d: RADIUS: Received from id 3 172.16.1.5:1812, Access-Accept, len 26
1w0d:         Attribute 8 6 FFFFFFFF
1w0d: RADIUS: saved authorization data for user F312D8 at CB4820
1w0d: AAA/AUTHEN (3388747900): status = PASS
1w0d: AAA/ACCT/EXEC/START User switch-telnet, port tty1
1w0d: AAA/ACCT/EXEC: Found list "vty"
1w0d: AAA/ACCT/EXEC/START User switch-telnet, Port tty1,
        task_id=1 timezone=UTC service=shell
1w0d: AAA/ACCT: user switch-telnet, acct type 0 (1188583497): Method=radius
  (radius)
1w0d: RADIUS: ustruct sharecount=3
1w0d: RADIUS: find_server: Server 172.16.1.5 skipped: wrong type.
1w0d: RADIUS: find_server: Server 172.16.1.5 skipped: wrong type.
1w0d: RADIUS: Initial Transmit tty1 id 4 172.16.1.6:1813, Accounting-Request,
  len 99
1w0d:         Attribute 4 6 AC100134
1w0d:         Attribute 5 6 00000001
1w0d:         Attribute 61 6 00000005
1w0d:         Attribute 1 15 73776974
1w0d:         Attribute 31 12 3137322E
1w0d:         Attribute 40 6 00000001
1w0d:         Attribute 45 6 00000001
1w0d:         Attribute 6 6 00000007
1w0d:         Attribute 44 10 30303030
1w0d:         Attribute 41 6 00000000
sw2#
1w0d: RADIUS: Retransmit id 4
1w0d: RADIUS: acct-delay-time for 8003754C (at 800375A9) now 5
```

5 Configure user **switch-telnet** password **cisco** on CiscoSecure ACS and switch2. See Figure 5-12 for users configured in ACS.

6 See Figure 5-13 for ACS NAS settings.

Figure 5-12 *User Settings on CiscoSecure ACS*

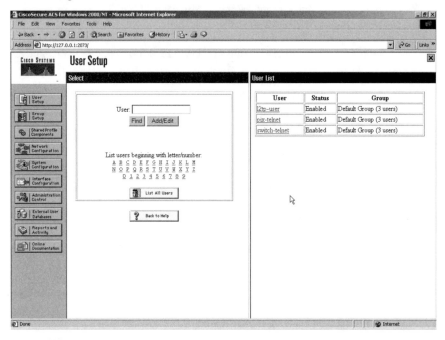

Figure 5-13 *NAS Settings on CiscoSecure ACS*

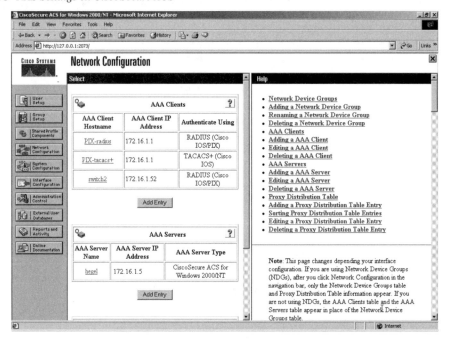

7.2: AAA on PIX

1 Configure PIX management using Telnet, and configure authentication using TACACS+, as demonstrated in the following example:

```
PIX(config)# show aaa
aaa authentication telnet console TACACS+

PIX(config)# show aaa-server
aaa-server TACACS+ protocol tacacs+
aaa-server TACACS+ (inside) host 172.16.1.5 cisco timeout 5
aaa-server RADIUS protocol radius
aaa-server RADIUS (inside) host 172.16.1.5 cisco timeout 5
aaa-server LOCAL protocol local

PIX(config)# show telnet
172.16.1.0 255.255.255.0 inside



R1#ping 172.16.1.1

Type escape sequence to abort.
Sending 5, 100-byte ICMP Echos to 172.16.1.1, timeout is 2 seconds:
!!!!!
Success rate is 100 percent (5/5), round-trip min/avg/max = 1/2/4 ms
R1#
R1#
R1#telnet 172.16.1.1
Trying 172.16.1.1 ... Open


User Access Verification

Username: pix-telnet
Password: cisco
Type help or '?' for a list of available commands.
PIX>
PIX> enable
Password: cisco
PIX#
PIX#
```

2 Configure PIX for Telnet from network 172.16.1.0/24 only.

3 Configure user **pix-telnet** password **cisco** in CiscoSecure ACS. Refer to Figure 5-12 for users configured in ACS.

   4 Refer to Figure 5-13 for ACS NAS settings.

   5 Do not configure any authentication for the console.

   6 No fallback method is configurable on PIX. Refer to the following document to gain
   access to PIX when the AAA server is down:

   www.cisco.com/warp/public/110/authtopix.shtml#gainingdown

NOTE   For more info on PIX management, see

              www.cisco.com/warp/public/110/authtopix.shtml

Section 8.0: Advanced Security

8.1: Perimeter Security

   1 Deny all inbound traceroute on R5 on Frame Relay link (173.5.1.128/25).

   2 One of the two ICMP messages that traceroute receives is the message **port unreachable**.
   The second one is the message **time exceeded** (TTL is 0).

   3 Configure the egress ACL to deny ICMP port-unreachable and time-exceeded, as
   demonstrated in the following example:

```
! <Snip from R5 config>
interface Serial1/0
 ip address 173.5.1.129 255.255.255.128
 ip access-group 103 out
!
access-list 103 deny    icmp any any port-unreachable
access-list 103 deny    icmp any any time-exceeded
access-list 103 permit ip any any
!
```

   4 Traceroute through R5 toward Frame Relay network to R6, R7, and VLAN4, and R8 will
   work OK with the solution in the configuration for item 3. The example following item 5
   shows the results of the traceroute.

   5 Verify traceroute from R8 to R2 and vice versa, as demonstrated in the following example:

```
! Traceroute successful from R8 to R2 before applying ACL on R5.

R8#traceroute 81.18.1.2

Type escape sequence to abort.
Tracing the route to 81.18.1.2
```

```
  1 173.5.1.3 0 msec
    173.5.1.2 0 msec
    173.5.1.3 4 msec
  2 173.5.1.129 40 msec 36 msec 40 msec
  3 10.1.1.2 92 msec 88 msec 92 msec
  4 81.18.1.2 92 msec *  88 msec
R8#




! Traceroute fail from R8 to R2 after applying ACL on R5.
R8#traceroute 81.18.1.2

Type escape sequence to abort.
Tracing the route to 81.18.1.2

  1 173.5.1.2 0 msec
    173.5.1.3 4 msec
    173.5.1.2 0 msec
  2 173.5.1.129 40 msec 36 msec 36 msec
  3 *  *  *
  4 *  *  *
  5 *  *  *
  6
R8#
R8#




! Traceroute successful from R2 to R8 after applying ACL on R5.
R2#traceroute 173.5.1.1

Type escape sequence to abort.
Tracing the route to 173.5.1.1

  1 81.18.1.3 4 msec 4 msec 4 msec
  2 10.1.1.1 44 msec 48 msec 48 msec
  3 173.5.1.130 80 msec
    173.5.1.131 80 msec
    173.5.1.130 84 msec
  4 173.5.1.1 80 msec *  80 msec
R2#




R5#show access-lists 103
Extended IP access list 103
    deny icmp any any port-unreachable (9 matches)
```

```
deny icmp any any time-exceeded (6 matches)
permit ip any any (6 matches)
R5#
```

NOTE   For more information on how traceroute works, see the following URLs:

www.cisco.com/warp/public/105/traceroute.shtml

www.informatik.uni-trier.de/~smith/networks/tspec.html

8.2: Access Restriction

1   Configure a route map on R8 to match for network 181.1.1.0/24 and set the output interface to null. This will black hole all packets for this destination without having to use an ACL, as demonstrated in the following example:

```
hostname R8
!
access-list 1 permit 181.1.1.0 0.0.0.255
route-map black-hole permit 10
 match ip address 1
 set interface Null0
!
```

8.3: Access Control

1   Configure the **strict** option on the PIX FTP **fixup** command to prevent web browsers from sending embedded commands in FTP requests, as demonstrated in the following example:

```
<Snip from PIX config>
fixup protocol ftp strict 21
```

2   The **strict** option only lets an FTP server generate the **227** command and only lets an FTP client generate the **PORT** command. The **227** and **PORT** commands are checked to ensure they do not appear in an error string.

Section 9.0: IP Services and Protocol-Independent Features

9.1: Network Address Translation (NAT)

1   Tricky NAT question. Configure NAT on both R6 and R7 for redundancy, as a packet from VLAN-4 can use either the R6 or R7 path, as demonstrated in the following example:

```
! Configure static NAT on R6 and R7 (same on both routers).
! <Snip from R6 config>
```

```
interface Ethernet0/0
 ip address 173.5.1.2 255.255.255.128
 ip nat inside
!
interface Serial1/0
 ip address 173.5.1.130 255.255.255.128
 ip nat outside
!
ip nat inside source static 173.5.1.40 173.5.1.135
ip nat outside source static 173.5.1.136 173.5.1.41


R6#show ip nat translations
Pro Inside global     Inside local     Outside local     Outside global
--- 173.5.1.135       173.5.1.40       ---               ---
--- ---               ---              173.5.1.41        173.5.1.136
R6#
```

NOTE   See the following URL for more info on NAT local and global definitions:

www.cisco.com/warp/public/556/8.html#defall

9.2: DHCP

1 Configure R1 as a DHCP server for clients in VLAN-2.

2 Exclude static IP addresses 172.16.1.1 through 172.16.1.5, already used in the topology diagram, as per Figure 5-1.

3 Disable DHCP conflict logging.

4 Configure a DHCP pool to assign IP address 172.16.1.100 based on host name mapping **LAB5**, as demonstrated in the example following item 5.

5 Configure another DHCP pool for all the other clients to get an IP address from the 172.16.1.0/24 range. Remember to assign the default gateway IP, 172.16.1.2, as demonstrated in the following example:

```
hostname R1
!
no ip dhcp conflict logging
ip dhcp excluded-address 172.16.1.100
ip dhcp excluded-address 172.16.1.1 172.16.1.5
!
ip dhcp pool LAB5
   host 172.16.1.100 255.255.255.0
```

```
        client-name LAB5
        default-router 172.16.1.2
    !
    ip dhcp pool ALL
        import all
        network 172.16.1.0 255.255.255.0
        default-router 172.16.1.2
    !
```

9.3: UDP Broadcast Forwarding

1 Configure R6 and R7 to forward UDP broadcasts to server 173.5.1.52 in VLAN-4.

2 Enable custom application for UDP port 2050 and disable standard UDP NetBIOS name service 137, as demonstrated in the following example:

```
! Configure same on R6 and R7 VLAN-4 interface.
! <Snip from R7 config>
interface Ethernet0/0
 ip address 173.5.1.3 255.255.255.128
 ip helper-address 173.5.1.52
 !
no ip forward-protocol udp netbios-ns
ip forward-protocol udp 2050
```

3 UDP broadcasts by default are not forwarded by the router.

9.4: Traffic-Based Accounting

1 Configure MAC-based IP accounting on R1 on the VLAN-2 interface (Ethernet0/0), as demonstrated in the example following item 3.

2 The MAC address accounting feature provides accounting stats for IP traffic based on the source and destination MAC addresses on a LAN interface.

3 Verify MAC accounting information using the **show interface mac** command, as demonstrated in the following example:

```
interface Ethernet0/0
 ip address 172.16.1.2 255.255.255.0
 ip accounting mac-address input
 ip accounting mac-address output
 !
```

```
R1#show interfaces ethernet 0/0 mac-accounting
Ethernet0/0
  Input  (510 free)
    0090.2742.fd94(156):  44 packets, 5435 bytes, last: 325970ms ago
```

```
      0007.5057.e27f(157):   44 packets, 4184 bytes, last: 10597ms ago
                     Total:   88 packets, 9619 bytes
Output  (509 free)
      0100.5e00.0009(86 ):   31 packets, 3286 bytes, last: 23274ms ago
      0090.2742.fd94(156):   28 packets, 2072 bytes, last: 354541ms ago
      0007.5057.e27f(157):   15 packets, 1110 bytes, last: 375595ms ago
                     Total:   74 packets, 6468 bytes
```

Section 10.0: Security Violations

10.1: Smurf Attack

1 Use the Port ACL feature on 3550s to block ICMP on Switch1.

2 Port ACL can be used to apply on the Layer-2 interface of the switch.

3 Port ACLs are applied on interfaces for inbound traffic only. Configure ACL on switch1 to deny ICMP and permit everything. Apply the ACL to Fastethernet0/4 on switch1, where AAA/CA server is connected as shown in Table 5-1. The example that follows shows this configuration:

```
hostname sw1
!
interface FastEthernet0/4
 switchport access vlan 2
 switchport mode access
 no ip address
 ip access-group 101 in
!
access-list 101 deny   icmp any any
access-list 101 permit ip any any
```

NOTE   For more information, see the following URL:

www.cisco.com/univercd/cc/td/doc/product/lan/c3550/12112cea/3550scg/swacl.htm#xtocid4

10.2: Basic VLAN Hopping Attack

1 The attacker can fool a switch by pretending to be a switch wanting to become a trunk peer.

2 This kind of attack requires a "trunking-favorable" setting, such as Auto, to succeed. If the attacker succeeds in negotiating trunk with a switch, it can send and receive traffic on all VLANs configured.

3 The best way to prevent a basic VLAN hopping attack is to turn off trunking on all ports except the ones that specifically require it.

4 Disable Auto-Trunking by making it into an access port on all unused ports on switch2. Also change the VLAN from native VLAN1 used by trunk ports to a VLAN not used for anything else, as demonstrated in the following example:

NOTE You can use the **interface range** command to execute a command on multiple ports at the same time.

```
sw2#config terminal
Enter configuration commands, one per line.  End with CNTL/Z.
sw2(config)#interface range FastEthernet 0/7 - 24
sw2(config-if-range)#switchport mode access
sw2(config-if-range)#switchport access vlan 5
sw2(config-if-range)#end
sw2#

! Default Status of an unused port
sw2#show interface fa0/10 switchport
Name: Fa0/10
Switchport: Enabled
Administrative Mode: dynamic desirable
Operational Mode: down
Administrative Trunking Encapsulation: negotiate
Negotiation of Trunking: On
Access Mode VLAN: 1 (default)
Trunking Native Mode VLAN: 1 (default)
Administrative private-vlan host-association: none
Administrative private-vlan mapping: none
Operational private-vlan: none
Trunking VLANs Enabled: ALL
Pruning VLANs Enabled: 2-1001

Protected: false
Unknown unicast blocked: disabled
Unknown multicast blocked: disabled


Voice VLAN: none (Inactive)
Appliance trust: none
sw2#
```

```
! Default status of a port here is 'dynamic desirable'.
! Desirable means: "I'm willing to become a VLAN trunk; are you interested?"
! This State is used when the switch is interested in being a trunk.
! Bad idea, never leave an unused port in desirable state.


! Status after making change i.e. disable trunking (making it an access port)
! and put into a VLAN with no trunk ports.
sw2#show interface fa0/10 switchport
Name: Fa0/10
Switchport: Enabled
Administrative Mode: static access
Operational Mode: down
Administrative Trunking Encapsulation: negotiate
Negotiation of Trunking: Off
Access Mode VLAN: 5 (Null-VLAN)
Trunking Native Mode VLAN: 1 (default)
Administrative private-vlan host-association: none
Administrative private-vlan mapping: none
Operational private-vlan: none
Trunking VLANs Enabled: ALL
Pruning VLANs Enabled: 2-1001


Protected: false
Unknown unicast blocked: disabled
Unknown multicast blocked: disabled


Voice VLAN: none (Inactive)
Appliance trust: none
sw2#
```

5 Best practice is to *always* use a dedicated VLAN for trunk ports. Do not use VLAN 1 for trunk ports or anything. The following example demonstrates changing Native VLAN for trunk ports and setting all other user ports to nontrunking.

```
<Snip from Switch2>
! Create a new separate VLAN for all Trunk ports; choose any number.
! See VLAN10 below;
sw2#show vlan brief

VLAN Name                             Status    Ports
---- -------------------------------- --------  -------------------------------
1    default                          active    Gi0/1, Gi0/2
2    VLAN-2                           active    Fa0/6
3    VLAN-3                           active    Fa0/2, Fa0/3
```

```
4    VLAN-4                    active  Fa0/4, Fa0/5
5    Null-VLAN                 active  Fa0/7, Fa0/8, Fa0/9, Fa0/10
                                       Fa0/11, Fa0/12, Fa0/13, Fa0/14
                                       Fa0/15, Fa0/16, Fa0/17, Fa0/18
                                       Fa0/19, Fa0/20, Fa0/21, Fa0/22
                                       Fa0/23, Fa0/24
10   Native-VLAN-for-Trunk     active
1002 fddi-default              active
1003 token-ring-default        active
1004 fddinet-default           active
1005 trnet-default             active
sw2#
sw2(config)#interface Fastethernet 0/1
sw2(config-if)#switchport trunk native vlan ?
  <1-4094>  VLAN ID of the native VLAN when this port is in trunking mode

sw2(config-if)#switchport trunk native vlan 10
sw2(config-if)#end
sw2#show interface Fastethernet 0/1 switchport
Name: Fa0/1
Switchport: Enabled
Administrative Mode: trunk
Operational Mode: trunk
Administrative Trunking Encapsulation: isl
Operational Trunking Encapsulation: isl
Negotiation of Trunking: On
Access Mode VLAN: 1 (default)
Trunking Native Mode VLAN: 10 (Native-VLAN-for-Trunk)
Administrative private-vlan host-association: none
Administrative private-vlan mapping: none
Operational private-vlan: none
Trunking VLANs Enabled: ALL
Pruning VLANs Enabled: 2-1001

Protected: false
Unknown unicast blocked: disabled
Unknown multicast blocked: disabled


Voice VLAN: none (Inactive)
Appliance trust: none
sw2#
```

```
! <Snip from Switch1>
sw1#show interfaces Fastethernet 0/1 switchport
Name: Fa0/1
Switchport: Enabled
Administrative Mode: trunk
Operational Mode: trunk
Administrative Trunking Encapsulation: isl
Operational Trunking Encapsulation: isl
Negotiation of Trunking: On
Access Mode VLAN: 1 (default)
Trunking Native Mode VLAN: 10 (Native-VLAN-for-Trunk)
Administrative private-vlan host-association: none
Administrative private-vlan mapping: none
Operational private-vlan: none
Trunking VLANs Enabled: ALL
Pruning VLANs Enabled: 2-1001


Protected: false
Unknown unicast blocked: disabled
Unknown multicast blocked: disabled


Voice VLAN: none (Inactive)
Appliance trust: none
sw1#
```

CHAPTER **6**

Practice Lab 6

One of the biggest challenges in the CCIE Lab is precise and accurate interpretation of the requirements of questions. Candidates must learn to interpret the questions accurately and understand exactly what is required. If the question is not clear, approach the proctor for clarification.

Due to this inaccurate interpretation problem, most candidates are unsuccessful in passing the exam, as they appear to have misattempted the test and do not fulfill the requirements of the question.

Although every candidate is technically sound and knowledgeable, it is the art of understanding the question, clear objectives, and hidden restrictions that leads to answering these questions correctly.

One of the main objectives of this book is addressing this very aspect. The exercises are crafted with hidden tricks/gotchas and require a close look, understanding each part of the test and identifying the best approach. This book develops and improves interpretation skills required to pass the CCIE Lab.

The lab is marked out of 100 points. You must complete the lab within 8 hours and obtain a minimum of 80 points to pass. As with all labs, this test has been written such that you should be able to complete all questions, including initial configuration (that is, IP addressing), within 8 hours, excluding cabling time. Allow up to 1 hour for cabling, using the provided instructions and observing the general guidelines. You can use any combination of routers as long as you fulfill the needs of the topology diagram. It is not compulsory to use routers of the same model.

NOTE   The real CCIE Lab does not require you to do any cabling or IP addressing.

Equipment List

- 8 routers with the following specifications (all routers are to be loaded with Cisco IOS Software Release 12.1(T) except for R5—see the following note):

    R1 — 2 Ethernet (with IP Plus image)

    R2 — 1 Ethernet, 1 BRI, 1 serial (with IP Plus + IOS Firewall image)

    R3 — 1 Ethernet, 1 serial (with IP Plus image)

R4 — 1 Ethernet, 1 BRI, 5 serials (with IP Plus image)

R5 — 1 Ethernet, 3 serials (with IP Plus + IPSec 56 image)

NOTE R5 needs to be loaded with 12.2(11)T or higher and R2 with any latest 12.0 mainline available. This is due to some specific tasks in the exercises to follow.

R6 — 1 Ethernet, 1 serial (with IP Plus + IPSec 56 image)

R7 — 2 Ethernet, 1 ATM (with IP Plus image)

R8 — 2 Ethernet, 1 ATM (with IP Plus image)

- 2 switches (3550)
- 1 PIX with 2 interfaces (version 6.x with DES enabled)
- 1 Cisco Intrusion Detection System (IDS) 42xx appliance (new version 4.x)
- 2 PCs:

  Windows 2000 Server with CiscoSecure ACS 3.x+

  Test PC with Cisco VPN Client 3.x software

General Guidelines

- Do not configure any static/default routes unless otherwise specified/required.
- Use DLCIs provided in the diagram.
- Use the IP addressing scheme provided in the diagram; do not change any IP addressing unless otherwise specified. In the CCIE Lab, initial configurations are loaded, and therefore IP addresses are not to be changed. In this book, each chapter has a separate lab topology with different IP addressing, so each chapter needs to be recabled and all IP addresses need to be redone from the previous chapter.
- Use **cisco** as the password for any authentication string, enable-password, and TACACS+/RADIUS key or for any other purpose unless otherwise specified.
- Add additional loopbacks as specified during this lab.
- Configure VLANs on Switch 1 and Switch 2 as per the diagram in Figure 6-1.
- All routers should be able to ping any interface in the network using the *optimal* path.
- Do not use any external resources or answers provided in this book when attempting the lab.
- Do not configure any authentication or authorization on the console and aux ports.

NOTE The real CCIE Lab exams are hands-on structures similar to this book. Each configuration exercise has preassigned point values. The candidate must obtain a minimum mark of 80% to pass. This book provides you with a similar structure to give you a better understanding and experience. For more information on CCIE exam structure, see this URL:

www.cisco.com/warp/customer/625/ccie/exam_preparation/preparation.html

---

Setting Up the Lab

You can use any combination of routers as long as you fulfill the topology diagram, outlined in Figure 6-1. It is not compulsory to use the same model of routers.

Figure 6-1   *Lab Topology Diagram*

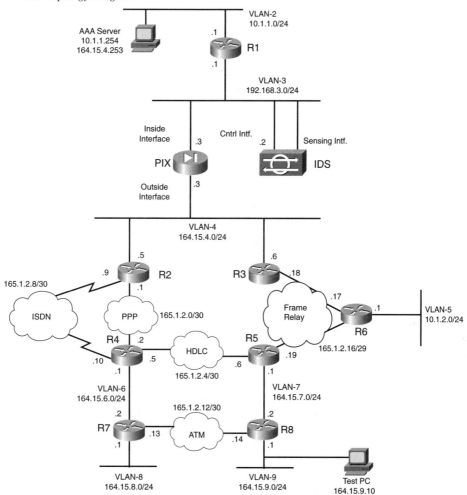

Frame Relay DLCI Information

Configure R4 as a Frame Relay switch and use Figure 6-2 for DLCI information. Only DLCIs indicated in Figure 6-2 should be mapped on the routers.

Routing Protocol Information

Use Figure 6-3 to configure all routing protocols.

Figure 6-2 *Frame Relay DLCI Diagram*

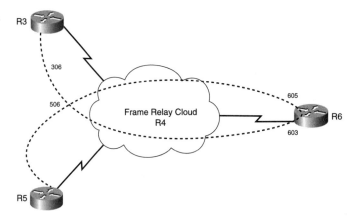

Figure 6-3 *Routing Protocol Information*

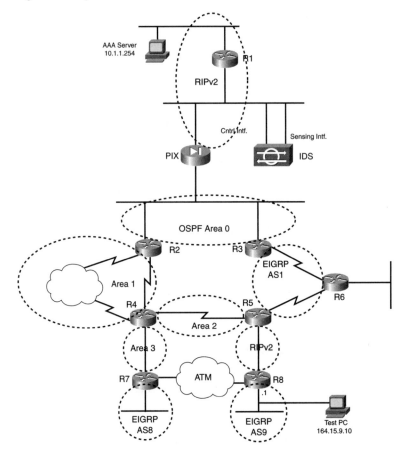

BGP Information

Use Figure 6-4 to configure BGP.

Figure 6-4 *BGP Information*

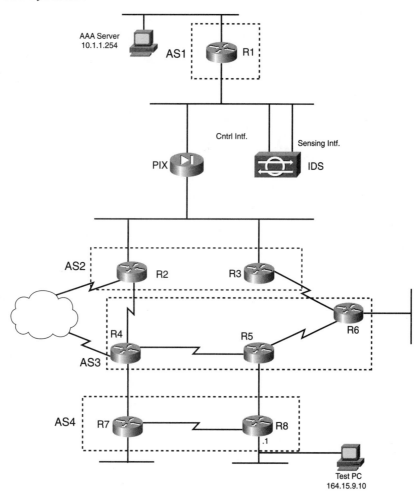

Cabling Instructions

Use Tables 6-1 and 6-2 for cabling all devices in your topology. It is not a must to use the same type or sequence of interface. You may use any combination of interface(s) as long as you fulfill the requirement.

Table 6-1   *Cabling Instructions (Ethernet)*

Ethernet Cabling	VLAN	Switch1	Switch2
Trunk port		Port 1	Port 1
R1-Fastethernet0/0	3	Port 2	
R1-Fastethernet0/1	2		Port 2
R2-Ethernet0	4	Port 3	
R3-Ethernet0/0	4		Port 3
PIX—outside-E0	4		Port 4
PIX—inside-E1	3		Port 5
VPN3000-Private (not used in this lab)	3	Port 4	
VPN3000-Public (not used in this lab)	4		Port 6
IDS Sensing	3	Port 5	
IDS Command and Control	3		Port 7
R4-Ethernet0/0	6	Port 6	
R5-Fastethernet0/0	7	Port 7	
R6-Ethernet0/0	5	Port 8	
R7-Fastethernet0/0	6		Port 8
R7-Fastethernet0/1	8	Port 9	
R8-Ethernet1/0	7		Port 9
R8-Ethernet1/1	9		Port 10
AAA Server	2	Port 10	
Test PC	9	Port 11	

Table 6-2   *Cabling Instructions (Serial)*

Back-to-Back Cabling	DTE-End	DCE-End
R3-to-frsw*	R3-serial0/0	R4-serial1/0
R5-to-frsw*	R5-serial1/0	R4-serial1/1
R6-to-frsw*	R6-serial1/0	R4-serial1/2
R4-to-R2	R2-serial0	R4-serial1/3
R4-to-R5	R5-serial1/1	R4-serial1/4

*frsw = Frame Relay switch R4

Practice Lab 6 Exercises

Chapter 6 introduces Cisco IDS version 4.0. Use the reference links provided in the verification section for more information.

The steps in each exercise are not necessarily intended to be completed in the order indicated. They can be done in any order of preference or as you feel appropriate. There may be situations where the steps have intentionally been written in incorrect order to cause a problem. You have to identify the best approach and fulfill all the requirements.

Section 1.0: Basic Configuration (15 points)

1.1: IP Addressing (2 points)

1 Redraw a detailed topology with all necessary information.

2 Configure IP addressing as shown in Figure 6-1.

3 Make sure you can ping all devices.

4 Configure the following loopbacks:

Loopback-1 11.11.11.11/24 on R1

Loopback-1 22.22.22.22/24 on R2

Loopback-1 33.33.33.33/24 on R3

Loopback-1 44.44.44.44/24 on R4

Loopback-1 55.55.55.55/24 on R5

Loopback-2 155.155.155.155/24 on R5

Loopback-1 66.66.66.66/24 on R6

Loopback-1 77.77.77.77/24 on R7

Loopback-1 88.88.88.88/24 on R8

Loopback-2 188.188.188.188/24 on R8

1.2: Frame Relay Configuration (3 points)

1 Configure R4 as a Frame Relay switch using the DLCI information provided for Frame Relay routing in Figure 6-2.

2 Configure Frame Relay between R3, R5, and R6. Configure a multipoint subinterface on R6 only. See Table 6-2 for link information.

3 Do not configure subinterfaces on any other router.

4 Make sure you are able to ping your own IP address on the Frame Relay interface.

    5 Configure VC-based traffic shaping on R6 for traffic rate for a Committed Information Rate (CIR) of 64 kbps and a peak rate of 128 kbps.

    6 Configure adaptive traffic rate adjustment for backward explicit congestion notifications.

1.3: Serial Configuration (3 points)

    1 Configure serial links between R4 and R2 as shown in Figure 6-1 with PPP encapsulation.

    2 Configure AAA for local authentication and authorization for PPP. R2 should use host name **router2**.

    3 Configure serial links between R4 and R5 as shown in Figure 6-1 with HDLC encapsulation.

    4 Do not configure subinterfaces.

1.4: LAN Switch Configuration (4 points)

    1 Configure both switches with VLANs as shown in Table 6-1.

    2 Configure ISL trunking between the two switches. Port 1 on both switches is connected for trunking. Configure native VLAN for trunk ports to VLAN-100.

    3 Configure VTP domain **lab6** with strong authentication.

    4 Using the built-in Switch database management templates, optimize memory resources on the switch by configuring both switches to be used as a Layer 2 device only, with no routing allowed—that is, disable routing capability on the switch. Do not use the **no ip routing** command to achieve this task.

1.5: ATM Configuration (3 points)

    1 Configure back-to-back ATM between R7 and R8.

    2 Configure ATM PVC on both ends to be same, as there is no ATM switch in between. Configure VPI=0 and VCI=78.

    3 Configure static maps.

NOTE   Define transmit clock source on one end using **atm clock INTERNAL**.

Section 2.0: Routing Configuration (25 points)

2.1: OSPF (5 points)

    1 Configure OSPF areas as shown in Figure 6-3.

    2 Hardcode OSPF router IDs as $x.x.x.x$, where x is the router number.

3 Configure MD5 authentication for all areas.

4 Configure virtual links where necessary using MD5 authentication.

2.2: EIGRP (4 points)

1 Configure EIGRP AS-1 between R3, R5, and R6 in the Frame Relay network 165.1.2.16/29.

2 Configure strong authentication for EIGRP AS-1.

3 Configure a static default route on R6 to null0. Configure R6 to advertise the default route to spokes, R3 and R5. Do not use summarization.

4 Configure R7 and R8 with EIGRP AS8 and AS9 for VLAN8 and VLAN9 networks. Redistribute accordingly.

5 Configure EIGRP AS 1 on R6 to use 40% of the available bandwidth. Do not use **bandwidth** to achieve this task.

2.3: RIP (3 points)

1 Configure RIPv2 between PIX and R1 using MD5 authentication.

2 Configure RIPv2 between R5 and R8 using clear text authentication. Redistribute RIP on R5 accordingly.

3 Do not configure the default route on PIX.

4 R1 should learn the default route from PIX.

5 Advertise Loopback-1 and VLAN2 networks on R1 in RIPv2.

2.4: BGP (13 points)

2.4.1: Basic BGP Configuration (3 points)

1 Configure BGP peers as shown in Figure 6-4.

2 Configure R1 in AS 1 to peer with R2 and R3 in AS 2. Configure PIX static and conduits accordingly.

3 Do not use any update source for BGP peers.

4 Configure R2 and R3 in AS2.

5 Configure R4, R5, and R6 in AS3.

6 Configure R7 and R8 in AS4 on the ATM link.

7 Configure R2 eBGP connections to R1 and R4.

8 Configure R3 eBGP connections to R1 and R6.

9 Configure R7 eBGP connection to R4.

10 Configure R8 eBGP connection to R5.

11 Advertise Loopback-1 on all BGP speakers.

2.4.2: BGP Conditional Advertisement (3 points)

1 Advertise Loopback2 on R8 in BGP.

2 Configure R5 to advertise Loopback2 of R8 to R4 and R6 only if Loopback1 of R8 is present in the BGP table.

2.4.3: BGP Path Selection (4 points)

1 R4 should reach Loopback1 of R7 via R8. R5 should reach Loopback1 of R8 via R7.

2 Do not use local preference, MED, weight, or any filtering mechanism.

3 Do not configure R4 or R5 to achieve this task.

2.4.4: BGP Route Filtering (3 points)

1 Configure filtering such that R1 should not receive any routes originated in AS3 from R3.

2 Do not use route maps, network lists, prefix lists, or distribute lists.

Section 3.0: ISDN Configuration (7 points)

3.1: Basic ISDN (3 points)

1 Configure ISDN on R2 and R4.

2 Use network 165.1.2.8/30.

3 Advertise ISDN network in Area 1 using strong authentication.

ISDN information:

BRI number on R2 is 99047132

BRI number on R4 is 99047265

Switch-type = basic-net3

3.2: PPP Callback (4 points)

1 Configure PPP callback using RADIUS server in VLAN2.

2 R2 should call back R4.

3 Configure static NAT translation and conduits on PIX for the AAA server behind R1 to achieve this task, as shown in Figure 6-1.

4 Configure PPP callback client for outbound calls not to send a challenge to the callback server.

5 Configure the callback server to disconnect the call for any unauthorized users; this should happen before the callback sequence occurs.

Section 4.0: PIX Configuration (6 points)

4.1: Basic PIX Configuration (3 points)

1 Configure host name PIX with inside/outside IP address, as shown in Figure 6-1.

2 Configure RIP for the inside interface using MD5 authentication.

3 Configure RIP to advertise the default route to inside (R1) but not the outside.

4 Do not configure ACL on interface(s); use conduits instead.

5 Configure PAT translation to 164.15.4.254 for all networks behind PIX to be able to ping any networks outside the PIX.

6 Configure static NAT translation for R1 FastEthernet0/0 — 192.168.3.1 to 164.15.4.10 for BGP peering. Configure conduit(s) to permit BGP connection from R2 and R3 only.

7 Configure static NAT translation for Loopback1 of R1 to itself.

8 Configure a static default route on PIX.

4.2: Advanced PIX Configuration (3 points)

1 Configure PIX to send SNMP traps to SNMP server 192.168.3.10.

2 Configure SNMP community string **cisco123**.

3 Configure PIX logging accordingly.

4 SNMP server should not be able to poll from the PIX.

Section 5.0: IPSec/PPTP Configuration (10 points)

5.1: IPSec LAN-to-LAN Router-to-PIX (4 points)

1 Configure IPSec LAN-to-LAN between R6 and PIX for VLAN5 and VLAN2 networks, respectively.

2   Configure preshared with all other parameters accordingly.

3   Configure a static route for network 10.1.1.0/24 if required.

5.2: IPSec Remote Access to Router (3 points)

1   Configure Remote Access VPN client to R5 for Test PC in VLAN9.

2   Configure MD5 hashing and Diffie Hellman group 2.

3   Configure group **3000client** with password **cisco123**.

4   Configure client authentication using local username **cisco** password **cisco**.

5   Configure the VPN client to receive IP addresses in the range 172.16.1.1–172.16.1.10 and DNS server IP 164.15.7.100 and WINS server IP 164.15.7.200 from the router.

6   The client should use the tunnel to access Loopback2 of R5 only. All other outbound traffic should be unencrypted.

7   Do not configure any static route on R5 to achieve this task.

5.3: PPTP to PIX with RADIUS Authentication and MPPE Encryption (3 points)

1   Configure PPTP Remote Access to PIX for Test PC in VLAN9.

2   Configure MS-CHAP authentication and 40-bit MPPE encryption.

3   Configure RADIUS authentication for PPTP clients.

4   Configure IP pool on PIX 192.168.1.1–192.168.1.10 for PPTP clients.

5   Configure a username **pptp-user**, password **cisco** on CiscoSecure ACS.

6   Configure a user in ACS with appropriate attribute settings for MPPE encryption.

Section 6.0: IOS Firewall Configuration (6 points)

6.1: Context-Based Access Control (CBAC) (3 points)

1   Configure CBAC on R2 to protect VLAN4.

2   Inspect all common connection-oriented protocols.

3   Apply egress ACL on unprotected interface(s) only.

4   Allow ICMP explicitly.

6.2: Advanced Context-Based Access Control (CBAC) (3 points)

1 Configure CBAC to allow Java applets from 164.0.0.0/8 and 165.0.0.0/8 networks only.

2 Servers in protected zones should not exceed 200 concurrent embryonic connections. Offending hosts should be blocked for 1 hour.

Section 7.0: AAA (4 points)

7.1: AAA on the Router (4 points)

1 Configure TACACS+ authentication and authorization on R2 for management.

2 Configure accounting for shell and commands.

3 Configure user **r2-telnet**, password **cisco** on CiscoSecure ACS.

4 Configure TACACS+ to maintain a single TCP open connection with the AAA server.

5 All routers should be able to Telnet R2.

6 Configure PIX accordingly.

Section 8.0: Advanced Security (7 points)

8.1: ROMMON Security (3 points)

1 Disable password recovery on R1 to prevent a person with physical access to the router(s) from viewing the configuration file and setting the configuration register to ignore the startup configuration.

8.2: Access Control (2 points)

1 Configure PIX to reset denied TCP packets that terminate at the PIX's least-secure interface.

2 Note that by default, these packets are silently discarded.

8.3: Access Restriction (2 points)

1 Configure access restriction on R3 in VLAN4.

2 R3 should be able to Telnet R2 but not vice versa.

3 All other routers should be able to Telnet to R3.

Section 9.0: IP Services and Protocol-Independent Features (12 points)

9.1: Network Address Translation (NAT) (4 points)

1   Configure NAT on PIX for VLAN2 to 164.15.4.20.

2   Configure NAT on R6 for VLAN5 to 165.1.2.20.

3   IPSec LAN-to-LAN between R6 and PIX for these networks should not be affected.

9.2: HSRP (3 points)

1   Configure secure HSRP between R2 and R3 for redundancy.

2   Configure Virtual IP 164.15.4.100.

3   Monitor the Frame Relay link on R3. In the event of FR going down, R2 should take the Active role.

9.3: Translation Timeout Improvements (1 point)

1   Configure PIX to free up translation slot(s) after 1 hour of idle time.

9.4: Congestion Management—QoS (4 points)

1   Control congestion on R6 by configuring queuing using the following parameters:

   * IP packets with a byte count greater than 1500 are assigned a low-priority queue level.

   * IP packets originating on or destined for TCP port 23 are assigned a medium-priority queue level.

   * IP packets entering on interface Ethernet 0/0 (VLAN5) have medium priority.

   * All IP routing protocols configured on R6 have high priority.

   * All other IP packets assigned have a high-priority queue level.

2   Select a queuing type that ensures guaranteed timely delivery.

3   Increase Telnet performance in Section 7.1 by reducing the size of the TCP/IP headers. The router is experiencing a large percentage of small packets for excessive Telnet connections.

Section 10.0: Security Violations (8 points)

10.1: DoS Attack (4 points)

1 A web server was attacked on the network.

2 The nature of the attack could not be characterized.

3 Sniffing data collected is the only forensic evidence available to determine the nature of the attack.

4 Assume R7-Loopback1 (77.77.77.77) is the web server in this question.

5 Analyze the sniffer captures provided in Figures 6-5a through 6-5d and characterize the attack. Determine the best possible method to prevent such an attack in the future.

6 Note the attack is from a random source IP. You cannot configure ACL or any other method for Layer 3 or Layer 4 information provided in the sniffer captures.

7 Do not configure any ACL on any interface to achieve this task.

Figure 6-5a *Attack Sniff Capture 1*

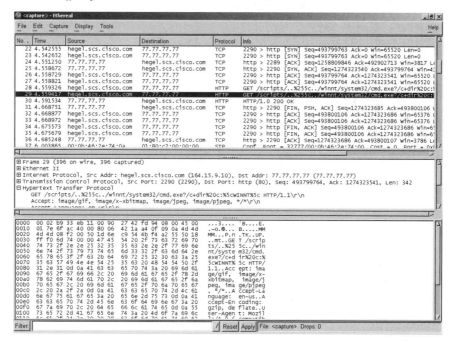

Figure 6-5b *Attack Sniff Capture 2*

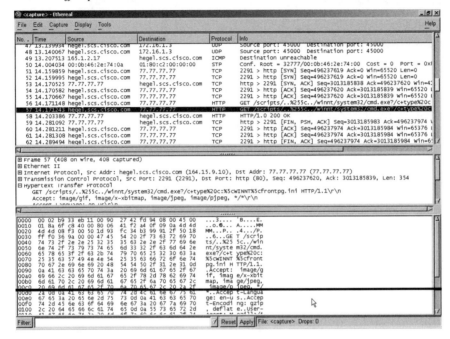

Figure 6-5c *Attack Sniff Capture 3*

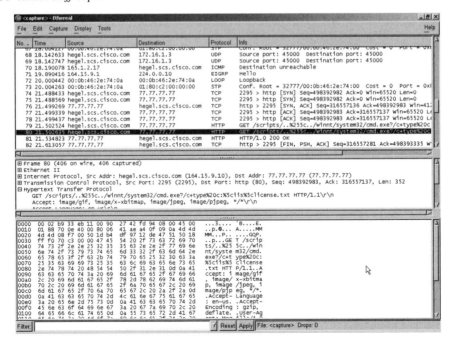

Figure 6-5d *Attack Sniff Capture 4*

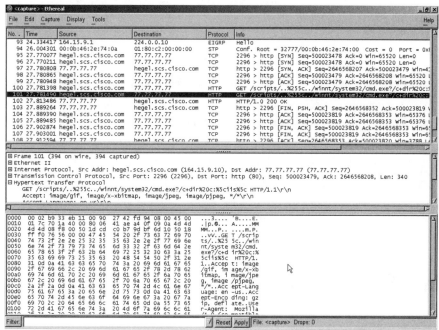

10.2: IDS Blocking (Shunning) (4 points)

1 Configure Cisco IDS sensor (version 4.0) as shown in Figure 6-1.

2 Configure the Command and Control interface with IP address 192.168.3.2 in VLAN-3.

3 Configure IDS to protect the web server. Assume R1-Loopback1 (11.11.11.11) to be the web server. Configure access to the web server accordingly.

4 Initialize the sensor from the console. Configure IP address, default gateway, and host name **sensor1** accordingly.

5 Use IDM (IDS Device Manager) to configure other parameters and IEV (IDS Event Viewer) to receive alarms from the sensor.

6 Configure IDS for port 8080 for IDM (web browsing) to the sensor. Default is 443.

7 Configure IDS for Telnet management from VLAN2 and VLAN3 networks only.

8 Identify and tune a built-in signature for the unique pattern that matches the sniffer captures shown in Figures 6-5a through 6-5d to combat similar attacks. Make sure it is High severity. Configure this signature for shunning, blocking all sources of these attacks.

NOTE	If you do not have IDS version 4.0, use a sensor with version 3.x, configure all parameters as appropriate, and complete the remaining tasks in the preceding exercise.

Verification, Hints, and Troubleshooting Tips

Some parts of the exercises can be tricky and may impact other sections. Well-thought-out techniques require approaching each part of the lab.

Always redraw a detailed diagram, and highlight each aspect of the network so that it is easy to visualize the big picture with all the necessary information on one page.

The hints provided here are to be used as a guideline and address some or all parts of the corresponding exercise question. They are not listed in any order. You can always use an alternative approach to address the exercise as long as you fulfill the requirements and do not violate any known or unknown restrictions.

Section 1.0: Basic Configuration

1.1: IP Addressing

1 Redraw a detailed topology. This helps you visualize the entire topology with all the necessary information and eases the troubleshooting process.

2 Configure IP addressing as shown in Figure 6-1.

3 Configure loopback(s) as indicated. All loopbacks will be used in exercises to follow.

4 Make sure you can ping all devices after you finish each individual exercise and toward the end of all the exercises.

1.2: Frame Relay Configuration

1 Configure R4 as a Frame Relay switch using the DLCI information provided for Frame Relay routing in Figure 6-2.

2 Configure Frame Relay between R3, R5, and R6. Configure subinterface(s) on R6 only. See Table 6-2 for link information.

3 Do not configure subinterfaces on any other router.

4 To ping your own IP address on the Frame Relay interface, configure a static map for your own IP address.

5   Configure traffic shaping on R6 on a per VC based for traffic rate for CIR of 64 kbps and a peak rate of 128 kbps. Refer to the example following item 7.

6   Configure adaptive traffic rate adjustment for BECN. Refer to the example following item 7.

7   Remember to enable traffic shaping on the main FR interface for all PVCs and SVCs as demonstrated in the following example:

```
hostname r6
!
interface Serial1/0
 frame-relay traffic-shaping
!
interface Serial1/0.1 multipoint
 ip address 165.1.2.17 255.255.255.248
 frame-relay class lab6
!
map-class frame-relay lab6
 frame-relay traffic-rate 64000 128000
 frame-relay adaptive-shaping becn
```

NOTE   See this URL for pinging your own interface in Frame Relay:

www.cisco.com/warp/public/125/12.html#pingyourself

See these URLs for Frame Relay traffic shaping:

www.cisco.com/warp/public/125/12.html#topic10

www.cisco.com/univercd/cc/td/doc/product/software/ios122/122newft/122t/122t4/ft_afrts.htm

1.3: Serial Configuration

1   Serial links between R4 and R2 are connected back-to-back, no Frame Relay. See Figure 6-1 to configure with PPP encapsulation.

2   Configure AAA and local authentication and authorization for PPP. Configure R2 to send CHAP host name **router2**. Configure username **router2** on R4 and username **r4** on R2, as demonstrated in the following example:

```
! <Snip from R2>
hostname r2
!
aaa new-model
aaa authentication ppp default local
aaa authorization network default local
```

```
!
username r4 password 0 cisco
!
interface Serial0
 ip address 165.1.2.1 255.255.255.252
 encapsulation ppp
 ppp authentication chap
 ppp chap hostname router2

! <snip from R4>
hostname r4
!
!
username router2 password 0 cisco

aaa new-model
aaa authentication ppp default local
aaa authorization network default local
!
interface Serial1/3
 ip address 165.1.2.2 255.255.255.252
 encapsulation ppp
 clockrate 56000
 ppp authentication chap
```

3 Serial links between R4 and R5 are also connected back-to-back, as shown in Figure 6-1. Use the default HDLC encapsulation.

4 Do not configure subinterfaces.

1.4: LAN Switch Configuration

1 Configure VLANs on both switches as shown in Table 6-1.

2 Configure ISL trunking between the two switches on Port 1 and configure native VLAN for trunk ports to VLAN-100, as demonstrated in the following example:

```
! <Snip from Switch1>
interface FastEthernet0/1
 switchport trunk encapsulation isl
 switchport trunk native vlan 100
 switchport mode trunk

! <Snip from Switch2>
interface FastEthernet0/1
 switchport trunk encapsulation isl
 switchport trunk native vlan 100
 switchport mode trunk
```

3 Configure VTP domain **lab6** with password **cisco**.

4 3550s have built-in switch database management (SDM) templates, which can be used to optimize memory resources on the switch. Configure the SDM "VLAN" template on both switches for Layer 2 functionality only. Configure the SDM "VLAN" template, disabling routing capability in the switch. The following example demonstrates how to configure and verify SDM templates:

```
! <snip from Switch1>
sw1(config)#sdm prefer vlan
Changes to the running SDM preferences have been stored, but cannot take
effect until the next reload.
Use 'show sdm prefer' to see what SDM preference is currently active.

NOTE: Use caution with 'sdm prefer vlan', as any current Layer3 configuration
data will not be saved after a reload.
sw1(config)#
sw1(config)#exit
sw1#
sw1#reload
Proceed with reload? [confirm]

! After reloading the switch;
sw1#show sdm prefer
 The current template is the vlan template.
 The selected template optimizes the resources in
 the switch to support this level of features for
 8 routed interfaces and 1K VLANs.

 number of unicast mac addresses:   8K
 number of igmp groups:             1K
 number of qos aces:                1K
 number of security aces:           1K
 number of unicast routes:          0
 number of multicast routes:        0
```

NOTE   You need to reboot the switches for changes to take effect.

NOTE   For more information on Switch Database Management (SDM) templates, see the following URL:

www.cisco.com/univercd/cc/td/doc/product/lan/c3550/12113ea1/3550scg
/swadmin.htm#1171047

1.5: ATM Configuration

1 Configure back-to-back ATM between R7 and R8.

2 For back-to-back connection, you need to configure one end with **atm clock INTERNAL** for clock source.

3 Configure ATM PVC on both ends to be the same, as there is no ATM switch in between. Configure VPI=0 and VCI=78.

4 Configure static maps to peer address with broadcast.

Section 2.0: Routing Configuration

2.1: OSPF

1 Configure OSPF areas as shown in Figure 6-3.

2 Configure MD5 authentication for all areas.

3 Hardcode OSPF router IDs (see the example following item 4).

4 Configure an OSPF virtual link between R2 and R4 using MD5 authentication, as demonstrated in the following example:

```
hostname r2
!
router ospf 110
 router-id 2.2.2.2
 log-adjacency-changes
 area 0 authentication message-digest
 area 1 authentication message-digest
 area 1 virtual-link 4.4.4.4 message-digest-key 1 md5 7 02050D480809
 network 164.15.4.0 0.0.0.255 area 0
 network 165.1.2.0 0.0.0.3 area 1
 network 165.1.2.8 0.0.0.3 area 1
!

r2#show ip ospf virtual-links
Virtual Link OSPF_VL0 to router 4.4.4.4 is up
  Run as demand circuit
  DoNotAge LSA allowed.
  Transit area 1, via interface Serial0, Cost of using 64
  Transmit Delay is 1 sec, State POINT_TO_POINT,
  Timer intervals configured, Hello 10, Dead 40, Wait 40, Retransmit 5
    Hello due in 00:00:01
    Adjacency State FULL (Hello suppressed)
```

```
Message digest authentication enabled
   Youngest key id is 1
r2#


r2#show ip ospf neighbor

Neighbor ID      Pri  State        Dead Time   Address       Interface
3.3.3.3            1  FULL/DR      00:00:34    164.15.4.6    Ethernet0
4.4.4.4            1  FULL/  -     00:00:35    165.1.2.2     Serial0
r2#


hostname r4
!
router ospf 110
 router-id 4.4.4.4
 log-adjacency-changes
 area 0 authentication message-digest
 area 1 authentication message-digest
 area 1 virtual-link 2.2.2.2 message-digest-key 1 md5 cisco
 area 2 authentication message-digest
 area 3 authentication message-digest
 network 164.15.6.0 0.0.0.255 area 3
 network 165.1.2.0 0.0.0.3 area 1
 network 165.1.2.4 0.0.0.3 area 2
 network 165.1.2.8 0.0.0.3 area 1


r4#show ip ospf virtual-links
Virtual Link OSPF_VL0 to router 2.2.2.2 is up
  Run as demand circuit
  DoNotAge LSA allowed.
  Transit area 1, via interface Serial1/3, Cost of using 781
  Transmit Delay is 1 sec, State POINT_TO_POINT,
  Timer intervals configured, Hello 10, Dead 40, Wait 40, Retransmit 5
    Hello due in 00:00:06
    Adjacency State FULL (Hello suppressed)
    Index 1/1, retransmission queue length 0, number of retransmission 1
    First 0x0(0)/0x0(0) Next 0x0(0)/0x0(0)
    Last retransmission scan length is 1, maximum is 1
    Last retransmission scan time is 0 msec, maximum is 0 msec
  Message digest authentication enabled
   Youngest key id is 1
r4#
```

```
r4#show ip ospf neighbor

Neighbor ID     Pri   State       Dead Time   Address       Interface
2.2.2.2          1    FULL/  -    00:00:35    165.1.2.1     Serial1/3
5.5.5.5          1    FULL/  -    00:00:35    165.1.2.6     Serial1/4
7.7.7.7          1    FULL/DR     00:00:38    164.15.6.2    Ethernet0/0
r4#
```

2.2: EIGRP

1   Configure EIGRP AS-1 between R3, R5, and R6 in the Frame Relay network 165.1.2.16/29.
    A hidden issue is that due to the Frame Relay hub-and-spoke issue, the hub will not
    advertise routes learned from spoke(s) due to **split-horizon** being enabled. That is, R6
    (hub) will not advertise EIGRP routes from R3 to R5 and vice versa. The workaround is
    to disable split horizon on the Frame Relay link on R6. Again, EIGRP split horizon is
    disabled using **no ip split-horizon eigrp** *AS#*. See the following example:

```
hostname r6
!
interface Serial1/0.1 multipoint
 ip address 165.1.2.17 255.255.255.248
 no ip directed-broadcast
 ip bandwidth-percent eigrp 1 40
 ip authentication mode eigrp 1 md5
 ip authentication key-chain eigrp 1 lab6
 no ip split-horizon eigrp 1
 frame-relay map ip 165.1.2.17 603 broadcast
 frame-relay map ip 165.1.2.18 603 broadcast
 frame-relay map ip 165.1.2.19 605 broadcast
 no frame-relay inverse-arp
```

2   Configure MD5 authentication for EIGRP AS-1.

3   Configure a static default route on R6 to null0. Redistribute static into EIGRP 1 for spokes
    to learn.

4   Another hidden issue. For the rest of the network to learn Frame Relay network
    165.1.2.16/29, redistribute connected on R3 and R5.

5   Configure EIGRP AS8 and AS9 for networks in VLAN-8 and VLAN-9 on R7 and R8.
    Redistribute EIGRP on R7 and R8 accordingly.

6   Configure bandwidth utilization in EIGRP AS 1 on R6 to use 40% of the bandwidth, as
    demonstrated in the configuration following item 1.

2.3: RIP

1 Configure RIPv2 on PIX and R1 using MD5 authentication. Advertise Loopback-1 on R1 in RIPv2.

2 Configure RIPv2 on R5 and R8 using clear text authentication. Redistribute RIP on R5 into OSPF and EIGRP and vice versa. Remember, three-way redistribution doesn't work. Also redistribute OSPF into EIGRP. See the example following item 3.

3 You also need to redistribute connected on R5 into OSPF for others to learn FR and VLAN7 network. See redistribution into OSPF for connected networks in the following example:

```
hostname r5
!
router eigrp 1
 redistribute ospf 110
 redistribute rip
 network 55.55.55.0 0.0.0.255
 network 165.1.2.16 0.0.0.7
 default-metric 10000 1000 255 1 1500
 no auto-summary
 no eigrp log-neighbor-changes
!
router ospf 110
 router-id 5.5.5.5
 log-adjacency-changes
 area 2 authentication message-digest
 redistribute connected metric 1 subnets route-map conn
 redistribute rip metric 1 subnets
 network 165.1.2.4 0.0.0.3 area 2
!
router rip
 version 2
 redistribute eigrp 1 metric 1
 redistribute ospf 110 metric 1
 passive-interface Serial1/0
 passive-interface Serial1/1
 network 164.15.0.0
 no auto-summary
!
access-list 1 permit 165.1.2.16 0.0.0.7
access-list 1 permit 164.15.7.0 0.0.0.255
!
route-map conn permit 10
 match ip address 1
!
```

4 Configure PIX to advertise the default route to R1.

5 Advertise Loopback-1 and VLAN2 networks on R1 in RIPv2.

2.4: BGP

2.4.1: Basic BGP Configuration

1 Configure BGP peers as shown in Figure 6-4.

2 Do not use any update source for BGP peers.

3 Configure R1 in AS1 to peer with R2 and R3. Configure PIX static and conduits accordingly, as demonstrated in the example that follows (remember to configure next hop on R2 and R3 to NATed address on PIX):

```
PIX(config)# show static
static (inside,outside) 164.15.4.10 192.168.3.1 netmask 255.255.255.255 0 0

PIX(config)# show conduit
conduit permit icmp any any (hitcnt=20)
conduit permit tcp host 164.15.4.10 eq bgp host 164.15.4.5 (hitcnt=1)
conduit permit tcp host 164.15.4.10 eq bgp host 164.15.4.6 (hitcnt=1)
```

4 Configure R2 in AS2 to peer with R3 and R4.

5 Configure R3 in AS2 to peer with R1, R2, and R6.

6 Configure R4 in AS3 to peer with R2 , R5, and R7.

7 Configure R5 in AS3 to peer with R4, R6, and R8.

8 Configure R6 in AS3 to peer with R3 and R5. Make sure you configure next-hop-self for R3 and R5 peer.

9 Configure R7 in AS4 to peer with R4 and R8.

10 Configure R8 in AS4 to peer with R5 and R7.

11 Advertise Loopback-1 on all BGP speakers.

2.4.2: BGP Conditional Advertisement

1 Advertise Loopback2 on R8 in BGP.

2 Configure R5 for conditional advertisement for Loopback2 of R8 to R4 and R6, as demonstrated in the following example:

```
hostname r5
!
```

```
router bgp 3
 bgp router-id 5.5.5.5
 neighbor 165.1.2.5 remote-as 3
 neighbor 165.1.2.5 route-reflector-client
 neighbor 165.1.2.5 advertise-map conditional-advertisement exist-map
   check-route-from-R8
 neighbor 165.1.2.17 remote-as 3
 neighbor 165.1.2.17 route-reflector-client
 neighbor 165.1.2.17 advertise-map conditional-advertisement exist-map
   check-route-from-R8
 no auto-summary
!
access-list 10 permit 88.88.88.0 0.0.0.255
access-list 11 permit 188.188.188.0 0.0.0.255
!
route-map conditional-advertisement permit 10
 match ip address 11
!
route-map check-route-from-R8 permit 10
 match ip address 10
!
```

3 Verify by shutting down Loopback1 on R8. R5 will then *not* advertise Loopback2 of R8 to its neighbors R4 and R6 due to the absence of Loopback1 of R8.

NOTE   The BGP Conditional Route Injection feature is supported by all platforms in Cisco IOS Release 12.2(11)T or higher that support BGP.

2.4.3: BGP Path Selection

1 R4 should reach Loopback1 of R7 via R8. R5 should reach Loopback1 of R8 via R7.

2 Configure AS-PATH prepend on R7 and R8.

3 See the following example to configure as-path prepend on R7:

```
hostname r7
!
router bgp 4
 bgp router-id 7.7.7.7
 network 77.77.77.0 mask 255.255.255.0
 neighbor 164.15.6.1 remote-as 3
 neighbor 164.15.6.1 route-map set-prepend out
 neighbor 165.1.2.14 remote-as 4
 no auto-summary
!
```

```
access-list 1 permit 77.77.77.0 0.0.0.255
!
route-map set-prepend permit 10
 match ip address 1
 set as-path prepend 4 4
!
route-map set-prepend permit 20


! BGP table on R4 before AS-PATH prepend on R7.
r4#show ip bgp
BGP table version is 32, local router ID is 4.4.4.4
Status codes: s suppressed, d damped, h history, * valid, > best,
  i - internal,
               r RIB-failure
Origin codes: i - IGP, e - EGP, ? - incomplete

   Network          Next Hop         Metric LocPrf Weight Path
 * i22.22.22.0/24   165.1.2.18              100      0 2 i
 *>                 165.1.2.1        0               0 2 i
 * i33.33.33.0/24   165.1.2.18       0      100      0 2 i
 *>                 165.1.2.1                        0 2 i
 *> 44.44.44.0/24   0.0.0.0          0           32768 i
 *>i55.55.55.0/24   165.1.2.6        0      100      0 i
 *>i66.66.66.0/24   165.1.2.17       0      100      0 i
 * i77.77.77.0/24   165.1.2.6               100      0 4 i
 *>                 164.15.6.2       0               0 4 i
 * i88.88.88.0/24   164.15.7.2       0      100      0 4 i
 *>                 164.15.6.2                       0 4 i
 * i188.188.188.0/24 164.15.7.2      0      100      0 4 i
 *>                 164.15.6.2                       0 4 i


! BGP table on R4 after AS-PATH prepend on R7.
r4#show ip bgp
BGP table version is 72, local router ID is 4.4.4.4
Status codes: s suppressed, d damped, h history, * valid, > best,
  i - internal,
               r RIB-failure
Origin codes: i - IGP, e - EGP, ? - incomplete

   Network          Next Hop         Metric LocPrf Weight Path
 * i22.22.22.0/24   165.1.2.18              100      0 2 i
 *>                 165.1.2.1        0               0 2 i
 * i33.33.33.0/24   165.1.2.18       0      100      0 2 i
 *>                 165.1.2.1                        0 2 i
```

```
*> 44.44.44.0/24    0.0.0.0               0            32768 i
*>i55.55.55.0/24    165.1.2.6             0     100       0 i
*>i66.66.66.0/24    165.1.2.17            0     100       0 i
*>i77.77.77.0/24    165.1.2.6                   100       0 4 i
*                   164.15.6.2            0             0 4 4 4 i
*> 88.88.88.0/24    164.15.6.2                         0 4 i
* i188.188.188.0/24 165.1.2.6             0     100     0 4 i
*>                  164.15.6.2                         0 4 i
```

4 See the following example to configure as-path prepend on R8:

```
hostname r8
!
router bgp 4
 bgp router-id 8.8.8.8
 network 88.88.88.0 mask 255.255.255.0
 network 188.188.188.0 mask 255.255.255.0
 neighbor 164.15.7.1 remote-as 3
 neighbor 164.15.7.1 route-map set-prepend out
 neighbor 165.1.2.13 remote-as 4
 no auto-summary
!
access-list 1 permit 88.88.88.0 0.0.0.255
!
route-map set-prepend permit 10
 match ip address 1
 set as-path prepend 4 4
!
route-map set-prepend permit 20
```

```
! BGP table on R5 before AS-PATH prepend on R8.
r5#show ip bgp
BGP table version is 57, local router ID is 5.5.5.5
Status codes: s suppressed, d damped, h history, * valid, > best,
  i - internal,
                r RIB-failure
Origin codes: i - IGP, e - EGP, ? - incomplete

    Network          Next Hop          Metric LocPrf Weight Path
*>i22.22.22.0/24    165.1.2.18                100       0 2 i
* i                 165.1.2.1            0     100       0 2 i
*>i33.33.33.0/24    165.1.2.18           0     100       0 2 i
* i                 165.1.2.1                  100       0 2 i
*>i44.44.44.0/24    165.1.2.5            0     100       0 i
*> 55.55.55.0/24    0.0.0.0              0            32768 i
*>i66.66.66.0/24    165.1.2.17           0     100       0 i
```

```
*> 77.77.77.0/24    164.15.7.2                       0 4 i
* i                 164.15.6.2          0     100     0 4 i
*> 88.88.88.0/24    164.15.7.2          0             0 4 i
* i                 164.15.6.2                100     0 4 i
*> 188.188.188.0/24 164.15.7.2          0             0 4 i
* i                 164.15.6.2                100     0 4 i


! BGP table on R5 after AS-PATH prepend on R8.
r5#show ip bgp
BGP table version is 10, local router ID is 5.5.5.5
Status codes: s suppressed, d damped, h history, * valid, > best,
  i - internal,
                r RIB-failure
Origin codes: i - IGP, e - EGP, ? - incomplete

    Network           Next Hop          Metric LocPrf Weight Path
* i22.22.22.0/24      165.1.2.1           0     100     0 2 i
*>i                   165.1.2.18               100     0 2 i
* i33.33.33.0/24      165.1.2.1                100     0 2 i
*>i                   165.1.2.18          0     100     0 2 i
*>i44.44.44.0/24      165.1.2.5           0     100     0 i
*> 55.55.55.0/24      0.0.0.0             0          32768 i
*>i66.66.66.0/24      165.1.2.17          0     100     0 i
*> 77.77.77.0/24      164.15.7.2                        0 4 i
*  88.88.88.0/24      164.15.7.2          0             0 4 4 4 i
*>i                   164.15.6.2                100     0 4 i
*> 188.188.188.0/24   164.15.7.2          0             0 4 i
* i                   164.15.6.2                100     0 4 i
```

2.4.4: BGP Route Filtering

1 Configure filtering on R1 not to receive any routes originated in AS3 from R3 using as-path ACL with filter list. Refer to the example following item 2.

2 Note that the emphasis is on originated AS3 routes, such as Loopback1s on AS3 routers—R4, R5, and R6. All other routes traversed R3 having AS3 in as-path (such as Loopback1 of R7 and R8) should be visible. See the BGP table on R1 in the following example after applying the filter list:

```
hostname r1
!
router bgp 1
 bgp router-id 1.1.1.1
 network 11.11.11.0 mask 255.255.255.0
 neighbor 164.15.4.5 remote-as 2
```

```
neighbor 164.15.4.5 ebgp-multihop 255
neighbor 164.15.4.6 remote-as 2
neighbor 164.15.4.6 ebgp-multihop 255
neighbor 164.15.4.6 filter-list 1 in
no auto-summary
!
ip as-path access-list 1 deny _3$
ip as-path access-list 1 permit .*
!
route-map filter-AS3-routes-from-R3 permit 10
 match as-path 1
!
route-map filter-AS3-routes-from-R3 permit 20
!
```

```
! BGP table on R1 before applying the filter-list.
r1#show ip bgp
BGP table version is 10, local router ID is 1.1.1.1
Status codes: s suppressed, d damped, h history, * valid, > best, i - internal
Origin codes: i - IGP, e - EGP, ? - incomplete
```

Network	Next Hop	Metric	LocPrf	Weight	Path
*> 11.11.11.0/24	0.0.0.0	0		32768	i
* 22.22.22.0/24	164.15.4.5			0	2 i
*>	164.15.4.5	0		0	2 i
* 33.33.33.0/24	164.15.4.6	0		0	2 i
*>	164.15.4.6			0	2 i
* 44.44.44.0/24	164.15.4.6			0	2 3 i
*>	164.15.4.5			0	2 3 i
* 55.55.55.0/24	164.15.4.6			0	2 3 i
*>	164.15.4.5			0	2 3 i
* 66.66.66.0/24	164.15.4.6			0	2 3 i
*>	164.15.4.5			0	2 3 i
* 77.77.77.0/24	164.15.4.6			0	2 3 4 i
*>	164.15.4.5			0	2 3 4 i
* 88.88.88.0/24	164.15.4.6			0	2 3 4 i
*>	164.15.4.5			0	2 3 4 i
* 188.188.188.0/24	164.15.4.6			0	2 3 4 i
*>	164.15.4.5			0	2 3 4 i

```
! BGP table on R1 after applying the filter-list.
r1#show ip bgp
BGP table version is 10, local router ID is 1.1.1.1
```

```
Status codes: s suppressed, d damped, h history, * valid, > best, i - internal
Origin codes: i - IGP, e - EGP, ? - incomplete

     Network            Next Hop          Metric LocPrf Weight Path
*>  11.11.11.0/24      0.0.0.0                0           32768 i
*   22.22.22.0/24      164.15.4.5                            0 2 i
*>                     164.15.4.5             0               0 2 i
*   33.33.33.0/24      164.15.4.6             0               0 2 i
*>                     164.15.4.6                            0 2 i
*>  44.44.44.0/24      164.15.4.5                            0 2 3 i
*>  55.55.55.0/24      164.15.4.5                            0 2 3 i
*>  66.66.66.0/24      164.15.4.5                            0 2 3 i
*   77.77.77.0/24      164.15.4.6                            0 2 3 4 i
*>                     164.15.4.5                            0 2 3 4 i
*   88.88.88.0/24      164.15.4.6                            0 2 3 4 i
*>                     164.15.4.5                            0 2 3 4 i
*   188.188.188.0/24   164.15.4.6                            0 2 3 4 i
*>                     164.15.4.5                            0 2 3 4 i
```

Section 3.0: ISDN Configuration

3.1: Basic ISDN

1 Configure ISDN between R2 and R4 using network 165.1.2.8/30.

2 Advertise ISDN network in Area 1 using MD5 authentication.

3 Remember, you need to configure ACL and CBAC on ISDN (BRI) interface on R2 for Section 6.1. See the example following item 3 in Section 6.1 in the pages that follow.

3.2: PPP Callback

1 Configure PPP callback using the RADIUS server in VLAN2, as demonstrated in the example following item 4.

2 Configure R2 as a callback server and R4 as a callback client.

3 Configure static NAT translation and conduits on PIX for AAA server, as demonstrated in the following example:

```
PIX(config)# show static
static (inside,outside) 164.15.4.253 10.1.1.254 netmask 255.255.255.255 0 0

PIX(config)# show conduit
conduit permit icmp any any (hitcnt=607)
conduit permit udp host 164.15.4.253 eq radius host 22.22.22.22 (hitcnt=3)
```

4 Configure PPP CHAP authentication with the **callin** option on the callback client so that it does not send a challenge to the callback server, as demonstrated in the following example:

```
! <Callback server (R2) configuration>
hostname r2
!
aaa new-model
aaa authentication login vty tacacs+ none
aaa authentication ppp default local
aaa authentication ppp isdn radius local
aaa authorization exec vty tacacs+ none
aaa authorization network default local
aaa authorization network isdn radius local
enable password 7 02050D480809
!
username r4 password 7 14141B180F0B
!
interface BRI0
 ip address 165.1.2.9 255.255.255.252
 ip access-group 101 in
 no ip directed-broadcast
 ip inspect lab6 out
 encapsulation ppp
 ip ospf message-digest-key 1 md5 7 1511021F0725
 dialer callback-secure
 dialer idle-timeout 900
 dialer map ip 165.1.2.2 name r4 class lab6 broadcast 99047265
 dialer-group 1
 isdn switch-type basic-net3
 no peer default ip address
 no fair-queue
 no cdp enable
 ppp callback accept
 ppp authentication chap isdn
 ppp authorization isdn
!
ip radius source-interface Loopback1
!
map-class dialer lab6
 dialer callback-server username
!
access-list 199 deny    ospf any any
access-list 199 deny    eigrp any any
access-list 199 deny    tcp any any eq bgp
access-list 199 deny    tcp any eq bgp any
access-list 199 permit ip any any
!
```

```
dialer-list 1 protocol ip list 199
!
radius-server host 164.15.4.253 auth-port 1645 acct-port 1646
radius-server key cisco


! <Callback client (R4) configuration>
hostname r4
!
username r2 password 0 cisco
!
interface BRI0/0
 ip address 165.1.2.10 255.255.255.252
 encapsulation ppp
 ip ospf message-digest-key 1 md5 cisco
 dialer idle-timeout 900
 dialer map ip 165.1.2.9 name r2 broadcast 99047132
 dialer-group 1
 isdn switch-type basic-net3
 no peer default ip address
 no fair-queue
 no cdp enable
 ppp callback request
 ppp authentication chap callin
!
dialer-list 1 protocol ip permit
!
```

5 Dialstring needs to be downloaded and applied from the AAA (RADIUS) server.

6 Configure the **dialer callback-secure** command on the callback server. This will disconnect any unauthorized users before callback.

7 On the AAA server (RADIUS) attribute configuration, the Cisco AVPair lcp:send-secret=cisco is needed during authentication of the callback. If you do not include this AVPair, you must configure the remote router's CHAP username and password locally on the callback server.

NOTE   You must configure the following attributes for RADIUS callback to work. Syntax may vary from RADIUS servers. See Figures 6-6a and 6-6b for ACS settings:

Cisco-AVPair = "lcp:callback-dialstring=99047265"

Cisco-AVPair = "lcp:send-secret=cisco"

---

8 See the username **r4** settings in Figures 6-6a and 6-6b and callback attribute settings on CiscoSecure ACS.

Figure 6-6a *Username r4 for PPP Callback in ACS*

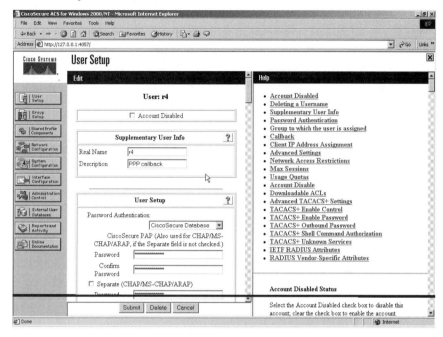

Figure 6-6b *PPP Callback Attributes*

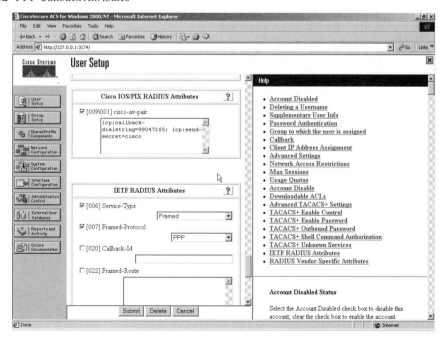

9 Verify by shutting the PPP link between R2 and R4, as demonstrated in the following example:

```
! <Debugs and show output from R2-callback-server>
r2#show debug
Dial on demand:
  Dial on demand events debugging is on
Callback:
  Callback activity debugging is on

4d01h: %LINK-3-UPDOWN: Interface BRI0:1, changed state to up
4d01h: BR0:1 DDR: PPP callback Callback server starting to r4 99047265
4d01h: BR0:1 DDR: disconnecting call
4d01h:  isdn_Call_disconnect()

4d01h: %LINK-3-UPDOWN: Interface BRI0:1, changed state to down
4d01h: BR0:1 DDR: disconnecting call
4d01h:  isdn_Call_disconnect()

4d01h: BR0:1 DDR: disconnecting call
r2#
r2#
r2#
4d01h: DDR: Callback timer expired
4d01h: BR0 DDR: beginning callback to r4 99047265
4d01h: BR0 DDR: Attempting to dial 99047265
4d01h: DDR: Freeing callback to r4 99047265
4d01h: %LINK-3-UPDOWN: Interface BRI0:1, changed state to up
4d01h: %ISDN-6-CONNECT: Interface BRI0:1 is now connected to 99047265
4d01h: %LINEPROTO-5-UPDOWN: Line protocol on Interface BRI0:1, changed state
   to up
4d01h: %OSPF-5-ADJCHG: Process 110, Nbr 4.4.4.4 on BRI0 from DOWN to INIT,
   Received Hello
4d01h: %ISDN-6-CONNECT: Interface BRI0:1 is now connected to 99047265 r4
4d01h: %OSPF-5-ADJCHG: Process 110, Nbr 4.4.4.4 on BRI0 from INIT to 2WAY,
   2-Way Received
4d01h: %OSPF-5-ADJCHG: Process 110, Nbr 4.4.4.4 on BRI0 from 2WAY to EXSTART,
   AdjOK?
4d01h: %OSPF-5-ADJCHG: Process 110, Nbr 4.4.4.4 on BRI0 from EXSTART to
   EXCHANGE, Negotiation Done
4d01h: %OSPF-5-ADJCHG: Process 110, Nbr 4.4.4.4 on BRI0 from EXCHANGE to
   LOADING, Exchange Done
4d01h: %OSPF-5-ADJCHG: Process 110, Nbr 4.4.4.4 on BRI0 from LOADING to FULL,
   Loading Done
r2#
r2#
r2#show dialer
```

```
BRI0 - dialer type = ISDN

Dial String      Successes   Failures   Last called   Last status
99047265             16          2       00:00:18      successful
0 incoming call(s) have been screened.
0 incoming call(s) rejected for callback.


BRI0:1 - dialer type = ISDN
Idle timer (900 secs), Fast idle timer (20 secs)
Wait for carrier (30 secs), Re-enable (15 secs)
Dialer state is data link layer up
Dial reason: Callback return call
Time until disconnect 883 secs
Connected to 99047265 (r4)


BRI0:2 - dialer type = ISDN
Idle timer (900 secs), Fast idle timer (20 secs)
Wait for carrier (30 secs), Re-enable (15 secs)
Dialer state is idle
```

r2#**show isdn active**
```
--------------------------------------------------------------------
                        ISDN ACTIVE CALLS
--------------------------------------------------------------------
History table has a maximum of 100 entries.
History table data is retained for a maximum of 15 Minutes.
--------------------------------------------------------------------
Call  Calling   Called   Remote Seconds Seconds Seconds Charges
Type  Number    Number   Name   Used    Left    Idle    Units/Currency
--------------------------------------------------------------------
Out             99047265   r4     24      875     24      0
--------------------------------------------------------------------
```

r2#**show ip ospf neighbor**
```
Neighbor ID    Pri   State       Dead Time   Address      Interface
4.4.4.4         1    FULL/  -     00:00:34    165.1.2.10   BRI0
3.3.3.3         1    FULL/DR      00:00:39    164.15.4.6   Ethernet0
r2#
```

```
! <Debugs and show output from R4-callback-client>
```
r4#**show debug**
```
Dial on demand:
  Dial on demand events debugging is on
Callback:
  Callback activity debugging is on
```

```
r4#
*Mar 16 22:59:20.686: BR0/0 DDR: Dialing cause ip (s=165.1.2.10, d=165.1.2.9)
*Mar 16 22:59:20.686: BR0/0 DDR: Attempting to dial 99047132
*Mar 16 22:59:22.044: %LINK-3-UPDOWN: Interface BRI0/0:2, changed state to up
*Mar 16 22:59:22.153: BR0/0:2 DDR: Callback negotiated - Disconnecting
*Mar 16 22:59:22.153: DDR: Callback client for r2 99047132 created
*Mar 16 22:59:22.553: %ISDN-6-CONNECT: Interface BRI0/0:2 is now connected
   to 99047132
*Mar 16 22:59:22.557: %LINK-3-UPDOWN: Interface BRI0/0:2, changed state to
   down
*Mar 16 22:59:22.565: BR0/0:2 DDR: disconnecting call
r4#
r4#
*Mar 16 22:59:38.007: %LINK-3-UPDOWN: Interface BRI0/0:2, changed state to up
*Mar 16 22:59:38.660: BR0/0:2 DDR: Remote name for r2
*Mar 16 22:59:38.708: BR0/0:2 DDR: Callback received from r2 99047132
*Mar 16 22:59:38.708: DDR: Freeing callback to r2 99047132
*Mar 16 22:59:38.756: BR0/0:2 DDR: dialer protocol up
*Mar 16 22:59:39.709: %LINEPROTO-5-UPDOWN: Line protocol on Interface
   BRI0/0:2, changed state to up
*Mar 16 22:59:44.013: %ISDN-6-CONNECT: Interface BRI0/0:2 is now connected
   to 99047132 r2

r4#show dialer

BRI0/0 - dialer type = ISDN

Dial String      Successes    Failures    Last DNIS   Last status
99047132              147        16365     00:00:35       successful
0 incoming call(s) have been screened.
0 incoming call(s) rejected for callback.


BRI0/0:1 - dialer type = ISDN
Idle timer (900 secs), Fast idle timer (20 secs)
Wait for carrier (30 secs), Re-enable (15 secs)
Dialer state is idle

BRI0/0:2 - dialer type = ISDN
Idle timer (900 secs), Fast idle timer (20 secs)
Wait for carrier (30 secs), Re-enable (15 secs)
Dialer state is data link layer up
Time until disconnect 894 secs
Connected to 99047132 (r2)
```

```
r4#show isdn active
- - - - - - - - - - - - - - - - - - - - - - - - - - - - - - - - - - - - - - - - - - - - -
                              ISDN ACTIVE CALLS
- - - - - - - - - - - - - - - - - - - - - - - - - - - - - - - - - - - - - - - - - - - - -
Call  Calling   Called   Remote Seconds Seconds  Seconds  Charges
Type  Number    Number   Name   Used    Left     Idle     Units/Currency
- - - - - - - - - - - - - - - - - - - - - - - - - - - - - - - - - - - - - - - - - - - - -
In    ---N/A---  99047265  r2      21      898       1
- - - - - - - - - - - - - - - - - - - - - - - - - - - - - - - - - - - - - - - - - - - - -


r4#show ip ospf neighbor

Neighbor ID    Pri  State        Dead Time   Address       Interface
2.2.2.2         1   FULL/  -     00:00:36    165.1.2.9     BRI0/0
5.5.5.5         1   FULL/  -     00:00:32    165.1.2.6     Serial1/4
7.7.7.7         1   FULL/DR      00:00:35    164.15.6.2    Ethernet0/0
```

NOTE   See the following URLs for PPP Callback as a reference:

www.cisco.com/univercd/cc/td/doc/product/software/ios120/12cgcr/dial_r/drprt7
/drcalldd.htm

www.cisco.com/en/US/partner/tech/tk713/tk507
/technologies_configuration_example09186a00800946ff.shtml

www.cisco.com/warp/customer/793/access_dial/isdn-ppp-callback.html

---

Section 4.0: PIX Configuration

4.1: Basic PIX Configuration

1 Configure the PIX inside/outside IP address as shown in Figure 6-1.

2 Configure RIP for the inside interface using MD5 authentication, as demonstrated in the configuration after item 6.

3 Configure RIP to advertise the default route to inside (R1) but not the outside.

4 Do not configure ACL on interface(s); use conduits instead, as demonstrated in the configuration after item 6.

5 Configure PAT translation to 164.15.4.254 for all networks behind PIX to be able to ping any networks outside the PIX, as demonstrated in the configuration after item 6.

6   Configure static NAT translation for R1 FastEthernet0/0 - 192.168.3.1 to 164.15.4.10 for
BGP peering. Configure conduit(s) to permit BGP connection from R2 and R3 only. The
example that follows shows the configuration for the tasks in items 2, 4, 5, and 6.

```
PIX(config)# show rip
rip inside passive version 2 authentication md5 cisco 1
rip inside default version 2 authentication md5 cisco 1

PIX(config)# show nat
nat (inside) 1 0.0.0.0 0.0.0.0 0 0

PIX(config)# show global
global (outside) 1 164.15.4.254

PIX(config)# show static
static (inside,outside) 164.15.4.10 192.168.3.1 netmask 255.255.255.255 0 0
static (inside,outside) 11.11.11.11 11.11.11.11 netmask 255.255.255.255 0 0

PIX(config)# show conduit
conduit permit icmp any any (hitcnt=72)
conduit permit tcp host 164.15.4.10 eq bgp host 164.15.4.5 (hitcnt=3)
conduit permit tcp host 164.15.4.10 eq bgp host 164.15.4.6 (hitcnt=7)
```

7   Configure static NAT translation for Loopback1 of R1 to itself.

8   Configure a static default route to HSRP address 164.15.4.100 as per Section 9.2.

4.2: Advanced PIX Configuration

1   Configure PIX to send SNMP traps to server 192.168.3.10 with community string
cisco123.

2   Configure the server to send traps only and not to be able to poll, as demonstrated in the
following example:

```
PIX(config)# show snmp
snmp-server host inside 192.168.3.10 trap
no snmp-server location
no snmp-server contact
snmp-server community cisco123
snmp-server enable traps
```

3   Configure PIX history logging and enable logging.

Section 5.0: IPSec/PPTP Configuration

5.1: IPSec LAN-to-LAN Router-to-PIX

1 Configure LAN-to-LAN IPSec between R6 and PIX for the VLAN5 and VLAN2 networks, respectively.

2 Use preshared with other parameters as you feel appropriate, as demonstrated in the following example:

```
! <R6 configuration>
hostname r6
!
crypto isakmp policy 10
 authentication pre-share
 group 2
crypto isakmp key cisco address 164.15.4.3
!
!
crypto ipsec transform-set lab6 esp-des esp-md5-hmac
!
!
crypto map lab6 10 ipsec-isakmp
 set peer 164.15.4.3
 set transform-set lab6
 match address 101
!
interface Serial1/0.1 multipoint
 ip address 165.1.2.17 255.255.255.248
 crypto map lab6


! <PIX configuration>
hostname PIX
!
access-list nonat permit ip 10.1.1.0 255.255.255.0 10.1.2.0 255.255.255.0
access-list 101 permit ip 10.1.1.0 255.255.255.0 10.1.2.0 255.255.255.0
nat (inside) 0 access-list nonat
sysopt connection permit-ipsec
crypto ipsec transform-set lab6 esp-des esp-md5-hmac
crypto map lab6 10 ipsec-isakmp
crypto map lab6 10 match address 101
crypto map lab6 10 set peer 165.1.2.17
crypto map lab6 10 set transform-set lab6
crypto map lab6 interface outside
```

```
isakmp enable outside
isakmp key cisco address 165.1.2.17 netmask 255.255.255.255
isakmp policy 10 authentication pre-share
isakmp policy 10 encryption des
isakmp policy 10 hash sha
isakmp policy 10 group 2
isakmp policy 10 lifetime 86400
```

5.2: IPSec Remote Access to Router

1 Configure the remote access VPN client to R5 for Test PC in VLAN9. Use MD5 hashing and DH group 2. See the example following item 5.

2 Configure groupname **3000client** with password **cisco123**. See the example following item 5.

3 Configure AAA authentication and authorization for the client using local username **cisco** password **cisco**. See the example following item 5.

4 Configure IP pool 172.16.1.1–172.16.1.10 for the VPN client. See the example following item 5.

5 Configure split tunneling for the client to use the tunnel to access Loopback2 of R5 only. The example that follows shows this configuration as well as that for the tasks in items 1 through 4.

```
hostname r5
!
aaa new-model
aaa authentication login aaa local
aaa authorization network aaa local
!
username cisco password 0 cisco
!
crypto isakmp policy 10
 hash md5
 authentication pre-share
 group 2
!
crypto isakmp client configuration group 3000client
 key cisco123
 dns 164.15.7.100
 wins 164.15.7.200
 domain cisco.com
 pool vpnpool
 acl 155
!
```

```
crypto ipsec transform-set lab6 esp-3des esp-md5-hmac
!
crypto dynamic-map lab6dynmap 10
 set transform-set lab6
 reverse-route
!
crypto map lab6 client authentication list aaa
crypto map lab6 isakmp authorization list aaa
crypto map lab6 client configuration address respond
crypto map lab6 10 ipsec-isakmp dynamic lab6dynmap
!
interface Loopback2
 ip address 155.155.155.155 255.255.255.0
!
interface FastEthernet0/0
 ip address 164.15.7.1 255.255.255.0
 ip rip authentication key-chain lab6
 no ip route-cache
 no ip mroute-cache
 duplex auto
 speed auto
 crypto map lab6
!
ip local pool vpnpool 172.16.1.1 172.16.1.10
!
access-list 155 permit ip 155.155.155.0 0.0.0.255 172.16.1.0 0.0.0.255
!
```

6 Configure reverse-route injection (RRI) for routing reply packets to use the egress interface where crypto map is applied. RRI dynamically adds a route when the client is connected. See the example that follows:

```
r5#show ip route static
     172.16.0.0/32 is subnetted, 1 subnets
S       172.16.1.1 [1/0] via 0.0.0.0, FastEthernet0/0
r5#
```

7 Make sure you can ping loopback2 of R5 and any other network in the lab. Verify VPN client connection statistics; see Figures 6-7a through 6-7c.

NOTE   See this URL for a sample configuration:

www.cisco.com/warp/customer/707/ios_usr_rad.html

Figure 6-7a *VPN Client Connection Status—General Stats*

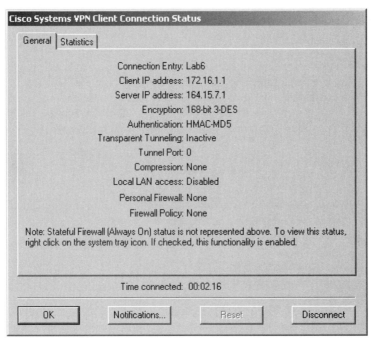

Figure 6-7b *VPN Client Connection Status—Statistics*

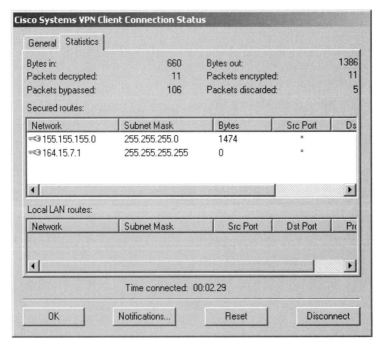

Figure 6-7c *VPN Client Connection—Pinging Loopback2 of R5 and Other Networks (Split Tunnel)*

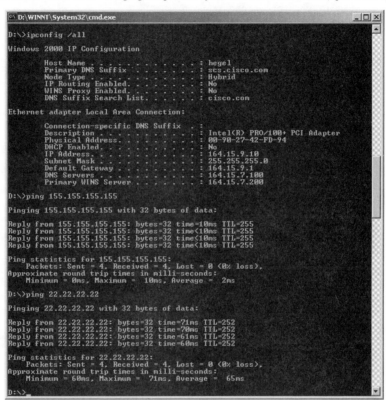

NOTE   Pinging 155.155.155.155 Loopback2 of R5 is encrypted; all other traffic is unencrypted via the split tunnel.

5.3: PPTP to PIX with RADIUS Authentication and MPPE Encryption

1 Configure PPTP remote access to PIX for Test PC in VLAN9.

2 Configure MS-CHAP authentication and 40-bit MPPE encryption and RADIUS authentication as demonstrated in the following example:

```
access-list nonat permit ip 192.168.3.0 255.255.255.0 192.168.1.0
  255.255.255.0
ip local pool pptp-pool 192.168.1.1-192.168.1.10
nat (inside) 0 access-list nonat
aaa-server ACS protocol radius
```

```
aaa-server ACS (inside) host 10.1.1.254 cisco timeout 10
sysopt connection permit-pptp
vpdn group 1 accept dialin pptp
vpdn group 1 ppp authentication pap
vpdn group 1 ppp authentication chap
vpdn group 1 ppp authentication mschap
vpdn group 1 ppp encryption mppe 40
vpdn group 1 client configuration address local pptp-pool
vpdn group 1 client authentication aaa ACS
vpdn group 1 pptp echo 60
vpdn enable outside
```

3 Configure IP pool on PIX 192.168.1.1-192.168.1.10 for PPTP clients.

4 Configure a username **pptp-user**, password **cisco** on CiscoSecure ACS with appropriate attribute settings for MPPE encryption. See Figures 6-8a through 6-8d for user settings on CiscoSecure ACS.

Figure 6-8a *Network Configuration: PIX Entry for Section 5.3*

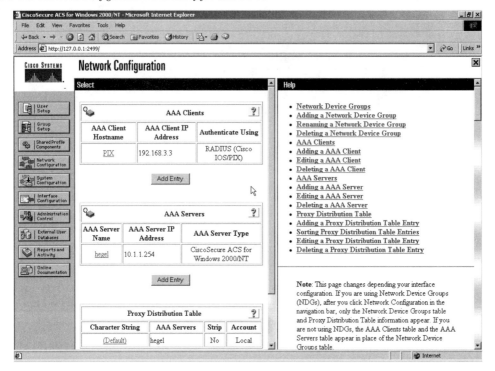

Figure 6-8b *Interface Configuration to Enable PPTP Attributes*

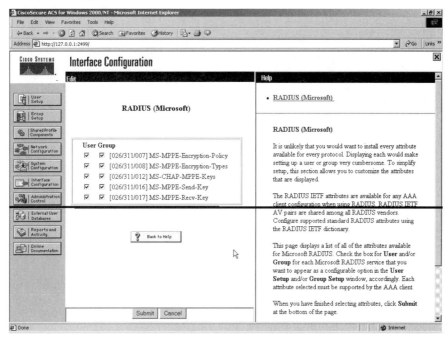

Figure 6-8c *Add User pptp-user for PPTP Authentication*

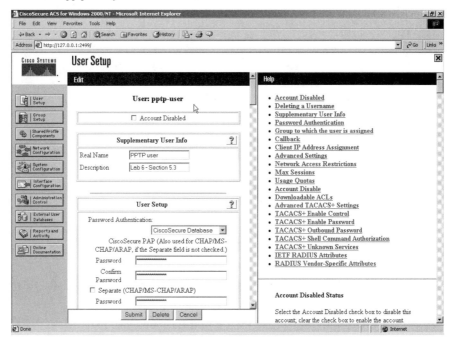

Figure 6-8d *RADIUS MPPE Attribute Settings for User pptp-user*

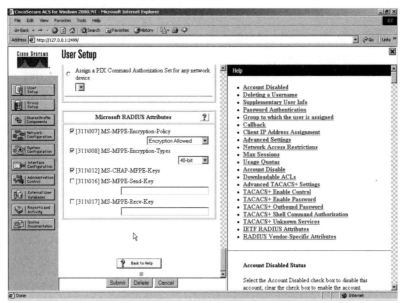

5 Verify on PIX to confirm your configuration is working properly, as demonstrated in the following example:

```
PIX(config)# show vpdn

PPTP Tunnel and Session Information (Total tunnels=1 sessions=1)

Tunnel id 5, remote id is 5, 1 active sessions
  Tunnel state is estabd, time since event change 15 secs
  remote   Internet Address 164.15.9.10, port 1042
  Local    Internet Address 164.15.4.3, port 1723
  16 packets sent, 100 received, 744 bytes sent, 7084 received

Call id 5 is up on tunnel id 5
Remote Internet Address is 164.15.9.10
  Session username is pptp-user, state is estabd
    Time since event change 315 secs, interface outside
    Remote call id is 16384
    PPP interface id is 1
    16 packets sent, 100 received, 744 bytes sent, 7084 received
    Seq 17, Ack 99, Ack_Rcvd 16, peer RWS 64
    0 out of order packets
```

6 Verify on PPTP client (Test PC) by pinging R1-192.168.3.1. Check the PPTP connection using **ipconfig/all**. See Figure 6-9.

7 Verify on Reports in ACS for Passed Authentication. See Figure 6-10.

Figure 6-9   *Capture from PPTP Client Connection from Test PC*

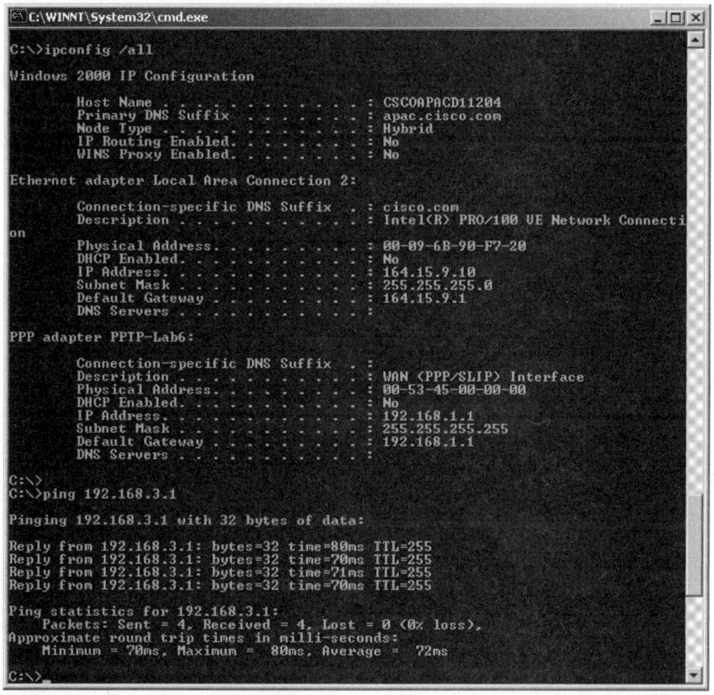

Figure 6-10   *ACS Reports for Passed Authentication*

NOTE	See the following URLs for more information to configure PPTP on PIX:
	www.cisco.com/warp/public/110/pptppix.html
	www.cisco.com/univercd/cc/td/doc/product/iaabu/pix/pix_sw/v_53/config /advanced.htm#1020296

Section 6.0: IOS Firewall Configuration

6.1: Context-Based Access Control (CBAC)

1 Configure CBAC on R2 to protect VLAN4.

2 Inspect all common connection-oriented protocols and apply egress ACL on the serial link and inspect outbound. Verify that CBAC works. The following example demonstrates all of these tasks:

```
hostname r2
!
ip inspect name lab6 ftp
ip inspect name lab6 http
ip inspect name lab6 smtp
ip inspect name lab6 sqlnet
ip inspect name lab6 tcp
!
interface Serial0
 ip address 165.1.2.1 255.255.255.252
 ip access-group 101 in
 ip inspect lab6 out
!
interface BRI0
 ip address 165.1.2.9 255.255.255.252
 ip access-group 101 in
 ip inspect lab6 out
!
access-list 101 permit ospf any any
access-list 101 permit tcp any any eq bgp
access-list 101 permit icmp any any
access-list 101 deny   ip any any


! Verify CBAC by telnetting from behind R2 i.e. from R3 to R4
r3#telnet 165.1.2.2
Trying 165.1.2.2 ... Open
```

```
User Access Verification

Username: router2
Password: cisco

r4>exit

[Connection to 165.1.2.2 closed by foreign host]
r3#



! Verify CBAC session table and dynamic ACL created as follows;
r2#show ip inspect sessions
Established Sessions
 Session 2795D0 (164.15.4.6:11035)=>(165.1.2.2:23) tcp SIS_OPEN


r2#show access-lists 101
Extended IP access list 101
    permit tcp host 165.1.2.2 eq telnet host 164.15.4.6 eq 11035 (20 matches)
    permit ospf any any (452 matches)
    permit tcp any any eq bgp (90 matches)
    permit icmp any any (222 matches)
    deny ip any any (12 matches)
```

3 Hidden issue: You also need to apply ACL and inspection on the ISDN interface in the event the serial goes down, as per Section 3.0. Make sure that CBAC works when ISDN is up. See the following example:

```
! To verify, trigger ISDN to come up by shutting down serial link on R4 to R2.
r2#show isdn active
------------------------------------------------------------------------
                          ISDN ACTIVE CALLS
------------------------------------------------------------------------
Call   Calling   Called   Remote  Seconds Seconds Seconds Charges
Type   Number    Number   Name    Used    Left    Idle    Units/Currency
------------------------------------------------------------------------
Out              99047265  r4      90      898     1       0
------------------------------------------------------------------------

r2#
r2#show ip ospf neighbor

Neighbor ID    Pri   State        Dead Time   Address      Interface
3.3.3.3          1   FULL/BDR     00:00:38    164.15.4.6   Ethernet0
4.4.4.4          1   FULL/ -      00:00:38    165.1.2.10   BRI0
r2#
```

```
! Now, Telnet from behind R2 i.e. from R3 to R4
r3#telnet 165.1.2.10
Trying 165.1.2.10 ... Open


User Access Verification

Username: router2
Password: cisco

r4>exit

[Connection to 165.1.2.10 closed by foreign host]
r3#


! Verify CBAC session table and dynamic ACL created as follows;
r2#show ip inspect sessions
Half-open Sessions
 Session 7FB8BC (164.15.4.6:11037)=>(165.1.2.10:23) tcp SIS_OPENING


r2#show access-lists 101
Extended IP access list 101
    permit tcp host 165.1.2.10 eq telnet host 164.15.4.6 eq 11037
    permit ospf any any (495 matches)
    permit tcp any any eq bgp (93 matches)
    permit icmp any any (232 matches)
    deny ip any any (12 matches)
```

4 Permit ICMP explicitly in the ACL, as ICMP protocol inspection is not supported in older
   IOS versions. ICMP protocol can be inspected in newer IOS versions. This feature was
   introduced into IOS from Release 12.2(15)T.

NOTE   See the following URL for Firewall Stateful Inspection of ICMP protocol:

www.cisco.com/univercd/cc/td/doc/product/software/ios122/122newft/122limit/122y
/122yu11/ftfwicmp.htm

6.2: Advanced Context-Based Access Control (CBAC)

1 Allow Java applets from 164.0.0.0/8 and 165.0.0.0/8 network(s) only, as demonstrated in
   the example following item 2.

2 Configure CBAC for TCP half-open sessions on per-host to 200 concurrent embryonic connections. Offending hosts are to be blocked for 1 hour, as demonstrated in the following example:

```
hostname r2
!
ip inspect name lab6 http java-list 6
ip inspect tcp max-incomplete host 200 block-time 60
!
access-list 6 permit 164.0.0.0 0.255.255.255
access-list 6 permit 165.0.0.0 0.255.255.255
```

Section 7.0: AAA

7.1: AAA on the Router

1 Configure TACACS+ authentication and authorization on R2.

2 Configure EXEC and commands accounting.

3 Configure TACACS+ single-connection on R2 and ACS to maintain a single open TCP connection, as demonstrated in the example following item 4.

4 Hidden issue: For all routers to be able to Telnet R2, you need to open a hole in ACL configured on R2, as demonstrated in the following example:

```
hostname r2
!
aaa new-model
aaa authentication login vty tacacs+ none
aaa authentication login con none
aaa authentication ppp default local
aaa authentication ppp isdn radius local
aaa authorization exec vty tacacs+ none
aaa authorization exec con none
aaa authorization network default local
aaa authorization network isdn radius local
aaa accounting exec default start-stop tacacs+
aaa accounting exec con none
aaa accounting commands 1 default start-stop tacacs+
aaa accounting commands 1 con none
aaa accounting commands 15 default start-stop tacacs+
aaa accounting commands 15 con none
!
interface Serial0
 ip address 165.1.2.1 255.255.255.252
```

```
 ip access-group 101 in
 no ip directed-broadcast
 ip inspect lab6 out
 encapsulation ppp
 ip tcp header-compression
 ip ospf message-digest-key 1 md5 7 121A0C041104
 ppp authentication chap
 ppp chap hostname router2
!
interface BRI0
 ip address 165.1.2.9 255.255.255.252
 ip access-group 101 in
 no ip directed-broadcast
 ip inspect lab6 out
 encapsulation ppp
 ip ospf message-digest-key 1 md5 7 1511021F0725
 dialer callback-secure
 dialer idle-timeout 900
 dialer map ip 165.1.2.2 name r4 class lab6 broadcast 99047265
 dialer-group 1
 isdn switch-type basic-net3
 no peer default ip address
 no fair-queue
 no cdp enable
 ppp callback accept
 ppp authentication chap isdn
 ppp authorization isdn
!
access-list 101 permit ospf any any
access-list 101 permit tcp any any eq bgp
access-list 101 permit icmp any any
access-list 101 permit tcp any any eq telnet
access-list 101 deny   ip any any
!
tacacs-server host 164.15.4.253 single-connection
tacacs-server key cisco
!
line con 0
 exec-timeout 0 0
 authorization exec con
 accounting commands 1 con
 accounting commands 15 con
 accounting exec con
 login authentication con
 transport input none
```

```
 escape-character 27
line vty 0 4
 password 7 1511021F0725
 authorization exec vty
 login authentication vty
!
end
```

```
r2#show access-lists 101
Extended IP access list 101
    permit ospf any any (10 matches)
    permit tcp any any eq bgp (2 matches)
    permit icmp any any (11 matches)
    permit tcp any any eq telnet (56 matches)
    deny ip any any
```

5   Configure PIX accordingly, as demonstrated in the following example:

```
PIX(config)# show conduit
conduit permit tcp host 164.15.4.253 eq tacacs host 164.15.4.5 (hitcnt=3)
```

```
PIX(config)# show static
static (inside,outside) 164.15.4.253 10.1.1.254 netmask 255.255.255.255 0 0
```

6   Configure user **r2-telnet** password **cisco** on CiscoSecure ACS.

7   Verify TACACS+ single-connection works using **debug** and **show** commands, as
    demonstrated in the example that follows. The router is maintaining a single TCP connection
    for every AAA request. It is not creating separate TCP three-way handshake/connection for
    each AAA request.

```
r2#show debug
General OS:
  TACACS access control debugging is on
  AAA Authentication debugging is on
  AAA Authorization debugging is on
  AAA Accounting debugging is on
TCP:
  TCP special event debugging is on
r2#
r2#
04:07:25: TCP0: state was LISTEN -> SYNRCVD [23 -> 164.15.4.6(11045)]
04:07:25: TCP0: Connection to 164.15.4.6:11045, received MSS 1460, MSS is 516
04:07:25: TCP: sending SYN, seq 3321423846, ack 1221867257
04:07:25: TCP0: Connection to 164.15.4.6:11045, advertising MSS 1460
04:07:25: TCP0: state was SYNRCVD -> ESTAB [23 -> 164.15.4.6(11045)]
04:07:25: TCB00B27EE8 setting property TCP_TOS (11) 88C0BC
04:07:25: AAA: parse name=tty2 idb type=-1 tty=-1
```

```
04:07:25: AAA: name=tty2 flags=0x11 type=5 shelf=0 slot=0 adapter=0 port=2
channel=0
04:07:25: AAA/AUTHEN: create_user (0xAC93FC) user='' ruser='' port='tty2'
rem_addr='164.15.4.6' authen_type=ASCII service=LOGIN priv=1
04:07:25: AAA/AUTHEN/START (453364680): port='tty2' list='vty' action=LOGIN
service=LOGIN
04:07:25: AAA/AUTHEN/START (453364680): found list vty
04:07:25: AAA/AUTHEN/START (453364680): Method=TACACS+
04:07:25: TAC+: send AUTHEN/START packet ver=192 id=453364680
04:07:25: TAC+: Using default tacacs server list.
04:07:25: TAC+: 164.15.4.253 (453364680) AUTHEN/START/LOGIN/ASCII queued
04:07:26: TAC+: (453364680) AUTHEN/START/LOGIN/ASCII processed
04:07:26: TAC+: ver=192 id=453364680 received AUTHEN status = GETUSER
04:07:26: AAA/AUTHEN (453364680): status = GETUSER
04:07:31: AAA/AUTHEN/CONT (453364680): continue_login (user='(undef)')
04:07:31: AAA/AUTHEN (453364680): status = GETUSER
04:07:31: AAA/AUTHEN (453364680): Method=TACACS+
04:07:31: TAC+: send AUTHEN/CONT packet id=453364680
04:07:31: TAC+: 164.15.4.253 (453364680) AUTHEN/CONT queued
04:07:32: TAC+: (453364680) AUTHEN/CONT processed
04:07:32: TAC+: ver=192 id=453364680 received AUTHEN status = GETPASS
04:07:32: AAA/AUTHEN (453364680): status = GETPASS
04:07:32: AAA/AUTHEN/CONT (453364680): continue_login (user='r2-telnet')
04:07:32: AAA/AUTHEN (453364680): status = GETPASS
04:07:32: AAA/AUTHEN (453364680): Method=TACACS+
04:07:32: TAC+: send AUTHEN/CONT packet id=453364680
04:07:32: TAC+: 164.15.4.253 (453364680) AUTHEN/CONT queued
04:07:32: TAC+: (453364680) AUTHEN/CONT processed
04:07:32: TAC+: ver=192 id=453364680 received AUTHEN status = PASS
04:07:32: AAA/AUTHEN (453364680): status = PASS
04:07:32: AAA/AUTHOR/EXEC (945293474): Port='tty2' list='vty' service=EXEC
04:07:32: AAA/AUTHOR/EXEC:   (945293474) user='r2-telnet'
04:07:32: AAA/AUTHOR/EXEC:   (945293474) send AV service=shell
04:07:32: AAA/AUTHOR/EXEC:   (945293474) send AV cmd*
04:07:32: AAA/AUTHOR/EXEC (945293474) found list "vty"
04:07:32: AAA/AUTHOR/EXEC:   (945293474) Method=TACACS+
04:07:32: AAA/AUTHOR/TAC+:   (945293474): user=r2-telnet
04:07:32: AAA/AUTHOR/TAC+:   (945293474): send AV service=shell
04:07:32: AAA/AUTHOR/TAC+:   (945293474): send AV cmd*
04:07:32: TAC+: 164.15.4.253 (945293474) AUTHOR/START queued
04:07:33: TAC+: (945293474) AUTHOR/START processed
04:07:33: TAC+: (945293474): received author response status = PASS_ADD
04:07:33: AAA/AUTHOR (945293474): Post authorization status = PASS_ADD
04:07:33: AAA/AUTHOR/EXEC: Processing AV service=shell
04:07:33: AAA/AUTHOR/EXEC: Processing AV cmd*
04:07:33: AAA/AUTHOR/EXEC: Processing AV priv-lvl=15
```

```
04:07:33: AAA/AUTHOR/EXEC: Authorization successful
04:07:33: AAA/ACCT/EXEC/START User r2-telnet, port tty2
04:07:33: AAA/ACCT/EXEC: Found list "default"
04:07:33: TAC+: 164.15.4.253 (2766450909) ACCT/REQUEST/START queued
04:07:33: TAC+: (2766450909) ACCT/REQUEST/START processed
04:07:33: TAC+: (2766450909): received acct response status = SUCCESS
r2#
r2#
04:07:42: AAA/ACCT/CMD: User r2-telnet, Port tty2, Priv 15:
          "show running-config <cr>"
04:07:42: AAA/ACCT/CMD: Found list "default"
04:07:42: TAC+: 164.15.4.253 (195719254) ACCT/REQUEST/STOP queued
04:07:42: TAC+: (195719254) ACCT/REQUEST/STOP processed
04:07:42: TAC+: (195719254): received acct response status = SUCCESS
r2#
r2#
04:07:52: AAA/ACCT/CMD: User r2-telnet, Port tty2, Priv 15:
          "write memory <cr>"
04:07:52: AAA/ACCT/CMD: Found list "default"
04:07:52: TAC+: 164.15.4.253 (3149635897) ACCT/REQUEST/STOP queued
04:07:52: TAC+: (3149635897) ACCT/REQUEST/STOP processed
04:07:52: TAC+: (3149635897): received acct response status = SUCCESS
r2#
r2#show tcp brief
TCB        Local Address           Foreign Address         (state)
00B26EA8   164.15.4.5.11003        164.15.4.253.49         ESTAB
00B27898   165.1.2.1.179           165.1.2.2.13788         ESTAB
00A14AFC   164.15.4.5.11000        164.15.4.6.179          ESTAB
00A141F8   164.15.4.5.11001        164.15.4.10.179         ESTAB
00B27EE8   164.15.4.5.23           164.15.4.6.11045        ESTAB
r2#
r2#
04:08:14: AAA/ACCT/CMD: User r2-telnet, Port tty2, Priv 1:
          "show clock <cr>"
04:08:14: AAA/ACCT/CMD: Found list "default"
04:08:14: TAC+: 164.15.4.253 (2173307971) ACCT/REQUEST/STOP queued
04:08:14: TAC+: (2173307971) ACCT/REQUEST/STOP processed
04:08:14: TAC+: (2173307971): received acct response status = SUCCESS
r2#
04:08:19: AAA/ACCT/EXEC/STOP: cannot retrieve modem speed
04:08:19: AAA/ACCT/EXEC/STOP User r2-telnet, Port tty2:
          task_id=33 timezone=UTC service=shell disc-cause=1 disc-cause-
            ext=1020 elapsed_time=46 nas-rx-speed=307364018
            nas-tx-speed=1927544894
04:08:19: TAC+: 164.15.4.253 (4082150891) ACCT/REQUEST/STOP queued
04:08:19: TAC+: (4082150891) ACCT/REQUEST/STOP processed
```

```
04:08:19: TAC+: (4082150891): received acct response status = SUCCESS
04:08:19: AAA/AUTHEN: free_user (0xAC93FC) user='r2-telnet' ruser=''
  port='tty2' rem_addr='164.15.4.6' authen_type=ASCII service=LOGIN priv=1
04:08:19: TCP2: state was ESTAB -> FINWAIT1 [23 -> 164.15.4.6(11045)]
04:08:19: TCP2: sending FIN
04:08:19: TCP2: state was FINWAIT1 -> FINWAIT2 [23 -> 164.15.4.6(11045)]
04:08:19: TCP2: FIN processed
04:08:19: TCP2: state was FINWAIT2 -> TIMEWAIT [23 -> 164.15.4.6(11045)]
r2#
r2#show tcp brief
TCB       Local Address       Foreign Address        (state)
00B26EA8  164.15.4.5.11003    164.15.4.253.49        ESTAB
00B27898  165.1.2.1.179       165.1.2.2.13788        ESTAB
00A14AFC  164.15.4.5.11000    164.15.4.6.179         ESTAB
00A141F8  164.15.4.5.11001    164.15.4.10.179        ESTAB
00B27EE8  164.15.4.5.23       164.15.4.6.11045       TIMEWAIT
r2#
```

8 See Figures 6-11a and 6-11b for network settings on CiscoSecure ACS for TACACS+ single-connect.

Figure 6-11a *Network Settings for TACACS+ Single-Connect on ACS*

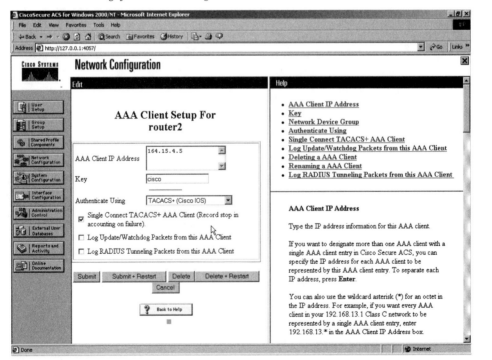

Figure 6-11b *AAA Clients on ACS*

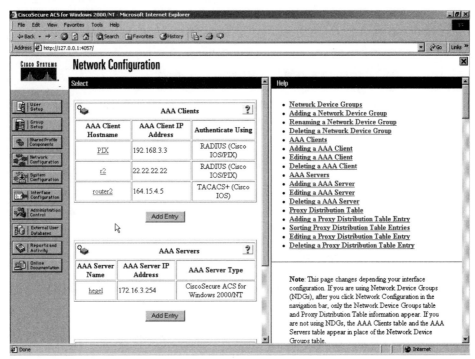

NOTE TACACS+ single connection is deprecated in newer IOS versions—see bug ID CSCdv86920.

R2 is configured for RADIUS and TACACS+ at the same time. Use different host names. Host names do not necessarily need to match on the device with ACS settings.

Section 8.0: Advanced Security

8.1: ROMMON Security

CAUTION **Disclaimer**: The author and Cisco Press are not liable for any damage to routers when using this feature. Please use this feature with extreme caution, and read all related materials and the following recovery procedure.

1 The 2600/3600 series (and newer versions of ROMMON for the 1700 series) all have what is known as a "ROMMON security" feature.

2 ROMMON security is designed to prevent a person with physical access to the router (2600 or 3600) from viewing the configuration file.

3 ROMMON security disables access to the ROMMON so that a person cannot set the configuration register to ignore the startup configuration. See the example that follows:

```
Router(config)#no service password-recovery
WARNING:
Executing this command will disable password recovery mechanism.
Do not execute this command without another plan for
password recovery.

Are you sure you want to continue? [yes/no]: yes
Router(config)#

! Upon system boot, the 3600 will display a message warning the user
! that password recovery is disabled:
System Bootstrap, Version 11.1(4675) [kluk 143], INTERIM SOFTWARE
Copyright (c) 1994-1996 by cisco Systems, Inc.
C3600 processor with 32768 Kbytes of main memory
Main memory is configured to 64 bit mode with parity disabled

PASSWORD RECOVERY FUNCTIONALITY IS DISABLED
program load complete, entry point: 0x80008000, size: 0x2733f4
```

NOTE The ROMMON Security feature is not enabled via the config register, but rather with a global configuration command: **no service password-recovery**. This will turn on ROMMON security and prevent the router from responding to a break sequence on boot-up.

Risks: If a router is configured with **no service password-recovery**, this disables all access to the ROMMON. If there is not a valid IOS image in Flash in the router, the user will not be able to use the **ROMMON XMODEM** command to load a new Flash image. To fix the router, you must get a new IOS image on a Flash SIMM or on a PCMCIA card (3600 only).

To minimize this risk, a customer who uses ROMMON security should also use dual Flash bank memory and put a backup IOS image in a separate partition.

On the 3640 and 3660, in an emergency you can remove the NVRAM and reseat it. The NVRAM is implemented using battery backed-up SRAM. Removing the SRAM will erase the contents of NVRAM, which contains the **no service password-recovery** configuration. The NVRAM chip is located on the motherboard of the 3640 next to the PCMCIA connector. The silkscreen on the motherboard will identify it as "NVRAM." Please be sure to use proper anti-static procedures when handling the NVRAM.

The 1700, 2600, and 3620 use an EEPROM to hold the configuration. The EEPROM does not erase when you remove it.

Dependencies: The boot bits in the configuration register must not be set to 0x0 (boot to ROMMON) or 0x1. The "ignore" config bit must not be set. If the configuration register settings aren't correct, the router will print this error message:

```
Router(config)#config-register 0x3920
Router(config)#no service password-recovery
Please setup auto boot using config-register first.
```

Recovery procedure: If a user uses this feature and loses the enable password, use following method to erase the entire contents of NVRAM:

Step 1   Boot the system and wait until after the system decompresses the IOS image:

```
Self decompressing the image : ###############################
################]
```

Step 2   Press Break within 5 seconds.

The 3600 will ask if you want to reset the router to the factory default configuration:

```
PASSWORD RECOVERY IS DISABLED.
Do you want to reset the router to factory default
configuration and proceed [y/n] ? y
```

Step 3   Reset the router configuration to factory default.

NOTE   Consult the following URLs for more information:

www.cisco.com/warp/customer/701/59.html

www.cisco.com/warp/customer/130/recovery_c2600.html

www.cisco.com/warp/customer/130/recovery_c3600.html

www.cisco.com/warp/customer/130/xmodem_generic.html

www.cisco.com/warp/customer/130/sw_upgrade_proc_ram.shtml

8.2: Access Control

1   Configure **service resetoutside** on PIX to reset denied TCP packets that terminate at the least-secure (outside) interface.

2   By default, these packets are silently discarded.

3   The **resetoutside** option is highly recommended with dynamic or static interface Port Address Translation (PAT).

4   Actively resetting these connections avoids the 30-second timeout delay.

NOTE   For more information, consult the following URL:

www.cisco.com/univercd/cc/td/doc/product/iaabu/pix/pix_62/cmdref/s.htm#1045404

8.3: Access Restriction

1 Configure an access list on R3 to restrict Telnet access from R2.

2 Configure the **established** keyword for R3 to be able to Telnet R2 but not vice versa, as demonstrated in the following example:

```
hostname r3
!
interface Ethernet0/0
 ip address 164.15.4.6 255.255.255.0
 ip access-group 110 in
!
access-list 110 permit tcp host 164.15.4.5 host 164.15.4.6 established
access-list 110 deny  tcp host 164.15.4.5 host 164.15.4.6 eq telnet
access-list 110 permit ip any any


! Telnet from R2 to R3 successful after applying ACL.
r3#telnet 164.15.4.5
Trying 164.15.4.5 ... Open

r2>
r2>


! Telnet from R2 to R3 fails after applying ACL.
r2#telnet 164.15.4.6
Trying 164.15.4.6 ...
% Destination unreachable; gateway or host down
r2#


! Verify counters on ACL on R3.
r3#show access-lists 110
Extended IP access list 110
    permit tcp host 164.15.4.5 host 164.15.4.6 established (50 matches)
    deny tcp host 164.15.4.5 host 164.15.4.6 eq telnet (2 matches)
    permit ip any any (210 matches)
```

Section 9.0: IP Services and Protocol-Independent Features

9.1: Network Address Translation (NAT)

1 Configure NAT on PIX for VLAN2 to 164.15.4.20, as demonstrated in the following example:

```
access-list nonat permit ip 10.1.1.0 255.255.255.0 10.1.2.0 255.255.255.0
nat (inside) 0 access-list nonat
nat (inside) 2 10.1.1.0 255.255.255.0 0 0
nat (inside) 1 0.0.0.0 0.0.0.0 0 0
global (outside) 1 164.15.4.254
global (outside) 2 164.15.4.20



! Ping from R1 to anywhere on the network sourcing from VLAN2 network.
! eg 22.22.22.22

r1#ping ip
Target IP address: 22.22.22.22
Repeat count [5]:
Datagram size [100]:
Timeout in seconds [2]:
Extended commands [n]: y
Source address or interface: 10.1.1.1
Type of service [0]:
Set DF bit in IP header? [no]:
Validate reply data? [no]:
Data pattern [0xABCD]:
Loose, Strict, Record, Timestamp, Verbose[none]:
Sweep range of sizes [n]:
Type escape sequence to abort.
Sending 5, 100-byte ICMP Echos to 22.22.22.22, timeout is 2 seconds:
!!!!!
Success rate is 100 percent (5/5), round-trip min/avg/max = 4/7/8 ms

r1#debug ip nat
6d00h: ICMP: echo reply rcvd, src 22.22.22.22, dst 10.1.1.1
6d00h: ICMP: echo reply rcvd, src 22.22.22.22, dst 10.1.1.1
6d00h: ICMP: echo reply rcvd, src 22.22.22.22, dst 10.1.1.1
6d00h: ICMP: echo reply rcvd, src 22.22.22.22, dst 10.1.1.1
6d00h: ICMP: echo reply rcvd, src 22.22.22.22, dst 10.1.1.1
```

```
! Verify on PIX if network 10.1.1.0/24 was NATed correctly.
PIX(config)# show xlate
7 in use, 44 most used
PAT Global 164.15.4.20(3) Local 10.1.1.1 ICMP id 3427
PAT Global 164.15.4.20(2) Local 10.1.1.1 ICMP id 3426
PAT Global 164.15.4.20(1) Local 10.1.1.1 ICMP id 3425
PAT Global 164.15.4.20(0) Local 10.1.1.1 ICMP id 3424
PAT Global 164.15.4.20(4) Local 10.1.1.1 ICMP id 3428
Global 164.15.4.10 Local 192.168.3.1
```

2 Configure NAT on R6 for VLAN5 to 165.1.2.20, as demonstrated in the following example:

```
hostname r6
!
interface Ethernet0/0
 ip address 10.1.2.1 255.255.255.0
 ip nat inside
!
interface Serial1/0.1 multipoint
 ip address 165.1.2.17 255.255.255.248
 ip nat outside
 crypto map lab6
!
ip nat pool lab6 165.1.2.20 165.1.2.20 netmask 255.255.255.0
ip nat inside source route-map nonat pool lab6 overload
!
access-list 102 deny   ip 10.1.2.0 0.0.0.255 10.1.1.0 0.0.0.255
access-list 102 permit ip 10.1.2.0 0.0.0.255 any
!
route-map nonat permit 10
 match ip address 102
!


! Ping from R6 to anywhere on the network sourcing from VLAN5 network.
r6#ping ip
Target IP address: 165.1.2.19
Repeat count [5]:
Datagram size [100]:
Timeout in seconds [2]:
Extended commands [n]: y
Source address or interface: 10.1.2.1
Type of service [0]:
Set DF bit in IP header? [no]:
Validate reply data? [no]:
Data pattern [0xABCD]:
```

```
Loose, Strict, Record, Timestamp, Verbose[none]:
Sweep range of sizes [n]:
Type escape sequence to abort.
Sending 5, 100-byte ICMP Echos to 165.1.2.19, timeout is 2 seconds:
!!!!!
Success rate is 100 percent (5/5), round-trip min/avg/max = 64/66/68 ms
```

! Verify NAT translation
r6#**show ip nat translations**
```
Pro Inside global      Inside local      Outside local      Outside global
icmp 165.1.2.20:3139   10.1.2.1:3139     165.1.2.19:3139    165.1.2.19:3139
icmp 165.1.2.20:3140   10.1.2.1:3140     165.1.2.19:3140    165.1.2.19:3140
icmp 165.1.2.20:3141   10.1.2.1:3141     165.1.2.19:3141    165.1.2.19:3141
icmp 165.1.2.20:3142   10.1.2.1:3142     165.1.2.19:3142    165.1.2.19:3142
icmp 165.1.2.20:3143   10.1.2.1:3143     165.1.2.19:3143    165.1.2.19:3143
```

r6#**ping ip**
```
Target IP address: 33.33.33.33
Repeat count [5]:
Datagram size [100]:
Timeout in seconds [2]:
Extended commands [n]: y
Source address or interface: 10.1.2.1
Type of service [0]:
Set DF bit in IP header? [no]:
Validate reply data? [no]:
Data pattern [0xABCD]:
Loose, Strict, Record, Timestamp, Verbose[none]:
Sweep range of sizes [n]:
Type escape sequence to abort.
Sending 5, 100-byte ICMP Echos to 33.33.33.33, timeout is 2 seconds:
!!!!!
Success rate is 100 percent (5/5), round-trip min/avg/max = 64/67/68 ms
```

! Verify NAT translation
r6#**show ip nat translations**
```
Pro Inside global      Inside local      Outside local      Outside global
icmp 165.1.2.20:1617   10.1.2.1:1617     33.33.33.33:1617   33.33.33.33:1617
icmp 165.1.2.20:1618   10.1.2.1:1618     33.33.33.33:1618   33.33.33.33:1618
icmp 165.1.2.20:1619   10.1.2.1:1619     33.33.33.33:1619   33.33.33.33:1619
```

```
icmp 165.1.2.20:1620   10.1.2.1:1620    33.33.33.33:1620   33.33.33.33:1620
icmp 165.1.2.20:1621   10.1.2.1:1621    33.33.33.33:1621   33.33.33.33:1621
```

3 Configure **nonat** on PIX and R6 for IPSec LAN-to-LAN between R6 and PIX. See PIX and R6 configuration in the examples for items 1 and 2.

4 Hidden issue: You need to configure static DLCI mapping for 165.1.2.20 on R3 and R5 to 306 and 506, respectively, as demonstrated in the following example:

```
r3#show frame map
Serial0/0 (up): ip 165.1.2.17 dlci 306(0x132,0x4C20), static,
               broadcast,
               CISCO, status defined, active
Serial0/0 (up): ip 165.1.2.18 dlci 306(0x132,0x4C20), static,
               broadcast,
               CISCO, status defined, active
Serial0/0 (up): ip 165.1.2.20 dlci 306(0x132,0x4C20), static,
               broadcast,
               CISCO, status defined, active


r6#show frame map
Serial1/0.1 (up): ip 165.1.2.17 dlci 603(0x25B,0x94B0), static,
               broadcast,
               CISCO, status defined, active
Serial1/0.1 (up): ip 165.1.2.18 dlci 603(0x25B,0x94B0), static,
               broadcast,
               CISCO, status defined, active
Serial1/0.1 (up): ip 165.1.2.19 dlci 605(0x25D,0x94D0), static,
               broadcast,
               CISCO, status defined, active
```

9.2: HSRP

1 Configure HSRP between R2 and R3 for redundancy, as demonstrated in the example following item 3.

2 Configure virtual IP 164.15.4.100. Remember, this should also be configured as the default gateway on the PIX.

3 Configure authentication using password **cisco**, as demonstrated in the following example:

```
! <Snip from R3 config>
hostname r3
!
interface Ethernet0/0
 ip address 164.15.4.6 255.255.255.0
```

```
 no ip redirects
 no ip directed-broadcast
 ip ospf message-digest-key 1 md5 cisco
 standby 1 priority 105 preempt
 standby 1 authentication cisco
 standby 1 ip 164.15.4.100
 standby 1 track Serial0/0
```

r3#**show standby**
```
Ethernet0/0 - Group 1
  Local state is Active, priority 105, may preempt
  Hellotime 3 holdtime 10
  Next hello sent in 00:00:02.045
  Hot standby IP address is 164.15.4.100 configured
  Active router is local
  Standby router is 164.15.4.5 expires in 00:00:09
  Standby virtual mac address is 0000.0c07.ac01
  Tracking interface states for 1 interface, 1 up:
    Up   Serial0/0
r3#
```

```
! <Snip from R2 config>
hostname r2
!
interface Ethernet0
 ip address 164.15.4.5 255.255.255.0
 ip ospf message-digest-key 1 md5 cisco
 standby 1 preempt
 standby 1 authentication cisco
 standby 1 ip 164.15.4.100
```

r2#**show standby**
```
Ethernet0 - Group 1
  Local state is Standby, priority 100, may preempt
  Hellotime 3 holdtime 10
  Next hello sent in 00:00:00.550
  Hot standby IP address is 164.15.4.100 configured
  Active router is 164.15.4.6 expires in 00:00:07, priority 105
  Standby router is local
  4 state changes, last state change 00:05:10
r2#
```

4 Configure interface tracking on R3 for the FR link (Serial 0/0), and configure Priority 105, because when the interface is down, it penalizes 10 points, so the priority will be dropped to 95 on R3, and R2 will preemptively take the Active role, having default priority 100. When the Serial interface is up, the priority is back to the normal 105 on R3 and preemptively takes the Active role again. The following example shows the verification of this configuration:

```
! Shutdown the serial link (FR) on R3
r3#config terminal
Enter configuration commands, one per line.  End with CNTL/Z.
r3(config)#interface serial 0/0
r3(config-if)#shutdown
r3(config-if)#
3d05h: %STANDBY-6-STATECHANGE: Standby: 1: Ethernet0/0 state Active
  -> Speak
3d05h: %LINK-5-CHANGED: Interface Serial0/0, changed state to
  administratively down
3d05h: %LINEPROTO-5-UPDOWN: Line protocol on Interface Serial0/0, changed
  state to down
3d05h: %STANDBY-6-STATECHANGE: Standby: 1: Ethernet0/0 state Speak
  -> Standby
r3(config-if)#
r3(config-if)#end
r3#
r3#
r3#show standby
Ethernet0/0 - Group 1
  Local state is Standby, priority 95, may preempt
  Hellotime 3 holdtime 10
  Next hello sent in 00:00:02.259
  Hot standby IP address is 164.15.4.100 configured
  Active router is 164.15.4.5 expires in 00:00:09
  Standby router is local
  Standby virtual mac address is 0000.0c07.ac01
  Tracking interface states for 1 interface, 0 up:
    Down Serial0/0


! R2 now ACTIVE
1w0d: %STANDBY-6-STATECHANGE: Standby: 1: Ethernet0 state Active  -> Speak
1w0d: %STANDBY-6-STATECHANGE: Standby: 1: Ethernet0 state Speak   -> Standby
1w0d: %STANDBY-6-STATECHANGE: Standby: 1: Ethernet0 state Standby -> Active
r2#
r2#show standby
Ethernet0 - Group 1
  Local state is Active, priority 100, may preempt
  Hellotime 3 holdtime 10
```

```
Next hello sent in 00:00:00.036
Hot standby IP address is 164.15.4.100 configured
Active router is local
Standby router is 164.15.4.6 expires in 00:00:07
Standby virtual mac address is 0000.0c07.ac01
8 state changes, last state change 00:00:30


! Un-Shut the serial link (FR) on R3
r3#config terminal
Enter configuration commands, one per line.  End with CNTL/Z.
r3(config)#interface serial 0/0
r3(config-if)#no shutdown
r3(config-if)#
3d05h: %STANDBY-6-STATECHANGE: Standby: 1: Ethernet0/0 state Standby
  -> Active
3d05h: %LINK-3-UPDOWN: Interface Serial0/0, changed state to up
3d05h: %LINEPROTO-5-UPDOWN: Line protocol on Interface Serial0/0, changed
  state to up
r3(config-if)#end
r3#show standby
Ethernet0/0 - Group 1
  Local state is Active, priority 105, may preempt
  Hellotime 3 holdtime 10
  Next hello sent in 00:00:02.875
  Hot standby IP address is 164.15.4.100 configured
  Active router is local
  Standby router is 164.15.4.5 expires in 00:00:08
  Standby virtual mac address is 0000.0c07.ac01
  Tracking interface states for 1 interface, 1 up:
    Up   Serial0/0


! R2 now STANDBY
1w0d: %STANDBY-6-STATECHANGE: Standby: 1: Ethernet0 state Active -> Speak
1w0d: %STANDBY-6-STATECHANGE: Standby: 1: Ethernet0 state Speak  -> Standby
r2#show standby
Ethernet0 - Group 1
  Local state is Standby, priority 100, may preempt
  Hellotime 3 holdtime 10
  Next hello sent in 00:00:00.104
  Hot standby IP address is 164.15.4.100 configured
  Active router is 164.15.4.6 expires in 00:00:08, priority 105
  Standby router is local
  10 state changes, last state change 00:00:51
```

9.3: Translation Timeout Improvements

1 Configure xlate timeout on PIX to 1 hour using the **timeout** command (the default is
3 hours), as demonstrated in the following example:

```
! Default xlate timeout.
PIX(config)# show timeout
timeout xlate 3:00:00
timeout conn 1:00:00 half-closed 0:10:00 udp 0:02:00 rpc 0:10:00 h323 0:05:00
  sip 0:30:00 sip_media 0:02:00
timeout uauth 0:05:00 absolute


! Change using 'timeout' command shown below.
PIX(config)# timeout xlate 1:00:00
PIX(config)# show timeout
timeout xlate 1:00:00
timeout conn 1:00:00 half-closed 0:10:00 udp 0:02:00 rpc 0:10:00 h323 0:05:00
  sip 0:30:00 sip_media 0:02:00
timeout uauth 0:05:00 absolute
```

9.4: Congestion Management—QoS

1 Configure priority queuing on R6 to control congestion, as demonstrated in the following
example:

```
hostname r6
!
interface Serial1/0
 no ip address
 no ip directed-broadcast
 encapsulation frame-relay
 no ip mroute-cache
 priority-group 1
!
access-list 110 permit eigrp any any
!
priority-list 1 protocol ip low gt 1500
priority-list 1 protocol ip medium tcp telnet
priority-list 1 interface Ethernet0/0 medium
priority-list 1 protocol ip high list 110


r6#show queueing priority
Current priority queue configuration:
```

```
List    Queue  Args
1       low    protocol ip           gt 1500
1       medium protocol ip           tcp port telnet
1       medium interface Ethernet0/0
1       high   protocol ip           list 110
```

2 Apply the **priority-group** to the main interface.

3 Verify that queuing is working, as demonstrated in the following example:

```
! <Queue count before Ping; note the low queue count is zero (0)>
r6#show queueing interface serial 1/0
Interface Serial1/0 queueing strategy: priority


Output queue utilization (queue/count)
        high/11 medium/0 normal/235164 low/0


r6#ping ip
Target IP address: 22.22.22.22
Repeat count [5]:
Datagram size [100]: 2000
Timeout in seconds [2]:
Extended commands [n]:
Sweep range of sizes [n]:
Type escape sequence to abort.
Sending 5, 2000-byte ICMP Echos to 22.22.22.22, timeout is 2 seconds:
!!!!!
Success rate is 100 percent (5/5), round-trip min/avg/max = 1024/1036/1048 ms


! <Queue count after pinging with large packets, See the low count increase>
r6#show queueing interface serial 1/0
Interface Serial1/0 queueing strategy: priority


Output queue utilization (queue/count)
        high/18 medium/0 normal/235181 low/5


! <Queue count before Telnet; note the medium count is zero (0)>
r6#show queueing interface serial 1/0
Interface Serial1/0 queueing strategy: priority


Output queue utilization (queue/count)
        high/28 medium/0 normal/235198 low/5


! <Telnet from R6 to anywhere on the network>
```

```
r6#telnet 164.15.4.5
Trying 164.15.4.5 ... Open

Username: r2-telnet
Password: cisco

r2#exit

[Connection to 164.15.4.5 closed by foreign host]
r6#


! <Queue count after Telnet, See the medium count increase>
r6#show queueing interface serial 1/0
Interface Serial1/0 queueing strategy: priority

Output queue utilization (queue/count)
          high/37 medium/46 normal/235214 low/5
```

4 To increase Telnet performance in Section 7.1, configure R2 and R4 for TCP header
   compression to reduce the size of the headers.

5 The TCP header compression technique only compresses the TCP header; it has no effect
   on UDP packets or other protocol headers. It is supported on serial lines using High-Level
   Data Link Control (HDLC) or PPP encapsulation. Note that you must enable compression
   on both ends of a serial connection (R2 and R4). See the following example:

NOTE   You can assign only one queuing mechanism type to an interface.

```
! <Snip from R2 config>
hostname r2
!
interface Serial0
 ip address 165.1.2.1 255.255.255.252
 ip tcp header-compression


! <Snip from R4 config>
hostname r4
!
```

```
interface Serial1/3
 ip address 165.1.2.2 255.255.255.252
 ip tcp header-compression


! <Verify on R2>
r2#show ip interface serial 0
Serial0 is up, line protocol is up
  Internet address is 165.1.2.1/30
  TCP/IP header compression is enabled and compressing

! <Verify on R4>
r4#show ip interface serial 1/3
Serial1/3 is up, line protocol is up
  Internet address is 165.1.2.2/30
  TCP/IP header compression is enabled and compressing
```

NOTE   See the following URLs for more info on priority queuing (PQ) and other techniques to tune IP performance on a router:

www.cisco.com/univercd/cc/td/doc/product/software/ios122/122cgcr/fqos_c/fqcprt2/qcfconmg.htm#48685

www.cisco.com/univercd/cc/td/doc/product/software/ios122/122cgcr/fqos_c/fqcprt2/qcfconmg.htm#23965

www.cisco.com/univercd/cc/td/doc/product/software/ios122/122cgcr/fqos_c/fqcprt2/qcfpq.htm

www.cisco.com/univercd/cc/td/doc/product/software/ios122/122cgcr/fipr_c/ipcprt1/1cfip.htm#15478

Section 10.0: Security Violations

10.1: DoS Attack

1 A web server (R7 in this case) was attacked on the network.

2 The nature of the attack could not be characterized.

3 Analyze the forensic evidence sniffer captures collected at the time of the attack, as shown previously in Figures 6-5a through 6-5d.

4 The attack was targeted to the web server on port 80.

5 Notice a unique pattern in all the GET requests—the use of **cmd.exe** to penetrate /browse through it. **cmd.exe** is the command shell access in Windows.

6 As mentioned, the attack is from a random source IP. You cannot configure any ACL on Layer 3 or Layer 4 information provided in sniffer captures, as per the restriction.

7 Mitigate this attack by classifying inbound packets on entry points on R7 (VLAN-6 and ATM link) with the class-based marking feature. Then, use Policy-Based Routing to black hole these packets to null0, as demonstrated in the example that follows. Make a discard decision at the ingress interface of the router.

```
hostname r7
!
class-map match-any http-attack
  match protocol http url "*cmd.exe*"
!
policy-map mark-inbound-packets
  class http-attack
    set ip dscp 1
!
interface FastEthernet0/0
 ip address 164.15.6.2 255.255.255.0
 ip policy route-map null_policy_route
!
interface ATM3/0
 ip address 165.1.2.13 255.255.255.252
 ip policy route-map null_policy_route
!
access-list 101 permit ip any any dscp 1
!
route-map null_policy_route permit 10
 match ip address 101
 set interface Null0
```

NOTE   See this URL to mitigate the "Code Red" worm. See Method B in particular, as used in this task. www.cisco.com/warp/public/63/nbar_acl_codered.shtml

10.2: IDS Blocking (Shunning)

1 Configure the Cisco IDS sensor as shown in Figure 6-1.

2 Initialize the sensor using the **setup** command from the sensor console. Configure host name **sensor1** with IP address 192.168.3.2 in VLAN-3. See the URL on the last page of this chapter for more details on initializing the sensor.

3 When using the **setup** command to initialize, configure the web server port to 8080; the default is 443.

4 Hidden issue: Configure the default gateway to be R1 (192.168.3.1) and not PIX (192.168.3.3), as PIX does not route packets from the same interface.

5 Configure SPAN on switch1 to monitor the R1 (VLAN3) interface, as demonstrated in the example that follows:

```
hostname sw1
!
monitor session 1 source interface Fa0/2
monitor session 1 destination interface Fa0/5


sw1#show monitor session 1
Session 1
- - - - - - - - - -
 Type        : Local Session
Source Ports:
     RX Only:        None
     TX Only:        None
     Both:           Fa0/2
Source VLANs:
     RX Only:        None
     TX Only:        None
     Both:           None
Source RSPAN VLAN: None
Destination Ports: Fa0/5
     Encapsulation: Native
             Ingress: Disabled
Reflector Port:     None
Filter VLANs:       None
Dest RSPAN VLAN:    None
```

6 Verify that the sensor is configured correctly for the sensing interface and the command and control interface, as demonstrated in the example that follows:

```
! By default, on some 42xx appliances, the sensing interface is
! configured to use int2 and not int0. Check the documentation.
! You can change this from the sensor console as follows
! Before changing the port;
sensor1# show interfaces
command-control is up
   Internet address is 192.168.3.2, subnet mask is 255.255.255.0, telnet is
      enabled.
   Hardware is eth1, tx

Network Statistics
   eth1      Link encap:Ethernet  HWaddr 00:06:5B:ED:59:B4
             inet addr:192.168.3.2  Bcast:192.168.3.255  Mask:255.255.255.0
             UP BROADCAST RUNNING MULTICAST  MTU:1500  Metric:1
             RX packets:58940 errors:0 dropped:0 overruns:0 frame:0
             TX packets:6067 errors:0 dropped:0 overruns:0 carrier:0
             collisions:0 txqueuelen:100
             RX bytes:4714133 (4.4 Mb)  TX bytes:2948632 (2.8 Mb)
             Interrupt:16 Base address:0xdcc0 Memory:feb20000-feb40000

Group 0 is up
   Sensing ports int2
   Logical virtual sensor configuration: virtualSensor
   Logical alarm channel configuration:  virtualAlarm

VirtualSensor0
   General Statistics for this Virtual Sensor
      Number of seconds since a reset of the statistics = 18
      Total number of packets processed since reset = 0
      Total number of IP packets processed since reset = 0
      Total number of packets that were not IP processed since reset = 0
      Total number of TCP packets processed since reset = 0
      Total number of UDP packets processed since reset = 0
      Total number of ICMP packets processed since reset = 0
      Total number of packets that were not TCP, UDP, or ICMP processed since
         reset = 0
      Total number of ARP packets processed since reset = 0
      Total number of ISL encapsulated packets processed since reset = 0
      Total number of 802.1q encapsulated packets processed since reset = 0
      Total number of packets with bad IP checksums processed since reset = 0
      Total number of packets with bad layer 4 checksums processed since reset = 0
      Total number of bytes processed since reset = 0
```

```
    The rate of packets per second since reset = 0
    The rate of bytes per second since reset = 0
    The average bytes per packet since reset = 0
Fragment Reassembly Unit Statistics for this Virtual Sensor
    Number of fragments currently in FRU = 0
    Number of datagrams currently in FRU = 0
    Number of fragments received since reset = 0
    Number of complete datagrams reassembled since reset = 0
    Number of incomplete datagrams abandoned since reset = 0
    Number of fragments discarded since reset = 0
Statistics for the TCP Stream Reassembly Unit
    Current Statistics for the TCP Stream Reassembly Unit
        TCP streams currently in the embryonic state = 0
        TCP streams currently in the established state = 0
        TCP streams currently in the closing state = 0
        TCP streams currently in the system = 0
        TCP Packets currently queued for reassembly = 0
    Cumulative Statistics for the TCP Stream Reassembly Unit since reset
        TCP streams that have been tracked since last reset = 0
        TCP streams that had a gap in the sequence jumped = 0
        TCP streams that was abandoned due to a gap in the sequence = 0
        TCP packets that arrived out of sequence order for their stream = 0
        TCP packets that arrived out of state order for their stream = 0
        The rate of TCP connections tracked per second since reset = 0
The Signature Database Statistics.
    The Number of each type of node active in the system (can not be reset)
        Total nodes active = 0
        TCP nodes keyed on both IP addresses and both ports = 0
        UDP nodes keyed on both IP addresses and both ports = 0
        IP nodes keyed on both IP addresses = 0
    The number of each type of node inserted since reset
        Total nodes inserted = 0
        TCP nodes keyed on both IP addresses and both ports = 0
        UDP nodes keyed on both IP addresses and both ports = 0
        IP nodes keyed on both IP addresses = 0
    The rate of nodes per second for each time since reset
        Nodes per second = 0
        TCP nodes keyed on both IP addresses and both ports per second = 0
        UDP nodes keyed on both IP addresses and both ports per second = 0
        IP nodes keyed on both IP addresses per second = 0
    The number of root nodes forced to expire because of memory constraints
        TCP nodes keyed on both IP addresses and both ports = 0
```

```
        Alarm Statistics for this Virtual Sensor
           Number of alarms triggered by events = 1
           Number of alarms excluded by filters = 0
           Number of alarms removed by summarizer = 0
           Number of alarms sent to the Event Store = 1

Sensing int0 is down
   Hardware is eth0, TX
   Reset port

Sensing int1 is up
   Hardware is eth1, TX
   Reset port
   Command control port

Sensing int2 is up
   Hardware is eth2, SX
   Reset port

MAC statistics from the IntelPro interface
   Link = down
   Speed = N/A
   Duplex = N/A
   State = up
   Rx_Packets = 0
   Tx_Packets = 0
   Rx_Bytes = 0
   Tx_Bytes = 0
   Rx_Errors = 0
   Tx_Errors = 0
   Rx_Dropped = 0
   Tx_Dropped = 0
   Multicast = 0
   Collisions = 0
   Rx_Length_Errors = 0
   Rx_Over_Errors = 0
   Rx_CRC_Errors = 0
   Rx_Frame_Errors = 0
   Rx_FIFO_Errors = 0
   Rx_Missed_Errors = 0
   Tx_Aborted_Errors = 0
   Tx_Carrier_Errors = 0
   Tx_FIFO_Errors = 0
   Tx_Heartbeat_Errors = 0
```

```
              Tx_Window_Errors = 0
              Tx_Abort_Late_Coll = 0
              Tx_Deferred_Ok = 0
              Tx_Single_Coll_Ok = 0
              Tx_Multi_Coll_Ok = 0
              Rx_Long_Length_Errors = 0
              Rx_Short_Length_Errors = 0
              Rx_Align_Errors = 0
              Rx_Flow_Control_XON = 0
              Rx_Flow_Control_XOFF = 0
              Tx_Flow_Control_XON = 0
              Tx_Flow_Control_XOFF = 0
              Rx_CSum_Offload_Good = 0
              Rx_CSum_Offload_Errors = 0
              PHY_Media_Type = Fiber
              Dropped Packet Percent = 0

      sensor1#




      ! <Change the sensing interface as follows ;>
      sensor1# configure terminal
      sensor1(config)# interface group 0
      sensor1(config-ifg)# no sensing-interface int2
      sensor1(config-ifg)# sensing-interface int0
      sensor1(config-ifg)# exit
      sensor1(config)# exit
      sensor1# show interfaces
      command-control is up
        Internet address is 192.168.3.2, subnet mask is 255.255.255.0, telnet is
          enabled.
        Hardware is eth1, tx

Network Statistics
      eth1      Link encap:Ethernet  HWaddr 00:06:5B:ED:59:B4
                inet addr:192.168.3.2  Bcast:192.168.3.255  Mask:255.255.255.0
                UP BROADCAST RUNNING MULTICAST  MTU:1500  Metric:1
                RX packets:59248 errors:0 dropped:0 overruns:0 frame:0
                TX packets:6254 errors:0 dropped:0 overruns:0 carrier:0
                collisions:0 txqueuelen:100
                RX bytes:4735280 (4.5 Mb)  TX bytes:2968052 (2.8 Mb)
                Interrupt:16 Base address:0xdcc0 Memory:feb20000-feb40000
```

```
Group 0 is up
  Sensing ports int0
  Logical virtual sensor configuration: virtualSensor
  Logical alarm channel configuration:  virtualAlarm

VirtualSensor0
  General Statistics for this Virtual Sensor
    Number of seconds since a reset of the statistics = 44
    Total number of packets processed since reset = 113
    Total number of IP packets processed since reset = 74
    Total number of packets that were not IP processed since reset = 39
    Total number of TCP packets processed since reset = 70
    Total number of UDP packets processed since reset = 4
    Total number of ICMP packets processed since reset = 0
    Total number of packets that were not TCP, UDP, or ICMP processed since
      reset = 0
    Total number of ARP packets processed since reset = 2
    Total number of ISL encapsulated packets processed since reset = 0
    Total number of 802.1q encapsulated packets processed since reset = 0
    Total number of packets with bad IP checksums processed since reset = 0
    Total number of packets with bad layer 4 checksums processed since reset = 0
    Total number of bytes processed since reset = 7771
    The rate of packets per second since reset = 2
    The rate of bytes per second since reset = 176
    The average bytes per packet since reset = 68
  Fragment Reassembly Unit Statistics for this Virtual Sensor
    Number of fragments currently in FRU = 0
    Number of datagrams currently in FRU = 0
    Number of fragments received since reset = 0
    Number of complete datagrams reassembled since reset = 0
    Number of incomplete datagrams abandoned since reset = 0
    Number of fragments discarded since reset = 0
  Statistics for the TCP Stream Reassembly Unit
    Current Statistics for the TCP Stream Reassembly Unit
      TCP streams currently in the embryonic state = 0
      TCP streams currently in the established state = 0
      TCP streams currently in the closing state = 0
      TCP streams currently in the system = 1
      TCP Packets currently queued for reassembly = 0
    Cumulative Statistics for the TCP Stream Reassembly Unit since reset
      TCP streams that have been tracked since last reset = 4
      TCP streams that had a gap in the sequence jumped = 0
      TCP streams that was abandoned due to a gap in the sequence = 0
      TCP packets that arrived out of sequence order for their stream = 0
```

```
                  TCP packets that arrived out of state order for their stream = 70
                  The rate of TCP connections tracked per second since reset = 0
          The Signature Database Statistics.
             The Number of each type of node active in the system (can not be reset)
                  Total nodes active = 38
                  TCP nodes keyed on both IP addresses and both ports = 3
                  UDP nodes keyed on both IP addresses and both ports = 2
                  IP nodes keyed on both IP addresses = 6
             The number of each type of node inserted since reset
                  Total nodes inserted = 50
                  TCP nodes keyed on both IP addresses and both ports = 4
                  UDP nodes keyed on both IP addresses and both ports = 4
                  IP nodes keyed on both IP addresses = 7
             The rate of nodes per second for each time since reset
                  Nodes per second = 1
                  TCP nodes keyed on both IP addresses and both ports per second = 0
                  UDP nodes keyed on both IP addresses and both ports per second = 0
                  IP nodes keyed on both IP addresses per second = 0
             The number of root nodes forced to expire because of memory constraints
                  TCP nodes keyed on both IP addresses and both ports = 0
          Alarm Statistics for this Virtual Sensor
             Number of alarms triggered by events = 1
             Number of alarms excluded by filters = 0
             Number of alarms removed by summarizer = 0
             Number of alarms sent to the Event Store = 1

Sensing int0 is up
   Hardware is eth0, TX
   Reset port

MAC statistics from the IntelPro interface
      Link = up
      Speed = 100
      Duplex = Full
      State = up
      Rx_Packets = 1433
      Tx_Packets = 0
      Rx_Bytes = 118744
      Tx_Bytes = 0
      Rx_Errors = 0
      Tx_Errors = 0
      Rx_Dropped = 0
      Tx_Dropped = 0
      Multicast = 285
```

```
        Collisions = 0
        Rx_Length_Errors = 0
        Rx_Over_Errors = 0
        Rx_CRC_Errors = 0
        Rx_Frame_Errors = 0
        Rx_FIFO_Errors = 0
        Rx_Missed_Errors = 0
        Tx_Aborted_Errors = 0
        Tx_Carrier_Errors = 0
        Tx_FIFO_Errors = 0
        Tx_Heartbeat_Errors = 0
        Tx_Window_Errors = 0
        Tx_Abort_Late_Coll = 0
        Tx_Deferred_Ok = 0
        Tx_Single_Coll_Ok = 0
        Tx_Multi_Coll_Ok = 0
        Rx_Long_Length_Errors = 0
        Rx_Short_Length_Errors = 0
        Rx_Align_Errors = 0
        Rx_Flow_Control_XON = 0
        Rx_Flow_Control_XOFF = 0
        Tx_Flow_Control_XON = 0
        Tx_Flow_Control_XOFF = 0
        Rx_CSum_Offload_Good = 857
        Rx_CSum_Offload_Errors = 0
        PHY_Media_Type = Copper
        Dropped Packet Percent = 0

Sensing int1 is up
   Hardware is eth1, TX
   Reset port
   Command control port

Sensing int2 is down
   Hardware is eth2, SX
   Reset port

sensor1#
```

7 Use IDM (IDS Device Manager) to configure other parameters, and install IEV (IDS Event Viewer) on the AAA server to receive alarms from the sensor.

8 Using IDM, enable IDS Telnet access for VLAN2 (10.1.1.0) and VLAN3 (192.168.3.0) networks only, as demonstrated in Figure 6-12.

Figure 6-12 *Allow Host Setting for VLAN2 and VLAN3 Networks*

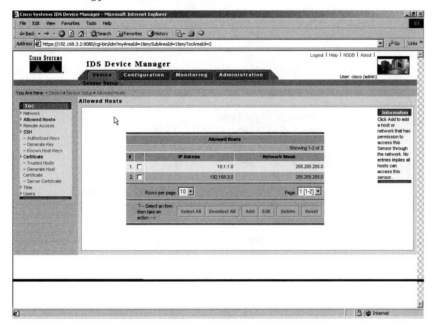

9 Configure PIX static translation for 11.11.11.11 and conduit accordingly, as demonstrated in the example that follows:

```
PIX(config)# show conduit
conduit permit tcp host 11.11.11.11 eq www any (hitcnt=34)


PIX(config)# show static
static (inside,outside) 11.11.11.11 11.11.11.11 netmask 255.255.255.255 0 0
```

10 Enable the HTTP server on R1.

11 Verify that the sensor is receiving packets and events. Enable ICMP echo and echo-reply signature for HIGH severity. Ping from anywhere on the network to 11.11.11.11. You should start receiving alarms. See the example that follows:

```
!  Enable ICMP signature for HIGH severity using IDM
! Signature Configuration mode. Ping from anywhere on the
! network to 11.11.11.11 and verify on sensor as follows:

sensor1# show events

evAlert: eventId=1050202358373315320 severity=high
  originator:
    hostId: sensor1
```

```
      appName: sensorApp
      appInstanceId: 980
   time: 2003/04/24 20:20:11 2003/04/24 20:20:11 UTC
   interfaceGroup: 0
   vlan: 0
   signature: sigId=2004 sigName=ICMP Echo Req subSigId=0 version=S37
   participants:
     attack:
       attacker: proxy=false
         addr: locality=OUT 164.15.4.6
       victim:
         addr: locality=OUT 11.11.11.11

evAlert: eventId=1050202358373315321 severity=high
  originator:
    hostId: sensor1
    appName: sensorApp
    appInstanceId: 980
   time: 2003/04/24 20:20:11 2003/04/24 20:20:11 UTC
   interfaceGroup: 0
   vlan: 0
   signature: sigId=2000 sigName=ICMP Echo Rply subSigId=0 version=S37
   participants:
     attack:
       attacker: proxy=false
         addr: locality=OUT 11.11.11.11
       victim:
         addr: locality=OUT 164.15.4.6

<press Ctrl-C to exit>
sensor1#


! <Also use following command to verify number of events triggered.>
sensor1# show statistics eventStore
Event store statistics
   General information about the event store
      The current number of open subscriptions = 0
      The number of events lost by subscriptions and queries = 1
      The number of queries issued = 5
      The number of times the event store circular buffer has wrapped = 0
   Number of events of each type currently stored
      Debug events = 0
      Status events = 11
      Log transaction events = 223
      Shun request events = 0
```

```
            Error events, warning = 1
            Error events, error = 15
            Error events, fatal = 0
            Alert events, informational = 6
            Alert events, low = 0
            Alert events, medium = 0
            Alert events, high = 6
    sensor1#
```

12 The built-in signature for the unique pattern that matches the sniffer captures shown in Figures 6-5a through 6-5d is SigID 5081. Configure blocking (shun) for this signature.

13 Using IDM, edit signature ID 5081, which is for cmd.exe access. By default it is Medium severity. Browse from Test PC to 11.11.11.11 with the following in the URL:

http://11.11.11.11/scripts/..%255c../winnt/system32/cmd.exe?/c+dir%20c.

14 IDS will detect the execution of cmd.exe in the HTTP GET request and trigger signature 5081. Run the **show events alert** command on the sensor before browsing; you will see the alarm trigger on console.

15 Use the IDM to modify the signature to High and browse again. See Figures 6-13a and 6-13b. Check on the sensor using **show events alert high**. This should show HIGH alerts only, as demonstrated in the example that follows:

```
    sensor1# show events alert high

    evAlert: eventId=1050202358373315428 severity=high
      originator:
        hostId: sensor1
        appName: sensorApp
        appInstanceId: 980
      time: 2003/04/24 21:46:43 2003/04/24 21:46:43 UTC
      interfaceGroup: 0
      vlan: 0
    signature: sigId=5081 sigName=WWW WinNT cmd.exe access subSigId=0
      version=S37/system32/cmd.exe
      context:
        fromAttacker: R0VUIC9zY3JpcHRzLy4uJTI1NWMuLi93aW5udC9zeXN0ZW0zMi9jbWQuZXhl
    Py9jK2RpciUyMGM6JTVjaWlzJTVjIEhUVFAvMS4xDQ==
      participants:
        attack:
        attacker: proxy=false
          addr: locality=OUT 164.15.9.10
          port: 3069
        victim:
          addr: locality=OUT 11.11.11.11
          port: 80
    <press Ctrl-C to exit>
    sensor1#
```

Figure 6-13a *Blocking (Shun) Configuration Using IDM—Interface Configuration*

Figure 6-13b *Blocking (Shun) Configuration Using IDM—Interface Configuration*

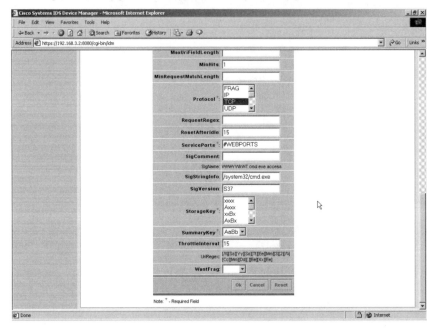

16 Configure blocking (shunning) for signature ID 5081. Configure blocking parameters for the R1 Fastethernet0/0 (VLAN3) interface. See Figures 6-14a through 6-14c.

Figure 6-14a *Blocking (Shun) Configuration Using IDM—Add Logical Device*

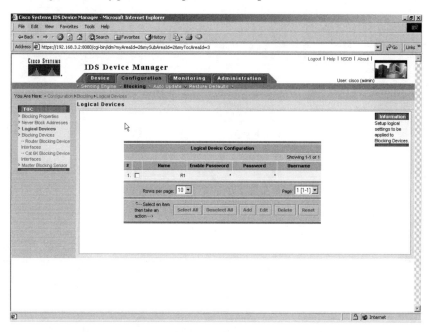

Figure 6-14b *Blocking (Shun) Configuration Using IDM—Add Blocking Device (R1)*

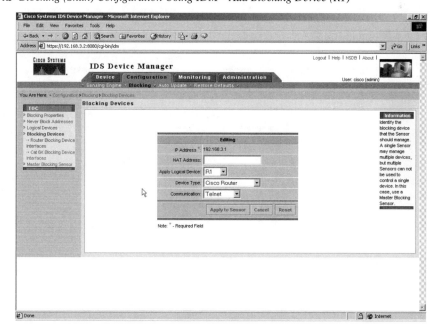

Figure 6-14c *Blocking (Shun) Configuration Using IDM—Interface Configuration*

17 Verify the shunning configuration by launching an attack, and check on R1 for dynamic
ACL for **deny** statements, as demonstrated in the example that follows:

```
! Browse to R1 (11.11.11.11) from Test PC in VLAN9. Then, check
! dynamic ACL entry on R1. Refer to the following URLs
! http://11.11.11.11/scripts/..%255c../winnt/system32/cmd.exe?/c+dir%20c:
! or
! http://11.11.11.11/scripts/..%255c../winnt/system32/cmd.exe?
  /c+dir%20c:%5c
! or
! http://11.11.11.11/scripts/..%255c../winnt/system32/cmd.exe?
  /c+dir%20c:%5cWINNT%5c
r1#show access-lists
Extended IP access list IDS_FastEthernet0/0_in_1
    permit ip host 192.168.3.2 any (203 matches)
    deny ip host 164.15.9.10 any (18 matches)
    permit ip any any (44 matches)
r1#
```

```
! <snip from R1 configuration>
hostname r1
!
interface FastEthernet0/0
 ip address 192.168.3.1 255.255.255.0
 ip access-group IDS_FastEthernet0/0_in_1 in
!


! <Verify sensor configuration for blocking>
sensor1# show statistics NetworkAccess
Current Configuration
   AllowSensorShun = false
   ShunMaxEntries = 100
   NetDevice
      Type = Cisco
      IP = 192.168.3.1
      NATAddr = 0.0.0.0
      Communications = telnet
      ShunInterface
         InterfaceName = FastEthernet0/0
         InterfaceDirection = in
State
   ShunEnable = true
   NetDevice
      IP = 192.168.3.1
      AclSupport = uses Named ACLs
      State = Active
sensor1#
```

18 Another hidden issue: For some devices (VLAN6 or VLAN8) in the network to be able to browse to 11.11.11.11, make sure you permit web traffic to host 11.11.11.11 in the ingress ACL configured on R2 for Section 6.1. See the example that follows.

NOTE   The sensor software is nearly completely rearchitected for version 4.0. The legacy Postoffice protocol that uses UDP port 45000 has been replaced with the Remote Data Exchange Protocol (RDEP). RDEP uses the HTTP/HTTPS protocol to communicate XML documents between the sensor and external systems. Alarms and configuration are communicated using RDEP, which is based on the HTTP/HTTPS and XML open standards. Providing a secure, open system that uses standard communication protocols allows greater internal and third-party integration.

```
hostname r2
!
interface Serial0
 ip address 165.1.2.1 255.255.255.252
 ip access-group 101 in
!
interface BRI0
 ip address 165.1.2.9 255.255.255.252
 ip access-group 101 in
!

access-list 101 permit ospf any any
access-list 101 permit tcp any any eq bgp
access-list 101 permit icmp any any
access-list 101 permit tcp any any eq telnet
access-list 101 permit tcp any host 11.11.11.11 eq www
access-list 101 deny    ip any any

r2#show access-lists 101
Extended IP access list 101
    permit ospf any any (1845 matches)
    permit tcp any any eq bgp (457 matches)
    permit icmp any any (367 matches)
    permit tcp any any eq telnet (70 matches)
    permit tcp any host 11.11.11.11 eq www (7 matches)
    deny ip any any (3 matches)
r2#
```

NOTE	The default username and password are both **cisco**. You will be prompted to change the password when you first log in. The sensor is configured to force the use of strong passwords (not based on dictionary words) at least eight characters long.
	If you are upgrading an IDS-4220-E or IDS-4230-FE, you must swap the network cables. The former command and control interface is now the sniffing interface. See the documentation for more information.

NOTE	Use the following URLs for reference for IDS version 4.0 configuration:
	Initializing the Sensor
	www.cisco.com/univercd/cc/td/doc/product/iaabu/csids/csids9/hwguide/hwchap4.htm#363980
	Quick Start Guide
	www.cisco.com/univercd/cc/td/doc/product/iaabu/csids/csids9/15282_01.htm
	Upgrading IDS software version 3.1 to version 4.0
	www.cisco.com/univercd/cc/td/doc/product/iaabu/csids/csids9/15284_02.htm#1023416
	New features in Version 4.0
	www.cisco.com/univercd/cc/td/doc/product/iaabu/csids/csids9/15284_02.htm#1050016
	IDS 4.0 Documentation home page
	www.cisco.com/univercd/cc/td/doc/product/iaabu/csids/csids9/index.htm

CHAPTER 7

Practice Lab 7

Any ending can also be viewed as the beginning of something new, and such is the intent of this final lab. From the time when you started your journey preparing for your CCIE Security Lab exam, this book will serve to mark the end of your preparation and give you the self-confidence and assurance for the readiness to appear for the real lab that you have been long waiting for. Good luck to you.

The lab is marked out of 100 points. You must complete the lab within 8 hours and obtain a minimum of 80 points to pass. As with all labs, this test has been written such that you should be able to complete all questions, including initial configuration (that is, IP addressing), within 8 hours, excluding cabling time. Allow up to one hour for cabling, using the provided instructions and observing the general guidelines. You can use any combination of routers as long as you fulfill the needs of the topology diagram in Figure 7-1. It is not compulsory to use routers of the same model.

NOTE   The real CCIE Lab does not require you to do any cabling or IP addressing.

Equipment List

- 8 routers with the following specifications (all routers are to be loaded with Cisco IOS Software 12.1(T) train, with the exception of Load 12.2(13)T1 or higher on R6):

    R1 — 2 Ethernet (with IP Plus image)

    R2 — 1 Ethernet, 1 BRI, 1 serial (with IP Plus + IPSec 56 image)

    R3 — 1 Ethernet, 1 serial (with IP Plus image)

    R4 — 1 Ethernet, 1 serial (with IP Plus image)

    R5 — 2 Ethernet, 1 ATM (with IP Plus + IOS Firewall)

    R6 — 1 Ethernet, 1 BRI (with IP Plus + IOS Firewall + IPSec 56 image)

    R7 — 2 Ethernet, 1 ATM (with IP Plus image)

    R8 — 2 Ethernet (with IP Plus image)

- 1 switch (3550)
- 1 PIX with 2 interfaces (version 6.x with DES enabled)
- 1 VPN3000 concentrator (version 3.6.x)
- 2 PCs:

    Windows 2000 Server with CiscoSecure ACS 3.x+

    Test PC with Cisco VPN Client 3.x software

General Guidelines

- Do not configure any static/default routes unless otherwise specified/required.
- Use DLCIs provided in the diagram.
- Use the IP addressing scheme provided in the diagram; do not change any IP addressing unless otherwise specified.
- Use **cisco** as the password for any authentication string, enable-password, and TACACS+/ RADIUS key or for any other purpose unless otherwise specified.
- Add additional loopbacks as specified during this lab.
- Configure VLANs on Sw1 as per Figure 7-1.
- All routers should be able to ping any interface in the network using the *optimal* path.
- Do not use any external resources or answers provided in this book when attempting the lab.
- Do not configure any authentication or authorization on the console and aux ports.

NOTE   The real CCIE Lab exams are hands-on structures similar to this book. Each configuration exercise has preassigned point values. The candidate must obtain a minimum mark of 80% to pass. This book provides you with a similar structure to give you a better understanding and experience. For more information on CCIE exam structure, see

www.cisco.com/warp/customer/625/ccie/exam_preparation/preparation.html

---

Setting Up the Lab

You can use any combination of routers as long as you fulfill the topology diagram, outlined in Figure 7-1. It is not compulsory to use the same model of routers.

Frame Relay DLCI Information

Configure R6 as a Frame Relay switch and use Figure 7-2 for DLCI information. No additional dynamic DLCIs are allowed for this exercise.

Figure 7-1   *Lab Topology Diagram*

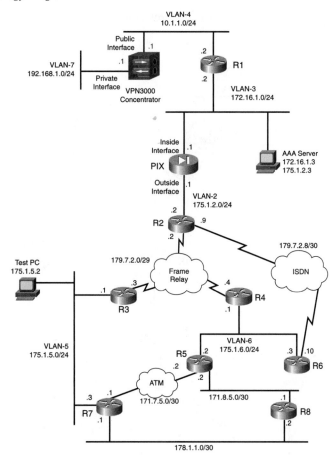

Figure 7-2   *Frame Relay DLCI Diagram*

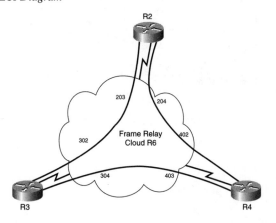

Routing Protocol Information

Use Figure 7-3 to configure all routing protocols.

Figure 7-3 *Routing Protocol Information*

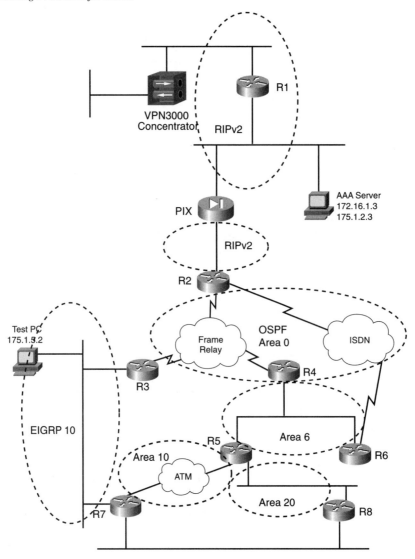

BGP Information

Use Figure 7-4 to configure BGP.

Figure 7-4   *BGP Information*

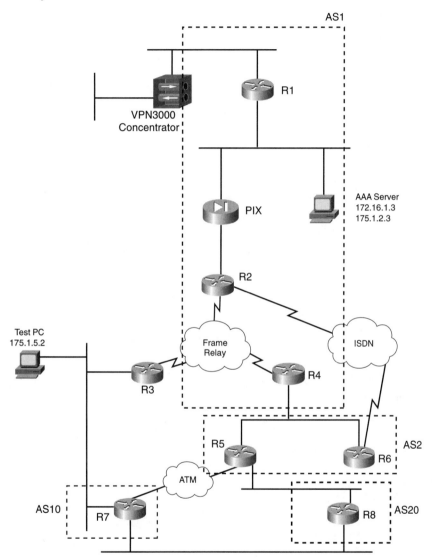

Cabling Instructions

Use Tables 7-1, 7-2, and 7-3 for cabling all devices in your topology. It is not a must to use the same type or sequence of interface. You may use any combination of interfaces as long as you fulfill the requirement.

Table 7-1 *Cabling Instructions (Ethernet)*

Ethernet Cabling	VLAN	Switch1
VPN3000-Private	7	Port 1
VPN3000-Public	4	Port 2
R1-Fastethernet0/0	4	Port 3
R1-Fastethernet1/0	3	Port 4
AAA Server	3	Port 5
PIX—inside-E1	3	Port 6
PIX—outside-E0	2	Port 7
R2-Ethernet0	2	Port 8
R3-Ethernet0/0	5	Port 9
Test PC	5	Port 10
R4-Ethernet0/0	6	Port 11
R5-Ethernet1/0	6	Port 12
R6-Ethernet0/0	6	Port 13
R7-FastEthernet0/1	5	Port 14

Table 7-2 *Cabling Instructions (Serial)*

Back-to-Back Cabling	DTE-End	DCE-End
R2-to-frsw*	R2-serial0	R6-serial1/0
R3-to-frsw*	R3-serial0/0	R6-serial1/1
R4-to-frsw*	R4-serial1/0	R6-serial1/2

*frsw = Frame Relay switch R6

Table 7-3 *Cabling Instructions (Ethernet)*

Back-to-Back Ethernet Cabling		
R5-to-R8	R5-Ethernet1/1	R8-FastEthernet0/0
R7-to-R8	R7-FastEthernet0/0	R8-FastEthernet0/1

Practice Lab 7 Exercises

This chapter is the last lab in this book.

The steps in each exercise are not necessarily intended to be completed in the order indicated. They can be done in any order of preference or as you feel appropriate. There may be situations where the steps have been intentionally written incorrectly to create problems. You have to identify the best approach and fulfill all the requirements.

Section 1.0: Basic Configuration (15 points)

1.1: IP Addressing (3 points)

1 Redraw a detailed topology with all necessary information.

2 Configure IP addressing as shown in Figure 7-1.

3 Make sure you can ping all devices.

4 Configure the static default route on R1 to PIX.

5 Configure two static default routes on R5, one to R7 and another to R8.

6 Configure all routers to learn the default gateway dynamically.

7 Configure the static default route on the VPN3000 concentrator to R1. Do not configure any routing protocol on the concentrator. Manage the concentrator from the AAA server using HTTPS and not HTTP.

1.2: Frame Relay Configuration (4 points)

1 Configure R6 as a Frame Relay switch using the DLCI information provided for Frame Relay routing in Figure 7-2.

2 Configure a full-mesh Frame Relay network between R2, R3, and R4.

3 Do not configure subinterface(s) on any router.

1.3: LAN Switch Configuration (4 points)

1 Configure switch1 with the VLAN information provided in Table 7-1.

2 Configure strict security for VLAN3 devices. In the event of a security breach, the switch should shut down the port.

3 Configure the Switch1 management interface in VLAN5 with IP 175.1.5.25/24. Configure a static default route.

1.4: ATM Configuration (3 points)

1 Configure back-to-back ATM between R5 and R7.

2 Configure ATM PVC on both ends to be the same, as there is no ATM switch in between. Configure VPI=0 and VCI=700.

3 Configure static maps.

NOTE   Define transmit clock source on one end using **atm clock INTERNAL**.

1.5: Ethernet Back-to-Back Configuration (1 point)

1 Configure R5, R7, and R8 back-to-back Ethernet cabling as per Table 7-3. Do not use the switch VLANs. Use cross-over cable.

Section 2.0: Routing Configuration (20 points)

2.1: OSPF (4 points)

1 Configure OSPF as shown in Figure 7-3.

2 Do not change the default network type on the Frame Relay network.

3 Redistribute where necessary. Make sure all networks appear on all routers using the optimal path.

4 Configure clear-text authentication.

5 R8 must not learn any OSPF routes from neighbor R5. Do not configure a distribute list or passive interface on any routers to achieve this task.

2.2: EIGRP (3 points)

1 Configure EIGRP AS 10 on R3 and R7 as shown in Figure 7-3. Advertise the VLAN5 network in EIGRP.

2 Make sure all routers can ping the Test PC.

3 Redistribute EIGRP into OSPF on R3 and R7.

4 Configure strong authentication.

5 R4 and R5 should reach the VLAN5 network via R3 and not R5. Do not change any Admin Distance or Metric/cost. Do not configure any policy routing to achieve this task.

2.3: RIP (3 points)

1 Configure RIP between R1, R2, and PIX as shown in Figure 7-3.

2 Configure clear-text authentication.

3 Do not advertise the default gateway to R2 using RIP.

2.4: BGP (10 points)

2.4.1: Basic BGP Configuration (3 points)

1 Configure BGP as shown in Figure 7-4.

2 Configure R1, R2, and R4 in AS1.

3 Configure R4 to peer with R5 and R6 in AS2.

4 Configure R5 to peer with R7 and R8 in AS10 and AS20, respectively.

5 Do not use update source for any peering.

6 Hardcode the BGP router ID to x.x.x.x (where x is the router number).

7 Advertise network 178.1.1.0 on R7 and R8 in BGP.

8 Configure Loopback1 with 11.11.11.11/24 on R1. Advertise Loopback1 on R1 in BGP. Make sure all routers see Loopback1.

9 Configure Loopback1 with 44.44.44.44/24 on R4. Advertise Loopback1 on R4 in BGP. Make sure all routers see Loopback1.

2.4.2: BGP Summarization (3 points)

1 Configure null routes on R7 for networks 177.1.1.0, 177.1.3.0, 177.1.4.0, 177.1.7.0, and 177.1.11.0. All these networks are Class C. Advertise these networks in BGP on R7.

2 Summarize all these networks beyond R5. All individual routes must be marked **s** for suppressed in the R5 BGP table.

3 All routers should see only one route for these networks. Do not summarize to a full Class B. All routers beyond R5 except R6 should see the individual route 177.1.11.0 from R7.

2.4.3: BGP Conditional Advertisement (4 points)

1 Configure Loopback1 on R6 with 66.66.66.66/24.

2 Configure R6 to advertise Loopback1 to R5 only if Loopback1 of R4 is absent from the BGP table on R6.

3 Do not use any filtering mechanism such as a filter list, prefix list, or distribute list to achieve this task.

Section 3.0: ISDN Configuration (6 points)

3.1: Basic ISDN (3 points)

1 Configure ISDN on R2 and R6.

2 Use network 179.7.2.8/30.

3 Advertise the ISDN network in Area 0 using clear-text authentication.

4 Do not configure any legacy commands.

ISDN information:

BRI number on R2 is 99047132

BRI number on R6 is 99047265

Switch-type = basic-net3

3.2: Dial Backup (3 points)

1 Configure DDR between R2 and R6 when *any* interface on R4 goes down.

2 Do not configure **use backup interface** or **ospf demand-circuit** to achieve this task.

Section 4.0: PIX Configuration (7 points)

4.1: Basic PIX Configuration (3 points)

1 Configure PIX bootstrap configuration.

2 Configure static translation for AAA server with the IP addresses shown in Figure 7-1. Configure ACL accordingly.

3 Configure RIP for R1 and R2 as per Section 2.3.

4 Configure a static default route on PIX to R2.

4.2: Advanced PIX Configuration (4 points)

1 Filter all Java applets and ActiveX controls that return to the AAA server from an outbound HTTP connection.

2 Configure filtering for all users except AAA server to prevent outbound users from accessing World Wide Web URLs using a WebSense filtering application server 175.1.5.23 on VLAN5 based on the company security policy. When the

WebSense server is unavailable, let all outbound connections pass through PIX without filtering.

3 Block all outbound HTTP connections destined for a proxy server that listens on port 8080.

Section 5.0: IPSec/PPTP Configuration (10 points)

5.1: IPSec LAN-to-LAN Router-to-VPN3000 (4 points)

1 Add a new Loopback1 on R2 with an IP address of 192.168.2.1/24. This loopback will serve as a private network on R1 to be encrypted.

2 Configure a LAN-to-LAN IPSec tunnel between R2 and the VPN3000 concentrator for networks 192.168.2.0/24 and 192.168.1.0/24, respectively.

3 Configure preshared authentication with all other parameters as appropriate.

4 Configure the VPN3000 concentrator with IP addressing as shown in Figure 7-1. Configure the default route to R1.

5 The VPN3000 concentrator should not peer to R2 with IP address 175.1.2.2.

6 Do not add any static routes to achieve this task.

5.2: IPSec Remote Access to the Router (3 points)

1 Configure remote access — VPN client to R6 for Test PC in VLAN5.

2 Configure group **lab7-group** with password **cisco123**.

3 Configure client authentication using local username **vpnuser** password **cisco**.

4 Configure the VPN client to receive IP addresses in the range 172.16.10.1–172.16.10.50.

5 VPN Client (Test PC) should use the tunnel to access Loopback1 of R6 only. All other outbound traffic should be unencrypted.

6 Do not configure any static route on R6 to achieve this task.

5.3: PPTP to Router with Local Authentication (3 points)

1 Configure PPTP remote access to R1 for Test PC in VLAN5.

2 Configure MS-CHAP authentication. Configure local authentication for PPTP clients. Configure username **pptpuser** password **cisco**.

3 Configure an IP pool on R1 172.16.11.1–172.16.11.50 for PPTP clients.

  4 Configure static NAT translation on PIX for R1 (172.16.1.2–175.1.2.20) and ACL accordingly to achieve this task.

  5 Do not configure any MPPE encryption.

  6 Configure ACL such that the PPTP client when connected to R1 should not be able to ping anything. All other traffic should be permitted explicitly.

Section 6.0: IOS Firewall Configuration (8 points)

6.1: Context-Based Access Control (CBAC) (5 points)

  1 Configure R5 with IOS Firewall to protect VLAN6.

  2 Configure the firewall to monitor all TCP and UDP traffic.

  3 The R7 ATM network should be able to Telnet, ping, and FTP to all networks beyond R5 and should not be able to initiate any traffic to the Frame Relay network.

  4 The VLAN2 network should not be able to ping the R7 ATM link, but not vice versa.

  5 Configure the number of existing half-open sessions that will cause the firewall to start deleting half-open sessions at 1500 and to stop deleting at 1200 sessions.

  6 Configure 20 seconds for a TCP session to reach the established state before the firewall starts dropping the session.

6.2: Intrusion Detection System (IDS) (3 points)

  1 Configure IDS on R6 to protect against attacks using the following parameters:

  Remote host 175.1.2.3

  Remote HostID 3

  Local host 175.1.6.3

  Local HostID 1

  Org ID 100

  Postoffice protocol UDP 45000

  2 Configure IDS to send events to the syslog server and IDS management center 175.1.2.3 (AAA server). Configure PIX accordingly.

  3 Syslog reports lots of false positive alarms, as shown in the following syslog snip from R6. Disable this alarm from said source.

```
*Mar 15 03:10:14.597: %IDS-4-ICMP_FRAGMENT_SIG: Sig:2150:Fragmented ICMP
    Traffic - from 175.1.5.2 to 175.1.6.3
*Mar 15 03:10:44.658: %IDS-4-ICMP_FRAGMENT_SIG: Sig:2150:Fragmented ICMP
    Traffic - from 175.1.5.2 to 175.1.6.3
```

```
*Mar 15 03:11:14.767: %IDS-4-ICMP_FRAGMENT_SIG: Sig:2150:Fragmented ICMP
   Traffic - from 175.1.5.2 to 175.1.6.3
*Mar 15 03:11:44.901: %IDS-4-ICMP_FRAGMENT_SIG: Sig:2150:Fragmented ICMP
   Traffic - from 175.1.5.2 to 175.1.6.3
```

Section 7.0: AAA (8 points)

7.1: AAA on the Router (4 points)

1 Configure R7 router management with TACACS+ using AAA server, as shown in Figure 7-1.

2 Configure PIX translation and ACL accordingly.

3 Configure authentication for Telnet traffic only.

4 Configure username **lab7-telnet** with password **cisco** on CiscoSecure ACS and local router database for fallback.

5 Configure command authorization and assign said user with a privilege of level 5.

6 Privilege level 5 users should be able to see the current configuration and ping devices on the network only. Log all these events.

7 Log session timings for this user for billing purposes.

7.2: AAA on the Switch (4 points)

1 Configure switch1 management with RADIUS using the AAA server, as shown in Figure 7-1.

2 Configure PIX translation and ACL accordingly.

3 Configure authentication for Telnet traffic only.

4 Configure username **switch-telnet** with password **cisco** on CiscoSecure ACS and the local switch database for fallback.

5 Log session timings for this user for billing purposes.

Section 8.0: Advanced Security (8 points)

8.1: Perimeter Security (3 points)

1 R2 has experienced TCP-based DoS attacks in the past to a DNS server in VLAN2.

2 Configure R2 to prevent this attack. Do not use CAR to achieve this task.

8.2: Access Control (3 points)

1 Provide Telnet access to R1 for all users between 9:00 a.m. and 5:00 p.m. Monday through Friday only.

2 Configure local authentication for Telnet with username **ADMIN** password **cisco**.

8.3: Access Restriction (2 points)

1 A local host behind PIX 10.1.1.10 starts a TCP connection using source port 1515 to a foreign host 175.1.6.10 on any destination port.

2 PIX is denying this connection for a custom-based application on this server, which has return traffic on ports other than those used for originating the connection when establishing the session.

3 Configure PIX to allow packets from the foreign host 175.1.6.10 source port 2525 back to local host 10.1.1.10 destination port 5252 instead of 1515.

Section 9.0: IP Services and Protocol-Independent Features (10 points)

9.1: NTP (3 points)

1 Configure R7 as the NTP server with R2 and Sw1 as clients.

2 Configure strong authentication.

3 Make sure Switch1 is always NTP synchronized.

9.2: Congestion Management—QoS (4 points)

1 Configure QoS on the R4 WAN link for the following traffic in the following order:

   a. All Telnet traffic

   b. OSPF Routing protocol

   c. All ICMP traffic to VLAN6

   d. All web traffic

   e. All other traffic

2 Select a QoS technique that works in round-robin fashion, giving each queue a fair bandwidth share.

3 Increase the byte count to 2000 for the web traffic queue.

4 Configure the ICMP queue to be able to hold 40 packets enqueued at any time.

9.3: HSRP (3 points)

1 Sw1 should always be reachable in case any router interface(s) in VLAN5 go down.

2 Configure Virtual IP 175.1.5.250 with authentication.

Section 10.0: Security Violations (8 points)

10.1: DoS Attack (4 points)

1 An intruder can potentially compromise a router and use it as a launch pad to attack other devices on the network.

2 Assume R3 is compromised and an attacker is launching an ICMP flood attack to R2.

3 Use an appropriate method on R3 to prevent this.

4 Do not configure an ACL on any interface on R2 or R3 to achieve this task.

5 Make sure R2 is able to ping R3.

10.2: High CPU Caused by an Attack (4 points)

1 R8 is experiencing a HIGH CPU, causing flaps in BGP and OSPF neighbors.

2 It has been noticed that there are an unusually high number of logs related to RSHELL. See the snip from the following router log. These seem to be the main cause of the issue.

```
.May 20 20:22:01.204 GMT-3: %RCMD-4-RSHPORTATTEMPT: Attempted to connect to
   RSHELL from 1.1.1.1
.May 20 20:22:01.244 GMT-3: %RCMD-4-RSHPORTATTEMPT: Attempted to connect to
   RSHELL from 2.2.2.2
.May 20 20:22:01.244 GMT-3: %RCMD-4-RSHPORTATTEMPT: Attempted to connect to
   RSHELL from 3.3.3.3
```

3 All the IP addresses trying to connect to the RSHELL port are invalid.

4 Prevent this from happening again.

5 Do not configure the router to use rsh.

Verification, Hints, and Troubleshooting Tips

An important thing to remember is to divide each section (exercises) into an appropriate timeslot. Do your math and make sure you don't spend more than the planned allotted time for a given task. By allocating each section a fair timeslot, you are essentially planning the entire lab and distributing resources effectively. If you get stuck on any part of the lab, try to leave it for later and move on, as you might discover that moving on will solve issues you were not able to address earlier.

Always redraw a detailed diagram, and highlight each aspect of the network so that it is easy to visualize the big picture with all necessary information on one page.

The hints provided here are to be used as a guideline and address some or all parts of the corresponding exercise question. They are not listed in any order. You can always use an alternative approach to address the exercise as long as you fulfill the requirements and do not violate any known or unknown restrictions.

Section 1.0: Basic Configuration

1.1: IP Addressing

1 Redraw a detailed topology with all necessary information.

2 Configure IP addressing as shown in Figure 7-1.

3 Configure the static default route on R1 to PIX.

4 Configure the static default route on PIX to R2.

5 Configure OSPF to originate the default route on R5 for all other routers to learn DG dynamically.

6 Configure the default route on the VPN3000 concentrator to R1. Do not configure any routing protocol on the concentrator.

7 Manage the concentrator from the AAA server using HTTPS and not HTTP. See Figure 7-5.

1.2: Frame Relay Configuration

1 Configure R6 as the Frame Relay switch using the DLCI information provided for Frame Relay routing in Figure 7-2.

2 Configure static maps on R2, R3, and R4.

3 Do not configure subinterface(s) on any router.

Figure 7-5   *VPN3000—Filter Rules for HTTPS on the Public Interface*

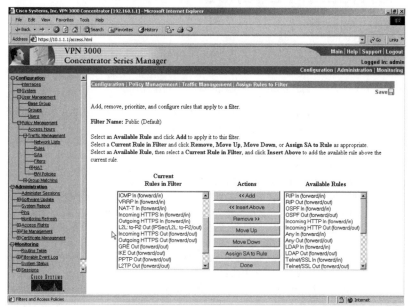

1.3: LAN Switch Configuration

1 Configure sw1 with the VLAN information provided in Table 7-1.

2 Configure port security for all interfaces on VLAN3 devices.

3 Configure **shutdown** as action for violation.

4 Configure the VLAN5 interface on Switch1 for management with IP 175.1.5.25/24. Configure a static default route to 175.1.5.250 (the HSRP address).

1.4: ATM Configuration

1 Configure back-to-back ATM between R5 and R7.

2 Configure ATM PVC on both ends to be the same, as there is no ATM switch in between. Configure VPI/VCI 0/700.

3 Configure static maps on both ends.

4 Configure transmit clock source on one end using **atm clock INTERNAL**.

1.5: Ethernet Back-to-Back Configuration

1 Configure back-to-back Ethernet using cross-over cable between R5 <-> R8 and R7 <-> R8, as per Table 7-3. Do not use the switch VLANs.

Section 2.0: Routing Configuration

2.1: OSPF

1   Configure OSPF as shown in Figure 7-3.

2   Do not change the default network type on the Frame Relay network.

3   Configure Unicast OSPF on R2, R3, and R4 using the **neighbor** command, as the Frame
Relay network by default is NON-BROADCAST:

```
r2#show ip ospf interface
Serial0 is up, line protocol is up
  Internet Address 179.7.2.2/29, Area 0
  Process ID 110, Router ID 2.2.2.2, Network Type NON_BROADCAST, Cost: 64
  Transmit Delay is 1 sec, State DROTHER, Priority 1
  Designated Router (ID) 3.3.3.3, Interface address 179.7.2.3
  Backup Designated router (ID) 4.4.4.4, Interface address 179.7.2.4
  Timer intervals configured, Hello 30, Dead 120, Wait 120, Retransmit 5
    Hello due in 00:00:01
  Index 1/1, flood queue length 0
  Next 0x0(0)/0x0(0)
  Last flood scan length is 1, maximum is 1
  Last flood scan time is 4 msec, maximum is 4 msec
  Neighbor Count is 2, Adjacent neighbor count is 2
    Adjacent with neighbor 4.4.4.4  (Backup Designated Router)
    Adjacent with neighbor 3.3.3.3  (Designated Router)
  Suppress hello for 0 neighbor(s)
  Simple password authentication enabled


<snip from R2>
router ospf 110
 router-id 2.2.2.2
 log-adjacency-changes
 area 0 authentication
 redistribute rip metric 1 subnets
 network 179.7.2.0 0.0.0.7 area 0
 neighbor 179.7.2.4 priority 1
 neighbor 179.7.2.3 priority 1


<snip from R3>
router ospf 110
 router-id 3.3.3.3
 area 0 authentication
```

```
    redistribute eigrp 10 metric 1 subnets
    network 179.7.2.0 0.0.0.7 area 0
    neighbor 179.7.2.2 priority 1
    neighbor 179.7.2.4 priority 1


<snip from R4>
router ospf 110
 router-id 4.4.4.4
 area 0 authentication
 area 6 authentication
 area 6 virtual-link 5.5.5.5 authentication-key 7 094F471A1A0A
 network 175.1.6.0 0.0.0.255 area 6
 network 179.7.2.0 0.0.0.7 area 0
 neighbor 179.7.2.2 priority 1
 neighbor 179.7.2.3 priority 1
```

4 Change the default network type on the ATM link from non-broadcast to point-to-point:

```
<snip from R5>
interface ATM0/0
 ip address 171.7.5.2 255.255.255.252
 ip ospf authentication-key 7 094F471A1A0A
 ip ospf network point-to-point
 no atm ilmi-keepalive
 pvc 0 0/700
  protocol ip 171.7.5.1 broadcast
  broadcast
  encapsulation aal5snap


<OSPF network type before changing the default>
r5#show ip ospf interface
ATM0/0 is up, line protocol is up
  Internet Address 171.7.5.2/30, Area 10
  Process ID 110, Router ID 5.5.5.5, Network Type NON_BROADCAST, Cost: 1
  Transmit Delay is 1 sec, State DR, Priority 1
  Designated Router (ID) 5.5.5.5, Interface address 171.7.5.2
  No backup designated router on this network
  Timer intervals configured, Hello 30, Dead 120, Wait 120, Retransmit 5
    Hello due in 00:00:02
  Index 1/2, flood queue length 0
  Next 0x0(0)/0x0(0)
  Last flood scan length is 0, maximum is 0
  Last flood scan time is 0 msec, maximum is 0 msec
```

```
  Neighbor Count is 0, Adjacent neighbor count is 0
  Suppress hello for 0 neighbor(s)
  Simple password authentication enabled


<OSPF network type after changing the default>
r5#show ip ospf interface
ATM0/0 is up, line protocol is up
  Internet Address 171.7.5.2/30, Area 10
  Process ID 110, Router ID 5.5.5.5, Network Type POINT_TO_POINT, Cost: 1
  Transmit Delay is 1 sec, State POINT_TO_POINT,
  Timer intervals configured, Hello 10, Dead 40, Wait 40, Retransmit 5
    Hello due in 00:00:00
  Index 1/2, flood queue length 0
  Next 0x0(0)/0x0(0)
  Last flood scan length is 1, maximum is 1
  Last flood scan time is 0 msec, maximum is 0 msec
  Neighbor Count is 1, Adjacent neighbor count is 1
    Adjacent with neighbor 7.7.7.7
  Suppress hello for 0 neighbor(s)
  Simple password authentication enabled
```

5 Configure clear-text authentication for all areas and virtual links.

6 Redistribute OSPF and RIP mutually on R2.

7 Configure a virtual link between R4 and R5 using clear-text authentication, as demonstrated in the example following item 8.

8 Hidden issue: You need to configure another virtual link between R5 and R6 for redundancy of the ISDN link:

```
<snip from R4>
router ospf 110
 router-id 4.4.4.4
 area 0 authentication
 area 6 authentication
 area 6 virtual-link 5.5.5.5 authentication-key 7 094F471A1A0A

<snip from R5>
router ospf 110
 router-id 5.5.5.5
 area 0 authentication
 area 6 authentication
 area 6 virtual-link 6.6.6.6 authentication-key 7 13061E010803
 area 6 virtual-link 4.4.4.4 authentication-key 7 110A1016141D
 area 10 authentication
 area 20 authentication
```

```
<snip from R6>
router ospf 110
 router-id 6.6.6.6
 area 0 authentication
 area 6 authentication
 area 6 virtual-link 5.5.5.5 authentication-key 7 110A1016141D
```

9 Configure R5 to originate the default route.

10 To filter OSPF routes for R8, configure **ospf database-filter** on R5 to stop advertising LSAs, but continue to advertise Hello packets so that adjacency is always established:

```
<snip from R5>
hostname r5
!
interface Ethernet1/1
 ip address 171.8.5.2 255.255.255.0
 ip ospf database-filter all out



<R8 routing table before applying database-filter on R5>
r8#show ip route ospf
      171.7.0.0/30 is subnetted, 1 subnets
O IA    171.7.5.0 [110/11] via 171.8.5.2, 00:00:50, FastEthernet0/0
      175.1.0.0/24 is subnetted, 3 subnets
O IA    175.1.6.0 [110/11] via 171.8.5.2, 00:00:50, FastEthernet0/0
O E1    175.1.5.0 [110/12] via 171.8.5.2, 00:00:40, FastEthernet0/0
O E2    175.1.2.0 [110/1] via 171.8.5.2, 00:00:40, FastEthernet0/0
      179.7.0.0/29 is subnetted, 1 subnets
O IA    179.7.2.0 [110/75] via 171.8.5.2, 00:00:50, FastEthernet0/0
O*E2 0.0.0.0/0 [110/1] via 171.8.5.2, 00:00:40, FastEthernet0/0



<R8 routing table after applying database-filter on R5>
r8#show debug
IP routing:
  IP routing debugging is on



2w6d: RT: del 179.7.2.0/29 via 171.8.5.2, ospf metric [110/75]
2w6d: RT: delete subnet route to 179.7.2.0/29
2w6d: RT: delete network route to 179.7.0.0
2w6d: RT: del 175.1.6.0/24 via 171.8.5.2, ospf metric [110/11]
2w6d: RT: delete subnet route to 175.1.6.0/24
2w6d: RT: del 171.7.5.0/30 via 171.8.5.2, ospf metric [110/11]
```

```
2w6d: RT: delete subnet route to 171.7.5.0/30
2w6d: RT: delete network route to 171.7.0.0
2w6d: RT: del 175.1.5.0/24 via 171.8.5.2, ospf metric [110/12]
2w6d: RT: delete subnet route to 175.1.5.0/24
2w6d: RT: del 175.1.2.0/24 via 171.8.5.2, ospf metric [110/1]
2w6d: RT: delete subnet route to 175.1.2.0/24
2w6d: RT: delete network route to 175.1.0.0
2w6d: RT: del 0.0.0.0 via 171.8.5.2, ospf metric [110/1]
2w6d: RT: delete network route to 0.0.0.0
r8#
r8#
r8#show ip route ospf
<no routes>
r8#


<Neighbor still UP>
r8#show ip ospf neighbor

Neighbor ID     Pri   State       Dead Time   Address       Interface
5.5.5.5          1    FULL/BDR    00:00:36    171.8.5.2     FastEthernet0/0
```

2.2: EIGRP

1 Configure EIGRP AS-10 between R3 and R7 with MD5 authentication, as shown in Figure 7-3.

2 Advertise the VLAN5 network in EIGRP.

3 Redistribute EIGRP into OSPF on R3 and R7.

4 For R4 and R5 to reach VLAN5 network via R3, configure metric-type 1 in OSPF redistribution on R3. Metric type 1 routes have preference over Metric type 2 routes. By default, OSPF redistributes as Metric type 2 unless explicitly configured otherwise:

```
<snip from R3 config>
router ospf 110
 router-id 3.3.3.3
 redistribute eigrp 10 metric 1 metric-type 1 subnets

r4#show debug
IP routing:
  IP routing debugging is on


3d01h: RT: del 175.1.5.0/24 via 175.1.6.2, ospf metric [110/1]
3d01h: RT: add 175.1.5.0/24 via 179.7.2.3, ospf metric [110/65]
```

```
<R4 routing table before changing metric type, check the next-hop address for
   175.1.5.0>
r4#show ip route ospf
      171.7.0.0/16 is variably subnetted, 2 subnets, 2 masks
O IA    171.7.5.0/30 [110/12] via 175.1.6.2, 00:13:38, Ethernet0/0
O IA    171.7.5.0/24 [110/11] via 175.1.6.2, 00:13:38, Ethernet0/0
      171.8.0.0/24 is subnetted, 1 subnets
O IA    171.8.5.0 [110/20] via 175.1.6.2, 00:13:38, Ethernet0/0
      175.1.0.0/24 is subnetted, 3 subnets
O E2    175.1.5.0 [110/1] via 175.1.6.2, 00:13:38, Ethernet0/0
O E2    175.1.2.0 [110/1] via 179.7.2.2, 00:13:38, Serial1/0

<R4 routing table after changing metric type, check the next-hop address for
   175.1.5.0>
r4#show ip route ospf
      171.7.0.0/16 is variably subnetted, 2 subnets, 2 masks
O IA    171.7.5.0/30 [110/12] via 175.1.6.2, 00:14:32, Ethernet0/0
O IA    171.7.5.0/24 [110/11] via 175.1.6.2, 00:14:32, Ethernet0/0
      171.8.0.0/24 is subnetted, 1 subnets
O IA    171.8.5.0 [110/20] via 175.1.6.2, 00:14:32, Ethernet0/0
      175.1.0.0/24 is subnetted, 3 subnets
O E1    175.1.5.0 [110/65] via 179.7.2.3, 00:00:11, Serial1/0
O E2    175.1.2.0 [110/1] via 179.7.2.2, 00:14:32, Serial1/0
```

2.3: RIP

1 Configure RIP on R1, R2, and PIX with clear-text authentication.

2 Advertise the default gateway to R1 from PIX using RIP.

3 Redistribute RIP and OSPF mutually on R2.

4 Make sure PIX receives all routes via RIP.

2.4: BGP

2.4.1: Basic BGP Configuration

1 Configure BGP as shown in Figure 7-4.

2 Configure R2 as Route-Reflector for R1 and R4 as its clients.

3 Do not use update source for any peering.

4 Use the **bgp router-id** command to hardcode BGP router IDs.

5 Advertise network 178.1.1.0 on R7 and R8 in BGP.

6 Advertise Loopback1 in BGP on R1 and R4.

2.4.2: BGP Summarization

1 Configure null routes on R7 as indicated. Advertise these networks in BGP on R7.

2 Summarize on R5 using the **aggregate** command with the **summary-only** keyword, as demonstrated in the example following item 3.

3 Unsuppress network 177.1.11.0 using a route map for neighbor R4 so that the individual route gets advertised:

```
<snip from R5>
router bgp 2
 no synchronization
 bgp router-id 5.5.5.5
 aggregate-address 177.1.0.0 255.255.240.0 summary-only
 neighbor 171.7.5.1 remote-as 10
 neighbor 171.8.5.1 remote-as 20
 neighbor 175.1.6.1 remote-as 1
 neighbor 175.1.6.1 unsuppress-map unsuppress-null
 neighbor 175.1.6.3 remote-as 2
 no auto-summary
!
access-list 2 permit 177.1.11.0 0.0.0.255
!
route-map unsuppress-null permit 10
 match ip address 2


<BGP table on R5, all individual routes marked with 's'>
r5#show ip bgp
BGP table version is 33, local router ID is 5.5.5.5
Status codes: s suppressed, d damped, h history, * valid, > best, i - internal
Origin codes: i - IGP, e - EGP, ? - incomplete

   Network          Next Hop          Metric LocPrf Weight Path
 * i11.11.11.0/24   175.1.6.1                 100      0 1 i
 *>                 175.1.6.1                          0 1 i
 *> 44.44.44.0/24   175.1.6.1              0            0 1 i
 * i                175.1.6.1              0   100      0 1 i
 *> 177.1.0.0/20    0.0.0.0                        32768 i
 s> 177.1.1.0/24    171.7.5.1             0            0 10 i
 s> 177.1.3.0/24    171.7.5.1             0            0 10 i
 s> 177.1.4.0/24    171.7.5.1             0            0 10 i
 s> 177.1.7.0/24    171.7.5.1             0            0 10 i
 s> 177.1.11.0/24   171.7.5.1             0            0 10 i
 *  178.1.1.0/30    171.8.5.1             0            0 20 i
 *>                 171.7.5.1             0            0 10 i
```

```
<snip from R4, see the individual route present>
r4#show ip bgp
BGP table version is 128, local router ID is 4.4.4.4
Status codes: s suppressed, d damped, h history, * valid, > best, i - internal
Origin codes: i - IGP, e - EGP, ? - incomplete

     Network          Next Hop          Metric LocPrf Weight Path
 *>i11.11.11.0/24     172.16.1.2             0    100      0 i
 *> 44.44.44.0/24     0.0.0.0                0         32768 i
 *  177.1.0.0/20      175.1.6.2                          0 2 i
 *>                   175.1.6.2                          0 2 i
 *> 177.1.11.0/24     175.1.6.2                          0 2 10 i
 *  178.1.1.0/30      175.1.6.3                          0 2 10 i
 *>                   175.1.6.2                          0 2 10 i


<snip from R6, see the individual route absent>
r6#show ip bgp
BGP table version is 121, local router ID is 6.6.6.6
Status codes: s suppressed, d damped, h history, * valid, > best,
  i - internal,
                r RIB-failure
Origin codes: i - IGP, e - EGP, ? - incomplete

     Network          Next Hop          Metric LocPrf Weight Path
 *  i11.11.11.0/24    175.1.6.1                   100      0 1 i
 *>                   175.1.6.1                            0 1 i
 *  i44.44.44.0/24    175.1.6.1              0    100      0 1 i
 *>                   175.1.6.1              0            0 1 i
 *>i177.1.0.0/20      175.1.6.2                   100      0 i
 *>i178.1.1.0/30      171.7.5.1              0    100      0 10 i
```

4   This individual route will be advertised to R4, and eventually from there R4 will advertise to R6, but as R6 will see its own AS number in the route, it will drop/discard it and will not insert it in the BGP table. So you don't have to do anything to prevent this route to R6.

2.4.3: BGP Conditional Advertisement

1   Configure Loopback1 on R6 with 66.66.66.66/24, as demonstrated in the example following item 2.

2   Configure conditional advertisement on R6 to advertise Loopback1 to R5 only if Loopback1 of R4 (44.44.44.0) is absent from the BGP table on R6:

```
<snip from R6>
router bgp 2
 no synchronization
```

```
bgp router-id 6.6.6.6
network 66.66.66.0 mask 255.255.255.0
neighbor 175.1.6.1 remote-as 1
neighbor 175.1.6.2 remote-as 2
neighbor 175.1.6.2 advertise-map advertise non-exist-map check-exist-route
no auto-summary
!
access-list 1 permit 44.44.44.0 0.0.0.255
access-list 2 permit 66.66.66.0 0.0.0.255
!
route-map check-exist-route permit 10
 match ip address 1
!
route-map advertise permit 10
 match ip address 2
!


! Verify Conditional advertisement using following show and debug outputs.

<Advertised routes to R5, note 66.66.66.0 is not advertised>
r6#show ip bgp neighbors 175.1.6.2 advertised-routes
BGP table version is 168, local router ID is 6.6.6.6
Status codes: s suppressed, d damped, h history, * valid, > best,
  i - internal,
              r RIB-failure
Origin codes: i - IGP, e - EGP, ? - incomplete

   Network          Next Hop        Metric LocPrf Weight Path
*> 11.11.11.0/24    175.1.6.1                        0 1 i
*> 44.44.44.0/24    175.1.6.1            0            0 1 i


<Verify Conditional Advertise state>
r6#show ip bgp neighbors 175.1.6.2
BGP neighbor is 175.1.6.2,  remote AS 2, internal link
  BGP version 4, remote router ID 5.5.5.5
  BGP state = Established, up for 1w2d
  Last read 00:00:33, hold time is 180, keepalive interval is 60 seconds
    Neighbor capabilities:
    Route refresh: advertised and received(old & new)
    Address family IPv4 Unicast: advertised and received
    IPv4 MPLS Label capability:
  Received 14501 messages, 0 notifications, 0 in queue
  Sent 14468 messages, 0 notifications, 0 in queue
  Default minimum time between advertisement runs is 5 seconds
```

```
   For address family: IPv4 Unicast
    BGP table version 163, neighbor version 163
    Index 2, Offset 0, Mask 0x4
    Route refresh request: received 0, sent 0
    Condition-map check-exist-route, Advertise-map advertise, status: Withdraw
    4 accepted prefixes consume 192 bytes
    Prefix advertised 38, suppressed 0, withdrawn 12

    Connections established 12; dropped 11
    Last reset 1w2d, due to Peer closed the session
  Connection state is ESTAB, I/O status: 1, unread input bytes: 0
  Local host: 175.1.6.3, Local port: 179
  Foreign host: 175.1.6.2, Foreign port: 11030
```

```
<Note that this is not advertised to R5>
r6#show ip bgp 66.66.66.0
BGP routing table entry for 66.66.66.0/24, version 161
Paths: (1 available, best #1, table Default-IP-Routing-Table)
  Advertised to non peer-group peers:
  175.1.6.1
  Local
    0.0.0.0 from 0.0.0.0 (6.6.6.6)
      Origin IGP, metric 0, localpref 100, weight 32768, valid, sourced,
      local, best
```

```
<Shutdown Loopback1 on R4, and enable following debugs on R6 and monitor>
r6#debug ip bgp updates
r6#
r6#show debug
IP routing:
  BGP updates debugging is on

*Mar 14 22:09:28.987: BPG(0): Condition check-exist-route changes to
    Advertise
*Mar 14 22:09:29.015: BGP(0): net 66.66.66.0/24 matches ADV MAP advertise:
    bump version to 166
*Mar 14 22:09:29.936: BGP(0): nettable_walker 66.66.66.0/24 route sourced
    locally
*Mar 14 22:09:29.936: BGP(0): 175.1.6.1 computing updates, afi 0, neighbor
    version 165, table version 166, starting at 0.0.0.0
*Mar 14 22:09:29.936: BGP(0): 175.1.6.1 skip UPDATE 66.66.66.0/24 (chgflags:
    0x0), next 0.0.0.0, path
*Mar 14 22:09:29.936: BGP(0): 175.1.6.1 update run completed, afi 0, ran for
    0ms, neighbor version 165, start version 166, throttled to 166
```

```
*Mar 14 22:09:29.936: BGP(0): 175.1.6.2 computing updates, afi 0, neighbor
    version 165, table version 166, starting at 0.0.0.0
*Mar 14 22:09:29.940: BGP(0): 175.1.6.2 66.66.66.0/24 matches advertise map
    advertise, state: Advertise
*Mar 14 22:09:29.940: BGP(0): 175.1.6.2 send UPDATE (format) 66.66.66.0/24,
    next 175.1.6.3, metric 0, path
*Mar 14 22:09:29.940: BGP(0): 175.1.6.2 1 updates enqueued (average=55,
    maximum=55)
*Mar 14 22:09:29.940: BGP(0): 175.1.6.2 update run completed, afi 0, ran for
    0ms, neighbor version 165, start version 166, throttled to 166


<Routes advertised to R5, note 66.66.66.0 is now advertised>
r6#show ip bgp neighbors 175.1.6.2 advertised-routes
BGP table version is 166, local router ID is 6.6.6.6
Status codes: s suppressed, d damped, h history, * valid, > best,
    i - internal,
                r RIB-failure
Origin codes: i - IGP, e - EGP, ? - incomplete

   Network          Next Hop          Metric LocPrf Weight Path
*> 11.11.11.0/24    175.1.6.1                           0 1 i
*> 66.66.66.0/24    0.0.0.0                0         32768 i
r6#


<Verify Conditional Advertise state>
r6#show ip bgp neighbors 175.1.6.2
BGP neighbor is 175.1.6.2,  remote AS 2, internal link
  BGP version 4, remote router ID 5.5.5.5
  BGP state = Established, up for 1w2d
  Last read 00:00:19, hold time is 180, keepalive interval is 60 seconds
  Neighbor capabilities:
    Route refresh: advertised and received(old & new)
    Address family IPv4 Unicast: advertised and received
    IPv4 MPLS Label capability:
  Received 14505 messages, 0 notifications, 0 in queue
  Sent 14473 messages, 0 notifications, 0 in queue
  Default minimum time between advertisement runs is 5 seconds

 For address family: IPv4 Unicast
  BGP table version 166, neighbor version 166
  Index 2, Offset 0, Mask 0x4
  Route refresh request: received 0, sent 0
  Condition-map check-exist-route, Advertise-map advertise, status: Advertise
  3 accepted prefixes consume 144 bytes
  Prefix advertised 39, suppressed 0, withdrawn 13
```

```
    Connections established 12; dropped 11
    Last reset 1w2d, due to Peer closed the session
Connection state is ESTAB, I/O status: 1, unread input bytes: 0
Local host: 175.1.6.3, Local port: 179
Foreign host: 175.1.6.2, Foreign port: 11030


<Note now that 66.66.66.0 is advertised to R5>
r6#show ip bgp 66.66.66.0
BGP routing table entry for 66.66.66.0/24, version 166
Paths: (1 available, best #1, table Default-IP-Routing-Table)
  Advertised to non peer-group peers:
  175.1.6.1 175.1.6.2
  Local
    0.0.0.0 from 0.0.0.0 (6.6.6.6)
      Origin IGP, metric 0, localpref 100, weight 32768, valid, sourced,
      local, best



<Verify BGP table on R5>
r5#show debugging
IP routing:
  IP routing debugging is on
r5#
1w6d: RT: add 66.66.66.0/24 via 175.1.6.3, bgp metric [200/0]

r5#show ip bgp
BGP table version is 76, local router ID is 5.5.5.5
Status codes: s suppressed, d damped, h history, * valid, > best, i - internal
Origin codes: i - IGP, e - EGP, ? - incomplete


    Network          Next Hop         Metric LocPrf Weight Path
 *  i11.11.11.0/24   175.1.6.1               100      0 1 i
 *>                  175.1.6.1                        0 1 i
 *>i66.66.66.0/24    175.1.6.3         0     100      0 i
 *> 177.1.0.0/20     0.0.0.0                      32768 i
 s> 177.1.1.0/24     171.7.5.1         0            0 10 i
 s> 177.1.3.0/24     171.7.5.1         0            0 10 i
 s> 177.1.4.0/24     171.7.5.1         0            0 10 i
 s> 177.1.7.0/24     171.7.5.1         0            0 10 i
 s> 177.1.11.0/24    171.7.5.1         0            0 10 i
 *  178.1.1.0/30     171.7.5.1         0            0 10 i
 *>                  171.8.5.1         0            0 20 i
r5#
```

NOTE	See the following URLs for more info on conditional advertisement:
	www.cisco.com/univercd/cc/td/doc/product/software/ios120/12cgcr/np1_r/1rprt1/
	1rbgp.htm#1051695
	www.cisco.com/warp/customer/459/cond_adv.html

NOTE	There are a couple of known bugs relating to BGP and conditional advertisement.
	For more information, see bugs CSCdp18563 (registered customers only) and CSCdp20320 (registered customers only) in the Bug Toolkit.
	R6 is loaded with IOS version 12.2(13)T1 in this lab.

Section 3.0: ISDN Configuration

3.1: Basic ISDN

1   Configure ISDN on R2 and R6 for DDR as per Figure 7-1.

2   Advertise ISDN network in Area 0 using clear-text authentication.

3   Configure the Dialer interface on both routers, and do not use any legacy commands.

3.2: Dial Backup

1   Configure DDR Backup using Dialer-Watch on R2 and R6 to come up when "any" interface on R4 goes down.

2   Identify unique routes learned via R4 to be configured as watched routes. In the absence of a watched route from the routing table, DDR will kick in and bring up the ISDN.

3   See the following example for R2 and R6 configuration:

```
<snip from R2 config>
hostname r2
!
interface Dialer1
 ip address 179.7.2.9 255.255.255.252
 encapsulation ppp
 ip ospf authentication-key 7 05080F1C2243
 dialer pool 1
```

```
dialer remote-name r6
dialer string 99047265
dialer watch-group 1
dialer-group 1
ppp authentication chap
!
access-list 101 deny    ospf any any
access-list 101 permit ip any any
!
dialer watch-list 1 ip 44.44.44.0 255.255.255.0
dialer-list 1 protocol ip list 101


<snip from R6 config>
hostname r6
!
interface Dialer1
 ip address 179.7.2.10 255.255.255.252
 ip audit lab7 in
 encapsulation ppp
 ip ospf authentication-key 7 045802150C2E
 dialer pool 1
 dialer remote-name r2
 dialer string 99047132
 dialer watch-group 1
 dialer-group 1
 ppp authentication chap
!
access-list 199 deny    ospf any any
access-list 199 permit ip any any
!
dialer watch-list 1 ip 11.11.11.0 255.255.255.0
dialer-list 1 protocol ip list 199
```

4 See the following examples from R2 and R6, respectively, to test and verify DDR using
dialer-watch.

```
! Test and verify DDR using dialer-watch, Shutdown Serial1/0 on R4 (Frame
  Relay link to R2)
r2#show debugging
Dial on demand:
  Dial on demand events debugging is on

2w6d: DDR: Dialer Watch: watch-group = 1
2w6d: DDR:          network 44.44.44.0/255.255.255.0 DOWN,
```

```
2w6d: DDR:          primary DOWN
2w6d: DDR: Dialer Watch: Dial Reason: Primary of group 1 DOWN
2w6d: DDR: Dialer Watch: watch-group = 1,
2w6d: BR0 DDR: rotor dialout [priority]
2w6d: DDR:          dialing secondary by dialer string 99047265 on Di1
2w6d: BR0 DDR: Attempting to dial 99047265
2w6d: %LINK-3-UPDOWN: Interface BRI0:1, changed state to up
2w6d: BR0:1 DDR: Dialer Watch: resetting call in progress
2w6d: BR0:1: interface must be fifo queue, force fifo
2w6d: %DIALER-6-BIND: Interface BR0:1 bound to profile Di1
2w6d: BR0:1 DDR: dialer protocol up
2w6d: %LINEPROTO-5-UPDOWN: Line protocol on Interface BRI0:1, changed state
   to up
2w6d: %ISDN-6-CONNECT: Interface BRI0:1 is now connected to 99047265 r6
2w6d: %OSPF-5-ADJCHG: Process 110, Nbr 6.6.6.6 on Dialer1 from LOADING to
   FULL, Loading Done
```

```
r2#show ip route
Codes: C - connected, S - static, I - IGRP, R - RIP, M - mobile, B - BGP
       D - EIGRP, EX - EIGRP external, O - OSPF, IA - OSPF inter area
       N1 - OSPF NSSA external type 1, N2 - OSPF NSSA external type 2
       E1 - OSPF external type 1, E2 - OSPF external type 2, E - EGP
       i - IS-IS, L1 - IS-IS level-1, L2 - IS-IS level-2, ia - IS-IS inter area
       * - candidate default, U - per-user static route, o - ODR
       P - periodic downloaded static route

Gateway of last resort is 179.7.2.10 to network 0.0.0.0

     171.7.0.0/30 is subnetted, 1 subnets
O IA    171.7.5.0 [110/1796] via 179.7.2.10, 00:00:03, Dialer1
     171.8.0.0/24 is subnetted, 1 subnets
O IA    171.8.5.0 [110/1805] via 179.7.2.10, 00:00:03, Dialer1
     175.1.0.0/24 is subnetted, 3 subnets
O IA    175.1.6.0 [110/1795] via 179.7.2.10, 00:00:03, Dialer1
O E1    175.1.5.0 [110/65] via 179.7.2.3, 00:00:03, Serial0
C       175.1.2.0 is directly connected, Ethernet0
     179.7.0.0/16 is variably subnetted, 3 subnets, 3 masks
C       179.7.2.0/29 is directly connected, Serial0
C       179.7.2.10/32 is directly connected, Dialer1
C       179.7.2.8/30 is directly connected, Dialer1
     178.1.0.0/30 is subnetted, 1 subnets
O E1    178.1.1.0 [110/1797] via 179.7.2.10, 00:00:04, Dialer1
     11.0.0.0/24 is subnetted, 1 subnets
```

```
B       11.11.11.0 [200/0] via 172.16.1.2, 00:00:22
C    192.168.2.0/24 is directly connected, Loopback1
O*E2 0.0.0.0/0 [110/1] via 179.7.2.10, 00:00:04, Dialer1
```

r2#**show ip ospf neighbor**

Neighbor ID	Pri	State	Dead Time	Address	Interface
6.6.6.6	1	FULL/ -	00:00:33	179.7.2.10	Dialer1
N/A	1	ATTEMPT/DROTHER	-	179.7.2.4	Serial0
3.3.3.3	1	FULL/DR	00:01:30	179.7.2.3	Serial0

r2#**show isdn active**

```
-----------------------------------------------------------------
                        ISDN ACTIVE CALLS
-----------------------------------------------------------------
```

Call Type	Calling Number	Called Number	Remote Name	Seconds Used	Seconds Left	Seconds Idle	Charges Units/Currency
Out		99047265	r6	36	110	9	0

```
-----------------------------------------------------------------
```

r2#**show dialer**

```
BRI0 - dialer type = ISDN

Dial String      Successes    Failures    Last DNIS    Last status
0 incoming call(s) have been screened.
0 incoming call(s) rejected for callback.

BRI0:1 - dialer type = ISDN
Idle timer (120 secs), Fast idle timer (20 secs)
Wait for carrier (30 secs), Re-enable (15 secs)
Dialer state is data link layer up
Dial reason: Dialing on watched route loss
Interface bound to profile Di1
Time until disconnect 107 secs
Current call connected 00:00:41
Connected to 99047265 (r6)

BRI0:2 - dialer type = ISDN
Idle timer (120 secs), Fast idle timer (20 secs)
Wait for carrier (30 secs), Re-enable (15 secs)
Dialer state is idle
```

```
Di1 - dialer type = DIALER PROFILE
Idle timer (120 secs), Fast idle timer (20 secs)
Wait for carrier (30 secs), Re-enable (15 secs)
Dialer state is data link layer up
Number of active calls = 1

Dial String     Successes    Failures    Last DNIS   Last status
99047265               2           0    00:00:44     successful   Default
```

```
! When Serial1/0 comes up on R4, BGP converges and watched-route is UP, hence
  ISDN goes down.
2#
2w6d: %BGP-5-ADJCHANGE: neighbor 179.7.2.4 Up
```

```
r2#show ip bgp
BGP table version is 85, local router ID is 2.2.2.2
Status codes: s suppressed, d damped, h history, * valid, > best, i - internal
Origin codes: i - IGP, e - EGP, ? - incomplete

    Network          Next Hop          Metric LocPrf Weight Path
*>i11.11.11.0/24     172.16.1.2             0    100      0 i
*>i44.44.44.0/24     179.7.2.4              0    100      0 i
*>i66.66.66.0/24     175.1.6.3              0    100      0 2 i
*>i177.1.0.0/20      175.1.6.2                   100      0 2 i
*>i177.1.11.0/24     175.1.6.2                   100      0 2 10 i
*>i178.1.1.0/30      175.1.6.2                   100      0 2 20 i
```

```
2w6d: %ISDN-6-DISCONNECT: Interface BRI0:1  disconnected from 99047265 r6,
    call lasted 190 seconds
2w6d: %LINK-3-UPDOWN: Interface BRI0:1, changed state to down
2w6d: BR0 DDR: has total 2 call(s), dial_out 0, dial_in 0
2w6d: BR0:1 DDR: disconnecting call
2w6d: BR0:1 DDR: Dialer Watch: resetting call in progress
2w6d: DDR: Dialer Watch: watch-group = 1
2w6d: DDR:        network 44.44.44.0/255.255.255.0 UP,
2w6d: DDR:        primary UP
2w6d: %DIALER-6-UNBIND: Interface BR0:1 unbound from profile Di1
2w6d: %LINEPROTO-5-UPDOWN: Line protocol on Interface BRI0:1, changed state
    to down
```

```
! Test and verify DDR using dialer-watch, Shutdown Ethernet0/0 on R4 (VLAN6)
r6#show debugging
Dial on demand:
  Dial on demand events debugging is on
```

```
*Mar 21 22:54:54.494: DDR: Dialer Watch: watch-group = 1
*Mar 21 22:54:54.494: DDR:          network 11.11.11.0/255.255.255.0 DOWN,
*Mar 21 22:54:54.494: DDR:              primary DOWN
*Mar 21 22:54:54.494: DDR: Dialer Watch: Dial Reason: Primary of group 1 DOWN
*Mar 21 22:54:54.494: DDR: Dialer Watch: watch-group = 1,
*Mar 21 22:54:54.494: BR0/0 DDR: rotor dialout [priority]
*Mar 21 22:54:54.498: DDR:      dialing secondary by dialer string 99047132
   on Di1
*Mar 21 22:54:54.498: BR0/0 DDR: Attempting to dial 99047132
*Mar 21 22:54:54.782: %ISDN-6-LAYER2UP: Layer 2 for Interface BR0/0, TEI 65
   changed to up
*Mar 21 22:54:56.645: %LINK-3-UPDOWN: Interface BRI0/0:1, changed state to up
*Mar 21 22:54:56.649: BR0/0:1 DDR: Dialer Watch: resetting call in progress
*Mar 21 22:54:56.649: BR0/0:1: interface must be fifo queue, force fifo
*Mar 21 22:54:56.649: %DIALER-6-BIND: Interface BR0/0:1 bound to profile Di1
*Mar 21 22:54:56.725: BR0/0:1 DDR: Remote name for r2
*Mar 21 22:54:56.746: BR0/0:1 DDR: dialer protocol up
*Mar 21 22:54:57.727: %LINEPROTO-5-UPDOWN: Line protocol on Interface BRI0/
   0:1, changed state to up
*Mar 21 22:55:02.655: %ISDN-6-CONNECT: Interface BRI0/0:1 is now connected
   to 99047132 r2
*Mar 21 22:55:03.440: %OSPF-5-ADJCHG: Process 110, Nbr 2.2.2.2 on Dialer1
   from LOADING to FULL, Loading Done


r6#show ip route
Codes: C - connected, S - static, R - RIP, M - mobile, B - BGP
       D - EIGRP, EX - EIGRP external, O - OSPF, IA - OSPF inter area
       N1 - OSPF NSSA external type 1, N2 - OSPF NSSA external type 2
       E1 - OSPF external type 1, E2 - OSPF external type 2
       i - IS-IS, L1 - IS-IS level-1, L2 - IS-IS level-2, ia - IS-IS inter area
       * - candidate default, U - per-user static route, o - ODR
       P - periodic downloaded static route

Gateway of last resort is 175.1.6.2 to network 0.0.0.0

     171.7.0.0/30 is subnetted, 1 subnets
O IA    171.7.5.0 [110/11] via 175.1.6.2, 00:01:40, Ethernet0/0
     171.8.0.0/24 is subnetted, 1 subnets
O IA    171.8.5.0 [110/20] via 175.1.6.2, 00:01:40, Ethernet0/0
     175.1.0.0/24 is subnetted, 3 subnets
C       175.1.6.0 is directly connected, Ethernet0/0
O E1    175.1.5.0 [110/12] via 175.1.6.2, 00:01:30, Ethernet0/0
O E2    175.1.2.0 [110/1] via 179.7.2.9, 00:01:30, Dialer1
     66.0.0.0/24 is subnetted, 1 subnets
C       66.66.66.0 is directly connected, Loopback1
     179.7.0.0/16 is variably subnetted, 3 subnets, 3 masks
```

```
O       179.7.2.0/29 [110/1849] via 179.7.2.9, 00:01:41, Dialer1
C       179.7.2.8/30 is directly connected, Dialer1
C       179.7.2.9/32 is directly connected, Dialer1
    178.1.0.0/30 is subnetted, 1 subnets
O E1    178.1.1.0 [110/12] via 175.1.6.2, 00:01:31, Ethernet0/0
    177.1.0.0/20 is subnetted, 1 subnets
B       177.1.0.0 [200/0] via 175.1.6.2, 1w0d
O*E2 0.0.0.0/0 [110/1] via 175.1.6.2, 00:01:31, Ethernet0/0
```

```
r6#show ip ospf neighbor
```

Neighbor ID	Pri	State	Dead Time	Address	Interface
2.2.2.2	1	FULL/ -	00:00:33	179.7.2.9	Dialer1
5.5.5.5	1	FULL/BDR	00:00:35	175.1.6.2	Ethernet0/0

```
r6#show isdn active
------------------------------------------------------------------------
                         ISDN ACTIVE CALLS
------------------------------------------------------------------------
Call   Calling  Called   Remote  Seconds  Seconds  Seconds  Charges
Type   Number   Number   Name    Used     Left     Idle     Units/Currency
------------------------------------------------------------------------
Out ---N/A---   99047132 r2      28       109      10       0
------------------------------------------------------------------------
```

```
r6#show dialer

BRI0/0 - dialer type = ISDN

Dial String      Successes   Failures    Last DNIS   Last status
0 incoming call(s) have been screened.
0 incoming call(s) rejected for callback.

BRI0/0:1 - dialer type = ISDN
Idle timer (120 secs), Fast idle timer (20 secs)
Wait for carrier (30 secs), Re-enable (15 secs)
Dialer state is data link layer up
Dial reason: Dialing on watched route loss
Interface bound to profile Di1
Time until disconnect 106 secs
Current call connected 00:00:30
Connected to 99047132 (r2)
```

```
BRI0/0:2 - dialer type = ISDN
Idle timer (120 secs), Fast idle timer (20 secs)
Wait for carrier (30 secs), Re-enable (15 secs)
Dialer state is idle

Di1 - dialer type = DIALER PROFILE
Idle timer (120 secs), Fast idle timer (20 secs)
Wait for carrier (30 secs), Re-enable (15 secs)
Dialer state is data link layer up
Number of active calls = 1


Dial String      Successes    Failures   Last DNIS   Last status
99047132                 1           0    00:00:35    successful    Default
```

! When Ethernet0/0 comes up on R4, BGP converges and watched-route is UP,
  hence ISDN goes down

```
r6#
*Mar 21 22:59:26.031: %BGP-5-ADJCHANGE: neighbor 175.1.6.1 Up
r6#show ip bgp
BGP table version is 207, local router ID is 6.6.6.6
Status codes: s suppressed, d damped, h history, * valid, > best,
  i - internal,
                r RIB-failure
Origin codes: i - IGP, e - EGP, ? - incomplete

    Network          Next Hop        Metric LocPrf Weight Path
 *  i11.11.11.0/24   175.1.6.1              100       0 1 i
 *>                  175.1.6.1                        0 1 i
 *  i44.44.44.0/24   175.1.6.1          0   100       0 1 i
 *>                  175.1.6.1          0             0 1 i
 *> 66.66.66.0/24    0.0.0.0            0         32768 i
 *>i177.1.0.0/20     175.1.6.2              100       0 i
 *>i178.1.1.0/30     171.8.5.1          0   100       0 20 i


*Mar 21 23:00:48.150: %ISDN-6-DISCONNECT: Interface BRI0/0:1  disconnected
    from 99047132 r2, call lasted 351 seconds
*Mar 21 23:00:48.154: %LINK-3-UPDOWN: Interface BRI0/0:1, changed state to
    down
*Mar 21 23:00:48.154: BR0/0 DDR: has total 0 call(s), dial_out 0, dial_in 0
*Mar 21 23:00:48.158: %DIALER-6-UNBIND: Interface BR0/0:1 unbound from
    profile Di1
```

```
*Mar 21 23:00:48.166: BR0/0:1 DDR: disconnecting call
*Mar 21 23:00:48.166: BR0/0:1 DDR: Dialer Watch: resetting call in progress
*Mar 21 23:00:48.166: DDR: Dialer Watch: watch-group = 1
*Mar 21 23:00:48.166: DDR:         network 11.11.11.0/255.255.255.0 UP,
*Mar 21 23:00:48.166: DDR:         primary UP
*Mar 21 23:00:49.155: %LINEPROTO-5-UPDOWN: Line protocol on Interface BRI0/
    0:1, changed state to down
```

NOTE   For more info on dial backup using Dialer Watch, refer to the following URLs:

www.cisco.com/univercd/cc/td/doc/product/software/ios121/121cgcr/dialts_c/dtsprt6/
dcdbakdw.htm

www.cisco.com/warp/customer/129/bri-backup-map-watch.html

www.cisco.com/warp/customer/793/access_dial/ddr_dialer_profile.html

---

Section 4.0: PIX Configuration

4.1: Basic PIX Configuration

1 Configure the PIX IP address as shown in Figure 7-1.

2 Configure static NAT translation for the AAA server with the IP addresses shown in Figure 7-1. Configure ACL accordingly.

3 Configure RIP for R1 and R2 as per Section 2.3 with clear-text authentication.

4 Configure a static default route on PIX to R2.

4.2: Advanced PIX Configuration

1 Configure a filter to deny Java applets and ActiveX controls that return to the AAA server from an outbound HTTP connection:

```
filter activex 80 172.16.1.3 255.255.255.255 0.0.0.0 0.0.0.0
filter java 80 172.16.1.3 255.255.255.255 0.0.0.0 0.0.0.0
```

2 Configure a filter for all users except the AAA server to prevent outbound users from accessing World Wide Web URLs based on the company security policy. See the example following item 5.

3 Configure a WebSense filtering application server 175.1.5.23 on VLAN5. See the example following item 5.

4 Allow all outbound web connections when the WebSense server is unavailable. See the example following item 5.

5   Configure proxy-block for all outbound HTTP connections destined for a proxy server that listens on port 8080:

```
url-server (outside) host 175.1.5.23
filter url except 172.16.1.3 255.255.255.255 0.0.0.0 0.0.0.0 allow
filter url http 0.0.0.0 0.0.0.0 0.0.0.0 0.0.0.0 allow
filter url 8080 0 0 0 0 proxy-block
```

6   The **filter** command on PIX blocks the HTML <object> tag and comments it out within the HTML web page.

NOTE   For more information on the PIX **filter** command, refer to www.cisco.com/univercd/cc/td/doc/product/iaabu/pix/pix_62/cmdref/df.htm#1039734

Section 5.0: IPSec/PPTP Configuration

5.1: IPSec LAN-to-LAN Router-to-VPN3000

1   Configure a LAN-to-LAN IPSec tunnel between R2 and the VPN3000 concentrator.

2   The VPN3000 concentrator is behind R1. Configure the default route to R1.

3   Configure Loopback1 on R2 with 192.168.2.1/24.

4   The IPSec tunnel is to protect the VPN3000 concentrator and R2 networks on 172.16.1.0/24 to 172.16.2.0/24, respectively.

5   Configure preshared authentication with all other parameters as appropriate.

6   The tricky part is that the VPN3000 concentrator should not peer to R2 with IP address 175.1.2.2.

7   You need to configure bidirectional NAT on PIX for R2 IP 175.1.2.2 to an IP in VLAN3:

```
pixfirewall(config)# show static
static (inside,outside) 175.1.2.5 10.1.1.1 netmask 255.255.255.255 0 0
static (outside,inside) 172.16.1.10 175.1.2.2 netmask 255.255.255.255 0 0
```

8   Hidden issue: Once you configure bidirectional NAT, the BGP session between R1 and R2 will break/fail since R1 was configured to peer to R2 IP address 175.1.2.2. Change BGP peering to the NATed IP address 172.16.1.10:

```
router bgp 1
 no synchronization
 bgp router-id 1.1.1.1
 network 11.11.11.0 mask 255.255.255.0
```

```
neighbor 172.16.1.10 remote-as 1
no auto-summary
!
```

```
r1#show ip bgp summary
BGP router identifier 1.1.1.1, local AS number 1
BGP table version is 179, main routing table version 179
6 network entries and 6 paths using 798 bytes of memory
5 BGP path attribute entries using 260 bytes of memory
1 BGP rrinfo entries using 24 bytes of memory
2 BGP AS-PATH entries using 48 bytes of memory
0 BGP route-map cache entries using 0 bytes of memory
0 BGP filter-list cache entries using 0 bytes of memory
BGP activity 68/250 prefixes, 88/82 paths, scan interval 15 secs
```

```
Neighbor       V  AS  MsgRcvd MsgSent TblVer InQ OutQ Up/Down    State/PfxRcd
172.16.1.10    4  1   20      17      179    0   0    00:13:23   5
```

9 Configure LAN-to-LAN configuration on the VPN3000 concentrator, as shown in Figures 7-6a through 7-6d.

Figure 7-6a *LAN-to-LAN Configuration on VPN3000 (Define Peer, Preshared, IKE Proposal)*

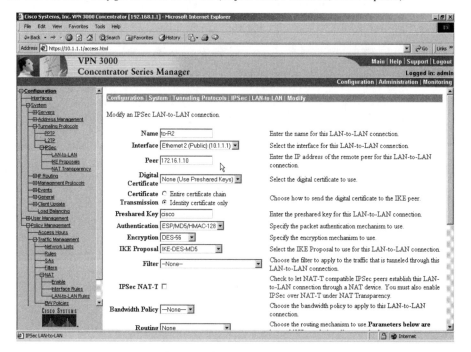

Figure 7-6b *LAN-to-LAN Configuration on VPN3000 (Define Local and Remote Networks)*

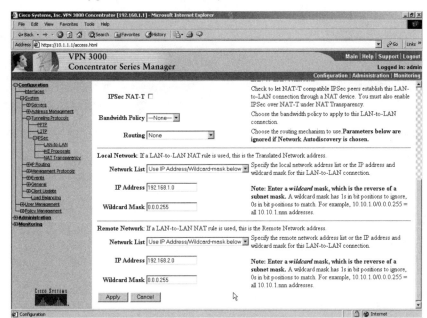

Figure 7-6c *LAN-to-LAN Configuration on VPN3000 (Filter Rules Created for L2L and Applied to Interface)*

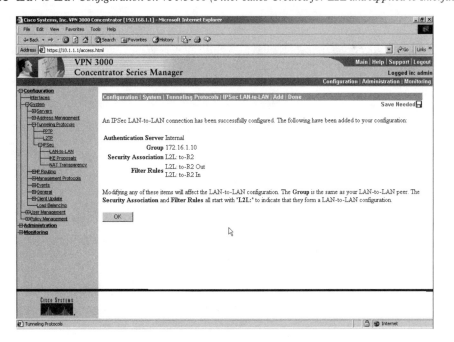

Figure 7-6d *LAN-to-LAN Configuration on VPN3000 (Modify)*

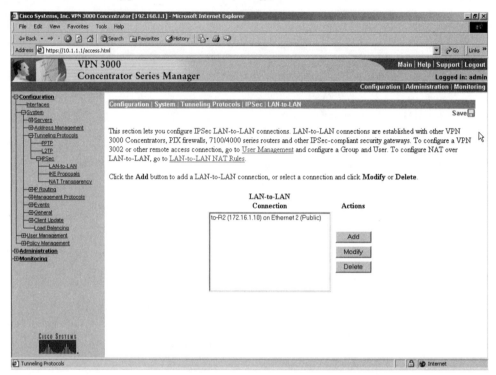

10 Another hidden issue: R2 has a default gateway via the serial interface to R4, which is not the interface where the crypto map is applied. The crypto map is applied on Ethernet0 on R2, so we need a static route for network 192.168.1.0/24 or a default route that is via the interface where the crypto map is applied.

11 The workaround is to configure policy routing for IPSec ACL and set the next hop to Ethernet0, where the crypto map is applied:

```
<snip from R2>
interface Ethernet0
 ip address 175.1.2.2 255.255.255.0
 ip policy route-map next-hop
 crypto map lab7
!
ip local policy route-map next-hop
!
access-list 110 permit ip 192.168.2.0 0.0.0.255 192.168.1.0 0.0.0.255
!
```

```
route-map next-hop permit 10
 match ip address 110
 set interface Ethernet0
 !
```

12 Configure IPSec R2 as follows:

```
hostname r2
!
logging rate-limit console 10 except errors
enable password 7 14141B180F0B
!
ip subnet-zero
no ip finger
ip tcp synwait-time 5
no ip domain-lookup
!
!
key chain lab7
 key 1
  key-string 7 104D000A0618
!
!
crypto isakmp policy 10
 hash md5
 authentication pre-share
crypto isakmp key cisco address 175.1.2.5
!
!
crypto ipsec transform-set lab7 esp-des esp-md5-hmac
!
crypto map lab7 10 ipsec-isakmp
 set peer 175.1.2.5
 set transform-set lab7
 match address 110
!
!
interface Ethernet0
 ip address 175.1.2.2 255.255.255.0
 crypto map lab7
!
access-list 110 permit ip 192.168.2.0 0.0.0.255 192.168.1.0 0.0.0.255
!
```

13 Verify IPSec configuration by pinging 192.168.1.1 from R2 sourcing from 192.168.2.1 (loopback1). Verify tunnel on R2 and concentrator. See the example that follows and Figures 7-7a and 7-7b.

```
r2#show crypto engine connections active

   ID Interface        IP-Address      State  Algorithm          Encrypt Decrypt
    1 <none>           <none>          set    HMAC_MD5+DES_56_CB        0       0
 2000 Ethernet0        175.1.2.2       set    HMAC_MD5+DES_56_CB        0     102
 2001 Ethernet0        175.1.2.2       set    HMAC_MD5+DES_56_CB      102       0


r2#show crypto isakmp sa
     dst            src            state        conn-id   slot
 175.1.2.5      175.1.2.2          QM_IDLE         1        0


r2#show crypto ipsec sa

interface: Ethernet0
    Crypto map tag: lab7, local addr. 175.1.2.2

    local  ident (addr/mask/prot/port): (192.168.2.0/255.255.255.0/0/0)
    remote ident (addr/mask/prot/port): (192.168.1.0/255.255.255.0/0/0)
    current_peer: 175.1.2.5
      PERMIT, flags={origin_is_acl,}
     #pkts encaps: 102, #pkts encrypt: 102, #pkts digest 102
     #pkts decaps: 102, #pkts decrypt: 102, #pkts verify 102
     #pkts compressed: 0, #pkts decompressed: 0
     #pkts not compressed: 0, #pkts compr. failed: 0, #pkts decompress failed: 0
     #send errors 3, #recv errors 0

     local crypto endpt.: 175.1.2.2, remote crypto endpt.: 175.1.2.5
     path mtu 1500, media mtu 1500
     current outbound spi: 60E2746B

     inbound esp sas:
      spi: 0xF319CC16(4078554134)
        transform: esp-des esp-md5-hmac ,
        in use settings ={Tunnel, }
        slot: 0, conn id: 2000, flow_id: 1, crypto map: lab7
        sa timing: remaining key lifetime (k/sec): (4607987/3389)
        IV size: 8 bytes
        replay detection support: Y
```

```
inbound ah sas:

inbound pcp sas:

outbound esp sas:
 spi: 0x60E2746B(1625453675)
   transform: esp-des esp-md5-hmac ,
   in use settings ={Tunnel, }
   slot: 0, conn id: 2001, flow_id: 2, crypto map: lab7
   sa timing: remaining key lifetime (k/sec): (4607984/3389)
   IV size: 8 bytes
   replay detection support: Y

outbound ah sas:

outbound pcp sas:
```

Figure 7-7a *VPN3000: Monitoring LAN-to-LAN Connection (Session Summary)*

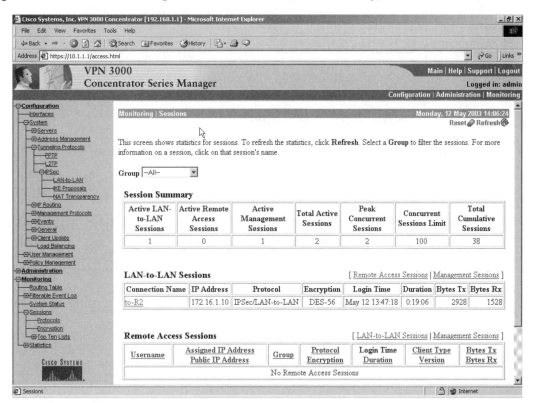

Figure 7-7b *VPN3000: Monitoring LAN-to-LAN Connection (Session Detail)*

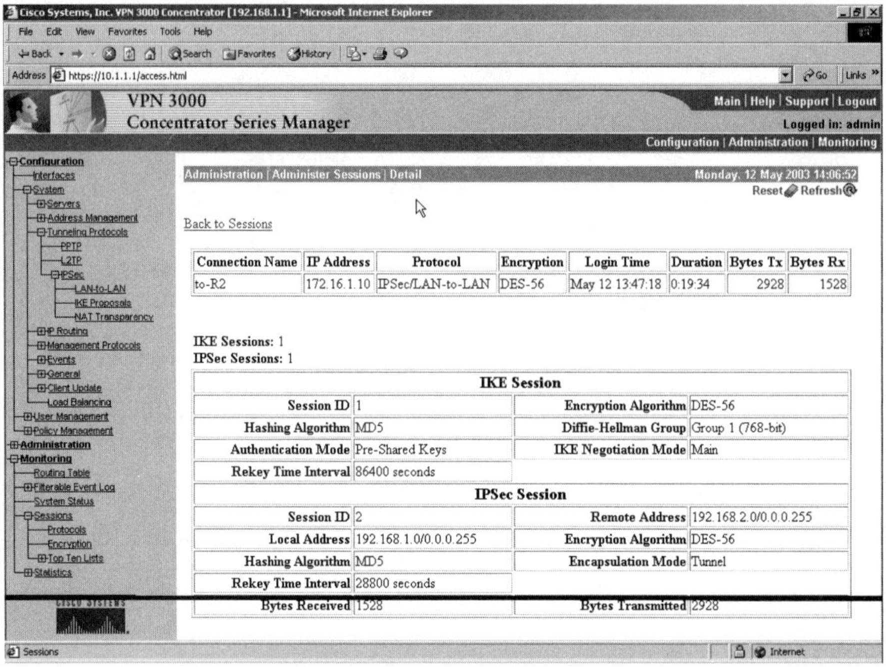

5.2: IPSec Remote Access to Router

1 Configure R6 as a VPN server for remote access VPN client Test PC in VLAN5.

2 Configure group **lab7-group** with password **cisco123**.

3 Configure AAA on R6 for VPN client authentication using local username **vpnuser** password **cisco**.

4 Configure an IP pool on R6 for the VPN client in the range 172.16.10.1 to 172.16.10.50.

5 Configure split tunneling on R6 such that VPN clients use the IPSec tunnel to access Loopback1 of R6 only. All other outbound traffic should be unencrypted.

6 See the following example for VPN server configuration on R6:

```
hostname r6
!
username vpnuser password cisco
!
aaa new-model
!
!
aaa authentication login vpn local
aaa authorization network vpn local
```

```
!
crypto isakmp policy 10
 hash md5
 authentication pre-share
 group 2
!
crypto isakmp client configuration group lab7-group
 key cisco123
 pool vpnpool
 acl 101
!
!
crypto ipsec transform-set lab7 esp-3des esp-md5-hmac
!
crypto dynamic-map lab7dyn 10
 set transform-set lab7
 reverse-route
!
!
crypto map lab7 client authentication list vpn
crypto map lab7 isakmp authorization list vpn
crypto map lab7 client configuration address respond
crypto map lab7 10 ipsec-isakmp dynamic lab7dyn
!
interface Ethernet0/0
 ip address 175.1.6.3 255.255.255.0
 crypto map lab7
!
ip local pool vpnpool 172.16.10.1 172.16.10.50
!
access-list 101 permit ip 66.66.66.0 0.0.0.255 172.16.10.0 0.0.0.255
!
```

```
<Launch VPN client connection from Test PC in VLAN5.
Verify VPN Client connection on R6>
```

r6#**show crypto engine connections active**

ID	Interface	IP-Address	State	Algorithm	Encrypt	Decrypt
2	Ethernet0/0	175.1.6.3	set	HMAC_MD5+DES_56_CB	0	0
2000	Ethernet0/0	175.1.6.3	set	HMAC_MD5+3DES_56_C	0	0
2001	Ethernet0/0	175.1.6.3	set	HMAC_MD5+3DES_56_C	0	0
2002	Ethernet0/0	175.1.6.3	set	HMAC_MD5+3DES_56_C	0	7
2003	Ethernet0/0	175.1.6.3	set	HMAC_MD5+3DES_56_C	7	0

```
r6#show crypto isakmp sa
dst              src            state         conn-id   slot
175.1.6.3        175.1.5.2      QM_IDLE             2       0

r6#show crypto ipsec sa

interface: Ethernet0/0
   Crypto map tag: lab7, local addr. 175.1.6.3

   local  ident (addr/mask/prot/port): (175.1.6.3/255.255.255.255/0/0)
   remote ident (addr/mask/prot/port): (172.16.10.2/255.255.255.255/0/0)
   current_peer: 175.1.5.2:500
     PERMIT, flags={}
   #pkts encaps: 0, #pkts encrypt: 0, #pkts digest 0
   #pkts decaps: 0, #pkts decrypt: 0, #pkts verify 0
   #pkts compressed: 0, #pkts decompressed: 0
   #pkts not compressed: 0, #pkts compr. failed: 0
   #pkts not decompressed: 0, #pkts decompress failed: 0
   #send errors 0, #recv errors 0

     local crypto endpt.: 175.1.6.3, remote crypto endpt.: 175.1.5.2
     path mtu 1500, media mtu 1500
     current outbound spi: 2245A5F4

     inbound esp sas:
      spi: 0xC41DDE7D(3290291837)
        transform: esp-3des esp-md5-hmac ,
        in use settings ={Tunnel, }
        slot: 0, conn id: 2000, flow_id: 1, crypto map: lab7
        sa timing: remaining key lifetime (k/sec): (4608000/3409)
        IV size: 8 bytes
        replay detection support: Y

     inbound ah sas:

     inbound pcp sas:

     outbound esp sas:
      spi: 0x2245A5F4(574989812)
        transform: esp-3des esp-md5-hmac ,
        in use settings ={Tunnel, }
        slot: 0, conn id: 2001, flow_id: 2, crypto map: lab7
        sa timing: remaining key lifetime (k/sec): (4608000/3409)
        IV size: 8 bytes
        replay detection support: Y
```

```
    outbound ah sas:

    outbound pcp sas:

local  ident (addr/mask/prot/port): (66.66.66.0/255.255.255.0/0/0)
remote ident (addr/mask/prot/port): (172.16.10.2/255.255.255.255/0/0)
current_peer: 175.1.5.2:500
  PERMIT, flags={}
 #pkts encaps: 7, #pkts encrypt: 7, #pkts digest 7
 #pkts decaps: 7, #pkts decrypt: 7, #pkts verify 7
 #pkts compressed: 0, #pkts decompressed: 0
 #pkts not compressed: 0, #pkts compr. failed: 0
 #pkts not decompressed: 0, #pkts decompress failed: 0
 #send errors 0, #recv errors 0

   local crypto endpt.: 175.1.6.3, remote crypto endpt.: 175.1.5.2
   path mtu 1500, media mtu 1500
   current outbound spi: D8B44B68

   inbound esp sas:
    spi: 0xD6035966(3590543718)
      transform: esp-3des esp-md5-hmac ,
      in use settings ={Tunnel, }
      slot: 0, conn id: 2002, flow_id: 3, crypto map: lab7
      sa timing: remaining key lifetime (k/sec): (4607999/3415)
      IV size: 8 bytes
      replay detection support: Y

   inbound ah sas:

   inbound pcp sas:

   outbound esp sas:
    spi: 0xD8B44B68(3635694440)
      transform: esp-3des esp-md5-hmac ,
      in use settings ={Tunnel, }
      slot: 0, conn id: 2003, flow_id: 4, crypto map: lab7
      sa timing: remaining key lifetime (k/sec): (4607999/3412)
      IV size: 8 bytes
      replay detection support: Y

   outbound ah sas:

   outbound pcp sas:
```

7 Verify the client connection from Test PC in VLAN 5. See Figures 7-8a and 7-8b.

Figure 7-8a *VPN Client Connection (General)*

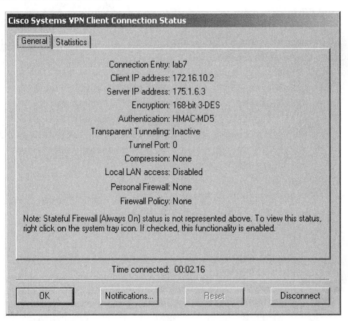

Figure 7-8b *VPN Client Connection (Statistics)*

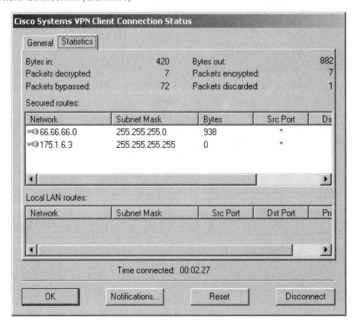

8 Make sure you can ping Loopback1 of R6 and all other networks. Verify in the VPN client connection that only Loopback1 traffic is encrypted. See Figure 7-9.

Figure 7-9 *VPN Client Ping Split-Tunnel Network*

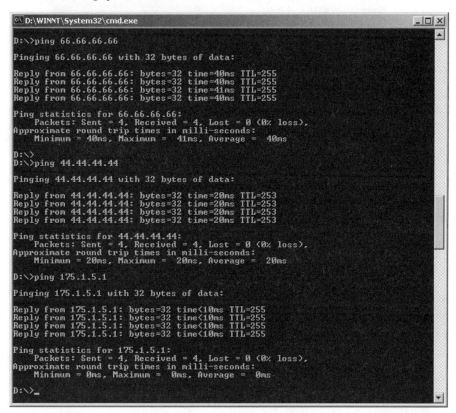

5.3: PPTP to Router with Local Authentication

1 Configure PPTP remote access to R1 for the Test PC in VLAN5.

2 Configure R1 as the PPTP server, as demonstrated in the example following item 3.

3 Configure ACL to deny ICMP and permit everything. Apply this ACL to the Virtual-Template interface:

```
hostname r1
!
aaa new-model
aaa authentication ppp pptp local
!
username pptpuser password cisco
!
```

```
vpdn enable
!
vpdn-group 1
! Default PPTP VPDN group
 accept-dialin
  protocol pptp
  virtual-template 1
!
interface Virtual-Template1
 ip unnumbered FastEthernet1/0
 ip access-group 101 in
 peer default ip address pool pptp-pool
 ppp authentication ms-chap pptp
!

ip local pool pptp-pool 172.16.11.1 172.16.11.50
!
access-list 101 deny    icmp any any
access-list 101 permit ip any any
```

<Launch PPTP client connection from Test PC in VLAN5.
Verify PPTP session>

r1#**show vpdn session**

PPTP Session Information Total tunnels 1 sessions 1

LocID	RemID	TunID	Intf	Username	State	Last Chg
16	49152	16	Vi1	pptpuser	estabd	00:02:40

r1#**show users**

Line	User	Host(s)	Idle	Location
* 0 con 0		idle	00:00:00	
Vi1	pptpuser	Virtual PPP (PPTP)	00:00:03	

  Interface User   Mode   Idle Peer Address

r1#**show ip interface virtual-access 1**
Virtual-Access1 is up, line protocol is up
  Interface is unnumbered. Using address of FastEthernet1/0 (172.16.1.2)
  Broadcast address is 255.255.255.255
  Peer address is 172.16.11.1
  MTU is 1500 bytes
  Helper address is not set

```
        Directed broadcast forwarding is disabled
        Multicast reserved groups joined: 224.0.0.9
        Outgoing access list is not set
        Inbound  access list is 101
        Proxy ARP is enabled
        Security level is default
        Split horizon is enabled
<output truncated>


r1#show access-lists 101
Extended IP access list 101
        deny icmp any any (12 matches)
        permit ip any any (130 matches)
```

4 Configure MS-CHAP authentication with no MPPE encryption.

5 Hint: By default, a client DUN created on the PC is configured to encrypt all data. You need to disable this in the Properties, Security tab by unchecking **Require data encryption**.

6 Configure local authentication for PPTP clients. Configure a username **pptpuser** password **cisco** on R1.

7 Configure an IP pool on R1 172.16.11.1–172.16.11.50 for PPTP clients.

8 Configure static NAT translation on PIX for R1 and ACL accordingly:

```
pixfirewall(config)# show static
static (inside,outside) 175.1.2.20 172.16.1.2 netmask 255.255.255.255 0 0

pixfirewall(config)# show access-list
access-list 101 permit icmp any any (hitcnt=44441)
access-list 101 permit tcp host 175.1.5.2 host 175.1.2.20 eq 1723 (hitcnt=17)
access-list 101 permit gre host 175.1.5.2 host 175.1.2.20 (hitcnt=811)
```

Section 6.0: IOS Firewall Configuration

6.1: Context-Based Access Control (CBAC)

1 Configure IOS Firewall—CBAC on R5 to protect VLAN6.

2 Configure inspection to monitor all TCP and UDP traffic.

3 Configure ACL on R6 such that the R7 ATM network can Telnet, ping, and FTP to all networks beyond R5 and should not be able to initiate any traffic to the Frame Relay network.

4 Additionally, any device in the VLAN2 network should not be able to ping the R7 ATM link, but R7 should be able to ping R3. See ACL 101 configured on R5 in the example following item 6.

5 Tune default firewall parameters for the number of existing half-open sessions that will cause the firewall to start deleting half-open sessions at 1500 and to stop deleting at 1200 sessions, as demonstrated in the example following item 6.

6 Configure the TCP syn-wait time to 20 seconds for a session to reach the established state before the firewall starts dropping the session:

```
hostname r5
!
ip inspect max-incomplete high 1500
ip inspect max-incomplete low 1200
ip inspect one-minute high 1500
ip inspect one-minute low 1200
ip inspect tcp synwait-time 20
ip inspect name lab7 tcp
ip inspect name lab7 udp
!
interface ATM0/0
 ip address 171.7.5.2 255.255.255.252
 ip access-group 101 in
 ip ospf authentication-key 7 094F471A1A0A
 ip ospf network point-to-point
 no atm ilmi-keepalive
 pvc 0 0/700
  protocol ip 171.7.5.1 broadcast
  broadcast
  encapsulation aal5snap
  !
!
interface Ethernet1/0
 bandwidth 155000
 ip address 175.1.6.2 255.255.255.0
 ip inspect lab7 in
 ip ospf authentication-key 7 14141B180F0B
 half-duplex
!
access-list 101 deny    ip any 179.7.2.0 0.0.0.7
access-list 101 deny    icmp any 175.1.2.0 0.0.0.255 echo-reply
access-list 101 permit icmp any any
access-list 101 permit tcp any any eq telnet
access-list 101 permit tcp any any eq ftp
access-list 101 permit tcp any any eq ftp-data
access-list 101 permit ospf any any
access-list 101 permit tcp any any eq bgp
!
```

```
r5#show ip inspect config
Session audit trail is disabled
Session alert is enabled
one-minute (sampling period) thresholds are [1200:1500] connections
max-incomplete sessions thresholds are [1200:1500]
max-incomplete tcp connections per host is 50. Block-time 0 minute.
tcp synwait-time is 20 sec -- tcp finwait-time is 5 sec
tcp idle-time is 3600 sec -- udp idle-time is 30 sec
dns-timeout is 5 sec
Inspection Rule Configuration
 Inspection name lab7
    tcp alert is on audit-trail is off timeout 3600
    udp alert is on audit-trail is off timeout 30
```

7 Verify ACL and CBAC configurations:

```
<Verify by telnetting from R4 to R7, check session table and dynamic ACL entry
on R5>
r5#show ip inspect sessions
Established Sessions
 Session 62D34A24 (175.1.6.1:11039)=>(171.7.5.1:23) tcp SIS_OPEN


r5#show access-lists 101
Extended IP access list 101
    permit tcp host 171.7.5.1 eq telnet host 175.1.6.1 eq 11039 (27 matches)
    deny ip any 179.7.2.0 0.0.0.7 (29 matches)
    deny icmp any 175.1.2.0 0.0.0.255 echo-reply (10 matches)
    permit icmp any any (10 matches)
    permit tcp any any eq telnet (90 matches)
    permit tcp any any eq ftp
    permit tcp any any eq ftp-data
    permit ospf any any (33 matches)
    permit tcp any any eq bgp (12 matches)
    permit tcp host 171.7.5.1 host 175.1.2.3 eq tacacs (22 matches)
    permit udp host 175.1.5.25 host 175.1.2.3 eq 1812


<Extended ping fail from R2-VLAN2 interface to R7>
r2#show ip interface brief
Interface       IP-Address      OK? Method Status                 Protocol
BRI0            unassigned      YES unset  up                     up
BRI0:1          unassigned      YES unset  down                   down
BRI0:2          unassigned      YES unset  down                   down
Dialer1         179.7.2.9       YES manual up                     up
Ethernet0       175.1.2.2       YES manual up                     up
Loopback1       192.168.2.1     YES manual up                     up
Serial0         179.7.2.2       YES manual up                     up
Serial1         unassigned      YES unset  administratively down  down
```

```
r2#ping ip
Target IP address: 171.7.5.1
Repeat count [5]:
Datagram size [100]:
Timeout in seconds [2]:
Extended commands [n]: y
Source address or interface: 175.1.2.2
Type of service [0]:
Set DF bit in IP header? [no]:
Validate reply data? [no]:
Data pattern [0xABCD]:
Loose, Strict, Record, Timestamp, Verbose[none]:
Sweep range of sizes [n]:
Type escape sequence to abort.
Sending 5, 100-byte ICMP Echos to 171.7.5.1, timeout is 2 seconds:
.....
Success rate is 0 percent (0/5)
r2#


<Successful ping from R7 to R2-VLAN2 interface>
r7#ping 175.1.2.2

Type escape sequence to abort.
Sending 5, 100-byte ICMP Echos to 175.1.2.2, timeout is 2 seconds:
!!!!!
Success rate is 100 percent (5/5), round-trip min/avg/max = 68/68/68 ms
r7#


<Verify ACL counters on R5>
r5#show access-lists 101
Extended IP access list 101
    deny ip any 179.7.2.0 0.0.0.7 (29 matches)
    deny icmp any 175.1.2.0 0.0.0.255 echo-reply (26 matches)
    permit icmp any any (15 matches)
    permit tcp any any eq telnet (90 matches)
    permit tcp any any eq ftp
    permit tcp any any eq ftp-data
    permit ospf any any (79 matches)
    permit tcp any any eq bgp (26 matches)
    permit tcp host 171.7.5.1 host 175.1.2.3 eq tacacs (22 matches)
    permit udp host 175.1.5.25 host 175.1.2.3 eq 1812
```

NOTE	See this URL for more info on configuring CBAC:
	www.cisco.com/univercd/cc/td/doc/product/software/ios120/120newft/120t/120t5/iosfw2/iosfw2_2.htm

6.2: Intrusion Detection System (IDS)

1 Configure IDS on R6 to protect against attacks using the parameters specified in the question, as demonstrated in the example following item 4.

2 Configure both Ethernet and ISDN interfaces for IDS.

3 Configure IDS to send events to the syslog server and IDS management center 175.1.2.3 (AAA server).

4 Tune signature 2150 using ACL to deny from host 175.1.5.2. Verify by sending large ICMP packets from Test PC and R4 or R2:

```
hostname r6
!
ip audit notify nr-director
ip audit notify log
ip audit po max-events 100
ip audit po remote hostid 3 orgid 100 rmtaddress 175.1.2.3 localaddress
   175.1.6.3 port 45000 preference 1 timeout 5 application director
   ip audit po local hostid 1 orgid 100
ip audit signature 2150 list 5
ip audit name lab7 info action alarm
ip audit name lab7 attack action alarm drop reset
!
interface Ethernet0/0
 ip address 175.1.6.3 255.255.255.0
 ip audit lab7 in
!
interface Dialer1
 ip address 179.7.2.10 255.255.255.252
 ip audit lab7 in

access-list 5 deny    175.1.5.2
access-list 5 permit any

r6#show ip audit configuration
Event notification through syslog is enabled
Event notification through Net Director is enabled
Default action(s) for info signatures is alarm
Default action(s) for attack signatures is alarm
```

```
Default threshold of recipients for spam signature is 250
Signature 2150 list 5
PostOffice:HostID:0 OrgID:0 Msg dropped:0
          :Curr Event Buf Size:0  Configured:100
Post Office is not enabled - No connections are active
Audit Rule Configuration
 Audit name lab7
    info actions alarm
    attack actions alarm drop reset

r6#show access-lists 5
Standard IP access list 5
    deny   175.1.5.2 (377 matches)
    permit any (42 matches)
```

5 Configure PIX with static translation and ACL to permit Postoffice protocol UDP/45000 and Syslog port UDP/514:

```
pixfirewall# show static
static (inside,outside) 175.1.2.3 172.16.1.3 netmask 255.255.255.255 0 0

pixfirewall# show access-list
access-list 101 permit udp host 175.1.6.3 host 175.1.2.3 eq 45000
access-list 101 permit udp host 175.1.6.3 host 175.1.2.3 eq syslog
```

NOTE   See this URL for more info on configuring IDS:

www.cisco.com/univercd/cc/td/doc/product/software/ios120/120newft/120t/120t5/iosfw2/ios_ids.htm

Section 7.0: AAA

7.1: AAA on the Router

1 Configure R7 router management with TACACS+ using the AAA server, as shown in Figure 7-1.

2 Configure PIX translation and ACL accordingly:

```
pixfirewall(config)# show static
static (inside,outside) 175.1.2.3 172.16.1.3 netmask 255.255.255.255 0 0

pixfirewall(config)# show access-list
access-list 101 permit tcp host 171.7.5.1 host 175.1.2.3 eq tacacs
  (hitcnt=81)
```

3 Hidden issue: There is ingress ACL on the R5 ATM link. You need to allow TCP/49 from R7 to the AAA server:

```
r5#show access-lists 101
Extended IP access list 101
    permit udp host 171.7.5.1 eq ntp host 179.7.2.2 eq ntp (1 match)
    deny ip any 179.7.2.0 0.0.0.7 (18 matches)
    deny icmp any 175.1.2.0 0.0.0.255 echo-reply (10 matches)
    permit icmp any any (30 matches)
    permit tcp any any eq telnet (85 matches)
    permit tcp any any eq ftp
    permit tcp any any eq ftp-data
    permit ospf any any (210 matches)
    permit tcp any any eq bgp (67 matches)
    permit tcp host 171.7.5.1 host 175.1.2.3 eq tacacs (220 matches)
```

4 Configure a named method list for Telnet and apply to vty for authentication, authorization, and accounting. Make sure this method falls back to local in the event the AAA server is down. The example following item 13 demonstrates this.

5 Configure a named method list for the console and apply it to the console with no authentication, authorization, or accounting.

6 Configure username **lab7-telnet** with password **cisco** on CiscoSecure ACS with privileges accordingly. See Figures 7-10a through 7-10c.

Figure 7-10a *User lab7-telnet Setting on ACS*

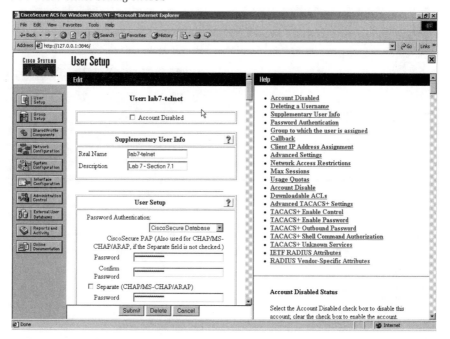

Figure 7-10b *User lab7-telnet Setting on ACS (Shell Exec and Privilege Level)*

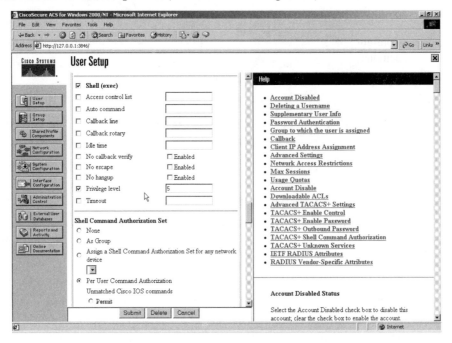

Figure 7-10c *User lab7-telnet Setting on ACS (Command Authorization Set)*

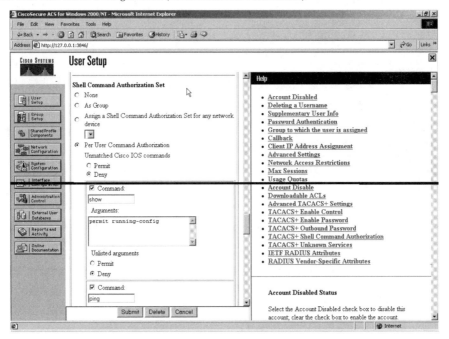

7 Configure the same username, **lab7-telnet**, on the R7 local database for fallback.

8 Configure command authorization and assign said user with a privilege of level 5.

9 Configure the router to assign **show run** and **ping** commands to privilege level 5, as demonstrated in the example following item 13.

10 Configure command level 5 accounting to log all these events.

11 Configure EXEC (shell) accounting for start and stop time.

12 Make sure the console does not have any authentication, authorization, or accounting.

13 The complete AAA configuration on R7 is as follows:

```
hostname r7
!
aaa new-model
aaa authentication login vty group tacacs+ local
aaa authentication login con none
aaa authorization exec vty group tacacs+ local
aaa authorization exec con none
aaa authorization commands 1 con none
aaa authorization commands 5 vty group tacacs+ local
aaa authorization commands 5 con none
aaa authorization commands 15 con none
aaa accounting exec vty start-stop group tacacs+
aaa accounting exec con none
aaa accounting commands 5 vty start-stop group tacacs+
aaa accounting commands 5 con none
!
username lab7-telnet privilege 5 password 7 045802150C2E
!
tacacs-server host 175.1.2.3
tacacs-server key cisco
!
!
privilege exec level 5 show running-config
privilege exec level 5 ping
!
line con 0
 exec-timeout 0 0
 authorization commands 1 con
 authorization commands 5 con
 authorization commands 15 con
 authorization exec con
 accounting commands 5 con
```

```
            accounting exec vty
            login authentication con
            transport input none
            escape-character 27
            !
            line vty 0 4
            password 7 14141B180F0B
            authorization commands 5 vty
            authorization exec vty
            accounting commands 5 vty
            accounting exec vty
            login authentication vty
            !
            end
```

14 See Figure 7-11 for TACACS+ accounting start-stop time records for billing purposes on CiscoSecure ACS.

Figure 7-11 *TACACS+ Accounting for Session Start-Stop Time (Billing Purposes)*

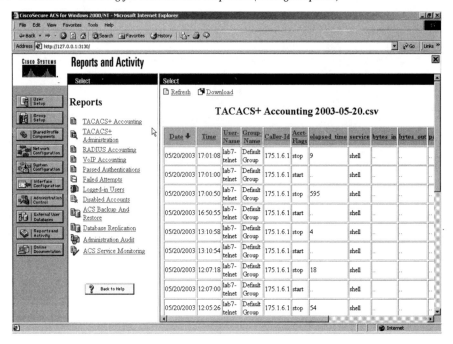

15 See Figure 7-12a for TACACS+ administration for command authorization on CiscoSecure ACS and Figure 7-12b for failed attempts of command authorization on CiscoSecure ACS.

Figure 7-12a *TACACS+ Administration for Command Authorization*

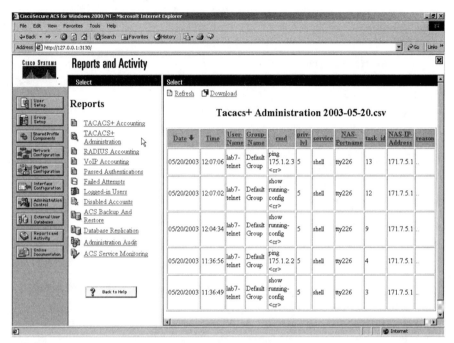

Figure 7-12b *Failed Attempts for Command Authorization*

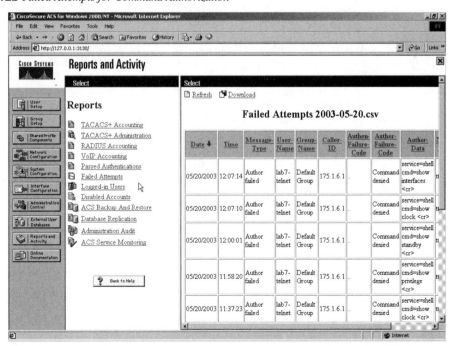

7.2: AAA on the Switch

1 Configure switch1 management with RADIUS using the AAA server, as shown in Figure 7-1.

2 Configure PIX translation and ACL accordingly:

```
pixfirewall(config)# show static
static (inside,outside) 175.1.2.3 172.16.1.3 netmask 255.255.255.255 0 0

pixfirewall(config)# show access-list
access-list 101 permit udp host 175.1.5.25 host 175.1.2.3 eq 1812 (hitcnt=3)
access-list 101 permit udp host 175.1.5.25 host 175.1.2.3 eq 1813 (hitcnt=2)
```

3 Hidden issue: There is ingress ACL on the R5 ATM link. You need to allow UDP/1812-1813 from switch1 to the AAA server:

```
r5#show access-lists 101
Extended IP access list 101
    deny ip any 179.7.2.0 0.0.0.7 (29 matches)
    deny icmp any 175.1.2.0 0.0.0.255 echo-reply (26 matches)
    permit icmp any any (15 matches)
    permit tcp any any eq telnet (90 matches)
    permit tcp any any eq ftp
    permit tcp any any eq ftp-data
    permit ospf any any (106 matches)
    permit tcp any any eq bgp (34 matches)
    permit tcp host 171.7.5.1 host 175.1.2.3 eq tacacs (56 matches)
    permit udp host 175.1.5.25 host 175.1.2.3 eq 1812 (4 matches)
    permit udp host 175.1.5.25 host 175.1.2.3 eq 1813 (10 matches)
```

4 Configure a named method list for Telnet and apply to vty for authentication, authorization, and accounting. Make sure this method falls back to local in the event the AAA server is down. See the example following item 9.

5 Configure a named method list for the console and apply it to the console with no authentication, authorization, or accounting.

6 Configure username **switch-telnet** with password **cisco** on CiscoSecure ACS.

7 Configure the same username, **switch-telnet**, on the switch1 local database for fallback.

8 Configure EXEC accounting to log session timings for billing purposes.

9 The complete AAA configuration on Switch1 is as follows:

```
hostname sw1
!
aaa new-model
aaa authentication login vty group radius local
aaa authentication login con none
aaa authorization exec vty group radius local
aaa authorization exec con none
```

```
aaa accounting exec vty start-stop group radius
aaa accounting exec con none
!
username switch-telnet password 7 1511021F0725

!
radius-server host 175.1.2.3 auth-port 1812 acct-port 1813
radius-server retransmit 3
radius-server key cisco
!
line con 0
 exec-timeout 0 0
 authorization exec con
 accounting exec vty
 login authentication con
line vty 0 4
 password 7 14141B180F0B
 authorization exec vty
 accounting exec vty
 login authentication vty
!
end
```

10 See Figure 7-13 to verify RADIUS accounting and Figure 7-14 for NAS configuration on CiscoSecure ACS.

Figure 7-13 *RADIUS Accounting for Session Start-Stop Time (Billing Purposes)*

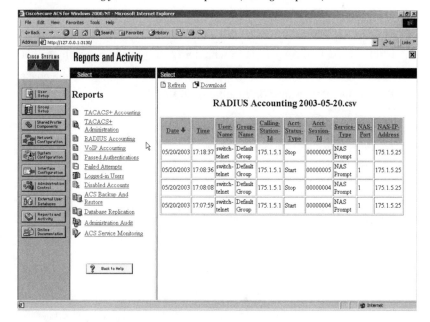

Figure 7-14 *Network Configuration on CiscoSecure ACS*

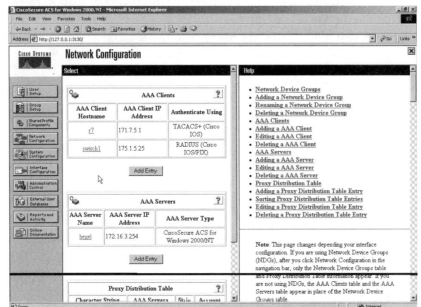

Section 8.0: Advanced Security

8.1: Perimeter Security

1 Configure ACL to deny TCP/53 with a SYN flag to prevent such an attack, as demonstrated in the example following item 2.

2 Permit any DNS request originating from VLAN2:

```
hostname r2
!
interface Serial0
 ip address 179.7.2.2 255.255.255.248
 ip access-group 199 in
!
access-list 199 permit tcp any any eq domain established
access-list 199 deny   tcp any any eq domain syn
access-list 199 permit ip any any
!
```

```
! Verify by telnetting from R3 to R2 on port 53
r3#telnet 179.7.2.2 53
Trying 179.7.2.2, 53 ...
% Destination unreachable; gateway or host down

r3#

! Check ACL counters on R2
r2#show access-lists 199
Extended IP access list 199
    permit tcp any any eq domain established
    deny tcp any any eq domain syn (46 matches)
    permit ip any any (52 matches)
```

3 DNS uses TCP port 53 for zone transfer and UDP port 53 for lookups.

4 In other words, this task requires permitting any zone transfers from the VLAN2 server to the Internet but not vice versa. The zone transfer TCP/53 port can be exploited and used to attack DNS servers.

8.2: Access Control

1 Configure time-based ACL to provide Telnet access to R1 for all users between 9:00 a.m. and 5:00 p.m. Monday through Friday only, as demonstrated in the example following item 2.

2 Configure local authentication for Telnet with username **ADMIN** password **cisco**:

```
hostname r1
!
aaa new-model
aaa authentication login vty local-case
!
username ADMIN password 7 00071A150754
!
access-list 110 permit tcp any any eq telnet time-range work-hours
!
!
line vty 0 4
 access-class 110 in
 login authentication vty
!
time-range work-hours
 periodic weekdays 9:00 to 17:00
!
end
```

```
Verify Telnet from R2 to R1.
r1#clock set 14:40:00 May 21 2003
r1#show clock
14:40:12.319 AST Wed May 21 2003

r1#who
    Line        User        Host(s)              Idle        Location
*  0 con 0                  idle                 00:00:00
   66 vty 0     ADMIN       idle                 00:00:09 172.16.1.10

   Interface  User       Mode               Idle Peer Address

r1#show time-range
time-range entry: work-hours (active)
   periodic weekdays 9:00 to 17:00
   used in: IP ACL entry

r1#show access-lists 110
Extended IP access list 110
    permit tcp any any eq telnet time-range work-hours (active) (2 matches)


! Change the clock to something not between 9:00am to 5:00pm
r1#clock set 2:40:00 May 21 2003
r1#show clock
02:40:02.987 AST Wed May 21 2003

r1#who
    Line        User        Host(s)              Idle        Location
*  0 con 0                  idle                 00:00:00

   Interface  User       Mode               Idle Peer Address

r1#show time-range
time-range entry: work-hours (inactive)
   periodic weekdays 9:00 to 17:00
   used in: IP ACL entry

r1#show access-lists 110
Extended IP access list 110
    permit tcp any any eq telnet time-range work-hours (inactive) (2 matches)
```

3 Hidden issue: Configure case-sensitive local authentication, as user ADMIN is in uppercase and password is in lowercase. This provides added security.

4   Configure PIX with static NAT and ACL to achieve this task:

```
pixfirewall(config)# show static
static (inside,outside) 175.1.2.20 172.16.1.2 netmask 255.255.255.255 0 0

pixfirewall(config)# show access-list
access-list 101 permit tcp any host 175.1.2.20 eq telnet (hitcnt=7)
```

8.3: Access Restriction

1   Any connection initiated from the local host to remote destinations will be allowed back on the same ports. If the remote destination changes the ports in between, the PIX will deny it, as it will not match with its session table.

2   Use the **established** command to permit return connections on ports other than those used for the originating connection based on an established connection.

3   The source port in this case is 1515, so the remote destination should have return traffic destined for port 1515. But in this case, the return traffic is changed to destination port 5252.

4   Here's how you configure the **established** command to allow this change of ports:

```
pixfirewall#show established
established tcp 1515 0 permitto tcp 5252 permitfrom tcp 2525
```

5   The IP addresses given are hypothetical and do not apply in the **established** command. The **established** command requires Layer 4 parameters only.

Section 9.0: IP Services and Protocol-Independent Features

9.1: NTP

1   Configure R7 as the NTP server with R2 and Switch1 as clients with MD5 authentication, as demonstrated in the example following item 3.

2   Configure clock and time zone accordingly.

3   Hidden trick: The NTP master must be configured on R3 and R7 for Switch1 redundancy. Configure Virtual IP as the NTP server on Switch1:

```
<snip from R7>
ntp authentication-key 1 md5 02050D480809 7
ntp master
end
```

```
r7#show ntp status
Clock is synchronized, stratum 8, reference is 127.127.7.1
nominal freq is 250.0000 Hz, actual freq is 250.0000 Hz, precision is 2**24
reference time is C2724021.6452EDE7 (03:23:45.391 AST Mon May 19 2003)
clock offset is 0.0000 msec, root delay is 0.00 msec
root dispersion is 0.02 msec, peer dispersion is 0.02 msec

r7#show ntp associations detail
127.127.7.1 configured, our_master, sane, valid, stratum 7
ref ID 127.127.7.1, time C2724021.6452EDE7 (03:23:45.391 AST Mon May 19 2003)
our mode active, peer mode passive, our poll intvl 64, peer poll intvl 64
root delay 0.00 msec, root disp 0.00, reach 377, sync dist 0.015
delay 0.00 msec, offset 0.0000 msec, dispersion 0.02
precision 2**18, version 3
org time C2724021.6452EDE7 (03:23:45.391 AST Mon May 19 2003)
rcv time C2724021.6452EDE7 (03:23:45.391 AST Mon May 19 2003)
xmt time C2724021.64529CCA (03:23:45.391 AST Mon May 19 2003)
filtdelay =     0.00    0.00    0.00    0.00    0.00    0.00    0.00    0.00
filtoffset =    0.00    0.00    0.00    0.00    0.00    0.00    0.00    0.00
filterror =     0.02    0.99    1.97    2.94    3.92    4.90    5.87    6.85
Reference clock status:  Running normally
Timecode:


<Snip from R3>
ntp authentication-key 1 md5 094F471A1A0A 7
ntp master
end


r3#show ntp status
Clock is synchronized, stratum 8, reference is 127.127.7.1
nominal freq is 249.5901 Hz, actual freq is 249.5901 Hz, precision is 2**16
reference time is C27240BD.E5C8D674 (03:26:21.897 AST Mon May 19 2003)
clock offset is 0.0000 msec, root delay is 0.00 msec
root dispersion is 0.02 msec, peer dispersion is 0.02 msec


r3#show ntp associations detail
127.127.7.1 configured, our_master, sane, valid, stratum 7
ref ID 127.127.7.1, time C27240BD.E5C8D674 (03:26:21.897 AST Mon May 19 2003)
our mode active, peer mode passive, our poll intvl 64, peer poll intvl 64
root delay 0.00 msec, root disp 0.00, reach 377, sync dist 0.015
delay 0.00 msec, offset 0.0000 msec, dispersion 0.02
precision 2**16, version 3
```

```
org time C27240BD.E5C8D674 (03:26:21.897 AST Mon May 19 2003)
rcv time C27240BD.E5C8D674 (03:26:21.897 AST Mon May 19 2003)
xmt time C27240BD.E5C7FA10 (03:26:21.897 AST Mon May 19 2003)
filtdelay =     0.00    0.00    0.00    0.00    0.00    0.00    0.00    0.00
filtoffset =    0.00    0.00    0.00    0.00    0.00    0.00    0.00    0.00
filterror =     0.02    0.99    1.97    2.94    3.92    4.90    5.87    6.85
Reference clock status:  Running normally
Timecode:

<Snip from R2>
ntp authentication-key 1 md5 110A1016141D 7
ntp authenticate
ntp trusted-key 1
ntp clock-period 17179918
ntp server 171.7.5.1 key 1
end
```

r2#**show ntp status**
```
Clock is synchronized, stratum 9, reference is 171.7.5.1
nominal freq is 250.0000 Hz, actual freq is 249.9993 Hz, precision is 2**19
reference time is C2724054.77E33BEE (03:24:36.468 AST Mon May 19 2003)
clock offset is -6.3133 msec, root delay is 72.54 msec
root dispersion is 6.65 msec, peer dispersion is 0.31 msec
```

r2#**show ntp associations detail**
```
171.7.5.1 configured, authenticated, our_master, sane, valid, stratum 8
ref ID 127.127.7.1, time C2724021.6452EDE7 (03:23:45.391 AST Mon May 19 2003)
our mode client, peer mode server, our poll intvl 64, peer poll intvl 64
root delay 0.00 msec, root disp 0.03, reach 377, sync dist 36.606
delay 72.54 msec, offset -6.3133 msec, dispersion 0.31
precision 2**24, version 3
org time C2724054.6CFC45C4 (03:24:36.425 AST Mon May 19 2003)
rcv time C2724054.77E33BEE (03:24:36.468 AST Mon May 19 2003)
xmt time C2724054.6544C93F (03:24:36.395 AST Mon May 19 2003)
filtdelay =    72.54   72.25   72.95   74.94   72.71   72.36   74.13   72.68
filtoffset =   -6.31   -6.05   -6.26   -7.14   -5.87   -5.80   -4.63   -5.44
filterror =     0.02    0.99    1.97    2.94    3.92    4.90    5.87    6.85

<Snip from Switch1>
ntp authentication-key 1 md5 13061E010803 7
ntp authenticate
ntp trusted-key 1
ntp clock-period 17179866
ntp server 175.1.5.250 key 1
end
```

```
sw1#show ntp status
Clock is synchronized, stratum 9, reference is 175.1.5.250
nominal freq is 250.0000 Hz, actual freq is 250.0000 Hz, precision is 2**18
reference time is C272405E.720AEDCB (03:24:46.445 AST Mon May 19 2003)
clock offset is -0.0838 msec, root delay is 0.67 msec
root dispersion is 0.14 msec, peer dispersion is 0.02 msec

sw1#show ntp associations detail
175.1.5.250 configured, authenticated, our_master, sane, valid, stratum 8
ref ID 127.127.7.1, time C2724021.6452EDE7 (03:23:45.391 AST Mon May 19 2003)
our mode client, peer mode server, our poll intvl 64, peer poll intvl 64
root delay 0.00 msec, root disp 0.03, reach 377, sync dist 0.381
delay 0.67 msec, offset -0.0838 msec, dispersion 0.02
precision 2**24, version 3
org time C272405E.71EF38BF (03:24:46.445 AST Mon May 19 2003)
rcv time C272405E.720AEDCB (03:24:46.445 AST Mon May 19 2003)
xmt time C272405E.71D2918E (03:24:46.444 AST Mon May 19 2003)
filtdelay =    0.67     0.63     0.63     0.61     0.60     0.66     0.61     0.60
filtoffset =  -0.08    -0.10    -0.08    -0.08    -0.08    -0.08    -0.10    -0.09
filterror =    0.02     0.99     1.97     2.94     3.92     4.90     5.87     6.85
```

9.2: Congestion Management—QoS

1 Configure custom queuing on R4 (FR interface) for the following in this order:

   a. All Telnet traffic to queue 1

   b. OSPF Routing protocol to queue 2

   c. All ICMP traffic to VLAN6 to queue 3

   d. All web traffic to queue 4

   e. All other traffic to queue 5

2 Custom queuing allows fairness not provided with priority queuing.

3 Specify the maximum number of packets allowed in each custom queue as follows.

4 Increase the byte count to 2000 for queue 4 for web traffic.

5 Configure queue 3 for ICMP; change the queue length limit from the default 20 packets to 40 packets.

6 The following example shows the complete configuration:

```
hostname r4
!
interface Serial1/0
 ip address 179.7.2.4 255.255.255.248
```

```
 encapsulation frame-relay
 custom-queue-list 1
!
access-list 102 permit ospf any any
access-list 103 permit icmp any 175.1.6.0 0.0.0.255
!
queue-list 1 protocol ip 1 tcp telnet
queue-list 1 protocol ip 2 list 102
queue-list 1 protocol ip 3 list 103
queue-list 1 protocol ip 4 tcp www
queue-list 1 default 5
queue-list 1 queue 3 limit 40
queue-list 1 queue 4 byte-count 2000
```

r4#**show queueing custom**
```
Current custom queue configuration:

List   Queue   Args
1      5       default
1      1       protocol ip        tcp port telnet
1      2       protocol ip        list 102
1      3       protocol ip        list 103
1      4       protocol ip        tcp port www
1      3       limit 40
1      4       byte-count 2000
```

r4#**show interfaces serial 1/0**
```
Serial1/0 is up, line protocol is up
  Hardware is cxBus Serial
  Internet address is 179.7.2.4/29
  MTU 1500 bytes, BW 1544 Kbit, DLY 20000 usec,
     reliability 255/255, txload 1/255, rxload 1/255
  Encapsulation FRAME-RELAY, crc 16, loopback not set
  Keepalive set (10 sec)
  LMI enq sent  187894, LMI stat recvd 187892, LMI upd recvd 0, DTE LMI up
  LMI enq recvd 0, LMI stat sent  0, LMI upd sent  0
  LMI DLCI 1023  LMI type is CISCO  frame relay DTE
  Broadcast queue 0/64, broadcasts sent/dropped 0/0, interface broadcasts 0
  Last input 00:00:02, output 00:00:02, output hang never
  Last clearing of "show interface" counters 3w0d
  Input queue: 0/75/0 (size/max/drops); Total output drops: 0
  Queueing strategy: custom-list 1
  Output queues: (queue #: size/max/drops)
      0: 0/20/0 1: 0/20/0 2: 0/20/0 3: 0/40/0 4: 0/20/0
      5: 0/20/0 6: 0/20/0 7: 0/20/0 8: 0/20/0 9: 0/20/0
```

```
10: 0/20/0 11: 0/20/0 12: 0/20/0 13: 0/20/0 14: 0/20/0
15: 0/20/0 16: 0/20/0
```
```
5 minute input rate 0 bits/sec, 0 packets/sec
5 minute output rate 0 bits/sec, 0 packets/sec
    441332 packets input, 22720511 bytes, 0 no buffer
    Received 0 broadcasts, 0 runts, 0 giants, 0 throttles
    0 input errors, 0 CRC, 0 frame, 0 overrun, 0 ignored, 0 abort
    421900 packets output, 18204848 bytes, 0 underruns
    0 output errors, 0 collisions, 8 interface resets
    0 output buffer failures, 0 output buffers swapped out
    6 carrier transitions
    RTS up, CTS up, DTR up, DCD up, DSR up
```

9.3: HSRP

1 Configure HSRP on R3 and R7 such that Switch1 is always reachable in the event of any
router interface(s) in VLAN5 going down.

2 Configure HSRP Virtual IP 175.1.5.250 with authentication. Use password **cisco**:

```
<Snip from R3>
interface Ethernet0/0
 ip address 175.1.5.1 255.255.255.0
 standby 1 preempt
 standby 1 authentication cisco
 standby 1 ip 175.1.5.250


r3#show standby
Ethernet0/0 - Group 1
  Local state is Standby, priority 100, may preempt
  Hellotime 3 holdtime 10
  Next hello sent in 00:00:01.578
  Hot standby IP address is 175.1.5.250 configured
  Active router is 175.1.5.3 expires in 00:00:08
  Standby router is local
  Standby virtual mac address is 0000.0c07.ac01


<Snip from R7>
interface FastEthernet0/1
 ip address 175.1.5.3 255.255.255.0
 standby 1 preempt
 standby 1 authentication cisco
 standby 1 ip 175.1.5.250


r7#show standby
FastEthernet0/1 - Group 1
  Local state is Active, priority 100, may preempt
```

```
Hellotime 3 holdtime 10
Next hello sent in 00:00:00.606
Hot standby IP address is 175.1.5.250 configured
Active router is local
Standby router is 175.1.5.1 expires in 00:00:08
Standby virtual mac address is 0000.0c07.ac01
7 state changes, last state change 00:03:20
```

Section 10.0: Security Violations

10.1: DoS Attack

1 Configure policy routing on R3 to black-hole ICMP echo packets destined for R2:

```
hostname r3
!
ip local policy route-map null
!
access-list 110 deny    icmp host 179.7.2.3 host 179.7.2.2 echo-reply
access-list 110 permit icmp host 179.7.2.3 host 179.7.2.2
route-map null permit 10
 match ip address 110
 set interface Null0
```

2 Apply the policy in global mode, as packets originated in R3 hit the local policy map.

3 Verify ping from R3 to R2 and vice versa:

```
! Ping from R2 to R3 Fails.
r3#ping 179.7.2.2

Type escape sequence to abort.
Sending 5, 100-byte ICMP Echos to 179.7.2.2, timeout is 2 seconds:
.....
Success rate is 0 percent (0/5)
r3#

! Ping from R2 to R3 Success.
r2#ping 179.7.2.3

Type escape sequence to abort.
Sending 5, 100-byte ICMP Echos to 179.7.2.3, timeout is 2 seconds:
!!!!!
Success rate is 100 percent (5/5), round-trip min/avg/max = 68/68/68 ms
r2#
```

```
<Verify using following show commands>
r3#show route-map
route-map null, permit, sequence 10
  Match clauses:
    ip address (access-lists): 110
  Set clauses:
    interface Null0
  Policy routing matches: 214 packets, 20128 bytes

r3#show access-lists
Extended IP access list 110
    deny icmp host 179.7.2.3 host 179.7.2.2 echo-reply (30 matches)
    permit icmp host 179.7.2.3 host 179.7.2.2 (10 matches)
```

10.2: High CPU Caused by an Attack

1 R8 is experiencing a high CPU due to RSHELL attempts from spoofed IP addresses.

2 Remote shell (rsh) gives users the ability to execute commands remotely.

3 You can use rsh to execute commands on remote systems to which you have access; this can also be a router. When you issue the **rsh** command, a shell is started on the remote system. The shell allows you to execute commands on the remote system without having to log in to the target host.

4 Prevent this by configuring an ACL on all links to deny TCP/514 used for RSH:

```
hostname r8
!
interface FastEthernet0/0
 ip address 171.8.5.1 255.255.255.0
 ip access-group 101 in
!
interface FastEthernet0/1
 ip address 178.1.1.2 255.255.255.252
 ip access-group 101 in
!
access-list 101 deny    tcp any any eq cmd
access-list 101 permit ip any any
!

! Verify by configuring RSH on R8 as per URL below and test by
! executing any IOS command on R8 remotely from any router.
```

```
r8#show access-lists
Extended IP access list 101
    deny tcp any any eq cmd (16 matches)
    permit ip any any (22 matches)
```

NOTE   For more info on configuring a router to use rsh, see this URL:

www.cisco.com/univercd/cc/td/doc/product/software/ios120/12cgcr/fun_c/fcprt2/
fcaddfun.htm#4134

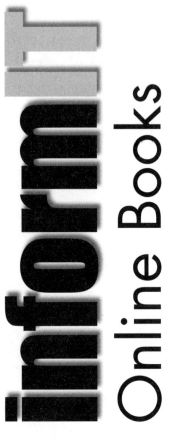